POVERTY IN THE UNITED STATES

An Encyclopedia of History, Politics, and Policy

POVERTY
IN THE
UNITED STATES

An Encyclopedia of History, Politics, and Policy

VOLUME 2 L–Z

edited by Gwendolyn Mink
and Alice O'Connor

A B C CLIO

Santa Barbara, California • Denver, Colorado • Oxford, England

Library of Congress Cataloging-in-Publication Data
Poverty in the United States : an encyclopedia of history, politics, and policy / Gwendolyn Mink and Alice O'Connor, editors.
p. cm.
Includes bibliographical references and index.
ISBN 1-57607-597-4 (hardback : alk. paper) — ISBN 1-57607-608-3 (e-book)
1. Poverty—United States—Encyclopedias. 2. Poor—United States—Encyclopedias. 3. Public welfare—United States—Encyclopedias.
I. Mink, Gwendolyn, 1952– II. O'Connor, Alice, 1958–
HC110.P6P598 2004
339.4'6'097303—dc22
2004017618

08 07 06 05 04 / 10 9 8 7 6 5 4 3 2 1

This book is also available on the World Wide Web as an eBook.
Visit abc-clio.com for details.

ABC-CLIO, Inc.
130 Cremona Drive, P.O. Box 1911
Santa Barbara, California 93116-1911

This book is printed on acid-free paper.
Manufactured in the United States of America

Contents

VOLUME 1

VOLUME 2

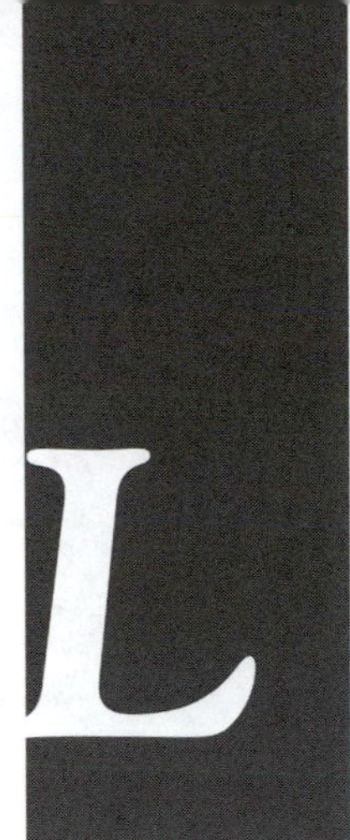

Labor Markets

Labor markets have historically played an important role in the experience of poverty and the distribution of economic opportunity in the United States, shaping the overall availability of jobs as well as wage levels, benefits, and possibilities for promotion. Labor market theories have also been prominent as explanations for poverty, in part reflecting the work-centered nature of U.S. social welfare policy.

Labor market theories of poverty attempt to address three main questions: (1) Why is there unemployment and underemployment (that is, why are people unable to work as many hours per week or as many weeks per year as they choose)? (2) What accounts for the very different valuations, and consequent pay levels, of different jobs? (3) Why are some people—and in particular, some socially significant *categories* of people, such as women or people of color—more likely to end up unemployed or in low-wage jobs? For as long as there have been labor markets in the United States, economists and others have put forward two conflicting types of theories about the answers to these questions. On the one hand, some have argued that labor markets are basically efficient and, in some fundamental sense, fair. This viewpoint favors *supply-side policies:* policies that remove restrictions on labor markets and help individuals to invest in skills. For the last 100 years, the predominant theory associated with this point of view has been neoclassical economics. On the other hand, critics have claimed that labor markets are inevitably greatly shaped by institutions distant from efficiency considerations, and often distant from fairness as well. These critics have championed *demand-side policies*, favoring enlightened regulation of wage levels and hiring and support for institutions designed to rectify power imbalances, such as unions. Over the last century, the critical view has been linked to radical (including Marxist) and institutionalist theories.

A glance at recent statistics establishes the link between labor markets and poverty in the United States. As Table 1 shows, adults who did no paid work in the previous year are far more likely to be in a household that fell below the poverty level than are those who worked year-round, full-time. Part-time and part-year workers fall between these two extremes, though closer to those who did no paid work at all. It is important to note that close to 3 percent of year-round, full-time workers live in poverty households: Sustained work at low wages can still leave a person and his or her household in poverty.

Why Is There Unemployment and Underemployment?

The average family in poverty worked a total of 1,112 hours in 1998, about half the 2,080 hours

Table 1

Poverty rates for adults, by amount of paid work, 1999

	Percent in poverty among those who:		
Age group	*Worked year-round, full-time*	*Worked part-time or part-year*	*No paid work*
All 16 and over	2.6%	13.1%	19.1%
Ages 25–64	2.3%	13.0%	26.4%

Source: U.S. Census Bureau 2000, Table 3.

that constitute year-round, full-time work for one person (Mishel, Bernstein, and Schmitt 2001, table 5.18). Although this low level of hours worked to some extent reflects deliberate choices (themselves influenced by other constraints such as child-rearing responsibilities or disability), unemployment and underemployment also limit work hours for poor families and individuals.

Until a third of the way through the twentieth century, the dominant explanation for unemployment was the classical view, holding that excessively high wages depress labor demand. The policy implication, which echoes down to this day, is that institutions maintaining higher wage levels, such as unions or minimum-wage laws, harm employment in the aggregate. Economists dismissed the possibility that aggregate demand might not be sufficient to absorb aggregate supply, citing Say's Law, that "supply creates its own demand."

When the Great Depression gripped the industrialized world during the 1930s, John Maynard Keynes's *General Theory of Employment, Interest, and Money* (1936) challenged this traditional consensus. Keynes argued that pessimistic expectations by capitalists, translated into anemic investments in plant and equipment, can become self-fulfilling, trapping an economy in a downturn. In these circumstances, Keynes argued, wage cutting simply aggravates the shortfall of demand, since it leaves workers with less money to spend on consumer goods. Instead, governments should use monetary policy (such as cutting interest rates) and, especially, fiscal policy (such as reducing taxes or expanding spending) to prime the pump of private consumer expenditure and to ensure full employment. Governments, including that of the United States, implemented this theory through social welfare spending and public works programs. World War II and postwar "military Keynesianism" (military spending aimed at job creation) carried this policy thread forward, although Congress backed away from an explicit commitment to guarantee *full* employment that had been embodied in early drafts of what became the Employment Act of 1946 (notably leaving out the "full" in the original title).

In the 1970s and 1980s, Keynesianism stumbled over the combination of stagnation and inflation in the United States (a possibility Keynes had discounted) and over the persistent high unemployment in western Europe that many attributed to classical causes—high wages and generous welfare payments. "New classical" economists revived the classical analysis of unemployment (Barro 1989). Equally important, huge federal deficits in the United States (run up by the tax cuts of the early 1980s combined with increased military spending) politically blocked proposals for substantial new tax cuts or spending programs, while antigovernment rhetoric undermined support for programs to create employment, such as the 1973 Comprehensive Employment and Training Act (CETA). By 2000, deficits had been replaced by surpluses, and a wide range of new empirical and theoretical research questioned classical accounts of unemployment (notably by David Blanchflower and Andrew Oswald [1994], who found that unemployment tends to be associated with *lower* wages rather than higher). Nonetheless, new classical economics continued to reign on campuses, and low unemployment at the outset of the twenty-first century blunted concerns about job creation, while a combination of economic recession and massive tax cuts soon re-created huge federal deficits, further constraining policy options.

*Under*employment's most readily measurable form is involuntary part-time employment—workers stuck in part-time jobs against their wills. Families of involuntary part-time workers are more likely to fall below the poverty line than are those of voluntary part-time workers, and both are far more likely to live in poverty than year-round, full-time workers. The causes of involuntary part-time employment are similar to those of unemployment. Indeed, fluctuations in the level of involuntary part-time employment track unemployment quite closely. However, involuntary part-time work has an added "classical" component, since employers typically offer part-time workers fewer fringe benefits and in some cases lower wages (Tilly 1996).

What Accounts for the Pay Levels of Different Jobs?

In 1999, $6.05 per hour marked the upper boundary of the lowest-paid 10 percent of U.S. wage earners (Mishel, Bernstein, and Schmitt 2001, table 2.6). If a person worked year-round, full-time at this wage, she or he would still fall $700 below the poverty line for a family of three. Indeed, the family-wide average hourly wage of families in poverty in 1998 was just slightly higher, at $6.16 (Mishel, Bernstein, and Schmitt 2001, table 5.18). At the other end, the lower boundary of the highest-paid 5 percent stood at $33.28 per hour. The highest-paid CEO in America in 2000, Citigroup's Sanford Weill, received $224.4 million in direct compensation for the year, which translates to about $72,000 per hour (assuming a sixty-hour week) (*Wall Street Journal* 2001). Clearly, differing wage levels contribute to extremes of wealth and poverty in the United States.

The leading theory of wage differences, that of neoclassical economics, puts forward an elegantly simple explanation: People are paid according to their productivity, or, more precisely, according to their *marginal revenue product*, meaning the amount they add to sales. The reasoning behind this theory is straightforward. As firms add more and more labor to a fixed stock of capital (machines, buildings, and so on), the added product gained from each added hour of labor eventually declines. Since firms maximize profits, they will keep adding labor as long as the amount of salable product yielded by an extra hour of labor exceeds the hourly wage, so that hiring one more hour of labor results in a net gain. They will stop adding labor precisely at the point at which the marginal revenue product equals the wage (see, for instance, Hamermesh 1986).

The question then becomes why some workers in some jobs are more productive than others. Neoclassical theorists point to two main factors: skill and the other resources a worker has to work with (for example, Baumol and Blinder 1991, ch. 36). Note that skill has two kinds of impacts. Certain *jobs* require more skill and involve greater productivity and therefore pay more. But even in two identical jobs, one *person* may bring more skill than another and therefore be more productive and earn more. As for other resources, neoclassical analysts posit that workers using more capital (more or better machines, faster computers, and the like) can be more productive. They often cite low capital-to-labor ratios to explain low pay levels in less-developed regions. Similarly, workers with more-able coworkers (better managers, more clever innovators) are more productive. The most important policy implication of this perspective is that wage differences are efficient. For example, firms offer higher wages to attract workers with higher skills, and the pay differential prompts workers to seek added education and training (Welch 1999). Neoclassical recommendations to reduce poverty include subsidizing the acquisition of general skills and facilitating capital inflow to or labor out-migration from depressed areas, such as mid-twentieth-century Appalachia.

Critical theorists take a different tack. Karl Marx himself concentrated primarily on the processes setting average wages for the working class, emphasizing workers' cost of subsistence and the class struggle. To the extent that he discussed wage differences, he accepted the neoclassical notion that they reflect skill differences (Marx [1867] 1967). But Marx's contemporary John Stuart Mill ([1848] 1929) wrote of "non-competing groups" in the labor market, for whom hiring and wages were governed by custom and institutions (such as guilds and professions) rather than by market competition. Institutionalist economists in the United States, most prominently represented in the early twentieth century by John R. Commons (1934), took Mill's proposition in two directions. They stressed the importance of institutions—including tangible organizations such as unions but also including more diffuse phenomena such as fairness norms—in regulating wages. And, more important for theorizing about poverty, they picked up the idea of segmented labor markets.

For much of the twentieth century, institutionalists, riveted by the momentous struggle to unionize the industrial workforce, focused broadly on how institutions affect wages. In the post–World War II years, however, renewed interest in issues of poverty and racial inequality sparked attention to segmentation, a term popularized by Peter Doeringer and Michael Piore (1971). The labor market segmentation perspective challenges the neoclassical notion of smooth, continuous trade-offs, holding that particular sets of characteristics or governing rules tend to be found together. This points to multiple, qualitative distinctions between good and bad jobs. Doeringer and Piore described the "secondary" segment as comprising jobs marked by low wages, high turnover, and arbitrary supervision and often by unpleasant working conditions (in contrast to well-paid, steady "primary"-sector jobs). These are the jobs of the working poor.

Theories of segmentation have typically adopted either functional or historical logics. Functional accounts, like neoclassical wage theory, focus on efficiency. For instance, some view the job ladders that characterize certain segments as incentive systems. The promise of advancement can help to deter shirking and to retain workers with valuable skills or proprietary knowledge. However, segmentation theorists appeal to history as well as efficiency. Historical accounts point to the enormous power of inertia enforced by both short-run efficiency (based in the familiarity of current ways of doing things) and the defense of vested interests. Sociologist Arthur Stinchcombe (1990, ch. 10) observed that many jobs still reflect the organizational forms of the era in which they were introduced; a case in point is the craft structures of the building trades. Struggles along class, race, and gender lines also weigh in. Neo-Marxists David Gordon, Richard Edwards, and Michael Reich (1982) attributed the initial homogenization and later segmentation of the U.S. proletariat to employers' efforts to assert control over their workforces, first by de-skilling the workers and later, in response to industrial unionism, by dividing them.

Policy advocates have used segmentation theory to argue for policies quite different from those implied by neoclassical productivity theory. The goal is to shift employment from secondary-sector jobs to primary-sector jobs, either by directly regulating the labor market (through devices such as the minimum wage or unions) or by industrial policies subsidizing better-paying, "high road" industries.

One hundred years ago, most economists held a mix of neoclassical and institutionalist views. But as the twentieth century wore on, the two theories diverged, for both methodological reasons (neoclassical tools became increasingly mathematical, whereas institutionalists relied on case studies) and ideological ones (institutionalists supported unionization and regulation of the labor market, whereas neoclassicals increasingly shunned these policies). The 1930s through the 1950s saw the zenith of institutionalist influence, both in the field of labor economics and in the corridors of power. Institutionalist arguments (along with powerful political considerations) underpinned Depression-era laws such as the Fair Labor Standards Act and the Wagner Act, as well as wartime regulation of industrial relations.

In the 1960s, neoclassical labor market analysis gained the upper hand. The elegant mathematical formulations developed by economists attracted scholars, as did the large data sets newly available for analysis with emerging computer technology. The sharp class struggles of the 1930s that had fueled institutionalist fortunes receded from the collective memory. Despite the flowering of segmentation theories in the 1960s and 1970s, the reigning analyses of labor markets and poverty remained neoclassically grounded (O'Connor 2001).

Beginning in the 1980s, neoclassical dominance took yet another turn. Encouraged by economist Gary Becker's application of neoclassical analysis to such "noneconomic" topics as marriage and childbearing (Becker 1976), orthodox economists used their tools to model labor market institutions. Interestingly, the conclusions and even policy recommendations of this "new information economics" sometimes replicate those of the institutionalists. For instance, Jeremy Bulow and Lawrence Summers (1986) used neoclassical incentive analysis to model a segmented labor market and concluded that policies subsidizing the primary sector would increase efficiency. Nonetheless, this and other neoclassical models are driven by efficiency considerations and by the assumption that rational individuals will pursue their own self-interest. Like older neoclassical models, they leave little space for acknowledging the influence of power, history, or culture.

Why Are Some People More Likely to End Up Unemployed or in Low-Wage Jobs?

Wage levels and unemployment rates differ markedly by gender, race, and ethnicity (see Table 2). As is well known, men in the United States earn higher average wages than women, whites and Asians earn more than Blacks and Latinos, and Latinos and, especially, Blacks suffer from higher unemployment. Relative poverty rates track these regularities in earnings (U.S. Census Bureau 2000).

Neoclassical theories explain who gets what job in much the same way that they explain pay differences across jobs—via differences in skills and therefore in potential productive capacities.

Table 2

Median hourly wage (1999) and unemployment rate (2000) by race, ethnicity, and gender

	White		*Black*		*Latino*		*Asian*	
	Men	*Women*	*Men*	*Women*	*Men*	*Women*	*Men*	*Women*
Median hourly wage	$13.90	$10.57	$10.78	$9.23	$11.03	$9.06	$14.67	$11.39
Unemployment rate	3.4%	3.6%	8.1%	7.2%	4.9%	6.7%	—	—

Note: Latinos can be of any racial group.

Source: Median wages from Mishel, Bernstein, and Schmitt 2001, Tables 2.25–26. Unemployment from U.S. Bureau of Labor Statistics, Employment and Earnings, January 2001, Tables 3 and 6.

Human capital theorists (Becker 1964) extended the basic productivity theory by reasoning that (1) a person would only defer earnings to obtain more education if the added learning increased his or her potential wage and (2) an employer would pay a higher wage to more educated workers only if they were indeed more productive (on average). Human capital theory has been applied not just to education but to a variety of parental investments and self-investments yielding higher productive returns, ranging from health care to reading bedtime stories. Others have pointed to—and argued about—the role of inherited abilities and the growing importance of "soft skills" such as motivation and style of interaction (Bowles, Gintis, and Osborne 2001; Moss and Tilly 2001). In general, orthodox economists have attributed most racial and ethnic differences in wages and unemployment to skill disparities, and policy advocates have used this analysis to bolster calls for better education for African Americans and Latinos. This explanation does not serve well for gender differences, since women now attain education on average slightly higher than men (and presumably inherit abilities similar to those of their brothers); more on this below.

At a polar opposite to hiring theories based on merit are those based on discrimination, espoused by critical theorists, including radicals, institutionalists, and feminists. Social scientists appeal to a variety of mechanisms to explain discrimination, including subconscious psychological attraction to those who are similar, conscious solidarity and defense of privilege, and employer-fomented divisions among workers. Critical theorists use discrimination to explain occupational segregation, such as that between men and women. To the extent that women or other groups are "crowded" into a restricted set of jobs, excess labor supply will drive down the wages offered to them. In addition, sociologist Paula England and colleagues (1994) have shown that a higher proportion of women in an occupational category are associated with lower average wages in that category, suggesting that the mix of job holders itself affects the valuation of the job.

The diagnosis of discrimination has led to three main policy prescriptions. First, and most straightforward, are laws—some dating as far back as the ratification of the Fourteenth Amendment to the Constitution in 1868—barring discrimination in hiring and wage setting and mandating affirmative action to offset the effects of past discrimination. Second, beginning in the 1970s, feminists observed that "equal pay for equal work" regulations help women little if they are located in different jobs than men, and consequently they have argued for pay equity—laws requiring equal pay for jobs of "comparable worth" as determined by a comparison of job characteristics (England 1992). Third, leaders of communities of color have called for community development to expand employment opportunities within those communities (Ferguson and Dickens 1999).

Neoclassical theorists have grappled with the concept of discrimination as well. As Becker (1957) pointed out, if employers indulge a "taste for discrimination," they are foregoing hiring the most productive workers or they are paying more than they must to obtain equally productive workers. This suggests that market competition will erode discrimination. Similarly, neoclassical theory is inclined toward the view that occupational segregation results from differing worker tastes or aptitudes rather than discrimination. However, theorists of *statistical discrimination* observed that it may be narrowly efficient—but not socially desirable—for employers to discriminate based on information about group averages or variances (for example, "Women do not stay at jobs as long on average," "African Americans on average have less skill") (Arrow 1973).

While skill and discrimination have loomed largest in theories of hiring, sociologists (and some economists) also highlight a variety of other exclusionary social structures. The *spatial mismatch theory* holds that residential segregation has cut many Blacks off from the jobs most appropriate to their skill levels, especially given increased suburbanization of manufacturing and retail jobs (Ihlanfeldt 1999). Noting that a large proportion of jobs are found through personal connections, some analysts have argued that less-effective social networks disadvantage the poor (Montgomery 1991). Feminists, assessing the high poverty rates of single mothers, have suggested that an important part of the problem is lack of flexibility in hours in the higher-paying jobs and, more generally, workplace demands that are biased toward the male-breadwinner household ideal (Albelda and Tilly 1997). Sociologist William Julius Wilson (1995) and others, echoing Gunnar Myrdal's (1944) notion of cumulative causation, have hypothesized that concentrated poverty unleashes a self-reinforcing cycle of social isolation, decreased orientation to work, and insufficient investment in skills. In its "culture of poverty" variant, this view converges with neoclassical concerns about skills, aptitudes, and work ethic (Mead 1992).

The academic and political fortunes of analyses linking poverty to labor market discrimination have largely followed those of the civil rights movement. Theories of discrimination saw an upturn of interest after World War II and then flourished during the 1960s and 1970s. Although theorizing and policymaking in this vein have continued, their influence has waned since the 1980s in the face of political and theoretical backlash and the claim that the Civil Rights Act of 1964 greatly diminished the extent of discrimination. Currently, most research and public policy attention focuses on skills.

Chris Tilly

See also: Capitalism; Economic Theories; Employment Policy; Income and Wage Inequality; Unemployment

References and Further Reading

Albelda, Randy, and Chris Tilly. 1997. *Glass Ceilings and Bottomless Pits: Women's Work, Women's Poverty*. Boston: South End Press.

Arrow, Kenneth. 1973. "The Theory of Discrimination." In *Discrimination in Labor Markets*, ed. Orley A. Ashenfelter and Albert Rees, 3–33. Princeton: Princeton University Press.

Barro, Robert J. 1989. *Modern Business Cycle Theory*. Cambridge, MA: Harvard University Press.

Baumol, William J., and Alan S. Blinder. 1991. *Economics: Principles and Policy*. 5th ed. New York: Harcourt Brace Jovanovich.

Becker, Gary S. 1957. *The Economics of Discrimination*. Chicago: University of Chicago Press.

———. 1964. *Human Capital: A Theoretical Analysis with Special Reference to Education*. New York: Columbia University Press, for National Bureau of Economic Research.

———. 1976. *The Economic Approach to Human Behavior*. Chicago: University of Chicago Press.

Blanchflower, David G., and Andrew J. Oswald. 1994. *The Wage Curve*. Cambridge: MIT Press.

Bowles, Samuel, Herbert Gintis, and Melissa Osborne. 2001. "The Determinants of Earnings: A Behavioral Approach." *Journal of Economic Literature* 39, no. 4: 1137–1176.

Bulow, Jeremy I., and Lawrence H. Summers. 1986. "A Theory of Dual Labor Markets with Application to Industrial Policy, Discrimination, and Keynesian Unemployment." *Journal of Labor Economics* 4: 376–414.

Commons, John R. 1934. *Institutional Economics: Its Place in Political Economy*. New York: Macmillan.

Doeringer, Peter B., and Michael J. Piore. 1971. *Internal Labor Markets and Manpower Analysis*. Lexington, MA: Heath.

England, Paula. 1992. *Comparable Worth. Theories and Evidence*. New York: Aldine.

England, Paula, Melissa S. Herbert, Barbara S. Kilbourne, Lori L. Reid, and Lori M. Megdal. 1994. "The Gendered Valuation of Occupations and Skills: Earnings in 1980 Census Occupations." *Social Forces* 73, no. 1: 65–99.

Ferguson, Ronald F., and William T. Dickens. 1999. *Urban Problems and Community Development*. Washington, DC: Brookings Institution.

Gordon, David M., Richard Edwards, and Michael Reich. 1982. *Segmented Work, Divided Workers. The Historical Transformations of Labor in the United States*. New York: Cambridge University Press.

Hamermesh, Daniel. 1986. "The Demand for Labor in the Long Run." In *Handbook of Labor Economics I*, ed. Orley Ashenfelter and Richard Layard, 429–471. Amsterdam: North-Holland.

Ihlanfeldt, Keith. 1999. "The Geography of Economic and Social Opportunity within Metropolitan Areas." In *Governance and Opportunity in Metropolitan* America, ed. Alan Altshuler, William Morrill, Harold Wolman, and Faith Mitchell, 213–252. Washington, DC: National Academy Press.

Keynes, John Maynard. [1936] 1964. *The General Theory of Employment, Interest, and Money*. New York and London: Harcourt Brace Jovanovich.

Marx, Karl. [1867] 1967. *Capital*. Vol. 1. New York: International Publishers.

Mead, Lawrence M. 1992. *The New Politics of Poverty: The Nonworking Poor in America*. New York: Basic Books.

Mill, John Stuart. [1848] 1929. *Principles of Political Economy*. London: Longmans, Green.

Mishel, Lawrence, Jared Bernstein, and John Schmitt. 2001. *The State of Working America, 2000–2001*. Ithaca, NY: Cornell University Press.

Montgomery, James D. 1991. "Social Networks and Labor Market Outcomes: Toward an Economic Analysis." *American Economic Review* 81: 1408–1418.

Moss, Philip, and Chris Tilly. 2001. *Stories Employers Tell: Race, Skill, and Hiring in America*. New York: Russell Sage Foundation.

Myrdal, Gunnar. 1944. *An American Dilemma: The Negro Problem and Modern Democracy*. With the assistance of Richard Sterner and Arnold Rose. New York: Harper.

O'Connor, Alice. 2001. *Poverty Knowledge: Social Science, Social Policy, and the Poor in Twentieth-Century U.S. History*. Princeton: Princeton University Press.

Solow, Robert M. 1990. *The Labor Market as a Social Institution*. Oxford: Blackwell.

Stinchcombe, Arthur L. 1990. *Information and Organizations*. Berkeley and Los Angeles: University of California Press.

Tilly, Chris. 1996. *Half a Job: Bad and Good Part-Time Jobs in a Changing Labor Market*. Philadelphia: Temple University Press.

U.S. Bureau of Labor Statistics. Various years. "Employment and Earnings." http://www.stats.bls.gov.

U.S. Census Bureau. 2000. *Poverty in the United States: 1999*. Current Population Reports, P60-210. Washington, DC: GPO. http://www.census.gov/hhes/www/poverty00.html.

Wall Street Journal. 2001. "Who Made the Biggest Bucks." April 12.

Welch, Finis. 1999. "In Defense of Inequality." *American Economic Review* 89, no. 2: 1–17.

Wilson, William Julius. 1995. *When Work Disappears: The World of the New Urban Poor*. New York: Knopf.

Labor Movement

See Agricultural and Farm Labor Organizing; American Association for Labor Legislation; Fair Labor Standards Act (FLSA); Service and Domestic Workers; Trade/Industrial Unions; Wagner Act

Latino/as

Latinos are both the largest minority group in the United States and one of the poorest. Moreover, their poverty is very responsive to economic fluctuations, making them more vulnerable to changes in the economy. The reasons for their poverty are as varied as the groups that make up the Latino population, but among the major explanatory factors are Latino migration patterns, high concentrations of workers in low-wage occupations, low levels of education, poor English proficiency, discrimination, and limited access to training programs and good educational facilities.

In 2001, there were 35.3 million Latinos in the United States, or 12.6 percent of the U.S. population. Latinos trace their heritage to a diverse set of countries. In 2000, 66 percent were of Mexican heritage, 14.5 percent were Central and South Americans, 9 percent were Puerto Ricans, and 4 percent were Cubans (Therrien and Ramirez 2001). Of the Central Americans, some of the largest groups were Salvadorans, Nicaraguans, and Guatemalans; among South Americans, there were a substantial number of persons of Peruvian, Argentinean, and Colombian descent. Among those from the Caribbean, there were a large number of people of Dominican descent.

This diversity is reflected in the geographical distribution of Latino subgroups. Mexicans were more concentrated in the West and the South,

Puerto Ricans and Dominicans in the Northeast, Cubans in the South. Those of Central and South American descent were more geographically dispersed, with large numbers in the West, the South, and the Northeast. But the Latino population has also grown in less traditionally Latino areas such as Georgia, Iowa, North Carolina, and Utah. Some cities, such as Boston and Chicago, have grown for the first time in decades partly because of Latino population growth. As a result of this population growth and dispersal, the economic and social outcomes of Latinos are likely to play an increasingly important role not only in specific regions but throughout the nation.

The outcomes to date suggest that the situation of many Latino families is precarious. The long economic boom of the 1990s pushed Latino poverty rates from some of their highest levels, in 1993, to some of their lowest since the mid-1970s, by 2000. Yet even in 2000, 30 percent of Latino children were poor (U.S. Census Bureau 2001). The economic downturn of 2001–2003 increased unemployment rates among Latinos, worsening economic circumstances for families (U.S. Bureau of Labor Statistics 2003).

Low levels of education are one of the most important factors explaining poor economic outcomes among U.S. Latinos. In 2000, 27 percent of Latinos over age twenty-five had fewer than nine years of education, and 43 percent of them had not completed high school (Therrien and Ramirez 2001). Low levels of educational attainment are especially problematic because the financial returns of an education have been rising steadily in the United States; as a result, income gaps between those with low and high levels of education have widened. But neighborhood segregation relegates Latinos to communities with underperforming schools that fail to provide adequate training to Latino children. Furthermore, tracking into vocational preparation or away from higher education limits the educational experience of Latinos and, in some cases, predetermines their outcomes.

English proficiency plays a critical role in social mobility. Indeed, some researchers have found that English proficiency has a greater effect than immigration status on the economic progress of immigrants (Capps, Ku, and Fix 2002). A lack of English proficiency has social consequences as well as economic ones; it isolates individuals and groups, limits their access to resources, and constrains their rights. For example, training programs are rarely available in immigrants' languages, limiting Latino access to such programs.

Another set of factors affecting Latino economic well-being is their migration patterns and U.S. immigration policy. Many Latino immigrants move back and forth between the United States and their country of origin in search of economic opportunity. This migration has allowed transnational relations to flourish, but it may also limit an immigrant's degree of economic mobility in the United States. Furthermore, a persistent flow of new Latino immigrants may keep wages down for previous waves of immigrants. However, U.S. immigration policy plays a critical role in patterning migration and its effects. Latinos who are in the United States as temporary immigrants do not have the possibility of readjusting their status, and others work in the United States for many years without legal documents. Given their status, it is almost impossible for many Latinos to move up the economic ladder, and they are forced to compete with new immigrants for the limited jobs at the bottom of the job queue.

Last, Latinos have some of the highest workforce participation rates of all racial and ethnic groups, but many are concentrated in low-skill jobs in the agricultural, service, construction, craft, repair, and transportation sectors. These jobs tend to be unstable and to have relatively high levels of unemployment, limited benefits, and low wages. As a result, only African Americans have a lower proportion of full-time, full-year employment. In addition to the educational and language issues mentioned above, part of the explanation for Latino occupational segregation is a lack of networks and ethnic job queues, and part is discriminatory practices in the labor market, both of which limit Latinos' access to training programs, investment opportunities, and promotions.

Belinda I. Reyes

See also: African Americans; Americanization Movement; Day Labor; Immigrants and Immigration; Immigration Policy; Migrant Labor/Farm Labor; Puerto Rican Migration; Racial Segregation; Refugee Policy

References and Further Reading

Bean, Frank D., and Marta Tienda. 1987. *The Hispanic Population of the United States*. New York: Russell Sage Foundation.

Capps, Randy, Leighton Ku, and Michael Fix. 2002. "How Are Immigrants Faring after Welfare Reform? Preliminary Evidence from LA and NYC." Washington, DC: Urban Institute.

Suro, Roberto, and B. Lindsay Lowell. 2002. *New Lows from New Highs: Latino Economic Losses in the Current Recession*. Pew Hispanic Center.

Therrien, Melissa, and Roberto R. Ramirez. 2001. *The Hispanics Population in the United States: Population Characteristics*. Current Population Report P20-535. Washington, DC: U.S. Census Bureau.

U.S. Bureau of Labor Statistics. 2003. "Table A-3. Employment Status of Hispanic or Latino Population by Sex and Age." Washington, DC: U.S. Division of Labor Statistics.

U.S. Census Bureau. 2001. *Current Population Survey, March 2000*. Ethnic and Hispanic Statistics Branch, Population Division. Washington, DC. Internet release date: March 6, 2001.

Legal Aid/Legal Services

Legal aid and legal services provide civil legal services, including individual legal representation, legislative advocacy, impact litigation, and community organizing, at low or no cost for poor people.

Since the inception of legal aid in the late nineteenth century, legal work for the poor has undergone significant changes. From its origin until 1965, legal work on behalf of poor people was funded with private monies, and those organizations engaged in the provision of legal services to the indigent were referred to as "legal aid" organizations. A major shift occurred in 1965, when the government federalized the provision of civil legal services to indigent people. After 1965, the term "legal services" was used to refer broadly to both the governmental agency that administered legal services and the local programs that received federal money to provide free civil legal assistance to low-income communities. Legal services programs reached the height of their success in the 1960s, but since then, they have suffered a backlash resulting in decreased funding and substantive restrictions on the type of work legal services lawyers can perform. The current status of the legal services system reflects an ongoing disagreement regarding the way legal assistance is provided to those in our society least able to gain access to justice.

The Origin of Legal Aid Societies in the United States (1876–1900)

In 1876, the German Legal Aid Society opened in New York City and became what is believed to be the first legal aid society in the United States. Originally designed to protect immigrants of German descent, the society provided free legal assistance to individuals who could not afford a lawyer. Following the path of the German Legal Aid Society, during the last quarter of the nineteenth century, privately funded legal aid societies began to emerge around the country in response to local needs. Operating on a grassroots level, early legal aid societies were largely unaware of similar work being done in other parts of the country.

The Beginning of the National Legal Aid Movement (1900–1920)

With the turn of the century and the onset of World War I, traditional sources of private funding decreased. In response, legal aid societies explored alternatives to reliance on private contributions, either becoming departments in existing charitable organizations or seeking local government funding. With these new forms of funding, the number of legal aid societies slowly increased nationwide between 1900 and 1919.

Then, in 1921, Reginald Heber Smith published a book entitled *Justice and the Poor* that compiled information on legal aid activities and advocated for legal aid on a national level. The book brought national attention to the previously local legal aid movement and united its advocates. Publication of Smith's book also brought mainstream lawyers and legal organizations into a national debate regarding the provision of free legal services to the indigent.

The New Deal Era and Beyond (1920–1960)

Given this new national debate, in 1921, the American Bar Association (ABA) formed a special committee on legal aid. However, ABA support for legal aid remained minimal throughout the 1930s, in part because of a concern that free legal services would take away increasingly scarce business from private practitioners.

In 1949, England passed a statute known as the British Legal Aid and Advice Scheme that created a legal aid system funded by the government. Passage of this act raised concern that the sentiment for government-funded legal services might spread from England to the United States. Fearing the potential for a socialist system of legal services in the United States, the ABA stepped up support for legal aid societies in the 1950s. This initial concern over legal aid societies funded by private charitable dollars versus state-sponsored provision of legal services set the stage for the ongoing struggle over the scope and conditions of free legal services to the indigent.

The War on Poverty Years: From Legal Aid to Legal Services (1960–1970)

From its inception in 1876 through the 1960s, legal aid was viewed as a mere private charity designed to placate the masses, to avert potential unrest, and, for the ABA, to increase the prestige of the bar. However, the Great Depression had raised awareness of the systemic causes and costs of economic inequality. During the 1960s, advocates began to argue that in the fight against inequality, poor people needed access to legal services.

Within this context, in the early 1960s, the Ford Foundation funded demonstration projects called "Gray Areas projects." Conceived as a strategic and innovative way to redress systemic inequality, Gray Areas projects were set up in New Haven, New York City, and Washington, D.C. The projects situated money in specific low-income neighborhoods and created decentralized service centers that provided a range of assistance, including consumer, medical, educational, and legal services. The Gray Areas projects played a crucial role in influencing the creation of a federal legal services program and foreshadowed the recurring battles over funding, politics, and independence of the legal aid/legal services movement.

Particularly influential was the New Haven Gray Areas project, which was forced to suspend operations only seven weeks after opening because of its involvement in a controversial case. After suspension of operations, Jean Cahn, one of the New Haven staff attorneys, and her husband, Edgar Cahn, wrote a law review article advocating federal government funding to establish neighborhood legal services. As the law review article was being written, President Lyndon B. Johnson announced the War on Poverty and formed the Office of Economic Opportunity (OEO), a new federal agency responsible for operating and overseeing the antipoverty programs.

Between 1964 and 1965, as federalization of

legal services became part of the national consciousness, the ABA debated whether or not to endorse federally funded legal services. After vigorous internal disagreement, in February 1965, under the leadership of then ABA president Lewis Powell, later to become a U.S. Supreme Court justice, the ABA adopted a resolution endorsing federal legal services. In 1965, the OEO initiated the Legal Services Programs, which administered federal money to local legal services programs nationwide. Thereafter, federal government funding for indigent civil legal assistance significantly increased, so that by 1967, there were approximately 300 legal services organizations receiving government grants totaling more than $40 million through the OEO Legal Services Program (Johnson 1974, 99).

Quickly utilizing these new resources, between 1967 and 1972, legal services attorneys focused on law reform work designed to change the systems that affected the lives of poor people. To support law reform work, the Legal Services Program created and funded "backup centers" and training programs. The backup centers, which were frequently housed at major law schools, and the educational programs were designed to support and assist in litigation of large cases that sought systemic changes. The law reform efforts proved so successful that between 1967 and 1972, the Supreme Court heard 219 cases filed by legal services attorneys involving the rights of the poor. Of these, 136 were decided by the Court and 73 resulted in favorable decisions (Huber 1976, 761). Many of these cases, which represented enormous substantive victories for poor people, have endured and remain landmark decisions (Redlich 1992, 753–754). Such success, however, had its costs, for conservative elites reacted negatively to the legal gains made on behalf of poor people. In response to these gains, some in Congress attempted in the late 1960s and early 1970s to restrict the program's activities.

The Debate over Independence (1970–1980)

Political pressure on the legal services program increased in the early 1970s when President Richard M. Nixon chose a staunch critic of the War on Poverty and legal services to head the OEO. The vulnerability of the organization to a backlash raised questions concerning its independence, and in 1971, the ABA and the President's Advisory Council on Executive Organization recommended the creation of a separate corporation to disperse legal services monies. Thus began a three-year battle over the independence of the legal services program.

Legislation introduced in Congress in 1971 sought the creation of a national Legal Services Corporation (LSC), which would make the legal services program independent of the executive branch of government. But President Nixon opposed the bill, due mainly to the decrease in executive control and oversight it represented. On the eve of his resignation in July 1974, President Nixon signed a compromise bill that created an independent LSC but defunded the backup centers and imposed minimal restrictions on the scope of work permitted by legal services lawyers. Over the next five years, funding for the LSC steadily increased.

Change in Political Climate: Retreat and Restructuring (1980–Present)

Governmental support for legal services abruptly changed in 1980 with the election of Ronald Reagan as president. In his 1982 budget, President Reagan called for the complete elimination of the LSC. The legal services board, law schools, the ABA, and judges expressed strong opposition, however, leading the president to suggest instead a block grant system of local legal aid provided by private attorneys and those willing to perform pro bono legal services. When he did not win approval for this proposal, President Reagan instead decreased funding,

Gideon v. Wainwright, *372 U.S. 335 (1963)*

Mr. Justice Black delivered the opinion of the Court.

Petitioner was charged in a Florida state court with having broken and entered a poolroom with intent to commit a misdemeanor. This offense is a felony under [372 U.S. 337] Florida law. Appearing in court without funds and without a lawyer, petitioner asked the court to appoint counsel for him, whereupon the following colloquy took place:

> The Court: Mr. Gideon, I am sorry, but I cannot appoint Counsel to represent you in this case. Under the laws of the State of Florida, the only time the Court can appoint Counsel to represent a Defendant is when that person is charged with a capital offense. I am sorry, but I will have to deny your request to appoint Counsel to defend you in this case.
>
> The Defendant: The United States Supreme Court says I am entitled to be represented by Counsel.

Put to trial before a jury, Gideon conducted his defense about as well as could be expected from a layman. He made an opening statement to the jury, cross-examined the State's witnesses, presented witnesses in his own defense, declined to testify himself, and made a short argument "emphasizing his innocence to the charge contained in the Information filed in this case." The jury returned a verdict of guilty, and petitioner was sentenced to serve five years in the state prison. Later, petitioner filed in the Florida Supreme Court this habeas corpus petition attacking his conviction and sentence on the ground that the trial court's refusal to appoint counsel for him denied him rights "guaranteed by the Constitution and the Bill of Rights by the United States Government." . . .

II

. . . We accept *Betts v. Brady*'s assumption, based as it was on our prior cases, that a provision of the Bill of Rights which is "fundamental and essential to a fair trial" is made obligatory upon the States by the Fourteenth Amendment. We think the Court in *Betts* was wrong, however, in concluding that the Sixth Amendment's guarantee of counsel is not one of these fundamental rights. . . .

The fact is that, in deciding as it did—that "appointment of counsel is not a fundamental right, [372 U.S. 344] essential to a fair trial"—the Court in *Betts v. Brady* made an abrupt break with its own well considered precedents. In returning to these old precedents, sounder, we believe, than the new, we but restore constitutional principles established to achieve a fair system of justice. Not only these precedents, but also reason and reflection, require us to recognize that, in our adversary system of criminal justice, any person haled into court, who is too poor to hire a lawyer, cannot be assured a fair trial unless counsel is provided for him. . . . The right of one charged with crime to counsel may not be deemed fundamental and essential to fair trials in some countries, but it is in ours. From the very beginning, our state and national constitutions and laws have laid great emphasis on procedural and substantive safeguards designed to assure fair trials before impartial tribunals in which every defendant stands equal before the law. This noble ideal cannot be realized if the poor man charged with crime has to face his accusers without a lawyer to assist him. . . .

Reversed.

increased restrictions, and appointed a hostile LSC board to oversee the organization.

This trend of antagonism toward legal services continued in the 1990s. In 1992, there was renewed congressional debate concerning the future of legal services. Although some advocated its elimination, others sought to severely restrict the work of legal services. Because Democrats still maintained some control in Congress, the 1992 bill to eliminate legal services was unsuccessful. However, in 1994, as Republicans gained control of both the House and the Senate for the first time in forty years, there were renewed calls for the elimination of legal services. In 1996, as Congress was debating the elimination of the LSC, legal services advocates determined that in order to maintain some funding they needed to concede and negotiate on the issue of restrictions. Thus, after debate, Congress passed and President Bill Clinton signed the Omnibus Consolidated Rescissions and Appropriations Act of 1996 (OCRAA), which decreased funding to legal services by 30 percent and imposed the most significant restrictions on the program to date.

The OCRAA restrictions prohibit government-funded legal services organizations from advocating or providing representation before legislative bodies and administrative rule-making proceedings, from litigating class-action lawsuits, from obtaining attorneys' fees, from representing certain categories of immigrants, from representing prisoners in civil litigation, and from representing people in certain claims, including abortion-related litigation, redistricting cases, and public housing cases where clients face eviction because of alleged drug-related crimes. In addition to these specific restrictions, legal services organizations are prohibited from using non-LSC funds to undertake activities for which LSC money is restricted. This so-called entity restriction and dramatically decreased funding forced legal services programs to change their structure. In larger cities, legal services providers split into two separate organizations, one performing unrestricted work with LSC money and the other utilizing the non-LSC money to engage in otherwise restricted work. It is within this context that legal services providers continue the traditions of providing invaluable legal assistance to those who would otherwise be unable to have access to the courts.

Christine N. Cimini

See also: Aid to Families with Dependent Children (ADC/AFDC); Community Organizing; Poverty Law; War on Poverty

References and Further Reading

Bellow, Gary. 1980. "Legal Aid in the United States." *Clearinghouse Review* 14: 337–345.

Brownell, Emery A. 1971. *Legal Aid in the United States*. Westport, CT: Greenwood Press.

Cahn, Jean, and Edgar Cahn. 1964. "The War on Poverty: A Civilian Perspective." *Yale Law Journal* 73: 1317–1352.

Huber, Stephen K. 1976. "Thou Shalt Not Ration Justice: A History and Bibliography of Legal Aid in America." *George Washington Law Review* 44: 754–774.

Johnson, Earl. 1974. *Justice and Reform*. New York: Russell Sage Foundation.

Merkel, Philip L. 1990. "At the Crossroads of Reform: The First Fifty Years of American Legal Aid, 1876–1926." *Houston Law Review* 27: 1–44.

Redlich, Allen. 1992. "Who Will Litigate Constitutional Issues for the Poor?" *Hastings Constitutional Law Quarterly* 19: 745–782.

Smith, Reginald Heber. 1921. *Justice and the Poor*. Boston: Merrymount Press.

Let Us Now Praise Famous Men, *James Agee and Walker Evans*

In 1936, author James Agee and photographer Walker Evans received an assignment from *Fortune* magazine to cover, both in words and in pictures, the plight of southern white tenant farmers (or sharecroppers). The end result was not—as originally intended—an article for the increasingly conservative *Fortune* magazine but a profoundly angry, self-conscious, and poetic book called *Let Us Now Praise Famous Men*, which was released in August 1939 to little fanfare and even less commercial success. By then, the Great Depression was over, and the book's power was lost on a nation whose focus had shifted to an impending war. Out of print only a few years after publication, the book was relegated to the obscure annals of journalistic history until its revival in the 1960s. Now considered a classic work of literary journalism, *Let Us Now Praise Famous Men* stands as a testament to the pain and suffering endured by impoverished sharecroppers during the Great Depression.

Agee and Evans drove to rural Alabama unsure of how to find a family of white tenant farmers who could be considered typical and who would also open their doors to their journalistic intrusions. But they were eventually able to win the trust of three families who accepted them and their project wholeheartedly. For two weeks, the journalists visited their homes to observe and take copious notes and pictures.

Although others before them wrote arguably exploitative exposés of rural poverty, Agee and Evans never failed to humanize their subjects. The prose and pictures never wavered from the truth, but the book managed to avoid privileged condescension and to portray the three tenant families with dignity.

The book is also an eclectic oddity, a complex and multilayered work of art containing many things seemingly unrelated to the coverage of Depression-era sharecroppers, including poems, confessional reveries, and lengthy sermons on the right way to listen to Beethoven. These oddities notwithstanding, *Let Us Now Praise Famous Men*, a title dripping with bitter irony, is at once a work of journalism simmering with outrage at the savage injustices heaped upon the American sharecropper, a confessional response to the pain and suffering one witnesses but is powerless to abate, and an unrelenting and truthful account of what these families had to withstand.

The abject living conditions of tenant farmers during the Great Depression attracted the attention not only of socially conscious journalists like Agee and Evans but also of policymakers, including President Franklin D. Roosevelt's administration. FDR appointed a Committee on Farm Tenancy to investigate this segment of the farming population, and the committee's report, released in February 1937, revealed a problem both widespread and stark: One half of the farmers in the South, a third in the North, and a quarter in the West were sharecroppers, most of whom endured the pain and insult of wretched poverty. The committee's eye-opening report led to the passage of the Bankhead-Jones Farm Tenant Act, which included provisions intended to help tenants become self-sufficient landowners.

Robert J. Lacey

See also: Picturing Poverty (I); Poor Whites; *Report on Economic Conditions of the South;* Rural Poverty; Sharecropping

References and Further Reading

Agee, James, and Walker Evans. [1939] 1988. Introduction by John Hersey, 1988. *Let Us Now Praise Famous Men*. Boston: Houghton Mifflin.

Maharidge, Dale, Michael Williamson, and Carl Mydans. 1989. *And Their Children after Them: The Legacy of* Let Us Now Praise Famous Men, *James Agee, Walker Evans, and the Rise and Fall of Cotton in the South*. New York: Pantheon Books.

Lewis, Oscar

See The Children of Sanchez; Poverty Research

Liberalism

A strongly contested political ideology in the United States, liberalism was the driving force behind the great expansion of the welfare state during the middle decades of the twentieth century. Despite its recent association with social welfare, however, the meaning of "liberalism" remains frustratingly hard to pin down, earning from political theorists and actors alike such descriptions as "diffuse," "protean," "divided," and "amorphous." In addition, when liberalism began and the extent to which it remains hegemonic in the United States are a matter of some debate. Although political elites formally rejected it as an ideology in the late twentieth century and scholars question its coherence as a belief system, its effects are everywhere to be seen. Liberalism is best characterized as a shifting set of values and institutional arrangements concerning the individual's relationship to society, to the economy, and to the state. What has remained constant in American liberalism, at least rhetorically, is the importance placed on the autonomy of equal individual human beings and, for most of its history, a commitment to reform. What has changed are the conceptions of the individual and of the barriers to the realization of the individual's autonomy.

One of the biggest challenges for understanding American liberalism is locating a coherent liberal tradition. As a political label, the term "liberal" appeared in the United States during the late nineteenth century, when it referred to a small political party called the Liberal Republicans (formed in 1872). The widespread use of "liberal" and "liberalism" came only with the emergence of an intellectual and political orientation self-defined as "liberal" during the New Deal in the 1930s. This self-acknowledged liberalism has since become known as "new liberalism" or "welfare state liberalism"—the phrase that best captures the way most Americans today think of liberalism.

Although liberalism was rarely used as a political label for much of American history, one can locate its antecedents in seventeenth-century British political thought and in the philosophy and institutional design of the early American republic. John Locke was the first to articulate a thoroughgoing liberal political theory. In his *Two Treatises of Government*, written primarily as a critique of monarchy, Locke asserted that men were born free, equal, and rational and that they therefore were capable of ruling themselves, politically and otherwise. From these assumptions followed Locke's idea of the contractual basis of political society: Men agree to give up their natural freedom under natural law in exchange for civil freedom under civil law, made and enforced by a government of their peers. This political structure was supposed to limit political arbitrariness and government abuse through the instruments of the written law, representative institutions like parliament, and institutional mechanisms such as the separation of powers. Ultimately, political power was checked by a right of revolution that could be invoked against a government that failed to protect people's God-given rights to life, liberty, and property.

The role of property in Locke's theory has sometimes been taken as evidence that Locke was primarily interested in securing the conditions for commercial capitalism rather than in promoting political liberty as such. Locke did speak of individuals as having an ownership right over both their own bodies and their labor (leading some to describe Locke's system as one of "possessive individualism"). But Locke's conception of property suggested a far broader domain of human entitlements: Human beings had, by the dictates of natural law, a moral right to their own life, freedom, and material possessions. If anything, property stood for the notion of self-determination or sovereignty. Locke's ideas about natural rights, the consent of the governed, and the immorality of arbitrary political power caught the imagination of American revolutionaries, who adopted an essentially Lockean vocabulary in their Declaration of Independence from the British. So too did the idea that individual autonomy stemmed from control over one's own productive property.

The second great plank of the Anglo-American liberal tradition is the idea that individual freedom depends upon a free-market economy. Inspired by Adam Smith's eighteenth-century political economy, this notion stressed the need for commercial dealings to be unfettered either by private monopolies or by too much government interference. A final element was religious toleration. These three doctrines of political, economic, and religious freedom came together in England to constitute classical liberalism, an ideology and political program that helped shape British politics for much of the nineteenth century. Hence, at the core of classical liberalism lay the protection of the rights and liberties of the autonomous individual and an endorsement of markets and of a government constrained by the rule of law.

Although sharing many of its values, the United States did not adopt British-style classical liberalism as an explicit political program; several things militated against this development. Republican ideals dating back to the Revolution stressed the virtues of citizenship, at times holding that the market-based economy should be placed in the service of political participation rather than being an end in itself. In addition, the slaveholding South required forms of political and economic coercion that were incongruous with the libertarian ethos of classical liberalism. Classical liberalism as such existed in the United States as a political force only for a brief moment during the Gilded Age of the 1870s and 1880s.

Facing large changes in the structure of American society and economy—particularly the emergence of large corporations and of social movements of laborites, populists, women, and African Americans demanding greater political inclusion and a more equitable distribution of social wealth—intellectuals and politicians adopted an extreme version of laissez-faire economics known as Social Darwinism. This creed held that poor, struggling individuals and prosperous corporations alike ought to be left alone to compete for survival. Corporations had "rights," the courts determined, just as did individuals, giving rise in the last quarter of the nineteenth century to a combination of a natural-rights jurisprudence and an antistatist politics. Social Darwinism quickly faded as a political ideal (though it persisted in certain intellectual circles and in the courts), as social scientists, reformers, and politicians, including Socialists, rejected the harsh individualism of laissez-faire. Foreshadowing aspects of twentieth-century liberalism, they praised the "coordinating power" of "state action" and railed against the arbitrary power of corporate monopolies.

Critics of laissez-faire recognized that the agents of integration and centralization, most importantly corporations, had displaced the property-owning sovereign individual as the locus of power in modern life. The newly interdependent individual required help from the government and from a robust civil society to maintain a semblance of autonomy. Social forces, not nature, God, or reason, determined who individuals were and their fate in life. Managing the complexity of modern life, moreover, required scientific and social scientific expertise. Between 1880 and 1920, then, Progressive reformers, according to the historian James Kloppenberg, "turned the old liberalism into a new liberalism, a moral and political argument for the welfare state based on a conception of the individual as a social being whose values are shaped by personal choices and cultural conditions" (Kloppenberg 1986, 299). The trope of an old liberalism, grounded in individual natural rights, in government constrained by law, and in the self-possessed individual, turned new is a familiar one. The goal of individual autonomy is probably the theme most commonly stressed by those who wish to link the two liberalisms. However, the fact that so much of the new liberalism, including its conception of the individual, is predicated on a rejection of the old complicates efforts to connect the two. Not surprisingly, scholars continue to debate the value of even positing a single liberal tradition.

The problem of continuity is exemplified by the politics of the New Deal, a self-avowedly liberal movement, which both drew on and transcended Progressivism. The conditions were set for a revaluation of the entire social order. Liberalism answered the call with "a theory of life," in philosopher John Dewey's words (Dewey [1935] 2000, 62). The label "liberal," which President Franklin D. Roosevelt gave to his New Deal, signified that the crisis of the Great Depression required a new vision of the role of government in American life. It indicated too a realism, not always present among Progressives, about the triumph of industrial capitalism over small-scale property ownership. To meet the crisis conditions, the new liberalism promoted unprecedented degrees of intervention in the economy by the federal government, including extra-constitutional emergency measures, the redistribution of wealth and resources, and expert management to direct these reforms. Roosevelt's measures were unusually popular with voters, who four times returned him to office. Most believed that New Deal liberalism would promote the good of society as a whole.

It was in the area of economic relations that New Deal liberalism made its biggest mark, criticizing the very market economy, albeit in radically changed form, that classical liberalism had once celebrated. The various cooperative and interventionist measures undertaken by the New Deal necessarily undermined economic autonomy but would stop short of outright socialist control of the economy. For example, the New Deal experimented with a form of corporatism in which tripartite bodies of business, labor, and government set wage rates and production levels. The New Deal also, via public works programs, provided what the capitalist market was no longer able to in sufficient numbers: jobs. Finally, liberalism addressed the appropriate means for reducing economic inequities, presenting itself as an alternative to communism and fascism. Of the two, often lumped together as "totalitarianism," communism proved to be the bigger challenge in the 1930s precisely because it was still attractive to many American reformers as a more egalitarian alternative to liberalism, and one that appeared to provide more economic security. Liberalism needed to rebut the idea that a violent revolution was the only way to achieve radical reform. Intellectuals responded by constructing an American "liberal tradition" to justify and limit potential anxiety over dramatic departures from existing institutional arrangements that the New Deal entailed.

Although continuing to view individuals as products of social forces, the new liberals simultaneously worried, unlike their Progressive forebears, about threats to individual autonomy by large organizations, whether public or private. Concern about overcentralization was one reason that the New Deal achieved only limited structural change, despite its significant and lasting reforms. Chief among these were the institutionalization of collective bargaining and programs such as Social Security and unemployment compensation. Although important, these changes aimed at providing a minimum standard of living for many Americans, not at fundamentally reworking capitalist institutions. An equally significant obstacle was the structure of American politics itself: the veto power that white southern Democrats held over congressional legislation. Concerned that far-reaching reform would undermine their interests, southern Democrats demanded that sharecropping and domestic labor, work largely performed by African Americans, be exempted from government programs. Equal opportunity and entitlements for Blacks, women, and other minorities would have to wait.

For almost two decades following World War II, political liberalism's critical edge was all but lost. Two conditions set the stage for a tamer liberalism: unprecedented prosperity and an ideologically charged Cold War. In the event, a "consensus" of sorts emerged among political elites that shunned all forms of collectivism, supported a modestly redistributive welfare state in which the government managed the now-prosperous economy indirectly through Keynesian policy, barred the most egregious civil rights violations, and rallied behind an extensive national security state, promoted as necessary to protect the freedom of Americans. Yet postwar liberalism was not simply a product of the Cold War. A new interest in individual rights and liberties, for example, was signaled initially by Roosevelt's call for a "second bill of rights" in 1944, in which he emphasized economic and social rights—to a living wage, health care, education, and protection from economic instability. An even bigger inspiration, and more indicative of the particular cast that postwar rights would take, was the UN Universal Declaration of Human Rights of 1948. Above all, the horrors of Nazi Germany fueled the quest for rights in the postwar period. Legal theorists and philosophers such as John Rawls sought an objective but nonmetaphysical basis for morality, while deeming insufficient the moral relativism implicit in the pragmatic ethics of Progressivism and the New Deal. New theories advanced the idea that morality was implicit in sound judgment and reasonable rules, promulgated by average human beings. Postwar rights discourse emanated from an essentially humanistic impulse. Rights were grounded not in God or in nature but in the concept of humanity itself: They were *human* rights.

The advocacy of rights was mainly an attempt to remedy flaws in the theory and practice of New Deal liberalism, principally by making the welfare state more egalitarian. This expansion of the welfare state characterized the next great moment of reform in the mid-1960s: President Lyndon B. Johnson's Great Society initiative, in which poor people and minorities were granted new rights and access to public resources through civil rights legislation and a War on Poverty that was fought through new programs such as Community Action, Legal Services, and Medicaid. Johnson's initiatives were greatly inspired by social movements: the civil rights movement of the 1950s and later feminism and the welfare rights movement. The social movements were composed of groups left out of the New Deal who took turns claiming rights and liberties already enjoyed by other Americans. For women, people of color, and other excluded groups, rights represented not an alternative to justice and equality but an expression of them—indeed, a precondition for meaningful political participation and autonomy. Other assertions of rights, such as rights to privacy and to protection from police, were responses to abuses of state power growing out of McCarthyism and to fears of totalitarian government.

These campaigns for individual rights, civil and political equality, and real economic opportunity had several consequences beyond their immediate goals. One was the exposure of a tension between rights and democracy; another was the legalizing of liberalism. Efforts to secure individual and, at times, group rights ran up against majoritarian democracy. Some such efforts were defeated in Congress; others were thwarted on the state and local levels. On the one hand, groups seeking greater inclusion and opportunities were already disenfranchised, either literally because they did not have the vote (such as African Americans in the South) or effectively because they did not have enough power to influence the political process. Pressuring the electoral system through mass action was one strategy for overcoming these difficulties. Another was to use the judicial system, which, although formally democratic, holds no pretense of being representative and is relatively insulated from deliberative democracy. Seeking justice from the courts when the legislatures had failed to act proved a controversial strategy, provoking hostility not just from those who resented the courts as havens for minorities but also from legal and political elites who worried, echoing the Progressives and the New Dealers, that "activist" courts were undermining democracy.

Thus began the sense, proffered first by liberals themselves, that liberalism was in crisis. Meanwhile, other forces were lining up to challenge what by the 1960s was perceived as a liberal hegemony in American politics and insti-

President Lyndon B. Johnson, Graduation Speech, University of Michigan, Ann Arbor, May 22, 1964

In the famous speech excerpted below, President Lyndon B. Johnson laid out a vision of a "Great Society," coining a phrase that would subsequently be associated with his expansive liberalism and challenging a new generation of college graduates to make it a reality.

. . . For a century we labored to settle and to subdue a continent. For half a century we called upon unbounded invention and untiring industry to create an order of plenty for all of our people.

The challenge of the next half century is whether we have the wisdom to use that wealth to enrich and elevate our national life, and to advance the quality of our American civilization.

Your imagination, your initiative, and your indignation will determine whether we build a society where progress is the servant of our needs, or a society where old values and new visions are buried under unbridled growth. For in your time we have the opportunity to move not only toward the rich society and the powerful society, but upward to the Great Society.

The Great Society rests on abundance and liberty for all. It demands an end to poverty and racial injustice, to which we are totally committed in our time. But that is just the beginning.

The Great Society is a place where every child can find knowledge to enrich his mind and to enlarge his talents. It is a place where leisure is a welcome chance to build and reflect, not a feared cause of boredom and restlessness. It is a place where the city of man serves not only the needs of the body and the demands of commerce but the desire for beauty and the hunger for community.

It is a place where man can renew contact with nature. It is a place which honors creation for its own sake and for what it adds to the understanding of the race. It is a place where men are more concerned with the quality of their goals than the quantity of their goods.

But most of all, the Great Society is not a safe harbor, a resting place, a final objective, a finished work. It is a challenge constantly renewed, beckoning us toward a destiny where the meaning of our lives matches the marvelous products of our labor. . . .

. . . For better or for worse, your generation has been appointed by history to deal with those problems and to lead America toward a new age. You have the chance never before afforded to any people in any age. You can help build a society where the demands of morality, and the needs of the spirit, can be realized in the life of the Nation.

So, will you join in the battle to give every citizen the full equality which God enjoins and the law requires, whatever his belief, or race, or the color of his skin?

Will you join in the battle to give every citizen an escape from the crushing weight of poverty?

Will you join in the battle to make it possible for all nations to live in enduring peace—as neighbors and not as mortal enemies?

Will you join in the battle to build the Great Society, to prove that our material progress is only the foundation on which we will build a richer life of mind and spirit?

There are those timid souls who say this battle cannot be won; that we are condemned to a soulless wealth. I do not agree. We have the power to shape the civilization that we want. But we need your will, your labor, your hearts, if we are to build that kind of society.

Those who came to this land sought to build more than just a new country. They sought a new world. So I have come here today to your campus to say that you can make their vision our reality. So let us from this moment begin our work so that in the future men will look back and say: It was then, after a long and weary way, that man turned the exploits of his genius to the full enrichment of his life.

tutions. Radical social movements in the 1960s, such as the New Left, blamed liberals and liberalism for a host of evils, among them the "liberal state," Vietnam, and quiescent labor unions. The election of Ronald Reagan in 1980 cemented the perception that liberalism had exhausted itself.

A conservative, "New Right" reaction to welfare state liberalism had begun much earlier, in response to the civil rights legislation and court victories of the 1960s. The presidential campaign of Barry Goldwater in 1964 and Richard M. Nixon's election in 1968 were both indicative of this turn, though Nixon was hardly a conservative on all matters. He greatly expanded the regulatory state, forming such agencies as the Environmental Protection Agency and the Occupational Safety and Health Administration. Nor was he afraid to intervene directly in the economy with such mechanisms as price controls. Nixon did adopt much of the cultural rhetoric of 1960s antiliberalism. In this view, government was seen as favoring some groups—minorities and the poor—over others in a zero-sum game and as overly responsive to the social movements and interest groups seeking greater equality. By the 1980s, antiliberalism had become for many a vague, if deeply felt, antipathy toward "big government," and Reagan took as his mandate the dismantling of much of the welfare state. When the Democratic Party finally returned to power in the 1990s, even it had disowned the liberal label and many of the programs of the regulatory welfare state. These self-described "New Democrats" took their cue in part from intellectuals formerly sympathetic to liberalism who had begun to criticize it under the banner of "communitarianism." The New Democrats felt that liberalism was too focused on absolute rights, leaving little room for political negotiation and moral suasion, and too enamored with centralized, command-and-control government. Nevertheless, liberalism remains a vibrant political philosophy in a constant process of adaptation to new challenges of cultural and ethnic diversity and economic inequality.

Anne Kornhauser

See also: Capitalism; Civil Rights Movement; New Right; Republicanism; Social Darwinism; War on Poverty; Welfare Capitalism; Welfare State

References and Further Reading

Brinkley, Alan. 1995. *The End of Reform: The New Deal in Recession and War*. New York: Knopf.

———. 2000. *Liberalism and Its Discontents*. Cambridge, MA: Harvard University Press.

Dewey, John. [1935] 2000. *Liberalism and Social Action*. Amherst, NY: Prometheus Books.

Gerstle, Gary. 1994. "The Protean Character of American Liberalism." *The American Historical Review* 99, no. 4: 1043–1073.

Kloppenberg, James T. 1986. *Uncertain Victory: Social Democracy and Progressivism in European and American Thought, 1870–1920*. New York: Oxford University Press.

———. 1998. *The Virtues of Liberalism*. New York: Oxford University Press.

Lowi, Theodore J. 1995. *The End of the Republican Era*. Norman: University of Oklahoma Press.

Rawls, John. 1971. *A Theory of Justice*. Cambridge, MA: Harvard University Press.

Ross, Dorothy. 1984. "Liberalism." In *Encyclopedia of American Political History: Studies of the Principal Movements and Ideas*, ed. Jack P. Greene, vol. 2, 750–763. New York: Scribner's.

Living-Wage Campaigns

Campaigns for a "living wage," which became a notable feature of state and local progressive politics during the 1990s, have revived much of the language and ideology first adopted by the working-class movement in the late nineteenth century. In the years after the Civil War, working-class leaders and social reformers largely abandoned their opposition to the wage system itself—or "wage slavery"—and instead embraced the idea that the quest for a "living wage" was itself a form of liberation. Unionists sought a wage high enough to allow an average-sized family to enjoy physical and mental health as well as dignity. Of course, many of these same

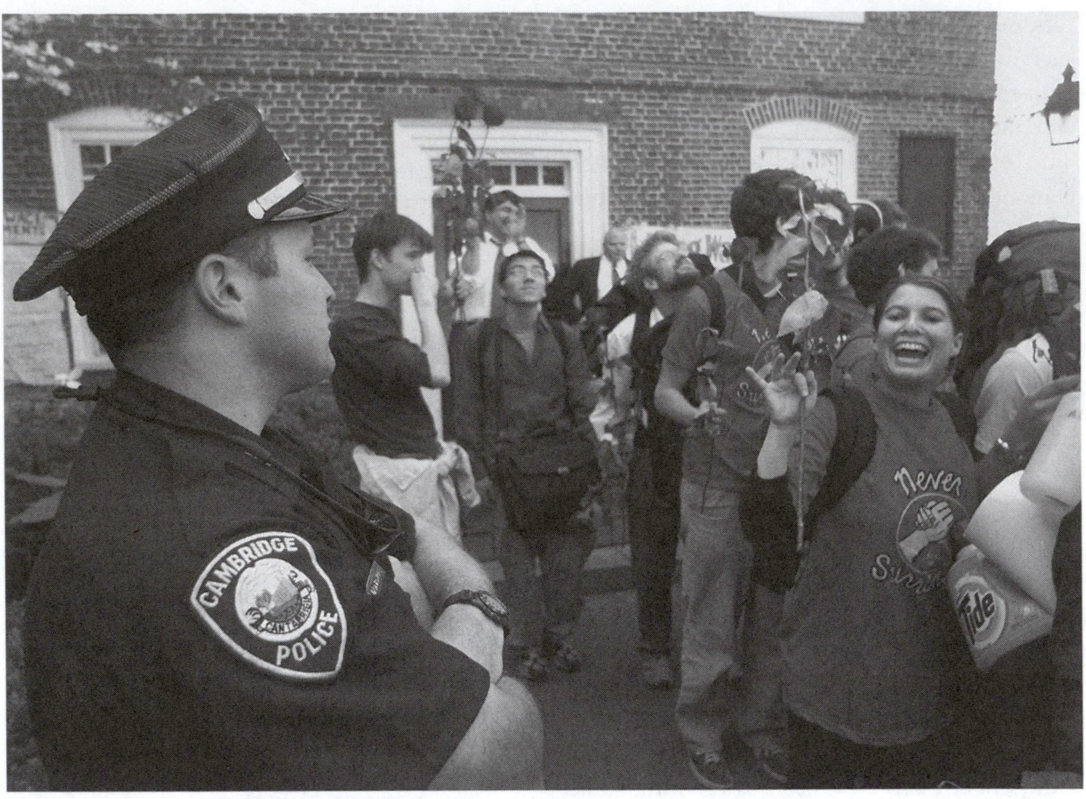

Cambridge, Massachusetts, police officer Steve Donahue (L) watches as Harvard University students end their 21-day sit-in and leave the university's Massachusetts Hall administration building, May 8, 2001. The demonstrators, who were demanding that Harvard pay a "living wage" of at least $10.25 an hour to its lowest-paid employees, gave up occupying the building after Harvard met several of their demands. (Reuters NewMedia/ Corbis)

laborite reformers held a highly radicalized and patriarchal understanding of the "living wage." Monsignor John Ryan's *Living Wage: Its Ethical and Economic Aspects*, an influential Progressive-Era tract, assumed that the family breadwinner was a male, and socialists like Jack London and unionists like Samuel Gompers believed that the "American standard" of living excluded Asian, African American, and Latino workers.

During the New Deal years and afterward, many reformers believed that something approaching a "living wage" had been achieved for the nation's working population. Mass unionization raised the living standards of millions of workers, including many in nonunion firms and institutions whose wage standards tracked collective bargaining in auto, steel, and other high-wage, well-organized industries. The federal minimum-wage law, first enacted in 1938, was too low and too narrow in its coverage to constitute a "living wage," but by 1968, it had been raised high enough to provide the income necessary to lift out of poverty a three-person family with one full-time breadwinner. Meanwhile, "prevailing-wage" statutes like the 1931 Bacon-Davis law, which covered construction workers on federally funded projects, ensured that most government entities would pay the prevailing wage, that is, the union wage, to contract construction workers.

By the 1990s, this system was in crisis. Trade union weakness deprived organized labor of the power to set regional or industry-wide wage standards, the minimum wage had lost 30 percent of its value since the late 1960s, and many government entities contracted out an increasing proportion of their work to low-wage, nonunion service firms. Indeed, the modern living-wage movement began in 1994 when clergy running food pantries in Baltimore found that a large proportion of those coming for aid held a regular job. Many worked full-time in privatized city jobs that had once been decently paid.

The Baltimore living-wage campaign was led by the Industrial Areas Foundation (IAF) and the American Federation of State, County, and Municipal Employees, in a coalition of community members, clergy, and unions that would become characteristic of most of the ninety city and county living-wage campaigns that followed during the next decade. The city of Baltimore announced that it could not require all employers to pay higher wages but that it could extend its prevailing wage law from construction to include private-sector firms holding service contracts with the city (covering janitors, bus drivers, security guards, and so on). Over four years, the plan raised wages from the minimum wage, then $4.35 an hour, to a level that enabled a family of four to meet the federal poverty line ($7.70 an hour in 1999).

The movement soon went nationwide. Given the stalemate in social policy at the national level and in most states, the fight for municipal living-wage ordinances proved a favorable terrain for progressive groups such as the Service Employees International Union, the Hotel Employees and Restaurant Employees Union (HERE), the IAF, and other local antipoverty groups. During the 1990s, a variety of ordinances were passed in many older industrial cities, including Boston, Duluth, Milwaukee, and New Haven, as well as in the high-cost-of-living cities of coastal California and the Pacific Northwest. The movement also became active on many college campuses, where living-wage advocates saw the university as the "government" entity that contracted out food, maintenance, parking, and security services. Few ordinances mandated higher wages for all workers in a city, but 85 percent covered government service contractors and about 40 percent called for higher wages for workers in firms that received economic assistance from a city or county. In Santa Monica, California, for example, where much beachfront infrastructure directly benefited local hotels, the living-wage ordinance applied to all large employers in the city's downtown tourist zone.

By the early twenty-first century, living-wage ordinances covered fewer than 50,000 workers, a minuscule proportion of the nation's huge poverty-level workforce. But these living-wage campaigns were nevertheless highly significant for three important reasons. First, they helped generate a new set of progressive coalitions at the state and local levels. The unions favored living-wage ordinances to forestall outsourcing and low-wage competition from nonunion firms, but they could not win without the community, religious, and economic development groups that often provided the key leaders of local living-wage movements. In the mid-twentieth century, these coalition partners had often been antagonistic, but now the labor movement was reinventing itself with their aid.

Second, the living-wage campaigns have had a substantial impact on local economic redevelopment efforts, focusing attention not only on the volume of jobs created by state and local incentives but on the quality of the jobs. Since tax incentives, rezonings, and outright subsidies have become so integral to urban redevelopment, the corporatist quid pro quo has increasingly involved higher-paying jobs.

And finally, the living-wage campaigns have been ideologically potent vehicles for the delegitimization of the laissez-faire economics that has returned to political ascendancy since the presidency of Ronald Reagan and for the valorization of the social and economic regulations necessary to the creation of a new generation of high-wage jobs. Living-wage ordinances have been bitterly opposed by service-sector employers and by conservative politicians and intellectuals, who argue that such laws will raise business costs, eliminate jobs, and increase municipal expenses. In response to such critiques, which apply to virtually all regulation of the labor market, including long-standing federal regulations governing minimum wages, job safety, and maximum hours, living-wage advocates like economists Robert Pollin and Robert Reich have conducted a series of empirical studies demonstrating that living-wage laws raise real incomes for covered employees, reduce turnover, and have little impact on city employment or cost of services.

Nelson Lichtenstein

See also: Fair Labor Standards Act (FLSA); Family Wage; Industrial Areas Foundation (IAF); Minimum Wage; Trade/Industrial Unions; "Working Poor"

References and Further Reading

Bernstein, Jared. 2000. "Higher Wages Lead to More Efficient Service Provision—The Impact of Living Wage Ordinances on the Public Contracting Process." Washington, DC: Economic Policy Institute.

Glickman, Lawrence. 1997. *A Living Wage: American Workers and the Making of Consumer Society*. Ithaca, NY: Cornell University Press.

Pollin, Robert, and Stephanie Luce. 1998. *The Living Wage: Building a Fair Economy*. New York: New Press.

Losing Ground, *Charles Murray*

With the publication in 1984 of *Losing Ground: American Social Policy 1950–1980*, Charles Murray established himself as the leading policy theorist of the New Right. He obtained this position by forcefully criticizing what he called a too liberal social welfare state. His later work, *The Bell Curve: Intelligence and Class Structure in American Life*, published in 1994 and coauthored with Richard Herrnstein, cemented his location in a conservative agenda committed to ending aid to poor, unmarried women with children. *The Bell Curve* reiterated themes running through *Losing Ground*. In *Losing Ground*, Murray condemned the programs of the Great Society years, arguing that they interfered with the natural order of things. That natural order required poor people to work hard for a living. Murray was especially harsh on Aid to Families with Dependent Children (AFDC), arguing that welfare was a strong disincentive for work.

Murray targeted his criticism against poor Black women and children. He was angered by the disproportionate number of Black welfare recipients, not because he objected to the racial distribution of poverty but because he blamed poverty among Blacks on their behaviors and calculations. In particular, he railed against young Black mothers for bearing "illegitimate" Black babies. Murray argued that the availability of welfare actually encouraged poor people to avoid work and promoted illegitimacy. Contending that the liberal welfare state agenda had been "disastrous" for poor people of all races but for poor Blacks especially, Murray called for the end of welfare.

Charles Murray also attacked affirmative action in *Losing Ground*, a theme he continued in *The Bell Curve*. In the latter book, he and Herrnstein resurrected the issue of inequality rooted in biological differences in intelligence. Although especially hard on African Americans, the two men were intent on articulating the point that a growing white underclass was the product of inferior intelligence.

Losing Ground and *The Bell Curve* prefigured the arguments for policy changes that would culminate in the dismantling of AFDC for poor women and children. These arguments congealed in the Republican agenda to eliminate welfare during the mid-1990s and continue to feed Republican initiatives to use social policy to promote marriage and compel work in the labor market.

Rose M. Brewer

See also: Family Structure; Racism; Welfare Policy/Welfare Reform

References and Further Reading

Herrnstein, Richard J., and Charles Murray. 1994. *The Bell Curve: Intelligence and Class Structure in American Life*. New York: Free Press.

Murray, Charles. 1984. *Losing Ground: American Social Policy 1950–1980*. New York: Basic Books.

Neubeck, Kenneth J., and Noel A. Cazenave. 2001. *Welfare Racism: Playing the Race Card against America's Poor*. New York: Routledge.

Lowell, Josephine Shaw

See Charity Organization Societies; *Public Relief and Private Charity*

Malthusianism

Malthusianism in its narrow sense designates the proposition, advanced by the English cleric Thomas Malthus in *An Essay on the Principle of Population* (1798), that human population advances geometrically while the food supply increases only arithmetically. This principle of population-to-food ratios assumed a world of scarcity or limited resources and posited that rapid population growth would inevitably lead to mass starvation and want. However, Malthusianism also dominated early-nineteenth-century Anglo-American discussions of poverty through three other, comparably controversial arguments that Malthus advanced along with his principle of ratios: (1) societies' lower classes were virtually doomed to poverty and misery because only such "positive" checks as famine, disease, and war were likely to bring their numbers into line with the available food supply; (2) the members of these classes were to blame for their condition because they failed to control their sexual appetites and reproductive propensity; (3) not only were needy laboring people not entitled to public poor relief, but such relief should be abolished because it only encouraged the irresponsible disposition of working-class families to produce more offspring than they could support. In subsequent editions of the *Essay on Population*, Malthus emended his arguments, in particular emphasizing that the lower classes could be taught to restrain their sexual activity and control their numbers. But despite acknowledgment that mass poverty and suffering might be averted by moral "preventive" checks, Malthusianism became identified as a fundamental component of the "dismal science" of classical economics. Its persisting influence, moreover, culminated in one of the watershed pieces of English legislation: the Poor Law Amendment Act of 1834, which sharply curtailed outdoor (that is, noninstitutional) assistance to the "able-bodied" poor.

In America as in England, there were eighteenth-century thinkers (notably Benjamin Franklin) who anticipated some of Malthus's arguments. But if only because the young republic was not faced with the magnitude of England's social problems—extensive unemployment, labor unrest, and spiraling poor-relief costs—neither the defense nor the denunciation of Malthusianism generated the same all-consuming intensity in the early-nineteenth-century United States. Nevertheless, both the controversies over Malthusianism and the actual impact of Malthus's arguments on poor-relief policy proved significant for the United States as well.

The escalating sectional conflict over southern Black slavery lent an indigenous dimension to the American controversies. Defenders of slavery and the southern social order above all embraced Malthusian population doctrine. Many of these invoked the slaves' supposed lack of "prudential restraint" to strengthen the case for slavery's expansion into new territories. Such pro-slavery Malthusians believed that confining the expanding slave population to the existing slave states would result either in the slaves' mass starvation, in race war, or even in the South's abandonment by an overwhelmed white population. Southerners also applied pro-slavery Malthusianism to criticize the social order of the free states. They predicted that as the nation's public domain was exhausted, a surplus population of rebellious wage laborers would continue to build in the North, much as it had in England.

Malthusianism generally met with a more hostile reception among commentators in the pre–Civil War North. This hostility stemmed in part from the overt pro-slavery uses made of Malthus's population principle. But it also reflected a more optimistic view of political economy and of the possibility of achieving and sustaining mass prosperity. Even as the nation's colleges commonly taught less pessimistic versions of classical economic doctrine, there arose an influential "American" school of political economy that unequivocally repudiated classical economics for denying God's benevolent intent and the natural "harmony of interests" existing among capital, labor, and other social entities. Malthus's population principle (along with David Ricardo's doctrine of rent), Henry Carey and others of this school argued, was not merely inapplicable to the land-abundant, labor-scarce, high-wage United States; it was wrong for all societies.

The Malthusian-classical economy-of-scarcity paradigm, the American school argued, should be thrown out along with the oppressive and "aristocratic" Old World arrangements that it sought to legitimate.

Yet there remained one particular sense in which Malthusianism, generally defined, did win substantial acceptance even in the antebellum North. The state officials and elite private citizens involved in poor-relief efforts may not have found any particular validity in Malthus's ratios. But, alarmed over the growing poverty and pauperism in New York and other urban centers, they embraced as overpowering truths the broader axioms of free-market competitive morality that underlay Malthusianism. These included the admonitions that the laboring poor must take responsibility for their own condition; that they should, with assistance from more enlightened classes, internalize the bourgeois values of self-discipline, sobriety, and foresight; and that outdoor relief for the able-bodied poor, by insulating them from the salutary prodding of physical want, morally debilitated laborers and increased the numbers of dependent poor. Reinforcing the older Protestant work ethic, Malthusianism bore at least indirect responsibility for the American, as well as the English, movement toward "well-regulated" almshouses and for the efforts in northern states particularly to abolish or drastically curtail public outdoor relief.

As class divisions hardened and social unrest grew in the post–Civil War period, both Malthusian population doctrine and Malthusian moralism made further inroads among the nation's political economists and other elite elements. In their defense of laissez-faire competitive individualism and economic discrepancies in Gilded Age America, leading conservative thinkers, such as William Graham Sumner, drew on Malthusian-Ricardian tenets (for example, the man-land ratio), again in tandem with the work ethic. The Malthusianism of such thinkers was itself influenced (although how profoundly is a matter of debate) by the newer scientific reasoning and terminology of Darwinian biology (for example, "the struggle for existence").

Like conservative Social Darwinism, overt Malthusianism fell into increasing disfavor with the ascendance of progressive reform thought, and during the early twentieth century the Malthusian specter of overpopulation was generally supplanted by recognition that science and technology could greatly amplify crop yields. However, Malthusianism in its broader meanings has never truly abandoned the field. To this day, criticisms of the "undeserving" poor, including claims that Black single mothers on welfare are promiscuous and sexually irresponsible, reflect Malthusianism's subliminal, persisting influence.

Jonathan A. Glickstein

See also: Deserving/Undeserving Poor; Poor Laws; Poorhouse/Almshouse; Relief; Self-Reliance; Slavery; Social Darwinism; Society for the Prevention of Pauperism; Speenhamland

References and Further Reading

Glickstein, Jonathan A. 2002. *American Exceptionalism, American Anxiety: Wages, Competition, and Degraded Labor in the Antebellum United States.* Charlottesville: University of Virginia Press.

Huston, James L. 1998. *Securing the Fruits of Labor: The American Concept of Wealth Distribution, 1765–1900.* Baton Rouge: Louisiana State University Press.

Spengler, Joseph J. 1933. "Population Doctrines in the United States." *Journal of Political Economy* 41 (August): 433–467; (October): 639–672.

Maternalism

The term "maternalism" refers to the ideology of early-twentieth-century women welfare reformers who contributed significantly to the development of American welfare. Studies of maternalism have revised conventional interpretations of the origins of the American welfare state, showing that key policies, such as the 1935 Social Security Act, did not develop merely in response to the Depression. Rather, their foundations were laid in the Progressive Era, when white middle-class women succeeded in enacting welfare programs specifically for women and children, even as efforts to secure universal entitlements, such as health care, failed. Although the maternalist movement waned in the 1920s, its leaders grew in influence during the New Deal. Maternalists gained unprecedented influence in the administration of President Franklin D. Roosevelt; in drafting portions of the Social Security Act, they made maternalist values a cornerstone of the American welfare state.

Maternalism was based on the nineteenth-century ideology of separate spheres, on the belief that childhood was a distinct stage of life, and on the conviction that women, as mothers and potential mothers, had a special ability—and responsibility—to protect children's welfare. It was made possible by economic and social changes, including new household technologies and a declining birthrate, that "freed" middle-class women for public caregiving and civic activism. Maternalist movements can be found throughout western Europe and the British Commonwealth, but they were particularly influential in the United States, where unions and courts rejected class-based welfare legislation and where a decentralized political structure and weak bureaucracy created a space for educated women to develop social welfare policy. Women's disenfranchisement was also an advantage, for it enabled female activists to present themselves as above politics while lobbying governments and designing policy.

Maternalism was a broad concept, but scholars have generally focused on two groups of mostly white activists: the members of women's clubs and voluntary associations, who numbered in the millions, and the tight-knit reform network that revolved around the U.S. Children's Bureau. The first group, members of the National Congress of Mothers and the General Federation of Women's Clubs, were less educated and more likely to be married than were their colleagues in the Children's Bureau network, but they were instrumental in waging maternalist campaigns at the state and local levels. By contrast, most national maternalist leaders, such as Children's Bureau chiefs Julia Lathrop and Grace Abbott and National Consumers League director Florence Kelley, were highly educated career women, often associated with social settlements. Taking advantage of the rhetoric of separate spheres, they presented themselves as "social mothers" or "social housekeepers" to expand their influence in politics and social work. Maternalists staffed local juvenile courts and child welfare organizations and state child health departments; the establishment of the U.S. Children's Bureau in 1912 also gave them a foothold in the federal government. Indeed, the entrance of women professionals into government service and social work was one of the most significant and long-lasting accomplishments of maternalism.

Historians debating the merits and legacy of maternalism have focused on three main issues. The first is the meaning and usefulness of the term. Although some scholars use "maternalism" broadly to refer to any political use of motherhood rhetoric, others draw a distinction between maternalism, with its emphasis on putting children first, and feminism, which was more individualistic and oriented to women's rights. Or they delineate differences within maternalism—for example, between the "sentimental maternalism" of the National Congress of Mothers and the more feminist or "progressive maternalism" of the Children's Bureau women. Others compare the maternalists who developed the American welfare state with those who opposed it, or question whether African American women reformers should be considered "maternalist."

A second debate has been over the legacy of maternalism. Was it progressive or conservative, feminist or antifeminist? Although some laud its potential for a more generous and caring welfare state, others underscore its class and race limitations. Scholars have been especially critical of its moralistic, class-bound ideas about family life. Most maternalists believed in the family-wage ideal—that fathers should earn enough money so that mothers could be full-time homemakers—and consequently objected to mothers working outside the home. As a result, they supported mothers' pensions, which provided partial support for a small number of children in

Special Message, *President Theodore Roosevelt,* 1909

To the Senate and House of Representatives: On January 25–26, 1909, there assembled in this city, on my invitation, a conference on the care of dependent children. . . .

Each of these children represents either a potential addition to the productive capacity and the enlightened citizenship of the nation, or, if allowed to suffer from neglect, a potential addition to the destructive forces of the community. The ranks of criminals and other enemies of society are recruited in an altogether undue proportion from children bereft of their natural homes and left without sufficient care.

Notwithstanding a wide diversity of views and methods represented in the conference, and notwithstanding the varying legislative enactments and policies of the States from which the members came, the conference, at the close of its sessions, unanimously adopted a series of declarations expressing the conclusions which they had reached. . . .

The keynote of the conference was expressed in these words:

Home life is the highest and finest product of civilization. Children should not be deprived of it except for urgent and compelling reasons.

Surely poverty alone should not disrupt the home. Parents of good character suffering from temporary misfortune, and above all, deserving mothers fairly well able to work but deprived of the support of the normal breadwinner, should be given such aid as may be necessary to enable them to maintain suitable homes for the rearing of their children. The widowed or deserted mother, if a good woman, willing to work and do her best, should ordinarily be helped in such fashion as will enable her to bring up her children herself in their natural home. Children from unfit homes, and children who have no homes, who must be cared for by charitable agencies, should, so far as practicable, be cared for in families.

"suitable" homes, over day nurseries or child care. They also supported legislative restrictions on night work, heavy lifting, and the number of hours wage-earning women (potential mothers) might work. Such legislation, although intended to protect mothers, often prevented women, whether or not they had children, from gaining economic independence and workplace equality.

Many scholars have emphasized maternalists' class and race bias. Most maternalist programs were predicated on the belief that "good mothering" was essential to child welfare, and they made cultural conformity to an American middle-class model of home life a principal goal. Mothers' pensions, for example, were limited to "deserving" mothers willing to let social workers teach them proper ("American") diet, dress, and child-rearing techniques. African American women, whose high rates of maternal employment often marked them as undeserving of aid, were disproportionately excluded from mothers' pensions. Similarly, the maternalist baby-saving campaigns, which aimed to lower infant and maternal mortality and which culminated in the 1921 Sheppard-Towner Act, emphasized the dangers of traditional midwives, "superstitious" healing rituals, and spicy food. Although designed by and for women, maternalist policies fostered women's dependence and were often paternalistic and controlling.

Although maternalist ideas were written into the Social Security Act, the movement itself began to decline in the mid-1920s. Club women's interest in welfare legislation faded, and social workers referred to their professional expertise, rather than motherhood, when asserting women's authority in the child welfare field. Since the 1930s, welfare activists have occasionally employed maternalist rhetoric, but never again with the same success.

Molly Ladd-Taylor

See also: Aid to Families with Dependent Children (ADC/AFDC); Maternalist Policy; National Congress of Mothers; U.S. Children's Bureau

References and Further Reading

Gordon, Linda. 1994. *Pitied but Not Entitled: Single Mothers and the Politics of Welfare*. New York: Free Press.

Koven, Seth, and Sonya Michel. 1993. *Mothers of a New World: Maternalist Politics and the Origins of Welfare States*. New York: Routledge.

Ladd-Taylor, Molly. 1994. *Mother-Work: Women, Child Welfare, and the State, 1890–1930*. Urbana: University of Illinois Press.

Mink, Gwendolyn. 1995. *The Wages of Motherhood: Inequality in the Welfare State, 1917–1942*. Ithaca, NY: Cornell University Press.

Skocpol, Theda. 1992. *Protecting Soldiers and Mothers: The Politics of Social Provision in the United States, 1870s–1920s*. Cambridge, MA: Harvard University Press.

Sklar, Kathryn Kish. 1995. *Florence Kelley and the Nation's Work: The Rise of Women's Political Culture, 1830–1900*. New Haven: Yale University Press.

Wilkinson, Patrick. 1999. "The Selfless and the Helpless: Maternalist Origins of the U.S. Welfare State." *Feminist Studies* 25 (Fall): 571–597.

Maternalist Policy

Maternalist policies, such as state mothers' pensions laws and maternal and child health services, were set in place during the Progressive Era and made national during the New Deal. Although the United States lagged behind European welfare states in developing universal entitlement programs, such as national health insurance, it participated in the international trend toward enacting social welfare policies specifically for women and children. Early-twentieth-century women reformers—dubbed "maternalists" by historians—accepted and even exalted women's responsibility for home and child care, and they endeavored to write "motherly" values, such as nurturing and compassion, into U.S. social policy. Mostly white and affluent or middle-class, they designed policies based on the principles that (1) children should be the nation's top priority, and (2) every child needed a "proper" home with a stay-at-home mother and a breadwinning father who earned a decent wage. Although rooted in nineteenth-century ideas about woman's place, these maternalist precepts were written into the 1935 Social Security Act and have framed American welfare policy ever since.

Maternalist ideas and activism flowed in many directions; maternalist policies, however, can be divided into three overlapping categories: child protection, social housekeeping, and maternal and child welfare. Institutions and measures specifically directed to children, such as kindergartens, juvenile courts, compulsory-education laws, and the regulation of child labor, were influenced by psychologist G. Stanley Hall's ideas about the importance of physical expression, play, and "mother love" to child development. But they also had an assimilationist objective: to teach "American" values and cultural norms to immigrant children and parents. By 1920, every state required school attendance, 10 percent of the nation's children attended kindergarten, and all but a few states had juvenile courts.

Social housekeeping was the second category of maternalist reform. Expanding the notions of "home" and "woman's sphere" to include the entire community, activist women justified their involvement in new professions like nursing and social work and in clubs, voluntary associations, and politics by invoking motherhood and women's supposed moral superiority. Maternalists disagreed over whether women should have the right to vote, but they all believed that women—"social mothers"—were needed to clean up political corruption. They worked for civil service reform and for pure food and drug laws, and they saw to it that maternalist policies enacted into law usually included a provision for female administrators.

The third category of maternalist reform, maternal and child welfare, has received the greatest amount of scholarly attention, for it continues to define women's place in the American welfare state. Many studies have focused on the U.S. Children's Bureau, the center of maternalist organizing and policy administration from the second decade of the twentieth century to the 1930s. The bureau was the brainchild of Lillian Wald, founder of New York's Henry Street Settlement, and Florence Kelley, director of the National Consumers League, and it grew out of decades of maternalist activism in women's clubs and social settlements. Its establishment in 1912 and the appointment of longtime Hull House resident Julia Lathrop as its first director gave maternalists a foothold in the federal government eight years before women had the right to vote. Lathrop used her extensive network among women activists to build a remarkably effective partnership between women's voluntary organizations and the federal government, combining social science research and political mobilization on behalf of child welfare. In the second decade of the twentieth century, the bureau published a series of studies that mobilized women around the issue of infant mortality. It also conducted research on the effects of child employment and administered the nation's first federal child labor law, the 1916 Keating-Owen Act, until the Supreme Court overturned it after nine months. The bureau failed to secure a child labor amendment to the Constitution despite a vigorous campaign, and it was not until the 1938 passage of the Fair Labor Standards Act—a bill that owed much to the efforts of Frances Perkins, the maternalist secretary of labor—that the United States banned most child labor.

Protective labor legislation for women workers has been another popular topic among historians of women and the welfare state, for it poses a question that remains relevant today: Can policies based on gender difference be an entering wedge for universal social programs, or are they inevitably discriminatory? Social democratic maternalists, such as Florence Kelley, supported sex-based labor laws in part because the courts struck down—and the American Federation of Labor opposed—most laws regulating the hours, wages, and safety conditions of adult men. In *Lochner v. New York* (198 U.S. 45 [1905]), for example, the Supreme Court ruled that a law mandating a maximum ten-hour workday for male bakers was unconstitutional because it denied them their freedom of contract. Three years after *Lochner*, however, the Supreme Court upheld the principle of protective legislation for women in *Muller v. Oregon* (208 U.S. 412 [1908]), a decision that owed much to the efforts of Kelley's National Consumers League. Future Supreme Court justice Louis Brandeis, brother-in-law of National Consumers League staffer Josephine Goldmark, argued the case, using his famous Brandeis Brief (developed largely by Goldmark) to convince the court that women's capacity to bear children—and populate the nation—placed the regulation of their work in the national interest. By 1925, all but four states limited women's working hours. Many also regulated rest periods, placed restrictions on nighttime employment and heavy lifting, and prohibited women from working in places deemed exceptionally dangerous or immoral. Kelley believed such protections would ease the physical burden on overworked women and would serve as an entering wedge to better labor standards for all workers. For the feminists who launched the Equal Rights Amendment (ERA) in 1923 and for many subsequent historians, however, sex-based labor laws that treated all women as mothers or potential mothers reinforced women's inequality. The debate over the ERA tore the women's movement apart. Although feminists saw the challenge to legalized gender difference as a crucial step toward women's rights—and pointed out that protective laws did not even apply to women of color who worked in agriculture or domestic service—maternalists objected that the ERA would overturn decades of work on behalf of wage-earning women. Tensions remained strong into the 1960s, even though workplace protections were extended to male industrial workers in 1938.

The underlying assumption behind protective legislation—that children needed mothers at home, not in the workforce—was also embedded in mothers' pensions, the most successful welfare reform of the Progressive Era. The first state mothers' pension law was enacted in Illinois in 1911; thirty-nine states passed similar laws within eight years. Maternalist organizations, especially the National Congress of Mothers, were the policy's most ardent supporters, for they saw mothers' pensions as protecting maternal custody rights and the dignity of poor widows. Not surprisingly, mothers' pensions also reflected maternalists' narrow understanding of children's needs. Pensions went only to "suitable" mothers willing to accept social work supervision and to bring their dietary, housekeeping, and child-rearing practices in line with "American" middle-class norms. Moreover, in spite of the claim that children needed full-time mothers, mothers' pensions were too meager to live on, and most states permitted—or required—recipients to work outside the home. Yet the belief that "good" mothers stayed home with their children kept reformers from endorsing child care programs or day nurseries that would support women in their capacity as wage earners. It also fostered discrimination against African American mothers, whose high rates of labor force participation often rendered them ineligible for aid. Defined as workers rather than caregivers, Black mothers faced the predicament that would come to haunt all welfare recipients: They were condemned as lazy nonworkers if they wanted to stay home with their children, but working outside the home made them "unfit" mothers.

The maternalist campaign against maternal and infant mortality, which culminated in the passage of America's first federal social welfare measure, was also based on middle-class notions about children's needs. Infant health (and, by extension, the health of pregnant women and new mothers) was the principal priority of the Children's Bureau in the second and third decades of the twentieth century. The bureau disseminated literature on prenatal and infant care, documented the economic causes of infant mortality, and coordinated local baby-saving campaigns. In 1918, the second year of World War I, 11 million women participated in the bureau's baby-saving drive. Three years later, Congress passed the Sheppard-Towner Maternity and Infancy Protection Act, the first "women's" bill to pass after women got the vote. Sheppard-Towner provided federal matching funds to the states for prenatal and child health clinics, for instruction in hygiene and nutrition, and for visiting nurses for pregnant women and new mothers. Mothers across the country were advised to seek medical care for childbirth and sick children, to use "American" child-rearing methods, and to refrain from feeding babies spicy food.

Despite Sheppard-Towner's modest provisions—Congress had rejected the Children's Bureau's efforts to secure medical and nursing care—conservative politicians and the American Medical Association painted the law as an attack on the family and a step toward "state medicine," and they forced its repeal in 1929. Federal funding for maternal and child health care was restored in Title V of the 1935 Social Security Act, but access to services was means-tested and was stigmatized as charity for the poor.

Ironically, although maternalism was rooted in nineteenth-century gender ideals, maternalist policies were not implemented at the federal level until the 1930s—just as mass unemployment, women's right to vote, and the growing proportion of women in the workforce showed maternalist ideas about separate spheres to be anachronistic. Still, most male and female New Dealers remained convinced that a breadwinning father was a child's greatest need. They designed programs, such as the Works Progress Administration, that promoted work and wage earning among men but gave little thought to public works or child care programs that would assist married women workers. In 1935, the Social Security Act instituted a two-track welfare system, with old-age and unemployment-insurance entitlements for male wage earners and means-tested charity, such as Aid to Dependent Children (ADC), for the "dependent" poor. Needy mothers and children were not entitled to ADC (as mothers' pensions were then called). Instead, aid was given only to the children of "deserving" mothers, and their mothers received no stipend at all. Despite modest changes over the years, the basic framework of ADC—wherein children's economic welfare is tied to the moral and cultural "suitability" of their mothers—endures.

Scholars have engaged in a vigorous debate over the extent to which maternalism was responsible for the failures of the U.S. welfare system. Did the maternalist commitment to sex-based policies, to American cultural norms, and to middle-class family norms produce the inequities in the two-track U.S. welfare state? Or are the shortcomings of American welfare due to political and economic circumstances beyond maternalists' control? Although some scholars stress the accomplishments of maternalists in the face of fierce opposition to progressive welfare reform, others underscore the limits of their all-white social network and middle-class perspective. Present-day antipoverty organizations continue to struggle over "maternalist" strategies. Some, like the Children's Defense Fund, have decided to put children first, while others place a greater priority on changing welfare and employment policies that would enhance mothers' wage-earning potential and economic independence. Still others advocate new welfare provisions that would recognize and support the caregiving work of mothers.

Molly Ladd-Taylor

See also: Aid to Families with Dependent Children (ADC/AFDC); Hull House; Maternalism; National Congress of Mothers; U.S. Children's Bureau; Welfare Policy/Welfare Reform

References and Further Reading

Goodwin, Joanne. 1997. *Gender and the Politics of Welfare Reform: Mothers' Pensions in Chicago, 1911–1929*. Chicago: University of Chicago Press.

Gordon, Linda. 1994. *Pitied but Not Entitled: Single Mothers and the Politics of Welfare*. New York: Free Press.

Koven, Seth, and Sonya Michel. 1993. *Mothers of a New World: Maternalist Politics and the Origins of Welfare States*. New York: Routledge.

Ladd-Taylor, Molly. 1994. *Mother-Work: Women, Child Welfare, and the State, 1890–1930*. Urbana: University of Illinois Press.

Michel, Sonya, and Robyn Rosen. 1992. "The Paradox of Maternalism: Elizabeth Lowell Putnam and the American Welfare State." *Gender and History* 4: 364–386.

Mink, Gwendolyn. 1995. *The Wages of Motherhood: Inequality in the Welfare State, 1917–1942*. Ithaca, NY: Cornell University Press.

Skocpol, Theda. 1992. *Protecting Soldiers and Mothers: The Politics of Social Provision in the United States, 1870s–1920s*. Cambridge, MA: Harvard University Press.

Sklar, Kathryn Kish. 1995. *Florence Kelley and the Nation's Work: The Rise of Women's Political Culture, 1830–1900*. New Haven: Yale University Press.

Wilkinson, Patrick. 1999. "The Selfless and the Helpless: Maternalist Origins of the U.S. Welfare State." *Feminist Studies* 25 (Fall): 571–597.

McWilliams, Carey

See Factories in the Field; Migrant Labor/Farm Labor

Means Testing and Universalism

Means testing and universalism are fundamental but opposite principles governing the eligibility of citizens for income, services, and other benefits in welfare states. Means testing, a legacy of the nineteenth-century poor laws, restricts benefits to applicants whose income and assets fall below an officially established threshold. Intrusive investigations are typically required to determine whether an individual's wages and assets are below the legal threshold. Universalism is based on the idea of common citizenship and social rights. Under universalism, public social welfare grants and services are available without restriction to all citizens regardless of social class, income, or status.

Though means testing is often justified as an efficient way to target income and services to needy people, it is used mainly to exclude people from social welfare programs. The nineteenth-century poor laws were written to sharply distinguish between paupers—those individuals unable to support themselves—and the able-bodied poor. Aid to the poor was thus conditioned on extreme want, and the measure of that want—the means test—stigmatized recipients as public burdens who lack independence and self-discipline. Means testing treats individuals as supplicants rather than as clients or beneficiaries with legitimate rights to social assistance. It can also lead to repeated investigations of applicants' personal lives, to behavioral requirements, and to other degrading practices that undermine recipients' self-respect. Defenders of means testing view these practices as necessary to make public aid to the poor less desirable than work.

Seeking to avoid the penury and stigmatization characteristic of means testing, universalistic social policies make equality the chief goal of welfare policy. Labor unions and labor-based political parties historically have embraced universalism for this reason. Universalism is valued not only because it is a fairer way to distribute public income transfers and services but also because it is thought to promote a common stake in the welfare state. Means testing is redistributive—that is one of its justifications—but it separates those who pay for public aid to the poor from those who benefit and thus inspires political opposition. Universalism distributes benefits and burdens to all citizens and inspires political support. Indeed, universalism is often defended as a tool to build political coalitions composed of different social classes and racial or ethnic groups and to promote social solidarity more generally.

As principles, means testing and universalism have offsetting virtues and vices. Means testing redistributes income to the poor, but it also may create work disincentives if benefits are reduced as individuals earn outside income or if benefits exceed wage levels. A generous means-tested policy may actually give individuals some leverage to bargain with employers in low-wage labor markets, which in turn leads to political pressure to keep means-tested benefits very low. Universal policies do not erode work incentives, but universalism is very expensive and much less effective than means testing in redistributing income and targeting benefits to the poor.

Universalism triumphed in Europe because of the strength of labor-based political parties and the support of the middle class. In the United States, by comparison, means testing is far more prevalent, reflecting the view that public aid should be sparing and reserved for the neediest. Public expenditures for means-tested policies in the United States are substantially higher than in almost all European countries. In Europe, moreover, means-tested policies are used to cover the gaps in universalistic social and health insurance, housing policies, and family allowances. This practice allows Europeans to embed means testing within politically popular universalistic programs. It amounts to redistribution within universalism and compensates for the inability of policymakers to infinitely expand costly universalistic programs.

In the United States, means-tested and universalistic policies define separate tiers in the welfare state. This separation goes back to the 1935 Social Security Act, which created a universal old-age insurance (Social Security) and unemployment compensation program for full-time workers and means-tested public assistance programs for the elderly and blind and for the children of widows (Aid to Dependent Children). Today, Social Security and Medicare cover almost all of the elderly, and means-tested policies for the elderly are used to supplement meager social insurance payments. Among nonelderly citizens, on the other hand, there is almost no overlap between individuals who receive means-tested benefits such as food stamps or other welfare programs and individuals who receive universal benefits such as unemployment compensation. Poor and middle-class citizens are treated very differently: Compared to people receiving universal benefits, recipients of means-tested aid receive lower, stigmatized benefits.

As a social welfare principle, universalism is ambiguous; in practice, many individuals are excluded from universalistic policies, either explicitly by law or implicitly. For example, the 1935 Social Security Act excluded farmworkers, domestic workers, and the self-employed, among other workers. Many of these workers were covered later by social insurance, but many more were excluded implicitly by requirements for extended attachment to the labor force. Those workers who experience low or intermittent employment—many women and members of racial minorities—are excluded, and if they do manage to gain entry, their benefits will be lower. Similarly, the policy permitting taxpayers to deduct interest payments on home mortgages from their taxable income, ostensibly a universalistic policy, implicitly excludes renters from what amounts to a significant and generous social welfare benefit.

Race and gender, not just social class, are defining features of means-tested and universalistic social welfare programs in the United States. These racial and gender divisions began when reformers during the Progressive Era advocated universalistic social insurance for male workers and created a very different program, mothers' pensions, for widows and their children. Unlike social insurance, mothers' pensions were locally controlled, encumbered with rules, and means-tested. Two-thirds of all African American workers were initially excluded from social insurance in the 1930s because they were employed as farmworkers or as domestic help. Poor African American workers had no choice but to turn to means-tested programs for help.

Although most African American families are covered today by Social Security, racial and gender divisions between means-tested and universalistic policies remain. Of those African Americans who receive a public cash transfer, almost three-quarters receive a means-tested benefit; by comparison, just under one-third of whites receiving an income transfer receive means-tested benefits. In universal programs, the pattern is just the opposite: About one-third of Blacks receive a non-means-tested benefit compared to three-quarters of whites (Brown et al. 2003, 98). Although women benefit from universalism in the United States, many women, particularly poor single mothers, must rely entirely on means-tested aid. These racial and gender divisions in the distribution of benefits reflect enduring labor market discrimination and unequal wages as well as the legacy of policy decisions.

Michael K. Brown

See also: Aid to Families with Dependent Children (ADC/AFDC); Poverty Line; Social Security Act of 1935

References and Further Reading

Baldwin, Peter. 1990. *The Politics of Social Solidarity: Class Bases of the European Welfare State, 1875–1975*. New York: Cambridge University Press.

Brown, Michael K. 1999. *Race, Money, and the American Welfare State*. Ithaca, NY: Cornell University Press.

Brown, Michael K., et al. 2003. *Whitewashing Race: The Myth of a Color-Blind Society*. Berkeley and Los Angeles: University of California Press.

Esping-Andersen, Gosta. 1990. *The Three Worlds of Welfare Capitalism*. Princeton: Princeton University Press.

Gordon, Linda. 1994. *Pitied but Not Entitled: Single Mothers and the History of Welfare, 1890–1935*. Cambridge, MA: Harvard University Press.

Katz, Michael B. 2001. *The Price of Citizenship: Redefining the American Welfare State*. New York: Henry Holt.

Medicaid

See Health Policy

Medicare

See Health Policy

Mental Health Policy

Mental health policy comprises the laws, regulations, court decisions, and programs by which government sustains, oversees, and supplements the delivery of mental health care services. The objectives of public policy in this sector include the prevention of mental health problems in the population, the treatment of mental illnesses in acute and chronic forms, and the provision of psychological, financial, and social supports to people with mental illnesses in various residential settings. According to this definition, mental health policy encompasses actions to maintain the mental health system, as well as those programs, such as health and disability insurance entitlements, that assist people with mental illnesses as part of a broader clientele (Rochefort 1997, 4–5). One of the earliest social welfare commitments in American society, policies in the mental health area have undergone tremendous growth and transformation over time. One constant, however, has been a mismatch between the level of need for mental health care and available resources, with marked inequalities of access for different social groups.

In the colonial era, people with mental illnesses who required public support were handled under the poor laws. Local officials relied on such practices as boarding disturbed individuals with neighbors and placing them in poorhouses and

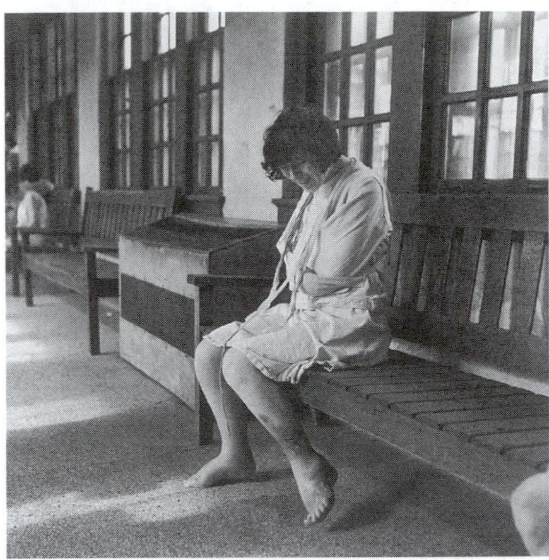

Woman in Straitjacket at a Psychiatric Hospital, Ohio, 1946. (Jerry Cooke/Corbis)

jails. The movement to establish specialized mental hospitals in the early 1800s began as reformers, such as Dorothea Dix of Massachusetts, uncovered the shocking inadequacies of these ad hoc arrangements. Dozens of mental institutions soon spread across the states under public and private auspices with the aim of providing patients with "moral treatment," or humane individualized care in a well-ordered environment.

During the late 1800s and early 1900s, however, a number of forces led to the deterioration of treatment and living conditions within public facilities. Population growth fueled overcrowding, legislatures neglected to fund the expansion and maintenance of state institutions as needed, and there was a steady accumulation of patients with dementias and other chronic disorders (Grob 1994, ch. 5). The influence of social status on mental health care grew especially pronounced during this period, both in public asylums' practice of determining treatments along class, ethnic, and racial lines and in the large gap in quality between public and private facilities (Grob 1994, 86–90).

The 1950s brought a major shift away from the long-term trend toward institutional treatment. After reaching a peak of 559,000 patients in 1955, the number of patients in state and county mental hospitals in the United States began a steep decline, falling more than 80 percent over the next four decades (Rochefort 1997, 216–217). The development of powerful new tranquilizing drugs was a causal factor, as were exposés of mental hospitals and court decisions favoring care in the "least restrictive" setting. Three important pieces of federal legislation in this period were the Community Mental Health Centers Act (1963), which expanded local mental health services; Medicaid (1965), which funded care in private nursing homes and general hospitals for many mentally ill persons; and Supplemental Security Income (1972), which gave financial support to patients living in the community. Yet a host of implementation problems marked this transition to the community, including the lack of low-cost supervised housing, poor coordination of services across different social welfare bureaucracies, and community opposition to mental health facilities. The emergence of the mentally ill as a distinct segment of the homeless—typical estimates range from one-quarter to one-third of this population—underscored the shortcomings of community mental health care in the nation's large urban centers (Rochefort 1997, 255–259).

Today's mental health reform agenda is multipronged. One major emphasis is on fashioning comprehensive systems of community support for people with severe and long-term mental disorders. This involves planning an array of mental health, substance abuse, health, housing, employment, and advocacy services, which are typically organized at the client level through a process known as case management. Assertive Community Treatment is one popular model that seeks to create "hospitals without walls" through use of multidisciplinary treatment teams accessing diverse resources on behalf of clients

Dorothea Dix Appealing for Federal Aid for the Mentally Ill, June 23, 1848

. . . I have myself seen more than nine thousand idiots, epileptics, and insane, in these United States, destitute of appropriate care and protection; and of this vast and most miserable company, sought out in jails, in poorhouses, and in private dwellings, there have been hundreds, nay, rather thousands, bound with galling chains, bowed beneath fetters and heavy iron balls, attached to drag-chains, lacerated with ropes, scourged with rods, and terrified beneath storms of profane execrations and cruel blows. . . .

[In an institution in New York state I viewed] a madman. The fierce command of his keeper brought him to the door, a hideous object; matted locks, and unshorn beard, a wild, wan countenance, disfigured by vilest uncleanliness; in a state of nudity, save the irritating incrustations derived from that dungeon, reeking with loathsome filth. There, without light, without pure air, without warmth, without cleansing, absolutely destitute of everything securing comfort or decency, was a human being—forlorn, abject, and disgusting, it is true, but not less of a human being—nay more, an immortal being, though the mind was fallen in ruins, and the soul was clothed in darkness. And who was he—this neglected, brutalized wretch? A burglar, a murderer, a miscreant, who for base, foul crimes had been condemned, by the justice of outraged laws and the righteous indignation of his fellow-men, to expiate offences by exclusion from his race, by privations and suffering extreme, yet not exceeding the measure and enormity of his misdeeds? No; this was no doomed criminal, festering in filth, wearing warily out of the warp of life in dreariest solitude and darkness. No, this was no criminal—"Only a crazy man."

Source: Dorothea Dix, "Memorial of D. L. Dix Praying a Grant of Land for the Relief and Support of the Indigent Curable and Incurable Insane in the United States, June 23, 1848" (U.S. Senate, "Senate Miscellaneous Document no. 150," 30th Cong., sess. 1). Reprinted in Edith Abbott, ed., *Some American Pioneers in Social Welfare: Select Documents with Editorial Notes* (1937. Reprint, New York: Russell and Russell, 1963), 108, 115.

(U.S. Department of Health and Human Services 1999, 286–287).

"Parity" insurance coverage is another leading issue in contemporary mental health policy. Historically, health insurers in the United States have restricted mental health benefits by placing limitations on services, by excluding particular diagnoses from covered illnesses, and by requiring that patients share more of the costs. By 2000, thirty-two states had passed laws to correct such forms of insurance discrimination, although with great inconsistency in the standards established for insurers and employers around the country (Hennessy and Goldman 2001, 60–62). Pro-parity groups are now intent on strengthening a federal parity statute passed in 1996 that contains many coverage gaps and enforcement loopholes.

The landmark U.S. Surgeon General's Report on Mental Health highlighted the prevalence of mental health problems among the nation's youth (U.S. Department of Health and Human Services 1999, 46). Estimates are that 20 percent of children and adolescents experience a psychiatric disorder each year and that as many as 9 percent of children ages nine to seventeen have serious emotional problems. However, only a minority of troubled children receive specialized treatment. Many innovative mental health services for children are being developed focusing on families, schools, foster care, court systems, and other environments. Yet gaps in the continuum of care are evident in the long waiting lists for children in many state mental health systems and in the high occupancy levels in hospital psychiatric units for children (Rochefort 1999, 19–22).

Interwoven with all of these issues—and sometimes exacerbating them—is the pervasive move toward managed care in the mental health sector over the past decade. Public and private health insurers alike have adopted, or contracted with, programs that make use of a range of reviewing and payment practices to control mental health services. Those questioning the appropriateness of this managed-care framework cite such problems as loss of confidentiality, denials of needed services, an overemphasis on drug-based treatments (as opposed to psychotherapy), and inadequate public regulation of for-profit managed-care companies. At the same time, however, managed care has been a vehicle for expanding the spectrum of mental health services in some health plans and for enhancing coordination and quality control. Managed care has also provided a powerful argument against predictions that mental health services would be overutilized under parity legislation. These two faces of managed mental health care—as object and instrument of reform—continue to define the movement in the early twenty-first century (Mechanic 1998).

Approximately 20 percent of Americans have a diagnosable mental disorder each year (U.S. Department of Health and Human Services 1999, 46). Direct and indirect costs of these problems exceeded $150 billion by the late-1990s and were felt within health, educational, social service, and criminal justice systems, as well as in the workplace (U.S. Department of Health and Human Services 1999, 49). Given its dynamic history and current social impact, mental health policy is of pivotal significance in the study of American social welfare.

David A. Rochefort

See also: Disability; Disability Policy; Health Policy; Homelessness; Poorhouse/Almshouse

References and Further Reading

Grob, Gerald N. 1994. *The Mad among Us: A History of the Care of America's Mentally Ill*. New York: Free Press.

Hennessy, Kevin D., and Howard H. Goldman. 2001. "Full Parity: Steps toward Treatment Equity for Mental and Addictive Disorders." *Health Affairs* 20, no. 4: 58–67.

Mechanic, David. 1998. *Mental Health and Social Policy: The Emergence of Managed Care*. Englewood Cliffs, NJ: Prentice-Hall.

Rochefort, David A. 1997. *From Poorhouses to Homelessness: Policy Analysis and Mental Health Care*. Westport, CT: Auburn House.

———. 1999. *Mental Health Care in Massachusetts*. Waltham, MA: Massachusetts Health Policy Forum. http://www.sihp.brandeis.edu/mhpf/issue_brief_8.pdf.

U.S. Department of Health and Human Services. 1999. *Mental Health: A Report of the Surgeon General*. Rockville, MD: U.S. Department of Health and Human Services, Substance Abuse and Mental Health Services Administration, Center for Mental Health Services, National Institutes of Health, National Institute of Mental Health.

Mexican American Legal Defense and Education Fund (MALDEF)

The Mexican American Legal Defense and Education Fund (MALDEF) addresses the ever-changing needs of the Latino community. MALDEF concentrates its efforts in the following areas: employment, education, immigration, political access, language, public resources, and equity issues.

Founded in the 1960s, MALDEF began its work in Texas during the civil rights era. Its initial efforts consisted of developing programs and policies that would encourage Mexican American students to participate in education and that would improve the schools. MALDEF's initial efforts focused on bilingual education, scholarships, and desegregation.

In 1966, a pivotal event redirected the organization's social activism efforts. A Mexican

American woman lost her leg in a work-related accident. MALDEF believed that the woman deserved at least $50,000 for the company's negligence. The issue was taken to court, but the woman's lawyers argued that since the jury that was to decide the case was all white, it was unlikely to give the woman a fair trial. The judge agreed, and placed two persons with Spanish surnames on the jury. But neither person was able to serve: One of them had been deceased for ten years, and the other was a noncitizen. As a result of this treatment—which was indicative of the judicial system's disregard for Latinos—MALDEF mounted a major battle to end jury discrimination in Texas and to improve the treatment of Mexican Americans in the judicial system, particularly in the Southwest.

Challenging long-standing judicial practices required substantial funding. In 1967, members of MALDEF met with the Ford Foundation to explain the problems that confronted Mexican Americans in the Southwest. They maintained that an organization that would represent and protect the needs of Latinos was a paramount necessity. The Ford Foundation agreed and granted MALDEF $2.2 million for civil rights litigation and $250,000 for scholarships for Latino law students. This grant established the organization and many of the principles it still practices today.

In 1968, the organization's first office was opened in San Antonio, Texas. MALDEF did not lack problems to tackle: Education, voting, employment discrimination, police brutality, prison reforms, land and water rights, and media and housing issues were but a few of the problematic areas.

Education was an early priority for MALDEF. In the Southwest, schools segregated or discriminated against Latino students in various ways. Up until the 1960s, for instance, Anglo students were able to transfer out of classes that were predominately Latino. Placement testing was another means of segregation, for the tests were biased against students for whom English was not a first language or who came from lower socioeconomic backgrounds. Further discrimination arose from the way schools were funded. School funding based on property taxes disadvantaged students in poor communities. Latino communities tended to be less well-off than Anglo communities, so their schools could not provide resources and opportunities equivalent to those of Anglo schools.

MALDEF fought discrimination in educational content as well as in educational access. Students read books that depicted Latinos in a negative light. MALDEF worked at changing some of these negative depictions. MALDEF also worked at improving bilingual education. A variety of challenges throughout the Southwest led to many curriculum changes within school districts, changes that improved the learning environment for Latino students. Today, the organization continues its efforts in education.

Before the 1970s, it was not uncommon for Latinos to be denied promotions and advancements in employment simply because they were not Anglo. In addition, employers often imposed unfair requirements on Latino employees who sought promotions. For example, Latino employees typically worked twice as long for a company as an Anglo counterpart would before being considered for promotion. As a result, Latinos were restricted to lower and less well-paid positions in the workforce. When they filed complaints of job discrimination, they often were terminated.

MALDEF secured civil rights and labor standards for Latinos in the workforce. The organization monitored employers and litigated against those who discriminated against employees simply because of their ethnicity. One issue that continues to be a legal challenge is the use of Spanish at work. Some employers mandate that workers speak English only. The issue of whether workers can speak Spanish during breaks has also been a point of contention.

The Voting Rights Act of 1965 (VRA)

encouraged minority participation in the political process. Before the VRA was enacted, racial, ethnic, and language-minority groups had to overcome numerous obstacles in order to participate in the political process. For instance, in some states, minorities had to pay poll taxes or pass literacy or English tests in order to vote. Many minorities were physically intimidated, threatened, or harmed when they sought to register, vote, or otherwise participate in the political process. Latinos were no exception.

MALDEF fought for VRA enforcement so that Latinos could be incorporated into the electoral system. For instance, MALDEF challenged policies that required annual voter registration of Latinos. The organization also challenged single-district voting schemes and poorly reapportioned districts. MALDEF was highly successful at increasing the overall number of Latino voters, particularly in the Southwest. The organization continues to promote political empowerment through its work on redistricting, voter registration, and voter fraud, to name but a few areas of activity.

MALDEF's greatest recent successes have come from its work on immigration. MALDEF fought to overturn California's Proposition 187, which would have ended education, health care, and social services to the state's undocumented immigrants. MALDEF also pursues national litigation on behalf of immigrants who are adversely affected by federal policy or lack of federal protections. For instance, MALDEF worked on the Nicaraguan Adjustment and Central American Relief Act (NACARA). Some Central American immigrants are in the United States on a temporary basis. These immigrants can be sent back to their country of origin when the United States deems conditions there are safe. Many immigrants are fearful of returning because they know that safety is a precarious condition in their home country. MALDEF, along with other immigrant advocate groups, has been able to extend the length of time these immigrants can stay in the United States.

MALDEF has also challenged the placement of immigrant detainees in detention facilities far from border communities or from their points of entry into the United States. In an ongoing challenge, MALDEF has worked to place such detainees nearer the Mexican border so that family members can track relatives in prison, visit them, and recruit legal assistance for them.

Lisa Magaña

See also: Chicana/o Movement; Latino/as

References and Further Reading

Grofman, Bernard. 1992. *Controversies in Minority Voting: The Voting Rights Act in Perspective*. Washington, DC: Brookings Institution.

Gutiérrez, José Angel. 1998. *The Making of a Chicano Militant: Lessons from Cristal*. Madison: University of Wisconsin Press.

Muñoz, Carlos. 1989. *Youth, Identity, Power: The Chicano Generation*. London and New York: Verso.

Navarro, Armando. 1995. *Mexican American Youth Organization: Avant-Garde of the Chicano Movement in Texas*. Austin: University of Texas Press.

———. 2000. *La Raza Unida Party: A Chicano Challenge to the U.S. Two-Party Dictatorship*. Philadelphia: Temple University Press.

Migrant Labor/Farm Labor

Although popular imagination pictures the migrant worker in a field of crops, migrant labor and farm labor are distinct historical phenomena. True, seasonal migrants have been an essential part of the labor force in agriculture, but they have also been vital to such industries as logging, mining, construction, railroads, food processing, and entertainment. Often the same workers have cycled through different industries piecing together a living out of an annual round of temporary jobs. Others have moved between industry and agriculture as family necessity, age, and opportunity dictate. Conversely, although most agricultural work is highly seasonal, family and local labor have often met the labor demands of farm operators. Whether agricultural or industrial, local or long-distance, migrant and farm labor have long been linked together by their close association with political battles over child labor, unionization, and the social safety net. They have also been important entry points to the U.S. labor market for immigrants, poor workers, women, and children.

During the nineteenth century, migrant families and individuals were closely associated with the advance of Euro-American settlement across North America. The frontier generation farmers cleared new land and grew grain for eastern markets, but they often moved on quickly to more inexpensive lands farther west, or into the cities. After the advent of the mechanical reaper, a seasonal migration of young men scouting land for their families and a few unemployed industrial workers were serving the expanding wheat farms of the Ohio and Mississippi River valleys by the 1870s. In the Rocky Mountain and Pacific Coast regions, mining, timber, and railroad construction relied heavily on seasonal migrant workers. On the newly opened lands of the northern plains and in California's Central Valley, railroad companies financed highly mechanized "bonanza" farms employing hundreds of workers at harvesttime. At the same time, high unemployment among urban workers sent large numbers of men on the road in search of work away from their hometowns, inspiring middle-class fears of a "tramp menace."

By the 1880s, an annual cycle of work—from summer work on railroads to fall harvesting to winter logging—supported a growing subculture of young immigrant and U.S.-born men who made their homes in the transient districts of Chicago, Minneapolis, Sacramento, Seattle, and other towns. These "hoboes" soon became the primary constituency of the Industrial Workers of the World, a militant union organized in 1905 that led successful campaigns to raise harvest wages in the Great Plains from 1915 to 1924 despite systematic repression by local, state, and federal officials. The union was also active in the Pacific Northwest's wheat and fruit harvests and in the seasonal round of farm labor that linked Arizona and coastal California. Although closely associated with extractive industries, the seasonal hobo migration also drew from the ranks of factory workers forced into the contingent labor market by the employment policies of meatpackers, railroads, and other industries. Other migrants were sons and daughters of farm families seeking resources to buy their own land and set up their own households. These migrant workers played a vital role in what historians have called "the discovery of unemployment" during the late nineteenth century as Americans debated whether poverty was caused by personal weaknesses or systemic economic failures.

Farm labor policies have long involved federal policy interventions. In addition to aiding in the repression of union organizations, the federal government provided essential funding in the early years of industrial agriculture through commodity price supports, tariffs, agricultural experiment stations, and other research funding. The emergence of the sugar beet industry, soon to employ a large number of migrant laborers, was the direct result of federal policies that sought to protect domestic sugar producers and to promote rural development. Land reclamation, damming, and irrigation projects in Florida, California, and the Pacific Northwest made farming possible in areas that formerly had been swamps or deserts. Meanwhile, federal policies directly and indirectly abetted the massive migration out of the southern states beginning in the 1930s. Federally supported experimentation with cotton hybrids that could grow in the drier California conditions broke the South's monopoly on cotton, while commodity price support programs led to the dispossession of thousands of families. When owners received federal payments to refrain from growing cotton, they often summarily evicted sharecropping families, a particularly acute problem in Arkansas and Missouri, where the Southern Tenant Farmers Union had made some progress in confronting

Latino migrant laborers harvest apples. (Corel Corp.)

exploitative conditions. All of this was part of a half-realized strategy to fight rural poverty by moving people off marginally productive land and into industrial employment. In the interim, the U.S. Farm Security Administration (FSA) built camps for migrant farmworkers to provide them with a modicum of modern living standards. John Steinbeck, author of *The Grapes of Wrath*, made a study of the FSA camps, which he depicted in his novel as clean, orderly, and benevolent alternatives to the camps set up by large private producers and which were popularized as such in the film version of the novel. Significantly, however, the federal government excluded agricultural laborers from the protections of the National Labor Relations Act, the Social Security Act, and the Fair Labor Standards Act.

With World War II, federal immigration and farm labor policy became more closely linked through the Bracero Program (1943–1964). With this program, migrant labor and farm labor became more closely associated because of labor market segmentation, augmented by the fact that braceros, at least nominally, could only work in agriculture. However, many braceros jumped their contracts in order to find work in other industries and settle into Mexican American communities. As a contract labor system, the Bracero Program undermined unionization efforts because workers could be deported through the collusion of employers and federal immigration agents. With the end of the program, farm unionization began anew, especially in California with the United Farm Workers, under the leadership of Cesar Chavez. By the 1970s, a farm labor movement closely associated with the Chicana/o movement emerged in midwestern farm states as well. Although these farm labor organizations have had some success in bargaining with large growers, labor market deregulation, repressive welfare policies, and intensified global migration of the 1980s and 1990s have increased the ranks of poor workers who continue to move about the country in search of work opportunities.

Frank Tobias Higbie

See also: Agricultural and Farm Labor Organizing; Bracero Program; Contingent Work; Day Labor; Deserving/Undeserving Poor; Dust Bowl Migration; *Factories in the Field; The Grapes of Wrath; Harvest of Shame;* Immigrants and Immigration; Immigration Policy; New Deal Farm Policy; Sharecropping; "Working Poor"

References and Further Reading

Daniel, Cletus. 1981. *Bitter Harvest: A History of California Farmworkers, 1870–1941*. Ithaca, NY: Cornell University Press.

Griffith, David, and Ed Kissam. 1995. *Working Poor: Farmworkers in the United States*. Philadelphia: Temple University Press.

Hahamovitch, Cindy. 1997. *The Fruits of Their Labor: Atlantic Coast Farmworkers and the Making of Migrant Poverty, 1870–1945*. Chapel Hill: University of North Carolina Press.

Higbie, Frank Tobias. 2003. *Indispensable Outcasts: Hobo Workers and Community in the American Midwest, 1880–1930*. Urbana: University of Illinois Press.

Valdés, Dennis Nodin. 1991. *Al Norte: Agricultural Workers in the Great Lakes Region, 1917–1970*. Austin: University of Texas Press.

Minimum Wage

The minimum wage is the smallest hourly wage that an employee may be paid as mandated by national law. As an employer mandate, it is designed to improve the wages, benefits, and employment conditions of unorganized workers. Established in U.S. federal law by the Fair Labor Standards Act (FLSA) of 1938, the minimum wage is considered a bedrock of labor-protective regulation and social welfare provision for less-skilled workers (for full-time and part-time workers in the private sector and in federal, state, and local governments). The immediate beneficiaries are by definition low-wage workers. Low-skilled workers in the South (for example, in the sawmill and apparel industries) were among the major beneficiaries of the initial legislation (which, in a bargain with southern Democrats, excluded agricultural and domestic workers until the 1960s). Today, minimum-wage workers are predominantly adult women (although a large proportion are teenagers) and are concentrated in the retail and service industries in such female-dominated jobs as cashiers and food preparers.

The Seventy-fifth Congress (well-known for the emergence of a conservative legislative coalition of southern Democrats and Republicans) established the federal minimum wage at an initial twenty-five cents per hour, to increase to thirty cents in 1944 and to forty cents in 1945. In the FLSA, Congress also defined the criteria that brought firms under its interstate commerce authority; specified industry, firm, and occupational exemptions; and retained statutory control over the magnitude and the timing of future adjustments. Congress, along with the president, revisits the minimum wage when exogenous economic changes (such as changes in the cost of living) or electoral conditions generate pressures to raise it. During the twentieth century, the minimum wage was increased nineteen times. In addition, the FLSA was amended eight times to extend coverage to more workers.

Historically, minimum-wage policy bargains have required political compromise among three groups in Congress: northern Democrats, generally representing more-urban, working-class, and politically liberal constituencies; southern Democrats, historically conservative, committed to racial segregation, antiunion, and resistant to federal regulation of any kind; and Republicans, who until the 1980s and the rise of the right wing of the party were dominated by more moderate, pro-business interests. For most of the period from 1938 to 1994, none of these players commanded a majority in Congress. Policy change resulted when members traded support and forged bargains over various provisions with other members and with the president in order to form an enacting coalition. Minimum-wage advocates, who controlled committee agendas, designed legislation to enact a change. Opponents typically preferred the status quo, allowing inflation to erode the value of the existing minimum wage. The outcome hinged upon the support of a third group, the moderates, whose preference for minor adjustment lay between the positions of the two ideological extremes. The bargain that emerged was an *intraparty* agreement between northern and southern Democrats, achieved by minimizing the scope and reducing the magnitude and/or extending the timing of any increase. Most recently, the 1996 Small Business Job Protection Act—representing a new *interparty* bargain between moderate Republicans and Democrats—was strategically allowed by the conservative House Republican leadership when a wage increase was linked with compensatory tax breaks for small business. Over the course of the twentieth century, no statutory action accounted for the most significant nonincremental policy change, as daily changes in the cost of living eroded the real value of the latest (nominal) minimum-wage increase. In addition, the congressional incremental phase-in over several years (that is, an escalator clause) of each minimum-wage increase was designed to minimize the magnitude of the annual wage cost that was imposed on businesses and to mitigate the potential adverse inflationary or employment effects.

As a tool of poverty alleviation, the minimum wage traditionally has been a mechanism to provide economic assistance to workers by effectively boosting their wages. Nevertheless, as an instrument of redistribution, it has long been a controversial political and policy issue; over the past few decades the minimum wage has failed to keep up with the cost of living and has lost value in real terms.

Supporters of the minimum wage argue that it does what it is supposed to: lift the wages of those workers with the least bargaining power. Its opponents, however, claim that it costs jobs by pricing low-wage workers out of the labor market and discouraging job creation. Although the claims of opponents have been challenged in empirical research, many use those claims to argue that raising the minimum wage is not necessarily the best way to aid the poor. The minimum wage can also benefit other workers indirectly, however, by making sure that the wage scale does not fall below reasonable standards of compensation, which is why the erosion of the minimum wage is also a sign of the declining political and economic position of wage labor. As the U.S. earnings distribution has widened and as wages at the bottom have eroded since the early 1970s, an increasing number of adults have become potential direct beneficiaries of minimum-wage legislation over the years.

Currently, covered nonexempt workers are entitled to a minimum wage of not less than $5.15 per hour, and this nominal value remains well below historic levels. The real value of today's minimum wage is 30 percent below its peak in 1968 and 24 percent below its level in 1979. The minimum wage reached its highest value in real terms in 1968, at $7.67 (in 1999 dollars). With five phased-in increases during the 1970s, its value held at approximately $6.60. The last increase of the 1970s left the inflation-adjusted value at $6.66. From 1981 through 1990, the nominal value did not change, eroding its real value at the end of the 1980s to $4.50. Although the nominal value was raised in two steps, from $3.35 to $3.60 in 1990 and to $4.25 in 1991, the value in real terms was still below its peak. By 1996, inflation had largely wiped out the 1990 increase, and the minimum wage adjusted for inflation reached a forty-year low (U.S. National Economic Council 2000, 2). In 1996, a two-step increase was enacted, lifting the minimum from $4.25 to $5.15, which was estimated to benefit 10 million workers. President George W. Bush recently proposed that states should be allowed to opt out of any federal increase. Currently, states can set a higher minimum wage, and ten states mandate minimum wages above the federal minimum floor (U.S. Department of Labor 2001).

In 1999, a full-time minimum-wage worker earned $157 less than the income required to reach the two-person family poverty threshold, whereas a full-time worker earning the minimum could have maintained a three-person family above the poverty threshold in 1969 and over most of the 1970s. During the 1980s, with no increases, the earning power of the minimum wage relative to the family poverty thresholds declined steadily, falling below the two-person threshold for the first time in 1985 and not rising above it again until 1997. At the same time, the Earned Income Tax Credit (EITC), which began in 1975 and was significantly expanded in 1993 and 2001, has softened the impact of a declining minimum wage. The average refundable tax credit, which provides payments even to families who owe no taxes, brought many minimum-wage workers supporting a family of two above the corresponding poverty threshold (U.S. Department of Labor 2001).

The minimum wage can improve the well-being of some low-wage workers. Some analysts confirm that an appropriately set minimum wage is likely to do more good (in redistribution) than harm in terms of employment and inflation (Freeman 1996). Others conclude that it is not the most efficient policy because it is not well targeted and because only about one-fifth of affected workers live in poor families (Mincy 1990, 1). However, a minimum wage is not the complete solution to poverty and low wages: Policies are also needed to augment the skills of the low-paid. Many believe that linking the minimum wage and the EITC creates an effective antipoverty measure, but it remains unclear whether the two will evolve as complements or substitutes in an effort to help working families.

Daniel P. Gitterman

See also: Earned Income Tax Credit (EITC); Fair Labor Standards Act (FLSA); Great Depression and New Deal; Poverty Line; "Working Poor"

References and Further Reading

Freeman, Richard. 1996. "The Minimum Wage as a Redistributive Tool." *The Economic Journal* 106 (May): 639–649.

Mincy, Ronald. 1990. "Raising the Minimum Wage: Effects on Family Poverty." *Monthly Labor Review* 113 (July): 18–25.

U.S. Department of Labor. 2001. *Minimum Wage and Overtime Hours under the Fair Labor Standards Act*. Washington, DC: Employment Standards Administration, Wages and Hours Division.

U.S. National Economic Council. 2000. *The Minimum Wage: Increasing the Reward for Work*. A report by the National Economic Council with the Assistance of the Council of Economic Advisers and the Office of the Chief Economist, U.S. Department of Labor. Washington, DC.

Missionaries

A missionary is an individual participating in a ministry commissioned by a religious organization to propagate its faith or carry on humanitarian work. Missionaries usually regulate their enterprise through a careful course of sermons and services given to convert the non-Christian or to quicken diminished faith. Throughout American history, missionaries have labored to assimilate non-Christians both at home and abroad to their worldview. They have been a critical component of settlement and colonialism, providing essential social networks for America's geographic and cultural expansion.

Since the arrival of colonists in America, missionary efforts have been an integral aspect of settlement. Whether it was Puritans preaching on Martha's Vineyard, Spanish Jesuits teaching the catechism to the Zuni, or Russians plying their orthodoxy in Alaska, Christian missionaries tackled the American wilderness with as much enthusiasm and stoic endurance as any frontiersman. For the monarchs and religious leaders funding these missions, spiritual and physical conquest were inseparable. In a commendation to Pedro Menéndez de Avilés, the leader of the original Catholic expedition to Florida in the 1560s, Philip II of Spain admired Menéndez's zeal "for the service of God Our Lord, and for the increase to the Royal Crown of these kingdoms" (Hutchison 1987, 17). Menéndez's converted natives were accountable as profits to the growing Spanish New World. The enduring colonial empire would simultaneously conquer and "save" its native subjects, easing the march of civilization with an education in the encroaching civilization.

Colonial missionary efforts were never merely about conversion. Missionaries labored to teach Native Americans the etiquette, literacy, and theology of their own culture. One of the earliest missions in America was founded in Massachusetts in 1646 by John Eliot, who attempted to ease the Native Americans into their new faith with a translation of the Bible into the local tongue. "I find it absolutely necessary to carry on civility with religion," Eliot noted in 1649 (Hutchison 1987, 15). Indeed, Eliot attempted to isolate native converts by placing them in "praying towns," where they could be fully immersed into Christian civilization.

By the mid-eighteenth century, Protestant revivals had consumed New England, causing a major theological shift from the Puritan emphasis on social covenant to an evangelical push for individual salvation. From this point forward, American Protestants saw evangelization of non-Christians as a responsibility placed upon a uniquely blessed people. Since the Puritans had arrived in the New World, there had existed a pervasive sense of America as a "chosen" nation. Now, after revolutions in government and theology, American Christians sought to fulfill this promise through an extension of their avid holiness into the world.

During the first half of the nineteenth century, missionary efforts were largely focused on resident non-Christians. In the South, missionaries from the Society for the Propagation of the Gospel in Foreign Parts (SPG) relentlessly pursued African slaves; members of the SPG believed slave conversion was a responsibility of slave ownership. They failed to convert many slaves, however, and it was not until Baptist and Methodist itinerant preachers spread across the rural South that Blacks began to convert in large numbers. The frontier was another site for evangelical success. Methodist circuit preachers, Bible-society agents, and medical missionaries mapped the American West. These itinerants not only attempted to convert "heathen" natives but also sought to civilize the western wilderness.

Alongside the Baptist and Methodist revivals of the antebellum era emerged the first national foreign mission societies. With their emphasis on the equality of all believers, the authority of charismatic leadership, and dramatic conversion rites, Baptist and Methodist missionaries were particularly skilled translators of Christendom. The "Great Century" of American missionary work was initiated and maintained by their assiduous efforts abroad, as these Protestants instituted their labor through the formation of the United Foreign Missionary Society, the American Board of Commissioners for Foreign Missions, the Baptist Board of Foreign Missions, and the Missionary Society of Connecticut. Following the multiple sectarian splits of the Civil War, missionary societies regrouped and redoubled their efforts, supporting missions throughout East and Southeast Asia, the South Pacific, Africa, and South America.

The 1888 founding of the Student Volunteer Movement, an organization focused on the recruitment of college-age volunteers, provided the organizational center for missionary activity. Prior to 1880, American missions abroad had been maintained by a relatively narrow sector of Protestant America. With the massive influx of young missionaries, missions became the central effort of American Christianity. The number of American foreign missionaries, which stood at 934 in 1890, reached nearly 5,000 a decade later and over 9,000 in 1915. This late-nineteenth-century missionary activity reflected the increased wealth of Protestant congregations, the general optimism of a prosperous nation, and a geopolitical obsession with imperial power. Missions provided—in the words of historian William Hutchison—the "moral equivalent" of imperialism (Hutchison 1987, 204), an on-the-ground translation of colonial power in religious terms.

The masses of young missionaries traveling abroad included a large cohort of women. By 1915, there were more than 3 million women on the membership rolls of some forty denominational missionary societies. Missionary activity offered American women a position of power and an opportunity for international adventure. In addition, theologians of missions suggested that missionary work was the special purview of women. Since the mid-nineteenth century, American evangelicals adhered to a theology of missions that attached special significance to the conversion of "heathen" mothers as the most efficient means of Christianizing heathen lands. The late-nineteenth-century "cult of true womanhood" further underlined this role, suggesting that the ideal woman was an "educated mother" extending her intelligent domesticity to manifold progeny.

The mid-twentieth century saw several shifts in American missionary activity. First, liberal Christians were increasingly critical of missions. Liberal belief in the sanctity of cultural pluralism suggested to many that the imperial element of mission work was inherently unethical. As liberals distanced themselves from this aspect of Christian work, Pentecostals, Mormons, and Catholics tackled the mission fields. Although Jesuits had been working as missionaries in America since the sixteenth century, in 1911, the Maryknoll Order established the first American-based Catholic missionary association, the American Foreign Missionary Society. Mormons and Pentecostals have seen enormous success abroad, with Pentecostal denominations growing at a faster rate internationally than any other Christian body.

It is easy to deride the missionary enterprise as a grotesque form of imperialism. However, it is important to recall the critical role missionaries played as cultural informants. During the nineteenth century, a vast majority of Americans derived their knowledge of non-Western people from the writings of missionaries. Moreover, missionaries abroad do not always pursue their "heathen" subjects with relentless and righteous ardor. Rather, many missionaries used their position to help local populations resist the encroachment of the more obtrusive colonial powers. Northern Baptists promoted indigenous autonomy and cultural distinctiveness within churches in Burma, and Methodist revivalists validated vernacular expressions of African spirituality. Although one must never lose sight of the primary motivation of missionaries—conversion—their relationships with native communities were and are nothing if not complex.

Kathryn Lofton

See also: Christian Fundamentalism; Colonial Period through the Early Republic; Social Gospel

References and Further Reading

Case, Jay Riley. 1999. "Conversion, Civilization, and Cultures in the Evangelical Missionary Mind, 1814–1906." Ph.D. diss., University of Notre Dame.

Chaney, Charles L. 1976. *The Birth of Missions in America*. South Pasadena, CA: William Carey Library.

Hutchison, William R. 1987. *Errand to the World: American Protestant Thought and Foreign Missions*. Chicago: University of Chicago Press.

Mothers of the South, *Margaret Hagood*

Margaret Hagood's *Mothers of the South* typifies the Depression-era interest in documenting contemporary social conditions as a means of influencing social change. Hagood, born in Georgia in 1907, earned a Ph.D. from the Institute for Research in Social Science at the University of North Carolina in 1937, where she studied with

Howard Odum, the leading southern social scientist of the era. Odum sought to train academics who would help solve the economic and social problems of the South. Hagood's dissertation relied on statistical analysis to determine how the high fertility of white southern women related to the region's economic difficulties. Her next study was a more personal examination of white tenant women. For over a year, Hagood interviewed hundreds of women about their lives, children, marriages, and farmwork. The resulting book, *Mothers of the South* (1939), was a generally sympathetic and thoughtful portrait of white farm women and the triple tasks of farm labor, household management, and child rearing they were performing. While echoing her male colleagues in criticizing the grueling labor conditions and political economy of southern sharecropping, she was unique—and pathbreaking—in acknowledging the gender inequities implicated in its patriarchal character. At the same time, in the interest of advocating better education and stricter birth control practices, Hagood suggested that the poverty and isolation of rural life were fostering a culturally backward population that—allowed to propagate unchecked—threatened the social health of the nation.

In 1940, Hagood, along with University of North Carolina–trained sociologist Harriet Herring and Farm Security Administration photographers Dorothea Lange and Marion Post, produced a documentary photography project on North Carolina. The photographs, featuring people of all classes, buildings of various kinds, and farmland, were exhibited at the University of North Carolina in 1940. Hagood viewed the exhibition as "an opportunity for us to demonstrate to ourselves and others some of the potentialities of Photography as a tool for social research" (Scott 1996, "Introduction," x).

The excerpt below demonstrates Hagood's mix of sympathy and worry directed at tenant women, typical of *Mothers of the South*.

Sarah Case

See also: Picturing Poverty (I); Poor Whites; Poverty Research; Rural Poverty; Sharecropping

. . . [T]he Southern tenant farm mothers compose a group who epitomize, as much as any, the results of the wastes and lags of the Region. They suffer the direct consequences of a long-continued cash crop economy; they undergo extreme social impoverishment from the lack and unequal distribution of institutional services; and they bear the brunt of a regional tradition—compounded of elements from religion, patriarchy, and aristocracy—which subjects them to class and sex discrimination. Moreover, they continue to augment the pathologies of the Region by their very functioning as they produce, at a ruinous cost to both the land and themselves, the cotton and tobacco by which the rural South still lives, and the children who are simultaneously the Region's greatest asset and most crucial problem. . . .

As a group for a unit of study in the broad research program on all the resources and wastes of the South, the tenant farm mothers embody many of the causes, processes, and effects of the general regional problems of an exploiting agriculture, overpopulation, general cultural retardation, chronological and technological lag. . . . our focus of attention is on these mothers as a unit of the present human resources of the South and as an important source of the future human resources of both the South and other regions of the United States.

Source: Margaret Jarman Hagood, *Mothers of the South: Portraiture of the White Tenant Farm Woman* (Chapel Hill: University of North Carolina Press, 1939; reprint, with introduction by Anne Firor Scott, Charlottesville: University of Virginia Press, 1996), 4–5.

Mothers' Pensions

See Aid to Families with Dependent Children (ADC/AFDC); Maternalism; Maternalist Policy; Progressive Era and 1920s; Welfare Policy/Welfare Reform

Moynihan, Daniel Patrick

See Family Structure; Moynihan Report; Poverty Research; Welfare Policy/Welfare Reform

Moynihan Report

The Moynihan Report is a government document, first released in 1965, that purported to explain the persistence of high rates of Black poverty by pointing to the "pathological" condition of the lower-class Negro family. Highly controversial as social policy and largely discredited as social science, the report is nevertheless invoked to this day as an authoritative document in poverty debates.

In the spring of 1965, Assistant Secretary of Labor Daniel Patrick Moynihan (who would later serve as a domestic policy adviser in the administration of President Richard M. Nixon and as Democratic senator from New York, 1977–2000) completed a "confidential" report intended to influence the government's post–civil rights–era "race" policies. The report, *The Negro Family: The Case for National Action*, argued that in the decade between the Supreme Court's school desegregation decision (*Brown v. Board of Education of Topeka, Kansas*, 347 U.S. 483) in 1954 and the passage of the 1964 Civil Rights Act, the United States had achieved the political, administrative, and judicial conditions to support full citizenship rights for Blacks. But, according to Moynihan, as long as the Negro (the prevailing term for African Americans in 1965) family remained mired in poverty and "pathology," this group would never be "equal" to other populations in the United States.

The Moynihan Report was eventually released into—and exacerbated—an explosive political context. Many Black activists and their white allies were increasingly frustrated that new antiracist laws and policies were not being enforced and that, as a result, African American families continued to experience discrimination and poverty shaped by institutional racism.

The report did not find fault with law enforcement or institutional policies, however. It faulted Negroes themselves. In Moynihan's view, in the hundred years since the Thirteenth Amendment to the U.S. Constitution ended slavery, the "disorganized" Black family—whose "disorganization" was originally the legacy of that slavery—had become more unstable than ever. Using descriptive data, including on Black rates of divorce and illegitimacy, on welfare "dependency," and on male unemployment and the percentages of Black youth found inadequate for the armed forces, Moynihan argued that such "pathological" social characteristics (1) created poverty, (2) sustained poverty, and (3) had achieved an "independent existence"; that is, they no longer depended on the legacy of slavery or institutional practices.

Progressive activists, scholars, and others were outraged by these arguments. In their view, the data showed unequal educational attainment but ignored unequal funding of inner-city schools. Nor had Moynihan presented data showing unequal race and class-based access to reproductive options when he defined Negro rates of illegitimacy as "pathological." He omitted information about widespread race-based wage differentials and hiring and firing practices; discrimination within housing, credit, and labor union arenas; law enforcement practices that targeted poor minorities; and other forms of institutional racism that locked African Americans into poverty.

Mainstream media responded to the report by referring to its "sensitive" treatment of difficult issues or by casting it as an illuminating exposé. Looking back on 1965, it bears mentioning that the passive, pathological image of Negro ghetto life in the report was sharply out of concert with the ever more militant phase of the civil rights movement then emerging. Similarly, Moynihan's excoriation of the "matriarchal" Negro family seems in retrospect to have been shaped by a kind of gender-status anxiety at the historical moment when various kinds of feminist activism were emerging. Thus, in a conclusion that at least some commentators at the time found questionable, Moynihan routinely used findings of Black female economic independence and comparative educational achievement as evidence of Black male emasculation—another symptom of the "pathology" Moynihan claimed to be documenting.

Despite the objections and counterarguments of African American activists and their allies in the 1960s, the report achieved the status of an iconic policy document. It has provided an enduring, if fallacious, argument for sharply constrained social spending, a strategy for "blaming the victim," and a model for "family values" rhetoric for the rest of the twentieth century and beyond.

Rickie Solinger

See also: Family Structure; *The Negro Family in the United States;* Poverty Research; Racial Segregation; Racism; "Underclass"; Welfare Policy/Welfare Reform

References and Further Reading

Bensonsmith, Dionne. 2002. "It's No Longer Just about Race: Social Constructions of American Citizenship in the Moynihan Report." In *Women's Work Is Never Done*, ed. Sylvia Bashevkin, 41–67. New York: Routledge.

Mink, Gwendolyn, and Rickie Solinger, eds. 2003. *Welfare: A Documentary History of U.S. Policy and Politics*. New York: New York University Press.

Murray, Charles

See Family Structure; *Losing Ground;* New Right

Mutual Aid

Mutual aid societies were a significant source of basic welfare services, especially insurance for illness, death, and funeral expenses, from the early nineteenth century until the growth of state services during the mid-twentieth century.

The earliest mutual aid societies were secret fraternal organizations such as the Masons, which supported members on an ad hoc basis. One fraternal group, the Odd Fellows, pioneered a more formalized mutual aid system, setting specific amounts for particular needs and establishing insurance as a benefit of membership paid for by annual dues. Just after the Civil War, the number of mutual aid societies in the United States mushroomed. Late-nineteenth-century groups combined the fraternal organizations' heritage of ritual and secrecy with a more sophisticated and generous distribution of aid. Although insurance remained their primary form of welfare, several operated orphanages, health clinics, hospitals, and homes for the elderly. One historian has estimated that by 1910, one-third of the American male population over the age of nineteen belonged to a fraternal organization (Beito 2000, 14). Women joined organizations as well, some specifically female, others open to both sexes. All mutual aid societies had some sort of selection criteria, usually based on sex, occupation, religion, or ethnicity.

Mutual aid societies appealed to Americans by providing needed aid while avoiding the stigma attached to charity or poor relief. By stressing such values as self-discipline, restraint, thrift, and temperance as well as a sense of shared responsibility, mutual aid societies allowed members to view their support as reinforcing rather than violating masculine ideals of independence. Further, government aid in this era was often inadequate and was usually limited to groups deemed "deserving," a stipulation that often functioned to exclude members of racial, ethnic, or religious minorities.

Indeed, mutual aid societies became popular among both African Americans and immigrant groups. The rise of fraternal societies coincided with the highest rate of immigration ever witnessed in the United States, from the late nineteenth to the early twentieth centuries, mostly from southern and eastern European countries. Ethnically based mutual aid societies provided financial support and a sense of community for newly arrived immigrants. Among African Americans, mutual aid societies represented self-help and racial pride. The membership of these societies cut across social classes, although leaders tended to come from the elite. Many included a religious component and served as civil rights societies as well as aid societies, providing a basis for organization both in local communities and nationwide.

In the 1920s, growth in membership slowed considerably as mutual aid societies suffered from the development of the commercial insurance industry, scandals of financial mismanagement within prominent societies, alternative demands on leisure time (including the radio and movies), and the slowdown of immigration. During the Depression, many members found it impossible to continue paying dues. Further, the extension of government services associated with the New Deal, especially Social Security, as well as the commercial companies' success in tying insurance to employment, made the aid functions of fraternal organizations less significant. Mutual aid societies suffered a dramatic drop in membership during the Depression, and numbers did not rise after the return to financial stability. Today, most fraternal organizations stress service to the local community rather than the provision of insurance and social welfare for members.

Sarah Case

See also: African American Migration; Charity; Community Chests; Immigrants and Immigration; Nonprofit Sector; Voluntarism

References and Further Reading

Beito, David. 2000. *From Mutual Aid to the Welfare State: Fraternal Societies and Social Services, 1890–1967*. Chapel Hill: University of North Carolina Press.

Cohen, Lizbeth. 1990. *Making a New Deal: Industrial Workers in Chicago, 1919–1939*. New York: Cambridge University Press.

Trotter, Joe William, Jr. 1990. *Coal, Class, and Color: Blacks in Southern West Virginia, 1915–32*. Urbana and Chicago: University of Illinois Press.

Nation of Islam

The Nation of Islam is a controversial religious movement with strong Black nationalist teachings that was established among poor Black southern migrants to Detroit in July 1930 by a mysterious person called Master Fard Muhammad. It has become the most enduring and strongest carrier of Black nationalism in U.S. society, producing a number of charismatic leaders such as Elijah Muhammad, Malcolm X, Muhammad Ali, Wallace Muhammad, and Louis Farrakhan. It also provided the foundations for the Black Power movement in the late 1960s. As a religious sect, the "Lost-Found Nation of Islam" survived several changes in leadership after Master Fard disappeared in 1934. Elijah Muhammad led the Nation from 1934 to 1975, and his son Wallace, who took over in 1975, produced a split in the membership by leading the majority of followers to orthodox, or Sunni, Islam. In 1978, Minister Louis Farrakhan led a rival faction to reestablish the Nation of Islam by emphasizing the teachings of Elijah Muhammad.

The major contributions of the Nation of Islam to the themes of poverty and social welfare lay in its religious ideology and in its attempts at the moral reformation of the marginalized Black poor. The teachings of Fard and Elijah Muhammad focused on a two-pronged attack upon the psyche and racial environment of Black people: "Know yourself" and "Do for self." The emphasis upon self-knowledge and self-identity was a critical consciousness-raising tool to affirm Blackness and African heritage in a society where both were denigrated. The task was to reverse the psychological valence of felt shame and worthlessness to one that saw Black people as "Allah's Chosen" and the "cream of the Planet Earth." The physical appearance of the Black Muslims reflected their confidence and pride; men in suits and bow ties acted as security guards or sold the Nation's newspapers on ghetto streets, and women in long, flowing white gowns and head coverings spoke at meetings.

The rallying cry of "Do for self" meant that alcoholics, drug addicts, prostitutes, and criminals had to clean themselves up and change their lives. It also meant that Black Muslims should not be dependent upon welfare or government aid but should work diligently to support themselves and their families through jobs or small businesses. Under Elijah Muhammad and Louis Farrakhan, members of the Nation have established thousands of small businesses—including grocery stores, bakeries, restaurants, bookstores, video and record shops, and cosmetic companies. In order to establish an independent economy for the Nation, members have bought farms to raise cattle and vegetable produce and have tried to set up their own banks and hospitals. The Nation's newspapers, Elijah Muhammad's *Muhammad Speaks* and Farrakhan's *Final Call*, also became fund-raising devices for individuals and mosques. C. Eric Lincoln aptly called the members of the Nation "Black puritans" because they worked hard, saved their money, and did not spend frivolously.

Farrakhan's highly successful Million Man March in 1995, in which close to 1 million Black people gathered in the largest crowd in the history of demonstrations in Washington, D.C., led to the establishment of an Economic Development Fund that proposes to build more schools, hospitals, farms, stores, airplanes, and good homes for members of the Nation.

The prisons, streets, and small Black storefront churches became recruiting grounds for ministers of the Nation like Malcolm X, who liked to "fish" for the souls of the poor. Under Farrakhan's leadership, members have been successful in getting rid of drug dealers in a number of public housing projects and private apartment buildings. The Nation has succeeded in organizing a peace pact between gang members in Los Angeles and those in several other cities. It has established a clinic for the treatment of AIDS patients in Washington, D.C. Under the leadership of Minister Abdullah Muhammad, the National Prison Reform Ministry has been established.

Farrakhan's messages of Black unity, self-knowledge, and economic independence and a biting critique of American society have struck a responsive chord among the Black masses. Rap groups and rappers like Public Enemy and Prince Akeem have helped popularize the appeal of the Nation, with songs such as "It Takes a Million to Hold Us Back" and "Coming Down Like Babylon."

Since 2000, Farrakhan has moved closer to Sunni Islam, instituting the Friday Jumu'ah prayer service and fasting during the lunar month of Ramadan. However, his focus is still on developing an Islam for Black people.

Lawrence H. Mamiya

See also: African American Migration; African Americans; Black Churches; Crime Policy; Islam

References and Further Reading

Gardell, Mattias. 1996. *In the Name of Elijah Muhammad: Minister Louis Farrakhan and the Nation of Islam*. Durham, NC: Duke University Press.

Lincoln, C. Eric. 1960. *The Black Muslims in America*. Boston: Beacon Press.

Mamiya, Lawrence H. 1982. "From Black Muslim to Bilalian: The Evolution of a Movement." *Journal for the Scientific Study of Religion* 21, no. 2 (June): 138–153.

———. 1999. "Louis Farrakhan, the Nation of Islam, and the Civil Rights Movement." In *Civil Rights in the United States*, ed. Waldo E. Martin and Patricia Sullivan, 271–272. New York: Macmillan.

National Association for the Advancement of Colored People (NAACP)

The National Association for the Advancement of Colored People (NAACP) is one of the oldest and largest civil rights organizations in the United States. The association was founded in New York City on February 12, 1909, the 100th anniversary of President Abraham Lincoln's birth, by white and Black activists who were outraged by the blatant violence and discrimination directed against Blacks in all parts of the country. During this time, Black men were being lynched, Black women were employed largely as maids and domestic servants, and the Black community lived in a state of extreme poverty. The founders of the NAACP, including Mary White Ovington, Oswald Garrison Villard, W. E. B. Du Bois, William English Walling, and Ida Wells-Barnett, believed that the situation of Blacks directly contradicted the ideals of the Declaration of Independence, the U.S. Constitution, and the Emancipation Proclamation.

The NAACP founders and early members wanted a militant alternative to the compromising posture of Tuskegee Institute founder Booker T. Washington, who downplayed citizenship rights while stressing industrial education and economic development for Blacks. From its earliest days, the NAACP has pursued multiple strategies to call national attention to the subordinate position of Blacks in American society. The group's activities have contributed to some of the most important legal, political, and social changes in American history.

In 1910, Du Bois was hired as director of publicity and research. In this capacity, he edited *The Crisis*, the NAACP's monthly publication. In it, he challenged race prejudice and ideas of Black inferiority and documented the atrocities and injustices occurring against Blacks. For more than two decades, Du Bois contributed singularly to the NAACP media tradition of strong condemnation of racism and passivity in the face of racial injustice. He also recorded the achievements of African Americans. *The Crisis* gained a circulation of more than 50,000 within its first decade.

The NAACP grew dramatically under the leadership of James Weldon Johnson, Walter White, and Roy Wilkins from the 1920s to the 1970s. Johnson, the organization's first Black secretary, used his many contacts in Black cultural, educational, and political circles to organize local branches. White, who used his fair complexion to "pass" as a white person and investigate lynching throughout the South, organized branches as he traveled and spoke out against racial discrimination against Blacks. Roy Wilkins investigated Black labor conditions in the South and publicized the brutal conditions of poverty and discrimination faced by Blacks throughout the country. Along with Johnson, White, and Wilkins, other organizational representatives met frequently with elected officials to present the findings of their investigations and to encourage the passage of legislation to end lynchings and other forms of blatant discrimination and violence against Blacks.

The NAACP also formed a legal committee and recruited such outstanding lawyers as Charles Hamilton Houston and Thurgood Marshall to challenge the many institutionalized forms of racial discrimination. More than any other group, the NAACP challenged the legality of racial discrimination and Jim Crow segregation in education, housing, transportation, government, and practically all other areas of American life. Although the NAACP Legal Defense and Educational Fund eventually became a separate organization, NAACP lawyers have won many legal victories over the years. The group's most famous legal triumph was the U.S. Supreme Court's unanimous 1954 decision in *Brown v. Board of Education of Topeka, Kansas* (347 U.S. 483) declaring "separate but equal" educational facilities unconstitutional.

The civil rights movement from the mid-1950s to the mid-1960s, strong support from President Lyndon B. Johnson, and key congressional leadership resulted in the passage of the Civil Rights Act of 1964 and the Voting Rights Act of 1965. This important federal legislation represented the culmination of decades of work by the NAACP and other civil rights organizations. Following widespread state and local resistance to the new laws, the NAACP protested and went to court to force racist public officials, especially in the South, to allow Blacks to vote and to end formal discrimination against Blacks. The election of President Richard M. Nixon in 1968 led to conservative public policies and a narrower interpretation of the new civil rights legislation. The NAACP disagreed with the Nixon administration's hostility to Johnson's Great Society and antipoverty programs.

Since the 1970s, the NAACP has worked actively toward the same goals that occupied earlier NAACP leaders: full equality for Blacks and the elimination of racial violence and discrimination against Blacks. The NAACP has used new instruments (that is, the civil rights legislation) to pursue the old goal of guaranteeing African Americans all the rights of and opportunities open to white Americans. The NAACP has continued to emphasize the legal struggle against white racism and Black subordination. The association has denounced and sought legal

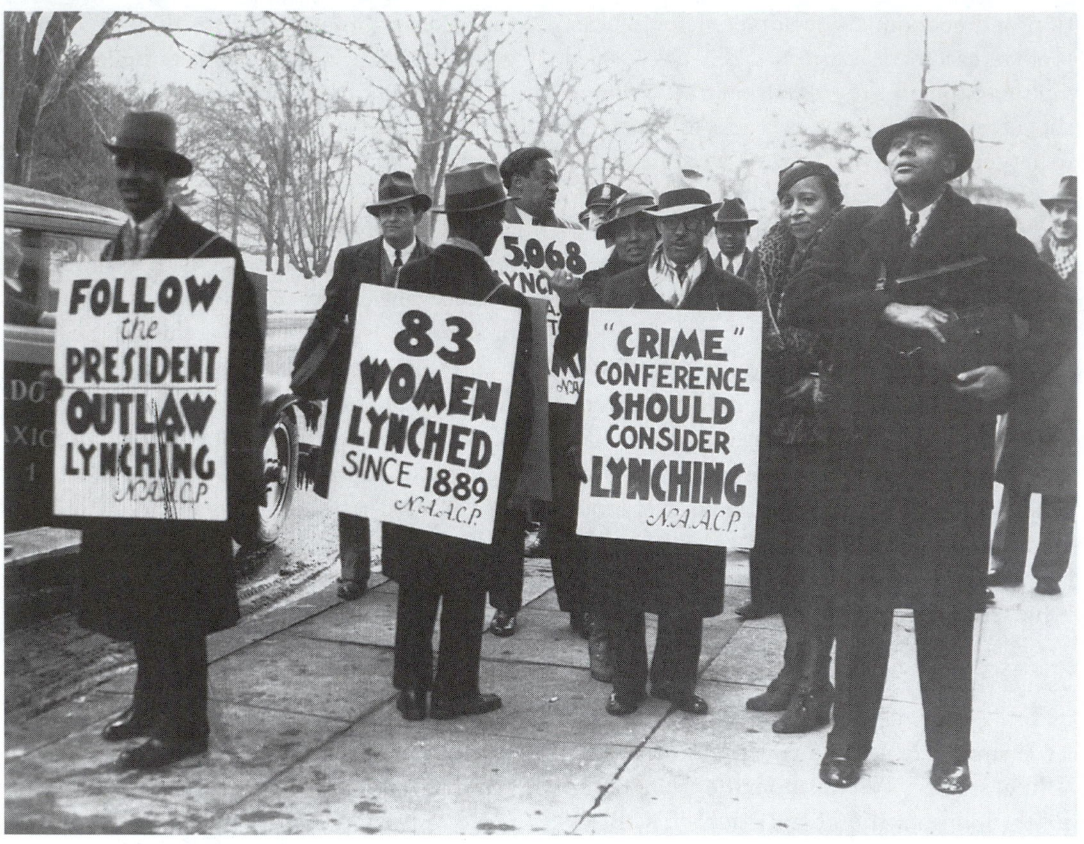

Members of the National Association for the Advancement of Colored People hold signs protesting the practice of lynching while a conference on crime takes place at the Capitol. Washington, D.C. (Corbis)

remedies to police brutality, the failure to achieve racial integration in schools, and the cutbacks in government programs (for example, affirmative action and contract set-asides) that benefited Blacks.

In addition to the legal struggle, the NAACP national leadership and department heads have attempted to increase employment, educational, and business opportunities for the Black community. The NAACP has worked with state and local governments, high schools and universities, business groups, fraternities and sororities, churches, and other institutions to inform African Americans about existing opportunities for advancement and to create those opportunities where they did not previously exist. NAACP presidents, such as Benjamin Hooks (1977–1993), Benjamin Chavis (1993–1994), and Kweisi Mfume (1996–present), as well as recent board chairs Myrlie Evers-Williams and Julian Bond, have continued the association's scholarship and test-preparation programs; Afro-American, Cultural, Technological and Scientific Olympics (ACT-SO); Fair Share agreements with businesses; prison programs; and voter education and registration programs. The NAACP has remained one of the most active Black political organizations in the post–civil rights period.

Ollie A. Johnson III

See also: Civil Rights Acts, 1964 and 1991; Civil

Rights Movement; Racial Segregation; Voting Rights Act, 1965

References and Further Reading

Kellogg, Charles F. 1967. *NAACP: A History of the National Association for the Advancement of Colored People, 1909–1920*. Vol. 1. Baltimore: Johns Hopkins University Press.

Watson, Denton L. 1990. *Lion in the Lobby: Clarence Mitchell, Jr.'s Struggle for the Passage of Civil Rights Laws*. New York: William Morrow.

Wedin, Carolyn. 1998. *Inheritors of the Spirit: Mary White Ovington and the Founding of the NAACP*. New York: John Wiley and Sons.

White, Walter. 1995. *A Man Called White: The Autobiography of Walter White*. Athens and London: University of Georgia Press.

National Association of Social Workers (NASW)

The largest and most prominent of U.S. social work organizations is the National Association of Social Workers (NASW), founded in 1955 to represent the professional interests of social work and to address the social structures and processes that generate economic, social, and political inequality.

Social work organizations are the associations founded to establish and maintain the standards of the social work profession, to support social workers through educational and professionalization activities, and, at times, to advocate on behalf of particular approaches to social policy and reform. Their development is part of the larger history of a profession that has undergone a great deal of change and internal contention over time, beginning with the initial emergence in the late nineteenth century of social work as a distinct profession with specific expertise and skills and the attendant rise of organizations designed to support particular aspects of the work social workers do. As early as 1874, social workers gathered under the auspices of the National Conference of Charities and Corrections, and in 1917, the National Social Workers Exchange provided support in job placement for social work positions for self-identified social workers.

As of August 2002, NASW had approximately 147,000 members. In an effort to consolidate amid the diversity and increased specialization within the field, it was formed through the amalgamation of a number of preexisting specialized social work organizations, including the American Association of Medical Social Workers (founded in 1918), the National Association of School Social Workers (1919), and the American Association of Psychiatric Social Workers (1926), and two study groups, the Association for the Study of Community Organization (1946) and the Social Work Research Group (1949) (Colby and Dziegielewski 2001).

Over the years, NASW has been pulled in various directions, reflecting long-standing tensions within the field over such core issues as the relative weights that social justice and social change should be given in professional practice. This issue is frequently referred to as the public-private debate or as the Jane Addams rank-and-file movement approach to practice versus the social casework approach. In contemporary times, this issue has been reignited over the role of private practice within the profession versus the historical commitment to working with the disadvantaged. The sociohistorical context has played an important role in this ongoing debate. NASW's members, and therefore the organization itself, were influenced by the social movements and events of the 1960s and became much more engaged in the political process through lobbying. Despite the movement of the larger U.S. culture to the right from the 1970s through the 1990s and its subsequent move to a more conservative social policy, NASW and the profession have continued to take a progressive stance by advocating for the rights of the less advantaged within the larger society and particularly for oppressed populations.

NASW has also been shaped by internal debates about qualifications for membership in the profession. Membership was initially limited to social workers with master's degrees in social work. In 1969, NASW opened membership to graduates of baccalaureate programs in social work whose programs were accredited by the Council on Social Work Education. NASW is currently the chosen professional home of bachelor's- and master's-level graduates from CSWE-accredited programs as well as of persons earning doctorates in social work and social welfare.

As currently defined, the overall mission of NASW is to work "to enhance the professional growth and development of its members, to create and maintain professional standards, and to advance sound social policies" (NASW). The newly formed organization brought professional unity to social workers engaged professionally in a variety of contexts. NASW has become, in effect, the voice of the profession and has chapters in all fifty states, the District of Columbia, Guam, Puerto Rico, and the U.S. Virgin Islands to carry out state and local activities on behalf of its members and clients. As of 1998, fully 80 percent of NASW's members were women. Fourteen percent of the organization's members identified themselves as ethnic minorities (Dolgoff and Feldstein 2000). Over the years since its founding, NASW has developed a professional association and a code of ethics and is active in the regulation and licensing of social workers in all fifty states, the District of Columbia, Puerto Rico, and the U.S. Virgin Islands.

NASW, its two affiliate organizations (the National Center for Public Policy and Practice and the NASW Communications Network), and its political action arm (Political Action and Candidate Election [PACE]) have engaged the public policy debate around the issues of welfare reform, AIDS, national health care, civil rights, and the prevention of violence.

PACE was established in 1975 by NASW as a political action committee to further NASW's policy agenda at the state and federal levels. PACE conducts research on political candidates and issues, endorses and financially supports political candidates, mobilizes voters by providing information and tools for engaging the political process, and promotes a legislative agenda on issues of importance to NASW. The Educational Legislative Action Network (ELAN), the predecessor lobbying arm of NASW formed in 1970, emerged from NASW's Ad Hoc Committee on Advocacy. This committee viewed advocacy as a constitutive element of social work practice. NASW also has a publishing arm, the NASW Press, which publishes the *NASW News* as well as scholarly journals, books, and reference materials.

In addition to NASW, an array of organizations have formed to represent the particular interests and visions of the nation's social workers. Some of these include the National Association of Black Social Workers (founded in 1968), the Association of Puerto Rican Social Service Workers (1968), the Asian American Social Workers (1968), and the Association of American Indian Social Workers (1971). Others, founded around subspecialty areas within the profession, include the Association for the Advancement of Social Work with Groups, the Association of Oncology Social Workers, the National Membership Committee on Psychoanalysis in Clinical Social Work, the North American Association of Christians in Social Work, the School Social Work Association of America, and the Association for Community Practice and Social Administration.

Susan A. Comerford

See also: Social Work

References and Further Reading

Colby, Ira, and Sophie Dziegielewski. 2001. *Social Work: The People's Profession*. Chicago: Lyceum Books.

Dolgoff, Ralph, and Donald Feldstein. 2000. *Understanding Social Welfare*. Boston: Allyn and Bacon.

Gortner, Harold, Julianne Mahler, and Jeanne Nicholson. 1987. *Organization Theory: A Public Perspective*. Chicago: Dorsey Press.

Jansson, Bruce S. 2001. *The Reluctant Welfare State*. Belmont, CA: Wadsworth.

NASW. Web site. http://www.naswdc.org/nasw/default.asp.

National Campaign for Jobs and Income Support

See Center for Community Change; Welfare Policy/Welfare Reform

National Congress of Mothers

The antecedent of today's National Parent-Teacher Association (PTA), the National Congress of Mothers played a major role in the expansion of public education and welfare services and in the popularization of parent education. Founded in 1897 by Alice McLellan Birney, the congress had 60,000 members by 1915 and was one of the most influential women's organizations in the United States. Theodore Roosevelt was a longtime member of its Advisory Council. In 1908, the congress changed its name to the National Congress of Mothers and Parent-Teacher Associations; in 1924, it dropped the word "mothers," a move that reflected the increasing authority of professional educators and maternalism's declining appeal. By 1930, the National Congress of Parents and Teachers had a membership of 1.5 million.

The ideology of the National Congress of Mothers was rooted in the concept of scientific motherhood, which held that women needed science and medical expertise to rear healthy children, and in the psychological theories of G. Stanley Hall. Applying Charles Darwin's theory

1905: The first board of managers of the National Congress of Mothers: Helen Lewis, Letitia G. Stevenson, Alice M. Birney, Phoebe A. Hearst, Mrs. William L. Wilson, Frances Benjamin Johnston, Clara B. Finley, Mrs. James H. McGill, Helen Birney, Cora E. Fuller, Mary Louisa Butler, and Harriet McLellan. (Library of Congress)

of evolution to child development, Hall argued that every child passed through stages that retraced the evolution of the human race. Members of the National Congress of Mothers embraced Hall's racialized view of child development and celebration of "natural" motherhood. Although most members were elite whites and most chapters were (like the public schools) racially segregated, the congress saw itself as speaking for women of all races and cultures. Prominent African Americans such as Frances Ellen Watkins Harper and Mary Church Terrell spoke at national conventions. A National Congress of Colored Parents and Teachers was established in 1926; it merged with the National PTA in 1970.

The work of the National Congress of Mothers was three-pronged: Members educated themselves about child psychology, they distributed information on scientific child rearing to the poor, and they took their "mother love" into the community, fund-raising for and running local school and child welfare programs until governments began to do so themselves. In the second decade of the twentieth century, typical projects included parent education; school hot lunch programs; fund-raising for playgrounds, music teachers, books, and school supplies; and lobbying governments for kindergartens, health clinics, and paved roads (to improve access to rural schools). The association also campaigned for juvenile courts and the abolition of child labor and was the major force in the crusade for mothers' pensions, which evolved into Aid to Dependent Children (welfare).

The Mothers Congress never took a stand on woman suffrage, but by the early 1920s, it was so closely associated with progressive causes that the notorious Spider Web Chart listed it, along with fourteen other women's organizations, as part of an international socialist-feminist-pacifist conspiracy. Subsequently, the congress turned away from child welfare to focus more narrowly on schools. Today, the National PTA's 6.5 million members remain vigorous advocates of public education, and its Web site still reflects the maternalist philosophy of putting "children first."

Molly Ladd-Taylor

See also: Aid to Families with Dependent Children (ADC/AFDC); Maternalism; Maternalist Policy

References and Further Reading

Ladd-Taylor, Molly. 1994. *Mother-Work: Women, Child Welfare, and the State, 1890–1930*. Urbana: University of Illinois Press.

Skocpol, Theda. 1994. *Protecting Soldiers and Mothers: The Political Origins of Social Policy in the United States*. Cambridge, MA: Harvard University Press.

National Congress of Neighborhood Women

Founded in Brooklyn, New York, in 1974, the National Congress of Neighborhood Women (NCNW) is an organization of working-class women that aims to meet the needs and strengthen the abilities and power base of poor and working-class women by helping them recognize and develop the strengths they already have and by teaching skills to enable them to take more-active roles in the revitalization of their neighborhoods and communities. NCNW-sponsored leadership-training programs for women from around the country led to the creation of numerous affiliate organizations in both urban and rural areas of the United States. NCNW also has developed into an international organization, forming part of the Grassroots Organizations Operating Together in Sisterhood (GROOTS), which NCNW helped found after the UN-sponsored International Women's Conference in Nairobi in 1985.

Jan Peterson had moved to Brooklyn in the early 1970s to direct a Comprehensive Employment and Training Act (CETA) antipoverty program in the Williamsburg-Greenpoint neighborhood. Believing that both the mainstream (largely middle-class-oriented) New York feminist organizations and the overwhelmingly male leadership of the local community were ignoring the needs and concerns of local working-class women, she hired local women through CETA to work on community improvement. Through formal and informal surveys of neighborhood women, they helped identify community concerns and began to organize to meet them. In Brooklyn, NCNW developed programs to train women in leadership skills, engaged in community planning exercises, established a college program in the community through Empire State College, organized to save a firehouse that the city planned to close, worked with others to preserve bus routes in the community and to institute new ones, called local politicians to account, helped rehabilitate an abandoned hospital into housing for low-income families, and engaged in numerous other activities that eventually drew together women from both Italian American and African American neighborhoods.

The centerpiece of NCNW's programs to develop women's leadership is the Leadership Support Group, which brings women together with their peers to share experiences, feelings, ideas, strategies, and skills. Recognizing that a significant part of women's experience, particularly in working-class communities in the United States, is to be alienated from ongoing structures and institutions of power and influence and to be subject to economic and social forces over which those communities have little control, they insisted that working-class women learn how to build bridges to others, who might seem unlike them, to overcome divisions based on race and ethnicity that have traditionally kept such communities apart from one another and in competition for limited resources. Ultimately, NCNW aims to unite women across differences in work to secure for all people decent jobs, wages, housing, and other life basics.

Martha Ackelsberg

See also: Community Organizing

References and Further Reading

Belenky, Mary Field, Lynne A. Bond, and Jacqueline S. Weinstock. 1997. "The National Congress of Neighborhood Women." In *A Tradition That Has No Name: Nurturing the Development of People, Families, and Communities*, ed. Mary Field Belenky, Lynne A. Bond, and Jacqueline S. Weinstock, 202–228. New York: Basic Books.

Susser, Ida. 1982. *Norman Street: Poverty and Politics in an Urban Neighborhood*. New York: Oxford University Press.

National Council of La Raza

The National Council of La Raza (NCLR) is the largest Latino advocacy organization in the United States. Established in 1968, the NCLR works to eradicate poverty, discrimination, and barriers that impede the overall quality of life for Latinos. In order to accomplish these goals, the NCLR directs its efforts toward four objectives. First, the agency's capacity-building initiative supports Latino community-based organizations that serve needs locally. Second, the NCLR conducts research and policy analyses on Latinos and Latino-related issues. Third, the organization supports and conducts research on international projects that may impact Latinos. Finally, the NCLR is very successful at public outreach and information dissemination, particularly to the media.

The NCLR serves all Hispanic groups within the United States. The organization has offices in thirty-nine states and the District of Columbia and Puerto Rico. The NCLR serves more than 20,000 organizations, reaching an astounding 3 million people. The organization is headquartered in Washington, D.C., and has field offices in Chicago, Los Angeles, Phoenix, and San Antonio.

The organization's policy think tank, the Policy Analysis Center, located in Washington, D.C., has an excellent reputation for research as well as for being politically nonpartisan. The think tank provides both primary and secondary research on such issues as immigration, education, housing, poverty, civil rights, foreign policy, and special populations. It has provided expert testimony not only on issues related to the Latino community but also on immigration, education, free trade, race relations, health policy, and tax reform, to name but a few. The NCLR works in conjunction with other organizations to carry out comprehensive and related projects and initiatives. The organization also assists Latinos through its use of "issue networks," which channel funding to HIV/AIDS, health, education, and leadership initiatives.

Currently, the NCLR is involved in eight programmatic priorities: education, health, housing and community economic development, employment and antipoverty, civil rights and immigration, leadership, media advocacy, and technological initiatives. These priorities are based on the strategic plan the organization implemented in 1995. These priorities have since been modified to accommodate the issues' changing importance. For instance, since the late 1990s, the organization has focused on immigration reform, given the anti-immigrant rhetoric that has prevailed.

The organization implemented a series of programs and policies with the intention of increasing overall educational attainment. The initiatives have been aimed at students ranging from the Head Start or preschool level to the high school level. The organization has also facilitated programs that encouraged financial and social support for students. The NCLR has created a community program that works with parents and teachers in order to improve further involvement in education. Encouraging educational participation, the NCLR facilitates afterschool programs and educational alternative programs. In one of their most ambitious projects, the NCLR tested low-cost, community-based educational models at forty-six sites in twenty states. The NCLR also serves as a lobbyist against cuts in funding for bilingual education and advocacy work and against the eradication of farmworker education.

In terms of health care, the NCLR administers programs that work at improving the eradication of four curable diseases: cardiovascular disease, diabetes, and breast and cervical cancer. The NCLR attempts to do this in a variety of ways, such as health care outreach and collaboration with health care agencies and practitioners. The organization facilitates research and conferences in order to educate the community on the risks of certain ailments.

The NCLR promotes improved community quality of life for Latinos. There are a variety of programs that the organization facilitates in order to accomplish this goal. For instance, the NCLR promotes programs for home ownership among low-income Latinos. It also works to establish strong ties to communities where Latinos reside, such as through technical assistance, leadership development, and programs to improve economic development. The organization also works to build empowerment strategies in conjunction with community leaders, such as assisting in creating community agendas and fellowships to encourage community leadership development.

Furthermore, the NCLR develops programs and policies that serve to eradicate unemployment and poverty, facilitating back-to-work programs and getting jobs for people who have been displaced. It works with AmeriCorps, assisting individuals with literacy and job preparedness. The organization also implements programs that help bridge the gap between welfare and getting back into the workforce. Other programs include working with businesses in order to get students into well-paying jobs after they complete their education. The NCLR works as a lobby group against proposed changes that would negatively impact Latinos.

Finally, the NCLR mobilizes the community by leadership development, media advocacy, and the promotion of positive images in the media. The Hispanic Leadership Development and Support Initiative educates, funds, disseminates information to, and trains Latino leaders. The program has targeted seniors, community activists, women, and youth. The NCLR's media advocacy projects encourage more-positive portrayals of Latinos in the media. It funded a series of important content analysis studies that examined the number and types of Latino characters on television and monitored how those characters were depicted. Finally, the organization also rewards individuals who have worked at establishing a positive image of Latinos. As the Latino population escalates, the NCLR continues to address the needs of the community.

Lisa Magaña

See also: Chicana/o Movement; Community Organizing; Latino/as

References and Further Reading

Garcia, C. 1974. *La Causa Política: A Chicano Politics Reader*. Notre Dame, IN: University of Notre Dame Press.

Marquez, B. 1993. *LULAC: The Evolution of a Mexican American Political Organization*. Austin: University of Texas Press.

Pachon, Harry, and Joan Moore. 1985. *Hispanics in the United States*. Englewood Cliffs, NJ: Prentice-Hall.

Shockley, J. 1974. *Chicano Revolt in a Texas Town*. Notre Dame, IN: University of Notre Dame Press.

National Labor Relations Act

See Wagner Act

National Lawyers Guild

The National Lawyers Guild is a legal membership organization that, since its founding in 1937, has sought to further a politically progressive, community-focused approach to the law and lawyering. The initial impetus for the Guild came from labor lawyers who had been involved in union struggles during the Great Depression and the New Deal. However, the first national meeting of the Guild attracted 600 lawyers from all over the country, including federal and state court judges, members of Congress, state governors, and law professors. In creating the Guild, these founding members intended to establish an alternative to the American Bar Association, which at the time was open only to whites and was dominated by the conservative legal establishment. Since the 1930s, Guild members have focused their efforts on protecting a wide range of individual civil rights and on poverty and immigration law.

An important aspect of the Guild's early work involved expanding access to legal services. In 1938, the Guild initiated a small-scale experiment to provide low-cost legal services to the poor and middle-class in Chicago and Philadelphia. Though limited, the experiment was a modest success; by 1949, the Philadelphia office was serving 4,200 clients annually. The Guild's neighborhood offices later served as models for the neighborhood legal services offices of the 1960s.

In the 1940s, the Guild went through several years of internal strife over whether the organization should formally condemn communism; in the end, it did not, choosing to remain open to all progressive lawyers. During the McCarthy era of the 1950s, the Guild played an important role in the defense of individuals targeted by the U.S. House of Representatives Un-American Activities Committee (HUAC). Guild members represented virtually every person subpoenaed to appear before the committee. The Guild itself was singled out by the HUAC as a subversive organization, resulting in the immediate resignation of over 700 members.

The Guild has repeatedly organized members to provide legal representation to those taking on unpopular progressive causes. For example, the Guild provided legal representation and support to the civil rights movement in the 1960s. In 1964, the Guild opened a law office in Jackson, Mississippi, to assist civil rights workers. Guild lawyers ultimately represented hundreds of freedom riders and civil rights activists.

Similarly, during the Vietnam War, the Guild offered legal assistance to those opposing the war for political, moral, or religious reasons. In 1971, three Guild-sponsored military law offices opened overseas to provide legal assistance to hundreds of military personnel facing U.S. Army proceedings. More recently, the Guild's immigration project, based in Boston, has spearheaded Guild representation of the undocumented, asylees, and refugees.

Though its membership has remained small, one of the Guild's particular strengths continues to be its organizing on law school campuses. More than 100 law schools have Guild chapters that serve as a progressive counterweight to conservative campus groups such as the Federalist Society.

Martha F. Davis

See also: Legal Aid/Legal Services; Poverty Law

References and Further Reading

Auerbach, Jerold S. 1976. *Unequal Justice: Lawyers and Social Change in Modern America*. New York: Oxford University Press.

Ginger, Ann Fagan, and Eugene M. Tobin, eds. 1988. *The National Lawyers Guild: From Roosevelt through Reagan*. Philadelphia: Temple University Press.

National Lawyers Guild Foundation. 1987. *A History of the National Lawyers Guild, 1937–1987*. New York: National Lawyers Guild.

Rabinowitz, Victor. 1996. *Unrepentant Leftist: A Lawyer's Memoir*. Urbana: University of Illinois Press.

National Service

See AmeriCorps; Peace Corps; Voluntarism; Volunteers in Service to America (VISTA)

National Urban League

The National Urban League (NUL) was created as a social service organization in 1910 in New York City to improve the socioeconomic situation of Blacks in the northern cities of the United States. Poverty and all of its related social ills were plaguing Blacks in heart-wrenching fashion in the early 1900s. During this period, many African Americans fled the South for the North in search of economic opportunities and political liberty. Competing with European immigrants for jobs, facing northern forms of racial discrimination, and often having few family members or friends for support, many Blacks were forced to survive in unhealthy and unsafe living and working conditions with limited income and in substandard housing.

Recognizing the numerous social crises in Black urban life, progressive social workers and liberal philanthropists created numerous organizations to provide social services to Blacks and facilitate their transition to life in the North's urban ghettos. The National Urban League (originally the National League on Urban Conditions among Negroes) resulted from the merging of the Committee on Urban Conditions among Negroes, the Committee for the Improvement of Industrial Conditions among Negroes, and the National League for the Protection of Colored Women. Dr. George Edmund Haynes, a pioneering African American social worker, and Mrs. Ruth Standish Baldwin, a wealthy white advocate for the poor, were two of the key founders and early leaders of the Urban League.

From the NUL's earliest days, its social workers conducted research into the housing, employment, health, education, and general living conditions of Blacks and the urban poor. Based on their findings, these social workers were able to direct information and resources to this vulnerable population. The NUL also played an important role in the training of Black social workers. Because of its effective work and the grim conditions facing Blacks throughout the country, the NUL expanded rapidly, and within a few decades it had affiliates in most major cities with a large Black population. The national leaders of the NUL lobbied government officials in the 1930s and 1940s to include Blacks in New Deal programs that promoted economic recovery and provided jobs to unemployed Americans. Continuing this tradition, Executive Director Lester Granger led the NUL during the 1940s and 1950s. A veteran of the NUL and a newspaper columnist, Granger was especially active in working to integrate the armed forces, defense industries, and trade unions during and after World War II. The NUL also lobbied and pressured major corporations, small private employers, and educational and job-training institutes to give Blacks equal opportunities.

From the mid-1950s to the mid-1960s, the civil rights movement's public and confrontational demands for an end to racial discrimination against Blacks created a new energy for social change in the United States. Whitney M. Young Jr. became the NUL's executive director in 1961 and moved swiftly to increase the organization's visibility in favor of civil rights. He defended the organization against charges that it was controlled by and responsive to white corporate elites. Young also called for a domestic Marshall Plan to eliminate poverty in the United States and to decrease the economic gap between whites and Blacks. He believed strongly that the federal government had a large positive role to play in improving the social welfare of its citizens.

In 1971, Young's successor, Vernon E. Jordan Jr., agreed with Young's views and actively engaged the federal government. During the 1970s, and especially during the presidency of Jimmy Carter, Jordan was able to increase the NUL's social service programs and activities. It partnered with the federal government to administer programs in the areas of housing, health, education, and minority business development. Under Jordan's leadership, it also began to publish its annual report, *The State of Black America*, in which outstanding social scientists, writers, and policy analysts examine the important economic, social, political, and cultural issues facing African Americans.

John E. Jacob became National Urban League president in 1982 and had the unenviable task of leading the organization during the republican presidencies of Ronald Reagan and George H. W. Bush (1981–1993). During the 1980s, the NUL lost most of its government funding and returned to the private sector for support to continue its programs and activities. These were very difficult years because Jacob and most National Urban League leaders and social workers believed that the Reagan administration's social policies increased poverty and decreased the quality of life for most African Americans. The NUL also established youth development programs and addressed such social issues as teenage pregnancy, single-mother families, drug abuse, and violent crime in urban Black communities.

Since 1994, Hugh B. Price has led the National Urban League. As president and chief executive officer, Price has successfully increased funding for the organization while restructuring it internally to eliminate annual budget deficits. The NUL now has more than 100 affiliates in thirty-four states and the District of Columbia. Price has challenged corporations and businesses to invest in urban America to provide jobs and regular incomes to those citizens who would otherwise continue to experience a lack of opportunities. The National Urban League is currently emphasizing the importance of partnerships among the private, public, and nonprofit sectors to provide resources, policies, and programs to reduce poverty and increase social welfare. Price is also encouraging African Americans to deepen their own strong traditions of philanthropy, community development, and self-empowerment.

Ollie A. Johnson III

See also: Civil Rights Movement; National Association for the Advancement of Colored People (NAACP); Urban Poverty

References and Further Reading

Dickerson, Dennis C. 1998. *Militant Mediator: Whit-*

ney M. Young, Jr. Lexington: University Press of Kentucky.

Parris, Guichard, and Lester Brooks. 1971. *Blacks in the City: A History of the National Urban League*. Boston: Little, Brown.

Weiss, Nancy J. 1974. *The National Urban League, 1910–1940*. New York: Oxford University Press.

———. 1989. *Whitney M. Young, Jr. and the Struggle for Civil Rights*. Princeton: Princeton University Press.

National Welfare Rights Organization (NWRO)

See Feminisms; Poor People's Campaign; Welfare Policy/Welfare Reform; Welfare Rights Movement

Native Americans/ American Indians

American Indians and Alaska Natives represent one of the smallest minority groups in the United States by population, but they have one of the highest rates of poverty and unemployment.

The shape of contemporary American Indian poverty and the social welfare system around it is rooted in historical experience. Although much controversy surrounds this point, generally accepted population estimates indicate that there were between 5 million and 7 million Indians in North America at the time of contact with European settlers. Indians comprised diverse cultures and political economies adapted to distinct ecological niches. Most tribal peoples approached poverty and social welfare as the responsibility of family, clan, and kinship groups, though some highly stratified societies developed elaborate tributary polities. Contact with European colonial powers across North America dramatically transformed the circumstances in which indigenous peoples lived. The trade and evangelization that came along with European settlement brought cultural transformation, changed gender roles, and unleashed epidemic diseases. The colonial presence also introduced conflicting attitudes toward land, production, and exchange, while the ravages of war and conquest increased Indian dependency, exacerbated poverty, and undermined traditional means of providing for the collective welfare.

Indian poverty grew more severe during the nineteenth century as the United States pursued a policy of establishing reservations through treaties and agreements. It was also during this period that the federal government effectively institutionalized the relationship of dependency it had long fostered by making programs of Indian social services, "civilization," and assimilation part of the Bureau of Indian Affairs (BIA). Subsequently, in response to the need for opening new land for non-Indian settlement and to the deplorable conditions on many reservations, the treaty period ended in 1871 and was followed by allotment shortly thereafter. Through the General Allotment Act of 1887 and other related legislation, the federal government broke up reservation lands into individually owned parcels. The resulting "surplus land" that went unallotted was then opened to homesteaders and corporations. Not all tribes' lands were allotted, but the consequences proved disastrous for those that were. Tribally owned land plummeted from 138 million acres in 1887 to 55 million acres in 1934 (Trosper 1996, 179). Much of the land that was retained proved insufficient for subsistence. Consequently, many Indians turned to leasing out their lands and subsurface mineral rights to outsiders as a means of survival.

By the 1930s, it became widely recognized that past policies had failed to improve the economic conditions in which Indian people lived and that the problem lay not, as legions of missionaries and reformers had claimed in the past, in Indian culture but in the systematic subordination of Indian tribal rights and access to economic opportunity. The *Meriam Report*, named for Department of Interior official Lewis Meriam, based on a comprehensive investigative survey conducted by a multidisciplinary team of researchers and released in 1928, revealed devastatingly high incidences of poverty, disease, and poor health on reservations. Moreover, with the beginning of the Indian New Deal—through passage of the Indian Reorganization Act of 1934—Indian culture was no longer targeted as the cause of poverty. Indians engaged in the full panoply of New Deal programs aimed at generating employment, from the Civilian Conservation Corps–Indian Division to the Works Progress Administration. Meanwhile, the Indian Reorganization Act instituted a means for the restoration of tribal self-governance, put an end to the allotment program, created a revolving loan fund for economic development, and advocated cultural preservation initiatives.

During the postwar period, the pendulum of federal social policy toward Indians swung between, on the one hand, efforts to erase their cultural distinction by fostering assimilation and, on the other, tribal self-determination. These policies were accompanied by parallel shifts in the official treatment of tribal land rights. During the 1950s, the federal government inaugurated a policy of termination. Enunciated in House Concurrent Resolution 108, the policy called for the severing of the federal government's trust relationships with tribes. When this occurred, treaties and agreements were no longer recognized as binding and Indian lands became legally indistinguishable from those held by non-Indians. Termination ultimately affected the lives of 13,263 Indian tribal members and removed 1.3 million acres of land from trust status (Prucha 1984, 1048). It also created a crisis for local and state welfare bureaucracies that were not prepared to provide services for this massive influx of impoverished people.

During the 1960s, with the failure of termination policies becoming more salient, Congress began to make Indian tribal governments eligible for area redevelopment, education, and health programs developed for the general population. With the War on Poverty, this emphasis on larger federal investments merged with the idea of community action and self-determination. The latter was then codified as federal policy with the signing of the Indian Self-Determination and Education Assistance Act of 1975. This act enabled tribes to contract for control over various programs administered by the

D. W. C. Duncan, Testimony to the Senate Regarding the Dawes Act, 1906

Under our old Cherokee regime I spent the early days of my life on the farm up here of 300 acres, and arranged to be comfortable in my old age; but the allotment scheme [limiting Cherokees to sixty acres of land] came along and struck me during the crop season, while my corn was ripening in full ear. I was looking forward to the crop of corn hopefully for some comforts to be derived from it during the months of the winter. . . . I have 60 acres of land left to me; the balance is all gone. I am an old man, not able to follow the plow as I used to when a boy. What am I going to do with it? For the last few years, since I have had my allotment, I have gone out there on that farm day after day. I have used the ax, the hoe, the spade, the plow, hour for hour, until fatigue would throw me exhausted upon the ground. Next day I repeated the operation, and let me tell you, Senators, I have exerted all my ability, all my industry, all my intelligence, if I have any, my will, my ambition, the love of my wife—all these agencies I have employed to make a living out of that 60 acres, and, God be my judge, I have not been able to do it.

Source: Senate Report 5013, 59th Cong. (1906), 2nd sess., part 1

Bureau of Indian Affairs and the Indian Health Service. The 1990s then witnessed the advent of "self-governance" whereby tribes compacted with the federal government in order to receive block grants to develop, implement, and administer programs in the areas of health, education, and social welfare.

Policies may have improved since the late 1970s, but poverty remains prevalent. Many tribes possess natural resources, while others have taken advantage of gaming and tourism. However, the remoteness of most reservations from large markets presents a structural barrier to economic development, state governments are often hostile to tribal initiatives, investment capital is difficult to obtain, and dependency on federal dollars persists. Reservation employment opportunities are seldom available outside the BIA or tribal government, and Indians continue to face discrimination when seeking nonreservation jobs. Another struggle revolves around securing hunting, fishing, and resource rights guaranteed in law by government-to-government treaties but often not realized in practice (Trosper 1996, 179–181). Finally, the gross mismanagement of individual money accounts by the BIA has recently led to multimillion-dollar legal suits seeking compensation.

Contemporary indices reveal that despite increased federal assistance, most of the 562 federally recognized tribal entities that qualify for BIA services remain underfunded, and few can afford not to be dependent on even these sums. In 2001, the unemployment rate within these tribes stood at 42 percent of the available labor force, while 33 percent of those employed earned wages below the poverty line. The figures for self-governance tribes that have entered into compacts with the federal government demonstrate that even the most recent policy and administrative reforms have yet to bring substantial economic changes (U.S. Department of the Interior, Bureau of Indian Affairs, Office of Tribal Services 2001, ii–iii). According to the 1990 census, in the twenty-five largest tribes, most Indians worked in service, administrative support, and manual labor occupations (U.S. Bureau of the Census 1995). Finally, while the degree of poverty among males continues to be high, census data further indicate that Indians have experienced the "feminization of poverty" no less than other groups have. Poverty among single-parent, female-headed households has risen since the mid-1970s (for statistics, see Snipp 1996, 178).

In order to alleviate poverty in Native America, the federal government will need to continue to support on- and off-reservation Indian communities with sustained social services. Meanwhile, tribes will continue to explore new strategies to promote long-term economic development and seek ways to diversify their economies. The long history of poverty and social welfare among Indians has shown, however, that tribes will not sacrifice their rights as sovereign nations in order to gain economic parity. Therefore, the continued shift toward compacting and self-governance, in addition to the retention of tribes' federal trust status, will play a crucial role in creating an administrative structure reflective of these larger economic aspirations.

Daniel M. Cobb

See also: Alaska Natives; Area Redevelopment Act; Great Depression and New Deal; Native Hawaiians; War on Poverty

References and Further Reading

Cornell, Stephen, and Joseph P. Kalt, eds. 1992. *What Can Tribes Do?: Strategies and Institutions in American Indian Economic Development*. American Indian Manual and Handbook Series, no. 4. Los Angeles: American Indian Studies Center.

Ogunwole, Stella U. 2002. "The American Indian and Alaska Native Population: 2000." *United States Census 2000*. Washington, DC: U.S. Census Bureau.

Prucha, Francis Paul. 1984. *The Great Father: The United States Government and the American Indians*. 2 vols. Unabridged. Lincoln: University of Nebraska Press.

Snipp, C. Matthew. 1996. "Economic Conditions." In *Native America in the Twentieth Century: An*

Encyclopedia, ed. Mary B. Davis, 175–179. New York: Garland Publishing.

Trosper, Ronald. 1996. "Economic Development." In *Native America in the Twentieth Century: An Encyclopedia*, ed. Mary B. Davis, 179–181. New York: Garland Publishing.

U.S. Bureau of the Census. 1995. "Selected Social and Economic Characteristics for the 25 Largest American Indian Tribes: 1990." http://www.census.gov/population/socdemo/race/indian/ailang2.txt.

U.S. Department of the Interior. Bureau of Indian Affairs. Office of Tribal Services. 2001. *American Indian Population and Labor Force Report, 2001*. Washington, DC: GPO.

Native Hawaiians

Tourism is Hawaii's big business. During the late 1990s, some 6 million tourists arrived every year, eager for a respite from their ordinary lives. Many are hungry for an authentic "Hawaiian" experience—a luau or local music in the hotel bar. Few know that Native Hawaiians, the indigenous people of the Hawaiian Islands, live in poverty in the midst of a land of plenty. It is a cruel irony that Native Hawaiians, who are prominently featured in tourism ads—as barely clad warriors and hula girls—are the poorest social group in the islands.

The 2000 census found 254,910 Native Hawaiians and part-Native Hawaiians, or 22 percent of the state population. This figure represents a major increase in the size of the Native Hawaiian population, which was listed as 12.5 percent of the state population in 1990 and 9.3 percent in 1970. No doubt the dramatic increase between 1990 and 2000 is due, in major part, to two significant changes in race and ethnicity categories new to the 2000 census. First, Native Hawaiians, who had previously been lumped together with Asian Americans, were given their own racial/ethnic identification category. Second, the 2000 census allowed persons of multiracial heritage to check off multiple categories of racial background.

By any measure one uses, Native Hawaiians are disproportionately represented in the state's welfare statistics. One of the most telling indications of Native Hawaiian poverty is the proportion of Native Hawaiians who received Aid to Families with Dependent Children (AFDC) for selected months from 1978 to 2000 (AFDC changed to Temporary Assistance for Needy Families [TANF] in 1996). In these two decades, Native Hawaiian recipients of AFDC accounted for at least 28 percent and as much as 34.6 percent of total AFDC recipients between 1978 and 2000. In 1999, Native Hawaiians accounted for 28.8 percent of AFDC cases, 25.91 percent of the food stamp recipients, 20.04 percent of general assistance cases, and 10.16 percent of aged, blind, and disabled cases in the state. In 1999, overall, Native Hawaiians made up more than a quarter (27.55 percent) of individuals receiving assistance from the department of human services.

Among families living below the poverty level, families on public assistance, and individuals living in persistent poverty, Native Hawaiians are the largest racial group.

Data on income and poverty for Native Hawaiians give us a better understanding of why Native Hawaiians are overrepresented in welfare services. At the beginning of the 1990s, approximately one-fifth of all Native Hawaiian families were earning under $15,000 a year. Moreover, average family income for Native Hawaiians was almost $9,000 below the average family income for the state of Hawaii. Also, Native Hawaiians were more likely to be poor across the board, but this was especially true for female-headed households. Even the fact of owning a home seems to be only a slight protection from poverty. In 1990, one-fifth of female households in owner-occupied units were below the poverty level, and almost one-quarter of all Native Hawaiians in owner-occupied homes received public assistance. More generally, among female-headed households, 35 percent of Native Hawaiians were below the poverty level, compared with non-Native Hawaiians, 20 percent of whom were below the poverty level.

The above pattern of income inequality and poverty among Native Hawaiians has been consistent over time. Indeed, even since the major welfare reform of 1996, there appears to be little change in the pattern for Native Hawaiians. The social ecology of poverty in the islands matches closely the geographic areas in which Native Hawaiians live. The poorest areas have the highest concentrations of Native Hawaiian people, and the wealthiest areas have the lowest concentrations of Native Hawaiians. The *State of Hawaii Data Book 1999* found that Native Hawaiians are concentrated in the state's poorest neighborhoods and census tracts, such as the Waianae Coast and Waimanalo area of Oahu and the town of Wailuku in Maui. These areas, which have the highest concentrations of Native Hawaiians, tend to be what are known as "Hawaiian Homelands." Hawaiian Homelands are small pockets of land, about 200,000 acres spread across the islands (out of 4 million total acres in the islands), that were set aside in 1921 under provisions of a congressional act known as the Hawaiian Homes Commission Act, for homesteading by Native Hawaiians with 50 percent or more Hawaiian ancestry.

Landownership is the linchpin for understanding inequality, poverty, and welfare dependency for Native Hawaiians. And the history of landownership in the islands dates back to the U.S. overthrow of the Hawaiian kingdom in 1893. The overthrow set in motion a series of land divisions and political relationships between the more recently arrived settlers and Native Hawaiians. Over time, these property and political relationships, like layers and layers of sediment, were laid down, beginning with the annexation of Hawaii by the United States and 1898 and continuing through the admission of the Aloha State to the union in 1959. The sedimented history of land in Hawaii from the Native Hawaiian perspective boils down to this: Native Hawaiians feel they are the rightful owners of approximately 2 million acres, or 50 percent, of the landmass of the state, which is currently held in trust for them or managed by the state government. The 2 million acres includes the Hawaiian Homelands and a more sizable amount of land held in the Ceded Lands Trust (1.8 million acres). The ceded lands are controlled by the state of Hawaii. Native Hawaiians maintain that given the legal improprieties of the 1893 overthrow, the ceded lands should be returned to them. However, the ceded lands are a significant source of state revenues, of which approximately one-fifth is designated to be set aside for the betterment of Native Hawaiians.

The political relationships of Native Hawaiians to both the federal government and the state of Hawaii are complex and unsettled, which makes Native Hawaiian access to their land difficult, almost impossible. One of the central issues is, Who counts as Native Hawaiian? Some agencies, like the Department of Hawaiian Homelands and the administration of some programs under the auspices of the Office of Hawaiian Affairs, target only those Hawaiians with 50 percent or more blood quantum. Other state agencies, including the U.S. Census Bureau and the Office of Hawaiian Affairs (OHA), target Native Hawaiians without regard to blood quantum. Native Hawaiians, many of whom prefer the name Kanaka Maoli ("the indigenous people of Hawaii"), also identify as an *indigenous* people rather than a *racial* group. The political difference between *indigenous* and *racial minority* is an extremely important one since federally recognized indigenous peoples enjoy rights—sovereign rights, for example—that are not available to minority groups. A recent ruling by the U.S. Supreme Court, *Rice v. Cayetano* (528 U.S. 495 [2000]), found that the right to vote for officers of OHA must be extended to non-Native Hawaiians, a ruling that in essence defined Native Hawaiians as a racial minority subject to civil rights laws that prohibit classifications on the basis of race. Native Hawaiians, however, maintain that they are *not* a racial group—in the way that Asian Americans, for example, are defined by the federal government—but, rather, are a unique indigenous people, a categorization that resembles the categorization the federal government uses for Native Americans. For example, in Hawaii, Kamehameha Schools, a well-known K–12 educational institution, until recently admitted only Native Hawaiians. However, as a result of the *Rice v. Cayetano* ruling, the school has recently, by court order, admitted a student whose Native Hawaiian ancestry records are inaccurate or unverifiable.

In sum, then, the poverty and welfare issues for Native Hawaiians, in particular the dependency of Native Hawaiians on state services, must be understood within the context of the overarching historical and political relationship of Native Hawaiians to the United States and to the state of Hawaii. That current political relationship reinforces poverty and inequality for Native Hawaiians, even as the tourists continue to arrive.

Dana Takagi

See also: Native Americans/American Indians

References and Further Reading

Cooper, George, and Gavan Dawes. 1985. *Land and Power in Hawaii: The Democratic Years*. Honolulu, HI: Benchmark Books.

Dougherty, Michael. 1992. *To Steal a Kingdom*. Waimanalo, HI: Island Style Press.

Eleihiwa, Lilikala Kame. 1992. *Native Land and Foreign Desires*. Honolulu, HI: Bishop Museum Press.

Kent, Noel. 1993. *Islands under the Influence*. Honolulu: University of Hawaii Press.

Trask, Haunani Kay. 1993. *From a Native Daughter: Colonialism and Sovereignty in Hawai'i*. Monroe, ME: Common Courage Press.

Nativism

See Americanization Movement; Immigrants and Immigration; Immigration Policy

The Negro Family in the United States, *E. Franklin Frazier*

E. Franklin Frazier's *Negro Family in the United States*, published in 1939, is a pioneering text in American sociology and African American studies. It was the first full-length treatment of the Negro family that repudiated prevailing assumptions about the biological inferiority of Africans and the normative superiority of American culture. It represents years of meticulous data collection by Frazier, who recorded the biographies and personal experiences of thousands of people who would otherwise have been ignored by historians and social scientists. The book addresses a wide variety of issues about the relationships among economics, racism, culture, and family life that are as relevant and pressing in the new millennium as they were prior to World War II.

Frazier's Career

Frazier (1894–1962) was an important member of a cohort of African American activists who, after World War I, came together from vastly different regions of the country to form the cutting edge of a social, political, and cultural movement that would irrevocably change conceptions of race and the politics of race relations.

Frazier is known for his contributions to American sociology, but as a child of working-class parents, growing up in segregated Baltimore, he had to take all kinds of jobs before settling into an academic career. After graduating from Howard University in 1916, Frazier eventually earned his doctoral degree in sociology from the University of Chicago in 1931, all the while supplementing his income with various teaching positions.

Between 1922 and 1927, he worked in Atlanta, teaching sociology at Morehouse College and directing the Atlanta School of Social Work. Almost single-handedly, he transformed the fledgling Atlanta School of Social Work into a professional program that attracted Black students from all over the country.

Frazier returned to the South in 1929 to take a job teaching sociology at Fisk University in Nashville, in part because academic doors in the North were closed to him. In 1934, he assumed the leadership of Howard University's sociology department and remained there for the rest of his career. For all his accomplishments—the first African American president of the American Sociological Association (1948), author of the first serious textbook on African Americans, *The Negro in the United States* (1949), consultant on global race relations to UNESCO (1951–1953)—Frazier was never offered a tenure-track job in a predominantly white university. Near the end of his life, he was targeted and harassed by the FBI and other intelligence agencies for his public support of progressive causes and such activists as Paul Robeson and W. E. B. Du Bois.

Contributions to Sociology and Social Work

Before leaving Atlanta in 1927, Frazier had begun his research on the history and development of the Negro family, a project that would form the basis of his doctoral dissertation at the University of Chicago (completed in 1931) and of his first three books—*The Negro Family in Chicago* (1932), *The Free Negro Family* (1932), and *The Negro Family in the United States* (1939). Frazier himself noted that his first interest in the topic predated his studies in Chicago and was sparked by reading Du Bois's 1908 study *The Negro American Family* and by working as a social worker in the South. *The Negro Family in the United States*, published in 1939, was a synthesis of several previous studies. His approach to studying the family was quite eclectic; his theoretical framework drew on history, sociology, social psychology, and African American studies.

Frazier explicitly set out to repudiate racist stereotypes about the monolithic nature of Black families. He focused extensively on the "disorganized" Negro family in all its historical contexts—under slavery, after Reconstruction, in rural areas, and in the metropolis. Frazier had a tendency to read the modern condition of the family after World War I back into the nineteenth-century slave experience. At times, he used "disorganization" in a normative sense, juxtaposed with "civilization"; occasionally he used it synonymously with "urbanization." With his continued reference to the chaos and disorganization in urban Black family patterns, Frazier seriously underestimated the resources, ingenuity, and organization of "demoralized" families. Moreover, he shared many of the prevailing assumptions of a Victorian-gendered morality, no doubt reinforced by his own conventional marriage and sexual division of household labor. Thus, he assumed that the nuclear family and patriarchal authority represent an evolutionary development and that masculine and feminine gender roles are naturally constituted rather than the result of a socially constructed and negotiated process.

However, it is a mistake to impose contemporary insights on Frazier's ideas of the 1920s and 1930s. When he began his research, the prevailing interpretations were racial and biological, and academic and professional circles assumed the superiority of an idealized, middle-class, nuclear family. Frazier was innovative in demonstrating the social consequences of racism: He showed that the problems of Negro families were socially constructed rather than culturally inherited and that family disorganization was created within and by Western civilization rather than by the failure of Africans to live up to American standards. Moreover, he did not regard the Negro family as permanently and uniformly disorganized by slavery and its aftermath. Frazier's family is, in fact, a broad spectrum of families, constantly in a process of change and reorganization, depending on a complex interrelationship of economic, cultural, and social forces. He was interested in the varieties of the family as an institution that, at different times and under different conditions, was sometimes disorganized and demoralized, sometimes tenacious and resourceful. His perspective on the family was genuinely interdisciplinary, and his solutions to family disorganization were similarly complex and multifaceted. Though he was more of an economic determinist than a social psychologist, he was opposed to one-dimensional approaches to social policy.

Many years after its publication, Frazier's *Negro Family in the United States* gained notoriety when it became the basis of Daniel P. Moynihan's controversial 1965 report, entitled *The Negro Family: A Case for National Action*, in which he argued that the lower-class Black family had become mired in a self-perpetuating "tangle of pathology" characterized by dominant matriarchs and emasculated, unemployed men. In the aftermath of the report and in the context of a resurgent cultural nationalism, some objected to Frazier's emphasis on the damage done by racism to family and community. The same controversy was revived in the 1980s with respect to the "underclass" debate. But prior to World War II, when Frazier was trying to document the pathology of race prejudice, such a view was a challenge to racist assumptions about the inherent inferiority of African Americans.

Frazier's study of the Negro family is worth revisiting because it broke the hold of racialized paradigms and opened up African American communities to the possibility of serious historical and sociological investigations. Frazier chronicled community life and everyday customs, sketching portraits of human diversity and articulating contradictions that challenged the prevailing reification of African American families as uniformly deviant and pathological. Since publication of *The Negro Family in the United States* in 1939, this area of study has been transformed by feminism and the women's movements and by complex new developments in African American history. But the problems that Frazier reported about over sixty years ago—the impact of racism on family life, the interconnection between economic inequality and personal problems, and the difficulty of preserving human relationships in a society based on exploitation and inequality—remain ever present.

Anthony M. Platt

See also: Family Structure; Moynihan Report; Poverty Research; Racism; *The Vanishing Black Family*

References and Further Reading

Billingsley, Andrew. 1988. *Black Families in White America*. New York: Simon and Schuster.

Frazier, E. Franklin. [1939] 2001. *The Negro Family in the United States*. Notre Dame, IN: Notre Dame Press.

Platt, Anthony M. 1991. *E. Franklin Frazier Reconsidered*. New Brunswick, NJ: Rutgers University Press.

New Deal Farm Policy

New Deal farm programs initially either ignored or actually exacerbated the plight of the rural poor during the 1930s. While struggling to restore the solvency of commercial agriculture, the New Deal began developing a second set of farm programs in 1935 to come to terms with the nation's deep-rooted rural poverty. These initiatives achieved, at best, a mixed record before they were eliminated during World War II. Nevertheless, with their short-lived vision of a more cooperative, small-scale, and less commercialized system of agricultural production, they constituted some of the boldest—and most controversial—experiments in U.S. social policy.

Of the 6.2 million farmers in 1930, roughly one-half produced 90 percent of all goods sold off the farm. The other half produced but 10 percent (Baker 1937, 4–5). Many farmers were either tenants and sharecroppers or debt-burdened landowners eking out livings on a few acres of depleted and barren soils with few tools, no power equipment, and little livestock. In addition, there were large numbers of struggling farm laborers and rural workers who moved back and forth from farm to nonfarm work. The rural poor were concentrated most heavily in the South, with its nearly 2 million tenant farmers and sharecroppers, but they were a national phenomenon. Wherever they lived, the rural poor subsisted on miserable diets with virtually no hope of achieving decent housing, health care, or education for their children.

Rural poverty before the New Deal went almost unnoticed in the United States. During the 1930s, however, searing accounts of the rural poor by writers such as Erskine Caldwell, John Steinbeck, and James Agee; brilliant photographs by documentary photographers such as Dorothea Lange; and protests of the unfair treatment of southern tenant farmers in the administration of New Deal farm programs contributed to the discovery of the degraded condition of millions of rural families.

Early New Deal farm programs such as the Agricultural Adjustment Administration (AAA) and the Farm Credit Administration were designed to save a battered system of commercial agriculture. The Farm Credit Administration reorganized and expanded the federally sponsored farm credit system, but since the system's production and mortgage loans required some form of security, they were unavailable to poorer farmers. The AAA sought to boost farm income, and its major emphasis was on implementing voluntary production controls by paying cooperating farmers to cut back on crop and livestock production. Most of the rural poor produced too few goods to benefit from AAA production controls. In much of the South, however, the AAA exacerbated rural poverty by encouraging cotton landlords either to claim excessive shares of the benefit payments at the expense of sharecroppers and tenants or to reduce the number of renters they furnished. The evictions and abuses inspired furious debates within the U.S. Department of Agriculture (USDA) over whether the AAA should protect poorer farmers or concentrate primarily on restoring prosperity to commercial agriculture. Outside the USDA, landlord abuses encouraged the formation of groups such as the Southern Tenant Farmers Union (STFU), which fought to protect tenants and liberalize New Deal farm programs.

More helpful to the rural poor was the New Deal's Federal Emergency Relief Administration (FERA), which was established to help state and local governments provide relief to the unemployed and the destitute. Within months, the FERA, and related agencies such as the Civil Works Administration, were supporting 1 million farmers and their families with jobs and monthly relief payments. In 1934, the FERA established a Division of Rural Rehabilitation and began making small loans and grants to distressed farmers as part of a larger program of rural rehabilitation.

As the plight of the rural poor gained greater attention, Congress and the New Deal confronted two policy choices. One was to include farmers and farmworkers under the various provisions of the Social Security Act (1935) and later measures such as the Fair Labor Standards Act (1938). Such a course, however, faced serious obstacles because of the costs involved, the limited administrative capacities for applying these acts to agriculture, and fierce opposition from politically powerful southern planters and farm interest groups. Instead, the New Deal pursued a second approach, which was to develop new farm programs aimed at keeping the rural poor on the land and creating new opportunities for landownership among tenants and marginal farmers. The first important attempt to formulate this second farm program began in 1935 with the Resettlement Administration (RA), which absorbed the FERA's Rural Rehabilitation program. In late 1936, President Franklin D. Roosevelt established the President's Committee on Farm Tenancy, and its report helped win passage of the Bankhead-Jones Farm Tenant Act of 1937. The Bankhead-

Jones Act authorized the creation of the Farm Security Administration (FSA), which was established within the U.S. Department of Agriculture, and the FSA in turn absorbed the Resettlement Administration. What emerged, fitfully, was an alternative farm program aimed at raising rural living standards by developing a system of small-hold farming.

One part of this alternative farm program was the building of government-sponsored rural communities. Such projects had been under way before 1935, but the Resettlement Administration under Rexford G. Tugwell embraced and expanded community building as an antidote to rural poverty. An important adviser to Roosevelt and an undersecretary in the Department of Agriculture, Tugwell was critical of the USDA and the AAA for slighting rural poverty. He envisioned the RA guiding the resettlement of poorer farmers off marginal land and onto more-productive farms and into model rural communities. By the second half of the 1930s, about 150 such projects were under way on government-purchased or government-leased land (Baldwin 1968, 214). A second part of the program was to make available long-term, low-interest loans to tenants and poorer farmers to allow them to purchase farms or expand existing farms. A third part of the program expanded the rehabilitation program begun by the FERA by supplying destitute farmers with small loans. These averaged only $240 in 1937 and climbed to $600 in 1940, and by 1943, 695,000 families—or about one-ninth of America's farm families—had received one or more rehabilitation loans. In addition to the loans, the RA and FSA made available direct grants that averaged about $20 per client and that totaled $136.5 million for 500,000 families by 1943 (Baldwin 1968, 200, 202).

The community-building projects, tenant land purchase programs, and rehabilitation loan and grant programs were part of a larger effort to create a viable system of small-scale farming. RA/FSA clients had to agree to accept home and farm supervision by agricultural and home demonstration agents, who encouraged diversified farming, home food production, and strategies for raising standards of living while minimizing market risks. In addition, the RA/FSA programs sought to improve rural economic and social conditions by developing cooperative and group associations. The agencies encouraged their resettled farmers and rehabilitation clients to form cooperative purchasing and sales associations; cooperative cotton gins, canneries, and other processing facilities; and cooperative farms and land-leasing associations and to group together for services, such as sharing the expenses for veterinarians or harvesting equipment. The RA/FSA also worked with public health officials to establish medical care associations to create prepayment medical, hospital, and dental care plans.

Farmer on the Farm Security Administration Bois d'Arc cooperative farm. Osage Farms, Missouri, November 1939. (Corbis)

The RA and FSA achieved, at best, limited

success. The most beneficial programs were the rehabilitation loans and grants, which kept thousands of rural families off relief rolls and allowed them to survive the Depression and the droughts of the 1930s. The resettlement projects built only 10,000 farm homes, were often beset with internal dissension, and incurred large financial losses (Conkin 1959, 331). The tenant farm purchase program was more successful, but it had funds for only a few thousand of the 150,000 to 175,000 applicants each year (Baldwin 1968, 199). Furthermore, because these programs were intended to be self-liquidating, the RA/FSA limited larger loans and resettlement to those farmers most likely to establish a profitable farm, which meant that most of the rural poor were prevented from obtaining assistance. Overall, RA/FSA spending was but a fraction of what the USDA spent on price support and production-control programs. The national administrators of the RA and the FSA sought to aid Black farmers, but at the local level, the programs limited access and benefits to African Americans. The discrimination notwithstanding, however, for those Black tenants and landowners who did obtain RA/FSA assistance, the programs enabled them to survive the 1930s and remain on their farms after the Great Depression.

By the early 1940s, the RA/FSA programs were under intense attack from anti–New Deal congressmen, farm interest groups such as the American Farm Bureau Federation, and the state extension services. The resettlement projects drew the brunt of the attack as critics charged they were wasteful and a first step toward a system of "socialist" agriculture. The Farm Bureau objected to government subsidies of poorer farmers while other USDA programs were trying to curtail production. Many state extension services resented and feared competition from the FSA agricultural agents. These forces combined during World War II first to slash the FSA budget and then to eliminate the agency in 1945.

It is doubtful that an attack on rural poverty based on resettlement and converting tenants into landowners could have aided most of the nation's rural poor during the 1930s. Nevertheless, the RA and FSA programs were well-meaning and hopeful experiments, and their demise hastened the elimination of small-scale farmers from American agriculture after 1945.

David E. Hamilton

See also: Agricultural and Farm Labor Organizing; Dust Bowl Migration; *The Grapes of Wrath;* Great Depression and New Deal; *Let Us Now Praise Famous Men;* Migrant Labor/Farm Labor; Picturing Poverty (I); *Report on Economic Conditions of the South;* Rural Poverty; Sharecropping; Tennessee Valley Authority

References and Further Reading

Baker, O. E. 1937. "A Graphic Summary of the Number, Size, Type of Farm, and Value of Products." U.S. Department of Agriculture, miscellaneous publication no. 266. Washington, DC: GPO.

Baldwin, Sidney. 1968. *Poverty and Politics: The Rise and Decline of the Farm Security Administration.* Chapel Hill: University of North Carolina Press.

Cannon, Brian Q. 1996. *Remaking the Agrarian Dream: New Deal Rural Resettlement in the Mountain West.* Albuquerque: University of New Mexico Press.

Conkin, Paul K. 1959. *Tomorrow a New World: The New Deal Community Program.* Ithaca, NY: Cornell University Press.

Grant, Michael Johnston. 2002. *Down and Out on the Family Farm: Rural Rehabilitation in the Great Plains, 1929–1945.* Lincoln: University of Nebraska Press.

New Left

Poverty and economic inequality were major concerns of the New Left, a politically radical movement of young people during the 1960s. The leading organization of the New Left, the Students for a Democratic Society (SDS), turned its attention to poverty early in the decade. Inspired by its own social democratic heritage, the civil rights movement, and the publication of Michael Harrington's *Other America*, SDS launched the Economic Research and Action Project (ERAP) in 1963. ERAP would investigate and organize around the problem of economic inequality and the potential for economic democracy in the United States. Although ERAP did sponsor research, action—specifically community organizing around economic issues—soon became its main focus. By bringing individuals living in the same residential area together to fight for their common interests, SDS hoped to build "an interracial movement of the poor" to abolish poverty in America. Over the next few years, New Left organizers established thirteen official ERAP projects in white, predominantly Black, and racially diverse neighborhoods. The largest, most successful, and longest-lasting projects were located in Boston, Chicago, Cleveland, and Newark. By 1967 and 1968, however, it was clear that ERAP had failed to spark a social movement of poor Americans, and the projects were disbanded. Nevertheless, ERAP participants in all these cities left a community organizing legacy of fighting against poverty that lasted well beyond the 1960s.

The strategy and goals behind ERAP's antipoverty activism were articulated in a 1964 SDS document entitled "An Interracial Movement of the Poor?" by Carl Wittman, a student leader at Swarthmore College who had experience in civil rights and community organizing, and Tom Hayden, a University of Michigan graduate and important leader of SDS. Synthesizing insights and lessons from the labor movement, the Old Left, and the civil rights movement, the document outlined a strategy for building an interracial movement of the poor to target the intertwined problems of poverty, racism, and the lack of democracy in the United States. Given the historical moment, before the second wave of feminism, women's issues were not part of ERAP's political agenda. Instead, Wittman, Hayden, and other ERAP planners sought to mobilize unemployed Black, white, and Latino men into community organizations in the urban North. Organization building, it was hoped, would overcome the experience of oppression and the so-called culture of poverty that left the poor feeling powerless, isolated, and alienated. Poor community residents could thus find their political voice and become a political force. These local organizations would then forge ties with the civil rights and labor movements in order to achieve a national presence.

From there, Wittman and Hayden wanted ERAP to effect a true "war on poverty," arguing that President Lyndon B. Johnson's War on Poverty would not be won because it was not radical enough, since it was not intended to redistribute power and wealth. More concretely, "An Interracial Movement of the Poor?" laid out two reform aims for ERAP to be accomplished through unemployment campaigns: national economic planning with democratic participation and full and fair employment or a guaranteed annual income from the state. This call for jobs, income, planning, and participation reflected the New Left's understanding that the expansion of public authority to resolve the problem of poverty needed to be accompanied by the extension of political participation, especially to the poor themselves. Material resources alone could not solve the problem of poverty; citizen participation and empowerment were necessary at both the community level and in national policymaking.

When they put their strategy into practice, however, New Left organizers encountered low-income-community residents who challenged their assumptions and aims. In contrast to the expectation of ERAP planners that men would be their constituency, neighborhood women provided much of the leadership and membership for the ERAP projects. In the course of fulfilling their caretaking duties, women struggled daily with community conditions and, indeed, identified problems as part of their domestic responsibilities. Women's prominence and activism, combined with New Left organizers' commitment to ensuring grassroots participation in the projects ("Let the People Decide" became the favorite ERAP slogan), meant project aims proliferated beyond ERAP's original goals. To meet the range of needs in these low-income neighborhoods, ERAP projects organized campaigns around welfare, housing conditions, urban renewal, children's welfare, and police brutality as well as unemployment. Emphasized in all of the projects were campaigns for greater citizen political participation, with which poverty and inequality could be successfully targeted. In the process, ERAP participants challenged the idea that poor people were second-class citizens because they lacked the economic independence deemed necessary for full citizenship.

Despite a few successes, such as a school lunch program in Cleveland, a food surplus program in Boston, and War on Poverty funding in Newark, ERAP's attempt to realize full political and social citizenship for poor Americans met with failure. Black, white, and Latino, poor and working-class community participants in ERAP may have found their voice and articulated how they defined the problems of and solutions to inner-city poverty in the 1960s. But their voices needed to be heard, and listening and dialogue were not forthcoming from elected and appointed officials. As a consequence, disillusionment and frustration set in and contributed greatly to the disbanding of the community projects in 1967 and 1968. Even so, ERAP can be credited with some successes. Like community organizing efforts before and since, the neighborhood projects concretely improved people's lives in small ways through offering services. They also provided a set of experiences for participants—both New Left organizers and community members—that had the more intangible benefits of political and personal growth and development. As it turned out, SDS's community organizing became an important site for the emergence of both the women's liberation and welfare rights movements. Finally, ERAP left its mark on the community organizing efforts that flourished in the 1970s and helped develop a national vocabulary that has been used to defend local neighborhoods in the decades since.

Jennifer Frost

See also: Citizenship; Civil Rights Movement; Community Organizing; *The Other America;* Urban Poverty; War on Poverty; Welfare Rights Movement

References and Further Reading

Evans, Sara. 1979. *Personal Politics: The Roots of Women's Liberation in the Civil Rights Movement and the New Left*. New York: Knopf.

Frost, Jennifer. 2001. *"An Interracial Movement of the Poor": Community Organizing and the New Left in the 1960s*. New York: New York University Press.

New Property

In a groundbreaking 1964 article entitled "The New Property," law professor Charles Reich theorized that government largesse, including welfare benefits, constituted a new form of property worthy of legal protection. According to Reich, government benefits of various types were transforming society in the United States by replacing more traditional forms of private property. Reich surveyed a variety of examples of government largesse enjoyed by increasing numbers of Americans, including government jobs, occupational licenses, franchises, contracts, subsidies, services, public resources, and welfare benefits (including Social Security, unemployment, Aid to Dependent Children, and veterans' benefits). He argued, for example, that Americans were relying more on social insurance and less on savings. But Reich was no advocate of the welfare state. Rather, he feared that increased dependence on such largesse threatened to enlarge government power at the expense of individual autonomy. To prevent such loss of liberty, Reich reasoned that government largesse required both procedural and substantive protections similar to those granted to more traditional forms of property. In short, Reich provided a functional framework for continued reliance on property—albeit in its new form—as an economic basis for protecting individual liberty in a society increasingly dominated by government largesse. Reich also foreshadowed themes soon to be prominent among antipoverty advocates and scholars, such as social construction, bureaucratization, privatization, and legalization.

Social Construction of Property

Reich first asserted that wealth or value is created by culture and society. But he acknowledged that property is created by law. After describing the various forms and functions of property, he revealed how property is itself socially constructed. He also described the distinctive system of law emerging to regulate government largesse. This regulatory system was recognizing both individual rights and government powers and was developing procedures for mediating between individual and government interests.

Bureaucratization and Privatization

"The New Property" sounded an early warning about the risks associated with this regulatory system, especially its bureaucratization and privatization. Reich recognized the danger to liberty posed by invasive and pervasive government regulation. He cited many examples demonstrating the absence of standards for constraining bureaucratic discretion and the tendency toward corruption. Reich also recognized that no meaningful distinction existed between the public and private spheres. He criticized the inequalities among private actors in their relations with government and the uses of government power for private gain and advantage.

To address his special concern about impairment of the Bill of Rights, Reich invoked the unconstitutional conditions doctrine, which prohibits the government from doing indirectly (via conditions on largesse) what it cannot do directly (for example, via criminal prohibitions). Citing the problem of caseworkers making unannounced searches of welfare recipients' homes, Reich argued that recipients should not be forced to "choose between their means of support and one of their constitutional rights" (Reich 1964, 762). Here Reich grounded his normative argument on constitutional theory, asserting that "[a] first principle should be that government must have no power to 'buy up' rights guaranteed by the Constitution" (Reich 1964, 779).

Legalization

As the means of addressing these inherent dangers, Reich proposed using law to limit conditions on government largesse. He recommended that government be limited substantively to imposing only those conditions sufficiently relevant to the purposes underlying the attached benefits and that both discretion and delegation be clearly guided and closely monitored. He also urged that all decisions regarding government largesse be subjected to fair procedures.

One year later, Reich elaborated on "The New Property" in a follow-up article, "Individual Rights and Social Welfare." Here, Reich posited that society is built around entitlements, that many entitlements flow from government, and that it is "only the poor whose entitlements, although recognized by public policy, have not been effectively enforced" (Reich 1965, 1255). The U.S. Supreme Court cited and relied on this reasoning in *Goldberg v. Kelly* (397 U.S. 254 [1970]). In that decision, the Court noted that welfare benefits are statutory entitlements for eligible recipients and are thus more like property, which cannot be taken by the government without due process of law. Based on this premise, the Court held that government could not terminate welfare benefits without first providing an evidentiary hearing. Thus, "The New Property" substantially altered administrative procedure, leading to individualized hearings nationwide for welfare recipients threatened with termination of benefits.

Two developments have limited the reach of *Goldberg v. Kelly* and thus of the practical impact of "The New Property." First, in *Mathews v. Eldridge* (424 U.S. 319 [1976]), the U.S. Supreme Court refused to require pretermination hearings for recipients of Social Security disability benefits, instead establishing a three-part test to determine what process is due for government benefits other than welfare. This test requires courts to balance the private interest affected, the risk of error under current procedures, the probable value of additional safeguards, and the government's interests. Second, in the Personal Responsibility and Work Opportunity Reconciliation Act of 1996, Congress asserted that no individual shall be entitled to benefits under the new federal welfare program, Temporary Assistance for Needy Families (TANF). Whether courts will view this "no entitlement" language as limiting the due process rights of welfare recipients remains to be seen, but at least one state appellate court has followed Reich's logic and prohibited the government from compromising TANF benefits without procedural due process protections (*Weston v. Cassata*, 37 P.3d 469 [Colo. Ct. App. 2001]).

"The New Property" undoubtedly will provoke continued debate as its premises challenge the postwelfare ideology increasingly popular today.

Julie A. Nice

See also: Poverty Law; Welfare Policy/Welfare Reform

References and Further Reading

Brooklyn Law Review, ed. 1990. "Symposium: The Legacy of *Goldberg v. Kelly*: A Twenty Year Perspective." *Brooklyn Law Review* 56: 729.

Cimini, Christine N. 2002. "Welfare Entitlements in the Era of Devolution." *Georgetown Journal on Poverty Law and Policy* 9: 89–139.

Diller, Matthew. 2000. "The Revolution of Welfare Administration: Rules, Devolution, and Entrepreneurial Government." *New York University Law Review* 75: 1121–1220.

Farina, Cynthia R. 1998. "On Misusing 'Revolution' and 'Reform': Procedural Due Process and the New Welfare Act." *Administrative Law Review* 50: 591–634.

Nice, Julie A., and Louise G. Trubek. 1997–1999. *Cases and Materials on Poverty Law: Theory and Practice*. St. Paul, MN: West Publishing Company.

Reich, Charles A. 1964. "The New Property." *Yale Law Journal* 73: 733–787.

———. 1965. "Individual Rights and Social Welfare: The Emerging Legal Issues." *Yale Law Journal* 74: 1245–1257.

New Right

The term "New Right" refers to a coalition of conservative activists, intellectuals, politicians, and religious leaders who gained media attention and political power in the United States in the last third of the twentieth century. Imbued with an intense—if not necessarily internally coherent—ideological commitment to free-market capitalism, Christian morality, "traditional" (that is, patriarchal) family values, and anti–"big government" individualism, the American New Right combined pro-market libertarians, disillusioned liberals, traditional conservatives, and the Christian Right. Together, these groups helped shift the focus of public debate about poverty and welfare from market failure to the dangers of welfare "dependency." The New Right built a powerful base in the Republican Party during the 1980s and 1990s. Blaming New Deal and Great Society liberalism for economic decline, excessive taxes, bloated bureaucracy, crime, expanding welfare rolls, and moral permissiveness, the New Right discredited the liberal and social democratic goals of achieving social equality through purposeful government action. With the help of conservative foundations, grassroots organizations, think tanks, and a reinvigorated business lobby, the movement also scored major legislative victories, including the passage of the Personal Responsibility and Work Opportunity Reconciliation Act (1996), which replaced Aid to Families with Dependent Children (AFDC) with Temporary Assistance for Needy Families (TANF), made work a requirement for receiving welfare, and devolved responsibility for social welfare programs to the states in the name of the "New Federalism."

The emergence of the New Right as a political movement can be traced to a group of hard-core conservative activists who, having watched the overwhelming defeat of their presidential candidate Barry Goldwater by Democrat Lyndon B. Johnson in 1964, vowed to recapture electoral politics for the conservative Right. Aided in these efforts by a politically potent backlash against the expansion of civil rights and social welfare instigated by Johnson's Great Society programs and against the civil rights, feminist, youth counterculture, and New Left activism of the 1960s, the New Right began to gain momentum in the early 1970s by appealing to the resentments and anxieties of an economically vulnerable white working class. It made inroads among political elites, including a group of once–left and liberal intellectuals, who came to be known as neoconservatives as they turned rightward for their ideas and politics. Daniel Patrick Moynihan's warnings about the looming "crisis" of the Black family and about exploding welfare rolls expressed a growing disillusionment among liberals with ambitious welfare programs, urban riots, surging crime rates, and the growth of an "underclass." Concerned about "moral decline," neoconservatives helped revive a moral discourse that ascribed poverty to the moral failings of the poor.

Economic crisis in the early 1970s favored the New Right activists who were building the organizational infrastructure for a political movement to counter the New Left proponents of greater social equality. Financially supported by corporations alarmed at the costs of promoting greater equality, newly created New Right think tanks like the Heritage Foundation and already-existing organizations like the American Enterprise Institute advocated government retrenchment, privatization, and curbs on welfare spending. Accusing feminists, liberals, Black radicals, gay and lesbian activists, and welfare rights advocates of endorsing immoral and irresponsible behavior, New Right intellectuals disseminated their views through grassroots networks, publications, and the mainstream media. George Gilder's *Sexual Suicide* (1974) argued that social policy should reinforce marriage rather than enabling poor mothers to live without male support. By the late 1970s, New Right arguments that welfare benefits constituted a "moral hazard" had gained increasing support in an economy where the majority of Americans were facing a declining or stagnant standard of living.

Christian Right organizations also played a central role in the political rise of the New Right, exerting influence in local battles over "sex education," the Equal Rights Amendment, gay rights, and Christian schools in the 1970s. Founded in 1979, the Moral Majority defended "family values," opposed sexual permissiveness and feminism, and accused an activist welfare state of usurping the roles of families, churches, and charitable organizations in the 1980s. Its successor, the Christian Coalition, continued these campaigns while gaining increasing strength in the Republican Party. These groups mobilized grassroots electoral support for conservative causes and candidates through television and direct mail while influencing the Republican Party platform and candidates to support their issues.

Reagan's presidential victory in 1980 played a particularly pivotal role in galvanizing the New Right's disparate components around an antiliberal social policy agenda. The Heritage Foundation's *Mandate for Leadership* (1980) advised the incoming administration to distinguish between the "worthy" and "unworthy" poor. Programs for the poor and AFDC, or welfare, in particular, were the first and most vulnerable targets. Cuts in benefits, stronger work requirements for welfare recipients, and a devolution to the states of authority for AFDC soon followed. Journalist Ken Auletta popularized the term "underclass" to describe a deviant subculture, and President Reagan attacked "welfare queens," implicitly stereotyped as African American women. Intellectuals at the Manhattan Institute and other think tanks, including George Gilder in his *Wealth and Poverty* (1981) and Charles Murray in his *Losing Ground: American Social Policy, 1950–1980* (1984), advocated a punitive approach to welfare provision to overcome the moral failings of welfare recipients, and Lawrence Mead's *Beyond Entitlement: The Social Obligations of Citizenship* (1986) criticized the welfare system for failing to set behavioral standards for the poor. Through expanded use of welfare waiver provisions, the Reagan and Bush (I) administrations permitted states to test new work and discipline-oriented programs that were developed, in part, by think tanks like the Hudson Institute and the Heritage Foundation and were funded by the John M. Olin Foundation and the Lynne and Harry Bradley Foundation.

In response to the increasing power of the New Right discourse about "welfarism," a group calling themselves "New Democrats" began to distance themselves from their party's historic commitments to organized labor, civil rights, and New Deal and Great Society social welfare, in part by focusing on the dangers of long-term reliance upon welfare and on the need to make the poor economically self-sufficient. Agreeing that welfare reduced the incentive to work, New Democrats advocated expanded child care provisions and income support but also advocated tougher work requirements to wean poor mothers off welfare. Their discursive support aided the passage of the Family Support Act (1988) endorsing workfare. As a leading New Democrat, Bill Clinton, the governor of Arkansas, advocated workfare. Riding on that record, he campaigned for the presidency in 1992 to end "welfare as we know it."

Aided by New Democrats, the New Right won control of the antipoverty agenda during the 1990s. Presaging the repeal of AFDC, Lawrence Mead's *New Politics of Poverty: The Nonworking Poor in America* (1992) characterized "dependency at the bottom of society" as the issue of the day (Mead 1992, ix) while denying that racism underlay the attacks on welfare. Charles Murray and Richard J. Herrnstein's *Bell Curve: Intelligence and Class Structure in American Life* (1994) placed welfare recipients in a discursive framework associated with addiction, disease, and genetic deficiencies as they lamented "chronic welfare dependency" (Murray and Herrnstein 1994, 196). As part of their 1994 "Contract with America," Republicans proposed legislation to replace AFDC with a time-limited, conditional, and disciplinary program of temporary assistance. Having won control of Congress, the Republicans set about enacting the relevant legislation. In 1996, Clinton signed the Personal Responsibility and Work Opportunity Reconciliation Act, bringing many long-standing New Right welfare reform objectives to fruition. The new law requires welfare recipients to find work or to participate in work programs, strictly limits the amount of time a family can receive welfare, repeals the federal guarantee of aid to families, and devolves welfare administration and discretion to the states while requiring states to enforce penalties against recipients who do not meet the new work and morality criteria of the federal law. The 1996 law also included a "charitable choice" provision to facilitate delegation of welfare administration and services to religious groups interested in the moral reeducation of the poor in keeping with its sponsors' ideological alliance with the Christian Right. Upon assuming the presidency in 2001, George W. Bush proposed to make federal funding even more accessible to "faith-based charities" and less supervised.

Avoiding any recognition that child rearing and domestic duties involves work, and ignoring market failures, a New Right discourse blaming immorality, irresponsibility, fatherlessness, and the welfare state for poverty and advocating work, sexual restraint, and marriage as the cure for poverty had become increasingly influential in the United States by the century's end due to the political strength and the astute media management of the New Right coalition.

Dolores E. Janiewski

See also: Christian Fundamentalism; Liberalism; *Losing Ground;* New Left; War on Poverty; Welfare Policy/Welfare Reform

References and Further Reading

Mead, Lawrence. 1992. *The New Politics of Poverty: The Nonworking Poor in America*. New York: Basic Books.

Mink, Gwendolyn. 1998. *Welfare's End*. Ithaca, NY: Cornell University Press.

Murray, Charles, and Richard J. Herrnstein. 1994. *The Bell Curve: Intelligence and Class Structure in American Life*. New York: Free Press.

Noble, Charles. 1997. *Welfare as We Knew It: A Political History of the American Welfare State*. New York: Oxford University Press.

Schram, Sanford F. 1995. *Words of Welfare: The Poverty of Social Science and the Social Science of Poverty*. Minneapolis: University of Minnesota Press.

Waddan, Alex. 1997. *The Politics of Social Welfare: The Collapse of the Centre and the Rise of the Right*. Brookfield, UK: Edward Elgar.

Night Comes to the Cumberlands: A Biography of a Depressed Area, *Harry Monroe Caudill*

For the generation of the 1960s, no other book fixed the image of Appalachia as a region of poverty and hopelessness quite as boldly as Harry Monroe Caudill's *Night Comes to the Cumberlands*. Published in the summer of 1963, within months of Michael Harrington's *Other America* and the creation of a special antipoverty task force within the Kennedy administration, *Night Comes to the Cumberlands* quickly became the definitive text on poverty in Appalachia among journalists, academics, and government bureaucrats concerned with economic inequality in America. Caudill's passionate portrayal of an old and predominantly white part of the nation's heartland, devastated by corporate greed, environmental abuse, and government neglect, helped shape the dialogue about poverty and economic growth evolving nationally and among key White House advisers. After reading an account of unemployed and destitute coal-mining families in eastern Kentucky by *New York Times* reporter Homer Bigart, who toured the mountains with Harry Caudill after reading the book, President John F. Kennedy committed himself to an antipoverty program for the 1964 session of Congress.

Caudill's Appalachia was a land of rich natural beauty and human heritage overwhelmed by mismanagement and shortsighted exploitation. The coal industry and corrupt politicians were largely to blame for turning the Appalachian landscape into a wasteland and mountaineers into a demoralized people, he thought. But Caudill also found within the local culture deficiencies that fueled ignorance, clannishness, and an eagerness to accept public relief. A predominantly absentee coal industry, he argued, had ravaged the land, stolen its wealth of natural resources, and left the people to survive on the dole. Only a massive government effort similar to the New Deal's Tennessee Valley Authority and the European Marshall Plan could restore growth, create jobs, and improve education and housing in this forgotten corner of America.

Caudill was a former Kentucky legislator and lawyer and a native of the region. His understanding of poverty in Appalachia mirrored the dual perspectives on poverty prevalent among postwar American liberals, at once blaming the structural inequalities in the region's political economy and the individual decisions and cultural values of the mountain people themselves. Embracing both the "culture of poverty" and the new economic theories of growth and human capital, *Night Comes to the Cumberlands* appealed to a wide spectrum of 1960s liberals and became the bible of antipoverty warriors and environmental activists in the region for decades to come. Subsequent generations of Appalachian scholars would take issue with Caudill's pejorative, almost eugenic view of the region's traditional culture, but *Night Comes to the Cumberlands* would remain a landmark study, defining for most of the nation the conditions and tragic history of one of America's most persistently distressed areas. Caudill subsequently published ten books and more than 100 articles on Appalachia. He died in 1990.

Ronald D. Eller

See also: Appalachia; *The Other America*; Picturing Poverty (I); Poor Whites; Rural Poverty; Tennessee Valley Authority

References and Further Reading

Couto, Richard. 1994. *An American Challenge: A Report on Economic Trends and Social Issues in Appalachia*. Dubuque, IA: Kendall Hunt Publishing.

Duncan, Cynthia M. 1999. *Worlds Apart: Why Poverty Persists in Rural America*. New Haven: Yale University Press.

Nonprofit Sector

Since the colonial era, nonprofit social welfare organizations have been an important part of America's response to poverty and social welfare needs. But since the 1960s, this nonprofit role has been fundamentally transformed due to extensive federal funding of social services, the emergence of new social movements, and a profound restructuring of public policy and public service delivery that together constitute a revolution in America's approach to addressing social problems. Nonprofit social service agencies are now more central to America's response to poverty and other social problems than ever before.

Background

The current configuration of nonprofit, public, and for-profit social service organizations has been shaped by developments and trends that go back to the earliest decades of the republic. In the colonial period, churches, voluntary organizations, neighbors, and relatives provided emergency or supplemental cash and in-kind assistance, counseling, and support for people in need. Few formal voluntary service agencies existed. But in the early 1800s, volunteer societies proliferated throughout the country to care for children, mothers, and the disadvantaged (Crenson 1998; Katz 1996; Trattner 1999; Smith and Lipsky 1993).

As the nineteenth century progressed, more and more voluntary service organizations emerged, especially serving children and youth (Crenson 1998; Warner 1989; Brown and McKeown 1997). Many of these organizations were founded through religious sponsorship and affiliation, reflecting the surge of immigrants into urban America in the late nineteenth century and the concomitant need to provide them with support and social care. For instance, the major expansion of Catholic Charities occurred during this period (Brown and McKeown 1997). Many of these sectarian agencies, especially those in urban areas, received public subsidies, although often these subsidies were very controversial politically. In the late nineteenth century, a number of other voluntary organizations with at least some faith and social care components were also established, including the YMCA, the YWCA, Goodwill Industries, Volunteers of America, and the Salvation Army.

With the growth of nonprofit service organizations in the nineteenth century, the administration of social care became increasingly complicated. Nonprofit organizations emerged as central to service provision in child welfare (including foster care, adoption, and residential care), relief of the poor through cash and in-kind assistance (usually as a supplement to the public sector), immigrant assistance, and recreation. Public subsidies of nonprofit organizations tended to be quite targeted, with child and family service agencies the principal beneficiaries, particularly in urban areas with substantial immigrant populations (Warner 1989; Smith and Lipsky 1993). Also, public organizations, including state and local institutions for the mentally ill and developmentally disabled and for delinquent youth, continued to grow in size and number. Poor farms and almshouses continued to be a central component of public assistance, especially for the poor elderly and disabled. Typically, these institutions were administered directly by counties and towns or were managed under a contract to a private entrepreneur (Vladeck 1980; Katz 1996).

During the first two decades of the twentieth century, the number of nonprofit social welfare agencies continued to grow, albeit at a modest pace. Perhaps the most notable new type of nonprofit agency was the settlement house, which represented a genuine departure from previous services: The staff and volunteers of settlement houses viewed social problems such as poverty and joblessness as rooted in the social and economic environment—a marked break with the previous conception of poverty as rooted in individual and moral failure. Given their focus on the community and social environment, settlement houses emphasized outreach activities, group and community programs, and programs to change the social norms of poor and especially immigrant communities. Typically, settlement houses depended on small private donations and fees; they rarely received direct public grants or subsidies (Chambers 1963; Fabricant and Fisher 2002).

This period also witnessed the establishment of the Community Chest, the predecessor organization of today's United Way. Chapters of the Community Chest were founded by leading members of the business and nonprofit sectors in communities across the country as federated fund-raising organizations; their goal was to enhance the overall efficiency of local services. The member agencies of the Community Chest agreed to abide by certain fund-raising practices, including a joint campaign whose proceeds would be distributed to the member agencies. Thus, member agencies agreed to relinquish some autonomy in exchange for the benefits of a consolidated fund-raising campaign. Established in Cleveland in 1914, the Community Chest movement grew slowly at first, but after World War I, it spread quickly throughout the country. By 1929, 329 cities and towns had autonomous Community Chest chapters, under the loose umbrella of the Community Chest name (Katz 1996; Brilliant 1990). In general, member agencies were the established, elite voluntary agencies of the community: the YMCA, the YWCA, the Red Cross, the Boy Scouts and Girl Scouts, and child and family service agencies. Most of these agencies did not receive public subsidies; their revenues came from the Community Chest campaigns, other private donations, and service fees.

The Depression of the 1930s created daunting problems for nonprofit and public social service agencies. Many nonprofit agencies were forced to close or merge, and many were simply overwhelmed with the demand for help from jobless and impoverished citizens. In response, the federal government created numerous relief programs, but most of these programs were temporary. Eventually, these programs closed, leaving the underlying structure of the nonprofit social services intact: a relatively small array of agencies in local communities primarily focused on child and family services, recreation, and emergency assistance. These agencies were largely dependent upon private charity and client fees, with some agencies receiving small public subsidies. The federal government had almost no presence in the nonprofit social service sector.

More permanent substantive change in the administration and mix of services began in the late 1940s and 1950s. The federal government created new grant-in-aid programs to encourage local governments to increase the quality and scope of an array of social and health services, including mental health, vocational rehabilitation, and child welfare services (Merriam 1955). Congress passed the Hill-Burton Act in 1946 for the support of hospital construction and renovation. This act proved a boon to nonprofit hospitals, which used the construction loans to significantly expand their capacity and the centrality of their role in health care. Public institutions for the mentally ill and developmentally disabled also used these loans to renovate their facilities (Vladeck 1980).

Nonetheless, change in social services was very slow and incremental, and most new programs were small and undercapitalized. During the 1950s, nonprofit social service agencies that were members of the Community Chest typically depended upon donations from the Chest for 50 percent or more of their income. Agencies outside the Community Chest umbrella depended upon modest private donations and fees from clients (Smith and Lipsky 1993). Public funding of nonprofit agencies tended to be on a small scale and restricted to specific service niches, such as residential programs for youth administered by long-standing agencies such as Lutheran Social Services and Catholic Charities. Most nonprofit social services remained clustered in the family and child services and emergency assistance categories.

The New Federal Social Role and Its Implications for Nonprofit Agencies

Despite modest changes in social policy in the 1940s and 1950s, nonprofit social services possessed relatively limited capacity to address poverty and the problems of the disadvantaged. Some analysts blamed this situation in part on the disengagement of private social welfare agencies from the poor as these agencies strove to become more professional (Cloward and Epstein 1965). Others, such as Alfred Kahn (1962), argued that only with a concerted commitment by the public sector to comprehensive social services would the needs of the poor be adequately addressed. The clear implication was that private agencies were trapped in part by their dependence on private charity and client fees, which created large obstacles to the ability of these agencies to serve the poor.

These arguments helped spur a more widespread effort to alter the role of nonprofit social welfare agencies within the social service delivery system as part of the federal government's War on Poverty in the 1960s. The federal initiatives of this period—driven in part by emergent social movements—had profound consequences for nonprofit social service delivery, including a tremendous growth in the number and diversity of nonprofit social welfare agencies and a shift from reliance on private donations and client fees to reliance on public financing.

Growth and Diversification of Services

During the 1960s, the federal government funded a broad array of new social services: senior services, community mental health services, community action programs, job training, rape crisis centers, domestic violence programs, counseling for the poor and the disabled, specialized foster care, home care for the disabled and elderly, and intensive preschool for disadvantaged children (Head Start).

The increased availability of federal funding for social services encouraged the establishment and growth of new nonprofit agencies. These new agencies were usually heavily dependent on government funding; many were outside the established network of Community Chest agencies that had formed the core of the nonprofit social service system in local communities. (Many of the established agencies eventually expanded their programs through government funding as well.) These new agencies quickly took their place as central actors on the local social service scene, especially in service areas that more traditional nonprofit agencies had largely eschewed, such as drug treatment and services for the disabled and mentally ill. Indeed, the new community action agencies, in their effort to mobilize the citizens to help the disadvantaged, often took a confrontational stance toward the more established local service agencies, both nonprofit and public.

The Shift from Private to Public Funding

Since the colonial era, nonprofit agencies had been greatly constrained in their ability to address poverty and other social problems by their dependence on private charity and client fees. But the advent of extensive federal funding fundamentally changed the revenue mix of nonprofit agencies. For instance, federal spending on a bundle of social services including child welfare, vocational rehabilitation, and nutrition assistance rose from $2.2 billion in 1970 to $8.7 billion in 1980 (Bixby 1999, 89). This sharp increase in funding boosted the government's share of nonprofit social agency funding to well over half. Concomitantly, the relative contribution of private fees and donations to the revenue stream of nonprofits fell dramatically (Lynn 2002; Smith and Lipsky 1993; Smith 2002). The growth in public support also reduced the relative role of the Community Chest and its successor organization, the United Way, in funding nonprofit social services. This decline continues to the present day, although local United Way chapters are increasingly important in convening key stakeholders in the community to help define pressing social service priorities.

For nonprofits, the rise in public funding also meant that their funding was usually accompanied by rules and regulations on programmatic standards, client eligibility, and the allocation of expenses. These regulations can be at variance with a nonprofit agency's original mission and focus, creating profound internal organizational challenges for these agencies (Smith and Lipsky 1993).

Since the 1980s, the role of nonprofit agencies in addressing social problems has been directly affected by a number of important public policy developments. In the early 1980s, President Ronald Reagan reduced federal funding for many nonprofit social welfare programs and devolved responsibility for many federal social programs to the states (Gutowski and Koshel 1982). Many nonprofit agencies were forced to substantially retrench during this period, leaving many of their clients without services.

But over time, federal funding of social services rose again for four key reasons. First, state governments, often with the support of federal officials and nonprofit executives, refinanced social services by tapping into other sources of federal financing, especially Medicaid, the matching federal/state health insurance program for the poor and disabled, which has been rising rapidly since the mid-1980s. Today, many key social welfare services provided by nonprofit agencies are substantially funded by Medicaid, including child welfare services (particularly counseling and residential treatment), mental health care, rehabilitation services, residential programs for the developmentally disabled and chronic mentally ill, and home care.

Second, many new federal funding programs for social services were created or additional funds were provided for existing programs in several important service categories, including AIDS services, domestic violence, AmeriCorps, job training, mental health, drug and alcohol treatment, home care, day care, and child protection. These services are delivered primarily by nonprofit agencies, with the exception of home care and day care, where for-profit agencies play a substantial role. In an important change, many federal departments that historically did not directly fund social services, such as the Departments of Justice, Education, and Housing and Urban Development (HUD), emerged in the 1980s and 1990s as major funders of local social service programs.

Third, welfare reform was passed in 1996 by Congress and implemented in 1997. This legislation replaced Aid to Families with Dependent Children (AFDC) and gave states much greater flexibility in the administration and spending of federal dollars under the new program, Temporary Assistance for Needy Families (TANF). Due to the work requirement of TANF and a rapidly growing domestic economy, the number of people receiving cash benefits plummeted nationwide. Many states spent the resulting savings on cash assistance (coupled with additional federal aid for social services) on a variety of welfare-related services. Many nonprofit agencies have thus found themselves in an unusual position: Most agencies stridently opposed welfare reform (because of the new restrictions on cash assistance), and at least some of their clients have lost cash benefits, but many agencies have received additional funding to provide job training, welfare-to-work aid, and child care. In a very real sense, the United States has essentially abolished cash assistance for the poor and replaced it with a mix of support services, primarily provided by nonprofit organizations, designed to move the poor into the labor force as quickly as possible. To an extent, nonprofit agencies focused on providing services to the poor now receive funds that were previously devoted to cash assistance.

The fourth and final factor contributing to the continued growth of nonprofit social welfare agencies and their role in social services is the diversification in the tools of government social support. While direct funding for social services remains the norm, new tools of social support have expanded, including tax credits, loans, and tax-exempt bonds. For instance, the federal child care tax credit has fueled the growth in demand for nonprofit (and for-profit) child care. Tax-exempt bond financing has been used by state and local governments to help nonprofit social service agencies with their capital needs.

Next Steps for Social Policy and Nonprofit Service Agencies

In many respects, the transformation of nonprofit social service agencies since the mid-1970s typifies America's unique approach to social policy. In other advanced industrial countries, personal social services such as child care, mental health care, and rehabilitation programs are championed by major political parties as an essential right of every citizen. Extensive networks of government-funded public social services exist as a consequence. The United States has been much more reluctant to enact entitlement programs in the area of social services. For example, the Social Services Block Grant (SSBG), created in 1981 as part of the Reagan cutbacks, was a symbol of the federal government's reluctant commitment to social services. (Most of this money is channeled to nonprofit social welfare agencies.) The decline of SSBG in real terms since 1981 demonstrates the enduring ambivalence about major federal support for extensive social services.

Yet the social needs remain, so policymakers and advocates have done an end-run around SSBG. Instead of focusing on SSBG, policymakers and advocates greatly expanded federal support for nonprofit social services through a variety of other routes. But this expansion carries with it great risks for nonprofit agencies. Relatively modest technical changes to existing law could have a major negative impact on funding for nonprofit social welfare agencies. (For example, changes to eligibility for Supplemental Security Income [SSI], a federal program for the disabled and elderly poor, could significantly reduce certain clients' eligibility for nonprofit services.) More generally, the substantial tax cuts implemented by the administration of President George W. Bush in 2001–2003 will sharply curb the revenues of the federal government in the coming years, creating a budget squeeze that will make it much more difficult to continue federal funding of many service programs. Also, the refinancing of social services through Medicaid and to a lesser extent Medicare means that the future of social services is now tied to the ongoing national debate on the role of the federal government in health care. Significant reform of Medicaid, for example, would have far-reaching effects on nonprofit social service agencies. Policy changes affecting the clients of nonprofit agencies, such as changes in eligibility for TANF and food stamps, can have a direct impact on the demand for nonprofit services. The restrictiveness of public and private funding today makes it very difficult for many nonprofits to respond to changes in client circumstances.

Further, the emphasis on performance and outcome measurement by government and private funders alike and the stepped-up competition for public and private funding have forced many nonprofits to wrestle with very complex issues pertaining to mission and their role in the community. This is all the more difficult given the broader debate under way in the United States about community service, voluntarism, and the community-building role of nonprofit organizations. Nonprofit social service agencies have a great opportunity to help rebuild distressed communities, stimulate more voluntarism, and provide a locus for community service activities. But these activities may conflict with the pressure to be accountable to funders or with the desire to ward off competitors who do not have the same type of community obligations. Successful nonprofit organizations will be those agencies that can use their community connections to their competitive advantage and at the same time develop the capability to be accountable to funders and their communities. The success of nonprofits in responding to social need also hinges upon the capacity and willingness of government to adequately fund nonprofit agencies and address the multiple needs of the poor and disadvantaged through income support and other social policies.

Steven Rathgeb Smith

See also: Charitable Choice; Charity; Community Chests; Community-Based Organizations; Mutual Aid; Philanthropy; Privatization; Salvation Army; Settlement Houses; Voluntarism; Young Men's Christian Association (YMCA); Young Women's Christian Association (YWCA)

References and Further Reading

Bixby, Anne Kallman. 1999. "Public Social Welfare Expenditures, Fiscal Year 1995." *Social Security Bulletin* 62, no. 2 (April): 86–94.

Brilliant, Eleanor L. 1990. *The United Way: Dilemmas of Organized Charity.* New York: Columbia University Press.

Brown, Dorothy M., and Elizabeth McKeown. 1997. *The Poor Belong to Us: Catholic Charities and American Welfare.* Cambridge, MA: Harvard University Press.

Chambers, Clarke A. 1963. *Seedtime for Reform: American Social Service and Social Action, 1918–1933.* Minneapolis: University of Minnesota Press.

Cloward, Richard A., and Irwin Epstein. 1965. "Private Social Welfare's Disengagement from the Poor: The Case of Family Adjustment Agencies." In *Social Welfare Institutions: A Sociological Reader,* ed. Mayer N. Zald, 623–644. New York: John Wiley and Sons.

Crenson, Matthew. 1998. *Building the Invisible Orphanage.* Cambridge, MA: Harvard University Press.

Fabricant, Michael B., and Robert Fisher. 2002. *Settlement Houses under Siege: The Struggle to Sustain Community Organizations in New York City.* New York: Columbia University Press.

Gutowski, M. F., and J. J. Koshel. 1982. "Social Services." In *The Reagan Experiment,* ed. John L. Palmer and Isabel V. Sawhill. Washington, DC: Urban Institute Press.

Kahn, Alfred J. 1962. "The Social Scene and the Planning of Services for Children." *Social Work* 7, no. 3 (July): 3–14.

Katz, Michael B. 1996. *In the Shadow of the Poorhouse: A Social History of Welfare in America.* New York: BasicBooks.

Lynn, Laurence E., Jr. 2002. "Social Services and the State: The Public Appropriation of Private Charity." *Social Service Review* 72, no. 1 (March): 58–82.

Merriam, Ida C. 1955. "Social Welfare Expenditures in the United States, 1934–54." *Social Security Bulletin* 18, no. 5 (October): 3–15.

Murdoch, Norman H. 1994. *Origins of the Salvation Army.* Knoxville: University of Tennessee Press.

Smith, Steven Rathgeb. 2002. "Social Services." In *The State of the Nonprofit Sector,* ed. Lester M. Salamon, 149–186. Washington, DC: Brookings Institution.

Smith, Steven Rathgeb, and Michael Lipsky. 1993. *Nonprofits for Hire: The Welfare State in the Age of Contracting.* Cambridge, MA: Harvard University Press.

Trattner, Walter I. 1999. *From Poor Law to Welfare State: A History of Social Welfare in America*. 6th ed. New York: Free Press.

Vladeck, Bruce. 1980. *Unloving Care: The Nursing Home Tragedy*. New York: Basic Books.

Warner, Amos G. 1989. *American Charities: A Study in Philanthropy and Economics*. New Brunswick, NJ: Transaction Books.

North Carolina Fund

Governor Terry Sanford established the North Carolina Fund in 1963 as an experiment in public-private cooperation. The fund grew out of a confluence of interests between a progressive young governor, who was searching for ways to improve educational and job opportunities for disadvantaged families, and Paul Ylvisaker, director of the Ford Foundation's Gray Areas project, which for a number of years had been addressing issues of poverty and racial justice in urban areas across the nation. With additional support from the Z. Smith Reynolds Foundation, the Mary Reynolds Babcock Foundation, and various agencies of the federal government, the fund employed a racially integrated staff and supported a variety of community development programs in rural and urban areas across the state.

The fund initially emphasized public education, but its focus quickly shifted to community action and manpower development programs. The fund supported eleven community action agencies, ten of which are still in operation. Reflecting the special needs of local constituencies, rural projects focused on economic stability, housing, and employment, while urban initiatives were more oriented toward problems of juvenile delinquency, health care, and illiteracy.

Child sitting on steps outside of house, North Carolina/Billy Barnes for the North Carolina Fund. (Library of Congress)

The fund developed a number of cutting-edge antipoverty interventions. The North Carolina Volunteers, a model for Volunteers in Service to America (VISTA), recruited over 300 college students, Black and white, men and women, to spend the summers of 1964 and 1965 working with local social service agencies on poverty-related issues. The Community Action Technicians program trained over 100 people from diverse socioeconomic backgrounds, including many grassroots leaders, to staff the eleven community action agencies supported by the fund. The fund also created nonprofit corporations that focused on specific policy areas: manpower development, education, low-income housing, and community economic development.

The fund's fortunes tracked those of the larger civil rights and antipoverty movements, both of which it sought to advance. The fund took seriously the need for the "maximum feasible participation of the poor" in antipoverty programs, and it worked to give the poor the institutional and financial footing from which to press their demands. This strategy helped unleash a wave of activism in poor communities across the state. Two of the most notable grassroots organizations supported by the fund were the United Organizations for Community Improvement in Durham and the People's Program on Poverty in Bertie, Halifax, Hertford, and Northampton Counties. As the poor began to organize, picket, and protest, however, local elites intensified their opposition to the fund and to the War on Poverty more generally.

In 1968, the fund's directors closed up shop, partly by design and partly because of tensions within the liberal coalition that had sustained both the civil rights victories of mid-decade and President Lyndon B. Johnson's vision of a Great Society. The fund's legacy, however, stretches far beyond its five-year life span. Involvement with the fund permanently altered the objectives of several North Carolina foundations; many of the community development organizations it spawned continue to shape public policy at the regional, state, and local levels, and a large number of fund veterans occupy key positions in both public and nonprofit social service agencies today.

Robert Korstad

See also: Community Development; Community Organizing; Community-Based Organizations; Volunteers in Service to America (VISTA); War on Poverty

References and Further Reading

Korstad, Robert, and James Leloudis. 1999. "Citizen Soldiers: The North Carolina Volunteers and the War on Poverty." *Law and Contemporary Problems* 62 (Autumn): 177–197.

Records of the North Carolina Fund. Southern Historical Collection, Manuscripts Department, Library of the University of North Carolina at Chapel Hill. An extensive inventory is available at http://www.lib.unc.edu/mss/inv/n/North_Carolina_Fund/.

NOW Legal Defense and Education Fund

From its inception in 1966, the National Organization for Women (NOW) has viewed litigation as a strategy to help women gain rights and access to economic opportunity. In 1970, NOW created a separate litigating and education entity, the NOW Legal Defense and Education Fund, eligible for tax-deductible contributions.

While NOW Legal Defense has always supported a wide array of women's rights endeavors, initially its legal work focused on employment discrimination cases and the implementation of Title IX of the 1972 Education Amendments, which barred sex discrimination in educational institutions. In 1979, NOW Legal Defense participated as amicus in *Califano v. Westcott* (443 U.S. 76), which successfully challenged discriminatory welfare policies, and in 1984 NOW Legal Defense also filed an amicus brief in the Washington State pay equity case *AFSCME v. State of Washington* (770 F.2d 1401 [9th Cir.]).

In 1993, NOW Legal Defense began a more aggressive defense of poor women's rights, which were threatened by growing interest in federal welfare reform. A class-action lawsuit challenged New Jersey's policy that refused additional welfare benefits to children born to mothers receiving public assistance (the "family cap"), arguing that such a policy worked to coerce the reproductive choices of poor women; NOW Legal Defense continues to wage this fight. NOW Legal Defense also asserted that state welfare laws that provided lower benefits to new residents discriminated against women who moved to escape violent relationships. The Supreme Court ultimately reaffirmed the position that differential welfare benefits for new state residents violated the U.S. Constitution (*Saenz v. Roe* [526 U.S. 489 (1999)]).

In 1996, the NOW Legal Defense and Education Fund lobbied against the proposed revision of the federal welfare program and helped to prevent a mandated "family cap" in the new statute. NOW Legal Defense drafted the language that offered protection to poor women affected by domestic violence. In 1999, NOW Legal Defense established a national coalition of activist organizations to develop a progressive agenda aimed at ending poverty.

In 2002, the coalition focused on the pending reauthorization of the 1996 law, with NOW Legal Defense coordinating lobbying efforts. In addition, NOW Legal Defense played a key role in drafting a progressive welfare reauthorization bill, which was introduced in the House of Representatives by Congressmember Patsy Mink.

A feminist leader in the early-twenty-first-century welfare debate, NOW Legal Defense advocated for poor mothers as their children's caregivers; it also argued against increased work requirements and for access to education and training, increases in federal funds for child care, rejection of heterosexual marriage promotion as a means to reduce poverty, additional assistance for recipients affected by domestic violence and other employment barriers, protection for the civil rights of program participants, and access to benefits for legal immigrants. Republican dominance of Congress, however, made enactment of progressive legislation unlikely.

NOW Legal Defense continues to litigate in this area to protect the rights of women forced to work for benefits, to oppose the family cap, and to ensure that eligible recipients get benefits to which they are entitled.

Cynthia Harrison

See also: Aid to Families with Dependent Children (ADC/AFDC); Civil Rights Acts, 1964 and 1991; Employment Policy; Feminisms; Gender Discrimination in the Labor Market; Sexism; Welfare Policy/Welfare Reform

References and Further Reading

NOW Legal Defense and Education Fund. "Fact Sheet on the Building Opportunities Bonus." http://www.nowldef.org/html/issues/wel/reastatement.shtml. Accessed January 14, 2004.

U.S. House of Representatives. 2002. *TANF Reauthorization Act of 2001*. HR 3113. 107th Cong., 2d sess.

Nutrition and Food Assistance

Nutrition and food assistance in the United States consists of a range of public and private programs designed to enable low-income and other "special needs" households to meet their most basic nutritional needs by providing vouchers, or food stamps, for food purchases, free food packages, and subsidized or free cooked meals. In fiscal year 2002 the U.S. government spent approximately $32.6 billion on eleven different programs to feed needy and hungry Americans. It is virtually impossible to determine the total number of individuals who benefit from one or more of these food programs, since each program tallies its own participation data without asking whether its clients are receiving food from other federal programs as well. Some programs do not count participants at all but, rather, report the number of meals served or pounds of food distributed. Nor is it clear that these programs reach all those in need: The U.S. Census Bureau estimates that in 2000, 33 million people in the United States lived in "food insecure" households, that is, households in which members were uncertain about their ability or unable to acquire adequate food on a regular basis to meet essential needs. But we know from surveys that many eligible people, including many who are classified as "food insecure," never enroll in any food program at all. Nevertheless, data from the individual programs show that the number of people who receive federal food assistance is substantial. The food stamp program, for example, served over 17 million people in 2001; the Special Supplemental Nutrition for Women, Infants, and Children (WIC) program served more than 7.3 million (see the accompanying table).

Table 1

Major federal food assistance programs: participation rates and cost, 2001

	# of participants	*$ cost*
Food Stamp Program	17,313*	17,797
National School Lunch	27,504	6,475
School Breakfast	7,792	1,450
Child/Adult Care Food	2,725	1,739
Summer Food Service	2,115	215
WIC	7,306	4,150
Commodity Supplemental	407	103
Elderly Feeding	—	152
Indian Reservations	113	68
TEFAP	—	377

Note: All figures, participants and dollars, in millions. Elderly Feeding and TEFAP report only meals served and pounds distributed, respectively.

In addition to the various federal food assistance programs, there exists an extensive parallel system of private, nonprofit food pantries, soup kitchens, and shelters. Perhaps as much as 15 percent of the food distributed by these street-level providers is federal surplus commodities or food purchased with federal government grants, primarily through the Emergency Food Assistance Program (TEFAP), but the rest is raised through donations by individuals, religious institutions, food-processing corporations, farmers, supermarkets, and restaurants. These private programs tend to fill a niche that federal programs do not reach: About half the clients of charitable food programs do not receive federal food stamps, and two-thirds of women with small children who visit pantries do not take advantage of the WIC program.

The largest nonprofit food assistance organization, Second Harvest, which oversees a network of more than 70,000 street-level food providers, estimates that its programs serve nearly one-tenth of the American population in any given year. The affiliates of Second Harvest represent only a portion of the food pantries and soup kitchens in the United States, however. Estimates suggest that there could be as many as an additional 150,000 food pantries, mostly associated with religious congregations.

The structure of federal food assistance to the needy is based on the foundation of a large entitlement program open to any eligible person—food stamps—and a number of smaller, specialized programs designed to provide assistance to particularly vulnerable or needy categories of people. The modern food stamp program dates from a 1961 pilot program initiated by President John F. Kennedy. In 1964, food stamps were made a permanent part of the federal government's range of social welfare programs.

The food stamp benefit—which now comes in the form of an electronic benefit card, similar to a bank debit card—is available to American citizens and a small number of eligible legal immigrants whose gross household income does not exceed 130 percent of the federal poverty line. The amount of the benefit, which in 2001 averaged just under $75 per person per month, is designed to cover the gap between 30 percent of a household's net cash income and the cost of the U.S. Department of Agriculture's Thrifty Food Plan.

The program reached its peak coverage in 1994, when more than 27 million people were receiving benefits. The 1996 welfare reform legislation (Personal Responsibility and Work Opportunity Reconciliation Act) cut off food stamp benefits for the vast majority of legal immigrants by making them ineligible. These eligibility restrictions, along with the economic boom at the end of the 1990s, reduced program participation substantially. For various reasons—lack of knowledge, inconvenience, pride—a substantial number of eligible people (perhaps as many as 35–40 percent) do not participate in the food stamp program. Participation is highest among people with incomes at or below the federal poverty level, women with young children, and African Americans. It is lowest among the elderly and those whose net incomes are just below the food stamp eligibility cutoff.

In addition to food stamps, designed to cover all segments of the needy population, the federal government maintains an array of targeted programs for children, the elderly poor, women with small children, and Native Americans. One rationale for these programs is that they provide food for certain groups of people who cannot easily buy food for themselves and thus cannot count on coverage from the food stamp program. Children are usually dependent on others in the household to buy and prepare sufficient food, but normal food gathering and preparation cannot be taken for granted in socially dysfunctional or poor households. Another rationale is that children's physical and cognitive development is especially vulnerable to nutritional deficits.

The School Lunch program, which dates from 1946, and the School Breakfast program, authorized in 1966, are the two major childhood nutrition programs. Both programs are open to all children, regardless of income, but low-income children receive free or reduced-price meals. Just under half of all school lunches served are free, while approximately 7 percent are reduced-price. Coverage of the needy population is far greater in the lunch than in the breakfast program. While the former serves nearly 28 million children, only about 8 million children take advantage of the breakfast program. This disparity is less a function of individual household decisions to enroll than it is of the decisions of a number of schools not to participate in the breakfast program.

Additional federal food programs provide aid for infants and children, up to age five, of low-income mothers (WIC), for young children in day care facilities (Child and Adult Care Food Program), and for schoolchildren during the summer vacation (Summer Food Service Program). Federal food programs, then, cover children from birth to the end of public schooling. Evaluations of these programs suggest that they increase the nutritional intake and quality of food for participating children without reducing household expenditures on food. Participation in these programs among eligible children is not universal, however. Even for school lunch, an estimated 5 million to 7 million children who could be eating free or reduced-price meals are not doing so.

Other groups targeted by special programs include lactating women (WIC), the elderly (Nutrition Service Incentive Program, which helps fund Meals on Wheels and food served in senior citizen centers), and Native American families who live far from retail food outlets where the food stamp electronic benefit transfer may be used (Food Distribution on Indian Reservations).

Even with the combination of a comprehensively designed federal food assistance system and a network of private, nonprofit food providers, as many as 3.3 million households actually experienced hunger at some point in 2000. Complex eligibility rules for public programs, skimpy program benefits, lack of commitment to outreach, occasionally punitive administration, inadequate funding of nonentitlement programs like WIC, and fluctuations in private donations of food to charitable pantries and soup kitchens all mean that a system capable of eliminating hunger nevertheless works imperfectly.

Peter Eisinger

See also: Antihunger Coalitions; Food Banks; Food Stamps; Hunger

References and Further Reading

America's Second Harvest. 2001. *Hunger in America 2001, National Report*. Chicago: Author.

Eisinger, Peter. 1998. *Toward an End to Hunger*. Washington, DC: Brookings Institution.

Poppendieck, Janet. 1998. *Sweet Charity?* New York: Viking.

U.S. Department of Agriculture. Web site. Economic Research Service, Food Security in the United States. http://www.ers.usda.gov/Briefing/FoodSecurity/.

Office of Economic Opportunity

See War on Poverty

Old Age

Throughout recorded history, people at advanced ages have felt helpless as strength waned and resources diminished. Many had to rely on family and neighbors for essentials. In the modern era, relief often came from public sources. In this context, a basic paradox characterizes the U.S. experience. Although older Americans were more likely to be economically vulnerable prior to 1935 than afterward, their fellow citizens paid scant attention to late-life poverty. Only after World War I, when senescence was equated with pauperism, did the nation begin to mobilize institutional support and enact policies (corporate, religious, labor, philanthropic, state, and federal) to ameliorate the situation.

Americans of all ages, not just the old, generally lived marginal existences during the first century of U.S. history. Only 49 percent of all adult males held property according to the First Direct Tax (1798), which inventoried every residence, barn, wharf, and mill in the country and set values for land in urban and rural areas. Economic inequality grew during the first decades of the nineteenth century (Soltow 1989, 41, 190). In 1850, only 40 percent of all adults over the age of twenty held any real property. Of the adult white population, 59 percent possessed no land. Economist Lee Soltow (1975, 22, 24) has stated that a third of the nation's population had only the clothes on their backs and the petty cash in their pockets. Intestacy was common: Many people died with nothing to distribute.

The risk of pauperism was not borne equally by all Americans. In terms of material wealth, those who tilled the soil probably were not God's chosen, as Thomas Jefferson declared in *Notes on the State of Virginia* (1787), yet as late as 1870, farmers were roughly twice as likely as nonfarmers to own property. Half of the adult males living in cities were poor (Soltow 1975, 34–35). Slavery denied African Americans the right to acquire or possess property. Despite some states' efforts to liberalize divorce and property laws in the 1840s, few married or single women owned businesses or property in their own name. Arriving without much money, most immigrants came to the United States ambitious to capitalize on opportunities unavailable in Europe or Mexico. America was extolled as a land of opportunity, particularly compared to Old World countries, where greater gaps existed between rich and poor. But few immigrants made fortunes approaching that of Andrew

Carnegie, the Scottish-born millionaire industrialist whose self-described rags-to-riches story became an emblem of the immigrant success story. (The top decile of U.S. property owners tended to be native-born men whose fathers had been well-to-do.) Business downturns, bad crops, disabilities, or just bad luck dashed middle-class citizens' hopes and dreams. Most Americans muddled through, content to improve prospects for their children.

That said, during the first century of U.S. history, most frugal, hardworking men did increase their wealth as they grew older. Individuals were most likely to acquire property between the ages of twenty and thirty. Cumulative increases in wealth were modest after the age of forty, but unless a tragedy (such as disability) required them to liquidate assets after middle age, older men typically retained the property they had acquired. Two-thirds of all men between the ages of sixty-five and sixty-nine held some real estate in 1870. (Thus one-third had none.) When no longer able to work, aged men transferred assets to obtain assistance. Women were more vulnerable than men to old-age poverty. So, too, were African Americans freed by masters unwilling to provide care for them in their declining years. Foreign-born persons who remained in the United States also risked a miserable old age, since they were less likely than native-born citizens to acquire property or secure better-paying jobs over their lives.

Such were the modal life-course patterns for ordinary people. Examining the latter years of some of the Virginia Dynasty underscores the fact that the hazards of economic misfortune threatened both rich and poor. George Washington was sixty-five when he left the presidency. He returned to his estate in Mount Vernon, which he had taken pains to maintain better than he had when he commanded Revolutionary soldiers. His land was rich and his properties were well located; he owned many slaves. Indeed, Washington was probably the second- or third-wealthiest man in the United States when he died in 1799. Thomas Jefferson was not so fortunate. The nation's third president, after age sixty-five, devoted himself to civic projects, such as founding the University of Virginia, when he left the White House in 1809. Although he had been affluent in youth, chronic illness and financial reversals plagued him until his death at age eighty-two. Jefferson mismanaged assets. He lost money when crops and banks failed, land prices fluctuated, and personal notes were forfeited. Only his death in 1826 spared Jefferson from seeing his possessions auctioned off to cover bad loans and mounting debts. Five years later, Monticello was sold in disrepair (Peterson 1962, 380). James Madison, crippled with rheumatism, was confined to one room in his latter days. James Monroe had to sell his family estate in Albemarle, Virginia, to pay his debts. If even these venerable

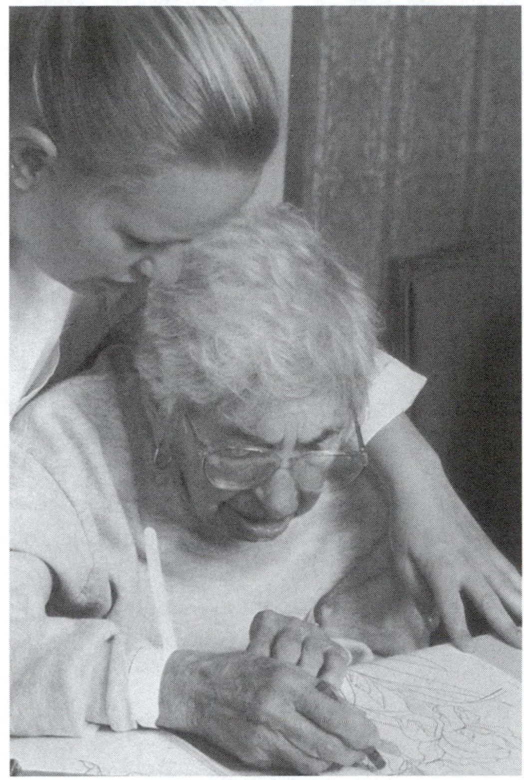

Adult with Art Therapist (Laura Dwight)

men faced financial ruin, it is little wonder that the specter of economic vulnerability—attributable to advanced age, declining health, financial losses, or all three—stalked their fellow citizens throughout their lives.

So what options existed for men and women in dire straits in their declining years? Census data indicate that most older people maintained independent households as long as possible. As late as 1895, only one-tenth of all native-born men and 13 percent of foreign-born males over the age of eighty in Massachusetts lived with strangers or were institutionalized (Achenbaum 1978, 76). Elderly women, in contrast, rarely were reported to be heads of households; roughly 70 percent lived with a child, a grandchild, or an in-law.

In keeping with tradition (and, in the colonial era, with British poor laws), the family was the primary source of charity to the aged. A 1692 Massachusetts Bay Colony act made kin legally as well as morally responsible for infirm and poor family members. By 1860, eighteen of the then thirty-three states had enacted measures to deal with dependency at all ages; another fourteen states had done so by 1914. None stipulated special provisions for the elderly, though Colorado, Kentucky, and Ohio made it a criminal offense not to care for an aged relative. Elder abuse doubtless was as prevalent in the past as it is today, yet most families made the necessary arrangements so that their parent(s) and grandparent(s) were not abandoned in old age.

Local communities were the next line of defense against poverty in old age for the elderly people legally residing in their jurisdiction (Haber and Gratton 1994, 118). Some places gave the aged poor food and firewood so that they could stay at home. Others bid out the needy to households willing to give them care economically. A few cities and counties erected almshouses to shelter anyone, including the old, who could not maintain his or her autonomy. Prior to the Civil War, men and women over sixty-five constituted about 16 percent to 25 percent of the almshouse population. As new institutions were created to care for the deaf, blind, orphans, and criminals, the percentage of older people in poorhouses soared: By 1910, roughly 45 percent of all native-born and 70 percent of all foreign-born almshouse inmates were at least sixty years old. Almshouses were notorious for their filth and sickness; going "Over the Hill to the Poorhouse," as Will Carleton wrote in a heart-wrenching poem (1871), was the option of last resort.

Religious groups and philanthropists offered alternatives to the public poorhouse. Protestant, Catholic, and Jewish congregations erected private facilities for the aged. Of the 1,200 such benevolent homes operating in 1939, roughly two-thirds were built between 1875 and 1919. As social work emerged as a profession, new regulations and standards for old-age homes went into effect. A few rich donors directed funds for the elderly. In 1905, through the Carnegie Foundation for the Advancement of Teaching, Andrew Carnegie set aside $10 million to ensure that college professors would be secure in their retirement. Benjamin Rose left $3 million in 1911 to assist the deserving, aged poor in Cleveland.

Some corporations (beginning with American Express in 1875) provided old-age pensions. They wanted to reward loyal aging employees and to ensure an efficient labor force. Yet by 1910, only sixty companies offered retirement plans—really gratuities, which were legally unenforceable. Unlike Britain, annuities attracted little interest in the United States. The American Federation of Labor, concerned with bread-and-butter issues for younger workers, voted against providing members old-age benefits in 1903. Thus only 1 percent of all American workers potentially had old-age-related benefits in 1914 (Achenbaum 1978, 83).

The major source of financial relief came from veterans' benefits. A U.S. Naval Home was established in 1833, a U.S. Soldiers Home in 1851. Elderly veterans of the American Revolution, the War of 1812, and the Mexican-American War belatedly received land or money; in 1840, 3.7 percent of all surviving soldiers and their widows over age sixty received military pensions. Beginning in the late 1870s, the Grand Army of the Republic lobbied for aging Union soldiers. The number of pensioners rose from 126,772 in 1886 to 921,083 in 1910, with disbursements increasing commensurately from $60 million to $160 million. In 1912, Congress granted a pension to every Yankee veteran over age sixty-two who had served at least ninety days in the war. Military pensions constituted 18 percent of the federal budget a year later. As part of the Civil War Pension Acts, the Act of May 11, 1912, was consistent with the growing conviction, confirmed by medical researchers, that old age itself was a disability (Cole 1992, 190).

Investigators began to document the extent and causes of old-age dependency. Although other subjects, such as the plight of children, attracted more attention, William D. P. Bliss in *The New Encyclopedia of Social Reform* (1908, 849) pronounced old age to have become one of the two or three major causes of pauperism. Lee Welling Squier's *Old Age Dependency in the United States* (1912), a pioneering work, was followed by studies by Lucille Eaves, Abraham Epstein, Robert Kelso, and Alice Willard Solenberger. New York and Massachusetts commissioned surveys. By the eve of the Great Depression, six states had enacted old-age assistance measures. Despite these innovations, military pensions remained the major support for Americans over age sixty-five: 82 percent of all beneficiaries and 80 percent of all funds expended in 1929 came from this single source.

The history of old-age dependency in the United States changed dramatically with the enactment of the Social Security Act (1935). Its expansion and liberalization—as well as the enactment of Medicare, Medicaid, the Older Americans Act, and Supplemental Security Income—meant that a smaller proportion of old people than of children lived below the federal poverty line (Katz 2001, 39, 237). Corporate pensions and private savings strengthened the safety net. Rather than celebrating success in the war against old-age dependency, however, conservative critics in the 1980s began to excoriate "the Greedy Geezers" and to urge privatization of old-age welfare. How ironic, for without Social Security, two-thirds of the elderly in the United States would be poor.

W. Andrew Achenbaum

See also: Ageism; Health Policy; Poorhouse/Almshouse; Social Security Act of 1935; Supplemental Security Income; Townsend Movement; Veterans' Assistance; Welfare Capitalism

References and Further Reading

Achenbaum, W. Andrew. 1978. *Old Age in the New Land: The American Experience since 1790*. Baltimore: Johns Hopkins University Press.

Bliss, William D. P. 1908. *The New Encyclopedia of Social Reform*. New York: Funk and Wagnalls.

Cole, Thomas R. 1992. *The Journey of Life: A Cultural History of Aging in America*. New York: Cambridge University Press.

Haber, Carole, and Brian Gratton. 1994. *Old Age and the Search for Security: An American Social History*. Bloomington: Indiana University Press.

Katz, Michael B. 2001. *The Price of Citizenship: Redefining America's Welfare State*. New York: Henry Holt.

Peterson, Merrill D. 1962. *The Jefferson Image in the American Mind*. New York: Oxford University Press.

Soltow, Lee. 1975. *Men and Wealth in the United States, 1850–1870*. New Haven: Yale University Press.

———. 1989. *Distribution of Wealth and Income in the United States in 1798*. Pittsburgh, PA: University of Pittsburgh Press.

Operation Breadbasket

In 1962, the Southern Christian Leadership Conference (SCLC) formed a subsidiary organization with the goal of putting "bread, money, and income into the baskets of Black and poor people." Operation Breadbasket used a number of different techniques to improve the low socioeconomic status of the Black communities in America, and, as it spread across the nation during the late 1960s, the program made concrete gains. Black consumers were organized to pressure companies to employ Blacks in proportion to their presence in the local population. In Atlanta, Georgia, the birthplace of Operation Breadbasket, their first large-scale campaign won a promise from local companies to create 5,000 jobs for Blacks over the next five years.

After initial organizing in the South, Chicago became the real hotbed of the organization's activities. Jesse Jackson helped found the Chicago chapter in 1966; his work there led Martin Luther King Jr., head of the SCLC, to appoint Jackson national director of Operation Breadbasket in 1967. The Chicago chapter's successes also indicate the extent of the challenge they confronted, for, though protests against local dairy and supermarket businesses to extract guarantees of future job creation and support for Black businesses did produce agreements with several large corporations, change was slow to come. It was not until 1970, when a second wave of demonstrations was launched to target the A&P supermarket chain (which had failed to deliver on its promise of 770 permanent and 1,200 summer jobs), that these guarantees began to be fulfilled.

Under Jackson's leadership, Operation Breadbasket became increasingly centered on Chicago and on Jackson's high-profile image. The program's focus expanded to cover a number of important projects, including running a free breakfast program and the Poor People's Campaign in Washington, D.C. (1968), battling against severe assaults on welfare spending, endorsing political candidates concerned with the needs of the Black community, and gaining space on local and national political agendas. In the face of these crucial initiatives, Operation Breadbasket was quickly overwhelmed, and by 1971, it was mired in obligations that simply overtaxed its already slight resources, as well as in charges of financial corruption. In addition, it was hindered by the perception that its orientation was more Chicago centered than national. Jackson finally left his position as head of Operation Breadbasket, dissolved its Chicago chapter, split from the SCLC, and formed Operation PUSH.

Operation Breadbasket continues to operate under the guidance of the SCLC, but on a much smaller scale than during the critical years of the 1960s. In its heyday, Operation Breadbasket allowed the Black communities of twelve major American cities to solidify the hard-won progress of the decade. By steadfastly boycotting and shaming companies that failed to employ Blacks in meaningful numbers, the program is estimated to have increased the income of the Chicago Black community by $2 million annually during the 1960s. And in seeking a proportional representation for Blacks in the workplace, the program's demands went well beyond subsequent affirmative action measures, which generally require only good-faith efforts to improve representation of minorities in workplaces and schools.

Rebecca K. Root

See also: Black Panther Party; Civil Rights Movement; Poor People's Campaign

References and Further Reading

Garrow, David, ed. 1989. *Chicago 1966: Housing Marches, Summit Negotiations, and Operation Breadbasket*. Brooklyn, NY: Carlson.

Peake, Thomas. 1987. *Keeping the Dream Alive: A History of the Southern Christian Leadership Conference from King to the 1980s*. New York: Lange.

Orphanages

For nearly a century, orphanages were one of the most prominent parts of charity in cities across the United States. They were built and managed by private religious and secular groups as well as by county and state governments, in the hope that they would rescue children from lives of

Constitution, By-laws, &c., of the Female Orphan Asylum of Portland, Maine (1828)

General Directions

From the first of April to the first of October, the Children shall rise at six o'clock, say their Prayers, wash themselves, comb their hair, make their beds, and clean their chambers; breakfast at seven; play or work in the garden until nine, when the governess shall read a chapter in the Bible and pray with them; attend school until twelve, dine at one, play until two, attend school until five, after which, play one hour. In the evening say their Prayers, go to bed at eight, wash their feet every night.

From the first of October to the first of April, the Children shall rise at seven o'clock, say their Prayers, wash themselves, comb their hair, make their beds and clean their chambers,—breakfast at eight, attend prayers, school and play hours as before. In the evening, say their Prayers, go to bed at Seven; and wash their feet once a week.

Source: From *Social Welfare: A History of the American Response to Need,* ed. June Axinn and Herman Levin, 2d ed. (White Plains, NY: Longman, 1982), 79.

poverty. Though still rare in the early nineteenth century, orphanages spread rapidly as urban centers grew and as immigrants flowed into them before and after the Civil War. Despite the name "orphanage," many of the children living within orphanages in the mid-nineteenth century had at least one living parent. By 1900, there were almost 1,000 orphanages spread across the country, but even so there were never enough orphanage beds to care for all the children in need of a home. Most children who entered orphanages in the early twentieth century had a family of some sort to return to, and most did so within a few years, as the family recovered from the death, illness, or unemployment that had driven it deep into poverty. The number of orphanages began to decline in the 1930s with the creation of Aid to Dependent Children, which allowed many needy children to remain with their mothers. In the 1990s, a few new orphanages were built, but group and family foster care had become the primary placement options for children removed from a poor single parent as well as for poor orphaned children.

In the early 1800s, a handful of orphanages were founded in the United States, mostly in northeastern cities. As cities grew in the decades after the American Revolution, they became home to an increasing concentration of poor people. Colonial methods of taking care of one's neighbors broke down, and one of the results was that some extremely poor children, most of them orphans, lived on urban streets. Concern about this new social problem led some reformers, many them middle-class Protestant women, to open small homes to care for these orphans.

These early orphanages provided shelter, food, and other basic needs for the children within them. They were usually associated with a religion: Some were broadly Protestant, while others were associated with a specific Protestant denomination. Between 1800 and 1830, a number of Catholic orphanages also appeared, run by nuns and seeking to care for Catholic orphans.

Orphanages were very much an institution for the poor. Most children who lost their parents had other family members who were willing and able to take them into their homes. This was also true of many orphans from families of modest means, but families living in dire poverty were less likely than other families to have relatives who were able to care for their children. Children from poor and working-class families, from families in the emerging middle class, and from affluent families were all orphaned, but in general it was only the poorest orphans who wound up being raised in orphanages.

Between the 1830s and the 1860s, two developments led to the creation of several hundred more orphanages, making them an increasingly familiar sight in the American landscape. The first development was the rising tide of immigration to the United States during these years, especially from Ireland and Germany. America's cities swelled with immigrants, who ranged from unskilled workers with limited economic opportunity to families of some means who were able to start their own businesses. The second development was tragic: In the early 1830s and again in the late 1840s, severe cholera epidemics swept through many American cities. These epidemics were especially destructive to families in working-class and poor communities, which had the worst sanitation and whose residents had little opportunity to escape the city when cholera arrived.

Cholera left many children, especially in these growing urban immigrant communities, as either orphans or "half-orphans"—children who had lost one parent and still had one living parent. Churches responded to the cholera epidemic of 1832–1833 by building dozens of new orphanages. These orphanages were more likely to be Catholic than in the past (though many were Protestant), and they tended to be somewhat bigger than earlier orphanages. Whereas the first wave of orphanages had usually simply been houses, now orphanage managers tried whenever possible to actually build more institutional structures in order to accommodate dozens of children at once. The numbers of children served increased as many orphanage managers responded to the destitution of poor families by accepting "half-orphans" as well as orphans. A family might need to ask an orphanage to take children in because one parent had died, because the father had become too ill to work, or because the mother fell too ill to care for her child. In almost all instances, families came to orphanages as their last resort.

Religious and ethnic pride played an important role in the growing orphanage movement, especially after the cholera epidemic of 1849. Many Catholic asylums were built with the express purpose of "saving" their children from Protestant orphanages. Their supporters feared, with some reason, that when Catholic children had nowhere else to turn except to a Protestant orphanage, they would be converted; hence building Catholic orphanages to care for Catholic children was not only a way to save the children from poverty and a life on the streets but also a way to save their souls. As more and different ethnic groups arrived in America later in the nineteenth century and during the early twentieth century, the same sort of logic played out within the Catholic community. Newly arriving Italian or Ukrainian Catholics, for example, had to rely on Irish Catholic orphanages when children in their community needed help, and so it became a point of both pride and ethnic solidarity to build an Italian or Ukrainian Catholic orphanage. The same logic would play out over and over during the next seventy years, as various ethnic groups built their own institutions so that the poorest children from their community would be raised within both the religious and cultural traditions of the community.

Children in these institutions had places to sleep and food to eat. Whether they had emotional shelter, however, varied from institution to institution and from child to child. Most orphanage managers were far more concerned with raising children to have a certain kind of moral sense and to be hard workers than they were with protecting children's emotional or psychological health. Orphanage children were almost always raised in a religious setting. School was usually held within the orphanage itself, as much to further children's religious education and to develop specific values in children as to give them a formal education. (This did not make orphanage schools terribly different from public schools of the mid-nineteenth century, which also tended to care as much about providing a moral upbringing as about how well children learned their reading, writing, and arithmetic lessons.) Most orphanage children also spent a considerable portion of the day working at chores around the institution, which were seen as job training for their later lives. Girls tended to be trained to be domestic servants—receiving skills also expected to help them if they became wives—and boys were trained as farmers or in a specific skill such as carpentry.

The terrible destruction and destitution brought to many communities by the Civil War filled orphanages to the bursting point in the 1860s and 1870s and helped lead both to the construction of dozens of new orphanages and to the expansion of many older institutions to care for more children. State governments also became involved in orphanages in the decades after the Civil War. Both New York and California adopted systems in which the government helped pay for the support of children in orphanages in those states. Several states, most notably Ohio, developed systems of county-based public orphanages to care for orphans, half-orphans, and even destitute children with living parents but no feasible home. Michigan led a number of states in developing "state public schools" that served as temporary orphanages before placing children out in people's homes.

By the late nineteenth century, the majority of children in most orphanages had either one or two living parents. This created a problem for orphanage managers, who in many cases wanted to separate their wards from their former lives of poverty, assuming that the children's families had been to blame for their poverty due to immoral behavior (such as excessive drinking) or to not having a proper work ethic. Whereas orphanage managers wanted to raise children within their walls and possibly place them out with families other than their own, the surviving parents or other family members of orphanage inmates wanted to reunite with the children once their family was more stable financially. The end result was that most children left orphanages after a stay of between one and three years, and their most common destination upon leaving was to return to their own families.

Orphanages faced a rising tide of criticism in the decades before and after 1900. The heart of these attacks was the belief that orphanages raised "institutional" children who were moved through the day by bells, marched in silence from one place to another, and never taught the kind of decision-making skills they would need once they were on their own. Paralleling this critique was another charging that orphanage children did not receive the kind of emotional warmth that a family could provide, that orphanages, no matter how hard they tried, could never really be homes for children in the best sense of the word.

There was some truth to these accusations. Some orphanages were harsh places, many staff members were poorly paid and untrained, and various kinds of abuse might be heaped on children by either staff or older inmates. At the same time, these attacks on orphanages combined with changes in society to lead to a noticeable improvement in how orphanages cared for their children. By the early twentieth century, many orphanages were helping their children interact with the outside world in a way that would have been considered undesirable by orphanage managers a half century earlier. Orphanage children became more likely to attend public schools, to go on outings to the city or the countryside, and to join the new groups that were forming, such as the Boy Scouts. As time passed, they had more and more contact with the outside and were less likely to be isolated behind asylum walls, especially after 1900.

In the 1890s, a consensus among charity workers (not including orphanage managers themselves) slowly began to develop that poor families should be helped to keep their children. If that was not possible, this consensus held, children should be cared for in other people's homes in what is now called foster care; orphanages should be a refuge of last resort. In the second decade of the twentieth century, many states passed mothers' pension laws that helped some destitute mothers keep their children at home. This idea was turned into a joint federal-state program in the New Deal's Aid to Dependent Children program, thus allowing many children with the kinds of family and financial problems that would once have led them to an orphanage to stay at home. At the same time, growing state agencies concerned with dependent children turned to foster care because it was less expensive than orphanage placement and was also considered healthier for children. Although orphanages provided alternatives to home care when the Great Depression ravaged families, the end of the orphanage era was at hand. Over the next few decades, orphanages would virtually all either close their doors, become foster care agencies, or shift from taking in children whose main problem was poverty to taking in children with serious behavioral or medical problems. Although a few conservative politicians during the 1990s called for reviving orphanages as an alternative to welfare and although the number of homeless children has been steadily rising, no actual return to orphanages as temporary homes for destitute children has occurred.

Timothy A. Hacsi

See also: Aid to Families with Dependent Children (ADC/AFDC); Catholic Church; Child Welfare; Child-Saving; Deserving/Undeserving Poor; Foster Care; Homelessness; Immigrants and Immigration; Protestant Denominations; Urban Poverty

References and Further Reading

Cmiel, Kenneth. 1995. *A Home of Another Kind: One Chicago Orphanage and the Tangle of Child Welfare*. Chicago: University of Chicago Press.

Crenson, Matthew A. 1998. *Building the Invisible Orphanage: A Prehistory of the American Welfare System*. Cambridge, MA: Harvard University Press.

Hacsi, Timothy A. 1997. *Second Home: Orphan Asylums and Poor Families in America*. Cambridge, MA: Harvard University Press.

Holt, Marilyn Irvin. 2001. *Indian Orphanages*. Lawrence: University Press of Kansas.

Zmora, Nurith. 1994. *Orphanages Reconsidered: Child Care Institutions in Progressive Era Baltimore*. Philadelphia: Temple University Press.

The Other America, *Michael Harrington*

In 1962, Michael Harrington published a short book on what was, until then, an obscure topic: *The Other America: Poverty in the United States*. He argued that there was an "invisible land" in the United States, consisting of 40 million to 50 million citizens whose income placed them below the poverty line: "the unskilled workers, the migrant farm workers, the aged, the minorities, and all others who live in the economic underworld of American life" (Harrington 1962, 2). This "other America" existed in rural isolation or in crowded urban slums where middle-class visitors seldom ventured. "That the poor are invisible is one of the most important things about them," Harrington wrote in his introductory chapter. "They are not simply neglected and forgotten as in the old rhetoric of reform; what is much worse, they are not seen" (Harrington 1962, 7).

Harrington's own background was far from that of the "other America" he described in his book. Born into a middle-class family in Saint Louis in 1928, he went on to graduate from Holy Cross College, attend Yale Law School, and receive a master's degree in literature from the University of Chicago, all by the time he turned twenty-one. But in 1951, his life took an unexpected turn when he joined Dorothy Day's Catholic Worker movement and spent two years caring for the poor in the Worker's "House of Hospitality" on New York's Lower East Side. Breaking with Catholicism, he joined the socialist movement, and by the early 1960s, he was a rising figure within the Socialist Party of America led by Norman Thomas.

Harrington's expectations for his book on poverty were modest; he hoped to sell at most a few thousand copies. Instead, the book went on to sell over a million copies and remains in print decades after its publication. *The Other America* awakened a generation of affluent Americans to the continued existence of a sizable population of poor people in the United States, and it helped spark the War on Poverty launched by President Lyndon B. Johnson in 1964.

Harrington's book also helped popularize the concept of the "culture of poverty." Poor people, he argued, were not simply confined to their status by inadequate incomes or bank accounts; rather, the poor were "people who lack education and skill, who have bad health, poor housing, low levels of aspiration and high levels of mental distress. . . . Each disability is the more intense because it exists within a web of disabilities" (Harrington 1962, 162). Harrington later came to criticize some of the uses to which the "culture of poverty" notion was put, especially by conservative opponents of social welfare programs. There is no question, though, that *The Other America* remains a landmark study of poverty in the United States. On the eve of the twenty-first century, *Time* magazine described it as one of the ten most influential nonfiction books published in the preceding century.

Maurice Isserman

See also: Catholic Worker Movement; Socialist Party; War on Poverty

References and Further Reading

Harrington, Michael. 1962. *The Other America: Poverty in the United States*. New York: Macmillan.

Isserman, Maurice. 2000. *The Other America: The Life of Michael Harrington*. New York: Public Affairs.

Pauperism

See Charity Organization Societies; Dependency; Poor Laws; *Poverty*; Society for the Prevention of Pauperism

Peace Corps

The Peace Corps is a federal agency, created in 1961, that sends American volunteers to poor and less-developed regions of the world to provide a range of educational, technical, and infrastructural assistance while also acting as unofficial goodwill ambassadors from the United States.

Americans "discovered" poverty abroad before they discovered it at home in the 1960s. The post–World War II decolonization of Africa and Asia, combined with competition for the support of these new nations during the Cold War, led the United States, Australia, Britain, and Canada all to develop youth volunteer programs to combat poverty in the third world.

President John F. Kennedy created the Peace Corps by executive order on March 1, 1961. He appointed R. Sargent Shriver (who would later go on to run the domestic War on Poverty) to head the agency, which became a popular symbol of Kennedy's "New Frontier." Within months, the Peace Corps began sending Americans abroad to work for two years in developing countries. Their purpose was to cement friendship with the third world, fight poverty, and promote peace. In doing so, the Peace Corps provided an opportunity for citizens to respond to the spirit of civic activism stimulated by the president when, in his 1961 inaugural address, he exhorted youth to "ask not what your country can do for you—but what you can do for your country." A key premise of the Peace Corps was that volunteers would live at the same level as the people whom they hoped to help, meaning that they would share the experience of poverty.

Sargent Shriver obtained authorization for the Peace Corps from Congress on September 22, 1961. The Peace Corps Act established three goals: "1) To help people of interested countries and areas in meeting their needs for trained manpower; 2) To help promote a better understanding of Americans on the part of the peoples served; and 3) To help promote a better understanding of other peoples on the part of Americans" (Executive Order 10924, 1961).

The first volunteers went to Ghana in August 1961. Volunteers to twelve additional countries in Africa, Asia, and Latin America followed immediately. There were 750 participants in the first year, and over 15,000 by 1965. Volunteers brought a wide range of professional skills

Peace Corps volunteers and villagers build a drinking-water well in Bihar, India, in 1967. (Library of Congress)

(from agronomy to zoology), but most were liberal arts graduates. They filled the largest program, which was elementary and secondary education. This component was strongest in Africa in response to the requests of recently decolonized nations. The Peace Corps also focused on community development, primarily in Latin America. This work, Kennedy believed, would help direct regional change into channels consistent with American strategic interests.

President Lyndon B. Johnson subsequently chose Shriver as the first director of the Office of Economic Opportunity because of his successful launching of the Peace Corps. To many, Shriver represented the potential for aggressive, optimistic leadership to produce quick results in the War on Poverty. In 1965, the Peace Corps became the model for Volunteers in Service to America (VISTA), a domestic program that sent volunteers to poor communities in the United States, also started by the Johnson administration.

The Peace Corps declined in the late 1960s as U.S. policies in Vietnam created disaffection among American youth. By the end of the war, the agency had shrunk by more than 50 percent. The Peace Corps retained its humanitarian mission, however, and continued sending an average of 6,000 volunteers abroad annually. By the turn of the twenty-first century, more than 150,000 Americans had served in 133 countries at the request of those nations.

Elizabeth Cobbs Hoffman

See also: U.S. Agency for International Development (AID); Voluntarism; Volunteers in Service to America (VISTA); War on Poverty

References and Further Reading

Fischer, Fritz. 1998. *Making Them Like Us: Peace Corps Volunteers in the 1960s*. Washington, DC: Smithsonian Institution Press.

Hoffman, Elizabeth Cobbs. 1998. *All You Need Is Love: The Peace Corps and the Spirit of the 1960s*. Cambridge, MA: Harvard University Press.
Rice, Gerard T. 1985. *The Bold Experiment*. Notre Dame, IN: University of Notre Dame Press.
Schwarz, Karen. 1991. *What You Can Do for Your Country*. New York: William Morrow.

Personal Responsibility and Work Opportunity Reconciliation Act (PRWORA)

See Aid to Families with Dependent Children (ADC/AFDC); Welfare Policy/Welfare Reform

The Philadelphia Negro, W. E. B. Du Bois

In 1897, W. E. B. Du Bois (1868–1963) was given a temporary post in the sociology department at the University of Pennsylvania to conduct a social survey of the Black community in Philadelphia. Du Bois, the first African American to receive a Ph.D. from Harvard University, carried out a study dauntingly broad in scope. He intended to learn as much as possible about Black life in Philadelphia—everything from Blacks' occupational and home lives to their recreational activities and relations with white citizens. After canvassing nearly every household in the Seventh Ward of Philadelphia, Du Bois found that the Black population, which at the time of the study was about 40,000, represented a "city within a city," a segregated group of people continually beset with the insults and hardships of racial discrimination and abject poverty. The result of his research was *The Philadelphia Negro* (1899), not only a detailed chronicle of Black living conditions but also a revealing analysis of the root causes of the chronic poverty encountered by households in the Seventh Ward.

Portrait of W. E. B. Du Bois. **The Philadelphia Negro** *(1899) examined the root causes of the chronic poverty encountered by households in the Seventh Ward of Philadelphia. (Corbis)*

Du Bois's painstaking and detailed investigation produced a portrait of a diverse, institutionally complex community struggling, with only limited success, to gain a stable foothold in Philadelphia's industrial and service economy. Using concepts and methods that were innovative at the time and that have since become standard in sociological and economic analysis, he documented the complex interplay of historical struggle, demographic change, racist attitudes among whites and immigrants, and discriminatory institutional practices that effectively ghettoized African Americans and kept them at the bottom of the socioeconomic ladder. His fieldwork also revealed the existence of serious social pathologies and health concerns within the Black community. Illiteracy, crime, alcoholism, and pauperism were rampant, the infant mortality rate was alarmingly high, and Blacks suffered disproportionately from consumption, diseases of the nervous system, and pneumonia. Although showing some disdain for the "improvident" behavior of the lower classes, Du Bois challenged prevailing racist ideology to show that Philadelphia Blacks were largely not responsible for these dire conditions. These conditions were the result of a racist system that denied Blacks the opportunities whites enjoyed and took for granted.

Du Bois found that Philadelphia Blacks were especially hard-pressed to find and keep gainful employment. Regardless of their training or credentials, Blacks could rarely hope to find much more than menial work. Black men were generally denied clerical or supervisory work except under extraordinary circumstances, could not get teaching jobs except at a few of the Black schools in the city, and, largely because of blatantly racist union practices, could only hope to find skilled work temporarily. Opportunities for Black women were even more limited. The three options open to them were domestic service, sewing, and married life.

When a Black person was fortunate enough to find a job, his or her hard-earned place was always vulnerable to the caprices of the employer or the economy. Du Bois found that employers rated Black employees not by their individual performance but as members of a group employers believed had a poor work ethic and inferior capabilities. As a result, Black men routinely earned less money than white men in the same position. In addition to being saddled with low-level jobs and poor wages, Blacks were often compelled to pay higher rents for worse housing. And if they had any disposable income left to spend, they often received reluctant (or even hostile) service in many restaurants, hotels, and stores, as well as in theaters and other places of recreation.

The result of these countless insults and injuries, according to Du Bois, was a general discouragement and bitterness in the Black community, a feeling of hopelessness that often fueled crime, recklessness, and dependency. Du Bois's conclusions were groundbreaking, and his book would become a classic in social science literature. Du Bois would go on to become a founder of the National Association for the Advancement of Colored People (NAACP) and a seminal voice on the problem of race in America.

Robert J. Lacey

See also: African American Migration; Poverty Research; Racial Segregation; Social Surveys; Urban Poverty

References and Further Reading

Katz, Michael B., and Thomas J. Sugrue, eds. 1998. *W. E. B. Dubois, Race, and the City:* The Philadelphia Negro *and Its Legacy*. Philadelphia: University of Pennsylvania Press.

Lewis, David Levering. 1994. *W. E. B. DuBois: Biography of a Race, 1868–1919*. New York: Henry Holt.

Philanthropy

Philanthropy, literally "love of one's fellow man," involves organized giving for improvement or for some benevolent or altruistic purpose and is related to charity. Both involve the donation of money or the volunteering of time to others less fortunate or viewed as needing intervention or improvement, but charity also comprises informal mutual helping, especially among poor people and in ethnic and racial communities. Philanthropy implies formal organization and larger-scale giving than charity and is a more modern phenomenon. Its twentieth-century form, the philanthropic foundation, reflects the increasing systematization and bureaucratization of modern life. Foundations, like other charitable entities, are nominally private, but government acknowledges their contribution to the public good by granting incorporation and tax exemption. Rather than focusing on poverty and its associated problems, twentieth-century foundations have directed the majority of their philanthropy to health, education, and religion (in that order), with arts and cultural organizations a distant fourth and human service organizations far behind.

The main characteristic of philanthropy, and what distinguishes it from publicly funded programs, is its voluntarism and thus its quirkiness. Philanthropy stems from the ideals, beliefs, enthusiasms, and prejudices of the giver. What counts are the donor's intentions, not the objective qualities of the recipient. In contrast, state provision is based on a system of entitlement (although administration of funds may be discretionary). Philanthropic ventures take shape according to the ideals and goals of the funders rather than the needs of recipients.

In colonial America, the relief of poverty was an obligation of citizenship, for the English poor laws obliged the inhabitants of each township to tax themselves for the support of the poor living in their midst. Publicly funded poor relief continued alongside private philanthropy and in dynamic relationship to it. In the nineteenth century, responsibility for the destitute remained a public charge that poor law officials (trustees) met by constructing dozens of specialized institutions to care for the insane, orphans, and the disabled.

Philanthropy in this early period can be seen in the altruism of a few wealthy people who founded colleges or benevolent institutions, often named after them. But in Benjamin Franklin's Philadelphia, the whole community developed philanthropic institutions for self-help and self-improvement, such as libraries and fire companies. Citizens also organized charitable institutions to aid the poor. Philanthropic efforts continued in the antebellum period, when wealthy white, urban elites, often inspired by evangelicalism and the ideal of stewardship, founded numerous charitable and benevolent associations that were then linked to one another in reform networks. Most scholars have focused on such philanthropy as part of the self-making of the middle and upper classes or as an arena for the reconstruction of Victorian class and gender relations. For example, Lori Ginzberg (1991) has described how unenfranchised middle- and upper-class women entered public work under the cloak of benevolence and care for their poorer sisters. However, few have attempted to assess the impact of this complex charitable intervention on poor families (exceptions are Gordon 1988 and Broder 2002).

Philanthropic ventures take shape under different historical conditions in different communities. In the era of Jim Crow and Black disenfranchisement (1877–1941), communities of color turned to private solutions when they did not receive their share of either government funding or mainstream philanthropic giving. Under the rubric of "self-help," "improvement," or "uplift," Black women organized to meet the critical needs of their communities. They raised funds to found institutions like Neighborhood House in Atlanta, or the Women's Improvement Club that supported Indianapolis's Flanner House, or Cleveland's Phillis Wheatley Association (Rouse 1989; Crocker 1992). This was philanthropy as reform politics, aimed to lift the race and elevate Black women as well as to meet the needs of communities ignored by segregationist politicians. Similarly, when Black Richmond, Virginia, banker Maggie Lena Walker gave $500 to activist-educator Nannie Burroughs, she engaged in philanthropy that was at once civic reform and racial uplift and a form of politics (Hine 1990, 76). In the ethnic and racial communities of Tampa, Florida, philanthropy also took many forms, from informal neighborly helping, to clubs and labor unions, to the benevolence dispensed by Anglo elites (Hewitt 1990).

Philanthropy underwent rapid change between the Civil War and the New Deal. While government continued its nominal obligation to support the "deserving poor," taxpayer-funded aid to the unemployed (called "outdoor relief") was stingy, erratic, and highly politicized. In New York City between 1875 and 1931, aid was cut off altogether in the name of reform. The primary response of philanthropy to the poor in this period was the charity organization society (COS), imported from England. Self-described reformers, COS advocates aimed to improve the administration of private charity using the model of the professionalizing field of medicine. They sought to base poor relief on the "scientific" diagnosis and treatment of need. The privately funded COS pioneered modern techniques of casework but opposed an expansion of welfare state responsibility, including mothers' pensions.

Foundation Philanthropy

Foundations were devised as a way to put private funds to public use while insulating the giver from direct appeals. Some were memorials created by the new rich and had perpetual funds dedicated to charitable or benevolent purposes. Modeled on business corporations but designed for public purposes, foundations were incorporated under state or federal law and administered by trustees appointed for life (Sealander 1997). The General Education Board (GEB) was set up by Standard Oil multimillionaire John D. Rockefeller Sr. (1839–1937) in 1903 to promote education in the United States "without distinction of sex, race or creed." The Carnegie Corporation was founded "by steelmaker Andrew Carnegie (1835–1919) to promote the advancement of knowledge" (Sealander 1997). Neither of those foundations focused primarily on poverty. Carnegie, who declared he would give away his entire fortune in his lifetime, made huge donations to world peace and to education: the Carnegie Foundation for the Advancement of Teaching (1905) and the Carnegie Endowment for International Peace (1911). Yet Carnegie's philanthropy also illustrates the personal and capricious character of philanthropy. Carnegie's gift of 2,800 libraries to communities across the nation showed he was more concerned about what he saw as cultural deprivation than about poverty. Rockefeller established several notable philanthropic foundations, including the Rockefeller Foundation (1911), for the "well-being of mankind throughout the world." His total philanthropic giving has been estimated at $245 million, but educational and health concerns, not poverty, absorbed the bulk of his giving.

It is difficult or impossible to gauge the impact on poverty of this vast spending. We know far more about the motivations of the givers than about the impact of their philanthropy. None of the major foundations adopted a goal of redistribution of wealth or viewed poverty as an economic problem. Foundation philanthropy nevertheless marked a significant response to poverty because foundations funded social science research and produced new knowledge about the poor, knowledge that was available to policymakers. When Margaret Olivia Sage (1828–1918) set aside $10 million in 1907 to endow the Russell Sage Foundation "for the improvement of the social and living conditions in the United States of America," she did not plan to give directly to the poor, but her foundation significantly advanced the study of poverty. It established the modern social work profession, funded innovative work on working families in the Pittsburgh district (the Pittsburgh Survey), and supported research on child labor, industrial relations, work accidents, housing, and consumer economics.

In the twentieth century, governments came to depend on foundation-supplied data on poverty and other issues. More recently, the foundations have become the institutional home of a sophisticated "poverty research industry" of sociologists, economists, and other experts, but the resulting data sometimes end up being used to frame policies that stigmatize the poor, especially poor women and people of color, rather than to construct better policies for poor families (O'Connor 2001).

Early-twentieth-century critics of foundations had feared them as "philanthropic trusts," undemocratic accumulations of great power and wealth standing in the way of reform. Populist opposition again found a voice in the congressional Patman Committee, chaired by a populist congressman, Wright Patman (D-Texas), and active throughout the 1960s. The resulting Tax Reform Act of 1969 demanded more public accountability from foundations, compelled them to be more open, and required a 6 percent annual payout of assets. New foundations sometimes tackled problems of "poverty amid plenty" that older ones had ignored. The Ford Foundation, established in 1936 by carmaker Henry Ford (1863–1947) gave millions to education, culture, and the arts and millions more to developing nations. In the early 1960s, encouraged by the liberal reformism of the Kennedy administration, Ford Foundation officials cooperated with antipoverty coalitions in programs to end race-based poverty in America's cities (Raynor 1999, 185; O'Connor 2001).

During the Reagan and Bush administrations of the 1980s and early 1990s, devolution of federal responsibility for social welfare to the states and cuts in government spending created pressure to shift responsibility for poverty from government to private philanthropy. By 1990, a huge nonprofit sector had developed, comprising by one calculation 8 percent of the gross domestic product and employing nearly 10 percent of the American workforce. In one year during the prosperous 1990s, Americans donated $143 billion to nonprofit organizations. Of this total, $109 billion was from individuals; $13 billion, from bequests; another $13 billion, from foundations; and $8 billion, from corporations ("Giving USA" 1998, 19–21). The size of this sector prompted conservatives to propose private philanthropy as a viable alternative to government for the delivery of social services. Religious organizations, they claimed, would do a better job serving the poor than government, and the retreat of government would release the pent-up charitable giving of the private sector. It is ironic that right-wing think tanks now support such "faith-based" (conservative evangelical) social agencies, for local, discretionary relief giving (direct service) was just the kind of retail philanthropy that foundations initially were designed to replace. Moreover, spending by nonprofits ("philanthropic spending") supplements but cannot replace government spending. Economist Lester Salamon draws attention to a shift in the focus of nonprofit social service agencies away from the problems of poor people. "Fewer than 30 percent of the agencies surveyed reported that the poor constitute half or more of the agency's clientele. By contrast, over half of the agencies reported serving few or no poor clients and over 60 percent of the resources went to the nonpoor," he writes. This finding was true for the human services in general. Salamon also found that government programs targeting the poor were far more effective than nonprofit ones. He predicted that cuts in government funding, rather than prompting a corresponding increase in private spending on the poor, would produce a decline (Salamon 1992, 171).

Moreover, nonprofits today rely on direct government support for one-fourth of their income. Thus, spending on the poor is not a matter of either-or, either government or private; instead, the two sectors are interdependent, or "synergistic," according to scholar Peter Dobkin Hall. Philanthropic giving for cultural and educational purposes—to found museums of art or concert halls, to support medical research, to fund colleges and schools—continues to exceed giving to the poor. Foundations continue to give far more to education and to scientific and medical research than to research on poverty and its associated problems: homelessness, unemployment, and low wages resulting from race or gender discrimination. New foundations created from the boom economy of the 1980s and 1990s include the Bill and Melinda Gates Foundation and the Packard Foundation (with assets in 1999 of $17 billion and $13 billion, respectively), with the Pew Charitable Trusts and the

Eli Lilly and Company Foundation not far behind (Dowie 2002, 194). The Bill and Melinda Gates Foundation philanthropy includes millions for AIDS research (*New York Times*, January 15, 2003). In January 2003, a donation of $8 million by auto insurance philanthropist Peter B. Lewis to the American Civil Liberties Union (ACLU) reminds us that philanthropy can be directed to liberal as well as to conservative ends.

Ruth Crocker

See also: Charity; Charity Organization Societies; Deserving/Undeserving Poor; Nonprofit Sector; Pittsburgh Survey; Poverty Research; Social Surveys

References and Further Reading

Broder, Sherri. 2002. *Tramps, Unfit Mothers, and Neglected Children: Negotiating the Family in 19th Century Philadelphia*. Philadelphia: University of Philadelphia Press.

Clotfelder, Charles, ed. 1992. *Who Benefits from the Nonprofit Sector?* Chicago: University of Chicago Press.

Crocker, Ruth. 1992. *Social Work and Social Order: The Settlement Movement in Two Industrialized Cities*. Urbana: University of Illinois Press.

———. 2002. "From Gift to Foundation: The Philanthropic Lives of Mrs. Russell Sage." In *Charity, Philanthropy, and Civility*, ed. Larry Friedman and Mark McGarvie, 199–216. New York: Cambridge University Press.

Dowie, Mark. 2002. *American Foundations: An Investigative History*. Cambridge: MIT Press.

Friedman, Larry, and Mark McGarvie, eds. 2002. *Charity, Philanthropy, and Civility in American History*. New York: Cambridge University Press.

Ginzberg, Lori D. 1991. *Women and the Work of Benevolence: Morality, Politics, and Class in the 19th Century United States*. New Haven: Yale University Press.

"Giving USA." 1998. Quoted in "Philanthropy in America: The Gospel of Wealth." *The Economist*, May 30: 19–21.

Gordon, Linda. 1988. *Heroes of Their Own Lives: The Politics and History of Family Violence*. New York: Viking.

Hall, Peter Dobkin. 1988. "Private Philanthropy and Public Policy: A Historical Appraisal." In *Philanthropy: Four Views*, ed. Robert Payton, 39–72. New Brunswick, NJ: Transaction Books.

Hewitt, Nancy A. 1990. "Charity or Mutual Aid? Two Perspectives on Latin Women's Philanthropy in Tampa, FL." In *Lady Bountiful Revisited: Women, Philanthropy, and Power*, ed. Kathleen D. McCarthy, 55–69. New Brunswick, NJ: Rutgers University Press.

Hine, Darlene Clark. 1990. "'We Specialize in the Wholly Impossible': The Philanthropic Work of Black Women." In *Lady Bountiful Revisited: Women, Philanthropy, and Power*, ed. Kathleen D. McCarthy, 70–93. New Brunswick, NJ: Rutgers University Press.

Katz, Michael, ed. 1993. *The "Underclass" Debate: Views from History*. Princeton: Princeton University Press.

Lagemann, Ellen, ed. 1999. *Philanthropic Foundations: New Scholarship, New Possibilities*. Bloomington: Indiana University Press.

McCarthy, Kathleen, D., ed. 1990. *Lady Bountiful Revisited: Women, Philanthropy, and Power*. New Brunswick, NJ: Rutgers University Press.

O'Connor, Alice. 2001. *Poverty Knowledge: Social Science, Social Policy, and the Poor in Twentieth-Century U.S. History*. Princeton: Princeton University Press.

Raynor, Gregory K. 1999. "The Ford Foundation's War on Poverty: Private Philanthropy and Race Relations in New York City, 1948–1968." In *Philanthropic Foundations: New Scholarship, New Possibilities*, ed. Ellen Lagemann, 195–228. Bloomington: Indiana University Press.

Rouse, Jacqueline Anne. 1989. *Lugenia Burns Hope, Black Southern Reformer*. Athens: University of Georgia Press.

Salamon, Lester M. 1992. "Social Services." In *Who Benefits from the Nonprofit Sector?*, ed. Charles Clotfelder, 134–173. Chicago: University of Chicago Press.

Sealander, Judith. 1997. *Private Wealth and Public Life: Foundation Philanthropy and the Reshaping of American Social Policy from the Progressive Era to the New Deal*. Baltimore: Johns Hopkins University Press.

Picturing Poverty (I) (1880–1960s)

Although images of poverty circulated in a variety of forms during the nineteenth century (in

Men gather in an alley called "Bandit's Roost" in Manhattan's Little Italy. Around the turn of the century, this part of Mulberry Bend was a notoriously dilapidated and dangerous section of the city. Photography by Jacob Riis. (Bettmann/Corbis)

chapbooks, penny magazines, and religious tracts), they are most commonly associated with what came to be known as the "social documentary" tradition of photography. Social documentary emerges at the intersection of a set of technical, economic, and political forces. The technical preconditions (emulsions capable of capturing movement, high-speed shutters, and the ability to reproduce photographs in books and newspapers) had coalesced by the late 1870s. We see the initial manifestation of a social documentary impulse in Great Britain. Henry Mayhew's *London Labour and the London Poor* was published in 1849–1850 with engravings drawn from Richard Beard's daguerreotypes. In 1868, photographer Thomas Annan was commissioned to document the slums of Glasgow, and by 1877, John Thomson had published *Street Life in London*, replete with images of the "crawlers" of Saint Giles. The technical innovations that allowed for the creation of images of the poor in situ coincided with the high point of Victorian-era industrialization and urbanization. These processes proved to be particularly unsettling in the United States, which had long held that its vast frontier would immunize it from the European "disease" of urban class conflict. This proved, of course, not

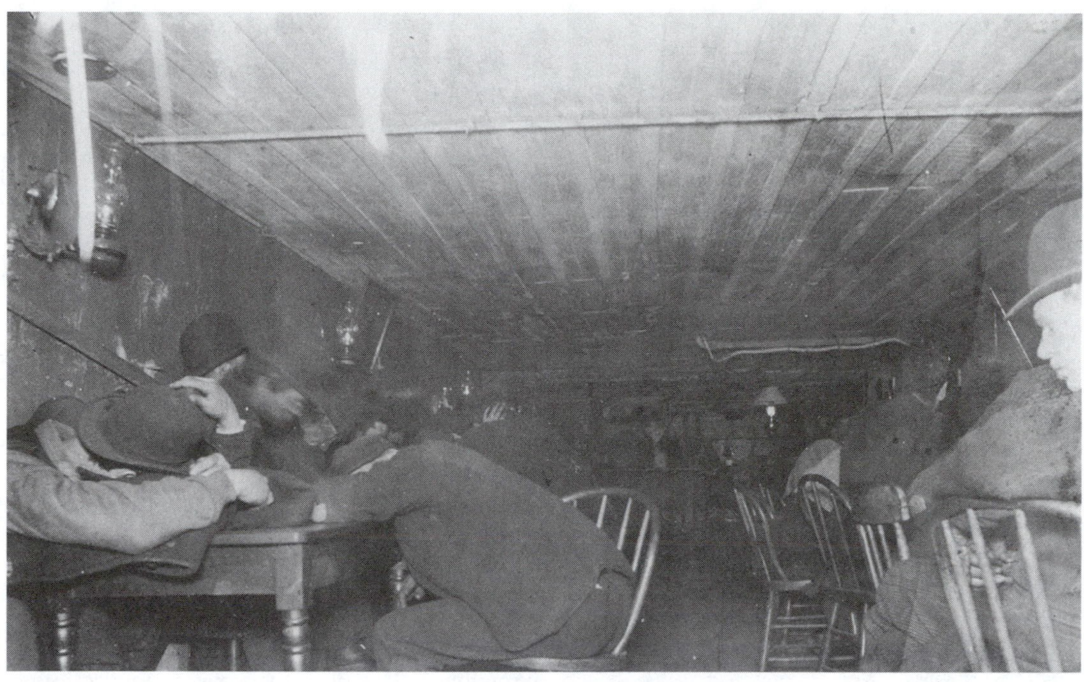

Jacob Riis, **An All Night Two Cent Restaurant,** *1890 (Museum of New York)*

to be the case, and in the period of intense industrialization following the Civil War, America's cities became home to an increasingly large immigrant working class.

This immigrant population transformed perceptions of the American city, or at least of its impoverished regions. Increasingly, the city was seen as a haven for disease (cholera, tuberculosis) and disorder (anarchism, labor organizing), even as the middle and upper classes were beginning their long march to the suburbs. The result was a growing spatial and psychological distance between the urban poor and the rich. This distance accounts in part for the frequent reliance on a quasi-colonialist rhetoric in nineteenth-century social documentary, in which the photographer casts himself as an intrepid explorer traversing the "dark continent" of East London or Lower Manhattan. The more sequestered and concentrated the poor became, the more imperative the demand to investigate, classify, and reveal them. This process of disclosure ran along a continuum from the dryly scientific (Charles Booth's seventeen-volume *Life and Labour of the People in London*, 1889–1903) to the frankly sensationalistic (Gustave Doré's *London: A Pilgrimage* or Charles Loring Brace's *The Dangerous Classes of New York and Twenty Years' Work among Them*, both 1872).

The social documentary tradition in America can be traced to the 1880s, when the Danish immigrant and police reporter Jacob A. Riis began using photographs of poor, mostly immigrant New Yorkers to proselytize for improvements in housing. Riis combined the quasi-scientific investigative approach pioneered by Mayhew with a finely tuned ability to excite his audiences' voyeuristic fascination with race and class "others." Making use of the new German technology of *blitzpulver*, "flash powder," Riis would often surprise his subjects while they

Lewis Hine, Portrait of an Immigrant, 1915 *(Bettmann/Corbis)*

were asleep or inebriated in dives and lodging houses. In order to galvanize public support, it was necessary for Riis to solicit the viewer's empathetic identification with the urban poor. At the same time, this humanitarian impulse was carefully balanced with a more self-interested appeal based on the potential threat (of crime, disease, and disorder) posed by immigrants confined in overcrowded tenements. We can identify a visual corollary for this frisson of danger in Riis's frequent use of the alley as a framing device. *Bandit's Roost* (1888) invites the viewer to enter the chaotic urban interior while simultaneously evoking a dangerous gauntlet, ringed by a phalanx of menacing slum dwellers.

Riis's lantern slide shows, newspaper articles, and books (for example, *How the Other Half Lives*, 1890) were part of a larger struggle to reform housing regulations in New York State, a struggle that led to the passage of the Tenement House Law of 1901. Fueled in part by the success of the tenement reform movement, New York's Russell Sage Foundation sponsored surveys of several American cities during the early twentieth century. In these projects, the overtly moralistic character of Victorian-era reform gave way to an environmentalist approach in which poverty was viewed as the product of a complex set of spatial and economic forces associated with city life. Early-twentieth-century surveys addressed a wide range of issues, from urban congestion to tuberculosis to women's labor to prison reform. All were seen as interrelated components of a larger social gestalt. The survey findings were presented in books as well as at public exhibitions that combined photographs, charts and graphs, dioramas, and models to generate support for specific legislative remedies. The rise of the survey methodology marks the transition to a professionalized approach to municipal reform. Riis's somewhat haphazard forays into the city, and his often-sensationalistic narratives of "the other half," were supplanted by more systematic techniques, epitomized by the six volumes of the Pittsburgh Survey of 1908.

The Pittsburgh Survey featured numerous photographs of the city's poor and working-class neighborhoods. Among the most powerful of these images were Lewis Hine's portraits of immigrant steelworkers. Whereas Riis was willing to indulge the not-so-subtle racism of his uptown audiences, Hine was determined to portray immigrants in a more dignified and compassionate manner. Although not immune to contemporary anxieties over the need to Americanize foreign-born workers, Hine's photographs (often borrowing formal conventions associated with art and middle-class portraiture) mark a significant break with the exoticizing stereotypes of his predecessors. At a time when immigrants were widely reviled in the press, Hine produced a series of photographs that portrayed new arrivals at Ellis Island not as parasitic

Lewis Hine, Girl Worker in Carolina Cotton Mill, 1908. *(Corbis)*

invaders but as more fully human, simultaneously hopeful and uncertain about their new lives in America. Hine was also active with the National Child Labor Committee, producing images of young workers in textile mills, mines, and factories throughout the United States during the second decade of the twentieth century. In his "work portraits" of the 1930s, Hine endeavored to show both men and women as skilled craftspeople, in control of complex machinery, at a time when Taylorist managerial literature portrayed the worker as little more than a brute laboring body.

By the early 1930s, America was entering the Great Depression. Beginning in 1933, President Franklin D. Roosevelt's New Deal programs represented the most sweeping political and economic reforms in the country's history. Among the groups hardest hit by the Depression were small farmers and farm laborers in the Midwest and the Southeast. The economic downturn, combined with an ongoing drought, forced tens of thousands of tenant families off the land in search of work. In 1935, the Resettlement Administration (RA) was established to coordinate New Deal rural relief, including debt adjustment programs, farm loans, and the creation of migrant camps and resettlement communities. In 1937, the RA became the Farm Security Administration (FSA). Roy Stryker, head of the "historical section–photographic" of the agency's Information Division, was respon-

Dorothea Lange, An eighteen-year-old mother and migrant agricultural worker from Oklahoma. Imperial Valley, California, ca. February–March 1937. (Corbis)

sible for commissioning images documenting the progress of New Deal agricultural programs. These were distributed free of charge to mainstream picture magazines, newspapers, and book publishers. Stryker recruited a remarkable team of young photographers, many of whom would go on to have distinguished careers in photojournalism and art, including Jack Delano, Walker Evans, Dorothea Lange, Russell Lee, Carl Mydans, Gordon Parks, Arthur Rothstein, Ben Shahn, John Vachon, and Marion Post Wolcott. Despite the severity of the Depression, FDR's policies remained deeply unpopular with many business and corporate leaders, who viewed them as dangerously socialistic. As a result, the FSA historical section under Stryker functioned as a kind of publicity office. It was necessary to provide photographic proof of both the severity of rural poverty and the efficacy of government programs designed to ameliorate it. This dual mission is reiterated in FSA imagery that shows, on the one hand, scenes of deserted farms and malnourished children and, on the other, images of happily "rehabilitated" FSA clients.

The relationship between the FSA and the rural poor was, however, somewhat more complex than this description suggests. Rural poverty was the result not simply of drought and depression but also of a larger process of agricultural modernization involving widespread mechanization and the centralization of farm ownership. For Stryker, the proper role of the government was not to retard the displace-

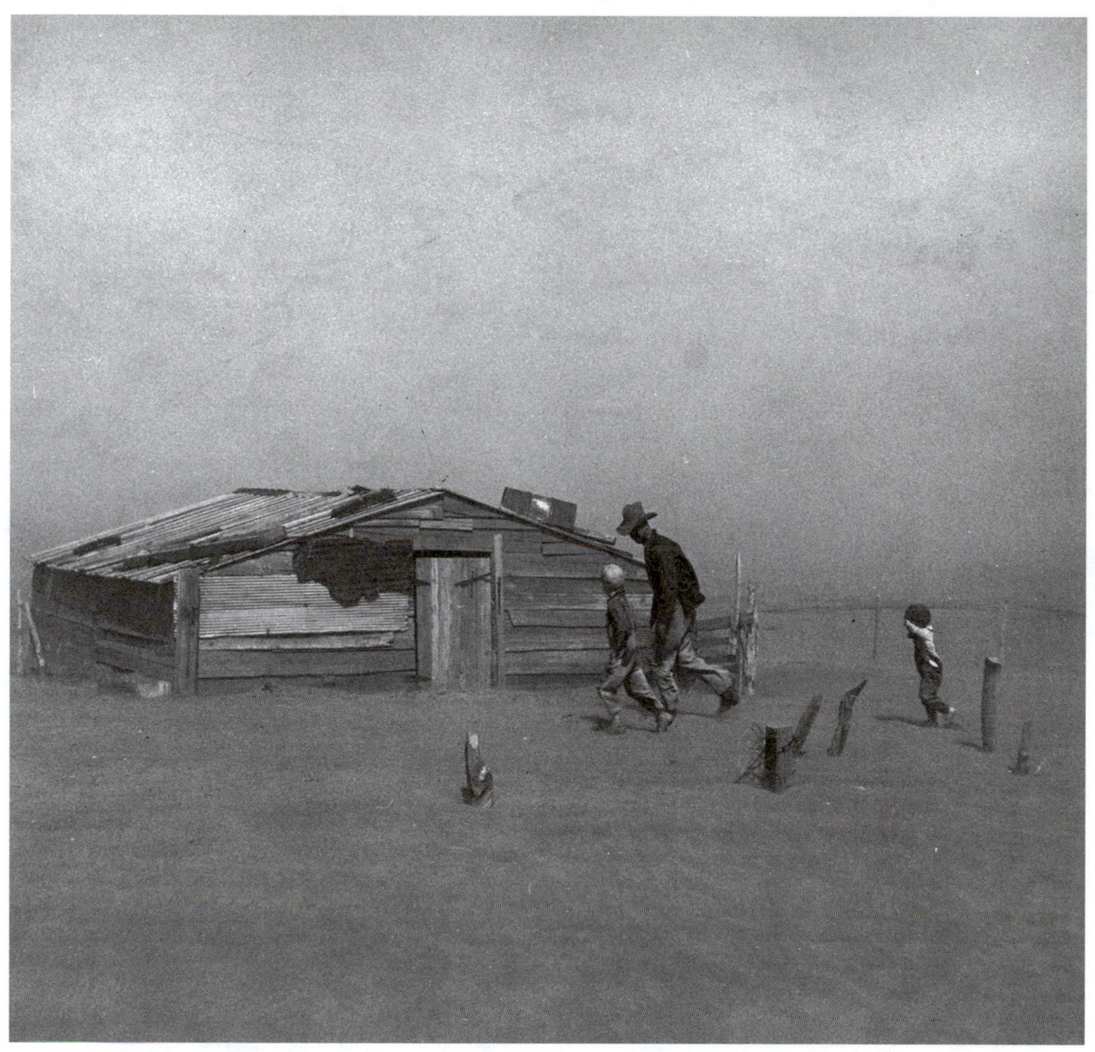

Arthur Rothstein, 1936. ***A farmer and his sons flee from an approaching dust storm in Oklahoma.*** **(Library of Congress)**

ment of tenants and sharecroppers but to rationalize it, to replace a process that was haphazard and chaotic with one that was orderly and humane. Farm families would be gradually adjusted to urban and suburban life through resettlement camps, job training, and Greenbelt incubator communities. Thus, despite the frequent paeans to America's yeoman farmer evident in New Deal literature and imagery, one of the primary effects of FSA policies was to further undermine small family farms. Stryker's photographers, who could observe the contradictions of FSA policies firsthand, tended to view the rural poor less as an inchoate mass to be managed and "rehabilitated" by the state than as individuals struggling through a traumatic and bewildering period in their lives. This movement between specificity and abstraction, between the immediacy of the photographic exchange and the pages of *Life*, was a frequent point of tension between Stryker and photographers, such as Dorothea Lange, who resented having their captions cut and their images edited to suit the shifting exigencies of FSA publicity and mass-circulation picture magazines.

The FSA was absorbed into the Office of War Information in 1943. It would be more than two decades before the photographic image would again play such a central role in debates over poverty and public policy. In his 1964 State of the Union address, President Lyndon B. Johnson declared "unconditional war on poverty," launching a plethora of programs and new federal agencies. Although there was some concern with the rural poor during the early 1960s, urban poverty, especially among African Americans, was the defining issue of Great Society–era public policy. The linkage to policy is most evident in a series of official commission reports produced in the aftermath of the riots that rocked America's cites between 1964 and 1968. The Governor's Commission on the Los Angeles Riots of 1965 published more than a hundred photos of the riot along with a color-coded map of deaths and property damage, evoking the lurid sensationalism of a Victorian penny dreadful. The 1967 National Advisory Commission on Civil Disorders was more sober, closer in tone to the Russell Sage Foundation's urban surveys, but the voyeuristic quality of the descriptions and photographs remained. By the 1960s, the inner city was a mysterious place to most white, middle-class Americans, and the photographic image was again called upon as a vicarious witness for viewers who were simultaneously fascinated and repelled by the spectacle of urban poverty. The riot reports, along with an ancillary literature of histrionic picture books and novels (*Anarchy Los Angeles*, *The Siege of Harlem*, and *Burn, Baby, Burn!*), generated an iconography of poverty that was both new and familiar, as Italian immigrants crowded into New York City tenements were replaced by African Americans crowded into the public housing projects of Chicago and Los Angeles. The reports reiterate the complex calculus of compassion and self-interest, fear of insurrection and outrage at the conditions that might spawn it, evident in Riis's work of almost a century before.

Grant H. Kester

See also: Child Labor; Dust Bowl Migration; Great Depression and New Deal; *How the Other Half Lives; Hull-House Maps and Papers;* Kerner Commission Report; *Let Us Now Praise Famous Men;* New Deal Farm Policy; Pittsburgh Survey; Social Surveys; *Survey* and *Survey Graphic*

References and Further Reading

Governor's Commission on the Los Angeles Riots. 1965. *Violence in the City—An End or a Beginning?* Los Angeles: Author.

Lange, Dorothea, and Paul Taylor. 1939. *An American Exodus: A Record of Human Erosion*. New York: Reynal and Hitchcock.

MacLeish, Archibald. 1938. *Land of the Free*. New York: Harcourt, Brace.

National Advisory Commission on Civil Disorders. 1968. *Report of the National Advisory Commission on Civil Disorders*. Introduction by Tom Wicker. New York: Bantam Books.

The Pittsburgh Survey. 1911. Ed. Paul Underwood Kellogg. 6 vols. New York: Charities Publication Committee.

Riis, Jacob A. 1890. *How the Other Half Lives: Studies among the Tenements of New York*. New York: Charles Scribner.

Picturing Poverty (II) (1960s–Present)

According to U.S. Census Bureau data, there were 32.9 million poor people living in the United States in 2001, and 22.7 million of them were white. These 22.7 million people accounted for slightly less than 10 percent of all whites. By contrast, 22.7 percent of Blacks and 21.4 percent of Hispanics were poor. In addition, 40.7 percent of the poor lived in central cities, as compared to 28.9 percent of all people in the United States. These data demonstrate that while there are more poor whites than nonwhites, Blacks and Hispanics are more likely to be poor, and poor people are more likely to live in urban areas. For many observers, these numbers describe a particular type of poverty that since the 1960s has become equated primarily with Blacks in a national discourse that often treats poverty and Blackness as synonymous. What began as an attempt to understand the seemingly intractable and highly concentrated poverty of Black inner-city communities from a range of perspectives had, by the 1990s, used the iconography of the ghetto not only to make poverty urban and Black but also to remove the majority of the poor from the national gaze. This partial picture of poverty came to tell a universal story of pathological behavior according to the norms and mores of a "culture of poverty" that eschews waged work, embraces crime, and exhibits family dysfunction. Trends in labor force participation and welfare receipt, in criminal offending and incarceration, and in the numbers of single-female-headed households bolster the connection between race and poverty that these "underclass" communities have come to represent. Based on this racialized picture of poverty, most Americans now support antipoverty initiatives aimed at reducing welfare dependency and crime, encouraging the formation of two-parent families, and discouraging extramarital childbearing.

Beginning in the 1960s, a number of events helped link race and poverty. Buoyed by recent legal victories intended to end racial segregation in public education, the civil rights movement pursued a racial justice mandate that included employment, housing, and access to voting for a population that was disproportionately poor. Urban rebellions from Watts to Newark further solidified this link, since much of the assessment of what had caused the riots and many of the recommendations for avoiding similar outbreaks in the future spoke directly to the need to address inner-city poverty. Moreover, research and studies from all political and ideological positions were influential not only in determining what social welfare policy should be but also in painting a picture of the poor, a picture that was largely urban and Black. Consequently, as the 1970s commenced, the prevailing picture of U.S. poverty featured single Black women and their dependent children in "matriarchal" families and communities and supported by government largesse. Although many Black single mothers were among the working poor, a significant number relied on government assistance to make ends meet.

According to the prevailing narrative of Black poverty, "matriarchal" families had been abandoned by husbands and fathers who were in turn replaced by government. Some contended that poor Black men's emasculation began with slavery, continued as a by-product of an understandable but unfortunate cultural adaptation, and was exacerbated by government programs that required them to be absent if their families were to be eligible for aid. The story continued: Without strong ties to familial dependents—who chose to rely on public assistance rather than on the work effort of individual men—these men opted for intermittently interrupted inner-city idleness. The only responsible adults to be found in these inner-city communities, it was thought, were the selfless matriarchs who had come to realize they were better off partnering with the government than with the poor men with whom they had children.

Although matriarchs were assumed to exist without adult men, there were other poor Black mothers whose presumed sexuality compromised their claims to public assistance. The fitness of their parenting and the suitability of their homes were questioned because of their relationships with men who were neither their legal husbands nor the biological fathers of their children. Many such women successfully maintained the division between their roles as mothers and as adult women engaged in consensual heterosexual relationships as they challenged the presumption that certain aspects of the latter necessarily compromised their ability to perform the duties of the former.

During the late 1970s and early 1980s, the matriarch and the sexual mother morphed into the welfare queen in public imagery. She was portrayed in political rhetoric and popular media as an irresponsible and immoral baby-making machine who defrauded the government, whether by collecting cash assistance to pay the note on her Cadillac or by having more children to collect more cash assistance. Unlike the selfless matriarch, she used welfare to finance her own conspicuous consumption at the expense of her dependent children. Like the sexual mother, she relied on the government for economic assistance while maintaining relationships with a series of men who eventually fathered more children they neither would nor could support. Unlike both the matriarch and the sexual mother, this popularly imagined welfare queen was apparently unable to raise her children, whom she unleashed to wreak havoc on her community and society. She also tied welfare to crime, for it was widely believed that she scammed the system, feigning need and taking money for nothing. The neoconservatism of the 1980s branded this welfare queen as willfully pathological and in need of a complete cultural, moral, and behavioral overhaul. She was responsible not only for the micro-dysfunction of herself and her family but also for the macro-dysfunction plaguing the increasingly marginalized inner-city communities in which she lived. She taught daughters to expect a life of government checks, baby daddies, and no marriage. She turned sons out onto the streets in search of male role models, for whom babies and baby mothers were unquestionable signs of virility and manhood. The availability of welfare was thought to retard the work ethic of "the underclass," plunging them deeper into the pathological culture of poverty. The imagery of the welfare queen, her family, and her community was indispensable to linking race, gender, class, and crime in the dominant national picture of poverty.

The poor were criminalized in two related ways. First, being visibly poor was seen as criminal because it was thought to be caused by conscious and deliberate choices to act in ways that were out of step with mainstream norms and mores regarding wage work, family structure, and reproduction. The high rates of unemployment, single-female-headed households, and extramarital childbirth in poor communities were thought to be driven by the culture of poverty, the mere adherence to which was deemed criminal. Second, visibly poor communities (particularly those in urban areas) were seen as dangerous public spaces that engendered criminals and criminal behavior. In this way, criminality and poverty were merged so that welfare rights and welfare participation were believed to facilitate pathological, poverty-causing behavior.

The merging of criminality, culpability, and poverty allowed the implementation of punitive measures and programs whose primary goal was to end the pathology of poverty by modifying behavior. Throughout the late 1980s and early 1990s, the federal government granted states waivers from federal welfare program requirements to enable them to experiment with stipulations and rules affecting reproduction, family structure, and waged work. Many of these experiments became codified in the 1996 Personal Responsibility and Work Opportunity Reconciliation Act, which relied heavily on the imagery of the Black inner city to support the criminalization of "the underclass" and its culture of poverty. Central to these punitive measures were stereotypes of the welfare queen, her man and her progeny, all of which seemed to justify making receipt of aid subject to conditions that would further stigmatize welfare receipt and demonize welfare recipients. The racialized picture of poverty that emerged made it easier to blame the poor for their poverty, linked poverty and criminality in ways that seemed to justify increasingly harsh measures intended to force the poor to behave differently, and allowed the government to substantially relieve itself of both obligations to the poor and responsibility to mitigate poverty. Despite the specificity of the Blackness on which this picture relies, the alleged pathology now transcends race to justify punishing those racial transgressors who choose to act like the Black and inner-city poor of "the underclass" (Crooms 2001).

Lisa A. Crooms

See also: African Americans; Aid to Families with Dependent Children (ADC/AFDC); Deserving/Undeserving Poor; Family Structure; Kerner Commission Report; Moynihan Report; 1940s to Present; Picturing Poverty (I); Racism; *Regulating the Poor;* "Underclass"; Urban Poverty; *The Vanishing Black Family;* Welfare Policy/Welfare Reform

References and Further Reading

Crooms, Lisa A. 2001. "The Mythical, Magical 'Underclass': Constructing Poverty in Race and Gender, Making the Public Private and the Private Public." *Journal of Gender, Race, and Justice* 5: 87–130.

Gilens, Martin. 1999. *Why Americans Hate Welfare: Race, Media, and the Politics of Anti-Poverty Policy.* Chicago: University of Chicago Press.

Kelley, Robin D. G. 1997. *Your Mama's Dysfunktional!: Fighting the Culture Wars in Urban America.* Boston: Beacon Press.

Kushnick, Louis, and James Jennings, eds. 1999. *A New Introduction to Poverty: The Role of Race, Power, and Politics.* New York: New York University Press.

Quadagno, Jill. 1994. *The Color of Welfare: How Racism Undermined the War on Poverty.* New York: Oxford University Press.

Roberts, Dorothy. 1997. *Killing the Black Body: Race, Reproduction, and the Meaning of Liberty.* New York: Vintage Books.

U.S. Census Bureau. http://www.census.gov/hhes/www/poverty.html.

Wilson, William Julius. 1996. *When Work Disappears: The World of the New Urban Poor.* New York: Knopf.

Pittsburgh Survey

Between 1907 and 1908, over seventy well-known social scientists, including Paul Kellogg, Florence Kelley, John R. Commons, Peter Roberts, Crystal Eastman, and Robert Woods, conducted an extensive social survey in Pittsburgh and nearby Homestead, Pennsylvania. The area seemed an ideal location for a thorough social survey because of the local prominence of the iron and steel industries. The project received generous funding from the Russell Sage Foundation. Between 1909 and 1914, the researchers published six large reports detailing their work, illustrated by photographs, including some by Lewis Hine. Four of the monographs focused on job accidents, on the steel industry, on mill-town life, and on low-paid female workers. The other two books collected essays on working conditions in the factories and on corruption in the local government.

Like other reformers of the Progressive Era, the survey team criticized the overwhelming influence of corporations on American life, blaming them for endangering the health and welfare of employees, damaging the environment, and corrupting local government. Although they blamed the iron and steel industries for most of Pittsburgh's social problems, the reformers also viewed Americanization of immigrant workers as an important aspect of civic improvement.

The Pittsburgh Survey was in many ways a major achievement in Progressive Era social investigation: multidisciplinary, methodologically sophisticated yet conducted with the participation of volunteers from the community and social welfare practitioners, and pitched to a broad general readership. It also served as a model for hundreds of community-based surveys in localities across the country. In other ways, however, the survey fell short of its most ambitious goal: reforming the city of Pittsburgh. Although the survey's authors believed they had provided city leaders an objective, clear-eyed overview of urban problems that needed attention, local city boosters and the press resented what they perceived as an overly negative portrait. Some of the survey investigators were also unable to transcend their own cultural biases to write about the immigrant workforce without stereotype and condescension. Still, the Pittsburgh Survey anticipated major urban reforms of the twentieth century, and it remains significant as a resource for studying the social conditions of early-twentieth-century industrial workers.

The excerpt below comes from an essay by Paul Kellogg, chief researcher of the survey.

Sarah Case

See also: Americanization Movement; Philanthropy; Poverty Research; Social Surveys; *Survey* and *Survey Graphic*

By minute specialization of jobs, by army-like organization, by keeping together a staff of highly paid regulars at the top, the industries of Pittsburgh are independent of the rank and file. Two-thirds of the steel workers are unskilled immigrants, and thousands of them in their ignorance of English are as uncomprehending as horses, if we may judge by the kind of Gee! Whoa! *and gesture commands that suffice for directing them. Specialization, elimination, speeding up,—these are inherently the aims of Pittsburgh business men, and the methods that turn out tons of shapes for the skilful [sic] workers of other cities to put into finished products. Without its marvelous framework of organization, eliminating dependence on personality in the masses and thereby rendering personality more indispensable in the captains, it would be impossible for Pittsburgh to convert its stream of labor into the most productive labor power known in modern industry. Large rewards for brains,—to overseers, manager's foremen, bosses, "pushers," and gang leaders in descending scale; heavy pressure toward equality of wages among the restless, changing, competitive rank and file,—these are the principles which Pittsburgh applies to the distribution of the wealth in the production of which she holds supremacy.*

Source: Paul Underwood Kellogg, ed., *Wage-Earning Pittsburgh* (New York: Russell Sage Foundation, 1914; reprint New York: Arno Press, 1974), 117.

Piven, Frances Fox

See Regulating the Poor; Welfare Rights Movement

Politics and Federal Policy

The politics and political processes of poverty and social welfare in the United States are linked to partisan politics; to labor, civil rights, antipoverty, and women's movements; to local, state, and national politics; and to legislative, administrative, and judicial politics. In addition, debates about poverty and social welfare are deeply racialized and gendered, that is, closely tied to racial and gender inequalities in income and political power, to gender and sexuality norms, and to ambivalent attitudes toward assistance to the poor and toward programs in aid of racial minorities.

The foundations of contemporary poverty politics were laid by the New Deal legislation of the 1930s. Up to that point, most antipoverty programs were administered by voluntary organizations, and the main sources of relief were almshouses or workhouses. In the late nineteenth and early twentieth centuries, some reformers advocated transforming the Civil War pension system into a universal system of benefits for "workingmen and their families." Others, notably women's organizations, advocated instead the nationalization of the mothers' pensions that many states had implemented (Skocpol 1992). There was little development of either option until the stock market crash of 1929 and the subsequent Great Depression forced poverty onto the national agenda. The Depression left over one-quarter of the American workforce unemployed, and unemployment rates were even higher among African Americans; in 1930, 50 percent of Blacks were unemployed.

President Herbert Hoover attempted to stimulate the economy with subsidies for industry, and private charities and local governments tried to assist the needy and the unemployed. However, none of these programs ended the Depression, and groups of unemployed people pressed for national relief. When Franklin D. Roosevelt was elected in 1932, he promised a "New Deal" to provide Americans with security from "the cradle to the grave." Beginning in 1933, the Federal Emergency Relief Administration (FERA) provided direct relief in the form of cash assistance, while the Civil Works Administration provided work relief (Patterson 1994). By 1935, however, the "dole" (or "handouts") had come under increasing criticism. The 1935 Social Security Act, therefore, distinguished between employable and unemployable recipients and made "social insurance" rather than welfare the main tool for combating poverty. The act laid out a four-part system of general assistance, work relief, categorical aid, and social insurance, providing old-age insurance and unemployment compensation, as well as Old Age Assistance and Aid to Dependent Children (ADC) for those outside the labor force. In addition to distinguishing between "deserving" and "undeserving" needy people, the law codified the regulation of women's personal lives, for ADC allowed states to tie eligibility for aid to such criteria as the "suitability" of the home and the "propriety" of the parent. Such criteria also amplified the ability of officials to discriminate based on race (Mink 1990).

Many New Deal policies responded to the increasingly strong and vocal labor movement. The Fair Labor Standards Act (FLSA) of 1938 enacted the first federal minimum wage, and the 1935 National Labor Relations Act (NLRA) granted workers the right to organize unions and to bargain collectively. Along with unions, civil rights and women's organizations also helped shape the New Deal. However, because the legislation was passed by a coalition of northern and southern Democrats, there were many racial inequities in New Deal programs. For example, neither the NLRA nor Social Security covered occupations commonly filled by Blacks, such as agricultural and domestic workers. Consequently, approximately two-thirds of Black workers were not initially covered (Hamilton and Hamilton 1992). Similarly, the FLSA and Social Security excluded many occupations dominated by women, such as many retail clerks and seasonal workers. In addition, women's entitlements and exclusions were tied to their roles as mothers, assumed their heterosexuality, and perpetuated their economic dependence on men. For example, the National Economy Act of 1933 legislated that a husband and wife could not both work for the federal government, including in work programs. Because men's salaries were higher, many women quit or refused federal jobs (Mink 1990). In addition, the categories of assistance that Blacks were eligible for were left to the discretion of state workers. Often, especially in the South, Blacks were therefore denied assistance. Nonetheless, the association of the Democratic Party with the antipoverty programs of the era precipitated a move by Black voters from the Republican Party, "the party of Lincoln," to the Democratic Party, "the party of the New Deal."

In the two decades following World War II, policymakers devoted scant attention to poverty, and the 1947 Taft-Hartley Act reduced much of the labor movement's power to press for economic reforms. Still, Social Security retirement pension coverage was expanded in the postwar era, the federal share of contributions to ADC was increased, cash assistance was extended to caregivers (usually mothers), and disability insurance was added to Social Security (Patterson 1994).

When John F. Kennedy was elected president in 1960, he owed his victory in several states to Black voters. Kennedy took office in the midst of rising civil rights activity and increased attention among civil rights activists to economic issues such as housing, jobs, welfare, and education (Quadagno 1994). Rather than confronting civil rights for Blacks directly and risking alienating white southern Democrats, however, Kennedy initiated antipoverty programs including the Manpower Development and Training Act (1962), which actually benefited whites more than it did Blacks.

Kennedy's assassination cut short his antipoverty endeavors. When Lyndon B. Johnson assumed office, he made poverty and civil rights domestic priorities. In 1964, Congress passed the Economic Opportunity Act (EOA), intended to address juvenile delinquency, civil rights, job training, and education. This law was the foundation of Johnson's War on Poverty and included such programs as Volunteers in Service to America (VISTA), Job Corps, College Work Study, and Head Start. In a significant departure from previous policy, the Office of Economic Opportunity (OEO) delegated authority to community action agencies to achieve "maximum feasible participation," to empower community organizations, and to attenuate the ability of local officials to discriminate against Blacks in the distribution of benefits. However, the level of community involvement ranged widely, from Chicago, where the Community Action Program (CAP) was controlled by Mayor Richard J. Daley's political machine, to Newark, where civil rights activists used the CAP to challenge the municipal government (Quadagno 1994). Moreover, funding for OEO was never adequate and was further reduced as opposition among local officials grew and spending for the Vietnam War increased.

Advocates also used the courts to establish rights for the poor. In 1968, *King v. Smith* (392 U.S. 309) struck down rules that denied benefits to the children of women who had sexual relationships, and *Shapiro v. Thompson* (394 U.S. 618 [1969]) struck down residency requirements for welfare benefits as abridging constitutional rights to interstate travel. *Goldberg v. Kelly* (397 U.S. 254 [1970]) upheld due process standards, mandating hearings for the termination of welfare benefits (Mink 1998). *Dandridge v. Williams* (397 U.S. 471 [1970]) sought unsuccessfully to make an equal protection argument against maximum grant limitations on family benefits.

Combined with direct action by groups such as the National Welfare Rights Organization (NWRO), the court successes helped to liberalize rules for Aid to Families with Dependent Children (AFDC, formerly ADC) and other benefits, increasing participation in welfare. Between 1961 and 1971, the number of individuals enrolled increased from 3.5 million to 11 million (Mink 1998). President Richard M. Nixon took office as this welfare rights movement was in full swing. Although Nixon abolished the OEO, he expanded the food stamp program, supported increases in Social Security, and added benefits for people with disabilities (Quadagno 1994). In addition, he proposed a Family Assistance Plan (FAP) that would have guaranteed a minimum income to low-income families while encouraging work. Though some hailed this proposal as a great improvement, it was very controversial, mainly because Nixon intended it to forge a coalition between southern conservatives and white working-class voters in the North. By the time of its demise in 1972, the FAP was opposed by southern conservatives, welfare activists such as the NWRO (which thought benefit levels were too low), and the U.S. Chamber of Commerce.

When Ronald Reagan assumed the presidency in 1981, he abolished or severely cut funding for many of Johnson's War on Poverty programs, including CAP, the Legal Services Corporation, and school lunches. He also tightened eligibility requirements for AFDC and food stamps, capped state spending for Medicaid, and cut the Comprehensive Employment and Training Act and federal subsidies for housing. In 1982, Congress made further cuts, increased workfare provisions, and further tightened AFDC eligibility requirements. Though poverty rose to the highest levels since 1963, participation in programs fell.

In addition to such cuts, the Reagan administration fomented public opposition to welfare by deploying racialized and gendered stereotypes such as that of the "welfare queen" who rides around in a Cadillac (Imig 1996). Liberal policymakers, though generally supportive of public assistance, did little to combat these stereotypes. In addition, Reagan-era cuts had rendered many welfare programs, in particular AFDC, less effective at lifting people out of poverty. By the late 1980s, there was a growing consensus that welfare had to be "reformed." In 1988, Congress passed the Family Security Act. Although the new law did not address the depreciation in the value of benefits, it imposed new education, training, or work requirements and toughened paternity and child support conditions (Amott 1990).

The effort to "reform" welfare gained momentum in 1993 when President Bill Clinton took office promising to "end welfare as we know it." When the Republican Party won a majority in the House of Representatives in 1994, Speaker Newt Gingrich unveiled a ten-point "Contract with America." Among the items on this agenda was reforming AFDC. Though Clinton did not support many of the provisions in the Republican-sponsored bill, in 1996 he signed the Personal Responsibility and Work Opportunity Reconciliation Act (PRWORA). This law ended AFDC, replacing it with the Temporary Assistance to Needy Families (TANF) program.

The TANF program made major changes in welfare. It ended the entitlement status welfare had held since the *King v. Smith* decision, imposed five-year time limits on benefits, and added work requirements, more restrictions on pursuing education while on public assistance, and an emphasis on marriage. The PRWORA also devolved many decisions to the states. Although the federal government sets key standards, states have the discretion, for example, to demand that recipients work outside the home earlier than required by federal law, to establish stricter time limits, to deny benefits if recipients fail to establish paternity, to deny certain benefits to noncitizens, and to require drug testing of recipients (Mink 1998).

In spite of the impact of the 1996 reforms on women and people of color, few feminist, African American, or Latino organizations and leaders made opposition to the PRWORA a priority (Mink 1998; Williams 1998). Six years later, however, women's, civil rights, and antipoverty organizations actively engaged debates surrounding the reauthorization of the TANF program. With grassroots groups, these organizations have spearheaded efforts against Republican calls for tougher work requirements and for marriage promotion programs. Gay, lesbian, bisexual, and transgender groups have also begun to work on welfare issues, addressing the fact that marriage promotion and paternity-establishment policies assume that all recipients are heterosexual.

Dara Z. Strolovitch

See also: Civil Rights Movement; Deserving/Undeserving Poor; Homophobia; Racism; Sexism; Social Security Act of 1935; War on Poverty; Welfare Policy/Welfare Reform; Welfare Rights Movement

References and Further Reading

Amott, Teresa. 1990. "Black Women and AFDC." In *Women, the State, and Welfare*, ed. Linda Gordon, 280–300. Madison: University of Wisconsin Press.

Hamilton, Donna, and Charles Hamilton. 1992. "The Dual Agenda of African American Organizations since the New Deal: Social Welfare Policies and Civil Rights." *Political Science Quarterly* 107: 435–453.

Imig, Douglas. 1996. *Poverty and Power*. Lincoln: University of Nebraska Press.

Mink, Gwendolyn. 1990. "The Lady and the Tramp." In *Women, the State, and Welfare*, ed. Linda Gordon, 92–122. Madison: University of Wisconsin Press.

———. 1998. *Welfare's End*. Ithaca, NY: Cornell University Press.

Patterson, James T. 1994. *America's Struggle against Poverty, 1900–1994*. Cambridge, MA: Harvard University Press.

Quadagno, Jill. 1994. *The Color of Welfare: How Racism Undermined the War on Poverty*. New York: Oxford.

Skocpol, Theda. 1992. *Protecting Soldiers and Mothers*. Cambridge, MA: Harvard University Press.

Williams, Linda. 1998. "Race and the Politics of Social Policy." In *The Social Divide*, ed. Margaret Weir, 417–463. Washington, DC: Brookings Institution.

Poor Laws

"Poor laws" is a term that refers to the collection of legal statutes, principles, and policies—including criminal penalties—that societies establish to regulate the behavior of poor people and to establish rules and restrictions for providing aid to the poor. Although poor laws have varied throughout history and in different countries, the Anglo-American poor law tradition has been singularly pronounced and enduring and continues to have a profound influence on social policy and politics to this day.

The English poor laws date back to a period of acute labor shortage in fourteenth-century England, during which the Statute of Laborers (1349) was passed prohibiting the giving of alms to "sturdy beggars" as a way of forcing those considered able-bodied to work (Trattner 1984). The prohibition, however, was continued even when labor was in surplus. It was recognized that certain categories of the poor were legitimately outside the labor market—the aged, the impotent, the sick, the feeble, and the lame. At first, the "worthy poor" were given licenses to beg in designated locations; later, publicly gathered alms were provided so they would not have to beg. The able-bodied, those "lusty or having limbs strong enough to labor," were kept in "continual labor." The various provisions were codified in the Elizabethan Poor Law (1601): The able-bodied must work, and the family was primarily responsible for the welfare of its members; relief was for community residents, not strangers (and under the 1662 Settlement Act, paupers could be forcibly returned to their original places of residence), and was administered at the local level, usually by the parish, and by established members of the community designated as "overseers" of the poor.

The foundational poor law distinction between the "deserving" and "undeserving" poor served a number of purposes. It aimed to save taxpayers money, never a minor consideration in welfare policy. It served to validate basic values. "Pauperism," the failure of the able-bodied to support themselves and their families without recourse to charity or public assistance, was designated a *moral* failure. Moreover, this moral failure was multidimensional. It was usually linked with other forms of deviant behavior—intemperance, vice, criminality, sexual promiscuity, or illegitimacy, all often imbued with racial and ethnic overtones. The goal of the English poor law principles was to ensure that the able-bodied did not slide into "pauperism." At the same time, by making provisions for public relief, they sought to stave off the threat of mass uprising in the face of widespread hunger and want. These basic English poor law principles significantly shaped welfare policy in colonial North America, and by the mid-seventeenth century, several colonies had enacted poor laws patterned after English legislation.

In the first decades of the nineteenth century, welfare in both England and the United States was in one of its periodic "crises." Underlying this sense of crisis were increasingly visible signs of poverty as both countries experienced periodic economic downturns, rapid urbanization, and industrialization along with the accompanying rises in the relief rolls, in perceived threats to the social order, in higher public relief expenditures, and in concerns about the supply of labor. Sidestepping the more fundamental roots of poverty, critics instead focused their energies on the poor laws themselves, which became subject to sustained reform campaigns on both sides of the Atlantic. The problem, as early reformers saw it, was that welfare was too difficult to administer in the field and had become too lax. Moreover, building on the ideas of English cleric Thomas Malthus, reformers argued that public relief only compounded the problems of poverty and pauperism by shielding the lower classes from the consequences of their own (mis)behavior and, in effect, encouraging them to have children and remain idle without suffering the consequences. By the 1830s, reform activism had culminated in important policy shifts, embodied in the Poor Law Amendment Act of 1834 in England and the wave of poorhouse construction in the United States. "Outdoor relief" was to be abolished. Henceforth, relief would only be given within the confines of the poorhouse. According to the logic of the reformers, the threat of being sent to the poorhouse would deter the able-bodied from seeking public assistance by making it contingent upon the loss of liberty and confinement in miserable conditions. Those who could not work still had to go to the poorhouse. Thus, the "deserving" poor were held "hostage" in order to enforce deterrence (Katz 1986, 32).

Eventually, the poorhouse reform movement proved too costly, cruel, and ineffective to sustain, and it was replaced by the presumably more humane doctrine of scientific charity. Nevertheless, the basic principle of the original poor law—and especially its distinction between the deserving and undeserving poor and its imperative to uphold the work ethic—remained. Charity, the new generation of poor law reformers argued, had several advantages over public assistance. Charity would be uncertain and up to the discretion of the donor, thus not weakening the work ethic. Moreover, private charities were more resistant to political pressure to liberalize benefits and more effective in exerting "those moral and religious influences that would prevent relief from degenerating into a mechanical pauperizing dole" (Trattner 1989, 86). Although the proposed measures were clothed in new theory, the assumptions as to the causes and cures of poverty remained the same. The task was to keep the poor from starving without breeding a class of paupers who chose to live off the public rather than to work. The goal of relief, therefore, was not primarily to relieve misery but rather to preserve—and enforce—the work ethic (Handler 1995, 17–20).

The Development of the American Welfare State

The poor law tradition continued to influence social provision through the early development of more systematic state and federal government policies, which continued to keep a careful check on aid recipients even as they gradually expanded the reach of public assistance. The characteristic feature of the American welfare state is its categorical nature: There are separate, distinct programs for specific categories of the poor. Categories began to develop in the nineteenth century with the start of separate state institutions for the blind, the deaf, and the insane. Next, institutions were created for poor Civil War orphans; they were not to be treated with the general mass of poor at the local level. This was followed by pensions for Civil War veterans, which grew into an extensive program before being abolished by progressive reformers at the turn of the century because of widespread corruption (Skocpol 1992). Workers' compensation was adopted during the first decades of the twentieth century.

During the nineteenth century, poor single mothers were considered no different from the general mass of undeserving poor, which meant that they had to work in the paid labor force. Toward the end of the century, children began to be distinguished as a separate category, and child protection laws were instituted to remove children from their impoverished mothers. At the same time, however, there was a growing number of social reformers, known as the child-savers, who claimed that if the mother was poor but otherwise fit and proper to raise the child, then perhaps it would be more conducive to child welfare to support the mother rather than to break up the home. This idea was endorsed in a White House conference in 1909, and in

1911, the first mothers' pension statute was enacted. By 1925, similar statutes had been enacted in almost all the states (Bell 1965, 6–7).

From its earliest days, ADC was an exercise in myth and ceremony. The myth was that poor mothers would be allowed to stay at home and take care of their children—hence the popular name "mothers' pension." The ceremony was that a small number of deserving white widows were helped; this validated the myth. The reality was that for most poor, single mothers and their children, at best, nothing had changed; at worst, they were stigmatized further by being excluded from the mothers' pension program. In contrast to welfare programs for the aged and the disabled (the "deserving poor"), which were administered by the local welfare departments, the mothers' pension programs were part of the local juvenile courts or county courts, which had jurisdiction over delinquent, neglected, and dependent children. Thus, the "fit and proper" mother was an alternative probation officer. Otherwise, the children could be removed from the home. In practice, mothers' pension programs remained small. Relatively few families were enrolled, recipients were predominantly white widows, and because benefits were rarely enough to live on, recipients were still pushed into the low-wage labor market to supplement the pensions (Bell 1965; Abramovitz 1988).

During the New Deal era, the Roosevelt administration concentrated more on old-age pensions, unemployment, and work programs than on welfare. Mothers' pensions, along with other state categorical programs, were incorporated into the Social Security Act of 1935 as Aid to Dependent Children (ADC, later Aid to Families with Dependent Children, or AFDC), as grants-in-aid, supported in part by the federal government and administered by the states. Thus, while establishing a federal role in relief provision, this landmark legislation preserved the poor law principle of localism. And yet, although state and local administrators still exercised considerable discretion over who did and who did not receive aid—through "suitable mother" standards, "man in the house" rules, and other such regulations—broader political and economic developments transformed welfare in ways that threatened to undermine age-old poor law prohibitions against aid to the "undeserving." Dramatic changes started to become evident in the 1950s and 1960s, as African Americans moved northward seeking civil rights and industrial rights, as the Democratic Party courted urban African Americans, and as the civil and legal rights revolutions encouraged more of those eligible for welfare to claim benefits—including growing proportions of divorced, separated, deserted, and never-married women and women of color. The federal courts and welfare rights activists forced open AFDC gates. For them, welfare had become a "right" rather than a matter of charitable or administrative discretion. Other observers, however, greeted the changes with growing alarm. To them, welfare was once again in a "crisis," which was captured in the "exploding" relief rolls. And once again the sense of crisis would eventually lead critics to reassert traditional poor law principles over a sustained period, culminating in a massive "reform" that, in 1996, would once again restrict cash relief and enforce work requirements for the "able-bodied," deny poor relief to the "undeserving" and to "outsiders," and devolve responsibility and authority in poor relief to the state and local levels.

From Welfare to Workfare

As one response to the so-called welfare crisis, the federal government, in 1967, enacted the Work Incentive Program (WIN), which combined both incentives and mandatory work requirements. All adults and children over age sixteen, with certain exceptions, were required to register and be referred to state employment services for training and employment services. But only 2–3 percent of the eligible recipients actually obtained jobs through WIN. The vast majority of eligible recipients were put on "administrative hold," and only 20 percent of those who were employed held their job for at least three months (Handler 1995, 58–59).

Nevertheless, the 1967 welfare "reforms" launched a thirty-year campaign to restore disciplinary controls characteristic of poor laws.

For the rest of the twentieth century, welfare (AFDC) remained a deeply divisive political issue. Although conservatives in both political parties led the charge for welfare discipline, some liberals eventually joined conservatives in demanding stiff work requirements. The emergence of antiwelfare New Democrats in the 1990s sealed the fate of AFDC. Himself a New Democrat, President Bill Clinton promised "to end welfare as we know it" during his quest for the White House. The promise was fulfilled with the passage of the Personal Responsibility and Work Opportunity Reconciliation Act of 1996 (PRWORA), which replaced AFDC with the Temporary Assistance to Needy Families (TANF) program. The legislation repealed the welfare entitlement and amplified state and local discretion over cash assistance through a block grant system of welfare funding. Work requirements, more stringent now than ever before, are strictly enforced through penalties and time limits. Welfare reform today is still in the shadow of the sturdy beggar.

Joel F. Handler and Danielle S. Seiden

See also: Aid to Families with Dependent Children (ADC/AFDC); Deserving/Undeserving Poor; Malthusianism; Poorhouse/Almshouse; Speenhamland; Vagrancy Laws/Settlement Laws/Residency Requirements; Welfare Policy/Welfare Reform

References and Further Reading

Abramovitz, Mimi. 1988. *Regulating the Lives of Women: Social Welfare Policy from Colonial Times to the Present*. Boston: South End Press.

Bell, Winifred. 1965. *Aid to Dependent Children*. New York: Columbia University Press.

Gordon, Linda. 1988. *Heroes of Their Own Lives: The Politics and History of Family Violence: Boston, 1880–1960*. New York: Viking.

Handler, Joel. 1995. *The Poverty of Welfare Reform*. New Haven: Yale University Press.

Handler, Joel, and Y. Hasenfeld. 1991. *The Moral Construction of Poverty: American Welfare Reform*. Newbury Park, CA: Sage.

Katz, Michael. 1986. *In the Shadow of the Poorhouse: A Social History of Welfare in America*. New York: Basic Books.

Kessler-Harris, Alice. 1982. *Out to Work: A History of Wage-Earning Women in the United States*. New York: Oxford University Press.

"Letters to the Secretary of State on the Subject of Pauperism." *Columbia Republican*. Quoted in *In the Shadow of the Poorhouse: A Social History of Welfare in America*, by Michael Katz, 6. New York: Basic Books, 1986.

Patterson, James. 1981. *America's Struggle against Poverty, 1900–1980*. Cambridge, MA: Harvard University Press.

Skocpol, Theda. 1992. *Protecting Soldiers and Mothers: The Political Origins of Social Policy in the United States*. Cambridge, MA: Harvard University Press.

Trattner, Walter. [1979, 1984] 1989. *From Poor Law to Welfare State: A History of Social Welfare in America*. 4th ed. New York: Free Press.

Poor People's Campaign

The Poor People's Campaign was organized in 1968 by the Southern Christian Leadership Conference (SCLC), a civil rights group, to draw attention to the plight of the poor and underprivileged. The campaign was designed to be not a one-day demonstration but an extended display of massive civil disobedience, with poor people from around the country erecting tents and living on the Mall in front of the Lincoln Memorial in Washington, D.C., until their demands were met. From mid-May until the end of June, when police destroyed poor people's homes in what SCLC called Resurrection City, several thousand people camped out in the nation's capital to dramatize their needs. The Poor People's Campaign consciously sought to draw in people from diverse racial, ethnic, and geographic backgrounds. It targeted institutionalized policies of racism, poverty, and militarism, contrasting the massive spending in Vietnam with the squalor in which most poor Americans lived. It demanded federal action to alleviate the poverty and suffering of the nation's neediest.

The central platform of the campaign, the Economic Bill of Rights, called for a $30 billion antipoverty package, which was to include a federal jobs program, housing for low-income families, an increase in welfare spending and education, a guaranteed annual income, and free food stamps for people out of work. The government, organizers charged, could easily afford to raise the standard of living of the poor. They argued that money to fight an unjust war killing civilians and soldiers halfway across the world was ill-spent and that those resources were sorely needed at home to alleviate the suffering of massive numbers of the nation's poor. They believed that poverty was the most pressing problem of the late 1960s.

Planned in 1967, the Poor People's Campaign signaled a shift in SCLC strategy away from civil rights toward economic inequality. Although most civil rights organizations, including SCLC, had included jobs and income as a part of their political platforms even in the early 1960s, the civil rights and voting rights campaigns dominated their organizing agendas. The Civil Rights Act of 1964, which ended de jure segregation, and the Voting Rights Act of 1965, which ensured equal access to the ballot, did not cure the poverty of many African Americans. But success in winning formal rights served to reinvigorate SCLC's commitment to eradicating the more intractable problem of poverty. Many activists immersed in the struggle to end racism realized that the legal victories had done little to counter the economic inequality that many African Americans experienced. Upon the suggestion of Marian Wright, the SCLC decided to organize a protest during which thousands of poor people from around the country would descend on the nation's capital to highlight their problems. SCLC hoped both to meet the needs of the poor and to undercut the rising radicalism and violence that were evident among some sectors of the Black Power movement.

Although spearheaded by SCLC, the campaign was the effort of a coalition of groups from around the country, including civil rights groups, welfare rights groups, churches, and labor unions. It was also a multiracial initiative and included Mexican Americans, Puerto Ricans, African Americans, Native Americans, and poor whites. The multiracial vision of the campaign, its grassroots character, and its protracted nature made the campaign particularly difficult to organize. SCLC staff were overwhelmed by the number of bureaucratic, bookkeeping, planning, coordinating, and logistical details of the campaign. They had to consider how to bring large numbers of poor people to the capital, raise money, publicize the event, register participants, build semisturdy homes, feed camp residents, provide medical care and sewage services—and the list went on.

The leadership of SCLC was also divided on the feasibility and wisdom of the campaign, with Bayard Rustin and Roy Wilkins expressing doubt. In addition, the campaign faced opposition from its outset. Many public officials and mainstream journalists felt that with the passage of the Civil Rights and Voting Rights Acts, the civil rights movement had succeeded and needed to disband. Others believed that racism was a regional problem, confined to the South, and that the new focus on poverty, which crossed geographic boundaries, was misplaced. Radicalization in the Black community also made organizing more difficult, for many African Americans had concluded that working within the system and pushing for legislative change was an ineffective strategy. All of these obstacles made raising money and coordinating the campaign difficult.

The assassination of Martin Luther King Jr. in April 1968 changed the course of the campaign. His death sparked a series of riots and uprisings in Baltimore, Chicago, Newark, Washington, D.C., and dozens of other communities

Unitarian Universalist Association, Poor People's Campaign, General Resolution, 1968

The Poor People's Campaign brought together a broad coalition of welfare rights, social justice, labor, and faith organizations, which pledged to work for its legislative goals, as indicated by the 1968 resolution of the Unitarian Universalist Association.

The Seventh General Assembly of the Unitarian Universalist Association urges support of the Poor People's Campaign of the Southern Christian Leadership Conference and endorses the following legislative goals sought by the Poor People's Campaign:

1. Meaningful jobs at adequate pay scales in both public and private sectors for the unemployed and the under-employed, with the government to be employer of last resort, and effective enforcement of anti-discrimination statutes;
2. A system of income maintenance, including a guaranteed minimum income for all, and family allowances modeled after the Canadian program;
3. Welfare payments brought up to realistically defined minimum levels, with punitive and family-disruptive qualifications rescinded;
4. Redoubled efforts at school desegregation and provision of quality education for all Americans from kindergarten through college;
5. A massive program of building and renovation to provide decent housing, both for the poor and for those on minimum income;
6. Adequate medical and dental care for all Americans to be implemented by a program of national health insurance;
7. Reform of the law enforcement and judicial system to eliminate all forms of discrimination against minority-group persons and those in poverty;
8. Eliminate subsidies to farmers for non-production of crops and increase government distribution of surplus food to the hungry.

around the country. His assassination led some African Americans to become even more disaffected and wary of peaceful efforts to change the system. The ensuing unrest also heightened anxiety among many white Americans, already fearful of urban protest. In addition, with King's death SCLC lost its central spokesperson and most effective mobilizer. More than other civil rights organizations, SCLC was a hierarchical organization, and King was the glue that held it together. At the same time, news of King's death led to an avalanche of donations to SCLC for the Poor People's Campaign. The campaign became for many people the best way to honor King's legacy. Under the direction of Ralph Abernathy, the new SCLC president, the campaign continued.

From all across the country, poor and homeless people converged on Washington in caravans, some in mule-drawn wagons, others in cars, buses, or pickups. Some came on foot and others, by train. A massive rally kicked off the campaign on May 12. The next day the first stake for Resurrection City was driven into the ground. Initially, Jesse Jackson managed this process; later, Hosea Williams took charge of running the city. During a six-week period, more than 6,000 residents were registered, but people came and left on a regular basis. Toward the end of the campaign, about 1,000 people lived in Resurrection City on the Mall. Residents of the so-called tent city camped out in prefabricated, A-frame homes made of plywood. They lived in the makeshift homes and used portable toilets. Because of SCLC's efforts, they had access to running water, electricity, and telephones. In addition to individual homes, there were dormitories as well as communal tents that housed a dining hall, a medical center, a "city hall," and a nursery. For some, life was more comfortable in Resurrection City than it had been in their rural shacks or dilapidated housing projects. They made daily visits to federal agencies, meeting with officials, pressing their demands but engaging only in nonviolent actions. They went to the Department of Agriculture; the Department of Health, Education, and Welfare; the Supreme Court; and the Department of Labor. In addition to being a means of protesting federal policy, Resurrection City was intended to be a multiracial model, where residents from different backgrounds, all equally poor, would share, cooperate, and live in harmony.

The multiracial character of the city proved to be a bigger problem than organizers expected. Most residents felt more comfortable with their own cultural, racial, and linguistic groups and resisted the integrated model that SCLC strove for. Provincialism and interracial tension prevailed. A focused agenda became more difficult to sustain, for each group was intent on pressing its own specific interests. In addition, small gangs of young people living in the encampment intimidated other residents, making life harder. Robberies, harassment, and violence demoralized many residents, and reports of the internal strife brought bad publicity to the campaign. In early June, seemingly nonstop rain dampened the homes as well as the spirits of the tent city's residents. The ground turned to mud, making life miserable for everyone. Finally, SCLC leadership increasingly came under criticism for staying in hotels and not spending more time with city residents. SCLC leaders came and went at their convenience. Few lived in Resurrection City, and many residents felt their absence and the consequent vacuum in leadership.

A major rally on June 19, which SCLC called Solidarity Day, brought out a crowd that police estimated at 50,000, although organizers believed that closer to 100,000 people attended. At the rally, an array of politicians, celebrities, and civil rights leaders, including Coretta Scott King, spoke of the continuing need to attack poverty. A few days after Solidarity Day, SCLC's permit to camp on the Mall expired. The next day, demonstrators who refused to leave were arrested, and some were tear-gassed, by park rangers and city police. Resurrection City was dismantled.

Although generally regarded as a failure by many historians, the Poor People's Campaign had mixed results. The encampment disbanded with most of its demands unmet. The negative publicity, internal conflicts within Resurrection City, and the lack of a strong national leadership left many residents feeling demoralized about the possibility of a broad national coalition. The campaign did little to resurrect SCLC's leadership in the wake of King's death. On the other hand, there were some minor victories. Federal officials promised to replace food commodities with food stamps, to make changes in welfare regulations, and to initiate a jobs program. Some of these reforms were implemented; others were not. Nevertheless, the direct access that many poor people had to high-level government officials exceeded many of their expectations. When confronted with demonstrators, federal officials often were sympathetic and expressed concern about the plight of the poor. In addition to these symbolic victories, the campaign solidified networks among antipoverty activists of different backgrounds and from around the country, and it reinvigorated the organizing of local activists. Many of these activists had been working and organizing to address poverty on the local level with little recognition or support from the major civil rights groups. The Poor People's Campaign brought their concerns front and center and propelled the issue of poverty into the national spotlight. Thus, despite its ostensible failures, the campaign marked a new phase in the Black freedom movement that addressed issues of poverty and that relied more on grassroots work than on national legislation.

Premilla Nadasen

See also: Civil Rights Movement; Citizens' Crusade Against Poverty (CCAP); Coxey's Army

References and Further Reading

Abernathy, Ralph. 1989. *And the Walls Came Tumbling Down*. New York: Harper and Row.

King, Martin Luther, Jr. 1998. *Autobiography of Martin Luther King, Jr.* New York: Warner Books.

Martin Luther King Jr. Papers Project at Stanford University. Web site. http://www.stanford.edu/group/King/. Last updated May 10, 2004.

McKnight, Gerald D. 1998. *The Last Crusade: Martin Luther King, Jr., the FBI, and the Poor People's Campaign*. Boulder, CO: Westview Press.

Poor Whites

Although most often associated with the rural South of the nineteenth and twentieth centuries, poor whites have existed throughout the United States in every period of American history. White poverty has generally been concentrated in rural areas of the United States, and as the nation's most persistently rural and impoverished region, the South has rightly been identified as the home of a significant poor white population in the United States. In a larger sense, however, whites have always, in terms of absolute numbers, made up the largest segment of the poor in the United States, even though poverty rates among the dominant white majority have remained relatively small compared to those among ethnic minorities, such as African Americans or Latinos. In 1993, for instance, 48 percent of those classified as poor by the federal government were white (Henwood 1997, 183). The representation of poor whites as a distinct race or ethnicity can largely be attributed to the characterizations of elite whites. Whether in the South or in the nation as a whole, these elites have typically denied that white impoverishment stemmed from economic factors, since such an admission would implicitly undermine the oft-repeated notion that the United States has been and remains a "classless" society. Rather, white elites have blamed the presence of white poverty in their midst on a variety of noneconomic factors, such as genetic defects caused by racial miscegenation or inbreeding and destructive traits such as drunkenness or laziness. As a result, poor whites, because they are white yet poor, have always generally been viewed as part of an "undeserving poor."

White poverty existed from the earliest days of European settlement of North America. In the seventeenth and eighteenth centuries, more than half of the white colonists arriving in the British colonies of North America came as indentured servants, most from England, Ireland, and Germany (Zinn 1995, 46). These individuals were bound to work for a landowner for a term of years in exchange for payment of the transatlantic passage and a promise of land at the indenture's end. Although some former servants did eventually prosper, the vast majority either perished before their term of service expired, returned to their country of origin, or became landless tenants.

In the first half of the nineteenth century, poor whites remained a significant part of the U.S. population, in both the North and the South. In the North, many poor whites found new economic opportunities in the region's emerging industries, though jobs frequently did not offer either a long-term guarantee of employment or wages sufficient for an existence above the poverty line. Many areas of the North also continued to have sizable rural, landless white populations, although throughout the nineteenth century, a number of these individuals seized new chances for landownership in the West. In the South, poor whites continued to struggle economically because of the growing

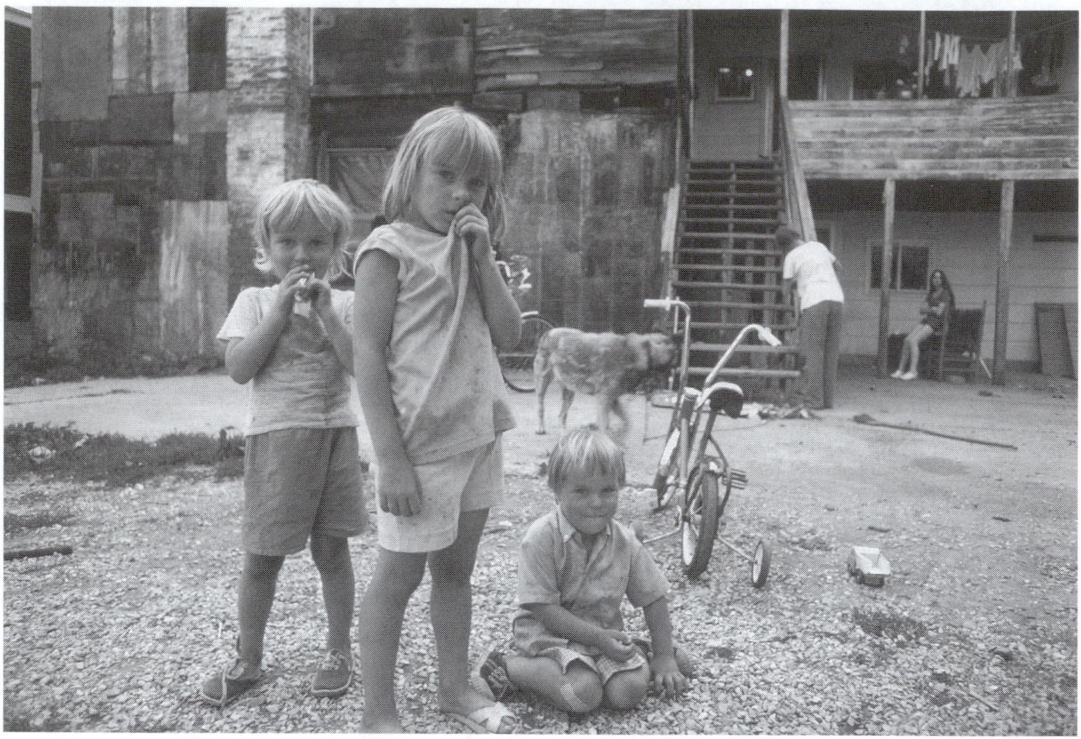

Children stand before old slum houses in a small Vermont town where unemployment is high due to a decline in industrial jobs. This town, with many tenement dwellings like this one, had the highest unemployment rating in the state in 1973. (Nathan Benn/Corbis)

importance of Black slavery in the region's economy. Quite simply, the existence of slavery limited the economic possibilities for the many whites who owned neither slaves nor land, a group that made up anywhere from 20 to 40 percent of the region's white households in the 1850s (Bolton 1994, 12, 85). Many of these poor whites remained permanently mired in poverty, struggling to survive by working in a variety of jobs—everything from laborer to tenant farmer to livestock tender to miner. They served as a casual, mobile labor force, plugging temporary labor shortages in an economy largely powered by African American slave labor. Elite white southerners admitted the existence of poor whites in their society, but planters would not attribute the presence of a poor white population to any economic factors because they believed slavery benefited all whites; rather, slave owners believed white poverty in a slave society resulted from cultural deficiencies or from racial impurities and incest in the bloodlines of certain white families.

After the Civil War, the number of poor whites in the South grew significantly. The independent white farmers, or yeomen, of the antebellum South increasingly became enmeshed in a one-crop (cotton) economy that dominated and impoverished the southern economy for almost a century after the Civil War. By 1900, over 40 percent of the region's white farmers toiled as tenant farmers or sharecroppers, while in the same year almost 100,000 whites worked in the cotton-mill villages that dotted the landscape of the southern Piedmont region (Ayers 1992, 111, 508). Neither form of work represented a path out of poverty. At the same time, sizable numbers of poor whites, like almost all African Americans in the region, were disenfranchised in the political transformations that swept the region in the late nineteenth and early twentieth centuries. As the southern economy diversified and became less agricultural and less rural in the half century after World War II, the number of poor whites declined in the region, though pockets of white poverty continue to exist, especially in the most isolated rural areas of the South. Since the Civil War, white poverty has also persisted in other parts of the United States, although there, poverty among ethnic minorities has been the more pressing problem.

The poor white stereotypes applied historically to southerners—as people who are ignorant, lazy, sexually promiscuous, and violent drunkards and who are largely responsible for their own poverty—are today used to describe the white poor nationwide. Poor whites continue to be identified with derisive labels, such as "redneck," "poor white trash," or simply "white trash." These characterizations continue to conceal the role that economic factors have played in creating poverty among even the most privileged group in U.S. society.

Charles C. Bolton

See also: Appalachia; Classism; Deserving/Undeserving Poor; Rural Poverty; Sharecropping

References and Further Reading

Ayers, Edward L. 1992. *The Promise of the New South: Life after Reconstruction*. New York: Oxford University Press.

Bolton, Charles C. 1994. *Poor Whites of the Antebellum South: Tenants and Laborers in Central North Carolina and Northeast Mississippi*. Durham, NC: Duke University Press.

Henwood, Doug. 1997. "Trash-O-Nomics." In *White Trash: Race and Class in America*, ed. Matt Wray and Annalee Newitz. New York: Routledge.

Wray, Matt, and Annalee Newitz, eds. 1997. *White Trash: Race and Class in America*. New York: Routledge.

Zinn, Howard. 1995. *A People's History of the United States, 1492–Present*. New York: HarperCollins.

Poorhouse/Almshouse

"Poorhouse" and "almshouse" are common terms for publicly subsidized institutions that proliferated in the nineteenth- and early-twentieth-century United States, nominally created to provide "indoor relief" for their destitute inmates but also meant to discipline the dependent poor or segregate them from the rest of society. These institutions were variously referred to as "the poorhouse," "the almshouse," "the lodging house," "the poor farm," and "the workhouse." Although poorhouses were present in larger towns in the American colonies since the 1600s, it was not until the nineteenth century that they became widespread; they had largely fallen into disuse by the 1940s. They housed a diverse range of people who had little in common but their poverty. They were temporary homes to infants and children as well as the elderly. The same poorhouse might house men and women; the sick and the able-bodied; the sane and those deemed insane; the deaf, blind, and epileptic; and "idiots." Also likely to be present were criminals and alcoholics, who were sometimes sentenced to labor in the workhouse as punishment for their offense. Although there were exceptions, most such institutions were grim, dirty, dilapidated, overcrowded, and ill funded. Residents were likely to be poorly fed, ill clothed (often in uniforms), and treated with brutality or indifference by staff who were often poorly trained and poorly paid. Sickness and disease, vermin, and lack of heat were common features of the nineteenth-century poorhouse. Overseers and superintendents of the poor, the city or county officials usually responsible for the provision of care for the poor, were also badly paid and little supervised. Some almshouses were paid a flat fee per inmate, thus offering them a financial incentive to keep their spending low.

The rise of the poorhouse as a preferred method of relief was very much a response to the rapid growth in "outdoor"—that is, noninstitutional—relief costs in the early nineteenth century. Based on the recommendations in a report of New York State's secretary of state, J. V. N. Yates, entitled "The Relief and Settlement of the Poor," the state legislature of New York passed the County Poorhouse Act in 1834. The act adopted poor-law reform principles that had recently been legislated in England: It demanded that all the dependent poor be defined as either "impotent" or "able"; it directed the county, not the town or municipality, to assume responsibility for managing and supervising relief programs; and it decreed that no able-bodied person between the ages of eighteen and fifty was to be eligible for any assistance except in the workhouse or the prison. Yates urged every county in the state to erect a poorhouse, and many did just that. Other cities and states followed New York's lead. A poorhouse was often established in the hope that it would offer a cheaper alternative to the growing expense of outdoor relief, in part by discouraging poor people from seeking public aid at all.

Work was often required from relief seekers in exchange for their food and shelter, whether the institution was called a workhouse or not. Some engaged their residents in "productive" work, in laundries, in small-goods manufacture, in woodcutting, or in agricultural production on farms in the hopes of making the poorhouse an economically efficient if not profitable way of providing poor relief. Others created make-work projects, like moving stones from one side of the yard to the other and then back again or forcing inmates to run on treadmills, supposedly as a way of inculcating the values and habits of hard work. Indeed, many such institutions saw enforced work as part of their rehabilitative mission, in the belief that poverty was a sign of moral or personal failure. Some required inmates to attend educational or motivational lectures; others imposed religious indoctrination.

Despite their often harsh and punitive conditions, poorhouses were frequently used strategically by the poor as a resource. Given the seasonal nature of unemployment throughout the period, for example, many men did depend upon the refuge of the poorhouse or the workhouse during the winter when employment was scarce. This in part explains why the number of men in the poorhouse tended to exceed the number of women there. Such use of poorhouses by able-bodied men drew the scorn and outrage of reformers and politicians, who characterized some local poorhouses as "winter resorts" for tramps, the newly emerging class of unemployed men who traveled the country in search of work. Families, too, made use of the poorhouse: In particularly dire times, parents would temporarily institutionalize their children until they could again afford to feed and care for them; married couples entered together when maintaining a home proved impossible. Pregnant and unmarried women shunned by their families or neighbors used the poorhouse as hospital and nursery. Most who used the poorhouse did so for brief periods of time and came and went at will. Perhaps no more than 20 to 25 percent of poorhouse inmates were there for one year or more, while two-fifths probably used the poorhouse for fewer than three weeks (Katz [1986] 1996). The poorhouse was also closely associated with and well used by immigrants. One study by Mary Roberts Smith (1895) of the San Francisco almshouse found that between 1869 and 1894, fewer than one in five inmates was native-born, and 68 percent of all female inmates were widows, reflecting the degree to which women were dependent upon male breadwinners.

The Dickensian poorhouse conditions described above were in some measure intentional: The poorhouse operated explicitly on the "less-eligibility" principle adopted from the English poor law—that is, relief should always be less desirable, or "less eligible," than the benefits that could be obtained from any work. The poorhouse was intended to be the most undesirable form of relief, so that it would provide aid only to those most desperately in need and deter the rest from seeking relief. Although the poorhouse loomed large as a warning and a threat to nineteenth-century Americans, in most locales in most years, more people nonetheless received aid outside an institution than within it.

The poorhouse ultimately declined primarily because, contrary to the hopes of many reformers, the almshouse, the workhouse, and the poorhouse were much more expensive than were the systems of paltry outdoor relief otherwise offered. And even when operated by private agencies, indoor relief institutions were generally operated with public funds. Public indoor relief expenditures more than doubled in New York from 1880 to 1891, and from the mid-1880s to the mid-1890s, they nearly tripled in Pennsylvania, doubled in Michigan, and rose fivefold in Wisconsin (Proceedings of the Conference 1887, Sched. B). The widespread devastation wrought and the need created by the depression of 1893 made dependence upon poorhouses prohibitively expensive, fueling growing calls for new and cheaper forms of aid.

The poorhouse also declined as a result of the growing efforts among reformers to better categorize and segregate the poor from one another and to create more specialized and more targeted forms of relief. Often these efforts were pursued through state boards of charities established after the Civil War to coordinate and regulate the growing number of relief institutions. From 1874 to 1875, about one-sixth of New York almshouse inmates were children; one-sixth were "old and destitute"; one-quarter were blind, deaf, epileptic, feebleminded, or otherwise "disabled"; and one-third were classified as insane. Yet by the mid-1890s, most almshouses were devoid of children, and by 1903, only 7 percent of all the institutionalized "insane" were in an almshouse (Hannon 1997, 425–427; Warner and Coolidge 1908, 196ff., and see esp. ch. 6, "The Almshouse and Its Inmates"). The poorhouse had given way to orphan asylums, foster homes, and juvenile reformatories for children, to insane asylums for the mentally ill (thanks in large measure to the efforts of mental health reformer Dorothea Dix), to separate institutions for men and women, and to new facilities for the blind, mute, deaf, alcoholic, feebleminded, and otherwise disabled. By the early 1900s, the poorhouse had become a refuge for the elderly—an old-age home that also served to remove those considered unproductive workers from the labor market (Katz 1983, [1986] 1996). Able-bodied men, especially immigrants and ethnic minorities, were increasingly denied access; they were found instead among the vast numbers of tramps and vagrants using police lodging houses or incarcerated and working in jails and prisons for violating the spate of new laws that criminalized begging or loitering. That said, even as late as the 1920s, children, the insane, and criminals could be found in significant numbers in some poorhouses.

After decades of decline, in part due to the expansion of other forms of available relief, in the 1970s, the United States witnessed the resurgence of the poorhouse in the form of the homeless shelter. By 2002, the number of children and families living in New York City shelters had reached record high levels: This total poorhouse population had climbed to over 32,000 people per night (Coalition for the Homeless 2002).

Stephen Pimpare

See also: Child-Saving; Crime Policy; Deserving/Undeserving Poor; Homelessness; Orphanages; Poor Laws; Relief; Vagrancy Laws/Settlement Laws/Residency Requirements

References and Further Reading

Coalition for the Homeless. 2002. "State of the Homeless 2002." February. New York: Author.

Hannon, Joan Underhill. 1997. "Shutting Down Welfare: Two Cases from America's Past." *Quarterly Review of Economics and Finance* 37, no. 2 (Summer): 419–438.

Katz, Michael. 1983. *Poverty and Policy in American History*. New York: Academic Press.

———. [1986] 1996. *In the Shadow of the Poorhouse: A Social History of Welfare in America*. Tenth Anniversary ed. New York: Basic Books.

Proceedings of the Conference of [Boards of Public] Charities and *Proceedings of the National Conference*

[of] on Charities and Correction[s]. 1874–1907. Published by the American Social Science Association (1874–1878); A. Williams and Co., Boston (1879–1881); Midland Publishing, Madison (1882); Geo. H. Ellis, Boston (1883–1903); Press of Fred. J. Heer (1904–1906); Press of Wm. B. Burford (1907).

Rothman, David J. 1971. *The Discovery of the Asylum: Social Order and Disorder in the New Republic*. Boston: Little, Brown.

Smith, Mary Roberts. 1895. "Almshouse Women: A Study of Two Hundred and Twenty-Eight Women in the City and County Almshouse of San Francisco." *Publications of the American Statistical Association* 4, no. 31 (September): 219–262.

Warner, Amos G., as revised by Mary Roberts Coolidge. 1908. *American Charities*. New York: Cromwell.

Populism

See Agrarian Movements; New Right; Nineteenth Century; Share Our Wealth

Poverty, Robert Hunter

Robert Hunter, born in 1874 in Indiana, became interested in economic problems after witnessing the effects of the depression of 1893. In his twenties, he worked at Chicago's Hull House, the country's most influential social settlement, and met socialist leaders while traveling in Europe. Both of these experiences influenced his thinking about the poor and economic inequality.

In 1904, Hunter published Poverty, a book that combined vivid descriptions of the dismal working and living conditions of the working poor with an innovative use of statistics. Hunter's main sympathies lay with the working poor of industrialized urban cities; he had little to say about southern poverty. Further, he voiced dismay with the nonworking poor, or "paupers," a group he viewed as morally deficient, idle, violent, and intemperate. In his book, Hunter made a sharp statistical as well as moral distinction between paupers—who were a small minority among poor people—and the vast majority of poor people who were hardworking, respectable men and women who barely survived on their meager incomes. Unlike many nineteenth-century social critics, Hunter viewed low wages and unemployment rather than individual failings as the chief causes of indigence among the working poor, and he advocated for government reform of industry rather than for individual uplift. Better wages, workers' compensation, industrial safety, improvements in public health and sanitation, a ban on child labor, and health benefits with employment were among the reforms Hunter supported.

In the excerpt below, Hunter describes the difficult lives of the urban industrial poor.

Sarah Case

See also: Poverty Line; Poverty Research; Settlement Houses; Social Surveys

In . . . cities and, indeed, everywhere, there are great districts of people who are up before dawn, who wash, dress, and eat breakfast, kiss wives and children, and hurry away to work or seek work. The world rests upon their shoulders; it moves by their muscle; everything would stop if, for any reason, they should decide not to go into the fields and factories and mines. But the world is so organized that they gain enough to live upon only when they work; should they cease, they are in destitution and hunger. The more fortunate of the laborers are but a few weeks from actual distress when the machines are stopped. Upon the skilled masses want is constantly pressing. As soon as employment ceases, suffering stares them in the face. They are the actual producers of wealth, who have no home nor any bit of soil which they may call their own. They are the millions who possess no tools and can work only by permission of another. In the main, they live miserable, they know not why. They work sore, yet gain nothing. They know the meaning of hunger and the dread of want. They love their wives and children. They try to retain their self-respect. They have some ambition. They give to neighbors in need, yet they are themselves the actual children of poverty.

Source: Robert Hunter, *Poverty* (New York: Macmillan, 1904; reprinted New York: Garrett Press, 1970), 4–5.

Poverty, Statistical Measure of

The statistical measure of poverty originated in the late nineteenth century to meet the need of developing social welfare programs to determine who needed aid. Statistical measures of poverty (1) are either direct or (more often) indirect, (2) use a relative or absolute standard, and (3) may vary by family composition, place, or both. Direct measurements of poverty measure consumption, and the subjects' *actual* levels of nutrition, health, and the like are assessed. However, since some people may choose to consume less but are not poor, it is far more common to measure poverty indirectly, by measuring the *capability* of income/resources to meet basic needs/necessities. "Relative" standards, such as "one-half of median income," refer to the income distribution as a whole (Fuchs 1967), whereas "absolute" standards are based on some standard of need. Absolute measures are much more common and can be descriptive (reflecting what the average or some subgroup spends), prescriptive (based on expert-derived standards of nutrition, housing, and so on), or some combination of the two.

Mollie Orshansky (1965) developed the most widely used statistical measure of poverty in the United States in the early 1960s, combining descriptive and prescriptive approaches. Orshansky's measure was adopted as the official federal poverty line (FPL) in the late 1960s as part of the federal government's War on Poverty. By the 1990s, the FPL had been compromised by being "frozen," and alternatives emerged to measure income adequacy or inadequacy more accurately. Key limitations and issues in the statistical measure of poverty include the exclusion of the homeless from poverty counts, treatment of noncash resources, the amount of variation by geography and household composition, equivalence scales, and the inclusion of new household costs and new understandings of "poverty." Although created initially by social reformers who abhorred the lack of necessities among the poor, most measures of poverty do not use actual consumption, except in developing countries where the majority of people live largely outside of a cash economy (making income measures meaningless). Most commonly, these consumption measures record levels of calorie consumption, health statistics, or such population-wide characteristics as infant mortality or adult literacy rates.

In a market economy, however, lack of consumption may reflect choice rather than lack of resources. If measured consumption were the criterion for categorizing subjects, someone who is dieting would be considered "poor" while someone who eats at a soup kitchen would not. Almost all statistical measures of poverty in the United States have been income—that is, indirect—rather than consumption—that is, direct measures—and are absolute rather than relative to the income distribution.

Developing a statistical measure of poverty required an important shift in thinking about the causes of poverty. Until the late nineteenth century, poverty was generally thought to be either an unexplained misfortune from God (as happened to the biblical character of Job) or the result of bad character. As theories of the social and economic roots of poverty emerged, charities and settlement houses, as well as public entities, needed to know who needed aid—especially among children.

Although some of the earliest poverty measures were based on detailed prescriptive or descriptive budgets, the first American investigator to attempt to measure the national extent of poverty, Robert Hunter in *Poverty* (1904), used only two thresholds (one each for the North and the South). Other early- and mid-twentieth-century measures of living standards were more detailed; the best known is the U.S. Department of Labor's Lower Living Standard for a City Worker. This standard was calculated for forty urban areas, for four regions, and as a national average (Johnson, Rogers, and Tan 2001). These family budgets were descriptive and were derived from actual consumption patterns.

The FPL developed by Orshansky is a combination of prescriptive and descriptive. The nutrition-standards-based food budget that underlies the FPL is prescriptive, while the multiplier of three (for all other costs) reflects the fact that families spent about one-third of their income on food, and therefore is descriptive.

Unfortunately, although the FPL is updated for inflation, it "freezes" the statistical measure of poverty in several ways: (1) The food budget has never been updated for changed nutritional standards. (2) Using the multiplier of three based on consumption patterns of the 1950s presumes that food continues to be about one-third of family expenditures. In fact, housing (and recently health care) costs have risen relatively faster than food, and spending on food now averages less than one-fifth of average budgets, even with increased consumption of food outside the home. (3) The FPL does not allow for new costs, particularly child care (since the assumption that mothers would remain in the home to care for children has changed and since increasing numbers of parents require out-of-home care) and taxes (particularly increases in payroll and income taxes). Not surprisingly, the FPL has failed to keep up with costs, so that even the U.S. Census Bureau now states that "the official poverty measure should be interpreted as a statistical yardstick rather than a complete description of what people and families need to live" (Dalaker 2001, 5). Over the four decades since its inception, the FPL has fallen from almost half to about 27 percent of median income.

There are three developments currently under way that seek to address the shortcomings of the FPL. First, public programs have begun to use multiples of the FPL to determine need. For example, applicants with incomes below 130 percent of the FPL would qualify for food stamps; applicants with incomes up to 300 percent of the FPL (depending upon the state) can qualify for child health insurance (State Child Health Insurance Plan [SCHIP] /Medicaid). Second, there have been numerous attempts to modify the FPL, culminating in a congressionally mandated study by the National Academy of Sciences, *Measuring Poverty* (Citro and Michael 1995), which summarized a wide range of research and made recommendations. Some of the recommendations are used in the "experimental" poverty measures published each year with the poverty statistics, but no changes have been made to the FPL. Third, both social scientists and advocates for the poor began to create alternatives, such as Basic Needs Budgets (Renwick and Bergmann 1993), "living wages," family needs budgets, and the Self-Sufficiency Standard (SSS) (Pearce 1996–2003).

The SSS measures how much it costs to live without subsidies and is calculated from the actual costs of housing, food, child care, and so on, using prescriptive numbers when available (such as nutrition standards) and descriptive numbers when not. The SSS does not impose equivalence scales by family size/composition or by geography. It calculates the SSS for seventy (or more) family types (reflecting child age as well as number of children and adults) and by county (or subcounty, data permitting). The budgets are "bare bones" (for example, there is no restaurant or take-out food in the food budget). The SSS has been adopted by some states, cities, and workforce development (training) councils to determine need/eligibility, to counsel clients, and to assess progress toward self-sufficiency.

Finally, there are several limits and issues in statistical measures of poverty. First, the measurement of the extent of poverty uses household samples. Those who are homeless—living in shelters, on the streets, or in nonhousing units (such as garages, cars, or camps)—are not counted, resulting in undercounting the poor by over 800,000 people, about one-fourth of whom are children (Burt et al. 2001). Second, using broader definitions of resources that include near cash (such as food stamps) and the value of noncash benefits (such as Medicaid or housing assistance) would reduce the count of the poor (using the FPL) by one or two percentage points. However, adding the value of certain benefits (such as employer-subsidized health care) as well as of difficult-to-assess resources (such as stock options and the mortgage interest deduction) would increase the incomes mainly of the nonpoor, increasing inequality and relative poverty, if not changing the absolute measures of poverty. Third, counting only after-tax income would decrease income and might increase the count of poor (depending on how indirect taxes, such as property taxes paid by landlords, are counted). Fourth, using a broader definition of needs that included what is necessary to participate in society socially, politically, and economically—what Amartya Sen (1983) calls "capability-functioning" needs—would affect the statistical measure of poverty, creating substantial variations between societies as well as between individuals in the measured level of poverty.

Diana M. Pearce

See also: Income and Wage Inequality; Living-Wage Campaigns; 1940s to Present; *Poverty*; Poverty Line; Poverty Research; "Working Poor"

References and Further Reading

Burt, Martha, Laudan Y. Aron, and Edgar Lee, with Jesse Valente. 2001. *Helping America's Homeless: Emergency Shelter or Affordable Housing?* Washington, DC: Urban Institute Press.

Citro, Constance F., and Robert T. Michael, eds. 1995. *Measuring Poverty: A New Approach*. Washington, DC: National Academy Press.

Dalaker, J. 2001. *Poverty in the United States: 2000*. U.S. Census Bureau Current Population Reports, series P60-214. Washington, DC: GPO.

Fisher, Gordon M. 1993. "From Hunter to Orshansky: An Overview of (Unofficial) Poverty Lines in the United States from 1904 to 1965." Unpublished paper. Available on the U.S. Census Bureau's Poverty Measurement Web site. http://www.census.gov/hhes/poverty/povmeas/papers/hstorsp4.html. Revised August 1997.

Fuchs, Victor. 1967. "Redefining Poverty and Redistributing Income." *Public Interest* 8 (Summer): 88–95.

Glennerster, Howard. 2002. "United States Poverty Studies and Poverty Measurement: The Past Twenty-Five Years." *Social Service Review* 76: 83–107.

Johnson, David S., John M. Rogers, and Lucilla Tan. 2001. "A Century of Family Budgets in the United States." *Monthly Labor Review*, May: 28–45.

Orshansky, Mollie. 1965. "Counting the Poor: Another Look at the Poverty Profile." *Social Security Bulletin* 28, no. 1: 3–29. Reprinted in *Social Security Bulletin* 51, no. 10 (1988): 25–51.

Pearce, Diana, with Jennifer Brooks. 1996–2003. *The Self-Sufficiency Standard for [34 States]*. Seattle: University of Washington. All state reports are available at http://www.sixstrategies.org.

Renwick, Trudi, and Barbara Bergmann. 1993. "A Budget-Based Definition of Poverty: With an Application to Single-Parent Families." *The Journal of Human Resources* 28, no. 1: 1–24.

Ruggles, Patricia. 1990. *Drawing the Line: Alternative Poverty Measures and Their Implications for Public Policy*. Washington, DC: Urban Institute Press.

Sen, Amartya. 1983. "Poor Relatively Speaking." *Oxford Economic Papers* 35, no. 2: 153–169.

Poverty Law

Poverty law encompasses a wide range of issues facing poor people, ranging from welfare to housing to environmental justice to education. In the United States, poverty law originated with efforts in the late nineteenth century to provide legal assistance to new immigrants. Through the early twentieth century, poverty law developed further, sponsored by local bar associations. In the 1960s, the federal government began providing limited funding to poverty lawyers to provide representation to the poor. State governments also often extended funding to poverty lawyers. Significantly, the body of poverty law that has developed through litigation and legislation underscores the disenfranchised status of poor people in society. In many instances—including, for example, cases involving privacy interests, family relationships, and workplace rights—being poor results in fewer legal rights. This is particularly true because poor people's resources so often derive from government rather than from private property, and the government is seldom held responsible to undertake any affirmative steps to protect the rights of citizens.

What Is Poverty Law?

Poverty law is a loosely defined area of law with changeable boundaries. Unlike the terms "bankruptcy law" and "maritime law," which refer to clear sets of statutes, transactions, or activities, the phrase "poverty law" refers to the status of the *individuals* subject to the law. An analog would be "left-handed people's law" or "blonde people's law." Such a body of law could cover the gamut of human behavior—everything affecting left-handed people, for example. But such a subcategory is only meaningful to the extent that it is different from the laws affecting right-handed people or brunettes. In other words, the phrase "poverty law" has a deeper meaning than merely "law affecting poor people." Rather, the assumption embedded in the phrase "poverty law" is that law affecting the poor is different from law affecting the nonpoor.

A threshold question in defining poverty law must be, Who is poor? There is no single answer, since there is a subjective element to determining what is necessary to subsist. Indeed, one factor in defining poverty is the extent of the gap between rich and poor in a society, rather than subsistence needs alone. The federal poverty line provides one definition of poverty, but many localities calculate different "standards of need" or "self-sufficiency" standards based on the particular state's cost of living. Moreover, the federal poverty line, developed in the 1960s based on then-current diets and lifestyles, has been criticized as antiquated and inadequate. Many people with incomes above the federal poverty line consider themselves poor and may be the subjects of poverty law.

There is little serious dispute that individuals receiving federal or state welfare assistance are poor. Further, welfare is unique to the poor; by definition, no wealthy people will be affected by the welfare system's rules. Because of this, welfare law is a core example of poverty law. Other government benefits, such as food stamps, public housing, legal services for the poor, unemployment insurance, and Social Security, are also generally considered within the realm of poverty law. Beyond these government benefits, poverty law might also address issues arising from low-wage work, gentrification of low-income neighborhoods, environmental justice, funding of public education, and special challenges facing low-income families such as child care, child support, and foster care.

The Origins of Poverty Law

The distinct legal treatment of the poor can be traced back at least to the seventeenth century, to the body of English laws known as the Elizabethan Poor Law (1601), which was adapted to the U.S. colonies. Those laws created particular rules applying to poor people that, among other things, established lines of responsibility for providing financial support to the poor, beginning with immediate relatives. In addition, influenced by British precedents, the early American poor laws made clear that American towns and parishes were responsible for their own poor. Many poor laws dealt with the treatment of poor people who attempted to travel across town, county, or state lines. Thus, poor laws varied from locality to locality, with some places providing workhouses for poor transients and others utilizing "outdoor relief" (that is, relief outside of such institutions as poorhouses), a predecessor of public welfare. Although these laws provided guidance as to how the poor should be treated, throughout the eighteenth and nineteenth centuries—and indeed, well into the twentieth century—poor relief was viewed as discretionary charity or largesse. As a legal matter, poor people were not deemed to have any enforceable rights to government support.

The distinct practice of poverty law in the United States began much later, with the creation of local legal aid societies in the late nineteenth century. These societies for the first time treated the poor not merely as passive subjects of special legal rules but as individuals who—like other citizens—might assert affirmative rights to fair treatment. This early version of poverty law was qualitatively different from poverty law today, however, because legal aid societies engaged in this practice saw their role as simply providing access to justice. In their view, giving poor people access to legal assistance in enforcing work contracts or negotiating housing needs would facilitate their integration into the social structures and institutions of society. In short, the legal establishment held to the laissez-faire notion that the law was class-blind.

The first legal aid society was created in New York City in 1876 by Edward Salomon, a former governor of Wisconsin, to assist poor German immigrants needing free legal aid and assistance. In 1889, the society's charter was amended to allow it to render free legal assistance to all. Nevertheless, the society's mission remained the same: to introduce immigrants to democracy by demonstrating the benefits of the rule of law. The society's caseload ran the gamut from real estate transactions to family issues. Many of the cases, however, involved unpaid wages arising from sweatshop employment.

Over the years, legal aid societies increasingly became a special project of the organized bar, augmented by pro bono assistance from private attorneys. By 1920, there were forty-one legal aid societies around the country. In 1923, the National Association of Legal Aid Organizations was formed. Most large cities had a local legal aid society by the end of the 1950s. Throughout this time, legal aid societies continued to see their role as apolitical: simply to provide advice and representation to the poor. Rather than aggressively pursuing their clients' rights in order to highlight the need for law reform or to achieve political ends to benefit their clients, most legal aid lawyers settled their clients' cases. From 1876 to 1965, legal aid society lawyers never appealed a case to the U.S. Supreme Court.

The practice of poverty law changed dramatically in the 1960s, when the civil rights movement, in combination with the War on Poverty, stimulated poverty rights organizing and encouraged lawyers to be much more aggressive on behalf of their low-income clients. At the same time, beginning in 1965, federal funding of legal services for the poor created a permanent cadre of lawyers dedicated to the practice of poverty law. Between 1963 and 1971, the number of lawyers for poor people rose by 650 percent to more than 2,500 nationwide. In contrast to earlier decades, dozens of poverty law cases were appealed to the U.S. Supreme Court. As a result, poverty law for the first time became an accepted area of legal study. Until 1965, no course on poverty law had ever been taught at an American law school. By 1967, poverty law courses were offered at thirty-six law schools.

The practice of poverty law in the 1960s bore scant resemblance to the poverty law practiced by legal aid society lawyers decades earlier. In an influential law review article, Edgar Cahn and Jean Cahn defined the role of a legal services lawyer as giving voice to a "civilian perspective" on the War on Poverty (Cahn and Cahn 1964, 1317). Another leader of the early legal services movement, Edward Sparer, argued that achieving social change should be the highest priority for poverty law offices.

King v. Smith, 392 U.S. 309 (1968)

Mr. Chief Justice Warren delivered the opinion of the Court.

. . . At issue is the validity of Alabama's so-called "substitute father" regulation, which denies AFDC payments to the children of a mother who "cohabits" in or outside her home with any single or married able-bodied man. . . .

I

. . . Under the Alabama regulation, an "able-bodied man, married or single, is considered a substitute father of all [392 U.S. 314] the children of the applicant . . . mother" in three different situations: (1) if "he lives in the home with the child's natural or adoptive mother for the purpose of cohabitation"; or (2) if "he visits [the home] frequently for the purpose of cohabiting with the child's natural or adoptive mother"; or (3) if "he does not frequent the home, but cohabits with the child's natural or adoptive mother elsewhere." . . . Whether the substitute father is actually the father of the children is irrelevant. It is also irrelevant whether he is legally obligated to support the children, and whether he does, in fact, contribute to their support. . . .

Between June, 1964, when Alabama's substitute father regulation became effective, and January, 1967, the total number of AFDC recipients in the State declined by about 20,000 persons, and the number of children recipients by about 16,000, or 22%. As applied in this case, the regulation has caused the termination of all AFDC payments to the appellees, Mrs. Sylvester Smith and her four minor children. . . .

Mr. Williams, the alleged "substitute father" of Mrs. Smith's children . . . is not legally obligated, under Alabama law, to support any of Mrs. Smith's [392 U.S. 316] children. . . .

II

The AFDC program is based on a scheme of cooperative federalism. . . . It is financed largely by the Federal Government, on a matching fund basis, and is administered by the States. . . .

One of the statutory requirements is that "aid to families with dependent children . . . shall be furnished with reasonable promptness to all eligible individuals. . . ." . . .

. . . There is no question that States have considerable latitude in allocating their AFDC resources, since each State is free to set its own standard of need . . . and to determine the level of benefits by the [392 U.S. 319] amount of funds it devotes to the program. . . . The appellees here, however, meet Alabama's need requirements; their alleged substitute father makes no contribution to their support, and they have been denied assistance solely on the basis of the substitute father regulation. . . .

Alabama's argument based on its interests in discouraging immorality and illegitimacy would have been quite relevant at one time in the history of the AFDC program. However, subsequent developments clearly establish that these state interests are

Underlying this change in the approach to poverty law practice was the recognition that poor people needed more than simple access to courts and lawyers and that poverty law should address the systemic differential treatment of the poor. The issue of unequal treatment of the poor was squarely addressed in an important article by Jacobus ten Broek, a law professor at the University of California, Berkeley. Writing in the *Stanford Law Review* in 1965, ten Broek argued that welfare laws create dual systems of family law in the United States, one set of laws for the indigent and another for everyone else. For example, under the welfare regime at the time, a man found to be cohabiting with a woman on welfare was deemed to be financially responsible for the woman's children, even if he was simply a boyfriend and the children were

not presently legitimate justifications for AFDC disqualification. Insofar as this or any similar regulation is based on the State's asserted interest in discouraging illicit sexual behavior and illegitimacy, it plainly conflicts with federal law and policy. . . .

In sum, Congress has determined that immorality and illegitimacy should be dealt with through rehabilitative measures, rather than measures that punish dependent children, and that protection of such children is the paramount goal of AFDC. . . .

III

The AFDC program was designed to meet a need unmet by programs providing employment for breadwinners. It was designed to protect . . . children in families without a "breadwinner," "wage earner," or "father." . . . To describe the sort of breadwinner that it had in mind, Congress employed the word [392 U.S. 329] "parent." . . . A child would be eligible for assistance if his parent was deceased, incapacitated or continually absent. . . .

It is clear . . . that Congress expected "breadwinners" who secured employment would support their children. This congressional expectation is most reasonably explained on the basis that the kind of breadwinner Congress had in mind was one who was legally obligated to support his children. We think it beyond reason to believe that Congress would have considered that providing employment for the paramour of a deserted mother would benefit the mother's children whom he was not obligated to support.

By a parity of reasoning, we think that Congress must have intended that the children in such a situation remain eligible for AFDC assistance notwithstanding their mother's impropriety. AFDC was intended to provide economic security for children whom Congress could not reasonably expect would be provided for by simply securing [392 U.S. 330] employment for family breadwinners. . . .

IV

. . . In denying AFDC assistance to appellees on the basis of this invalid regulation, Alabama has breached its federally imposed obligation to furnish "aid to families with dependent children . . . with reasonable promptness to all eligible individuals. . . ." . . . Our conclusion makes unnecessary consideration of appellees' equal protection claim, upon which we intimate no views.

. . . [N]o legitimate interest of the State of Alabama is defeated [392 U.S. 334] by the decision we announce today. The State's interest in discouraging illicit sexual behavior and illegitimacy may be protected by other means, subject to constitutional limitations, including state participation in AFDC rehabilitative programs. Its interest in economically allocating its limited AFDC resources may be protected by its undisputed power to set the level of benefits and the standard of need, and by its taking into account in determining whether a child is needy all actual and regular contributions to his support.

. . . We hold today only that Congress has made at least this one determination: that destitute children who are legally fatherless cannot be flatly denied federally funded assistance on the transparent fiction that they have a substitute father.

Affirmed.

from a prior relationship. Under the generally applicable family law, however, a mere boyfriend would not be deemed financially responsible for supporting his paramour's family. Ten Broek argued that this dual system violated constitutional equal protection principles.

The ultimate goals of poverty lawyers in this era were to increase resources available to poor people and to facilitate poor people's organizing. And this newly assertive practice of poverty law yielded a spate of significant cases, many of which reached the U.S. Supreme Court. Successful cases whittled away at the legal inequalities facing the poor. Even the unsuccessful cases nevertheless made a difference by bringing the differential treatment of the poor into sharp focus.

Wyman v. James (400 U.S. 309 [1971]) falls into the latter category. New York City welfare

Shapiro, Commissioner of Welfare of Connecticut, v. Thompson, *394 U.S. 618 (1969)*

Mr. Justice Brennan delivered the opinion of the Court.

II

There is no dispute that the effect of the waiting-period requirement in each case is to create two classes of needy resident families indistinguishable from each other except that one is composed of residents who have resided a year or more, and the second of residents who have resided less than a year, in the jurisdiction. On the basis of this sole difference the first class is granted and the second class is denied welfare aid upon which may depend the ability of the families to obtain the very means to subsist—food, shelter, and other necessities of life. . . .

III

Primarily, appellants justify the waiting-period requirement as a protective device to preserve the fiscal integrity of state public assistance programs. . . . This Court long ago recognized that the nature of our Federal Union and our constitutional concepts of personal liberty unite to require that all citizens be free to travel throughout the length and breadth of our land uninhibited by statutes, rules, or regulations which unreasonably burden or restrict this movement. . . .

Thus, the purpose of deterring the in-migration of indigents cannot serve as justification for the classification created by the one-year waiting period, since that purpose is constitutionally impermissible. If a law has "no other purpose . . . than to chill the assertion of constitutional rights by penalizing those who choose to exercise them, then it [is] patently unconstitutional." *United States v. Jackson*, 390 U.S. 570, 581 (1968).

Alternatively, appellants argue that even if it is impermissible for a State to attempt to deter the entry of all indigents, the challenged classification may be justified as a permissible state attempt to discourage those indigents who would enter the State solely to obtain larger benefits. We observe first that none of the statutes before us is tailored to serve that objective. . . .

More fundamentally, a State may no more try to fence out those indigents who seek higher welfare benefits than it may try to fence out indigents generally.

Implicit in any such distinction is the notion that indigents who enter a State with the hope of securing higher welfare benefits are somehow less deserving than indigents who do not take this consideration into account. But we do not perceive why a mother who is seeking to make a new life for herself and her children should be regarded as less deserving because she considers, among others factors, the level of a State's public assistance. Surely such a mother is no less deserving than a mother who moves into a particular State in order to take advantage of its better educational facilities.

Appellants argue further that the challenged classification may be sustained as an attempt to distinguish between new and old residents on the basis of the contribution they have made to the community through the payment of taxes.

. . . Appellants' reasoning would logically permit the State to bar new residents from schools, parks,

recipient Barbara James refused to allow a caseworker into her home to conduct a mandatory inspection. The mandatory inspection rule permitted inspections without a warrant and required such inspections as a prerequisite of receiving welfare benefits. In upholding the law, Justice Harry A. Blackmun wrote for the Supreme Court that no warrant was necessary because welfare benefits were merely charitable contributions from the state. According to the

and libraries or deprive them of police and fire protection. Indeed it would permit the State to apportion all benefits and services according to the past tax contributions of its citizens. The Equal Protection Clause prohibits such an apportionment of state services. . . .

IV

Appellants next advance as justification certain administrative and related governmental objectives allegedly served by the waiting-period requirement. They argue that the requirement (1) facilitates the planning of the welfare budget; (2) provides an objective test of residency; (3) minimizes the opportunity for recipients fraudulently to receive payments from more than one jurisdiction; and (4) encourages early entry of new residents into the labor force.

. . . [I]n moving from State to State or to the District of Columbia appellees were exercising a constitutional right, and any classification which serves to penalize the exercise of that right, unless shown to be necessary to promote a compelling governmental interest, is unconstitutional. . . .

The argument that the waiting-period requirement facilitates budget predictability is wholly unfounded. . . .

The argument that the waiting period serves as an administratively efficient rule of thumb for determining residency similarly will not withstand scrutiny. . . .

Similarly, there is no need for a State to use the one-year waiting period as a safeguard against fraudulent receipt of benefits; for less drastic means are available, and are employed, to minimize that hazard. . . .

We conclude therefore that appellants in these cases do not use and have no need to use the one-year requirement for the governmental purposes suggested. Thus, even under traditional equal protection tests a classification of welfare applicants according to whether they have lived in the State for one year would seem irrational and unconstitutional. But, of course, the traditional criteria do not apply in these cases. Since the classification here touches on the fundamental right of interstate movement, its constitutionality must be judged by the stricter standard of whether it promotes a compelling state interest. Under this standard, the waiting-period requirement clearly violates the Equal Protection Clause. . . .

V

Connecticut and Pennsylvania argue, however, that the constitutional challenge to the waiting-period requirements must fail because Congress expressly approved the imposition of the requirement by the States as part of the jointly funded AFDC program. . . .

. . . Congress enacted the directive to curb hardships resulting from lengthy residence requirements. Rather than constituting an approval or a prescription of the requirement in state plans, the directive was the means chosen by Congress to deny federal funding to any State which persisted in stipulating excessive residence requirements as a condition of the payment of benefits. . . .

Finally, even if it could be argued that the constitutionality of § 402 (b) is somehow at issue here, it follows from what we have said that the provision, insofar as it permits the one-year waiting-period requirement, would be unconstitutional. Congress may not authorize the States to violate the Equal Protection Clause. . . .

Accordingly, the judgments in Nos. 9, 33, and 34 are Affirmed.

Court, the state had to be permitted to monitor how its charitable funds were being used. If welfare recipients objected to such inspections on privacy grounds, Justice Blackmun concluded, they could simply forego support.

In contrast, *Goldberg v. Kelly* (397 U.S. 254 [1970]) expanded the rights of the poor. In that case, John Kelly argued that he should not be denied welfare benefits through an exercise of his caseworker's discretion absent an opportunity for

Goldberg v. Kelly, 397 U.S. 254 (1970)

Mr. Justice Brennan delivered the opinion of the Court.

The question for decision is whether a State that terminates public assistance payments to a particular recipient without affording him the opportunity for an evidentiary hearing prior to termination denies the recipient procedural due process in violation of the Due Process Clause of the Fourteenth Amendment.

I

. . .

[Welfare] benefits are a matter of statutory entitlement for persons qualified to receive them. Their termination involves state action that adjudicates important rights. The constitutional challenge cannot be answered by an argument that public assistance benefits are "a 'privilege,' and not a 'right.'" . . . The extent to which procedural due process [397 U.S. 263] must be afforded the recipient is influenced by the extent to which he may be "condemned to suffer grievous loss," . . . and depends upon whether the recipient's interest in avoiding that loss outweighs the governmental interest in summary adjudication. . . .

[W]hen welfare is discontinued, only a pre-termination evidentiary hearing provides the recipient with procedural due process. . . . For qualified recipients, welfare provides the means to obtain essential food, clothing, housing, and medical care. . . . Thus, the crucial factor in this context . . . is that termination of aid pending resolution of a controversy over eligibility may deprive an eligible recipient of the very means by which to live while he waits. Since he lacks independent resources, his situation becomes immediately desperate. His need to concentrate upon finding the means for daily subsistence, in turn, adversely affects his ability to seek redress from the welfare bureaucracy.

Moreover, important governmental interests are promoted by affording recipients a pre-termination evidentiary hearing. From its founding, the Nation's basic [397 U.S. 265] commitment has been to foster the dignity and wellbeing of all persons within its borders. We have come to recognize that forces not within the control of the poor contribute to their poverty. . . . Welfare, by meeting the basic demands of subsistence, can help bring within the reach of the poor the same opportunities that are available to others to participate meaningfully in the life of the community. At the same time, welfare guards against the societal malaise that may flow from a widespread sense of unjustified frustration and insecurity. Public assistance, then, is not mere charity, but a means to "promote the general Welfare, and secure the Blessings of Liberty to ourselves and our Posterity." The same governmental interests that counsel the provision of welfare, counsel as well its uninterrupted provision to those eligible to receive it; pre-termination evidentiary hearings are indispensable to that end.

Appellant . . . argues that the[re] are . . . countervailing governmental interests in conserving fiscal and administrative resources. These interests, the argument goes, justify the delay of any evidentiary hearing until after discontinuance of the grants. Summary adjudication protects the public fisc by

a hearing. The costs to a recipient of having subsistence benefits cut off were simply too great. The Supreme Court, in an opinion by Justice William J. Brennan Jr., upheld his claim, ruling that welfare recipients were entitled to pretermination hearings before losing their subsistence welfare benefits. This is one area where welfare recipients may be entitled to greater rights than the nonpoor, since the Court has limited pretermination hearings to instances involving subsistence benefits.

Outside of the welfare context, cases chal-

stopping payments promptly upon discovery of reason to believe that a recipient is no longer eligible. Since most terminations are accepted without challenge, summary adjudication also conserves both the fisc and administrative time and energy by reducing the number of evidentiary hearings actually held. [397 U.S. 266]

We agree with the District Court, however, that these governmental interests are not overriding in the welfare context. . . . [T]he interest of the eligible recipient in uninterrupted receipt of public assistance, coupled with the State's interest that his payments not be erroneously terminated, clearly outweighs the State's competing concern to prevent any increase in its fiscal and administrative burdens. . . .

II

We also agree with the District Court, however, that the pre-termination hearing need not take the form of a judicial or quasi-judicial trial. . . . We recognize, too, that both welfare authorities and recipients have an interest in relatively speedy resolution of questions of eligibility, that they are used to dealing with one another informally, and that some welfare departments have very burdensome caseloads. These considerations justify the limitation of the pre-termination hearing to minimum procedural safeguards, adapted to the particular characteristics of welfare recipients, and to the limited nature of the controversies to be resolved. . . .

In the present context, these principles require that a recipient have timely and adequate notice detailing the reasons for a [397 U.S. 268] proposed termination, and an effective opportunity to defend by confronting any adverse witnesses and by presenting his own arguments and evidence orally. . . .

The city's procedures presently do not permit recipients to appear personally, with or without counsel, before the official who finally determines continued eligibility. Thus, a recipient is not permitted to present evidence to that official orally, or to confront or cross-examine adverse witnesses. These omissions are fatal to the constitutional adequacy of the procedures. . . .

In almost every setting where important decisions turn on questions of fact, due process requires an opportunity to confront and cross-examine adverse witnesses. . . . Welfare recipients must therefore be given an opportunity to confront and cross-examine the witnesses relied on by the department. . . .

We do not say that counsel must be provided at the pre-termination hearing, but only that the recipient must be allowed to retain an attorney if he so desires. Counsel can help delineate the issues, present the factual contentions in an orderly manner, conduct cross-examination, and generally safeguard the [397 U.S. 271] interests of the recipient. . . .

Finally, the decisionmaker's conclusion as to a recipient's eligibility must rest solely on the legal rules and evidence adduced at the hearing. . . . And, of course, an impartial decisionmaker is essential. . . . We agree with the District Court that prior involvement in some aspects of a case will not necessarily bar a welfare official from acting as a decisionmaker. He should not, however, have participated in making the determination under review.

Affirmed.

lenging the right to Medicaid funding for abortion have raised the constitutional equal protection rights of poor women. In *Harris v. McRae* (448 U.S. 297 [1980]), for example, the Supreme Court examined whether the federal government could deny federal reimbursement for medically necessary abortions while extending Medicaid coverage for other medically necessary procedures. The Supreme Court ruled that the scheme did not deny equal protection rights to poor women since there was no affirmative government obligation to provide abortions. Poor

Dandridge v. Williams, 397 U.S. 471 (1970)

Mr. Justice Stewart delivered the opinion of the Court.

The regulation here in issue imposes upon the grant that any single family may receive an upper limit of $250 per month in certain counties and Baltimore City, and of $240 per month elsewhere in the State. The appellees all [397 U.S. 475] have large families, so that their standards of need, as computed by the State, substantially exceed the maximum grants that they actually receive under the regulation. The appellees urged in the District Court that the maximum grant limitation operates to discriminate against them merely because of the size of their families, in violation of the Equal Protection Clause of the Fourteenth Amendment. They claimed further that the regulation is incompatible with the purpose of the Social Security Act of 1935, as well as in conflict with its explicit provisions. . . .

I

. . . Although the appellees argue that the younger and more recently arrived children in such families are totally deprived of aid, a more realistic view is that the lot of the entire family is diminished because of the presence of additional children without any increase in payments. . . . Whether this per capita diminution is compatible with the statute is the question here. For the reasons that follow, we have concluded that the Maryland regulation is permissible under the federal law. . . .

Congress was itself cognizant of the limitations on state resources from the very outset of the federal welfare program. The first section of the Act, 42 U.S.C. § 601 (1964 ed., Supp. IV), provides that the Act is

> For the purpose of encouraging the care of dependent children in their own homes or in the homes of relatives by enabling each State to furnish financial assistance and rehabilitation and other services, as far as practicable under the conditions in such State, to needy dependent children and the parents or relatives with whom they are living . . . (Emphasis added.)

Thus, the starting point of the statutory analysis must be a recognition that the federal law gives each State great latitude in dispensing its available funds. . . .

Given Maryland's finite resources, its choice is either to support some families adequately and others less adequately or not to give sufficient support to any family. We see nothing in the federal statute that forbids a State to balance the stresses that uniform insufficiency of payments would impose on all families against the greater ability of large fami-

women who could not afford abortions were therefore in the same position with or without the Medicaid program. According to the Court, the constitutional freedom to choose an abortion does not require that government extend the resources to choose one—a ruling that preserves the stark inequality between women who can afford a legal abortion and poor women who cannot.

A major goal of poverty lawyers in the 1960s and 1970s was to establish poverty as a suspect class under the Constitution's equal protection clause. According poverty such a status would mean that classifications based on poverty would be permissible only if they were narrowly tailored to achieve an important government interest. Had this goal been achieved, it would have formed the basis for using the equal protection clause to challenge the dual treatment under family law noted by ten Broek as well as differential treatment in other areas where poor people were treated unequally. No court ever accepted this formulation. Instead, most courts have found that the government has broad dis-

lies—because of the inherent economics of scale—to accommodate their needs to diminished per capita payments. The strong policy of the statute in favor of preserving family units does not prevent a State from sustaining as many families as it can, and providing the largest families somewhat less than their ascertained per capita standard of need. Nor does the maximum grant system necessitate the dissolution of family bonds. For even if a parent should be inclined to increase his per capita family income by sending a child away, the federal law requires that the child, to be eligible for AFDC payments, must live with one of several enumerated relatives. The kinship tie may be attenuated, but it cannot be destroyed. . . .

Finally, Congress itself has acknowledged a full awareness of state maximum grant limitations. In the Amendments of 1967, Congress added to § 402(a) a subsection, 23 . . . [a] specific congressional recognition of the state maximum grant provisions. . . . The structure of specific maximums Congress left to the States, and the validity of any such structure must meet constitutional tests. However, the above amendment does make clear that Congress fully recognized that the Act permits maximum grant regulations.

II

Although a State may adopt a maximum grant system in allocating its funds available for AFDC payments without violating the Act, it may not, of course, impose a regime of invidious discrimination in violation of the Equal Protection Clause of the Fourteenth Amendment. . . .

In the area of economics and social welfare, a State does not violate the Equal Protection Clause merely because the classifications made by its laws are imperfect. . . .

Under this long-established meaning of the Equal Protection Clause, it is clear that the Maryland maximum grant regulation is constitutionally valid. . . . It is enough that a solid foundation for the regulation can be found in the State's legitimate interest in encouraging employment and in avoiding discrimination between welfare families and the families of the working poor. By combining a limit on the recipient's grant with permission to retain money earned, without reduction in the amount of the grant, Maryland provides an incentive to seek gainful employment. . . .

. . . [T]he intractable economic, social, and even philosophical problems presented by public welfare assistance programs are not the business of this Court. The Constitution may impose certain procedural safeguards upon systems of welfare administration. . . . But the Constitution does not empower this Court to second-guess state officials charged with the difficult responsibility of allocating limited public welfare funds among the myriad of potential recipients. . . .

The judgment is reversed.

cretion to apportion government benefits and that poverty classifications are permissible unless they are irrational.

Poverty Law Today

In the late twentieth century, the practice of poverty law changed again to move beyond litigation concerning constitutional equal protection and due process rights to innovative group litigation strategies, community-based representation, and client organizing and empowerment. At the same time, the substantive areas addressed by poverty law expand as lawyers continue to find new tools to wield on behalf of their clients.

One relatively new area of poverty law practice combines poverty law with environmental law to address environmental justice, that is, considerations of the extent to which the poor are disproportionately disadvantaged by unsafe or undesirable environmental practices. For example, environmental justice claims have been made on behalf of low-income, predominately minority communities challenging the placement of hazardous-waste dumps. Bringing these cases typically involves more than litigation but may not involve litigation at all. Identifying the impacts of the environmental issue in the community, organizing the community to raise its concerns, and working within the political process to address the issue have all been effective strategies. To the extent that litigation has resulted, the claims are rarely constitutional; instead, they involve violations of environmental or civil rights laws.

Challenges to inequities in public education funding are also representative of contemporary poverty law. Such challenges may be brought under state constitutional provisions guaranteeing education or equal protection as well as state statutory protections. Plaintiffs are typically inner-city schoolchildren, often members of a minority, who have allegedly been denied the right to an adequate education because funding formulas allow inner-city schools to languish. In bringing these cases, lawyers seek broad court-imposed remedies requiring states to redesign funding for public education to bring inner-city schools into line with suburban schools. Many of these suits have been successful, either as a result of a court order or through a settlement.

Poverty lawyers also increasingly utilize client empowerment strategies. For example, a legal group working with low-wage workers might provide literacy and job-skills classes to their clients while at the same time training them to advocate on their own behalf. If the group has identified particular legal issues—such as the failure to pay minimum wage—a range of strategies could be considered, of which litigation would only be one part. Other approaches might involve community pressure, publicity, or political tactics, perhaps in conjunction with a legal complaint to the National Labor Relations Board.

At first blush, it may appear that by emphasizing client empowerment, poverty law has come full circle, that, as in the days of legal aid societies, poverty lawyers are once again operating on a case-by-case basis to resolve the legal issues facing their clients. However, the new poverty lawyers—"rebellious lawyers," according to one commentator—are not satisfied by simply providing access to justice (Lopez 1992). Rather, they aim to transform a political system that supports class-based inequality by involving clients in problem solving and by empowering the poor beyond the specific issues at hand.

Finally, more traditional poverty law approaches utilizing class-action litigation have not been abandoned. For instance, after the enactment of welfare reform in 1996, states began reinstating restrictions on welfare recipients' travel reminiscent of those of the Elizabethan Poor Law. In particular, a number of states enacted laws to pay welfare benefits to recipients only at the level of the state from which they came, provided that level was lower. In 1999, the California version of this law was successfully challenged before the U.S. Supreme Court in *Saenz v. Roe* (526 U.S. 489). The Court found that the restrictions violated the federal constitutional right to travel. According to the Court, the ability to travel freely or to relocate across state lines is essential to the operation of our federal system.

The Future of Poverty Law

Poverty law has been controversial from the beginning, but it has been especially so since the inception of government funding. There is a long history of efforts by state and federal government to limit the scope of poverty law practice and therefore the access of poor people to lawyers, particularly because many legal grievances raised by the poor are leveled against the government. For example, in the 1960s, efforts were made to brand legal services lawyers as communists, thereby providing a basis for denying funding for their efforts. More recently, Congress imposed a number of restrictions on federally funded legal services lawyers. Among other things, they are barred from bringing class actions on behalf of clients, and they cannot engage in legislative advocacy on their clients' behalf. As in *Wyman v. James,* the rationale offered by Congress is that funding for legal services is charity and the government can therefore limit the funding as it chooses. Under this view, the government is under no obligation to fund lawyers to sue the government itself and could limit legal services lawyers to suits against private actors. Although this rationale has not been directly challenged, one of the federal restrictions—a ban on legal services' involvement in litigation challenging welfare reform—was struck down in 2001 by the U.S. Supreme Court on the ground that it violated lawyers' First Amendment rights.

Opponents of legal services for the poor have also targeted state methods of funding poverty lawyers, including the Interest on Lawyers Trust Accounts (IOLTA) programs. These programs, currently operating in every state, transfer interest accruing from pooled trust accounts into funds for legal services to the poor. Conservative legal groups have challenged IOLTA programs as unconstitutional takings, jeopardizing millions of dollars of funding for legal services nationwide.

Given the instability of government funding, poverty lawyers have long looked to other sources of support. Many foundations support poverty law initiatives. In addition, pro bono programs operated by bar associations generally focus on providing legal services for the poor in a wide range of areas. Some law schools mandate that students engage in pro bono work prior to graduation, and a few states monitor attorneys' pro bono contributions as part of their attorney licensing procedures.

These efforts certainly contribute to filling the needs of the poor for legal services in a range of areas. However, the efforts are limited. A significant environmental justice case, which may go on for years, will be beyond the scope of most pro bono efforts. Further, lawyers whose primary practice is in areas other than poverty law cannot be expected to develop an overall picture of poverty law that would enable them to operate strategically in advising clients or developing cases.

Beyond funding issues, the field of poverty law also faces substantive challenges in the twenty-first century. In particular, defining the affirmative role of government to address the needs of the poor continues to be a critical issue. In general, the federal courts have taken the position that constitutional protections constitute limits on government rather than affirmative obligations. For example, the government cannot deny welfare benefits without due process, but it is not required to provide the benefits in the first place. There are some exceptions to this doctrine—for instance, when the government has established a special relationship that creates a duty to act affirmatively. Such affirmative duties have been occasionally found in prisons or other settings where the government has undertaken to exercise exclusive control over an individual's circumstances.

Further, some state constitutions also incorporate affirmative obligations. Perhaps the signal example in the poverty law area is Article XVII of the New York State Constitution, which creates a state obligation to provide "aid and care to the needy." This provision has been interpreted to require that New York extend welfare benefits beyond the strict five-year time limits imposed on federal welfare benefits under the Personal Responsibility and Work Opportunities Reconciliation Act of 1996. In addition, the provision has been used as a basis for expanding housing support for low-income people in the state.

Increasingly, poverty rights activists seeking to establish affirmative governmental obligations have also turned to the provisions of international treaties and conventions. The International Covenant on Economic, Social, and Cultural Rights (ICESC) provides affirmative rights to basic subsistence support, housing,

Saenz v. Roe, *526 U.S. 489 (1999)*

Justice Stevens delivered the opinion of the Court.

I

. . . In 1992, in order to make a relatively modest reduction in its vast welfare budget, the California Legislature enacted § 11450.03 of the state Welfare and Institutions Code. That section sought to change the California AFDC program by limiting new residents, for the first year they live in California, to the benefits they would have received in the State of their prior residence. . . .

. . . [In 1996] PRWORA replaced the AFDC program with TANF. The new statute expressly authorizes any State that receives a block grant under TANF to "apply to a family the rules (including benefit amounts) of the [TANF] program . . . of another State if the family has moved to the State from the other State and has resided in the State for less than 12 months." . . .

II

On April 1, 1997, the two respondents filed this action in the Eastern District of California . . . challenging the constitutionality of PRWORA's approval of the durational residency requirement. . . .

III

The word "travel" is not found in the text of the Constitution. Yet the "constitutional right to travel from one State to another" is firmly embedded in our jurisprudence. . . .

In Shapiro, we reviewed the constitutionality of three statutory provisions that denied welfare assistance to residents . . . who had resided within those respective jurisdictions less than one year immediately preceding their applications for assistance. . . . [W]e began by noting that the Court had long "recognized that the nature of our Federal Union and our constitutional concepts of personal liberty unite to require that all citizens be free to travel throughout the length and breadth of our land uninhibited by statutes, rules, or regulations which unreasonably burden or restrict this movement." We squarely held that it was "constitutionally impermissible" for a State to enact durational residency requirements for the purpose of inhibiting the migration by needy persons into the State. . . . We further held that a classification that had the effect of imposing a penalty on the exercise of the right to travel violated the Equal Protection Clause "unless shown to be necessary to promote a compelling governmental interest," and that no such showing had been made. . . .

IV

The "right to travel" discussed in our cases embraces at least three different components. It protects the right of a citizen of one State to enter and to leave another State, the right to be treated as a welcome visitor rather than an unfriendly alien when temporarily present in the second State, and, for those travelers who elect to become permanent residents, the right to be treated like other citizens of that State. . . .

. . . What is at issue in this case, then, is th[e] third aspect of the right to travel—the right of the newly arrived citizen to the same privileges and immunities enjoyed by other citizens of the same State. That right is protected not only by the new arrival's status as a state citizen, but also by her status as a citizen of the United States. . . . That additional source of protection is plainly identified in the opening words of the Fourteenth Amendment:

"All persons born or naturalized in the United States, and subject to the jurisdiction thereof, are citizens of the United States and of the State wherein they reside. No State shall make or enforce any law which shall abridge the privileges or immunities of citizens of the United States; . . ." U.S. Const., Amdt. 14, § 1. . . .

. . . [I]t has always been common ground that this Clause protects the third component of the right to travel. Writing for the majority in the Slaughter-House Cases, Justice Miller explained that one of the privileges conferred by this Clause "is that a citizen of the United States can, of his own volition, become a citizen of any State of the Union by a bona fide residence therein, with the same rights as other citizens of that State." Id., at 80. . . .

That newly arrived citizens "have two political capacities, one state and one federal," adds special force to their claim that they have the same rights as others who share their citizenship. . . . Neither mere rationality nor some intermediate standard of review should be used to judge the constitutionality of a state rule that discriminates against some of its citizens because they have been domiciled in the State for less than a year. The appropriate standard may be more categorical than that articulated in *Shapiro*, see supra, at 8–9, but it is surely no less strict.

V

. . . [S]ince the right to travel embraces the citizen's right to be treated equally in her new State of residence, the discriminatory classification is itself a penalty.

It is undisputed that respondents and the members of the class that they represent are citizens of California and that their need for welfare benefits is unrelated to the length of time that they have resided in California. . . .

The classifications challenged in this case—and there are many—are defined entirely by (a) the period of residency in California and (b) the location of the prior residences of the disfavored class members. . . .

These classifications may not be justified by a purpose to deter welfare applicants from migrating to California for three reasons. First, although it is reasonable to assume that some persons may be motivated to move for the purpose of obtaining higher benefits, the empirical evidence reviewed by the District Judge, which takes into account the high cost of living in California, indicates that the number of such persons is quite small—surely not large enough to justify a burden on those who had no such motive. . . . Second, California has represented to the Court that the legislation was not enacted for any such reason. . . . Third, even if it were, as we squarely held in *Shapiro v. Thompson*, such a purpose would be unequivocally impermissible.

. . . California has . . . advanced an entirely fiscal justification for its multitiered scheme. . . . The question is not whether such saving is a legitimate purpose but whether the State may accomplish that end by the discriminatory means it has chosen. . . . [T]he Citizenship Clause of the Fourteenth Amendment expressly equates citizenship with residence. . . . It is equally clear that the Clause does not tolerate a hierarchy of 45 subclasses of similarly situated citizens based on the location of their prior residence. . . . Thus § 11450.03 is doubly vulnerable: Neither the duration of respondents' California residence, nor the identity of their prior States of residence, has any relevance to their need for benefits. Nor do those factors bear any relationship to the State's interest in making an equitable allocation of the funds to be distributed among its needy citizens. As in *Shapiro*, we reject any contributory rationale for the denial of benefits to new residents. . . .

. . . In short, the State's legitimate interest in saving money provides no justification for its decision to discriminate among equally eligible citizens.

VI

The question that remains is whether congressional approval of durational residency requirements in the 1996 amendment to the Social Security Act somehow resuscitates the constitutionality of § 11450.03. That question is readily answered, for we have consistently held that Congress may not authorize the States to violate the Fourteenth Amendment. . . . Moreover, the protection afforded to the citizen by the Citizenship Clause of that Amendment is a limitation on the powers of the National Government as well as the States. . . .

. . . Citizens of the United States, whether rich or poor, have the right to choose to be citizens "of the State wherein they reside." U.S. Const., Amdt. 14, § 1. The States, however, do not have any right to select their citizens. . . . The Fourteenth Amendment, like the Constitution itself, was, as Justice Cardozo put it, "framed upon the theory that the peoples of the several states must sink or swim together, and that in the long run prosperity and salvation are in union and not division." . . .

The judgment of the Court of Appeals is affirmed.

food, fair wages, and other necessities. The International Covenant on Civil and Political Rights (ICCPR) addresses democratic processes, including affirmative rights to due process and equal protection. The United States has not signed the ICESC, but it has signed and ratified the ICCPR. As antipoverty activists make global connections with poor people's movements internationally, international legal authorities will become an increasingly important part of poverty law.

Martha F. Davis

See also: Legal Aid/Legal Services; New Property; Poor Laws; Vagrancy Laws/Settlement Laws/Residency Requirements; War on Poverty; Welfare Law Center; Welfare Policy/Welfare Reform

References and Further Reading

Cahn, Edgar S., and Jean C. Cahn. 1964. "The War on Poverty: A Civilian Perspective." *Yale Law Journal* 73: 1317–1352.

Davis, Martha F. 1993. *Brutal Need: Lawyers and the Welfare Rights Movement, 1960–1973.* New Haven: Yale University Press.

Johnson, Earl, Jr. 1978. *Justice and Reform: The Formative Years of the American Legal Services Program.* New Brunswick, NJ: Transaction Books.

Law, Sylvia A. 1984. "Economic Justice." In *Our Endangered Rights: The ACLU Report on Civil Liberties Today*, ed. Norman Dorsen, 134–159. New York: Pantheon Books.

Lopez, Gerald. 1992. *Rebellious Lawyering: One Chicano's Vision of Progressive Law Practice.* Boulder, CO: Westview Press.

Nice, Julie A., and Louise G. Trubek. 1997. *Cases and Materials on Poverty Law: Theory and Practice.* Saint Paul, MN: West Publishing.

Poverty Line

A poverty line is a dollar figure (or figures) below which people experience economic deprivation or do not have a socially acceptable minimum standard of living. Poverty lines have been used to assess the adequacy of wages, to identify populations for whom ameliorative social policies should be developed, and to study the effects of public policies. Although embraced as a way to define poverty as an "objective," that is, quantifiable rather than moral, condition, poverty lines are also a reflection of broader social norms and have historically emerged out of efforts for social reform and political struggle. Many unofficial poverty lines were published in the United States during the Progressive Era, often based on standard budgets developed by social workers to assess the income levels necessary for families to meet basic needs. The federal government began using what is now its official poverty line in 1965 during the War on Poverty, based on the work of Social Security Administration analyst Mollie Orshansky. Reflecting widespread dissatisfaction with the official measure, a panel of social scientists proposed a new approach for developing an official poverty measure in 1995; this proposal is still being studied.

Unofficial poverty lines and income inadequacy measures were developed in the United States as early as 1871, when the first leaders of the Massachusetts Bureau of Statistics of Labor became the first known Americans to associate a specific dollar figure with the word "poverty" (Fisher 1997, 10, n58; Barrington and Fisher forthcoming). Many of these early measures took the form of "standard budgets"—lists of goods and services, including their costs, that a family of specified composition would need to live at a designated level of well-being. Successive poverty lines tended to rise in real terms as the real income of the general population increased—a phenomenon termed "the income elasticity of the poverty line" (Fisher 1992, 1997; Barrington and Fisher forthcoming).

The late-nineteenth- and early-twentieth-century measures differed in significant ways from the current poverty measure. One of the most significant differences is the fact that the earlier measures were commonly developed by social investigators, often female, acting as advocates of the disadvantaged rather than by academic social scientists. Developed as the United States was urbanizing and industrializing, they grew out of a context of labor conflict over wages and working conditions; concern about the living conditions of the low-paid, largely immigrant, industrial workforce; and rising inequality as the extremes of wealth and poverty became increasingly visible. During the Progressive Era and into the early 1920s, a growing number of income inadequacy lines and budgets were published, mostly by social workers and other advocates of unskilled workers, many of whom wanted these workers' wages to be set on the basis of basic family needs rather than on the basis of the supply and demand for labor considered as a commodity. Labor unions also used standard budgets (usually at above-poverty levels) in efforts to win higher wages. Although such standard budgets were generally established at the city or local level, Robert Hunter's influential 1904 book *Poverty* included the first (unofficial) poverty line for the whole nation: $460 for a family of five in the industrial North and $300 for the same family in the South. He used this measure to show that poverty was not confined to the "dependent" or "pauper" class. Large numbers of employed people were living below even a minimal standard of income, and their problems could be traced to fundamental inequities in industrial capitalism that would only be resolved through political struggle and reform.

Although numerous unofficial local budgets and other measures were published, the idea of a federal, officially sanctioned poverty line was much slower in coming. Federal agencies developed several low-income lines during the Great Depression, but none were given official status. In 1937, for instance, the Works Progress Administration published two standard budgets; the lower one, the emergency budget, was conceptually equivalent to the concept of poverty held in the 1960s. In 1949, a congressional subcommittee set an unofficial family low-income line of $2,000; this became the most commonly cited poverty line during most of the 1950s, a period of expanding general prosperity when few were paying attention to the still-widespread poverty problem in the United States. By the late 1950s, this postwar complacency was starting to change as books such as economist John Kenneth Galbraith's *Affluent Society* (1958) and activist Michael Harrington's *Other America* (1962) drew attention to the glaring contradiction of "poverty amidst plenty." These analyses signaled a major break in the tradition of calculating poverty lines: Instead of deriving them from standard budgets based on some measure of itemized living costs, analysts generally simply set "bottom-line" dollar figures, with more or less extensive supporting rationales. This was the practice followed in the analysis accompanying President Lyndon B. Johnson's declaration of a War on Poverty in January 1964, when the Council of Economic Advisors, in its 1964 *Economic Report of the President*, set a family poverty line of $3,000. This became the federal government's first (quasi-official) poverty line (Fisher 1992, 3–4; 1997, 32–34, 41–55).

Mollie Orshansky, a civil servant in the Social Security Administration (SSA), was disturbed that the new $3,000 poverty line was not adjusted by family size. In January 1965, she published an article analyzing the poverty population using thresholds adjusted by family size. Orshansky based her thresholds on what was known as the "economy food plan": the cheapest of the four food plans developed by the U.S. Department of Agriculture to present nutritionally adequate diets at different cost levels. Based on an Agriculture Department survey showing that families (at all income levels) spent about one-third of their after-tax monetary income on food in 1955, Orshansky calculated poverty thresholds for different family sizes by multiplying economy food plan costs by three. In presenting these thresholds, Orshansky emphasized that they were barely enough for a family to get by, leaving very little room for more than the most minimal provisions, and suggested that they should be used as a measure of income inadequacy, not of income adequacy.

Despite the problems acknowledged by Orshansky and others—and although her original intent had not been to develop a national poverty measure—the Office of Economic Opportunity, as the lead agency in the War on Poverty, adopted her thresholds as a working or quasi-official definition of poverty in May 1965, replacing the $3,000 figure. The U.S. Census Bureau began publishing poverty statistics based on Orshansky's thresholds in 1967.

As early as November 1965, SSA policymakers and analysts had begun advocating that the poverty thresholds be adjusted to reflect increases in general living standards. In 1968, an SSA plan to raise the thresholds modestly was rejected, but an interagency committee was appointed to reevaluate the thresholds. This committee decided to adjust the thresholds only for price changes reflected in the Consumer Price Index (CPI), and not for changes in general living standards. In 1969, the Bureau of the Budget designated the thresholds tied to the CPI as the federal government's official statistical definition of poverty.

Ever since the poverty thresholds and the Census Bureau income definition used with them were adopted, they have been criticized on various grounds. Critics have argued, on the one hand, that they seriously underestimate actual living costs (such as health care, housing, child care, transportation to work) and, on the other, that they do not account for noncash benefits in measuring family income (Ruggles 1990; Citro and Michael 1995). In 1992, in response to a congressional committee request, the National Research Council appointed a Panel on Poverty and Family Assistance to conduct a study to support a possible revision of the official poverty measure. In its 1995 report (Citro and Michael 1995), the panel proposed a new approach for developing an official U.S. poverty measure, although it did not propose a single set of poverty-threshold dollar figures. The panel proposed the development of a new poverty threshold for a reference family type, to be expressed as the cost of certain necessities, set within a dollar range based in part on consideration of standard budgets and relative and "subjective" poverty thresholds. The new threshold would be updated annually on a "quasi-relative" basis reflecting changes in actual expenditures for certain necessities. The panel deliberately adopted a resources (income) definition consistent with the concept underlying the poverty threshold, defining "resources" as the sum of money income from all sources plus the value of certain near-money benefits, minus taxes and certain expenses that cannot purchase goods and services included in the threshold concept.

The Census Bureau and other federal agencies are engaged in an ongoing study of experimental poverty measures based on the poverty panel's recommendations. This work, still in progress in 2004, is not expected to be completed for several years. Meanwhile, a growing number of analysts and advocates have turned once again to standard budgets and other alternative poverty measures in assessing the extent of need, the impact of social and economic policies, and the need for reform.

Gordon M. Fisher

[The views expressed in this entry are those of the author and do not represent the position of the U.S. Department of Health and Human Services.]

See also: *The Affluent Society; Economic Report of 1964; The Other America; Poverty;* Poverty, Statistical Measure of; Social Work; War on Poverty

References and Further Reading

Barrington, Linda, and Gordon M. Fisher. Forthcoming. "Poverty." In *Historical Statistics of the United States, Millennial Edition,* ed. Susan B. Carter, Scott S. Gartner, Michael R. Haines, Alan L. Olmstead, Richard Sutch, and Gavin Wright. New York: Cambridge University Press.

Citro, Constance F., and Robert T. Michael, eds. 1995. *Measuring Poverty: A New Approach.* Washington, DC: National Academy Press.

Fisher, Gordon M. 1992. "The Development and History of the Poverty Thresholds." *Social Security Bulletin* 55 (Winter): 3–14.

———. 1997. "From Hunter to Orshansky: An Overview of (Unofficial) Poverty Lines in the United States from 1904 to 1965." Unpublished paper. http://www.census.gov/hhes/poverty/povmeas/papers/hstorsp4.html. Revised August 1997.

Ruggles, Patricia. 1990. *Drawing the Line: Alternative Poverty Measures and Their Implications for Public Policy*. Washington, DC: Urban Institute Press.

Poverty Research

Broadly defined, poverty research is a wide-ranging field of study that encompasses inquiry into the social, economic, and political processes that generate inequality as well as more narrowly focused analyses of poor people and antipoverty programs. In the prosperous United States, where studying poverty has become a sizable research enterprise, poverty research can be sorted into three major, sometimes overlapping categories, each of which draws on a distinct historical tradition of research and action.

The first and, in the United States, largest and dominant category of poverty research consists of analyses of the socioeconomic characteristics and behavioral patterns of people in poverty or on welfare, as well as evaluations of social programs aimed at the poor. Conducted with funding from government, foundations, or scientific agencies, and often under the auspices of think tanks or university-based research institutes, this type of research has gained quasi-official status in the United States since the 1960s, when federal officials purposely set out to establish a contract research industry to serve the needs of the War on Poverty. That purpose, initially geared toward eliminating poverty, was soon overshadowed by the political demands of welfare reform. Grounded in the assumptions, methods, and concepts of neoclassical economics, poverty research is often highly technical, statistical, based on individual-level analysis, and for the most part does not subject the market or other institutions and cultural norms of mainstream society to critical scrutiny.

A second category is research situated within specific places—usually low-income communities or neighborhoods—that uses some combination of quantitative and qualitative or ethnographic research to capture the day-to-day realities, or the "human face," of poverty, to explore the conditions that foster it, and otherwise to situate the occurrence of poverty within the context of its immediate social and economic environment. Used in traditions that have looked upon poor communities as "laboratories" for exploring social "disorganization" and cultural deviance, community-based research originated in reform-oriented, Progressive-Era efforts to document the ravages of unregulated capitalism and labor market exploitation on community and family life; more recently, it has become a mainstay of social action research, in which community residents participate in setting and carrying out research agendas that reflect their priorities for change.

In contrast to studies that tend to isolate poverty as a somehow separate, self-contained subject of study, a third category of poverty research consists of more theoretical or more historical inquiries into the nature and incidence of poverty in relation to mainstream political economy, culture, and social relations. Such research tends not to focus exclusively on poor people and places; instead, it favors scrutinizing the policies, institutions, social practices, and cultural norms that generate disparities in material well-being. Although often drawing on the same types of empirical evidence that inform the other literatures, these studies frame the central question of poverty's underlying "causes" more broadly, going beyond the immediate circumstances of poor households or communities to the structural divisions of class, gender, and race and the political and economic dynamics that sustain them. Poverty, in this literature, is not a social or individual "pathology" or digression from the norm so much as it is a product of the normal workings of an unequally structured political economy and society.

For all their differences, these categories of research share certain characteristic features of the field. Thus, poverty research is largely an undertaking of relatively privileged, educated, middle-class professionals—mainly social scientists with academic training in economics, sociology, anthropology, history, or related fields—although it is at times conducted by community organizers and social reform activists and, occasionally, with the active participation of poor people. It also has an "applied" mission: Poverty research—in the eyes of most of its practitioners if not always in the views of the objects of its scrutiny—will help poor people by providing the knowledge for informed social policy or political action. In the United States, this notion has historically animated the development of an elaborate array of research methodologies and conceptual frameworks and, in the latter half of the twentieth century, the emergence of a substantial government- and foundation-funded research industry devoted to the study of poverty and its "causes, consequences, and cures." Although this research industry claims to produce value-free, politically neutral social science, in reality its increasingly narrow focus on the personal "deficits" and behavioral "deviance" of poor people has played an important role in the political revival of a very old idea: that the crux of the "poverty problem" rests in the individual and that the key to resolving it rests on ending welfare "dependency." Hence, an additional, if often unacknowledged, feature of poverty research: It is far more than a mere collection of facts and empirically or theoretically derived explanations; it is as much a product of specific historical developments—of the prevailing values, political and ideological struggles, social and economic relations, and cultural expectations of a given society—as is poverty itself. Indeed, the very notion of an "objective," social scientific, research-based understanding of poverty is itself rooted in a significant historical and ideological shift, away from the idea of poverty as a moral condition in need of moral redemption and toward a notion of poverty as a social condition, amenable to social intervention and reform.

Progressive-Era Roots

Although poor people have come under the scrutiny of socially designated investigators for centuries, it was not until the late nineteenth and early twentieth centuries that poverty research began to assume its modern form. Before then, investigations of poverty were largely equated with investigations of poor people, of their moral character and "deservingness" of some form of public assistance, and especially, of their propensity to "pauperism," or what is today referred to as "welfare dependency." Often conducted by members of the clergy or by the legions of (female) "friendly visitors" associated with local charities, such investigations were filtered through the biases of racial, ethnic, and class prejudice and the gender norms separating investigators from investigated, and above all through the conviction that insufficiently discriminating public assistance would promote laziness, intemperance, sexual license, and profligate childbearing among the poor. In the logic inspired by social theorist Thomas Malthus, it was feared that public assistance would protect the poor from the otherwise "natural" restraints of hunger, privation, or death. Rooted though they were in Protestant morality and an ethos of self-reliance, such prohibitions on relief also found powerful undergirding in classical liberalism, which in the United States of the industrializing Gilded Age took the form of an aggressively laissez-faire doctrine of unregulated capitalist development that relied on an abundance of low-wage labor for its wherewithal and that vehemently opposed relief.

It was against such powerful and pervasive cultural convictions that, beginning in the late nineteenth century and continuing throughout what became known as the era of progressive reform, a diverse array of intellectuals, reform activists, child welfare advocates, journalists, and social documentarians set out to bring a new understanding to the problem of poverty. Inspired by the work of British merchant and amateur statistician Charles Booth—whose massive, seventeen-volume study entitled *Life and Labour of the People in London* (1889–1903) was the basis of traveling exhibits around the world—American intellectuals and reformers associated with the settlement house movement launched a series of ambitious social surveys to document work and living conditions in the heavily immigrant, working-class neighborhoods of major industrial cities. Among the most famous were the *Hull-House Maps and Papers* (1895), which surveyed the neighborhood surrounding Chicago's Hull House settlement, and the six volumes (1909–1914) that resulted from the Pittsburgh Survey, an immense study of working-class Pittsburgh that, with substantial funding from the newly established Russell Sage Foundation, drew on dozens of nationally known experts as well as a large staff of paid and volunteer researchers. These and other surveys became the basis of traveling exhibits in which, through written, graphic, and photographic displays, investigators tied the incidence of such problems as poverty, delinquency, crime, and disease not to the personal failings of individuals but to the great social questions of the day: rapid urbanization, large-scale immigration, and, especially, the low wages, exploitative working conditions, and vast inequities wrought by unregulated capitalist growth. This emphasis on work and working conditions was echoed in Robert Hunter's *Poverty* (1904), the first national study of the subject based on official income data, among other sources. Confirming what other surveyors had found on the city level, Hunter reported that the vast majority of people living below his bare-bones measure of poverty were poor because of the low wages they earned or because of some related "social wrong."

Studies showed that it was no coincidence that the problems of low wages and labor exploitation were especially concentrated among "new" immigrants from southern and eastern Europe. These workers were less likely to be unionized, could more easily be exploited, were not yet proficient in English, and, in the biased eyes of the native-born, middle-class investigators, were culturally inclined to passive acceptance of their lot. Women and children were especially exploited as wage earners, as numerous investigations by maternalist and feminist reformers made clear, at least in part due to the prevailing ideology of the male breadwinner that helped justify their lower wages. It was up to the African American sociologist W. E. B. Du Bois, in his survey *The Philadelphia Negro* (1899), to reveal the deeply ingrained racial prejudices, pseudoscientific racial ideologies, and institutionalized practices that kept so many of the residents of Philadelphia's African American Seventh Ward in poverty and racially segregated housing and that shut them out of higher-paying employment.

In offering what historian Robert Bremner (1956) dubbed a "new view" of poverty, Progressive-Era social investigators were not necessarily abandoning the moral distinctions and understandings of the past. They, too, wrote of the dangers of "pauperism," drew distinctions between the "deserving" and "undeserving" poor, and at times wrote of immigrants as culturally, if not morally, deficient. But they were more significantly aiming to reframe the moral issue—from a focus on individual behaviors to one on the social and economic conditions that fostered them—and in the process to rechannel the direction of reform. And in shifting attention from the problem of "pauperism" to the much larger and underlying one of poverty, they were challenging the individualistic logic of laissez-faire. This did not make the Progressive social investigators any less committed to the rigors of "objective" social scientific research. It did, however, make them willing to subject a social order that many people treated as natural to the rigors of empirical research and to use such research as the basis of reform. In this sense, it is important to underscore the fact that the origins of poverty research can be traced to the reform movements of the late nineteenth and early twentieth centuries and to the overarching movement to make liberalism an ideology not of laissez faire but of reform.

As important as the new Progressive-Era view was in laying the groundwork for social scientific poverty research, several subsequent developments served to marginalize this early reform sensibility and to set the stage for the narrower type of inquiry that has come to dominate contemporary poverty research. Especially important was the growing professionalization of social investigation around an academic ideal modeled on the natural sciences—a development that tended to undercut the authority of the female and nonwhite investigators who continued to have limited access to academic opportunities. An equally significant and related factor was a turn away from the emphasis on political economy that had marked earlier studies toward the social psychological and cultural approaches of what came, after World War II, to be known as the behavioral sciences. Thus, in the urban neighborhood studies of the interwar Chicago school of sociology, poverty was understood not as a product of low wages and labor exploitation or, as Du Bois had argued, of an institutionalized economic, residential, and psychological color line, but as the result of the cultural backwardness and internal social "disorganization" experienced by immigrants and African Americans newly arrived in the industrial city from predominantly rural backgrounds. The implications of this shift in perspective were profound: Social disorganization and cultural "lag," not industrial capitalism, were at the root of the poverty problem; cultural assimilation and individual rehabilitation were the appropriate responses. And although social scientists such as E. Wight Bakke, in his Depression-era study of unemployed workers, would use this behavioral turn to explore the deep psychological costs of unemployment and to argue for labor reforms, with the return of prosperity, poverty research turned increasingly to the supposedly distinctive culture and psychology of the poor.

Poverty Research in the Affluent Society

Postwar politics and economy further encouraged the trend toward behavioral approaches to poverty research, as the experience of mass prosperity—including by a growing proportion of the white industrial working class—sent scholars in search of explanations for the paradox of poverty amid affluence. The vast expansion of government and foundation funding made the behavioral sciences the leading edge of social research as policymakers and government officials looked for individualized and therapeutic rather than structural solutions to social problems. Equally important was the influence of Cold War politics on postwar social science, which labeled as "subversive" or "socialistic" such ideas as universal health care and public housing and analyses that questioned capitalism or prevailing class, gender, and race relations. At the same time, it was in the course of Cold War–financed studies of "underdeveloped" communities in Mexico that anthropologist Oscar Lewis initially came up with the theory of a "culture of poverty." Conceptualized as an all-encompassing set of socially backward or deviant attitudes, psychological orientations, behaviors, and moral codes, the "culture of poverty" was held to keep whole classes of poor people isolated from mainstream society and to render them incapable of functioning in modernized industrial economies that required the self-reliance, work ethic, sexual morality, and ability to defer gratification that poor people supposedly lacked.

Based on highly problematic, culturally biased assumptions as well as on methods of observation and psychological testing that were later discredited, the idea of a "culture of poverty" and its many variations nevertheless became firmly established within liberal social science during the postwar years, and they were used to justify various social service–oriented interventions designed to "break the cycle of poverty." Similarly, the notion that African American poverty was rooted in some form of social "pathology"—specifically, in the female-headed, matriarchal family structure—was widely adopted in liberal social thought, even though the notion was subjected to well-documented criticism in the wake of then assistant secretary of labor Daniel Patrick Moynihan's report on the "crisis" of the Negro family in 1965. For a brief period, the culture of poverty became part of the critical discourse of the Left. As popularized by social democrat Michael Harrington in his influential book *The Other America* (1962), the imagery of a powerless, alienated class caught up in an endless cycle served as a broader critique of the political inadequacies of liberal social provision and of the skewed priorities of affluent America. In later years, well after some of their original proponents had abandoned them, these discredited yet still-influential theories would be adopted by conservatives to argue that social interventions such as welfare were only feeding the culture of poverty and ought to be abandoned in favor of more punitive work requirements, marriage promotion, and other policies to change the behavior of the poor. Thus, when in the 1980s left-liberal sociologist William Julius Wilson wrote about the emergence of an impoverished, culturally alienated urban "underclass" as a by-product of deindustrialization, long-term unemployment, and "social isolation," conservatives quickly embraced the notion as evidence of government-subsidized deviance on the part of the poor.

Despite the sensationalistic appeal of these cultural depictions, it was economists on the staff of President John F. Kennedy's Council of Economic Advisors in the early 1960s who emerged as the central players in developing a strategy for what later became the War on Poverty and in shaping the research it spawned. Committed to the principles of British economist John Maynard Keynes, they advocated a stronger federal role in stimulating economic growth and full employment, both of which they saw as key to understanding and fighting poverty. Confident of their ability to reduce—and ultimately to eliminate—poverty by keeping employment rates high, they minimized the problems of low wages, labor relations, discrimination, and structural transformation that had absorbed many Progressive-Era investigators (as well as their contemporaries on the liberal left) and focused instead on the "human capital" or skill deficiencies of poor people. Although defining poverty in the economic categories of employment and income and rejecting harder-to-measure psychological and cultural frames, they nevertheless shared something important with the cultural theorists: They made the study of poverty about measuring and analyzing the characteristics of poor people rather than about the social structures and processes shaping the distribution of income, opportunity, and wealth.

Nothing was more important to the course of poverty research than President Lyndon B. Johnson's declaration of an official War on Poverty in 1964. Adopting ideas from both the "culture of poverty" approach and the human capital approach, but also struck by the relative dearth of poverty research, officials at the newly created Office of Economic Opportunity (OEO) established the funding and the institutional basis for the poverty research industry and for its enormous growth in the decades to follow. Seeking to replicate the model of, and indeed actually recruiting analysts from, the postwar defense research industry, OEO created an office of research and program evaluation. Staffed heavily with economists trained in the methods of cost-benefit analysis, the office was created to generate the knowledge necessary for identifying the target, setting the goals, and ultimately winning the War on Poverty. Favoring "hard," quantitative data and research methods that could provide measurable indicators of program success, the OEO research office generated a surge of new research while also creating the institutional apparatus—the "think tanks that think for the poor"—that would quickly come to dominate and define poverty research. This approach to poverty research soon displaced—in the competition for funding, resources, and legitimacy—an alternative, more qualitative, and ultimately political model of research associated with the controversial Community Action Program. Marginalized though they were, these research strategies continued at the community level and have more recently been reinvigorated in participatory research and action projects.

With the demise of the official War on Poverty in the late 1960s and early 1970s, the priorities and agendas of the poverty research industry became increasingly driven by the politics of welfare reform. Initially focused on such provisions as the guaranteed income envisioned in the Nixon administration's Family Assistance Plan, poverty research soon shifted as the Reagan administration made the problem of welfare "dependency"—and the research dollars to explore it—a central organizing theme. Accompanying the conservative capture of the welfare debate, an explicitly conservative network of think tanks and research institutes developed to rival the more established Great Society poverty research industry. Although often couching their books and reports in the standard language of analytic research, conservatives mounted a moral and ideological attack on welfare, welfare recipients, and the poor more generally—appropriating, ironically, ideas about a "culture of poverty" and an "underclass" that had originated in liberal research. With books such as Charles Murray's *Losing Ground* (1984) and a steady stream of research briefs from the right-wing Heritage Foundation, American Enterprise Institute, and others, the focus of poverty research shifted even further away from income and need and toward welfare dependency, out-of-wedlock childbearing, and a host of behavioral "pathologies" as the key social problems to be resolved. In a return to the Malthusian, laissez-faire, moralistic logic that Progressive-Era social investigators had sought to challenge, this politically ascendant poverty research has provided a powerful rationale for policies that—while ignoring such issues as growing wage inequality and enduring discrimination—have made ending welfare and remoralizing poor people their sole goals. And although many of the scholars associated with the more liberally rooted poverty research industry do not necessarily subscribe to these views, their own narrow focus on the individual characteristics of poor people—reinforced by the spurt of funding for research on the extent of welfare "dependency" and the impact of recent welfare reform in bringing it to an end—has effectively accommodated the repauperization of the poverty issue orchestrated by the conservative Right.

Nevertheless, today as in the past, alternative, more broadly gauged and structurally oriented lines of inquiry have challenged the dominance of the narrowly construed study of poor people and welfare that has come to be designated as "objective," "scientific" poverty research. Participatory research is an essential component of a number of community-based organizations—such as the Applied Research Center (ARC) in Oakland, California—which combine social science with organizing to document the roots of poverty in the impact of globalization, economic restructuring, structural racism, and political disenfranchisement and to frame antipoverty policy as an issue of social and economic justice rather than of individual rehabilitation. Ethnographic research in urban and rural communities has also used a more "ground-up" perspective to cut through unexamined assumptions of cultural "pathology," instead documenting the variegated economic, social, and political strategies that shape daily life in low-income communities. A well-established literature has built on the theoretical insights of Frances Fox Piven and Richard Cloward—as well as on the sensibilities and experiences of the civil rights, labor, and welfare rights movements—to examine the political dimensions of poverty while reconceptualizing welfare as a political right. This and other, historical, research has tied poverty to major developments in political economy as well as to the related political struggles and policy choices that have shaped and dramatically reshaped the U.S. welfare state. The influence of feminist theory has been especially notable since the 1980s, illuminating the gendered nature of social and economic inequities perpetuated in labor markets, social policy, law, and family relations.

Significantly, these and other alternative approaches are often dismissed as "ideological" or "unscientific" in mainstream poverty research circles. In reality, however, what distinguishes them from more nominally "scientific" poverty research is not that they are less committed to the norms of social scientific evidence and objectivity but that they are willing to recognize the inherently and historically political and ideological nature of poverty research.

Alice O'Connor

See also: Applied Research Center; Deserving/Undeserving Poor; Malthusianism; New Right; Poverty, Statistical Measure of; Poverty Line; Social Surveys; "Underclass"; War on Poverty; Welfare Policy/Welfare Reform

References and Further Reading

Bremner, Robert. 1956. *From the Depths: The Discovery of Poverty in the United States*. New York: New York University Press.

Bulmer, Martin, Kevin Bales, and Kathryn Kish Sklar, eds. 1991. *The Social Survey in Historical Perspective, 1880–1940*. New York: Cambridge University Press.

Fitzpatrick, Ellen. 1990. *Endless Crusade: Women Social Scientists and Progressive Reform*. New York: Oxford University Press.

Gans, Herbert. 1995. *The War against the Poor: The Underclass and Antipoverty Policy*. New York: Basic Books.

Gordon, Linda. 1994. *Pitied but Not Entitled: Single Mothers and the History of Welfare*. New York: Free Press.

Katz, Michael B. 1989. *The Undeserving Poor: From the War on Poverty to the War on Welfare*. New York: Pantheon Books.

Lacey, Michael, and Mary O. Furner, eds. 1993. *The State and Social Investigation in Britain and the United States*. New York: Cambridge University Press.

Mink, Gwendolyn. 1995. *The Wages of Motherhood: Inequality in the Welfare State, 1917–1942*. Ithaca, NY: Cornell University Press.

O'Connor, Alice. 2001. *Poverty Knowledge: Social Science, Social Policy, and the Poor in Twentieth-Century U.S. History*. Princeton: Princeton University Press.

Piven, Frances Fox, and Richard Cloward. 1971. *Regulating the Poor: The Functions of Public Welfare*. New York: Random House.

Schram, Sanford F. 2002. *Praxis for the Poor: Piven and Cloward and the Future of Social Science in Social Welfare*. New York: New York University Press.

Privatization

Privatization is the process of transferring government functions to the private sector. State and local governments are increasingly paying private entities to deliver social services and welfare-related benefits. These private providers include small, community-based nonprofit organizations; large national nonprofit organizations such as the Salvation Army; large for-profit companies; and religious organizations. Although private entities have long aided the poor, after the enactment of the 1996 Personal Responsibility and Work Opportunity Reconciliation Act (PRWORA), welfare privatization has expanded in three significant ways. First, large for-profit companies have entered the field, competing for lucrative government contracts. Second, governments that choose to privatize must open up the process to religious organizations such as churches, synagogues, and mosques, an initiative commonly called "charitable choice." Third, private entities are not only delivering direct services (including substance abuse treatment, mental health counseling, job training, and the like) but are also taking over case-management functions, including decisions about eligibility and sanctions.

In most social welfare regimes, privatization takes one of two forms: (1) The government chooses to "contract out" services, or (2) the government gives welfare recipients vouchers that can be redeemed with private providers. Proponents of privatization generally argue that competition among providers results in cost savings as well as in increased efficiency and innovation. Alternatively, other proponents stress the value of having private community groups serve as a mediating force between government and its citizens. Opponents counter that government can best provide services in a uniform, nondiscriminatory manner and that private entities are susceptible to fraud, corruption, and conflicts of interest. Unions also point to the loss of higher-paying union jobs that result from privatization.

As described by then-president Bill Clinton, the PRWORA was designed to "end welfare as we know it." Not only did the PRWORA change the philosophy of welfare by making work a condition of benefits, but it also changed how welfare is delivered. The PRWORA pushed much of the authority over welfare administration from the federal government to the states, a process known as "devolution." The PRWORA also gave the states significant latitude to devolve their authority down to private providers. Under the PRWORA, frontline welfare workers no longer simply verify that applicants meet objective eligibility criteria and issue checks; instead, they exercise vast discretion in counseling clients to assist them in obtaining work. In privatized jurisdictions, this discretion rests in the hands of private employees. Notably, states are also privatizing other social services, particularly those related to children, such as foster care, adoption, and child support enforcement.

Historically, both government and private entities have played a role in poor relief in the United States, although their respective contributions have ebbed and flowed over the years, often in opposition to one another. There simply never was a mythic "golden age" during which private charity alone aided the poor. Until the twentieth century, most poor relief was provided at the local level by a mix of public and private efforts. The Great Depression brought the federal government into poor relief for the first time. In 1935, the Social Security Act created Aid to Dependent Children (ADC; later Aid to Families with Dependent Children, or AFDC), a federally funded, needs-based, cash-assistance program administered by the states (and replaced in 1996 by TANF).

However, federal funds did not extend to private groups until the 1960s, when President John F. Kennedy and President Lyndon B. Johnson emphasized a service-based strategy to help the poor obtain work through a vast network of private community action agencies. This initiative was short-lived, but it created an interdependent relationship between government and local providers that continues to this day. Currently, private providers deliver the bulk of government social services and, in turn, many receive the greatest share of their income from governments (Salamon 1995, 15).

The available evidence strongly suggests that privatization works best for straightforward municipal services such as trash collection and road paving and less well for complex social services (Donahue 1989, 217). In the latter type of programs, it is difficult to foster meaningful competition and to define measurable objectives. There are no large-scale studies comparing the results of private and government welfare programs, and such a study might be impossible given the largely decentralized nature of the current welfare system. As of 2002, most of the documented deficiencies in privatized welfare programs involved those run by for-profit companies, which have incentives to increase profits by pushing welfare beneficiaries out of programs and reducing service levels.

The legal consequences of privatization make it difficult for welfare beneficiaries and their advocates to remedy such problems. Unlike private entities, government agencies that deliver welfare benefits are subject to a wide variety of constraints on their discretion. For instance, government agencies must provide fair procedures before depriving persons of benefits. In addition, government records are subject to public review. Further, the government cannot violate the constitutional rights of social service beneficiaries, including their free speech rights, their rights against unlawful search and seizure, and their due process rights. Yet these principles of public law generally do not apply in privatized regimes (Gilman 2001, 641).

Although beneficiaries may have rights that arise from the contracts between the government and private providers, they have no right to be involved during the procurement process, when contracts are solicited, awarded, and negotiated. Given the lack of political and social capital in poor communities, these contracts rarely grant welfare recipients enforceable rights. Moreover, from a contract-management perspective, most local governments lack the expertise to draft contracts that define clear objectives and effectively measure outcomes. In jurisdictions that utilize vouchers, recipients may have even fewer enforceable rights, other than the "right" to go to another provider. Thus, in privatized jurisdictions, welfare recipients interact with employees of private companies who are insulated from public accountability and who exercise vast discretion. At the same time, recipients have fewer enforceable protections than they do in government-run jurisdictions.

Michele Estrin Gilman

See also: Charitable Choice; Community-Based Organizations; Nonprofit Sector; Voluntarism; War on Poverty; Welfare Administration; Welfare Policy/Welfare Reform

References and Further Reading

Donahue, John D. 1989. *The Privatization Decision*. New York: Basic Books.

Gilman, Michele Estrin. 2001. "Legal Accountability in an Era of Privatized Welfare." *California Law Review* 89 (May): 569–642.

National Center on Poverty Law. 2002. "The Implications of Privatization on Low-Income People." *Clearinghouse Review* 35 (January–February): 487–673.

Salamon, Lester M. 1995. *Partners in Public Service: Government-Nonprofit Relations in the Modern Welfare State*. Baltimore: Johns Hopkins University Press.

Progress and Poverty, *Henry George*

Like many Americans living in the depression-ravaged 1870s, Henry George (1839–1897) worried about the deleterious effects of industrial capitalism on American democracy. Why, he wondered, were the many indisputable benefits of industrial progress accompanied by an increase in the number of people living in poverty? Could the defining features of the nation's republican ideals and institutions—liberty, equality, and opportunity—endure in a society increasingly dominated by large corporations and powerful millionaires like Jay Gould and William K. Vanderbilt? Tormented by these questions and committed to answering them, in 1877 he began writing a book he titled *Progress and Poverty: An Inquiry into the Cause of Industrial Depressions and of Increase of Want with Increase of Wealth*. Published in 1879, it became the best-selling book on political economy in the nineteenth century.

George, a reform-minded newspaper editor living in California, had only a sixth-grade education. Nonetheless, he read widely, especially the classics of political economy, in preparation for writing his book. He was also an evangelical Christian who viewed his reform effort in almost messianic terms and laced much of *Progress and Poverty* with biblical references.

Developed over ten chapters and 534 pages, George's argument was that a major portion of the wealth created by society was being siphoned off by real estate speculators and land monopolists. They grew rich on these unearned profits while society's producers toiled in poverty with little opportunity for advancement. The solution, asserted George, was for the government to appropriate these profits through a uniform land-value tax, or what his supporters eventually took to calling the "single tax." With the rewards of speculation eliminated, undeveloped land and resources held by speculators would be sold to those seeking to develop it. Poverty would decline, and economic opportunity would once again flourish. Society would also benefit from increased tax revenues that would pay for parks, schools, libraries, and other public institutions.

Progress and Poverty attracted a wide readership among intellectuals, middle-class reformers, and wage earners in America and Great Britain. The latter were drawn more to George's vivid description of the ills plaguing Gilded Age society and his apocalyptic warnings against inaction than to his single-tax solution. In 1886, workers in New York City nominated George as the United Labor Party candidate for mayor; he nearly won. George's public career faded after that, but his middle-class followers formed Single Tax Clubs all across the country to promote his plan, a movement that eventually spread to Great Britain, Canada, Ireland, Australia, Denmark, and Hungary. The influence of *Progress and Poverty* also outlasted its author, shaping the consciousness of many prominent late-nineteenth- and early-twentieth-century reformers, including Jacob A. Riis, Ignatius Donnelly, Father John A. Ryan, and Robert La Follette.

Progress and Poverty remains in print today, and Henry George schools and Single Tax organizations operate in at least twenty-two countries.

Edward T. O'Donnell

See also: Capitalism; Debt; Economic Depression; Nineteenth Century; Property; Wealth

References and Further Reading

Andelson, Robert V., ed. 2004. *The Critics of Henry George: A Centenary Appraisal of Their Strictures on* Progress and Poverty. 2d rev. ed. Oxford: Blackwell.

Barker, Charles Albro. 1955. *Henry George*. New York: Oxford University Press.

O'Donnell, Edward T. 2004. *The Talisman of a Lost Hope: Henry George and Gilded Age America*. New York: Columbia University Press.

Property

Property can most simply be defined as enforceable claims to the uses and benefits of particular resources. Property has been implicated in the history of poverty and social welfare in several important ways. First, inequality in the distribution of property—and the benefits that accompany property ownership—is itself a major dimension of broader social and economic inequality in the United States. Second, despite various policies and institutions aimed at "democratizing" property in the form of home ownership, property ownership has historically been concentrated in the hands of wealthy individual and corporate owners and has become more so in recent decades. Third, large individual and corporate property owners have historically wielded considerable political power and influence, especially over policies (such as environmental regulation and tax policy) that may threaten their interests. Fourth, laws governing landownership and land use, enforcement of private restrictive covenants, and banking policies have historically excluded people on the basis of race and national origins from access to property. Such exclusions have had far-reaching repercussions, since property ownership and place of residence have served as gateways to such fundamental benefits of social citizenship as education. Finally, a substantial proportion of property ownership in colonial and pre–Civil War America was in the form of human bondage, or chattel slavery, with enormous and lasting consequences for African Americans' struggle for economic as well as political and social equality, consequences that are still being played out in contemporary social policy debates.

"Real property" refers to land and other natural resources; "personalty" or "personal property" refers to movable goods or claims to revenue from such "intangible" instruments as stocks, bonds, and commercial notes. "Private property" is the right of individuals or organizations to exclusive uses and benefits of resources. "Public property" is the rights held by government officials on behalf of a larger citizenry. "Common property" is the right of members of a community not to be excluded from the uses and benefits of resources. What constitutes legitimate enforceable claims to resources is a political question and has been subject to repeated contests in the United States. With the shift from an agrarian republic that mixed independent proprietorship and slavery to a corporate economy dominated by industrial and then financial capital, land gave way to revenues as the dominant form of property.

American rules governing property rights derive from English common law, although eight states, originally settled by French or Spanish colonists, adopted features of Continental civil law, including community property in marriage. Private property rights have never been absolute; they are subject to obligations (for example, a proprietor's duty not to use property in such a way as to injure the interests of a neighbor) and to government powers of taxation and regulation. Through most of the nineteenth century, southerners exercised common property rights for fishing, hunting, and grazing cattle, but fence laws ended these claims in the 1880s. Few common property rights survive today; communal irrigation systems in some villages in New Mexico are one exception. Public property is held at all levels of government; in 2000, the federal government owned 262 million acres, one-eighth of all American land (U.S. Bureau of Land Management 2003). Property has stood at the center of American political ideology from the outset. In the seventeenth century, English political theorist John Locke justified private property by arguing that since every man was endowed with property in his own labor, mixing this labor with unappropriated land entitled men to claim ownership. (Women were assumed to be dependent members of households headed by men; under the common law principle of coverture, a wife's property belonged to her husband, a rule that state legislatures ended in the mid-nineteenth century.) American Indians generally held common rights in land, which they used for both agriculture and hunting. English settlers, however, saw their own improvement of land as justifying its appropriation as private property once Indian lands had been taken by war or treaty. By the end of the eighteenth century, the Fifth Amendment of the U.S. Constitution recognized the primacy of private property rights by stating that property could not be taken by government without due process or just compensation; the Fourteenth Amendment (1868) extended this prohibition to state governments. For two centuries, Americans have debated what kinds of regulations are legitimate exercises of government's "police powers" on behalf of public safety and welfare and what regulations are "takings" that require due process and compensation.

In the early republic, property qualifications for voting were thought to confirm a man's capacity for political independence. In the 1820s and 1830s, state legislatures adopted universal white manhood suffrage while maintaining property qualifications for free Black men. The free labor ideology of antebellum farmers and artisans gained salience in direct contrast to the practice of chattel slavery in the South, where the plantation system relied on enslaved labor to produce cash crops of cotton, sugar, rice, and tobacco. By 1860, with ownership of slaves and land becoming highly concentrated, property in slaves represented nearly 60 percent of the wealth in the South (Wright 1978, 19). With the Civil War and the Thirteenth

Amendment (1865), 4 million people gained their freedom; in the absence of confiscation and redistribution of slave owners' land, however, the vast majority of freed people became agricultural wage workers (sharecroppers) or tenants, who had little bargaining power with white landowners and storekeepers.

The Republican Party courted the votes of northern farmers and artisans with the 1862 Homestead Act, which permitted settlers who improved land to claim 160 acres from the public domain in the trans-Mississippi West. At the same time, the Republican Congress joined state governments in granting land to railroads in order to subsidize construction of a transcontinental transportation system. In the late nineteenth century, farmers challenged corporate speculation and especially railroads' unilateral power over shipping rates, which were said to come at the expense of farmers' livelihood and the public good. In his 1879 *Progress and Poverty*, Henry George denounced the "unearned increment" collected by absentee land monopolists when values increased due to social development rather than owners' improvements.

Whatever the ideological appeal of independent proprietorship, nineteenth-century judges and lawyers also adopted utilitarian or instrumental conceptions of property in order to promote industrial development. English economist Jeremy Bentham had attacked the aura and power of the landed aristocracy by arguing that property rights were the product of policies rather than of natural law. Pragmatic American judges modified common law rules governing property rights—for example, principles of "first come, first serve" or prior appropriation—in order to encourage new industries, and western states also established new doctrines to govern rights to underground minerals or scarce water. Recognizing that multiple, overlapping claims often adhered in the same land or water, legal realists in the 1920s adopted the metaphor of property as a "bundle" of rights or claims that had to be sorted and weighed against one another.

Even after the proprietary agrarian economy had given way to a corporate industrial order, its legacy could be found in working-class families' self-built housing and in federal and state subsidies for home ownership. State legislatures passed laws exempting homesteads from seizure for debt, and in 1934, the Federal Housing Administration began insuring home mortgages to make housing more affordable. Federal income tax laws also permitted home owners to deduct the interest on mortgages. Such policies helped the United States achieve one of the highest rates of home ownership—two-thirds of all households in 2000—among industrial nations (U.S. Census Bureau 2003). In 1948, the Supreme Court ruled state enforcement of private restrictive racial covenants unconstitutional under the Fourteenth Amendment. The Federal Housing Administration and private lenders, however, continued to restrict access to home ownership for African Americans by "redlining," that is, denying mortgages to potential home buyers in neighborhoods with a high concentration of Black households. In 1968, the Fair Housing Act banned discrimination in the housing market.

Although many Americans continue to identify property with land, late-nineteenth-century industrialization turned personalty—especially claims on revenues—into the dominant form of property. Industrialists owned factories and tools as the means of production, and far from entitling a worker to ownership, labor could claim its value only through money wages or salaries. Business partnerships and especially incorporation allowed proprietors to pool capital and expand their enterprises. Railroads, extractive industries, and manufacturers that incorporated issued stock (shares of ownership) to investors, who were entitled to a share of the profits (dividends) and any increase in value of their stock upon sale (capital gains). Stockholders were also protected from liability for company debts beyond the value of their shares. Corporations also took loans from and paid interest to bondholders. Banks paid depositors interest for the use of capital held in savings accounts, and both private and institutional trustees managed investments for testamentary estates, one origin of mutual funds. Between 1880 and 1930, other forms of intangible property proliferated, especially insurance policies and pension plans. Although most working-class Americans had little savings, thousands of families contributed dues to fraternal associations (and by the 1910s were making weekly dime payments for industrial insurance policies) in order to secure burial and some assistance in the event of a wage earner's death.

Before the New Deal, government-distributed revenues were limited to pensions for veterans of the Union Army, mothers' pensions in some states, and unemployment insurance. Although private charities distributed relief, clients had no enforceable claims to these benefits. The 1935 Social Security Act expanded claims on government-managed property by setting up old-age insurance, assistance to people with disabilities, and aid to families, generally widows, with dependent children. Veterans' benefits were another form of federal "transfer payments," as these claims were called.

Legal theorists have designated claims to revenues, especially revenues channeled through government, the "new property." The constitutional status of rights in government transfer payments was established in 1970 when the U.S. Supreme Court ruled that welfare benefits could not be terminated (taken) without due process, that is, without hearings to determine the reason. Some theorists identified the "new property" with claims to job security (as enforced in suits against wrongful termination) as well as to job benefits. But in the 1980s and 1990s, revision of federal welfare policies, the decline of the labor movement, and management's emphasis on flexibility and turnover in employment eroded many claims to "new property." Still, to be propertyless in the contemporary United States is not only to lack income or assets but to lack access to benefits, whether secure employment, home finance, health insurance, government assistance, or retirement funds.

The corporate order, which separated a company's owners (stockholders) from its salaried managers, also distinguished property rights to a share of profits from powers of direct control. New devices—for example, stock options—were intended to realign corporate executives' and stockholders' mutual interest in profits. In the 1980s and 1990s, economic growth, and particularly the growth of revenues in any one company, was as often achieved through mergers and acquisitions as through more efficient production and distribution of goods. Some stockholders went to court to enforce their claims to the highest return, even if short-term profits came at the expense of a company's long-term growth.

Through its intangible forms and institutional management, property has become increasingly concentrated. By the mid-1990s, institutional investors (pension funds, insurance companies, mutual funds) controlled half the stock traded on the New York Stock Exchange (Seligman 1995, 485). Congress also promoted ordinary Americans' stake in institutional investments by granting tax benefits for Individual Retirement Accounts in 1974 and for employee contribution to 401(k) pension funds in 1981.

Other instruments reinforced the ascendancy of financial over real property. In 1960, Congress authorized real estate investment trusts (REITs), which allowed individuals to buy and sell publicly traded shares in land and buildings. The federally sponsored Government National Mortgage Association (Ginnie Mae) created a national mortgage market by selling shares in pooled home mortgages; and in the 1990s, commercial mortgage backed securities (CMBS) extended this practice to commercial real estate. These financial instruments increased the liquidity of real estate. Home owners, moreover, became adept at using real property to generate revenues by refinancing mortgages when interest rates dropped. With remarkable creativity, Americans also invented new properties that seem to mix the real and the intangible. Thus, in New York City, space over low-rise buildings was commodified as air or development rights that could be purchased by developers wanting to exceed zoning limits on building height. Companies whose emissions meet federal clean-air standards can sell "pollution rights" to companies whose emissions exceed those standards.

The environmental movement also placed new limits on how real property could be used in the late twentieth century. To counter environmental legislation of the 1970s, business groups supported a self-designated "property rights movement," which challenges government regulations by drawing on classical liberal rhetoric to identify private property with stewardship over natural resources. Although this movement itself demonstrates that property rights rest on conflicting political claims, it has avoided discussing the concentration of property in corporate institutions, on the one hand, or the diffusion of "stewardship" that comes with the intangible property, on the other. With the "democratization" of absentee ownership through financial instruments, millions of Americans claim the benefits of property with no knowledge of the specific sources of their income and little understanding of the consequences of its concentration. Meanwhile, some neoclassical theorists have suggested that the contemporary U.S. economy's emphasis on liquidity and transaction costs has so diminished traditional concepts of property rights that they can no longer be distinguished from rights to arrange economic claims and obligations through contracts. Nonetheless, however ambiguous its meanings or attenuated its forms, property remains central to American political ideology, and many Americans think of it as the foundation of political and personal freedom.

Elizabeth Blackmar

See also: Capitalism; Housing Policy; Income and Wage Inequality; Liberalism; New Property; *Progress and Poverty;* Slavery; Wealth; Wealth, Distribution/Concentration

References and Further Reading

Alexander, Gregory. 1997. *Commodity and Propriety: Competing Visions of Property in American Legal Thought, 1776–1970*. Chicago: University of Chicago Press.

Ely, James. 1998. *The Guardian of Every Other Right: A Constitutional History of Property Rights*. New York: Oxford University Press.

Glendon, Mary Ann. 1981. *The New Family and the New Property*. Boston: Butterworths.

Macpherson, C. B. 1978. *Property: Mainstream and Critical Positions*. Toronto: University of Toronto Press.

Seligman, Joel. 1995. "Another Unspecial Study: The SEC's Market 2000 Report and Competitive Developments in the United States Capital Markets." *Business Lawyer* 50: 485–526.

U.S. Bureau of Land Management. 2003. "Facts: Subsurface Acreage Managed by the BLM." http://www.blm.gov/nhp/facts/acres.htm.

U.S. Census Bureau. 2003. "Housing Vacancies and Homeownership Historical Tables." Table 14. http://www.census.gov/hhes/www/housing/hvs/historic/histt14.html.

Wolf, Peter M. 1981. *Land in America: Its Value, Use, and Control*. New York: Pantheon Books.

Wright, Gavin. 1978. *The Political Economy of the Cotton South: Households, Markets, and Wealth in the 19th Century*. New York: Norton.

———. 1986. *Old South, New South: Revolutions in the Southern Economy since the Civil War*. New York: Basic Books.

Protestant Denominations

Half of all Americans are Protestant, so it is difficult to generalize about American Protestant attitudes toward poverty or social policy (Layman and Pew Forum 2002). American religious freedom exacerbated the Protestant tendency for sects to multiply, creating a bewildering array of denominations sorted by class, race, region, and ethnic origin. Although individual Protestant denominations used to have distinct identities, the key distinction that emerged in the twentieth century is between conservative and liberal Protestants. Most theologically conservative Protestants are politically conservative. For them, poverty, like salvation, is individual, so conservative Protestants often frown on government social welfare programs. They prefer private charity, a traditional mission of the church. Liberal Protestants tend to see poverty as a social rather than just an individual problem and to support strong government social welfare programs.

Conservative Protestants

Conservatives include most *evangelicals*, those who had a "born-again" conversion experience and profess a personal relationship with Jesus, and *fundamentalists*, who claim that the Bible is the literal word of God. The two overlap, and both emphasize individual salvation through Jesus Christ.

Conservative Protestants organized in reaction to the liberal consensus that emerged in the twentieth century among the historic, or "mainline," Protestant denominations. Conservative Protestants' public advocacy typically focuses on sexual and moral issues such as pornography, homosexuality, premarital sex, and abortion. In the 1980s, organizations like the Moral Majority and the Christian Coalition forged an alliance with the Republican Party. Conservative Christians increasingly linked economic libertarianism—distrust of the federal government, opposition to taxes, and hostility to a social welfare state—with social conservatism. No matter how they feel about politics, however, conservative Protestants generally consider service to the poor to be a direct expression of Christian faith. One consortium, which does not nearly represent all conservative Protestant churches, is the National Association of Evangelicals (NAE). The NAE includes 43,000 congregations from fifty member denominations and other churches and organizations. Conservative denominations include the Southern Baptist Convention, the Assemblies of God, the Church of God, the Church of the Nazarene, and scores of others, as well as thousands of nondenominational Protestant churches, organizations, and campus ministries.

Liberal Protestants

The largest mainline liberal Protestant denominations are the United Methodist Church (8.5 million members), the Evangelical Lutheran Church in America (ELCA, 5.2 million), the Presbyterian Church (USA) (PCUSA, 2.6 million), the Episcopal Church (2.5 million), the American Baptist Churches in the USA (1.5 million), and the United Church of Christ (UCC, 1.5 million) (Wuthnow and Evans 2002, 4). Mainline Protestants' absolute numbers are about the same as in the 1940s, while evangelical Protestants' proportion of American Christians has rapidly grown.

Although mainline Protestants are theologically and economically diverse, they are better educated than the American average; 35 percent have a college or graduate degree, compared to 24 percent of the general population; 49 percent of those employed are professionals, managers, or business owners, compared to 26 percent of the labor force as a whole. Although individual views toward poverty vary, their denominations see poverty as a social-structural problem and support national social programs to address it. A key word for liberal Protestant responses to poverty is "justice": "Give justice to the weak and the orphan; maintain the right of the lowly and the destitute" (Ps. 82:3). Conservative Christians rarely use the term "justice" in speaking of poverty, for it suggests that current social arrangements might be systemically unjust. Liberal Protestants also advocate through affiliated groups, especially women's organizations. The largest is the United Methodist Women (UMW), whose priority is women's and children's issues, especially poverty. The liberal Protestant denominations have national public policy offices in Washington and staff appointed to lobby federal government officials on social welfare and other issues.

The mainline liberal Protestant denominations are united in the National Council of Churches (NCC), which includes thirty-six denominations and 140,000 congregations. Among its domestic priorities in 2000–2003 were universal health care, "environmental justice," "racial justice," "peace with justice," "justice for women," and a living wage. In 2000, the NCC launched a ten-year "mobilization to overcome poverty." Its president, Andrew Young, said, "The continued existence of poverty in the 21st century is the moral equivalent of slavery in the 19th century" (NCC 2000).

Since the 1980s, liberal Protestants seem to have less public visibility than do conservative Protestants on public policy issues, for multiple reasons. Although Christian conservatives were organized through the Republican Party, no elite has similarly organized liberal Protestants from above. Mainline denominations' Washington lobbying offices are chronically underfunded. Without powerful political mobilization, the most natural form of social action is local, and the most familiar and least controversial form of social action is charity rather than policy advocacy. Many mainline churches are part of faith-based community organizations affiliated with the Industrial Areas Foundation, the Pacific Institute for Community Organization (PICO) Network, the Gamaliel Foundation, or another organizing network. They organize and advocate on poor and working-class issues, but mostly at the local level. Liberal denominations' great challenge is to link local congregations to national policy advocacy.

History of Protestant Social Policy

Martin Luther's key theological claim was that salvation was gained by faith in God's grace rather than by "law" (the laws of the Hebrew Bible) or by "works" (virtuous actions or some other form of earning, as in the Catholic sale of indulgences). The emphasis on biblical rather than priestly authority led reformers to emphasize Christ's commandment to "love thy neighbor as thyself" (Matt. 22:39). The basis of reformers' social ethic was Christian "brotherly love." Taken to its revolutionary egalitarian extreme, this ideal helped justify the Peasants' War of 1525, in which peasants and artisans applied it to relations between noble and peasant. Some Protestant communities with a strong communal identity and sense of mutual obligation, such as sixteenth-century Zurich or the seventeenth-century Puritan Massachusetts Bay Colony, cared for their own poor (Wandel 1996).

The Radical Reformation saw the first of many Protestant utopian experiments whose social policy, among other things, was communistic. In 1534, in Münster, Germany, Anabaptists overturned the city government and property was shared. Subsequent egalitarian utopian attempts by Shakers, Mormons, Mennonites, and others flourished in the nineteenth-century United States (producing the Amana Church Society, the Harmony Society, the Oneida Community, and others).

Reformer John Calvin's views shaped American culture through the Puritan mission to create a "city on a hill." Based on a covenant with God, it would shine like a beacon to the world. Protestant revivalism, a distinctively American phenomenon, is characterized by traveling preachers who give religious services designed to renew religious fervor. The greatest periods of revivalism were the First and Second Great Awakenings (1720–1750 and 1780–1830, respectively).

American Protestantism is characterized by ironies. Protestant revivalism that, as did Luther himself, sought a private renewal of personal piety produced enthusiastic social reform movements. The Wesleyan idea that human will could influence salvation radically reversed the strict Puritan Calvinist belief in absolute predestination by God. This philosophy was more consistent with Americans' experience of their own agency in taming a continent. An optimistic culture of striving individualism could not resist this doctrine of *perfectionism*—improvement of self and society—that became a motor driving Protestant social reform and efforts to alleviate poverty. The belief that Christ would return after a millennium of social purification—*postmillennialism*—also inspired fervent movements to purify society. Protestants created the American voluntary association as we know it, beginning with the Connecticut Society for the Reformation of Morals (1813), which was swiftly followed by a host of temperance, abolition, and other reform societies.

As Protestant reformers sought to combat alcohol, they discovered its link to poverty. In 1850, the pioneering female Holiness preacher Phoebe Palmer founded the Five Points Mission in a New York City slum (Wandel 1996). Accelerating industrialization in the 1870s gave rise to the Social Gospel. Liberal Protestants responded to waves of poor immigrants and the widening gap between capitalists and laborers by seeking to bring about the Kingdom of God on earth through egalitarian social reform (Schmidt 1988).

Heidi J. Swarts

See also: Catholic Church; Charitable Choice; Charity Organization Societies; Christian Fundamentalism; Community Organizing; Industrial Areas Foundation (IAF); Liberalism; Quakers; Salvation Army; Social Gospel; Young Men's Christian Association (YMCA)

References and Further Reading

Layman, Geoffrey. 2001. *The Great Divide: Religious and Cultural Conflict in American Party Politics*. New York: Columbia University Press.

Layman, Geoffrey, and Pew Forum on Religion and Public Life. 2002. "Americans Struggle with Religion's Role at Home and Abroad." March 20. http://pewforum.org/publications/surveys/religion.pdf. Accessed June 17, 2003.

National Council of Churches (NCC). 2000. "NCC Launches 10-Year 'Mobilization to Overcome Poverty.'" November 17. http://www.ncccusa.org/news/2000GA/povaction.html. Accessed June 16, 2003.

Roof, Wade Clark, and William McKinney. 1987. *American Mainline Religion: Its Changing Shape and Future*. New Brunswick, NJ: Rutgers University Press.

Schmidt, Jean Miller. 1988. "Holiness and Perfection." In *Encyclopedia of the American Religious Experience*, ed. Charles H. Lippy and Peter W. Williams, vol. 3, 813–829. New York: Charles Scribner's Sons.

Wandel, Lee Palmer. 1996. "Social Ethics" and "Social Welfare." In *Oxford Encyclopedia of the Reformation*, ed. Hans J. Hillerbrand, 76–83. New York: Oxford University Press.

Wuthnow, Robert, and John H. Evans, eds. 2002. *The Quiet Hand of God: Faith-Based Activism and the Public Role of Mainline Protestantism*. Berkeley and Los Angeles: University of California Press.

Public Opinion

Public attitudes toward social policy in the United States can be viewed as a product of three underlying factors: (1) conflicts among widely held cultural values, (2) popular beliefs about government policies and social groups, and (3) the ways mass media and political elites frame policy-relevant information. Support for the modern welfare state runs weaker in the United States than in most Western democracies. Nevertheless, majorities consistently endorse government efforts to promote economic security and opportunity. The level of support for welfare provision varies considerably across social groups as well as across government programs. Most Americans, however, are not well informed about poverty and tend to approach social policy with a conflicted mixture of commitments to individualist, egalitarian, and humanitarian values. As a result, public opinion functions as both a cause and an effect of poverty politics. Mass preferences are often stable enough to impose constraints on policymakers, but these preferences can and do change in response to economic conditions and political campaigns.

Americans do not exhibit a principled opposition to government assistance. Public hostility toward "welfare handouts" may be highly visible, but it is an exception to the general rule (Gilens 1999). Americans favor maintaining or enhancing the vast majority of U.S. social programs. Most believe that government has a basic responsibility to shield individuals from destitution and to enlarge the scope of economic opportunity (Bobo and Smith 1994). Arrayed against these sentiments, however, is a powerful cultural belief system that affirms the widespread existence of opportunity, emphasizes the individual basis of achievement, and is relatively tolerant of economic inequalities (Kluegel and Smith 1986). The result is a complex political culture that offers resources to welfare advocates but, relative to western Europe, provides a comparatively weak context for demands for social rights.

Most Americans are poorly informed about poverty and social policy. In 1996, for example, polls reported that majorities supported welfare reform. On further questioning, however, half of those polled said they did not know what "reform" actually meant (Weaver 2000). In this instance and in others, public opinion is hampered not only by a lack of relevant facts but also by a surplus of inaccurate facts. Most Americans overestimate the percentage of the poor who are Black (Gilens 1999). They similarly overestimate the number of families on welfare, the size of cash benefits, the percentage of the budget spent on welfare, and the percentage of recipients who receive aid for an extended period of time (Kuklinski and Quirk 2000).

On the general question of what causes poverty, Americans are evenly divided. Approximately half believe that individuals are to blame for their own poverty, while the remainder emphasize forces beyond the individual's control (Demos 2002). In practice, though, beliefs about the origins of poverty tend to shift depending on a number of factors. One such factor is the "type" of poor person under consideration. When asked about a homeless person, for example, Americans tend to cite circumstances that the individual cannot control, such as mental illness; when asked about a welfare recipient, their explanations turn to immoral behavior, lack of hard work, and drug use (Bobo and Smith 1994). Societal conditions also exert an influence. During economic downturns, Americans become less likely to blame individuals for being poor (Gilens 1999). Finally, mass media stories also affect the public's assignment of blame. Stories that focus on specific low-income people are more likely to encourage personal attributions of blame than are news stories that focus on societal conditions (Iyengar 1990).

Support for social programs varies across subgroups of the U.S. population (Cook and Barrett 1992). Women and younger Americans are slightly more likely than men and older Americans to express support for the welfare state (Hasenfeld and Rafferty 1989). These gaps tend to be small, however, compared to those associated with race and socioeconomic status. Relative to other Americans, people of color and people with lower incomes are especially supportive of welfare programs (Hasenfeld and Rafferty 1989). These and other group-based differences may suggest to some that welfare opinions are rooted in self-interest. Direct evidence for this interpretation, however, has been scarce. Most analysts see self-interest as playing less of a role in forming welfare opinions than do life experiences and core values (Gilens 1999).

Social policy attitudes in the United States depend most directly on the interplay of two sets of core values. The first set fuels opposition to welfare programs. It includes individualist beliefs that each person should be responsible for his or her own economic status, antistatist beliefs that government cannot be trusted and should not grow too large, and commitments to the work ethic and "traditional" moral values. The second set consists of more supportive values such as egalitarianism (a normative commitment to equalities of opportunity, treatment, and status) and humanitarianism (the belief that each person has an ethical responsibility to assist those in need). Each value provides a somewhat distinctive basis for welfare opinion. Egalitarianism and humanitarianism, for instance, both promote a desire to assist the poor, but humanitarian values are less likely to foster support for income redistribution as an explicit governmental goal (Feldman and Steenbergen 2001).

Because these values tend to be deeply held, any one of them has the potential to serve as a stable anchor for policy preferences. In combination, however, they provide a dynamic basis for policy attitudes. Most Americans hold an ambivalent mixture of partially conflicting values—a desire to help the poor, for example, combined with a feeling that individuals should be responsible for their own well-being. The result is that public responses to poverty usually hinge on the specific ways Americans perceive government policies and their target groups. Such perceptions, of course, depend not only on the actual characteristics of policies and groups but also on the ways mass media and political advocates portray these characteristics.

The interplay of disparate values can easily be seen in the varying levels of public support for particular social programs. Americans are most likely to support programs they believe assist deserving beneficiaries, preserve personal responsibility and morality, protect or expand societal opportunities, and promote or reward hard work. Large majorities favor maintaining or increasing spending for programs such as Social Security, medical care, and education (Gilens 1999). There is somewhat less support for housing and employment programs, and support is lowest for programs that are linked to the goal of income redistribution or the label "welfare" (Hasenfeld and Rafferty 1989).

Public support runs strongest for programs perceived to offer universal benefits; more-targeted benefits, however, can elicit majority support when they are viewed as promoting opportunity or rewarding hard work and moral behavior (Gilens 1999). These same values help explain the public's relatively strong support for in-kind benefits such as food stamps and medical care. In-kind benefits are perceived as being more difficult to use for illicit or immoral activities than is cash income. In addition, in-kind benefits may be used to actively encourage preferred behaviors. A desire to promote employment, for example, has produced a strong public preference for making benefits such as child care, transportation allowances, and job training a central part of welfare reform (Gilens 1999). Income-maintenance programs that offer cash benefits to the poor tend to receive the least public support. In recent years, a majority of the public has supported making such benefits contingent on value-enforcing rules such as time limits, family caps, work requirements, and prohibitions on substance abuse (Gilens 1999).

The value basis of attitudes in this policy area can also be seen in the ways Americans distinguish among more and less "deserving" subgroups of the poor. Perceptions of group deservingness are arguably the strongest predictor of public support for welfare spending (Gilens 1999). Groups perceived as deserving assistance tend to be those who fulfill (or are exempted from) work expectations and who are not closely associated with racial or ethnic minorities. Contemporary Americans tend to place the elderly and people with disabilities in this category and hence support aid to these groups with little concern for questions of individual morality. By contrast, groups perceived as undeserving tend to include able-bodied individuals without jobs, single women perceived as violating sexual or reproductive norms, and racial minorities, whose poverty is viewed by many as a result of laziness and immoral behavior. Programs that disproportionately serve these groups tend to be less generous, more punitive, and more degrading—all of which serves to reinforce public scorn for their recipients and for the policies that aid them (Schram 1995).

In this regard, the impact of race merits special mention. Since the 1960s, the term "welfare" has come to function as a kind of code word for "undeserving Blacks." White Americans tend to believe that Black people make up the majority of poor families and welfare recipients. As a result, talk of "welfare" tends to evoke thoughts of African Americans, and beliefs about Black people shape images of welfare recipients. The old stereotype of Black laziness (a violation of individualism and the work ethic) is, today, the strongest predictor of whether a white person will view welfare recipients as undeserving, oppose welfare spending, and favor tough behavioral rules for program participants (Gilens 1999).

In all the preceding ways, contemporary public attitudes toward social policy are firmly rooted in values that are widely held in the United States. Conflict among these values, however, means that public attitudes depend greatly on how poverty and welfare issues get framed by political elites, mass media, and political activists. Political communications direct public attention toward particular groups of poor people, dimensions of poverty, and aspects of government policy. In doing so, they influence the specific beliefs people hold about the poor, and they affect the mix of values people bring to bear on questions of social provision (Iyengar 1990). Since the 1980s, political terms such as "the underclass" and "welfare dependency" have served as potent symbols making it easier to conceive, articulate, and accept opposition to assistance for the poor (Schram 1995). As historical and international comparisons demonstrate, however, opposing frames are available and can be quite effective at mobilizing public support.

In sum, public responses to poverty and social policy in the United States exhibit significant differences across groups and for specific policy designs. These responses reflect a stable and widely held set of values, but the interplay of these values allows for flexibility and—depending on how issues are framed—substantial shifts in public support over time and across programs. Accordingly, public opinion on social policy must be understood as both a source and an outcome of poverty politics in the United States.

Erin O'Brien and Joe Soss

See also: Dependency; Deserving/Undeserving Poor; Racism; "Underclass"; Welfare Policy/Welfare Reform; "Working Poor"

References and Further Reading

Bobo, Lawrence, and Ryan Smith. 1994. "Antipoverty Policy, Affirmative Action, and Racial Attitudes." In *Confronting Poverty*, ed. Shelton Danzinger, Gary Sandefur, and Daniel Weinburg, 365–395. Cambridge, MA: Harvard University Press.

Cook, Fay Lomax, and Edith J. Barrett. 1992. *Support for the American Welfare State: The Views of Congress and the Public*. New York: Columbia University Press.

Demos. 2002. "New Opportunities: Public Opinion on Poverty, Income Inequality, and Public Policy: 1996–2001." http://www.demos-usa.org/pubs/New_Opportunities.pdf. Cited May 15, 2002.

Feldman, Stanley, and Marco R. Steenbergen. 2001. "The Humanitarian Foundation for Public Support for Social Welfare." *American Journal of Political Science* 45, no. 3: 658–677.

Gilens, Martin. 1999. *Why Americans Hate Welfare; Race, Media, and the Politics of Antipoverty Policy*. New Haven: Yale University Press.

Hasenfeld, Yeheskel, and Jane Rafferty. 1989. "The Determinants of Public Attitudes Toward the Welfare State." *Social Forces* 67, no. 4: 1027–1048.

Iyengar, Shanto. 1990. "Framing Responsibility for Political Issues: The Case of Poverty." *Political Behavior* 12: 19–40.

Kluegel, J. R., and E. R. Smith. 1986. "Beliefs about Inequality: Americans' Views of What Is and What Ought to Be." In *Social Institutions and Social Change*. New York: A. de Gruyter.

Kuklinski, James H., and Paul J. Quirk. 2000. "Reconsidering the Rational Public: Cognition, Heuristics, and Mass Opinion." In *Elements of Reason: Cognition, Choice, and the Bounds of Rationality*, ed. A. Lupia, M. D. McCubbins, and S. L. Popkin, 153–182. New York: Cambridge University Press.

Schram, Sanford. 1995. *Words of Welfare: The Poverty of Social Science and the Social Science of Poverty*. Minneapolis: University of Minnesota Press.

Weaver, R. Kent. 2000. *Ending Welfare as We Know It*. Washington, DC: Brookings Institution.

Public Relief and Private Charity, *Josephine Shaw Lowell*

In the 1880s and 1890s, as president of the New York Charity Organisation Society (COS), Josephine Shaw Lowell sought to end public "outdoor" poor relief, or state-funded payments to needy families. Her influential role in the COS reflected the growing prominence of women in social welfare organizations in the late nineteenth century. Lowell, like other members of charity organization societies throughout the country, viewed poverty as primarily a moral rather than a material problem. Influenced by religious ideas of human corruptibility, Lowell believed that outdoor relief did little to cure poverty and instead encouraged idleness. She favored almshouses or workhouses that would "cure the individual, whether of sickness, insanity, intemperance, or simply of the tendency to be shiftless and lazy" (76). These institutions were to be sufficiently harsh to discourage all but the most needy. For those she believed could legitimately claim inability to work—such as the elderly without family or widows with young children—Lowell proposed private charitable donations coupled with supervisory visits intended to ensure that the character of recipients would be improved rather than further corrupted by such gifts. Lowell's view that government aid worsens rather than relieves poverty has been echoed by many antiwelfare critics in the twentieth century.

In the excerpts that follow, Lowell lays out her basic philosophy and "rules" for public and private charitable provision.

Sarah Case

See also: Charity; Charity Organization Societies; Poorhouse/Almshouse; Relief

We have, already, accepted in this paper the postulate that the community should save every one of its members from starvation, no matter how low or depraved such member may be, but we contend that the necessary relief should be surrounded by circumstances that shall not only repel every one, not in extremity, from accepting it, but which shall also insure a distinct moral and physical improvement on the part of all those who are forced to have recourse to it—that is, discipline and education should be inseparably associated with any system of poor relief.

. . . [O]ut-door relief is proved to be not only useless, as a means of relieving actual, existing suffering, but as active means of increasing present and future want and vice . . . [only] an institution . . . will be found to render possible the attainment of all the objects which should be aimed at by public relief.

. . . [I]nmates [of public institutions] shall have the necessaries of life, and besides being fed and clothed, they can be subjected to the best sanitary regulations, they can be kept clean and be required to live regularly, to work, to exercise, to sleep, as much or as little as is good for them, and this brings us to the second object, for in an institution the inmates besides being prevented from receiving moral harm, can be brought under such physical, moral, mental and industrial training as will eventually make them self-supporting. (67–69)

. . . [C]harity must tend to develop the moral nature of those it helps, and must not tend to injure others; . . .

. . . [T]he best way to help people is to help them to help themselves. . . . the main instrument to be depended on to raise the standard of decency, cleanliness, providence and morality among them must be personal influence, which means that . . . the educated and happy and good are to give some of their time regularly and as a duty, year in and year out, to the ignorant, the miserable and the vicious. (110–111)

Source: Josephine Shaw Lowell, *Public Relief and Private Charity* (New York: Arno Press, 1971; originally published New York and London: G. P. Putnam's Sons, 1884).

Public Works Administration

The Federal Emergency Administration of Public Works—commonly referred to as the Public Works Administration (PWA)—was the New Deal's first substantial effort to address the crisis of the Great Depression through the construction of public works projects. Created by Title II of the National Industrial Recovery Act (1933), the PWA attempted to increase productivity and employment in construction-related industries, a key economic sector. The stimulus provided by public works construction was originally intended to work in concert with the industrial codes enacted under the act's Title I, which tried to raise prices and wages by regulating competition. Although the PWA proved effective in generating infrastructure, critics of the agency charged that it was too slow and ineffective in reducing unemployment. In response to this criticism, President Franklin D. Roosevelt turned to parallel jobs and public works measures, including the short-lived Civil Works Administration (CWA) and, subsequently, the Works Progress Administration (WPA).

The PWA was based on the notion that government-funded public works projects could be deployed to counter drastic swings in the business cycle, an idea that was rooted in Progressive-Era ideas about the economy and the role of government in maintaining growth and stability. For example, the American Association for Labor Legislation, a prominent reform organization founded in 1906, had long advocated the maintenance of a "shelf" of plans and blueprints for public works projects, ready to be drawn upon in the event of an economic downturn. The Reconstruction Finance Corporation's division of self-liquidating public works, created under President Herbert Hoover in the early 1930s, operated in this spirit, funding projects such as bridges, dams, and toll roads that could generate revenue to pay for their construction. Upon its creation, the PWA incorporated many of the plans and personnel of this division into its own organization.

Under the direction of Secretary of the Interior Harold Ickes, the PWA built 34,508 projects costing over $6 billion, covering all but three counties of the United States. Economist John Kenneth Galbraith estimated that the PWA employed an average of 1,177,000 men each year between 1934 and 1938, after taking into account employment generated beyond the immediate construction site. Although the Federal Emergency Relief Administration (FERA) and the Civilian Conservation Corps (CCC) provided immediate relief and short-term work to the unemployed, the PWA operated by carefully reviewing plans submitted by states and localities and then commissioning selected projects to be constructed by private contractors. The PWA relied not on social welfare professionals but, rather, on people with a background in civil engineering and construction, drawing for its personnel on the Army Corps of Engineers, private engineers, and municipal officials with experience in public works construction. The PWA's Special Board for Public Works, which included such officials as Secretary of Labor Frances Perkins, was supervised by Ickes himself. Ickes and the Special Board evaluated proposed projects, and Ickes took the final decisions to regular meetings with President Roosevelt for his review.

Through a combination of direct appropriations and loans, the PWA funded 17,831 projects, costing $1.9 billion, built by federal agencies, and 16,677 projects, costing $4.2 billion, sponsored by nonfederal bodies. The construction of public buildings such as courthouses, post offices, auditoriums, armories, city halls, prisons, community centers, and government office buildings was a favored use of PWA funds. The PWA also sponsored the construction of streets, highways, and bridges. By July 1936, at least one PWA school project had been built in nearly half the nation's counties. Between 1933 and 1940, the PWA made possible about 80 percent of all sewer construction in the nation, allotting funds for more than 1,500 projects costing nearly half a billion dollars. The PWA also directed monies toward public housing projects, flood control and reclamation projects, a modernization program for the nation's railroads, and the construction of several vessels for the navy. Notable projects funded by the PWA include the overseas highway connecting Key West to mainland Florida, the Grand Coulee Dam in eastern Washington, the Triborough Bridge in New York City, and the San Francisco–Oakland Bay Bridge.

The PWA played a pioneering role in funding both nonfederal and federal hydroelectric projects. These nonfederal projects included California's Hetch Hetchy and Imperial hydroelectric projects, South Carolina's Santee-Cooper project, the Grand River Dam in Oklahoma, and the sprawling Lower Colorado River Authority as well as projects in Arizona, Idaho, Illinois, Maine, Michigan, Nebraska, Oregon, Utah, Virginia, and Washington. Federal projects included California's huge Shasta Dam, Montana's Fort Peck Dam, the Bonneville Dam project (covering Washington and Oregon), and the Tennessee Valley Authority, among others.

In addition to providing employment, the PWA's projects generated over $2.1 billion in orders for construction materials between 1933 and 1939. Items made from iron and steel, such as nails, rails, pipes, and structural steel, accounted for about one-third of these orders. Stone, clay, and glass products such as brick, cement, concrete, marble, and tile made up the same proportion of materials ordered, with the remainder of materials consisting of heavy machinery, wiring, lumber, and other products.

Concerned about the potential for public works to lead to waste and graft, Ickes was cautious about allotting federal monies, leading to much criticism that the PWA was simply moving too slowly to meet the crisis of the Depression. Responding to this criticism and to the harsh winter of 1933–1934, FDR gave more responsibility for fighting the Depression to Works Progress Administration head Harry Hopkins. Despite falling out of favor with President Roosevelt, Ickes remained in charge of the PWA through 1939, when the agency was placed under the auspices of the Federal Works Administration and its new head, former Rural Electrification administrator John Carmody.

Jason Scott Smith

See also: American Association for Labor Legislation; Capitalism; Civilian Conservation Corps (CCC); Employment Policy; Great Depression and New Deal; Housing Policy; Liberalism; Tennessee Valley Authority; Works Progress Administration (WPA)

References and Further Reading

Galbraith, John Kenneth, assisted by G. G. Johnson Jr. 1940. *The Economic Effects of the Federal Public Works Expenditures, 1933–1938*. Washington, DC: GPO.

Ickes, Harold L. 1935. *Back to Work: The Story of PWA*. New York: Macmillan.

Isakoff, Jack P. 1938. *The Public Works Administration*. Urbana: University of Illinois Press.

Public Works Administration. 1939. *America Builds: The Record of PWA*. Washington, DC: GPO.

Puerto Rican Migration

Puerto Ricans constitute the second largest Latino population in the United States and have historically experienced poverty rates among the nation's highest. The 2000 census showed nearly 3.5 million Puerto Ricans residing in the continental United States, up from 2.7 million in 1990 (a 24.9 percent increase). This is 9.6 percent of the Hispanic and 1.2 percent of the total U.S. population. Another 3.8 million live on the island of Puerto Rico. This geographic distribution between the Island and the mainland reflects the results of decades of shifting migration patterns—themselves influenced by the political and economic status of Puerto Rico vis-à-vis the United States—which have brought Island-born Puerto Ricans to major northeastern cities in response to the promise of better jobs and opportunities for themselves and their families. Although many migrants, especially in earlier generations, did experience better economic prospects and living standards, Puerto Ricans have also suffered the impact of economic restructuring, wage declines, and diminishing blue-collar and unionized job opportunities in their destination cities. Thus, migration has played an essential, if complicated, role in the social and economic fortunes of Puerto Ricans: An avenue to upward mobility as well as to economic hardship, the post–World War II migration made poverty among Puerto Ricans increasingly visible to Americans who knew little else about the Island or its culture.

The Puerto Rican population in the United States traces its origins back to Spanish colonial rule. The Island became a U.S. territory in 1898, as a result of the American invasion during the Spanish-American War. Puerto Ricans were granted U.S. citizenship in 1917. It was only in 1952 that the Island's official status changed from territory to "commonwealth." Although Puerto Rico is free to govern its internal affairs, the U.S. president and Congress retained veto power over all legislation and any amendments to the Puerto Rican Constitution.

Without visa or employment impediments, Puerto Ricans began migrating in small but steadily increasing numbers, especially after 1917. In part, they were responding to the increased demand for a domestic source of low-wage labor in the wake of World War I, more restrictive U.S. immigration laws, and the decline of European immigration. The migratory movement slackened somewhat during the Great Depression of the 1930s, when there was actually an interval of reverse migration from the mainland United States back to Puerto Rico.

By the end of World War II, however, the flow of migrants out of Puerto Rico had turned into a mass migration, establishing a pattern for a large segment of the Island's population. The postwar economic boom in the United States was a powerful draw for Puerto Ricans who, owing to rapid, federally sponsored urbanization and industrialization on the Island, were already being displaced from agricultural employment at a faster rate than the new economy could absorb. The stagnant agricultural sector set off major migrations, first to urban areas in Puerto Rico and then abroad. The process was accelerated by labor-recruitment strategies of U.S. firms on the Island and by systematic government-led dissemination of information about prospective jobs and higher wages.

The economic shifts that drove the postwar mass migration had some effect on the migrant population as well. The first major study of the Puerto Rican population in the United States in the postwar years dates from 1947. The 1950 survey carried out by C. Wright Mills, Clarence Senior, and Rose Goldsen of 5,000 New York Puerto Ricans revealed a largely urban skilled and semiskilled population, with previous work experience in manufacturing. These early migrants had educational and employment qualifications that exceeded those of the average Puerto Rican on the Island at that time.

By the late 1950s, however, relatively fewer migrants came from the Island's largest cities and most skilled groups, and a greater proportion were agricultural workers who had been displaced before World War II and who had little experience in manufacturing and less formal education than their predecessors. Although these migrants were readily absorbed as long as the demand for industrial workers kept growing, they were especially vulnerable to the downturns that were becoming increasingly evident in the domestic manufacturing sector by the 1970s.

In 1960, when close to two-thirds of the Puerto Rican population in the United States lived in New York City, one in two Puerto Rican men and three out of four Puerto Rican women working in the city worked in manufacturing. During the 1960s, and especially by the 1970s, however, the heavily urbanized Puerto Rican migrants were feeling the impact of displacement

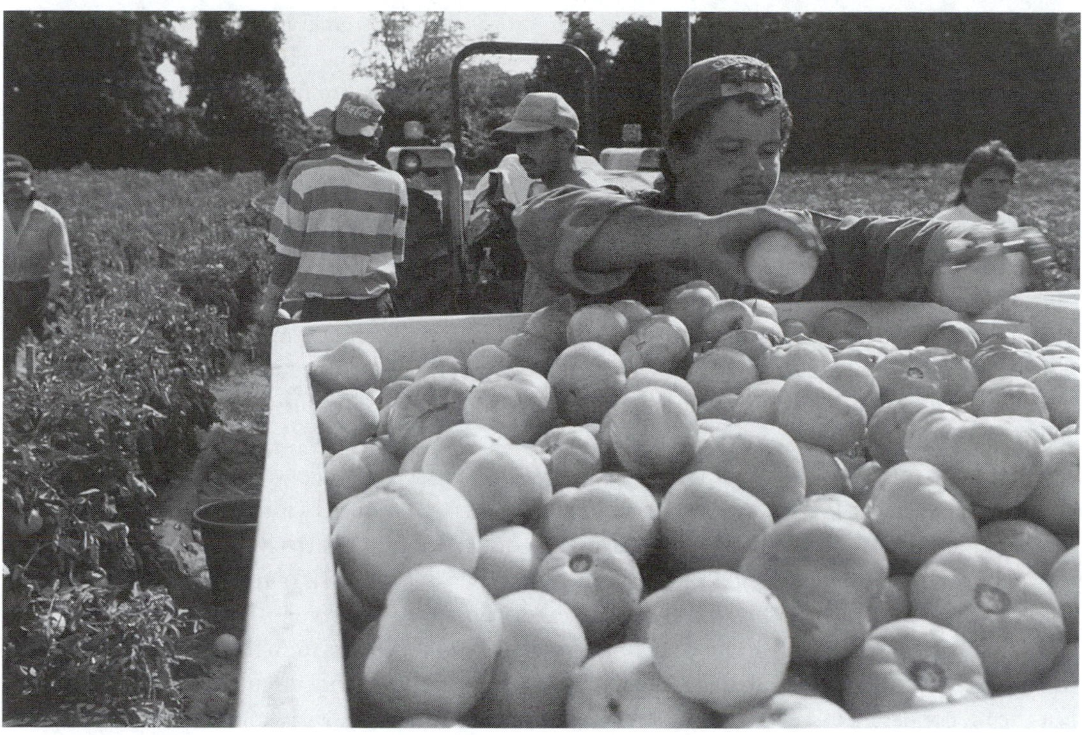

Puerto Rican migrant workers harvest tomatoes at Russel Marino Farm. (James Leynse/Corbis)

from goods-producing jobs and of declining employment opportunities as industries relocated. The long-term effects for Puerto Rican migrants—who had left the Island in search of improved opportunities—were devastating: increases in unemployment and joblessness, declines in earnings, and soaring poverty rates. With below-average schooling and less-than-fluent English, the primarily Island-born population could not easily move into new jobs in other expanding sectors of the economy (DeFreitas 1991). Throughout the 1970s, many returned to the Island. It was not until the 1980s, when unemployment (over 23 percent) and poverty (58 percent) shot up on the Island, that net out-migration resumed.

The 1980s presented a mixed picture for Puerto Rican migrants. On the one hand, the decade saw income growth, gains in earnings, increased female labor force participation, and improvements in educational attainment. On the other hand, the progress was not evenly shared. Those without a high school degree and with limited skills, many of them first-generation migrants from Puerto Rico, and those relocating in distressed postindustrial cities in the Northeast lost ground in terms of earnings, employment, and income during the decade. Thus, the good news was tempered by the reality of a growing polarization of socioeconomic outcomes—mirroring trends in the United States overall (Rivera-Batiz and Santiago 1995).

Studies of Puerto Rican migration patterns have consistently confirmed the centrality of labor market and other economic conditions in stimulating migrant flows and shaping migrants' economic prospects once relocated. Nevertheless, some observers have continued to invoke a series of pernicious ideas—beginning with anthropologist Oscar Lewis's widely discredited "culture of poverty"—to explain the persistence of high poverty rates among Puerto Ricans. Thus, the 1980s brought not only a resumption of migration but a renewal of extensive heated debate about the causes of persistent poverty among Puerto Ricans, who, like African Americans, were highly concentrated in racially segregated urban neighborhoods. Some argued that high rates of single-female family headship and increasing participation in government support programs for the poor, along with easy transit between the United States and the Island, prevented Puerto Ricans from developing a stronger attachment to the labor force and moving up the socioeconomic ladder. Others argued that certain locations, like New York, selectively attracted and retained those with poorer socioeconomic outcomes, which effectively slashed the chances of economic progress for the group and placed them along the ranks of an urban "underclass." But the preponderance of evidence suggests that increases in poverty for Puerto Ricans were more related to increases in unemployment and decreases in earning levels than to any such sociodemographic variables or cultural traits.

Empirical studies of the determinants of migration from the post–World War II era until the 1970s find that differences in employment and wages between the United States and Puerto Rico explain the migratory behavior of Puerto Ricans. Subsequent work, using census and passenger data, confirms the role of economic motives for migration during the more recent period, when unemployment on the Island reached double digits (over 23 percent in the early 1980s) and the poverty rate reached 58 percent.

Some analysts have argued that the failure of recent immigrants to quickly assimilate into U.S. culture and labor markets reflects a declining "quality" of immigrants. Others argue that there is no conclusive evidence that migration has become less selective over time. Nor is there evidence of a "brain drain" of professionals from the Island.

Moreover, studies have shown no significant differences in the characteristics of migrants (compared to nonmigrants) from 1955 to 1980, other than a relative increase in educational attainment level, reflecting the Island's improvements in education (Ortiz 1986).

Similarly, studies of the post-1980 wave of migrants indicate that the two most important factors contributing to the observed distribution of skills among migrants appear to be job offers and unemployment levels in Puerto Rico. Using 1982–1988 survey data from the Puerto Rican Planning Board, Edwin Meléndez (1994) found that the occupational distribution of emigrants and returnees mirrored the occupational distribution in Puerto Rico.

Separate analysis of the circulation behavior of Puerto Rican women—who represent at least half of all migrants from the Island—also refuted the perception that circular migration explains Puerto Ricans' disadvantaged economic position in the United States. Vilma Ortiz (1992) found limited support for the proposition that large numbers of Puerto Rican women are migrating back and forth between Puerto Rico and the United States. Not only had a majority of Puerto Rican women not migrated from Puerto Rico in the early 1980s, but also, among migrants, only a minority (6 percent) had had more than one migration experience.

Even if we look only at the U.S.-born children of Puerto Rican migrants, the economic gap between them and their non-Hispanic white counterparts remains substantial. Some authors have shown that a large share of the observed gap between average Puerto Rican and non-Hispanic white earnings can be accounted for by differences in education, work experience, and English-language ability. Undoubtedly, low educational attainment levels and English-language difficulties can have a strong negative effect, particularly for the Island-born. But not all of the economic gap between Puerto Ricans and non-Hispanic whites can be explained by traditional productivity differences. Other factors, such as discrimination, continue to play a role (see, for example, Darity, Guilkey, and Winfrey 1996; Meléndez, Carré, and Holvino 1995).

What would Puerto Rican and non-Hispanic white differences be if both groups had the same average characteristics? Using 1976 Survey of Income and Education data, Cordelia Reimers (1985) found that discrimination may account for as much as 18 percent of the wage gap between non-Hispanic white and Puerto Rican males; the difference was not significant for females. Nonetheless, standard economic criteria for measuring discrimination does not account for the role of other forms of (premarket) discrimination. For example, discrimination continues to limit housing options and residential choices of Puerto Ricans in the United States, as well as the quality of their education in urban public schools. Evidence of employment and wage discrimination also derives from employment testing or job audits that suggest that Latino job seekers experience widespread discrimination based on their ethnicity (Cross et al. 1990).

Although most Puerto Ricans in the United States continue to live in the Northeast, the 1990 and 2000 censuses provide evidence that a growing number of this population is moving away from large urban centers in traditional areas of settlement. At the same time, Puerto Ricans have both increased their presence in new areas and moved into smaller cities within the more traditional destinations. In the years ahead, it will be possible to assess whether changed patterns of migration, geographic dispersion, and occupational changes translate into more widely shared improvements in Puerto Ricans' economic well-being.

Aixa Cintron

See also: African American Migration; Immigrants and Immigration; Latino/as; "Underclass"; Urban Poverty

References and Further Reading

Cross, Harry, Gevieve Kenny, Jan Hall, and Wendy Zimmerman. 1990. *Employer Hiring Practices: Differential Treatment of Hispanics and Anglo Job Seekers*. Report 90-4. Washington, DC: Urban Institute Press.

Darity, William, Jr., David K. Guilkey, and William Winfrey. 1996. "Explaining Group Differences in Economic Performance among Racial and Ethnic Groups in the U.S.A.: The Data Examined." *The American Journal of Economics and Sociology* 55, no. 4: 411–425.

DeFreitas, Gregory. 1991. *Inequality at Work: Hispanics in the U.S. Labor Force*. New York: Oxford University Press.

Meléndez, Edwin. 1994. "Puerto Rican Migration and Occupational Selectivity." *International Migration Review* 28, no. 1 (Spring): 49–67.

Meléndez, Edwin, Françoise Carré, and Evangelina Holvino. 1995. "Latinos Need Not Apply: The Effects of Industrial Change and Workplace Discrimination on Latino Employment." *New England Journal of Public Policy* 11, no. 1: 87–115.

Mills, C. Wright, Clarence Senior, and Rose Goldsen. 1950. *The Puerto Rican Journey: New York's Newest Migrants*. New York: Harper and Row.

Ortiz, Vilma. 1986. "Changes in the Characteristics of Puerto Rican Migrants from 1955 to 1980." *International Migration Review* 20, no. 3: 612–628.

———. 1992. "Circular Migration and Employment among Puerto Rican Women." Paper presented at the Social Science Research Council Puerto Rican Poverty and Migration Conference. New York City, May 1.

Reimers, Cordelia. 1985. "A Comparative Analysis of the Wages of Hispanics, Blacks and Non-Hispanic Whites." In *Hispanics in the U.S. Economy*, ed. George J. Borjas and Marta Tienda, 27–75. Orlando, FL: Academic Press.

Rivera-Batiz, Francisco L., and Carlos Santiago. 1995. *Puerto Ricans in the United States: A Changing Reality*. Washington, DC: National Puerto Rican Coalition.

Tienda, Marta. 1989. "Puerto Ricans and the Underclass Debate." *Annals of the American Academy of Political and Social Sciences* 501: 105–119.

Puritans and Puritanism

The term "Puritan" identifies a member of a group of English Calvinists originating in the sixteenth century who sought to purge the Church of England of residual Catholic hierarchies. The word "Puritanism" refers to the generalized nexus of movements and theologies affiliated with Puritan religious dissent. Although the religion of the Puritans had virtually disappeared by the mid-nineteenth century, the ideologies propagated by the variant descendants of Puritanism endure into the contemporary era and continue to affect ideas about poverty and social obligations to the poor. Although the label "puritanical" is commonly associated with rigid, disciplinarian norms regarding sexuality, behavior, and work, Puritanism also embraced an ethic of moral stewardship that emphasized communal responsibility for the well-being of the poor. And while Puritans did not shy away from material wealth, they disapproved of the pursuit of wealth for its own sake and of its ostentatious manifestations, and they preached about the importance of personal humility and austerity.

"Puritan" was first used in the 1560s to describe those disappointed by the compromised Church of England established by Elizabeth I. During the reign of Elizabeth's successor, James I, the Puritans acquired an increasingly notorious profile following their intense lobby for ecclesiastical reform at the 1604 Hampton Court Conference. The Archbishop of Canterbury William Laud (1573–1645) attempted to quell growing Puritan enthusiasm through a systematic repression of their activities. Yet the archbishop's efforts were rebuffed by the brief Puritan dominance following the English Civil War (1642–1651)—also known as the Puritan Revolution—led by Oliver Cromwell. Internal strife led to a collapse of Cromwell's government, and after the Restoration (1660), many Puritans were forced to leave the Church of England.

This brief outline of British Puritan history fails to address the full complexity of the manifold Puritan positions. From the outset, Puritans disagreed about the amount of reform necessary to "purify" the Church of England. Some, known as "Presbyterians," merely sought to remove the hierarchy of bishops (the episcopacy). Others, like the Separatists and Congregationalists, also rejected certain rituals and membership allowances that they perceived as "human" constructs of the Catholic Church. For these critics, church was understood as a divine manifestation, *not* a human invention. The Separatist and Congregationalist Puritans held that church communities ought only to include the participation of those divinely called to join the congregation and should eliminate all decorative excesses representative of human involvement. Simplicity of worship and material austerity were signifying attributes of these Puritans.

The Separatists and Congregationalists constituted the majority of those who migrated to America during the early seventeenth century. Archbishop Laud's persecutions motivated many to seek a new context for their reformations. Thus, in 1628 a group of Congregationalists invested in a trading company, and by 1630 over 1,000 Puritan immigrants were able to settle in Massachusetts Bay Colony. Between 1630 and 1640, approximately 20,000 Puritans migrated to New England, making Puritanism the dominant religion in four American colonies (Plymouth, Massachusetts, New Haven, and Connecticut).

Although there were divergences among the Puritans, some general comments can be made about the theological and social facets of Puritanism. Puritanism was an intellectual descendent of Calvinism, a theological movement that emphasized the total depravity of man and the sainthood of all believers. Like Calvinism, Puritanism adhered to the belief that humans are sinners who cannot be saved unless God initiates the process of salvation. Yet Puritans were encouraged to ceaselessly emulate their own sainthood, even though only God could ordain their salvation. As historian Edmund S. Morgan explains, "Puritanism required that a man devote his life to seeking salvation but told him he was helpless to do anything but evil" (Morgan 1958, 7). Tireless labor and personal self-defamation were perceived as signs of Puritan sainthood. This display of saintliness is what has led many to caricature Puritans as cold and morally unbending. Although Puritans did advocate moral righteousness and personal discipline, they only did so because of a passionate devotion to their own perfection in the face of man's inherent sinfulness.

The defining social features of Puritanism were the focus on the local congregation, the centrality of a vernacular Bible, and the reifying maintenance of the biweekly sermons. Thus, the minister was in many ways the center of Puritan life, since it was he who directed the worship community, interpreted the scripture, and provided the sermons that explicated Puritan existence. The most famous statement of Puritan leadership was made even before the first immigrant disembarked. In the middle of the original oceanic crossing, John Winthrop (1588–1649) offered "A Model of Christian Charity" on the deck of the *Arabella*. Supervisor of the colonization effort, Winthrop used the format of the sermon to motivate endurance and moral excellence among the nascent Americans. "We must not content ourselves with usual ordinary means," Winthrop preached. "For we must consider that we shall be as a city upon a hill, the eyes of all people are upon us" (in Miller 1956, 83). In order to attain this model, Winthrop advocated a blueprint for a godly society premised on individual virtue and communal covenant.

Winthrop's dream of a "city upon a hill" established the primary metaphor for Anglo-American Puritan social life. Puritans' faith in the omnipresence of God's divine will, as well as their investment in God's manifold covenants among men and nations, served as motivation for their efforts to model reformed societies in New England that reflected the glory of God. The effort to form these cities led to the construction of New World governments more theocratic than democratic. Puritans believed in a society driven simultaneously by God's continuing providence and by his direct acts of creation. For Puritans, then, there was no separation between church and state, individual and the public; there was only the world made by God, righteous in its creation, denigrated and divided by the sinful hands of man. In "A Model of Christian Charity," Winthrop hoped that "every man might have need of each other" in the effort to resist residing in sin and that "hence they might be all knit more nearly together in the bond of brotherly affection" (in Miller 1956, 80). Man unified into congregation in an act of virtuous resistance against the selfish tyranny of individualism.

The idea of covenant was central to the maintenance of this stoic congregationalism. Puritans believed that God worked with people through covenants, or solemn agreements. Congregationalist Puritans, for example, argued that local churches are maintained when individuals concede to serving God's will through a communal covenant. Individual men were bound to God through a "covenant of grace" whereby God offers the salvation of Christ to those who exercise faith in Christ. Moreover, most Puritans also held that God formed covenants with nations. Although nations could possess divine blessing through the successful fulfillment of their covenant, individual countries would also suffer the wrath of God should they violate their national covenant. The covenant between God and nation was a tenuous one, dependent on the saintly fervor of citizens and rigorous adherence of congregations. "Downy beds make drowsy persons, but hard lodging keeps the eyes open," wrote Puritan poet Anne Bradstreet. "A prosperous state makes a secure Christian, but adversity makes him consider" (in Miller 1956, 277).

The adversity experienced by seventeenth-century Puritan settlers in the New World surely made them consider. The first generations of Puritans struggled with disease, war against the native inhabitants, and theological discord among the faithful. This turmoil only galvanized the colonies in their reformations, as if through their difficulties their saintliness was affirmed and their cause justified. Early American Puritans elaborated the terms of church membership, mandating a public confession of faith that became the prerequisite for church membership as well as for a voting role in the colony's government. Secular leaders were selected by virtue of their commitment to the scriptures, and their merit as leaders was ultimately interpreted in terms of their fulfillment of God's covenants. Thus, New England was not precisely a theocracy, for church and state authorities functioned through different institutional channels. However, the charismatic importance of the minister in both secular and ecclesiastical systems led to a blurring of governmental boundaries.

After 1650, Puritan church membership began to decline, and dissenting groups—like the Quakers and the Baptists—began to gain popularity. In 1684, the Massachusetts Bay Colony lost its charter, and the blended church-state authority that had ruled New England for nearly fifty years began to splinter. Historian Richard L. Bushman (1967) suggests that by 1690, there were no Puritans left in the New World; thereafter, there were only Yankees. Despite the denominational fragmentation and statistical decline of the Puritan religion, Puritanism as an ethical code and national metaphor has endured. Countless politicians evoke Puritan theology when they speak of America as a "city on a hill" or of the need for a "new covenant" between citizens and government. The Puritan emphasis on literacy and intellectual rationalism grounded American educational systems long before the Revolution, and their faith in a cooperative social covenant initiated a distinct self-understanding. Although many have stereotyped the Puritans as somber moralists, the theological complexity and historical significance of their reform movement cannot be denied.

Kathryn Lofton

See also: Colonial Period through the Early Republic; Protestant Denominations; Republicanism

References and Further Reading

Bushman, Richard L. 1967. *From Puritan to Yankee: Character and the Social Order in Connecticut, 1690–1765*. Cambridge, MA: Harvard University Press.

Miller, Perry. 1939. *The New England Mind.* Vol. 1, *The Seventeenth Century*. New York: Macmillan.

———. 1953. *The New England Mind.* Vol. 2, *From Colony to Province*. Cambridge, MA: Harvard University Press, 1953.

———, ed. 1956. *The American Puritans: Their Prose and Poetry*. New York: Columbia University Press.

Morgan, Edmund S. 1958. *The Puritan Dilemma: The Story of John Winthrop*. Boston: Little, Brown.

Stout, Harry S. 1986. *The New England Soul: Preaching and Religious Culture in Colonial New England.* New York: Oxford University Press.

Quakers (The Religious Society of Friends)

The Quakers, a group of radical Protestants also known as the Religious Society of Friends, descended from the seventeenth-century Puritan reformations in Great Britain. Following their migration to America, the Quakers briefly flourished in the Pennsylvania Colony. Although their numbers hover just over 100,000 members, Quakers exert a disproportionate moral influence in the United States as leading voices of pacifism and humanitarianism.

Quakers trace their origins to Pendle Hill in northeast England. At that spot, George Fox (1624–1691) received a vision from God in 1652. According to Fox's account, God told him, "There is one, even Christ Jesus, that can speak to thy condition." This message inspired Fox's advocacy of the doctrine of inner light. According to this theology, religious experience is an individual experience. Individuals can access religious truth and wisdom through the inner light of Christ present in the human soul. Christ "speaks" to man when his "light" enters human consciousness. This focus on the "inward light" of divine guidance would become the center of the Quaker religion.

For Fox and his followers, emphasis on the inner light was merely an extension of other Puritan reforms that attempted to cleanse the Church of England of all external doctrine and ritual and to refocus religious experience on the individual believer. However, church authorities—both Anglican and orthodox Puritan—perceived something far more subversive in the Religious Society of Friends. Quakers were expected to act in complete obedience to the inward light and to eschew any other doctrines, church structures, or ministerial recommendations. Moreover, Fox taught that Quakers should refuse to participate in any hierarchical etiquette (for example, kneeling before a king), since the inner light leveled men to equal status. The divine spirit could be anywhere, irrespective of class, gender, or race. This irreverence toward social status and institutionalized Christianity troubled secular and ecclesiastical leaders in England. From the outset, Quakers were persecuted for their beliefs, and early in the church's existence, many began to consider emigration to America.

However, even in the New World, Quakers faced intolerance. The very first Quakers to emigrate, Mary Fisher and Ann Austin, only remained in Massachusetts long enough to be charged with witchcraft and banned from the colonies. Puritan resistance to Quakers led to colonization of Rhode Island, which was for many years a safe haven for such religious outsiders as the Baptists and the Quakers. In 1681, William Penn (1644–1718), a wealthy British Quaker, received a charter from Charles II to repay a debt to the Penn family. This charter became the Pennsylvania Colony, known as the "Holy Experiment" in Quaker colonialism. By the late seventeenth century, Penn was already a well-known promoter of Quaker theology, having written the spiritual classic *No Cross, No Crown* (1669). With the Pennsylvania Colony, he attempted to enact the ideals he preached. Pennsylvania offered religious toleration to everyone and extended Quaker egalitarianism to include Native Americans, with whom Penn established fair trading relations.

Although Pennsylvania was a sanctuary open to all, it was primarily a Quaker colony, established to relieve the Quakers' oppression and sustain their style of life. In their effort to excise spiritual and material excess, Quakers adopted a simple style of dress and speech and modeled their communities using the principles of efficiency and austerity as their guides. Though spiritually motivated, this organizational tactic was monetarily beneficial. Pennsylvania, and in particular its capital, Philadelphia, was phenomenally prosperous. As one Quaker historian explained, factories and houses were built as "temples of holiness and righteousness, which God may delight in" (quoted in Tolles 1948, 63). Thus, Quakers constructed a successful capitalism based on theological devotion. In time, as historian Frederick B. Tolles noted, the "counting house became more important than the meeting house" (1948, 241–243) and the theological impetus for material success became more and more diluted. By the late nineteenth century, the obvious Quaker presence in Pennsylvania had disappeared.

Although their cultural dominance was in decline, Quakers maintained a strong social role in the United States. Quakers always exerted a moral influence disproportionate to their statistical numbers, for their theological disposition propelled them to social activism. Beginning in the seventeenth century, Quakers argued for the critical link between personal piety and social responsibility. Directed by their belief in the universal inner light, Quakers have persistently argued for the deconstruction of inequalities and social oppression. Quakers were central to the abolition of slavery; indeed, the Monthly Meeting of Friends in Germantown, Pennsylvania, published the first written public protest against slavery in 1688. For members of the Religious Society of Friends, the inviolability of an individual's conscience made slaveholding a clear sin. Quakers banned slaveholding among their members and were active managers of the Underground Railroad.

Aside from their prominence in abolition, Quakers were also active in movements for temperance, prison reform, and the abolition of poverty. Quakers were also heavily involved in the suffragette movement, with major leaders in the movement, including Susan B. Anthony and Lucretia Mott, claiming Quaker membership. As Quakers maintain no bounded church structure, social reform for them functions as a form of worship. In the twentieth century, members of the Religious Society of Friends focused their activist labors toward the end of war. Although Quakers were always pacifists, the horrors of modern warfare rejuvenated their quest to end organized violence between men. In 1917, Quakers founded the American Friends Service Committee to support Quakers and others in the maintenance of their witness for peace. The Friends Committee for National Legislation was formed as a lobbying organization based in Washington, D.C. Finally, throughout the Vietnam War, Quakers ran Civilian Public Service work camps to provide sites of alternative service for those claiming conscientious objector status.

Today, three groups of Quakers maintain organized membership rolls: the Friends United Meeting, which models its worship after mainline Protestant denominations, including liturgy and regular sermons; the Friends General Conference, a group that rejects all liturgy and maintains silence during worship services; and the

Evangelical Friends Alliance, which borrowed religious methods from revivalist tradition, including the practice of missions. Although diverse in worship patterns, these Quaker groups share a cultural life committed to social action and a ceaseless devotion to religious reform.

Kathryn Lofton

See also: Antihunger Coalitions

References and Further Reading

Bacon, Margaret Hope. 1969. *The Quiet Rebels: The Story of the Quakers in America*. New York: Basic Books.

Ingle, H. Larry. 1994. *First among Friends: George Fox and the Creation of Quakerism*. New York: Oxford University Press.

Tolles, Frederick B. 1948. *Meeting House and Counting House: The Quaker Merchants of Colonial Philadelphia, 1682–1763*. New York: Norton.

Trueblood, D. Elton. 1966. *The People Called Quakers*. New York: Harper and Row.

Racial Segregation

Racial segregation, whether it is de jure or de facto, is intended to order racial groups hierarchically through physical isolation or through the regulation of social interactions. It entails subordinating one racial group to another in a relationship of inferiority and superiority. In the United States, racial segregation has been used to establish white supremacy and to maintain white privilege by stigmatizing African Americans and other racial groups and by institutionalizing unequal access to social and economic resources. Today, residential segregation, or urban apartheid, has replaced legal segregation as one of the mainstays of racial inequality.

Legal, or de jure, segregation was characteristic mainly of the South, though many border states and some northern states had laws requiring segregated schools and prohibiting miscegenation. Southern laws mandating segregation date from the Black codes that were passed in many southern states after the Civil War but that only proliferated beginning in the 1880s. State legislatures passed segregation laws in order to minimize social and physical contact between Blacks and whites. These laws regulated contact in all public spaces: parks, libraries, hospitals, asylums, post offices, schools, public offices such as courthouses, and transportation, including all common carriers. Jim Crow laws were pervasive, extending to all realms of life: Georgia segregated prisoners, Louisiana required separate saloons for Blacks and whites, and even cemeteries were segregated.

Jim Crow laws underpinned political disenfranchisement and economic exploitation of Black workers. These laws stemmed partly from widespread fears of social equality among white southerners as a new Black middle class emerged after Reconstruction. It was no accident that Jim Crow first took hold in transportation. Railroads were the chief means of transportation in the South, and the one place where Blacks and whites, especially Black men and white women, would come together. Whites resented sitting in the same car with Blacks. Segregation was clearly connected to gender. Male preserves such as bars or racetracks were less likely to be segregated than were places where white women and Blacks could meet.

School segregation predated the proliferation of Jim Crow laws in the 1890s; southern laws mandating segregated schools go back to Reconstruction. Seventeen states had constitutional provisions requiring segregated schools; in addition, a handful of northern states permitted segregated schools. Schooling was separate and unequal. White southerners were callously indifferent to the plight of Black schoolchildren. Average per pupil expenditures for Black schools in the south were just 34 percent of expenditures for white schools, a ratio that did not appreciably change until the 1940s (Margo 1990). Black schoolchildren made do with fewer books, blackboards, and other equipment, and their schools were housed in dilapidated buildings.

The Supreme Court upheld Jim Crow laws in *Plessy v. Ferguson* (163 U.S. 537 [1896]), ruling that such laws did not violate either the Thirteenth or the Fourteenth Amendment to the Constitution. The majority held that segregation was a reasonable exercise of the police powers delegated to states. Ignoring the fact that segregation was intended to isolate and subordinate African Americans and that it was separate and unequal, the majority ruled that Jim Crow laws were not discriminatory. "Laws permitting, and even requiring, their separation," the majority wrote, "in places where they are liable to be brought into contact, do not necessarily imply the inferiority of either race to the other." Until Plessy was overruled in *Brown v. Board of Education of Topeka, Kansas* (347 U.S. 483 [1954]), segregation was not understood to be an act of discrimination.

Yet the Supreme Court did not uphold all segregation laws. After the turn of the twentieth century, many southern cities passed laws requiring segregated housing, only to have the Supreme Court rule in *Buchanan v. Warley* (245 U.S. 60 [1917]) that such laws were in violation of the 1866 Civil Rights Act, which gave Blacks the right to "inherit, purchase, lease, sell, hold, and convey real and personal property." In fact, levels of residential segregation in the South were much lower than in the North until the 1950s. In most southern cities, small concentrations of Blacks lived amid whites rather than in geographically isolated areas, as happened in the North. A unique settlement pattern in southern cities—whites living on avenues, Blacks in the alleys—and the pervasiveness of Jim Crow laws were the main reasons residential segregation in the South did not duplicate the northern pattern.

De facto segregation in the North was in many ways just as rigid and just as pervasive. Unlike southern segregation, northern segregation was based on isolation and confinement. Beginning in the 1920s, northern whites segregated residential neighborhoods by resisting the settlement of migrating Blacks in white areas through violent reprisals and racial covenants. The latter were private agreements used by real estate brokers and home-owner associations to maintain whites-only neighborhoods. Covenants required home buyers to agree that if they sold their homes, they would sell only to whites. Real estate agents used racial covenants as a marketing tool, selling the idea of white enclaves outside cities. After the Supreme Court upheld racial covenants in a 1926 opinion, *Corrigan v. Buckley* (271 U.S. 323), they became the mainstay of northern apartheid until they were overturned in *Shelley v. Kraemer* (334 U.S. 1 [1948]).

Before racial covenants were introduced and widely used, most African Americans in the North lived in neighborhoods that were predominantly white. By 1930, northern cities were segregated, although the average northern Black resident lived in a neighborhood that was still (barely) majority white. A few cities were already highly segregated by this time; in Chicago, for example, the average Black family lived in a neighborhood that was more than two-thirds Black. By 1970, this was true of all northern cities.

Industrial labor markets in both the North and the South were also sharply segregated for much of the twentieth century, but in very different ways. Southern industry was horizontally segregated; Blacks and whites worked in different industries—textile mills were lily white, whereas the lumber industry was completely Black. The northern pattern was based on exclusion and vertical segregation within industries. Migrating Blacks were typically denied access to industrial jobs until immigration was curtailed in the 1920s, and even then Black workers experienced higher unemployment rates than whites. Until the formation of the Congress of Industrial

Organizations (CIO) in the 1930s, Black workers were also denied access to unions or confined to segregated locals. And when Blacks did get jobs in northern factories, those jobs were typically the dirtiest and lowest paying.

Racial exclusion in manufacturing broke down during the World War II economic boom. Blacks made enormous strides in acquiring manufacturing jobs, yet most factories remained vertically segregated. In both regions, Blacks were concentrated in unskilled jobs because they were denied access to either skilled blue-collar jobs or white-collar jobs. Southern factories maintained segregated seniority lists that prevented Blacks from moving up the occupational hierarchy. Northern factories were less blatant about subordinating Black workers, but the segregation was no less effective. Indeed, northern urban labor markets were sharply segregated. Passage of the Civil Rights Act in the 1960s and the use of affirmative action to break down racially discriminatory job classifications and pay scales began to erode occupational segregation in both the North and the South.

The federal government used its authority as an instrument of segregation throughout much of the twentieth century. From President Woodrow Wilson's election in 1912 until the 1960s, most federal offices and jobs were rigidly segregated. However, the most important use of federal authority to entrench and expand segregation occurred after the 1940s when southerners used federal social policies to build a segregated welfare state in the South and whites in both regions used federal housing policies to consolidate racial apartheid in big cities.

Federal grants-in-aid subsidized Jim Crow beginning in the New Deal and continuing until passage of the 1964 Civil Rights Act. Especially egregious was the use of the 1946 Hill-Burton Act, which provided federal funds to build hospitals and other medical facilities after the war, to build segregated hospitals in the South. The law prohibited racial discrimination but permitted "separate but equal" facilities. Between 1946 and 1963, the federal government distributed $37 million to eighty-nine segregated medical facilities. Southerners also used veterans' programs and numerous other federal subsidies to gild a Jim Crow welfare state. They were stopped only by Title VI of the 1964 Civil Rights Act, which prohibited discriminatory allocation of federal funds. Henceforth, southern jurisdictions had to demonstrate that federal dollars were not being used to segregate African Americans. This law also enabled federal officials to begin dismantling segregated schools in the South twelve years after *Brown* by threatening to withhold grants-in-aid if school districts did not integrate schools.

Federal policies were crucial to the expansion of segregated housing in metropolitan areas throughout the country. In the thirty years after the Great Depression, a rigid pattern of residential segregation became a permanent feature of all big cities in both the North and the South. By 1970, 82 percent of Blacks in the thirty largest U.S. cities would have had to move to achieve a residential pattern that was considered "even" or integrated, that is, one in which all neighborhoods reflected the racial composition of a city (Massey and Denton 1993, 77). More than three-quarters of all African Americans in these cities lived in mostly Black neighborhoods, and one-third of all African Americans in the United States lived under conditions of hypersegregation, in geographically isolated, racially clustered neighborhoods.

Discrimination by real estate agents in local housing markets, aided by mortgage lenders' refusal to make loans in Black neighborhoods and by federal housing and urban renewal policies, produced a deeply embedded pattern of segregation within cities and between cities and suburbs. Federally insured home mortgages permitted whites to flee cities for entirely white suburbs, and they did so in large numbers. The Federal Housing Administration's underwriting policies steered mortgages to white suburbs and away from inner-city communities, fearing

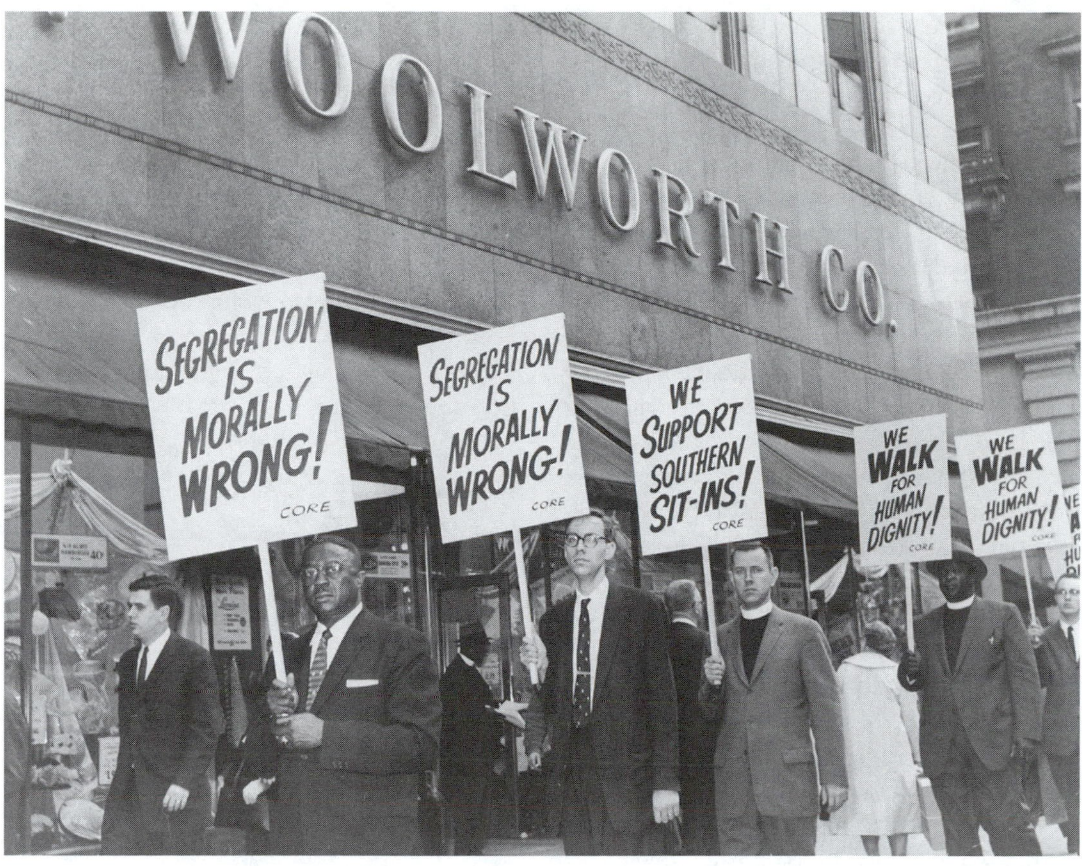

Picket line in front of F.W. Woolworth store in New York City, April 14, 1960, in protest of the store's lunch counter segregation at southern branches in its chain. The picketers, a majority of whom were ministers, were sponsored by a church committee on Woolworth's policies in cooperation with the Congress of Racial Equality. (Library of Congress)

that anything less than rigid segregation would undermine property values. The FHA's guidelines for mortgage lenders invoked explicit racial criteria and "could well have been culled from the Nuremberg laws," wrote Charles Abrams, a housing expert (Abrams 1955, 385).

At the same time, public officials used federally subsidized public housing and urban renewal programs to build rigidly contained racial ghettos in big cities. Downtown business interests and local politicians used public housing to remove Blacks from choice downtown properties slated for redevelopment. New public housing could not be dispersed because whites violently resisted residential integration, and local housing officials responded by building government-subsidized housing in Black neighborhoods, usually on sites abandoned by industry or white home owners. In some cases—Philadelphia, for example—city officials created racially segregated neighborhoods from scratch. Southerners used urban renewal and public housing to build barriers between Black and white neighborhoods. After 1950, the southern pattern of residential segregation resembled that in the North. Residential segregation has persisted despite passage of laws that make discrimination in housing markets illegal. The segregation index, the proportion of Blacks who would have to move to achieve integration, hardly changed between 1950 and 1990.

Entrenched residential segregation perpetuates racial inequality in three ways. First, outside the South, most schools remain highly segregated because of de facto segregation between northern cities and their suburbs. In *Milliken v. Bradley* (418 U.S. 717 [1974]), the Supreme Court rejected interjurisdictional remedies for metropolitan school segregation, such as busing, on the grounds that there was no evidence implicating suburban districts in de jure segregation. As the dissenters pointed out, this decision ignored the government policies that aided and abetted residential segregation. Today, Blacks and Latinos make up 85 percent of the enrollment in big-city school districts, and whites are the only group who attend schools in which the vast majority of students are of their own race.

Second, residential segregation is one of the main props of wealth inequality between Blacks and whites. Median Black net worth is a fraction of white net worth, and one of the main reasons is that white-owned housing is more valuable than Black-owned housing. The greater value of white-owned housing relative to Black-owned housing is due to white flight and segregation, which contributes to lower housing values and disinvestment in Black neighborhoods.

Finally, racially segregated cities intensify poverty. Jobs and economic investment have moved from central cities to the suburbs in the last half of the twentieth century, leaving African Americans locked into economically deteriorating, segregated neighborhoods. This spatial mismatch between jobs and residences is one of the key causes of persistently high African American poverty rates. Big-city racial ghettos also concentrate poverty geographically: The higher the level of segregation, the more likely poor Blacks are to live in neighborhoods that are disproportionately poor; poor whites, by contrast, are more likely to live in economically diverse areas. Racial segregation intensifies the effects of such economic and social changes as disinvestment; such effects are not apparent in integrated neighborhoods. One consequence is that Black and Latino students are far more likely to attend segregated schools in neighborhoods with concentrated poverty.

Racial segregation remains deeply entrenched in American society more than thirty-five years after the civil rights revolution. Jim Crow has been replaced by big-city ghettos as the most important contemporary form of racial separation and domination.

Michael K. Brown

See also: Civil Rights Acts, 1964 and 1991; Racism; Urban Poverty; Urban Renewal

References and Further Reading

Abrams, Charles. 1955. *Forbidden Neighbors: A Study of Prejudice in Housing*. New York: Harper and Brothers.

Hirsch, Arnold. 1998. *Making the Second Ghetto: Race and Housing in Chicago, 1940–1960*. Chicago: University of Chicago Press.

Johnson, Charles S. 1943. *Patterns of Negro Segregation*. New York: Harper and Brothers.

King, Desmond. 1995. *Separate and Unequal: Black Americans and the U.S. Federal Government*. New York: Oxford University Press.

Kluger, Richard. 1980. *Simple Justice: The History of* Brown v. Board of Education *and Black America's Struggle for Equality*. New York: Knopf.

Margo, Robert A. 1990. *Race and Schooling in the South, 1880–1950*. Chicago: University of Chicago Press.

Massey, Douglas, and Nancy Denton. 1993. *American Apartheid: Segregation and the Making of the Underclass*. Cambridge, MA: Harvard University Press.

Orfield, Gary, and Susan E. Eaton. 1996. *Dismantling Desegregation: The Quiet Reversal of* Brown v. Board of Education. New York: New Press.

Racism

Poverty in the United States, and the welfare policy response to it, cannot be fully understood without examining the role played by racism. Racism refers to beliefs and practices through which a dominant group systematically maintains privileges and advantages over other groups believed to be "racially" inferior. The latter are often identified by physical features such as skin color. In recent years, beliefs in biological racial inferiority have largely been replaced by beliefs in the cultural inferiority of such "minority" groups. Although evolutionary biologists hold that distinct races really do not exist and that there are no socially meaningful "racial" differences, racism rests upon these assumptions. Whites' racist beliefs and practices have primarily focused on people of African, Latin American, Asian, and Native American ancestry. Historically, women in these groups have faced "double jeopardy," being forced to deal simultaneously with both racism and sexism (Amott and Matthaei 1996). Although struggles against racism have met with notable successes in terms of achieving civil rights for many people of color, these struggles have failed to make similar inroads against their economic deprivation. In the period 1998–2000, non-Hispanic whites had an average poverty rate of 7.8 percent, in comparison to 23.9 percent for African Americans, 23.1 percent for Hispanics, and 25.9 percent for Native Americans. The rate for Asian Americans was 11.3 percent, close to but above the average poverty rate for whites (U.S. Census Bureau 2001, 7).

Racism is a major factor in the perpetuation of high rates of poverty among people of color, and it is expressed through a wide range of social institutions and personal interactions (Feagin 2001). Racial discrimination in housing markets segregates many people of color into locales in which few whites live. The local school systems on which many families of color depend are frequently poorly funded and substandard, and dropout rates are higher than in primarily white school districts. People of color must also contend with racial discrimination by employers. Residential isolation, poor schooling, and employer discrimination restrict many workers of color to unskilled, low-wage, service-sector jobs that usually carry few benefits and are often unstable or temporary. Even in prosperous times, unemployment rates are much higher for workers of color than for whites. Following economic slowdowns, workers of color have more difficulty becoming reemployed than do white workers.

The resulting chronic and harsh conditions of impoverishment among people of color pose difficult obstacles to forming permanent adult partnerships and thus undermine family and marital stability. People of color are seriously overrepresented not only in the U.S. poverty population but also among those in "extreme poverty" (that is, in households with incomes below 50 percent of the federally defined poverty line). Most impoverished families of color are headed by women. At best, U.S. welfare policy allows for very meager income assistance for such families and offers little help in escaping poverty, in part due to racism.

Racist beliefs and practices have long accompanied government programs that provide means-tested public assistance to poor families (Neubeck and Cazenave 2001). Racism in the realm of welfare has rested heavily upon stereotypes about the supposed laziness, immorality, and irresponsibility of people of color, particularly African American women. As a consequence, mothers of color have long been considered prime examples of the "undeserving poor" and held personally responsible for their own poverty.

The Social Security Act of 1935 established the first jointly funded federal-state welfare program for poor families. Yet for years, poor families of color in many locales were treated as undeserving and were either not given assistance for which they were eligible under the law or were given cash assistance in amounts lower than those being received by whites. White caseworkers denied aid to households of color if, in their opinion, mothers failed to provide a "suitable home" for their children or if they suspected that mothers were seeing (and thus allegedly receiving cash assistance from) a male. Families of color frequently had their welfare eligibility abruptly canceled when local farms or other employers wanted labor, regardless of the fact that the wages they paid and on which the families would be forced to depend were inadequate.

Many racially discriminatory policies and practices were altered in response to struggles by the civil rights and welfare rights movements of the 1960s. As a result, increasing numbers of impoverished families of color were able to get welfare assistance. Changes in legal standards and rules regarding nondiscrimination did not put an end to racism in welfare politics, however. Many politicians still employ subtle racist stereotypes of laziness and immorality among African Americans in condemning the alleged "welfare dependency" of recipients, stereotypes that the mass media have helped reinforce. It is telling that presidential candidate Ross Perot caused little political or public reaction when, in an appearance on a 1996 national television talk show, he stereotyped the typical young Black male as "a breeder who gets the woman pregnant and then she gets welfare" (quoted in Neubeck and Cazenave 2001, 156–157). Researchers have found that the mass media tend to use visual images of mothers of color with stories reporting negatively on welfare and its recipients but are more likely to use images of whites when poor people are being depicted positively (Gilens 1999).

Although whites and African Americans made up similar percentages of the nation's welfare rolls from the 1970s to the mid-1990s, political elites have successfully framed welfare as a "Black problem." It is true that people of color are disproportionately represented on the welfare rolls, but this is in large part due to the high rates of poverty and extreme poverty mentioned earlier. Yet a significant minority of whites believe that most or all welfare recipients are Black, including whites residing in states in which very few African Americans live (Gilens 1999). National survey data collected by the National Opinion Research Center (NORC) show that the majority of whites believe that African Americans are less likely to prefer to be self-supporting than are people who are racially like themselves (based on NORC data from the Roper Center, University of Connecticut).

Racist stereotypes have helped frame welfare reform discourse, leading to policy changes that deny impoverished families any entitlement to public assistance and place strict time limits on its receipt. Such stereotypes have also been used to justify ever more stringent work requirements for welfare recipients and efforts to promote marriage and discourage both abortion and out-of-wedlock births. Those states with the largest African American and Latino/a populations have the strictest welfare eligibility policies and the harshest penalties for violating welfare rules (Schram, Soss, and Fording 2003). Impoverished whites forced to rely on public assistance are also, along with poor people of color, negatively affected by the racism that restricts eligibility and holds down benefits.

Kenneth J. Neubeck

See also: Aid to Families with Dependent Children (ADC/AFDC); Deserving/Undeserving Poor; Racial Segregation; Sexism; Welfare Policy/Welfare Reform

References and Further Reading

Amott, Teresa, and Julie Matthaei. 1996. *Race, Gender, and Work: A Multi-Cultural Economic History of Women in the United States*. Rev. ed. Boston: South End Press.

Feagin, Joe R. 2001. *Racist America: Roots, Current Realities, and Future Reparations*. New York: Routledge.

Gilens, Martin. 1999. *Why Americans Hate Welfare: Race, Media, and the Politics of Anti-Poverty Policy*. Chicago: University of Chicago Press.

Neubeck, Kenneth J., and Noel A. Cazenave. 2001. *Welfare Racism: Playing the Race Card against America's Poor*. New York: Routledge.

Schram, Sanford F., Joe Soss, and Richard C. Fording, eds. 2003. *Race and the Politics of Welfare Reform*. Ann Arbor: University of Michigan Press.

U.S. Census Bureau. 2001. *Poverty in the United States: 2000*. Washington, DC: GPO.

Refugee Policy

U.S. refugee policy consists of a set of programs designed to protect and to meet the immediate needs of groups designated as "refugees." According to the definition adopted from the 1951 U.N. Refugee Convention, refugees are persons with a well-founded fear of persecution. Resettlement programs are designed to incorporate refugee groups into the social and economic fabric of the receiving community. Because some refugees continue to be poor and to combine public assistance with work activities to survive, the refugee resettlement program has been criticized for creating a new "underclass" of welfare dependents. Such cultural-behavioral explanations of poverty, however, fail to consider the disparities in the way refugee programs have been applied for different groups and the consequences of deindustrialization and a receding welfare state on the poor communities where most refugees resettle. Although it is the historic policy of the United States to admit persons of special humanitarian and foreign policy concern, once here, refugees experience the vagaries of the welfare system and the race, class, and gender hierarchies that produce social inequality.

After World War II, the international outrage at the lack of response to Nazi atrocities resulted in the admission to the United States of thousands of displaced Europeans. The first refugee legislation, the Displaced Persons Act of 1948, allowed legal resettlement beyond the restrictive immigration quotas, which since the early twentieth century had become increasingly more explicitly restrictive and biased against nonwhites and people of non-Anglo-Saxon national origin. However, it was the Soviet suppression of the Hungarian rebels in 1956 that led to what was to become the blueprint for future refugee resettlement policy, introducing a bias in favor of groups opposed to communist regimes—in particular those who could serve American strategic aims in the Cold War—while aiming to promote economic self-sufficiency among resettled refugees. To ensure the success of the Hungarian refugees, the federal government funded a network of voluntary and public organizations to provide cash assistance, social services, and job placement.

The refugee resettlement program was expanded in response to major events of the Cold War against communism, including the Cuban revolutionary reforms under Fidel Castro beginning in 1959 and the U.S. withdrawal from Vietnam with the fall of Saigon in 1975, both of which contributed to increased flows of refugees from communist regimes. These refugees benefited from the continuing Cold War; from the expansion of antipoverty, civil rights, and social welfare policies during the 1960s and 1970s; and from the Immigration Reform Act of 1965, which lifted racially motivated national origins quotas. The Cuban Refugee Act (1966) and the Indochina Migration and Refugee Assistance Act (1975) gave Cubans and Southeast Asians legal claims to refugee status and therefore entitled them to cash and medical assistance and social services to hasten adjustment to a new country. These refugee programs also emphasized job training and placement services. Most of those in the first waves of Cubans in the 1960s and of the Vietnamese in the 1970s were from the middle and professional classes and were familiar with U.S. institutions. In addition, many Cubans already had established family ties in the United States, which helped with adjustment. Some families prospered by utilizing capital they had escaped with and by taking advantage of the availability of federal business loans. Even with the advantages of their social and educational backgrounds and government support, many Cubans and Vietnamese experienced downward job mobility, and families required multiple wage earners to survive (Haines 1985, 18–22).

By the 1980s, the Cold War was waning, and social welfare policy was turning toward regulating poor people's behavior and preventing welfare dependency rather than improving structural conditions and opportunities. The passage of the Refugee Act of 1980 reflected these broader developments. The act was meant to standardize procedures for the regular flow of refugees and for emergency admission to the United States for any persons facing persecution. The act streamlined resettlement services through a newly formed Office of Refugee Resettlement (ORR). In the interest of reducing the possibility of welfare dependency, it limited refugee cash and medical assistance to the first thirty-six months of resettlement and limited reimbursements to states for Aid to Families with Dependent Children, Medicaid, and Supplemental Security Income to thirty-six months if these services were required after the expiration of refugee assistance. These measures brought an end to the federal government's previous practices of funding resettlement programs without any time limits and of reimbursing states for refugees on public assistance. Resettlement programs remained vulnerable to the domestic politics of welfare retrenchment and congressional budget cuts even after the passage of these restrictive measures. Since 1981, refugee cash and medical assistance has continued to be reduced; it currently allows eight months of assistance with no reimbursement to states. Thus, the Refugee Act of 1980—legislation meant to increase humanitarian involvement worldwide—has become another example of the effects of devolution and a retreat from social justice.

As changes in refugee and domestic policy unfolded, worldwide economic and political crises created significant refugee flows from Cambodia, Laos, Vietnam, Central America, Cuba, and the Caribbean, a situation that demanded humanitarian and diplomatic attention. However, each group experienced a different reception. The Mariel boat lift from Cuba in 1980 reveals the racial and class politics of refugee policy. Several interlocking factors contributed to the massive exodus of Cubans to the United States, including desires for family reunion, the economic crisis in Cuba in the 1970s, and the perception that opportunities were available in the United States. The Mariel Cubans included young, single men and women socialized during Castro's regime and a number of Black Cubans and former criminals and mental patients. Rather than granting the Mariel Cubans refugee status, President Jimmy Carter's administration created a special category of "entrant-status pending" to reduce the cost of resettlement and to quell criticism of the Cuban program. Although the Mariel Cubans lacked full refugee status, they fared better than do the Haitians, Dominicans, Guatemalans, and Salvadorans who are also seeking to escape political and economic oppression but who, because they are fleeing noncommunist governments, are considered "economic" migrants. The second, post-1980 wave of Southeast Asian refugees, on the other hand, benefited from the image of Asian immigrant success and the collective remorse for the Vietnam War.

Nevertheless, the second wave of Southeast Asian refugees experienced considerable hardship in the United States. This group consisted of diverse groups of Vietnamese boat people, Cambodian war victims of the Khmer Rouge, and the Hmong and Laotian operatives recruited by the United States to fight the Vietcong. Many Southeast Asians were young adults and children who had lived in refugee camps and had suffered traumas prior to their arrival. Even if the working-age adults possessed the skills or language capabilities to enter gainful employment immediately, they arrived as U.S. cities were experiencing the effects of economic recession and deindustrialization, and they faced greatly diminished availability of the jobs that had traditionally provided opportunities for immigrants and native-born populations to rise out of poverty. As a result, many Southeast Asian families combine welfare with low-wage and informal work to survive.

The poverty and perceived welfare dependency of refugees helped fuel the anti-immigrant elements of the 1996 Personal Responsibility and Work Opportunity Reconciliation Act. Even as legal immigrants, refugees and their children are subject to harsh new restrictions on eligibility for Temporary Assistance for Needy Families (TANF, the program that replaced Aid to Families with Dependent Children), food stamps, and Supplemental Security Income for the disabled. Those who do qualify for TANF are subject to TANF work requirements, which are especially burdensome to poor women with limited English proficiency.

Karen Quintiliani

See also: Asian Americans; Immigrants and Immigration; Immigration Policy; Latino/as; Welfare Policy/Welfare Reform

References and Further Reading

Haines, David W., ed. 1985. *Refugees in the United States: A Reference Handbook*. Westport, CT: Greenwood Press.

Hein, Jeremy. 1993. "Refugees, Immigrants, and the State." *Annual Review of Sociology* 19: 43–59.

Malkki, Lisa H. 1995. "Refugees and Exile: From 'Refugee Studies' to the National Order of Things." *Annual Review of Anthropology* 24: 495–523.

Newland, Kathleen. 1995. *U.S. Refugee Policy: Dilemmas and Directions*. Washington, DC: Carnegie Endowment for International Peace.

Tang, Eric. 2000. "Collateral Damage: Southeast Asian Poverty in the United States." *Social Text* 18, no. 1: 55–79.

Regulating the Poor, *Frances Fox Piven and Richard A. Cloward*

Frances Fox Piven and Richard A. Cloward's first book, *Regulating the Poor,* published in 1971, has remained in print for over thirty years and was reissued in 1992 in an updated edition. This book originally won the C. Wright Mills Award from the Society for the Study of Social Problems and over time has come to be considered a classic in the field of social theory.

In *Regulating the Poor,* Piven and Cloward most forcefully articulated a distinctive understanding of the political and economic role of welfare in capitalist society in general and in the United States in particular. For Piven and Cloward, welfare is a secondary institution calibrated to respond not to the needs of the poor but to the contradictory needs of the primary institutions of the capitalist political economy: on the one hand, to maintain a ready supply of people willing to take low-wage jobs by keeping welfare benefits low; on the other, to maintain political stability by placating poor people with more generous welfare benefits in times of social unrest. As such, welfare is itself wrapped in contradictions. Over time, the system would change not so much to get better as to swing, pendulum-like, to serve alternating political and economic objectives as conditions dictated. Thus, welfare could be used at some points in time to co-opt the poor and keep them from becoming radicalized and at others to push more people into the low-wage labor force.

Drawing on their earlier writings and building from this theoretical insight, Piven and Cloward emphasized that the possibilities for progressive change under these conditions were small, and that such change was only likely to occur to the extent that agitation from below could force more substantial concessions than policymakers would normally make. Piven and Cloward were in this sense neo-Marxists—dialectical thinkers who recognized the contradictory character of social formations such as welfare—and structuralists who recognized that the relationship of structure to agency did indeed constrain what was politically possible at any given point in time, but they were also perhaps more open to the capacity of actors to push for change than Marx himself had allowed.

When it was introduced, Piven and Cloward's perspective was a startling theoretical development in the historiography of social welfare. It single-handedly forced a reconsideration of the received wisdom in the field that the development of social welfare was a linear, cumulative developmental process that would lead to progress and greater inclusiveness over time. Instead, the tensions between what we can distinguish as "social assistance" and "social control" continued to move social welfare policy in a more cyclical fashion. Admittedly, with each swing of the pendulum from generosity back to retrenchment the method of social control could change. Medicalization in the 1990s, criminalization in the 1950s, demonization a century before: Each represents a different form for a different time in which the pendulum swung toward social control. Still, the old wine of social control was in new bottles of social construction.

Piven and Cloward's clear-eyed, realistic analysis in *Regulating the Poor* stripped away the sentimentality associated with social welfare as a kindly service toward the poor. Piven and Cloward demonstrated that social welfare, especially in the highly capitalistic United States, tended to be very much designed to ensure that people were offered only the limited assistance that was consistent with the needs of a hypercapitalist political economy. Their historical analysis showed that welfare tended to give more emphasis to political co-optation during times of political instability, such as during the Great Depression and the 1960s, and to place more emphasis on enforcing work norms during times of stability. Moreover, periods of liberalization are bound to be followed by retrenchment, in turn creating the conditions for opposition from those most adversely affected and leading to new periods of liberalization. Liberalization is not inevitable, however, and Piven and Cloward emphasized that important progressive social changes will only come about when those oppressed by these forms of power and control resist. Their moral for this saga is as pertinent now in a new era of welfare retrenchment as it was when they first began to develop their thesis in the 1960s.

Sanford F. Schram

See also: Aid to Families with Dependent Children (ADC/AFDC); Poor Laws; Relief; Speenhamland; Welfare Policy/Welfare Reform; Welfare Rights Movement; Welfare State

References and Further Reading

Piven, Frances Fox, and Richard A. Cloward. 1992. *Regulating the Poor: The Functions of Public Welfare*. Updated ed. New York: Vintage Books.

Schram, Sanford F. 2002. *Praxis for the Poor: Piven and Cloward and the Future of Social Science in Social Welfare*. New York: New York University Press.

Relief

Aid or assistance to the poor has been termed "poor relief," or, more disparagingly, "the dole." The term "welfare" has largely supplanted "relief" since the mid-twentieth century. Throughout most of American history, relief has been provided in two main forms. *Indoor relief* was assistance to the poor offered through an institutional residence: an almshouse, poorhouse, workhouse, orphanage, asylum, or homeless shelter. *Outdoor relief* or *out-relief* was the provision to poor people of aid that did not require their institutionalization. Although some outdoor relief has been provided in cash, much has been in-kind relief—aid in the form of goods or services (food, clothing, or fuel) or scrip or vouchers redeemable for select goods (in the late twentieth century through programs such as food stamps and housing assistance). *Work relief* has been another prominent form of relief, first widely used during the depression of 1893 in many large cities and later a prominent feature of the New Deal's emergency relief provisions. Private charity provided most poor relief until late in the 1800s, although it typically did so with public funds. Although indoor relief has historically been more expensive than outdoor relief, outdoor relief has been more contested and controversial.

After decades of modest change, public relief expenditures (especially for outdoor relief)

increased dramatically during and immediately after the Civil War as industrialization and urbanization increased the number of people unable to provide for themselves and their families. Nationwide, from 1850 to 1860, relief rolls rose 76 percent (Kiesling and Margo 1997). Many cities increased their poor-relief expenditures again in response to the deep depression of 1873–1878. Complaints abounded about the "indiscriminate charity," public and private both, that this depression called forth. With the late-century anti-relief charity organization societies often leading the charge, most of the largest American cities and many smaller ones abolished or substantially reduced their poor-relief programs. The late nineteenth century marks the first widespread and successful American assault on relief, with public outdoor relief the primary target. But this effort to eliminate or reform outdoor relief in cities was short-lived, for the next deep depression, in 1893, further expanded the ranks of the poor and unemployed and caused many cities to reinstate their outdoor relief programs and create innovative new programs to care for and placate the poor.

During the nineteenth century, state governments had assumed responsibility for the care of those poor without legal settlement, established asylums and other institutions, and created state boards of charity to coordinate the public and private relief programs within their jurisdictions, but the Progressive Era marked the real entrance of state governments into the arena of relief provision. New forms of categorical and means-tested relief programs were established to meet new needs and to care for those poor deemed most deserving. Between 1917 and 1920 alone, states enacted some 400 new relief provisions, and by 1931, all states but two had enacted mothers' or widows' pension programs. By 1928, public relief expenditures were three times the amount of private expenditures (Katz [1986] 1996, 215–216).

The Great Depression and the New Deal marked the entrance of the federal government into relief. The federal role had largely been limited to land grants to the states for indoor relief institutions and to pensions for veterans of the Revolutionary and Civil Wars. The response of President Franklin D. Roosevelt's administration to the Great Depression included a massive and unprecedented expansion of American relief, first as cash relief and then as work relief. By 1934, one-sixth of the American population was "on the dole," and by 1935, some 30 percent of the African American population was (Piven and Cloward [1971] 1993, 75–76). So great was this expansion of government provision of relief that by 1938, American relief as a percentage of gross domestic product exceeded that offered by Germany, the United Kingdom, France, Sweden, and others (Amenta 1998, 5). Nonetheless, relief still remained hotly contested, and even FDR voiced concern about the dangers of cash relief and the ways in which it "induces a spiritual and moral disintegration." Thus, he promised in 1935 in the State of the Union Address that "the federal government must and shall quit the business of relief." Though relief would never return to its prior local form, and despite the institutionalized insurance-style programs of the Social Security Act of 1935 (SSA), America did not retain its leadership in relief or welfare spending.

Using mothers' pensions as a policy model, Title IV-A of the SSA created Aid to Dependent Children (later Aid to Families with Dependent Children [AFDC]). This twentieth-century joint federal-state program offered cash relief primarily to women with children. After decades of consistent but relatively modest growth in this program, the 1960s saw a great expansion. Relief rolls grew 17 percent in the 1950s, but 107 percent from 1960 to 1969 (Piven and Cloward [1971] 1993, 183). State-run general assistance programs, which offered aid to men and women ineligible for AFDC, also grew, though more modestly. This relief expansion, however, marked the second great American assault on poor relief, one that had something in common with the nineteenth-century campaigns against the supposed expense, fraud, and "perverse incentives" of outdoor relief. Indeed, by the 1980s, many prominent politicians and policy intellectuals urged a return to the local, minimal, private charity of the nineteenth century. This second anti-relief campaign culminated in the "welfare reforms" of 1996. Once again, outdoor relief was the focal point for assaults upon public assistance to the poor.

Stephen Pimpare

See also: Aid to Families with Dependent Children (ADC/AFDC); Charity; Charity Organization Societies; Deserving/Undeserving Poor; General Assistance; Great Depression and New Deal; Maternalist Policy; Means Testing and Universalism; Poorhouse/Almshouse; Progressive Era and 1920s; Social Security Act of 1935; Welfare Policy/Welfare Reform

References and Further Reading

Amenta, Edwin. 1998. *Bold Relief: Institutional Politics and the Origins of Modern American Social Policy*. Princeton: Princeton University Press.

Katz, Michael B. [1986] 1996. *In the Shadow of the Poorhouse: A Social History of Welfare in America*. Tenth anniversary ed. New York: Basic Books.

Kiesling, L. Lynne, and Robert A. Margo. 1997. "Explaining the Rise in Antebellum Pauperism, 1850–1860: New Evidence." *Quarterly Review of Economics and Finance* 37, no. 2 (Summer): 405–418.

Piven, Frances Fox, and Richard A. Cloward. [1971] 1993. *Regulating the Poor: The Functions of Public Welfare*. New York: Vintage Books.

Religion

See Black Churches; Buddhism; Catholic Church; Charitable Choice; Christian Fundamentalism; Islam; Judaism; Missionaries; Protestant Denominations; Puritans and Puritanism; Quakers; Salvation Army; Social Gospel

Report on Economic Conditions of the South, *National Emergency Council*

In 1938, the U.S. National Emergency Council published the *Report on Economic Conditions of the South*. The *Report* sketched a devastating picture of southern poverty, asserting, in President Franklin D. Roosevelt's words, that "the South presents right now the nation's No. 1 economic problem—the nation's problem, not merely the South's" (Roosevelt 1938). The *Report* portrayed the South as a drag on the rest of the nation—a brake on efforts to relieve the Great Depression and develop American industry—and it offered a blueprint for national policy to develop the laggard region and uplift its people.

The *Report* condensed the condition of the South into fifteen brutally descriptive sections on topics from soil depletion to unsanitary housing, from deficient health care to meager sources of credit, each section delineating the region's backwardness and misery. In 1937, per capita income had reached barely half the standard for the rest of the nation. The South registered the nation's lowest industrial wages, farm income, and tangible assets. Those statistics translated into genuine suffering.

But the *Report* was never the straightforward presentation of facts it purported to be. It crystallized a new view of southern poverty, one that attributed the region's woes to paltry public services and an overreliance on agriculture and low-wage industry. This Depression-era conception barely considered the region's history of racial conflict, seeing economic uplift as the remedy not only for southern poverty but also for racial injustice and reactionary politics.

The *Report* signaled a shift in the direction of federal policy toward the South. The federal government embarked on the long-term sponsorship of southern economic growth, pursuing development along the lines favored by Roosevelt and southern New Dealers: the elimination of low-wage employment through a federal minimum-wage law, nationally financed improvements in education and public services, and encouragement for southern industrialization and economic modernization.

As part of FDR's program to liberalize the Democratic Party, the *Report* also marked an important watershed in national politics. FDR's so-called purge, an unsuccessful effort to unseat congressional opponents of the New Deal in the 1938 midterm elections, concentrated on defeating the recalcitrant conservative southerners in the president's own party. The president campaigned vigorously through the South, repeatedly citing the *Report*'s findings from the stump.

Hostility to the president's interference in the southern primaries intensified southern criticism of the *Report* and further cemented a political alliance between Republican opponents of the New Deal and conservative southern Democrats. While the *Report* encapsulated the prevailing view of regional poverty and of its causes, consequences, and cures, the ensuing controversy raised formidable obstacles to achieving the policy goals it envisioned.

Bruce J. Schulman

See also: Agricultural and Farm Labor Organizing; Fair Labor Standards Act (FLSA); New Deal Farm Policy; Rural Poverty; Tennessee Valley Authority

References and Further Reading

Carlton, David L., and Peter A. Coclanis. 1996. *Confronting Southern Poverty in the Great Depression: The Report on Economic Conditions of the South with Related Documents*. Boston: Bedford Books/St. Martin's Press.

———. 2003. *The South, the Nation, and the World: Perspectives on Southern Economic Development*. Charlottesville: University Press of Virginia.

Johnson, Guy. 1982. *Research in Service to Society: The First Fifty Years of the Institute for Research in Social Science*. Chapel Hill: University of North Carolina Press.

Report on Economic Conditions of the South (1938)

In the South, as elsewhere, the two most important economic endowments are its people and its physical resources. . . . In spite of the wealth of population and natural resource, the South is poor in the machinery for converting this wealth to the uses of its people. With 28 percent of the Nation's population, it has only 16 percent of the tangible assets, including factories, machines, and the tools with which people make their living. With more than half the country's farmers, the South has less than a fifth of the farm implements. Despite its coal, oil, gas, and water power, the region uses only 15 percent of the Nation's factory horsepower. Its potentialities have been neglected and its opportunities unrealized.

The paradox of the South is that while it is blessed by Nature with immense wealth, its people as a whole are the poorest in the country. Lacking industries of its own, the South has been forced to trade the richness of its soil, its minerals and forests, and the labor of its people for goods manufactured elsewhere. If the South received such goods in sufficient quantity to meet its needs, it might consider itself adequately paid.

Source: David L. Carlton and Peter A. Coclanis, *Confronting Southern Poverty in the Great Depression: The Report on Economic Conditions of the South with Related Documents* (Boston and New York: Bedford Books, 1996), 42–43, 45–47.

Roosevelt, Franklin D. 1938. "Address at Barnsville, GA, August 11, 1938." http://www.presidency.ucsb.edu/site/docs/pppus.php?admin=032&year=1938&id=101.

Schulman, Bruce J. 1991. *From Cotton Belt to Sunbelt: Federal Policy, Economic Development, and the*

Transformation of the South, 1938–1980. New York: Oxford University Press.

Reproductive Rights

"Reproductive rights" are a concept and a claim that feminists crafted to describe their political struggle for the legalization of abortion in the late 1960s and early 1970s. Since the mid-nineteenth century, when abortion was criminalized state by state, millions of women had secretly sought and obtained criminal abortions—if they could afford to, and if they knew where to go for help. Millions of others, often girls and women who were poor, had attempted self-abortion, frequently with disastrous results. By the middle to late 1960s, in the context of numerous human rights movements inspired by the civil rights movement for basic and full citizenship rights for African Americans in the United States, feminists began to speak out, arguing that without the right to control their own bodies and fertility, including by means of abortion, women in the United States could not be full citizens.

Many of the most highly visible of these feminists were white women, spokespersons of emergent national "reproductive rights" organizations such as the National Abortion Rights Action League (NARAL), or organizers of local, abortion-rights speak-outs. In the same era, feminist women of color (who, in the wake of the civil rights movement, could, for the first time, command some serious media attention for their politics) redefined the meaning of "reproductive rights" in ways that acknowledged how race and class created profoundly different reproductive experiences for different groups of women in the United States. Women of color, through such organizations as the National Black Women's Health Project, made the case that for "reproductive rights" to have real meaning for all women, including poor women, the concept had to encompass the right to reproductive health care. A right to reproductive health care would include access, without coercion, to contraception and to general reproductive medical services; the right and access to abortion services for women unable or unwilling to manage a pregnancy; and (most radically) the right and resources to enable a woman to carry a pregnancy to term and to be a mother, even if she lacked the resources enjoyed by middle-class women.

This last component of comprehensive "reproductive rights" aimed to redress local and national public policy initiatives mandating various punishments for poor mothers who received welfare benefits, such as compulsory birth control or sterilization, or loss of welfare benefits. These initiatives, which had been introduced in state legislatures in every region of the country, were predicated on the idea that poor women and maternity were incompatible.

Throughout the 1970s and 1980s, mainstream U.S. political culture reinforced this idea. After a series of Supreme Court decisions legalized general access to birth control and decriminalized abortion, many middle-class Americans came to believe more strongly than ever that a woman who became pregnant or stayed pregnant when she was poor was an illegitimate mother. Against this dominant view, many low-income women, women of color, and allies worked to expand the "reproductive rights" agenda beyond the right to legal abortion to include the claim that poor women have the right to be mothers, if and when they choose.

Paradoxically, at the same time that policymakers and politicians were pressuring poor women, often women of color, to suppress their fertility, the same public officials and a majority in the U.S. Supreme Court agreed that the right to abortion, guaranteed by *Roe v. Wade* (410 U.S. 113 [1973]), constituted a real right only for women who could pay for abortion services. The Hyde Amendment, adopted by Congress just three years after *Roe*, affirmed that the federal government, guarantor of abortion rights,

Katie Relf et al. v. Caspar W. Weinberger et al.

National Welfare Rights Organization v. Caspar W. Weinberger et al.

United States District Court for the District of Columbia
372 F. Supp. 1196
1974
Gesell, District Judge.

These two related cases, which have been consolidated with the consent of all parties, challenge the statutory authorization and constitutionality of regulations of the Department of Health, Education and Welfare (HEW) governing human sterilizations under programs and projects funded by the Department's Public Health Service and its Social and Rehabilitation Service. 39 Fed. Reg. 4730–34 (1974). Plaintiffs are the National Welfare Rights Organization (NWRO), suing on behalf of its 125,000 members, and five individual women, proceeding by class action on behalf of all poor persons subject to involuntary sterilization under the challenged regulations. Defendants are the Secretary of HEW, under whose authority the regulations were issued, 42 U.S.C. § 216, and two high-level HEW officials charged with the administration of federal family planning funds.

. . . Congress has authorized the funding of a full range of family planning services under two basic procedures. The Public Health Service administers federal grants to state health agencies and to public and private projects for the provision of family planning services to the poor, 42 U.S.C. §§ 300 et seq., 708(a), and the Social and Rehabilitation Service provides funds for such services under the Medicaid and Aid to Families of Dependent Children programs, 42 U.S.C. §§ 601 et seq., 1396 et seq.

Although there is no specific reference to sterilization in any of the family planning statutes nor in the legislative history surrounding their passage, the Secretary has considered sterilization to fall within the general statutory scheme and Congress has been made aware of this position. But until recently, there were no particular rules or regulations governing the circumstances under which sterilizations could be funded under these statutes.

Sterilization of females or males is irreversible. The total number of these sterilizations is clearly of national significance. . . . Over the last few years, an estimated 100,000 to 150,000 low-income persons have been sterilized annually under federally funded programs. . . .

Although Congress has been insistent that all family planning programs function on a purely voluntary basis, there is uncontroverted evidence in the record that minors and other incompetents have been sterilized with federal funds and that an indefinite number of poor people have been improperly coerced into accepting a sterilization operation under the threat that various federally supported welfare benefits would be withdrawn unless they submitted to irreversible sterilization. Patients receiving Medicaid assistance at childbirth are evidently the most frequent targets of this pressure. . . .

When such deplorable incidents began to receive nationwide public attention due to the experience of the Relf sisters in Alabama, the Secretary took steps to restrict the circumstances under which recipients of federal family planning funds could conduct sterilization operations. . . .

These regulations provide that projects and programs receiving PHS or SRS funds, whether for family planning or purely medical services, shall neither perform nor arrange for the performance of a nontherapeutic sterilization unless certain procedures are carried out. These vary depending upon whether the patient is, under state law, a legally competent adult, a legally competent person under the age of 18, a legally incompetent minor, or a mental incompetent. . . .

(continues)

Relf *and* National Welfare Rights Organization v. Caspar W. Weinberger et al. (continued)

Plaintiffs do not oppose the voluntary sterilization of poor persons under federally funded programs. However, they contend that these regulations are both illegal and arbitrary because they authorize involuntary sterilizations, without statutory or constitutional justification. They argue forcefully that sterilization of minors or mental incompetents is necessarily involuntary in the nature of things. Further, they claim that sterilization of competent adults under these regulations can be undertaken without ensuring that the request for sterilization is in actuality voluntary. The Secretary defends the regulations and insists that only "voluntary" sterilization is permitted under their terms. . . .

. . . The Supreme Court has repeatedly stated that the right of privacy entails the right of the individual "to be free from unwarranted governmental intrusion into matters so fundamentally affecting a person as the decision whether to bear or beget a child." . . . Involuntary sterilizations directly threaten that right . . . and plaintiffs correctly contend that the challenged regulations authorize such sterilizations. . . .

The Court must therefore proceed to the merits. While plaintiffs invoke both statutory and constitutional principles . . . the issues tendered may be readily resolved simply by resort to the underlying statutes. Accordingly, no occasion exists to consider the related constitutional claims.

. . . [T]he Court finds that . . . the challenged regulations are arbitrary and unreasonable in that they fail to implement the congressional command that federal family planning funds not be used to coerce indigent patients into submitting to sterilization. . . .

. . . Although the term "voluntary" is nowhere defined in the statutes under consideration, it is frequently encountered in the law. Even its dictionary definition assumes an exercise of free will and clearly precludes the existence of coercion or force. . . . And its use in the statutory and decisional law, at least when important human rights are at stake, entails a requirement that the individual have at his disposal the information necessary to make his decision and the mental competence to appreciate the significance of that information. . . .

No person who is mentally incompetent can meet these standards, nor can the consent of a representative, however sufficient under state law, impute voluntariness to the individual actually undergoing irreversible sterilization.

Minors would also appear to lack the knowledge, maturity and judgment to satisfy these standards with regard to such an important issue, what-

had no obligation to help a poor woman overcome the obstacle of poverty—her lack of money to pay for an abortion—that prevented her from exercising her newly won constitutional right. By the 1980s, abortion services, contraception, and access to new reproductive technologies and even to motherhood itself constituted the "reproductive rights" of middle-class women, while poor women often did not have access to the first three and were reviled if they achieved the last.

Over the course of the 1980s and 1990s, middle-class women spearheaded efforts to save *Roe* in an era of growing anti-abortion-rights politics. In these same decades, poor women and their allies responded to ever more complex and vibrant political assaults on the reproductive behavior of women who lacked economic resources. In the name of "reproductive rights," including the right to be a mother, welfare rights activists and others opposed abortion-funding restrictions, family cap legislation (which denied public assistance to children born to women already receiving welfare benefits and thus

ever may be their competence to rely on devices or medication that temporarily frustrates procreation. This is the reasoning that provides the basis for the nearly universal common law and statutory rule that minors and mental incompetents cannot consent to medical operations. . . .

The statutory references to minors and mental incompetents do not contradict this conclusion, for they appear only in the context of family planning services in general. Minors, for example, are not legally incompetent for all purposes, and many girls of child-bearing age are undoubtedly sufficiently aware of the relevant considerations to use temporary contraceptives that intrude far less on fundamental rights. However, the Secretary has not demonstrated and the Court cannot find that Congress deemed such children capable of voluntarily consenting to an irreversible operation involving the basic human right to procreate. Nor can the Court find, in the face of repeated warnings concerning voluntariness, that Congress authorized the imposition of such a serious deprivation upon mental incompetents at the will of an unspecified "representative."

The regulations also fail to provide the procedural safeguards necessary to ensure that even competent adults voluntarily request sterilization. . . . Even a fully informed individual cannot make a "voluntary" decision concerning sterilization if he has been subjected to coercion from doctors or project officers. Despite specific statutory language forbidding the recipients of federal family planning funds to threaten a cutoff of program benefits unless the individual submits to sterilization and despite clear evidence that such coercion is actually being applied, the challenged regulations contain no clear safeguard against this abuse.

In order to prevent express or implied threats, which would obviate the Secretary's entire framework of procedural safeguards, and to ensure compliance with the statutory language, the Court concludes that the regulations must also be amended to require that individuals seeking sterilization be orally informed at the very outset that no federal benefits can be withdrawn because of a failure to accept sterilization. . . .

. . . The dividing line between family planning and eugenics is murky. . . . Whatever might be the merits of limiting irresponsible reproduction, which each year places increasing numbers of unwanted or mentally defective children into tax-supported institutions, it is for Congress and not individual social workers and physicians to determine the manner in which federal funds should be used to support such a program. We should not drift into a policy which has unfathomed implications and which permanently deprives unwilling or immature citizens of their ability to procreate without adequate legal safeguards and a legislative determination of the appropriate standards in light of the general welfare and of individual rights.

increased the likelihood that poor pregnant women on welfare would seek abortions), and other attempts to constrain the childbearing of poor women.

In the last decades of the twentieth century, middle-class America cast poor women as potent symbols of misbehaving women, and many politicians built careers on the claim that such women, even in the era of "reproductive rights," did not qualify for these rights or for motherhood. A group of aggressively conservative Republicans spoke frequently in Congress and elsewhere in the 1990s about their solution to rampant illegitimate motherhood in America: Remove the children from their poor, single mothers' care and place them in orphanages or in the families of properly married, middle-class heterosexual couples, via adoption. The Personal Responsibility and Work Opportunity Reconciliation Act of 1996 ("welfare reform") encoded this proposition: Motherhood in the United States is now officially recognized as an economic status and a class privilege. Those who do not have enough money to pay for all the expenses associated

Harris, Secretary of Health and Human Services, v. McRae et al., *448 U.S. 297 (1980)*

This case presents statutory and constitutional questions concerning the public funding of abortions under Title XIX of the Social Security Act, commonly known as the "Medicaid" Act, and recent annual Appropriations Acts containing the so-called "Hyde Amendment." The statutory question is whether Title XIX requires a State that participates in the Medicaid program to fund the cost of medically necessary abortions for which federal reimbursement is unavailable under the Hyde Amendment. The constitutional question, which arises only if Title XIX imposes no such requirement, is whether the Hyde Amendment, by denying public funding for certain medically necessary abortions, contravenes the liberty or equal protection guarantees of the Due Process Clause of the Fifth Amendment, or either of the Religion Clauses of the First Amendment. . . .

Since the Congress that enacted Title XIX did not intend a participating State to assume a unilateral funding obligation for any health service in an approved Medicaid plan, it follows that Title XIX does not require a participating State to include in its plan any services for which a subsequent Congress has withheld federal funding. . . .

Having determined that Title XIX does not obligate a participating State to pay for those medically necessary abortions for which Congress has withheld federal funding, we must consider the constitutional validity of the Hyde Amendment. . . . We address first the appellees' argument that the Hyde Amendment, by restricting the availability of certain medically necessary abortions under Medicaid, impinges on the "liberty" protected by the Due Process Clause as recognized in *Roe v. Wade*, 410 U.S. 113, and its progeny. . . .

The Hyde Amendment . . . places no governmental obstacle in the path of a woman who chooses to terminate her pregnancy, but rather, by means of unequal subsidization of abortion and other medical services, encourages alternative activity deemed in the public interest. . . .

. . . [I]t simply does not follow that a woman's freedom of choice carries with it a constitutional entitlement to the financial resources to avail herself of the full range of protected choices. . . . [A]lthough government may not place obstacles in the path of a woman's exercise of her freedom of choice, it need not remove those not of its own creation. Indigency falls in the latter category. The fi-

with having and raising a child should not become mothers.

The era of "reproductive rights" has facilitated reproductive dignity for many women in the United States. Still, the slimmer a woman's economic resources, the slimmer her access to "reproductive rights": comprehensive reproductive health care, access to abortion services, and socially approved motherhood.

Rickie Solinger

See also: Adolescent Pregnancy; Adoption; Birth Control; Eugenics; Welfare Policy/Welfare Reform

References and Further Reading

Nelson, Jennifer. 2003. *Women of Color and the Reproductive Rights Movement*. New York: New York University Press.

Roberts, Dorothy. 1997. *Killing the Black Body: Reproduction, Race, and the Meaning of Liberty*. New York: Pantheon Books.

Solinger, Rickie. 1997. *Beggars and Choosers: How the Politics of Choice Shapes Adoption, Abortion, and Welfare in the United States*. New York: Hill and Wang.

nancial constraints that restrict an indigent woman's ability to enjoy the full range of constitutionally protected freedom of choice are the product not of governmental restrictions on access to abortions, but rather of her indigency. Although Congress has opted to subsidize medically necessary services generally, but not certain medically necessary abortions, the fact remains that the Hyde Amendment leaves an indigent woman with at least the same range of choice in deciding whether to obtain a medically necessary abortion as she would have had if Congress had chosen to subsidize no health care costs at all. We are thus not persuaded that the Hyde Amendment impinges on the constitutionally protected freedom of choice recognized in *Wade*. . . . Although the liberty protected by the Due Process Clause affords protection against unwarranted government interference with freedom of choice in the context of certain personal decisions, it does not confer an entitlement to such funds as may be necessary to realize all the advantages of that freedom. . . .

It remains to be determined whether the Hyde Amendment violates the equal protection component of the Fifth Amendment. This challenge is premised on the fact that, although federal reimbursement is available under Medicaid for medically necessary services generally, the Hyde Amendment does not permit federal reimbursement of all medically necessary abortions. The District Court held, and the appellees argue here, that this selective subsidization violates the constitutional guarantee of equal protection. The guarantee of equal protection under the Fifth Amendment is not a source of substantive rights or liberties . . . but rather a right to be free from invidious discrimination in statutory classifications and other governmental activity. . . .

. . . [W]e have already concluded that the Hyde Amendment violates no constitutionally protected substantive rights. We now conclude as well that it is not predicated on a constitutionally suspect classification. . . . [T]he principal impact of the Hyde Amendment falls on the indigent. But that fact does not itself render the funding restriction constitutionally invalid, for this Court has held repeatedly that poverty, standing alone, is not a suspect classification. See, e.g., *James v. Valtierra,* 402 U.S. 137. . . .

The remaining question then is whether the Hyde Amendment is rationally related to a legitimate governmental objective. . . . [T]he Hyde Amendment, by encouraging childbirth except in the most urgent circumstances, is rationally related to the legitimate governmental objective of protecting potential life. . . .

Republicanism

The term "republicanism" has two different but interrelated meanings, one institutional, one conceptual. Both meanings can be traced to the ancient Roman Republic and its privileging of *res publica,* "public things." Republicanism is an institutional ideal about how the political order should be structured, about who should rule and who should govern. Republicanism is also a conceptual or ethical ideal that insists that when self-interested and public-oriented values clash, as they always do in politics, the latter should triumph.

As an institutional idea, republicanism's irreducible core is its literal rejection of monarchy, the rule of one. Rulership is a public rather than a private thing, to be publicly shared by more than one solitary individual. How many more is not self-evident. The continuum runs from the oligarchic or aristocratic few to the democratic many. What is constant is that ruling is shared. This institutional republicanism has a lineage as old as the ancient Greek city-state; it stretches through the Roman Republic, medieval city-states like Venice, and the seventeenth-century English commonwealth; then moves across the Atlantic to the American founding.

Conceptually, republicanism is the conviction that concern for the community, for public things, is morally superior to concern for self, for self-interest. In this sense, republicanism is the general privileging of community over the individual. Aristotle and Cicero articulated the doctrine, and in their wake came the otherwise utterly incompatible collection of Thomas Aquinas, Niccolò Machiavelli, and Jean-Jacques Rousseau, and finally today's communitarians, with their criticisms of a liberalism that privileges the individual and self-interest.

From its core normative assumptions, a kind of republican economics has evolved, an economic tradition that is less competitive, more cooperative, and more communal and that sees economic life as serving moral public ends rather than amoral personal or individual ends. This "moral economy" tradition within republicanism has its roots in Aristotle and Aquinas and sees wages and prices not as market or profit driven but as "just" or "unjust." It sees subsistence economies as natural and growth economies as artificial. It validates private property but requires that such property serve communal needs. It insists that the poor be provided for and that no one starve; it values the care of and sharing with communal others more than the aggrandizement of self.

For Aquinas, it was moral for a man to violate the sanctity of private property, even to steal, if he needed to feed his starving family. John Winthrop, fleeing the British monarchy to settle in Massachusetts, told his fellow Puritans that "wee must be knitt together in this worke as one man, wee must entertain each other in brotherly affection. Wee must be willing to abridge our selves of our super fluities, for the supply of others necessities" (Winthrop 1838, 47).

These "republican economics" and the broader republican normative commitment to public responsibility and civic duty are a fundamental nonsocialist building block of the modern state's social welfare obligations. Since the eighteenth century in the Anglo-American world, they have had to confront the "liberal" economics of Adam Smith, which posit an amoral market economy in which self-interested "butchers, bakers, and brewers" (Smith 1887, 140) seek personal profit. Still, the revival of interest in republicanism in recent decades, especially among students of American political thought and among activist communitarians and other reformers, has made it an important alternative to liberal individualism as an ideological grounding of modern public welfare policy.

Isaac Kramnick

See also: End Poverty in California (EPIC); Liberalism; Nineteenth Century; Socialist Party

References and Further Reading

Kramnick, Isaac. 1990. *Republicanism and Bourgeois Radicalism: Political Ideology in Late Eighteenth Century England and America*. Ithaca, NY: Cornell University Press.

Pangle, Thomas L. 1988. *The Spirit of Modern Republicanism: The Moral Vision of the American Founders and the Philosophy of Locke*. Chicago: University of Chicago Press.

Pocock, J. G. A. 1975. *The Machiavellian Moment: Florentine Political Thought and the Atlantic Republican Tradition*. Princeton: Princeton University Press.

Smith, Adam. 1887. *An Inquiry into the Nature and Causes of the Wealth of Nations*. London: T. Nelson and Sons.

Winthrop, John. 1838. *A Modell of Christian Charity*. 3rd Series, vol. 7. Boston: Massachusetts Historical Society.

Resettlement Administration

See New Deal Farm Policy

Riis, Jacob

See How the Other Half Lives; Picturing Poverty (I)

Rural Poverty

Until the 1970s, rural poverty in the United States was associated with the struggle of rural families to eke a living out of the land, epitomized by James Agee and Walker Evans's classic account of Depression-era suffering, *Let Us Now Praise Famous Men*. These images of the rural poor lingered long after the Depression and influenced popular ideas about poverty. In fact, rural poverty persisted at rates higher than those found in urban centers until the end of the 1970s, when central-city poverty overtook rural poverty for the first time. This precipitated a decline in interest in rural poverty within academic and policy circles, and today there remains little specific policy to address the unique problems of rural poverty or its links to urban conditions. Nevertheless, at the beginning of the third millennium, rural poverty in the United States remains widespread and severe. In some regions and communities, the rates once again match or exceed those found in certain parts of central cities.

Background

The current obscurity of rural poverty reflects the greater visibility of urban problems and the common belief that rural poverty is a passing vestige of an old, resource-based economy that is less malignant and threatening to core societal values than is urban poverty. In part, popular attachment to mythical agrarian values, rooted in a distorted historical narrative, has idealized rural landscapes, social forms, and demographic characteristics. The images of the hardscrabble but self-reliant yeoman farmer or the small-town shopkeeper whose communities are characterized by mutual assistance have held sway in popular imagination despite their limited historical accuracy. The result is a nostalgic view of rural life that literally whitewashes rural poverty, presenting rural populations as white, working-class families, who are seen as less threatening to dominant values and elites.

There is an element of truth to these stereotypes. In the absence of other support systems, the rural poor tend to rely on family and extended kin when times are hard, and they are more likely to be white, working, and married than are the urban poor. Rural poverty, however, like rural society, is more complex and diverse, both socially and spatially, than is often acknowledged. Women, single-headed households, and children are increasingly overrepresented among the rural poor, resulting in a convergence between rural and urban poverty profiles. Racial and ethnic minorities are also among the most disadvantaged of the rural poor and have higher percentages living in poverty than their urban counterparts. This racial dimension to rural poverty manifests itself geographically; poverty has historically been concentrated in regions that suffer long-standing conditions of chronic economic underdevelopment and exploitation, often linked with racial and ethnic discrimination. Prominent examples include the plantation South, the Appalachian and Ozark highlands, Indian reservations, and the *colonias* of the Southwest (Billings and Blee 2000; Lyson and Falk 1993; Pickering 2000). Although the specific development patterns, political and economic histories, and population groups of these "forgotten places" have differed, all share the deprivations associated with impoverished places and class polarization.

For example, in rural Texas, where the dominant economy of the nineteenth century was built around cattle ranches, wealthy ranchers and merchants exploited Mexican laborers to ensure their own political and economic power. Over time, this evolved into a dominant urban merchant class and a political patronage system that kept the poor in their place while blaming them for their own condition (Maril 1989). In the postbellum plantation South, elite white planters opposed industrial and economic development in order to increase their political and economic control over the large but weak Black laboring class. The large number of laborers whose survival depended on plantation work kept wages down and landowners' profits up and contributed to the creation of a permanent stratified social system (Hyland and Timberlake 1993). In twentieth-century Appalachia, the mining industry assumed the role that agriculture had in the South, exploiting the region's resources while exerting absolute control over workers in mining camps (Eller 1982). Persistent poverty in these places is the legacy of white elite domination of a larger class, often made up of people of color.

In addition, the history of rural America has been the history of the adverse effects of economic restructuring both in persistently poor regions, with their unique development trajectories, and in the broader rural economy. For example, since the turn of the twentieth century, rural communities have been depopulated by the technological transformation of agricultural methods and the steady growth of corporate agriculture. Chronic crises of overproduction and deflation of land prices, such as the farm crisis of the 1980s, further impoverished the remaining agrarian sector. Even where demand for agricultural labor remains high, the result is to increase the ranks of the working poor. In the migrant farm labor sector, for example, wages are low, conditions are poor, and jobs are unstable, and rampant exploitation takes advantage of a vulnerable labor force composed of poorly educated and largely undocumented immigrants. Similarly, the dispersal of food-processing plants to rural areas—where they have relocated in search of lower-wage labor, as did textile factories before them—has contributed to the changing face of rural poverty by attracting a largely Hispanic immigrant workforce to predominantly white rural areas. Although most immigrants in search of jobs gravitate to the central cities, certain rural locales have become destination points for immigrants, particularly those of Hispanic origin, and those immigrants too often find themselves living in poverty.

Other rural sectors also have suffered severe economic reverses. Increasingly capital-intensive methods of resource extraction have reduced employment in coal and timber production. Resource depletion and environmental regulation threaten economies based on natural resources, such as coastal fisheries and northwest lumber. Rural manufacturing grew during the 1960s and 1970s as a result of rural industrial incentive policies that lured firms from the cities with the promise of cheap land and labor. But the areas that attracted such industries have since declined as firms have moved to offshore locations with even cheaper and more plentiful labor. These industries join the long exodus of textile mills and similar old-line manufacturing industries that have relocated their operations.

Such economic shifts also link rural and urban poverty. Rural people who found themselves unable to make a living off the land began migrating to the cities in the middle of the eighteenth century. Nineteenth-century urban industrialization offered job opportunities to new waves of rural migrants. In the twentieth century, particularly in the post–World War II era, the cataclysmic restructuring within agriculture—favoring large, high-yield producers and introducing labor-saving technology to the fields—resulted in the mass migration of rural southern Blacks to northern and midwestern cities. Drawn by the promise of industrial jobs yet facing discrimination and residential segregation once they got there, many migrants got caught in the rising poverty, joblessness, and ghettoization that came to characterize postwar cities and that were intensified by subsequent rounds of urban deindustrialization.

Explanations for Rural Poverty

Despite clear evidence documenting the impact of structural economic changes on high and persistent rates of rural poverty, explanations

Poor white children in the Ozark Mountains, near Bella Vista, Arkansas. Undated photo. (Bettmann/Corbis)

for the sources of rural poverty vary widely, ranging from the inadequacies of individuals to the inadequacies of local organizations to the failures and tyrannies of the world economy. There is an element of truth to all of these explanations, and efforts to polarize them as either/or theories, while often politically successful in driving policy, have had little explanatory value. The disadvantages that mark rural persons and places are real. Many rural peoples start life with few resources and with individual deficits, both cause and consequence of the failure of institutions and the operations of local and global structures that ignore or exploit these deficits.

The confusion of proximate causes with underlying explanations is expressed in the conflation of different ways of conceptualizing poverty, as either a social or a spatial phenomenon. A social conceptualization of poverty is concerned with poor people and their characteristics; a spatial conceptualization, with poor places and their attributes. The former approach focuses on the correlates of poverty for individuals: low levels of education, high rates of marital instability and nonmarital childbearing and child rearing, and weak labor force attachment. The latter approach examines patterns of spatial inequality and the characteristics of the economy in places with high rates of persistent poverty: low levels of human and social capital, inadequate social services, corrupt and paternalistic political institutions, and lack of good jobs, infrastructure, and investment. Although these characteristics are also present in poor urban places, they are arguably more encompassing in poor rural regions.

The factors that describe the conditions of poor persons and places, that restrict opportunity, and that perpetuate these conditions are outcomes of poverty. Their origins are found in the historical development of social and spatial relations. Thus "the road to poverty" (Billings and Blee 2000)—whether in rural Appalachia, Indian country, or anywhere in between—must be mapped using historical accounts that analyze the cumulative effects of culture, economy, and government policy. Each place has a unique development trajectory and a particular mix of external and internal exploitation of land and labor in collusion with local political repression and corruption, rigid class barriers, and livelihood practices that may enable survival but not mobility. Poverty persists in these places because the power structures that perpetuate these conditions remain unchallenged and unopposed and because the organizations and institutions designed to alleviate deprivation or to create mobility are missing or ineffective. Although the contemporary manifestations may appear to be a culture of poverty, or alternatively, an internal colony, invariably they are highly complex products of all these factors.

Current Developments in Rural Policy

Debates about the causes of poverty have important implications for where to apply leverage to effect change. Is it at the level of individual behavior? Or in community and regional economic development policies? Or in some combination of individual incentives and penalties to change behavior plus macroeconomic programs to create opportunity? Although all these different approaches can be found in past and present policies targeted at the rural poor, the United States has generally opted for efforts to change individual behavior rather than to change the structures that create and sustain poverty. As a result, it has missed opportunities to address unique place-specific problems.

There is virtually no policy that systematically addresses rural poverty or economic development in the United States. The two policies that have most affected rural poverty have been (1) social welfare policy in the form of national safety net programs and their local applications, and (2) the patchwork of industrial and agricultural policies that indirectly shape rural livelihoods. Neither of these policies or programs, however, has made a substantial difference in combating rural poverty. The former has had different impacts and meanings for rural places and peoples than for the urban poor, while the latter has benefited wealthy individual and corporate interests rather than the economic health of entire rural communities.

U.S. social welfare policy as it unfolded during the twentieth century created a highly gendered, raced, and geographically skewed safety net. For example, Social Security, the premier safety net program enacted during the New Deal, failed to cover farm labor, despite the very high rates of poverty in this sector at the time and in subsequent decades. Like similar exclusions from unemployment insurance, the Fair Labor Standards Act, and other labor-protective legislation of the 1930s, these provisions were made in an explicitly racial bargain with conservative southern Democrats, who were determined to maintain control over their heavily African American agricultural labor force. Also excluded from Social Security benefits were many rural women, who historically worked in unpaid reproductive, family, and informal labor.

Both the rules and the administration of safety net programs such as welfare have limited their effectiveness in rural areas. Although eligibility rules were nationally determined, benefit levels were set by the states and were administered locally. Not surprisingly, many of the places with the greatest levels of persistent rural poverty are in states with the least generous and most repressive welfare programs. Weak or corrupt program administration and the lack of information, transportation, and privacy that characterizes many small communities often result in services that are scarce, inconvenient, inaccessible, or stigmatized, decreasing the use of safety net programs by the rural poor.

In the case of the welfare reform legislation

of 1996, the stated intent to move welfare recipients into paid employment is more problematic in rural places, where jobs are limited and those paying a living wage even scarcer, where transportation and child care are lacking, and where the personal resources that potential workers bring to jobs are few. Moving rural residents into permanent employment presented challenges even during the long economic boom of the 1990s. What happens during a downturn is just beginning to emerge, and the history of welfare reform for rural poverty remains to be lived and chronicled.

Industrial and agricultural policies have also been ineffective at combating rural poverty, and systematic and comprehensive policies aimed at the structural problems of rural areas do not exist. Efforts to intervene in the farm economy, beginning in the Depression era, came under immediate assault and had little impact on the poorest rural residents. Later attempts during the War on Poverty to enact more comprehensive policy for poor rural farmers and their families was scaled back to a form that was far less reform minded than what had been initially sought (O'Connor 1992). As a result, the major form of rural economic policy has been commodity programs: crop subsidies and price supports. These programs primarily affect large-scale corporate agribusiness, typically making rich farmers richer while further disadvantaging small family farmers. Although these are in contention as globalization unfolds, to date there is little else on the horizon.

There have also been sporadic efforts to create economic development in some of the most persistently poor regions. Two mechanisms for doing this have been infrastructure investments—such as the Appalachian Regional Commission (established in 1965) and the more recent Delta Regional Commission—and the empowerment and enterprise zone programs of the 1990s. None of these, however, has focused effectively on problems of rural poverty, and in the wake of these programs, there has been little in the way of systematic policy or follow-up to determine their impact. As a result, a comprehensive place-based rural policy—as opposed to sectoral programs and interventions—remains controversial and without widespread support. It remains to be seen whether the twenty-first century will witness policy that makes inroads in tackling poverty in the most persistently poor rural places in the United States.

Ann R. Tickamyer, Cynthia M. Duncan, and Kara Heffernan

See also: African American Migration; Globalization and Deindustrialization; Income and Wage Inequality; Migrant Labor/Farm Labor; Sharecropping; Slavery; Urban Poverty; War on Poverty; Welfare Policy/Welfare Reform; "Working Poor"

References and Further Reading

Billings, Dwight B., and Kathleen M. Blee. 2000. *The Road to Poverty: The Making of Wealth and Hardship in Appalachia.* New York: Cambridge University Press.

Duncan, Cynthia M. 1999. *Worlds Apart: Why Poverty Persists in Rural America.* New Haven: Yale University Press.

Eller, Ronald D. 1982. *Miners, Millhands, and Mountaineers: Industrialization of the Appalachian South, 1880–1930.* Knoxville: University of Tennessee Press.

Hyland, Stanley, and Michael Timberlake. 1993. "The Mississippi Delta: Change or Continued Trouble?" In *Forgotten Places: Uneven Development in Rural America,* ed. T. A. Lyson and W. W. Falk, 76–101. Lawrence: University Press of Kansas.

Lichter, Daniel T., and Leif Jensen. 2002. "Rural America in Transition: Poverty and Welfare at the Turn of the Twenty-First Century." In *Rural Dimensions of Welfare Reform: Welfare, Food Assistance, and Poverty in Rural America,* ed. B. A. Weber, G. J. Duncan, and L. E. Whitener. Kalamazoo, MI: Upjohn Institute.

Lyson, Thomas A., and William W. Falk, eds. 1993. *Forgotten Places: Uneven Development and the Loss of Opportunity in Rural America.* Lawrence: University Press of Kansas.

Maril, Robert Lee. 1989. *Poorest of Americans: The Mexican Americans of the Lower Rio Grande Valley in Texas.* Notre Dame, IN: University of Notre Dame Press.

O'Connor, Alice. 1992. "Modernization and the Rural Poor: Some Lessons from History." In *Rural*

Poverty in America, ed. Cynthia M. Duncan, 215–233. Westport, CT: Auburn House.

Pickering, Kathleen. 2000. "Alternative Economic Strategies in Low-Income Rural Communities: TANF, Labor Migration, and the Case of the Pine Ridge Indian Reservation." *Rural Sociology* 56, no. 4: 148–167.

Rural Sociological Society Task Force on Persistent Rural Poverty. 1993. *Persistent Poverty in Rural America.* Boulder, CO: Westview Press.

Tickamyer, Ann, Julie White, Barry Tadlock, and Debra Henderson. 2002. "Where All the Counties Are above Average." In *Rural Dimensions of Welfare Reform: Welfare, Food Assistance, and Poverty in Rural America*, ed. B. A. Weber, G. J. Duncan, and L. E. Whitener. Kalamazoo, MI: Upjohn Institute.

S

Salvation Army

"Soup, soap and salvation," an early motto of the Salvation Army, captures the denomination's mission to succor bodies while saving souls. The Salvation Army began in London in 1865 as the Christian Mission, a religious outreach run by William Booth, an independent evangelist determined to convert the unchurched masses. Booth, whose theology was fundamentalist, did not intend to start a new Protestant denomination, but because he sought down-and-outers whom the churches ignored, his mission became a movement. In 1878, when Booth changed the group's name to the Salvation Army, he was already called "the General," and his new "army" rapidly adopted a military look and language. Its newspaper was the *War Cry,* its ministers were "officers," and its members were "soldiers."

According to Salvationist lore, the Army's social outreach began when Booth saw homeless men sleeping beneath London Bridge. Appalled by this stark evidence of poverty's toll, Booth ordered his son Bramwell to "do something." Though the tale is apocryphal, it illustrates Booth's commitment to "practical religion," a Christian response to human need. Booth first experimented with practical religion in the early 1870s, opening a string of inexpensive food shops throughout London. (The enterprise was too costly and he closed them after a few years.) In the 1880s, when the Army set up its first training college, Booth's daughter Emma took female "cadets" to work in the London slums. Rather than aggressively proselytizing the residents, the young women lived among them, seeking to win their trust through acts of service and compassion.

The Army, which came to New York in 1880, initially responded to indigence in an ad hoc manner. Within a decade of its arrival, it began a slum mission and a "rescue home" for "fallen women." But by 1890, William Booth decided a more systematic approach was needed. The result was *In Darkest England and the Way Out,* which sold 115,000 copies in its first year of publication. *In Darkest England* proposed the establishment of urban "salvage stations" to teach employment skills to the poor. Once prepared for work, clients would, hopefully, be "saved" and shipped to farm colonies in England and overseas. The plan was never put into practice (though there were three short-lived farm colonies in the United States), but the Army did develop myriad social services. During the dark days of the 1893 depression, the Army opened a woman's shelter in New York City that welcomed anyone who needed a bed. A few months later, a men's shelter was set up nearby, and Salvationist leaders announced plans for housing the needy nationwide. The Army required a minimal fee or a few hours' work from those who had no money, and they encouraged "guests" to

Portrait of the Salvation Army by W. P. Snyder (Library of Congress)

attend the nightly worship service. The Army's "handouts" were opposed by proponents of scientific philanthropy, a school of thought that believed in investigating all hardship cases and separating the "deserving" from the "undeserving" poor. From their perspective, the Army's activities reflected the worst kind of religious sentimentality. But Salvationists believed their methods allowed the poor to retain their dignity and improved chances for their redemption. Many of the early Social Gospel writers applauded the Army's efforts as a model for Christian philanthropy.

The Army continued expanding its social services network during the first two decades of the twentieth century. As a result of its humanitarian work during World War I, the public perception of the group shifted from that of an evangelical movement engaged in relief work to a religiously based philanthropic organization. Salvationists said their philanthropy was "nonsectarian," offered regardless of race, religion, or nationality. By the time of the Great Depression, the Army—one of the few service providers operating on a national scale—was in a key position to offer assistance. By early 1933, Salvationists were giving New York City's needy 100,000 meals and 25,000 lodgings free of charge each week. When the city ran out of beds, it asked the Army to provide more, and when coffee stations were needed around town, municipal leaders turned to the Army for assistance. The Army helped millions while maintaining its core beliefs. For example, judging that the dole undermined an individual's self-respect, Salvationists often asked recipients to work for their bed and bread. They tried to treat clients with dignity and to keep families intact. When the federal government began providing relief, it frequently partnered with the Army (which cared for 20 percent of the homeless and transient population nationwide). Still, throughout the 1930s and 1940s, Army funds came overwhelmingly from private sources.

During the post–World War II boom, private donors—grateful for the Army's help in the Depression and its work with the United Service Organization (USO)—gave generously. The increase in funds, combined with the professionalization of social work, had a profound impact on the organization. As programs expanded, so did the numbers of lay staff; between 1951 and 1961, the number of non-Salvationist clerical and social workers doubled. Since the Army was a movement based on the belief that service springs from religious conviction, this new development troubled some Salvationists. Likewise, some Salvationists saw as problematic the expansion of government funds for social service delivery, a trend that started in the 1960s and ballooned in the 1970s.

But the desire to help outweighed concerns about secularizing influences. With government assistance, the Army either began or expanded its work in probation supervision, low-cost housing, nutritional services, day care, and drug rehabilitation. On the one hand, the Army appeared to accept government regulations mandating strict separation between church and state. On the other hand, the Army regularly affirmed—in statements to donors as well as to its membership—its evangelical mission. Reading between the lines suggests that the Army tried to find a balance between its faith commitments and government requirements. Historically, the Army had accepted funds from anyone; William Booth believed that tainted money was washed clean in God's service. Yet accepting public money entailed special liabilities: Government agencies wanted to control the programs they financed, whereas Salvationists were accustomed to overseeing their own mix of religion and social service. Regulators asked the Army to separate the religious from the social aspects of their programs, calculating how much office space, utilities, and manpower went into each—a tedious task that also undermined the integrity of Salvationist theology. The passage of charitable choice legislation in 1996 improved the situation, permitting faith-based providers to maintain a religious environment in the context of service delivery. For its part, the Army decided to minimize its reliance on government funds by keeping those contracts to 15 percent of its budget.

In 2001, donors contributed $1.39 billion to the Army's $2.31 billion budget, which, in turn, subsidized such programs as residential alcoholic rehabilitation centers, shelters for transients, halfway houses for ex-convicts and ex–drug addicts, medical facilities, group homes, family programs, outreach programs to battered women and families with AIDS, thrift stores, employment bureaus, day care centers, prison work, and emergency relief. The Salvation Army in the United States is known for its abundant resources and diverse programs, despite its modest size of 581,000 members. There are about 3 million Salvationists worldwide.

Diane Winston

See also: Charitable Choice; Charity; Deserving/Undeserving Poor; Food Banks; Homelessness; Hunger; Missionaries; Nonprofit Sector; Philanthropy; Protestant Denominations; Social Gospel; Urban Poverty

References and Further Reading

McKinley, Edward H. 1995. *Marching to Glory: The History of the Salvation Army in the United States, 1880–1992*. Grand Rapids, MI: William B. Eerdmans.

Taiz, Lillian. 2001. *Hallelujah Lads and Lassies: Remaking the Salvation Army in America*. Chapel Hill: University of North Carolina Press.

Winston, Diane. 1999. *Red Hot and Righteous: The Urban Religion of the Salvation Army*. Cambridge, MA: Harvard University Press.

———. 2002. "Ballington (1857–1940) and Maud Booth (1865–1948), Founders of the Volunteers of America, and Evangeline Booth (1865–1950), Commander of the Salvation Army." In *Notable*

American Philanthropists: Biographies of Giving and Volunteering, ed. Robert T. Grimm Jr. Westport, CT: Greenwood and Onyx Press.

Scientific Charity

See Charity; Charity Organization Societies; Philanthropy; *Public Relief and Private Charity*; Society for the Prevention of Pauperism

Self-Reliance

The term "self-reliance" is used to describe (1) the material fact of self-support and (2) an attitude of willingness to be self-supporting. Self-reliance is framed as both an objective reality and a subjective state of mind. It is important to note these two ways of using the term because, in the postindustrial economy, very few individuals are objectively self-reliant throughout their lives. Instead, most individuals are economically entwined with the state in one form or another; for example, through subsidized property loans, educational grants, or Social Security payments. Very few individuals achieve the objective condition of permanent self-reliance. There does seem to be, however, a tacit or de facto sense of whether a given individual is "sufficiently self-reliant." Being "sufficiently self-reliant" is the unspoken standard to which the poor today are held. Yet given the difficulty of explicitly identifying what counts as "sufficiently self-reliant," self-reliance is best understood as a norm rather than an objective condition.

Despite the rarity of full material self-reliance in the postindustrial age, self-reliance as an ideal or norm dominates the contemporary American imagination. Self-reliance frames the relationship between the individual and the collective. As a norm, self-reliance suggests that the aim of the responsible citizen is to be as materially self-supporting as possible. In this context, self-reliance is the ethical injunction to refrain from relying excessively on one's community, to work as hard as one can, and to avoid being a burden. In this scenario, one must take as little as possible from the common stock. There are two justifications for this ethical stance: (1) If everyone adopts the attitude of minimizing one's use of relief, no one will be unduly impinged on by shirking or undeserving neighbors, and (2) if the provision of and reliance on common stock can be minimized, everyone's entanglement with public agencies will be minimized, and thus everyone's individual freedom will be maximized. These two assertions will be discussed in turn.

In contemporary social welfare debates, self-reliance is equated with paid employment. Wage work has become the marker of the will to self-reliance. Yet in the postindustrial capitalist context, not all workers are equally well positioned to move toward self-reliance via wage work. Barriers to self-reliance in the wage economy range from unpaid labor responsibilities—the necessity to care for young children or for disabled or elderly family members—to low skill levels, to transportation problems, to substance abuse problems, to bias in hiring practices. The ethic of self-reliance ought to be contextualized to take into account individual circumstances, particularly the circumstances of those who are engaged in the unpaid caregiving labor traditionally done by women. Those who devote time to unpaid caregiving labor have less capacity to achieve self-reliance via wage work, yet they are nevertheless engaged in social labor that is valuable to the community. And the ethic of self-reliance ought to take into account the structural constraints of the labor market, its failure to absorb all potential workers as wage earners, and the reality that a segment of the population will be unemployed at any given time.

Insofar as the norm of self-reliance aims to minimize engagement with public agencies, it is compelling to contemporary Americans in part because of a romanticized past that sentimentalizes the autonomous individual. In this vision, those who are most autonomous from government are most free, and those who are able to avoid interdependence are able to preserve their freedom. Those who idealize autonomy are skeptical about becoming overly involved in the dependency needs of their fellow citizens. This political fantasy of near-perfect autonomy is closely related to the myth of the idealized breadwinner, which combines the ideal of the maximally free male with the traditional division of labor between the sexes, so that women and children remain dependent on a "free" male citizen who supports them. This vision of self-reliance coupled with traditional gender roles is becoming increasingly remote as we see changes in the wage structure (there are fewer male-breadwinner jobs available that allow men to support a family on one paycheck) and changes in traditional family structure (there are fewer two-parent families).

Romantic ideals of autonomy have an important place in American political thought and underscore the link between limited government and individual freedom, but they may also cause one to lose sight of the legitimate needs of citizens who fail to manifest self-reliance. For instance, the self-reliance narratives associated with Ralph Waldo Emerson and American Transcendentalism prize autonomous thinking, individual inquiry, and a skepticism toward entanglements with traditional institutions. This frame can be important in the context of fostering freethinking democratic citizens. Yet Transcendentalist anxiety about interdependence can also engender an irrational fear of those in need and of the government institutions that support them and a phobia of other citizens' leeching or impinging on the self-reliant. The fear of excessively dependent subjects, the "undeserving poor," who are a burden to the collective is evidenced in critiques of welfare provision.

Those who are anxious about the dependency needs of their fellow citizens frequently believe that engendering greater material self-support begins with the cultivation of an attitude of self-reliance among the poor. This is personalized behavior modification as a hedge against poverty, and the core message to those in need is "try harder." This strategy is visible in several post-1996 welfare programs that require individual personal responsibility plans and that try to inculcate diligence, punctuality, reliability, and conformity to employer demands. The aim of this component of welfare reform is to reduce welfare dependence and to increase employment, clearly stated in the Temporary Assistance for Needy Families program's goal to "end the dependence of needy parents on government by promoting job preparation, work, and marriage" (Public Law 104-193, Title I, Part A, Sec. 401 [a][2]).

The ethic of self-reliance is also visible in the 1996 welfare reform legislation's elimination of aid to legal immigrants. Here we see a redeployment of the ideal of the self-sufficient citizen and, more importantly, the assertion that recent immigrants have a special responsibility to manifest self-reliance. The law states, "Self-sufficiency has been a basic principle of United States immigration law since this country's earliest immigration statutes" (Public Law 104-193, Title IV, Sec. 400 [1]). Legislators are clearly anxious to emphasize that resident aliens have a special responsibility to uphold the norm of self-reliance.

Anne M. Manuel

See also: Dependency; Deserving/Undeserving Poor; Family Structure; Family Wage; Immigrants and Immigration; Liberalism; Republicanism; Unemployment; Welfare Policy/Welfare Reform

References and Further Reading

Coontz, Stephanie. 1993. *The Way We Never Were: Family and the Nostalgia Trap*. New York: Basic Books.

Public Law 104-193. 1996. *Personal Responsibility and Work Opportunity Reconciliation Act*. 104th Cong., August 22.

Schram, Sanford. 2000. *After Welfare: The Culture of Post-Industrial Social Policy*. New York: New York University Press.

Service and Domestic Workers, Labor Organizing

In the wake of the decline in manufacturing in the United States from the 1970s through the turn of the twenty-first century, millions of jobs have been lost to low-cost foreign producers. Industrial job loss has devastated working-class communities throughout the United States as manufacturing jobs paying living wages have moved to lower-cost locations in Latin America and East Asia. Since the mid-1970s, basic manufacturing industries have been replaced by lower-paying health care, social services, domestic, food services, building maintenance, and other service-sector industries as the fastest-growing source of employment in the U.S. economy.

Within the burgeoning service sector, expanding demand for health and social services has played an especially significant role. With the growth of the health care industry and government support programs, service and domestic work has become a large and growing component of the service sector that now comprises more than two-thirds of all jobs in the United States. This shift has in turn had major implications for the labor movement, which in recent decades has come up against the limitations of traditional collective bargaining practices while seeing its most significant innovations in service-sector organizing.

The Rise of Services and Public-Sector Unions

Historically, public-sector service jobs have paid workers significantly higher wages than comparable private-sector jobs, primarily due to worker efforts to form public employee unions that create wage and benefit standards for low-skilled workers employed in public hospitals, municipal buildings, and public welfare offices. The American Federation of State, County, and Municipal Employees (AFSCME), chartered by the American Federation of Labor in Wisconsin in 1936, grew to become the nation's largest public-employee union by the early 1980s, largely due to the expansion of government social services. Nationwide, the union represents 1.3 million members employed in secretarial and clerical work, social work, maintenance, hospital and health care work, domestic work, food services, and corrections. By contrast, service workers in the private sector, now a growing segment of service work in the United States, have been typically unorganized due to greater resistance to unionization among private employers than among government managers.

The public sector, dominated by service workers, was the primary source of trade union growth from the 1950s to the 1970s. Even as union density in the private sector declined, public-sector union growth continued unabated into the early 1980s. The promise of greatly improved working conditions and higher wages and benefits through unionization encouraged vast numbers of workers to join public-sector unions during this period. In just over fifteen years, public-sector trade union membership in the United States swelled from slightly over 1 million in 1960 to over 3 million in 1976, accounting for over 80 percent of all trade union growth in the nation during the 1960s and 1970s.

Among fiscal conservatives, a strong backlash emerged against the rapid ascendancy of public-employee service unions as a social and political force in urban politics in the 1970s. They were disturbed by what they saw as the undue influence of public-employee unions on public policy. Collective bargaining by public-sector service unions, critics argued, imposed unfair costs on citizens by raising taxes to finance wage increases. Fiscal conservatives saw the influence of public-employee unions in the service sector as raising taxes on citizens and imposing high costs on local government budgets. In response to growing pressure for austerity budgets created by a series of urban fiscal crises, rising deficits, antigovernment ideology, and taxpayer revolts, the capacity of public-employee unions to negotiate from a position of strength declined considerably beginning in the mid-1970s. The worker activism of the 1960s and 1970s was followed by a period of labor conciliation, particularly in the aftermath of the municipal government fiscal crises in the mid-1970s and President Ronald Reagan's summary dismissal of striking air traffic controllers in 1981.

The growth of labor bureaucracies and their coalescence with management after the formation of public-employee unions further moderated labor demands and undercut wages, working conditions, and job security. After their unions were officially recognized by government authorities, many union leaders—once enthusiastic about mobilizing workers' demonstrations, petition drives, and strikes—tended to become moderate and accommodating in the face of employers' demands for concessions. In New York and other major cities, some leaders of public-employee unions offered little opposition to budget cuts that weakened their members' wages and job security.

Since the 1980s, public-sector union leaders have had great difficulty combating public authorities' efforts to restrain wages through budget cuts, privatization, mass layoffs, and programs of permanent job attrition. Even though studies have found that cities with public-sector service unions have no higher municipal budget costs than do cities without such unions, the right-wing drive to undermine labor standards and service workers' wages increased precipitously after 1980. Consequently, states and municipalities have continued to subcontract public health and social services to private and nonprofit employers paying substantially lower wages than those received by workers in public-employee unions.

The Working Poor

The growth of service work has contributed significantly to the expansion of the numbers of the working poor—full-time laborers earning too little to provide for such essentials as food, shelter, clothing, and health care. A key factor in the growth of low-wage services is privatization and the deterioration of the unionized public-sector jobs that have provided a large proportion of service employment since the 1960s. The growth in the private segment of service employment is relatively new, overturning decades of public-sector workers' efforts to improve their status through organizing into unions. Moreover, due to the rapid growth of private service work since the 1980s and the propensity for high turnover in this sector, continuity in the industry is limited, complicating efforts to organize workers into unions that may be able to provide higher-wage jobs.

Rising poverty among service workers also reflects the decline in government safeguards moderating the instabilities of the private labor market, including unemployment insurance and welfare benefits. The new welfare law established by the Personal Responsibility and Work Opportunity Reconciliation Act of 1996 has swelled the numbers of the working poor by forcing those on public assistance into workfare programs, that is, programs requiring work in exchange for public assistance. Although workfare ostensibly trains workers for eventual entry into the labor market, a majority of workers are pushed into low-wage service jobs as housekeepers, domestics, food service workers, and other service-sector workers, in jobs that do not provide living wages or health benefits. The growth of workfare in turn has significantly undermined the ability of labor unions representing service workers to maintain industrial standards in the public and private sectors. Privatization and outsourcing to low-wage employers paying workers much less than they would earn in public-sector jobs complicate service workers' efforts to maintain wage and work standards through their unions. Public-sector service jobs are frequently outsourced to private vendors, who are not accountable to prevailing collective bargaining agreements with government authorities.

Combating Service Cuts through Coalition Building

Amid the backlash against public-sector workers in the 1980s and 1990s, some union leaders have sought to cultivate potential allies among community members who are the recipients of the essential health care, education, and social services they provide. The primary objective is to form and join community-based coalitions around the complementary goals of improved working conditions and improved social and health care services for clients. Labor activist and scholar Paul Johnston (1994) argues that because service workers in the public sector are frequently legally constrained from striking and protesting in ways that private-sector workers are not, they must mobilize to defend and augment their power through building coalitions and movements beneficial to their members' interests.

Through the formation of labor-community alliances, service employee unions seek to influence state budgeting policies by pressing government officials to support services—such as improved health care and affordable housing—beneficial to union members and key community groups. This involves persuading the public and government officials of the significant work their members perform, even as they engage in more militant strategies against government cutbacks through public demonstrations along with community allies. Such strategies are designed to counter divisive management tactics that seek to pit the interests of unions and their members against the broader public interest. The labor-community organizing strategy is thus posed as an alternative to the management-labor cooperation promoted by union leaders and public officials in previous decades. By organizing members and the public around joint causes, the labor-community strategy encourages public-employee unions to politicize the collective bargaining process and wield the strike threat more effectively in bargaining with management.

Resisting Privatization and Organizing Outsourced Labor

The two leading contemporary service unions, the Service Employees International Union (SEIU) and AFSCME, have embraced the strategy of engaging labor-community alliances and membership mobilization. Ironically, though SEIU primarily represents private-sector workers and AFSCME represents public-sector unions, both labor organizations are appealing to federal, state, and local public officials to advance the interests of members and their clients. Since the late 1990s, SEIU—operating in the private and nonprofit sectors—has provided the most notable national example of a union advancing its members' interests through building community alliances. The union's New York State affiliate—SEIU Local 1199—has mobilized home-care workers and their clients since the late 1980s to improve wages and appalling working conditions through public demonstrations and by pressing government to provide higher subsidies. Nor has the decline of public-sector service jobs and the growth of private-sector jobs diminished worker interest in organizing and joining unions. Indeed, service-sector workers form the backbone of SEIU, a union that represents workers in two key sectors: building services and health care. The national union's leadership has devoted significant resources to unionization efforts in these two sectors and has gained the capacity to organize in major urban regions. Through the organization of 500,000 health care workers, SEIU membership has grown to 1.2 million. Much of the union's new growth is occurring among home-care, institutional health care, and domestic workers employed by private and nonprofit agencies, some subsidized by the federal and state governments, that provide care to the young and elderly. The union's Justice for Janitors campaign scored a major success in Los Angeles in 1989 through a dramatic mobilization of labor and community supporters, leading to subsequent organizing efforts throughout the nation.

The growth in the number of immigrant workers remains a major component of new organizing efforts in the service sector, especially the organization of domestic workers who care for the young and the old and who clean private homes and buildings. A large proportion of domestic workers are immigrant women of color who are not protected by federal and state labor laws and who are subject to racial and sex discrimination. Thus, unions must contend with the problem of organizing isolated workers in private homes who are struggling for the enforcement of standard legal protections provided to all other workers by federal and state law. A growing number are joining workers' centers that provide them with English-language education, labor law classes, and assistance with wage and discrimination claims against employers.

AFSCME too is mobilizing members to support increased funding for public institutions where its members are employed and to combat privatization efforts on municipal and state levels. The union is constrained by persistent efforts by fiscal conservatives to punish members through privatization and wage cuts. In the late 1990s, shocked by the scale of privatization and consequent harm to its members, the national union emerged from an era of relative passivity to more forcefully safeguard members' wages and job security in regions throughout the country. Moreover, AFSCME is reaching out to organize service workers now in the private sector and is now actively engaged in new organizing campaigns throughout the country.

Since the late 1990s, the march toward privatization has escalated turf battles among unions organizing low-wage service workers in the pub-

"Organizing Domestic Workers in Atlanta, Georgia," Dorothy Bolden, 1970

I started organizing the maids in 1968. . . . The salary of the maids was very low. They were working in model homes, beautiful homes, and they had a great deal of responsibility. . . . I would go around in the bus and ask the maids how they would feel about joining if we would organize, and they would say, "Oh, I'm for that." One day I took three ladies, and made a radio announcement. Told how we was getting together in the National Domestic Workers Union of America. I picked up many members that time, which was beautiful.

I had to meet with the maids every week to keep them encouraged, to keep the strength up. I was talking, and they was responding to my talk. . . .

You can't negotiate with private employers, private homes. You have to teach each maid how to negotiate. And this is the most important thing—communicating. I would tell them it was up to them to communicate. If I wanted a raise from you I wouldn't come in and hit you over your head and demand a raise—I would set out and talk to you and let you know how the living costs have gone up. . . . When the employers heard that we was unionizing, the wages went up to $12. . . . A lot of the maids got raises. They didn't get fired. Some of them quit because the lady wouldn't give them the money. When you unionize like this, on a private basis, and you're self-employed, your risk is that the one that doesn't join your union, she gets a good increase in salary. And this is the hardest part. And I told them we weren't going to be able to get in all the maids in Atlanta, but we could improve.

Source: Dorothy Bolden, taped interview with Gerda Lerner, 1970, in *Black Women in White America: A Documentary History,* ed. Gerda Lerner (New York: Vintage Books, 1972), 26–37.

lic sector. As AFSCME vocally opposes privatization of social services, SEIU supports living-wage campaigns targeting private and nonprofit workers. The two unions are operating on two fronts: AFSCME opposes privatization as an antiworker measure that targets the women and people of color who predominate in service-sector jobs. Although the union still seeks to represent private-sector workers, it sees privatization as eroding the quality of public-sector jobs and service delivery to clients.

SEIU puts its emphasis on creating municipal living-wage laws for public services already contracted out to private providers. Living-wage laws seek to ensure that services contracted out by government to the private sector provide workers with decent wages and benefits. The living-wage movement emerged in earnest during the mid-1990s and has grown slowly through the early 2000s. Fewer than 100,000 workers were covered by living-wage laws by 2002, but the strategy has gained strength as a larger number of municipalities have passed local ordinances. It remains to be seen whether the antiprivatization movement and living-wage movement will protect larger segments of service workers.

Immanuel Ness

See also: Agricultural and Farm Labor Organizing; Domestic Work; Fair Labor Standards Act (FLSA); Living-Wage Campaigns; Trade/Industrial Unions; Wagner Act; Workfare; "Working Poor"

References and Further Reading

Fink, Leon, and Brian Greenberg. 1989. *Upheaval in the Quiet Zone: A History of Hospital Workers' Union Local 1199*. Chicago: University of Illinois Press.

Hondagneu-Soleto, Pierrette. 2001. *Domestica: Immigrant Workers Cleaning and Caring in the Shadows of Affluence*. Berkeley and Los Angeles: University of California Press.

Johnston, Paul. 1994. *Success while Others Fail: Social Movement Unionism and the Public Workplace*. Ithaca, NY: Cornell University Press.

Maier, Mark H. 1987. *City Unions: Managing Discontent in New York City*. New Brunswick, NJ: Rutgers University Press.

Wellington, Harry H., and Ralph K. Winter. 1971. *The Unions and the Cities*. Washington, DC: Brookings Institution.

Zax, Jeffrey, and Casey Ichniowski. 1988. "The Effects of Public Sector Unionism on Pay, Employment, Department Budgets, and Municipal Expenditures." In *When Public Sector Workers Unionize*, ed. Richard B. Freeman and Casey Ichniowski. Chicago: University of Chicago Press.

Settlement Houses

Settlement houses are community institutions that house facilities and staff for recreational, arts, youth, social welfare, and community-enrichment activities. Now often called "neighborhood centers," there are probably 900 in the United States today and as many as 4,500 worldwide. The settlement house movement originated in Great Britain and the United States in the late 1880s as one expression of a new philosophy informing middle-class participation in voluntary social service to new and generally poor population clusters in industrial cities. Departing from a more punitive approach to providing goods and services to the poor, the settlement house founders held that middle- and upper-class volunteers would trade in the currency of character and would receive as well as give by serving these fellow citizens. By World War I, there were about 400 settlement houses across the United States, primarily in northeastern and midwestern cities.

Complicated ironies characterized British welfare thought in the imperial and capitalist mid-nineteenth century. In London, charity reform initially took the form of *charity organization*, pioneered by Octavia Hill, a disciple of John Ruskin, and W. H. Fremantle, an Anglican rector. Distressed by what she perceived as the moral vacuity and deleterious effects of unsystematic almsgiving, Hill experimented with reformed housing for the poor: rentals benevolently overseen by genteel volunteers who would help teach the tenants cleanliness and respon-

King Philip Settlement House, Fall River, Massachusetts. *Photo by Lewis W. Hine. (Library of Congress)*

sibility. The Charity Organisation Society (1869), inspired by Hill's work, offered benign supervision and systematic assessment of the needs of poor families. Charity initiatives cast a steely eye on the individual poor person, insisting that the "truly needy" demonstrate strong moral fiber as well as unavoidable misfortune. Both also drew on the moral philosophy of contemporary social organicist thinkers to implicate the nonpoor in improving the lives of the poor.

It remained to the Anglican priest Samuel Augustus Barnett and his spouse Henrietta to reject the punitive aspects of the new model of social welfare while magnifying its Christ-inspired service aspects. Toynbee Hall opened its doors in East London in 1884. It was named for Anglican scholar and Oxford don Arnold Toynbee, who inspired a generation of educated middle-class reformers to embrace the new approach. Canon Barnett called upon Oxford students to come share their class-based blessings in a "spirit of neighborliness." This first settlement was followed by almost fifty more in the United Kingdom before World War I.

Within a few years, American travelers to Great Britain encountered the settlements. Students and seekers, both men and women, these young people were inspired by the same texts and the same flavor of social issues as their British counterparts had been. Uneasy with the prosperity and increased cultural isolation of the middle classes, unable to exert social leadership in traditional ways, and challenged by new vocational opportunities, these individuals were eager and able to embark on an urban adventure. Jane Addams, Robert Woods, Stanton Coit, and Vida Scudder actually visited the English settlements. Other early leaders, such as Chicago's Graham Taylor, were fed by the travelers' reports as well as the transatlantic texts of Christian

Socialism. The founders of the American settlement movement became its leaders for the next forty years.

The first American settlements, in Boston, New York, and Chicago, followed the spirit of Barnett's dictum that the residents would learn from their new neighborhoods. Hull House, founded in 1889 by Jane Addams and Ellen Gates Starr in the heart of working-class Chicago, was the most widely known. For Addams, the settlement ideology was inseparable from her personal experience. A female college graduate who was resisting the traditional "family claim" (Addams 1893, 13), Addams was unwilling to pursue individual gain or personal culture without social responsibility. While building on traditional associations of women with nurturing and social service, Addams and the other women reformers of her generation used the settlement house movement to change the society into which American college women graduated. The young men who gravitated to settlement work were also unusual for their time. Often influenced by liberal Protestantism, many were searching for a vocation that was service-oriented without being traditionally religious and that would give expression to their liberal-to-radical political leanings. Settlement house men were also unusual in their pursuit of such traditionally "feminized" reform issues as children's well-being and sanitation. In the bustling, noisy, ethnically diverse urban neighborhoods, these college graduates learned unanticipated lessons about social morality, political expediency, cross-cultural encounters, and the lives of the working classes.

The settlement programs grew rapidly in the first two decades after their founding (the "Twenty Years" of Jane Addams's institutional memoir of Hull House). From scattered child drop-ins and underpopulated reading groups in the first year or two, both in-house and outreach programs multiplied. Settlement residents learned to solicit donations for the meeting rooms, playgrounds, art studios, theaters, clinics, and gymnasiums they built. In addition, settlers became their neighbors' advocates with existing agencies and pioneers of new agencies for sanitary services, education, labor standards, and child welfare at both local and federal levels. The settlement houses attracted reformers and university personnel. They became classrooms for post-1900 social work schools.

After their Progressive-Era beginnings, tangled up in the heady world of social reform, the settlements contracted, institutionalized, and reevaluated themselves during and after World War I. Settlements became less fluid and more identified with particular neighborhoods, activities, or religious groups. Settlement workers commuted to work rather than living in the houses, and full-time workers were more often paid as staff rather than housed as volunteers. Settlements sought annual funding with catchall agencies like the Community Chest and, later, United Way, which were designed to detect and shun controversial causes and persons. Surviving and evolving settlements have served the children and young people of their communities for over a century, in the latter part of that time primarily as activity centers rather than as the experimental stations they were formerly.

Mina Carson

See also: Americanization Movement; Charity Organization Societies; Community Chests; Deserving/Undeserving Poor; *Hull-House Maps and Papers*; Immigrants and Immigration; Philanthropy; Pittsburgh Survey; Progressive Era and 1920s; Social Gospel; Social Work; *Twenty Years at Hull-House*

References and Further Reading

Addams, Jane. 1893. "The Subjective Necessity for Social Settlements." In *Philanthropy and Social Progress: Seven Essays, Delivered before the School of Applied Ethics at Plymouth, Massachusetts during the Session of 1892*, 1–26. New York: Thomas Y. Crowell.

Blank, Barbara Trainin. 1998. "Settlement Houses: Old Idea in New Form Builds Communities." *The New Social Worker* 5, no. 3. http://www.socialworker.com/settleme.htm.

Carson, Mina. 1990. *Settlement Folk: Social Thought*

and the American Settlement Movement, 1885–1930. Chicago: University of Chicago Press.
Davis, Allen. 1967. *Spearheads for Reform: The Social Settlements and the Progressive Movement, 1890–1914*. New York: Oxford University Press.
Trolander, Judith. 1987. *Professionalism and Social Change: From the Settlement House Movement to Neighborhood Centers, 1886 to the Present*. New York: Columbia University Press.

Sexism

Sexism is a form of oppression that results in the subordination of women and girls on the basis of their biology or gender. There are several consequences that follow from this subordination, including the overrepresentation of women among the poor, inadequate provisions for women and girls in social welfare policy, and the treatment of poor single mothers as a "special case" of deviancy and social pathology that requires extraordinarily intrusive forms of governmental intervention. Given the complex nature of social structures, sexism never appears as a perfectly distinct phenomenon. Sexism is intertwined with other discriminatory forces, such as class exploitation, racism, and homophobia. As such, the effects of sexism are particularly devastating for women and girls who are located in the working class, in communities of color, and in the lesbian community.

The domestic labor thesis holds that women are more likely to be poor than men because women typically forgo educational achievement, job opportunities, and career development in order to care for their male partners, elderly parents, and children. From this perspective, women subsidize men, and society as a whole, by performing unpaid domestic labor. Where heterosexual women are concerned, the theory suggests that if a woman sacrifices her own life chances to support her male partner and family but then goes through a separation and divorce, her risk of impoverishment will be much greater than that of her former partner. Divorce settlements rarely generate enough compensation for these women; the vast majority of once-married mothers with children do not receive adequate child support payments. The domestic labor thesis obviously cannot account for the fact that lesbians who have never had male partners are overrepresented among the poorest of the poor. But the theory does shed light on the condition of many single mothers who are separated from their male partners, either by death or because of the breakdown in their relationship. The significant racial differences within the poor single-mother population, however, should not be neglected. Although divorce does lead to poverty for many white women, many poor single Black mothers who have left their male partners were already poor before their separation, because their male partners did not earn a living wage.

There are two types of sexist oppression in the workplace that affect women's income and wealth: exclusion and differentiation. Although discrimination against women in employment is illegal under Title VII of the 1964 Civil Rights Act, serious inequities nevertheless persist. Girls and women are often discouraged from pursuing the same educational opportunities and career paths as the males from their same class and age cohort. In these cases, they are informally excluded from the full-time paid workforce because of gender attributes or expectations assigned to them as women. Some girls and women actually are encouraged to seek paid employment, but not in the same jobs or along the same trajectories as their male counterparts. Treated differently than male workers with the same qualifications, these women are often funneled into specific employment sectors—such as service work, light manufacturing, and textiles—where low wages and unskilled dead-end jobs are common. Some of the most exploited women in these positions work in sweatshop conditions. Even among the women workers who earn a minimum wage, however, the risk of poverty is quite high. A household with two dependents that is led by a full-time, year-round worker who earns a minimum wage still falls well below the poverty line, and single women are far more likely than single men to have at least one dependent in their household.

Women often enter the employment market with the same qualifications as men. Although more men than women earn professional degrees, women surpass men in their rates of high school completion, college enrollment, and college graduation rates. Women are nevertheless typically paid less than equally qualified men and are often passed over for raises and promotions. Employers who do promote entry-level workers to supervisory and junior management positions often look for the social and psychological characteristics that are generally associated with typical male behavior, such as an assertive leadership style, and prefer to build familiar all-white-male mentoring networks and management environments. Because women workers often assume much greater burdens in child rearing and domestic labor than do their male counterparts, they often cannot pursue the activities that are needed to ensure they will earn a promotion and a better income. Qualified women are also often subjected to "mommy tracking" and "glass ceilings." Even when they are in fact available for overtime, on-the-job-training, travel, and other additional duties, they are often denied the opportunity to advance their careers because their employers assume that all women workers prioritize their families over their jobs.

The discriminatory treatment of women in the social welfare policy field is expressed in at least two ways. First, the needs of low-income women are often neglected, as social policy experts, legislators, and entire bureaucratic structures either privilege the needs of men over those of women, ignore the gendered bases of poverty, or expect women to conform to masculine policy assumptions. For example, key programs such as subsidized child care, which are common in other Western countries, would help poor women meet the care needs of their children when they leave them to work in the labor market. Yet child care is not guaranteed even though welfare policy requires poor women to work their way out of poverty in jobs outside the home.

A second way in which social welfare policy practices its sexism against poor women arises from stereotypes about their reproductive behavior and seeks to regulate sex and childbearing. Poor women of color, in particular, are treated by social welfare policy as irresponsible and sexually promiscuous deviants who cannot be trusted either to make proper fertility decisions or to raise their own children. Sexism has produced the dangerous myth that because poor women are social outlaws, strong moral policing and behavior modification components must be included within governmental poverty assistance programs. Although this myth can be easily refuted by social science data, it is nevertheless widely regarded as objective truth. As a result, sexist and racist ideology has become deeply normalized and institutionalized not only in American social welfare policy practices but also in the laws that govern income assistance, child removal, child support enforcement, and Medicaid.

Anna Marie Smith

See also: Child Care; Deserving/Undeserving Poor; Domestic Work; Family Structure; Foster Care; Gender Discrimination in the Labor Market; Reproductive Rights; *The Vanishing Black Family;* Welfare Policy/Welfare Reform; "Working Poor"

References and Further Reading

Barrett, Michèle. 1988. *Women's Oppression Today: The Marxist/Feminist Encounter*. London: Verso.

Ehrenreich, Barbara. 2001. *Nickel and Dimed: On (Not) Getting By in America*. New York: Metropolitan Books.

Eisenstein, Zillah. 1994. *The Color of Gender: Reimagining Democracy*. Berkeley and Los Angeles: University of California Press.

Mink, Gwendolyn. 1998. *Welfare's End*. Ithaca, NY: Cornell University Press.

Zinn, Maxine Baca. 1989. "Family, Race, and Poverty in the Eighties." *Signs* 14, no. 4: 856–874.

Share Our Wealth, 1935

For politicians such as Senator Huey Long of Louisiana, the severity of the Great Depression inspired radical plans to eliminate poverty. In 1934, the charismatic Senator Long began promoting a redistribution program he called "Share Our Wealth." As governor of Louisiana, Long had attacked entrenched corporate power, abolished the poll tax and property taxes on the poor, and built highways, hospitals, and public schools. He also created a powerful political machine that controlled the state's legislature and press and ruthlessly targeted political opponents. Elected to the Senate in 1930, Long supported Franklin D. Roosevelt's 1932 campaign, but he ultimately found the president's programs too moderate. His Share Our Wealth campaign proposed taxing the wealthy to ensure that no American's income was less than one-third or more than 300 times the national average. Long expected the plan to be the cornerstone of his campaign for the presidential election of 1936, but he was assassinated by a political opponent on September 9, 1935.

Sarah Case

See also: Bonus Army; End Poverty in California (EPIC); Great Depression and New Deal; Townsend Movement; Wealth; Wealth, Distribution/Concentration

Here is the sum and substance of the share-our-wealth movement:

1. *Every family to be furnished by the Government a homestead allowance, free of debt, of not less than one-third the average family wealth of the country. . . . No person to have a fortune of more than 100 to 300 times the average family fortune. . . .*
2. *The yearly income of every family shall be not less than one-third the average family income. . . .*
3. *To limit or regulate the hours of work to such an extent as to prevent over-production . . . [and] allow the maximum time to the workers for recreation, convenience, education, and luxuries of life. . . .*
4. *An old-age pension to the persons over 60.*
5. *To balance agricultural production with what can be consumed . . . include[ing] the preserving and storage of surplus commodities to be paid for and held by the Government . . . [without] destroying any of the things raised to eat or wear, nor [the] wholesale destruction of hogs, cattle, or milk.*
6. *To pay the veterans of our wars what we owe them and to care for their disabled.*
7. *Education and training for all children to be equal in opportunity in all schools, colleges, universities, and other institutions for training in the professions and vocations of life. . . .*
8. *The raising of revenue and taxes for the support of this program to come from the reduction of swollen fortunes from the top, as well as for the support of public works to give employment whenever there may be any slackening necessary in private enterprise.*

Source: Richard D. Polenberg, ed., *The Era of Franklin D. Roosevelt, 1933–1945: A Brief History with Documents* (Boston and New York: Bedford Books, 2000), 130–131.

Sharecropping

When approximately 4 million enslaved people were freed after the defeat of the Confederacy in the Civil War and the passage of the Fourteenth Amendment (1868) to the U.S. Constitution, a new system of land tenure soon emerged in the cotton plantation regions of the American South. This system was characterized by landless farmers, both Blacks and whites, working in families for a "share" of the crop. This share would be paid in the form of an advance in farm supplies and other provisions, with the remaining coming due at the end of the year when the crops were harvested. If farm families contributed only their labor to the arrangement, known as "sharecropping," they were usually paid around one-third of the crop as their share. If they contributed tools or animals in the bargain, known as "share tenanting," they worked for half or even two-thirds of the crop. Black farmers were typically sharecroppers, whereas white farmers in this arrangement were typically share tenants. In both cases, however, the system left the farmers mired in poverty and deeply indebted to the merchants who initially furnished supplies and other items on credit. This sharecropping system lasted until the 1940s, when it began to disappear as southern landowners replaced sharecroppers with wage laborers working mechanical cotton pickers.

Sharecropping took hold in the South for several interrelated social, political, and economic reasons. First, the failure of the federal government to provide the formerly enslaved with land, long-term and low-interest loans, and adequate protection immediately after the Civil War left them few resources with which to challenge their former masters. Second, most freedmen and freedwomen, as they were called at the time, refused to work in a slavelike system of gang labor under close supervision by white bosses. They wanted family farms of their own, or at least ones they could rent, and they wanted to farm them free of any immediate supervision. Third, although the U.S. Army tried to introduce a system of wage labor, poor crop yields due to the withdrawal of Black women and children from the fields, an infestation by army worms, flooding—especially in areas ravaged by the war—and scarce agricultural resources such as tools and mules to work the land doomed the wage system almost from the start. Also, it was too easy for unscrupulous planters to hold back on wage payments or to simply not pay at all. Finally, short supplies of credit and cash made it difficult in any case for wages to be paid until the crops were harvested. In this context, the Black farmers preferred—even insisted in many cases—that they work the land on shares. Supply merchants and many southern landlords began to look upon the share system as a way of sharing the risks of production with labor. As a result, sharecropping had emerged as the preferred form of land tenure throughout the cotton South by the 1880s.

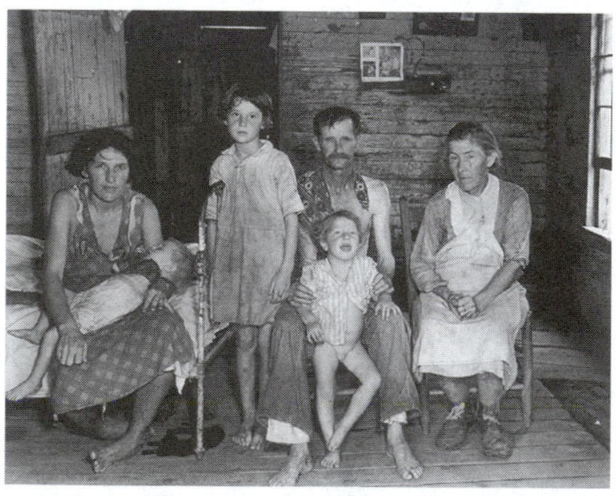

Alabama sharecropper Bud Fields and his family at home, 1935 (Library of Congress)

Tragically, sharecropping soon became an economic box from which there was no easy exit. And it entrapped within its walls white landowning farmers, who had lost their lands and independent farming status by the thousands by 1900. The mechanism of entrapment was simple enough. In order to cover their risks in advancing supplies to their sharecroppers and tenant farmers, landlords resorted to "furnishing merchants," many of whom were northern suppliers, who charged high interest rates for the supplies advanced in order to cover the risks involved. These furnishing merchants took liens on the crops of the farmers whom they supplied and required them in turn to grow only cotton on the land. This further reduced the croppers to the status of dependent farmers unable to even have garden crops on their places. Almost everything consumed by the helpless sharecroppers was purchased at inflated credit prices through the merchants' stores. Most southern states also passed crop-lien laws that gave the furnishing merchants first claim to the crops, before the claims of landlords for rent or workers for wages. As a result, landowners sometimes became merchants themselves, and many merchants became landowners, buying cheaply priced plantations from their profits as suppliers. And any sharecropper who might try to sneak his family away in order to avoid working another year, indebted to the store with no end in sight, could be arrested and forced to work, sometimes in chain gangs.

Scholars debate why the system became so firmly rooted in the South. Some emphasize the lack of a diversified economy in the postbellum South. With few jobs outside of plantation agriculture, sharecroppers had no alternatives. Others suggest that the ever-declining cotton prices made it nearly impossible for sharecroppers and tenants to work themselves out of their debts or to avoid the usurious credit prices they were charged. And most scholars point out that the Jim Crow racial context of the postbellum South, which pitted poor whites and Blacks against each other, offered no political means for challenging the system. If anything, southern white politicians used the "race issue" to perpetuate their power while poor southern whites lashed out at Blacks as scapegoats for their own miserable impoverishment. In this racially charged environment, any southern Blacks who protested the economic injustice of sharecropping risked beatings and horrible deaths by lynching.

Sharecropping as a system of southern agriculture began to break around the time of World War I. The prewar boll weevil infestation (which destroyed crops and resulted in record-breaking foreclosures of farmlands) and the overproduction of cotton (resulting in low cotton prices) in the 1920s created an economic crisis as landowners lost their farms to the banks. As a result, thousands of sharecroppers and tenants were displaced from the soil, causing a flood of southern Black refugees to northern cities. The fatal blow occurred, however, with the Great Depression of the 1930s. Ironically, a New Deal program aimed at paying farmers to cut back on crop production in order to increase crop prices finally killed sharecropping. Southern landowners refused to pass on the federal payments to the Black and white sharecroppers and tenants who worked their lands. Instead, they simply evicted them from their farms and plantations. In addition, many southern landowners used their federal crop payments to mechanize their plantations, especially in the rich delta lands of Mississippi, further reducing the need for sharecroppers after 1940. Thousands of Black sharecroppers joined the earlier stream of migrants to urban places in the North in a movement of people known as the Great Migration. By the mid-1950s, sharecropping as a system of labor had all but vanished from the scene.

Ronald L. F. Davis

See also: African American Migration; Freedmen's Aid; New Deal Farm Policy; *Report on Economic Conditions of the South*; Rural Poverty; Slavery

References and Further Reading

Jones, Jacqueline. 1992. *The Dispossessed: America's Underclasses from the Civil War to the Present*. New York: Basic Books.

Littwack, Leon. 1979. *Been in the Storm So Long: The Aftermath of Slavery*. New York: Knopf.

Woodman, Harold D. 1995. *New South, New Law: The Legal Foundation of Credit and Labor Relations in the Postbellum Agricultural South*. Baton Rouge: Louisiana State University Press.

Wright, Gavin. 1986. *Old South, New South: Revolutions in the Southern Economy since the Civil War*. New York: Basic Books.

Sheppard-Towner Infancy and Maternity Protection Act

See Health Policy; Maternalist Policy; Progressive Era and 1920s

Sinclair, Upton

See End Poverty in California (EPIC); *The Jungle*

Slavery

Slavery was both a contested symbol of dependency in pre–Civil War American political and social thought and an economic institution that directly or indirectly affected the lives of millions of Americans, Black and white. Ideologically, the relationship between poverty and slavery was prominently debated in three important periods: (1) the late seventeenth and early eighteenth centuries, when the racist ideology that accompanied slavery's first major expansion was culled from the matrix of contemporary attitudes toward the poor; (2) the era of the Revolution, when slavery functioned both as a symbol of tyranny and impoverishment and as an allegedly necessary means of containing threats from below; and (3) the antebellum era, when slavery was alternately attacked as a system of blighting poverty and defended as a form of poor relief that constituted a moral alternative to the "wage slavery" of free laborers in industrial capitalism. Although slavery was generally profitable in a narrow sense, it must be judged a broader economic failure in that its effects hindered industrialization and urbanization in the South until well into the twentieth century. Most important, slavery exacted an enormous human toll in lives that were subjected to the destructive effects of poor living standards and systematic violence. The persistence of poverty in the United States owes much to the slave South's deliberate maintenance of low educational and social welfare standards.

During the seventeenth century, North American slavery vied with indentured servitude and free wage work to satisfy the colonial demand for labor. Between the closing decades of the seventeenth century and the opening decades of the eighteenth century, a rise in the price of indentured servants and a decline in the price of slaves coincided with increasing European demand for Chesapeake-grown tobacco and the growth of an incipient rice industry in South Carolina. While in the northern colonies slavery never gained more than a marginal foothold, this confluence of developments encouraged the southern colonies to import more enslaved Blacks from Africa and the Caribbean.

The resulting increase in the slave population was accompanied by an expansion of the plantation system and a deterioration in the already-low living standards of Blacks. The plantation system, with its rigorous division of labor, disciplined organization of work gangs, overseer supervision, profit-driven work pace, and systematic use of violence, steadily replaced the seventeenth-century pattern of small-farm production, placed more control in planter hands, and kept the provision of welfare at a bare minimum, well below the living standard of typical white households. Revised slave codes, with provisions for branding, whipping, and mutilating recalcitrant slaves, reflected the new discipline. The new codes also put an end to the fluidity of seventeenth-century race relations by constructing a legal caste system that confined all Blacks to a status below that of the lowest whites.

Although the English were probably culturally predisposed to view dark-skinned Africans with contempt, the racial antipathy evident in the revised laws should be seen in the broader context of English attitudes toward poverty and

Enslaved people on the J. J. Smith plantation in Beaufort, South Carolina, in 1862 (Library of Congress)

labor. Economic thought during the expansion of English capitalism in the seventeenth century placed a new emphasis on increasing the productivity of the laboring classes in the race to augment national wealth and power vis-à-vis other competing nations. In such a climate of opinion grew proposals not only to incarcerate the poor in workhouses but also to enslave them as a method of combating their alleged tendency to prefer idleness and drunkenness to hard work, or "industry." Unwilling in practice to reduce the status of Anglo-European servants to perpetual, hereditary slavery, the planters who ruled the southern colonies proved less squeamish about enslaving a group of laborers whose skin color could readily mark them as inferior even to the white poor. Slavery thus became a palpable symbol of abject dependency, so much so that disgruntled colonial merchants in the mid-eighteenth century could portray English mercantile policy as an attempt at subjecting the colonies to a degrading slavery.

During the Revolutionary period, slavery faced both ideological and economic challenges to its continued existence. The egalitarian and antislavery implications of the natural rights doctrine in the Declaration of Independence posed a genuine threat to the legitimacy of slavery. Soon the northern states either abolished slavery outright or adopted some scheme of gradual emancipation, while in the upper South, manumissions increased and antislavery sentiment made genuine inroads. At the same time, the falling prices of tobacco and rice decreased the profitability of slave labor, while the indigo industry collapsed altogether from the impact of wartime disruptions.

In response to such challenges, most southerners defended the legitimacy of slavery. Although some, like Thomas Jefferson, agonized over the tyranny and injustice of slavery, most southern elites feared that emancipation would encourage lower-class disorder and result in a race war. Rather than extend "inalienable rights" to slaves, southerners at the Constitutional Convention ensured that the new Constitution sanctioned the right to own slave property and that such property served as a basis for southern political power in the new union of states.

Despite its fundamental violation of Revolutionary doctrine, slavery grew rapidly in the early nineteenth century. After Eli Whitney invented the cotton gin in 1793, cotton production rapidly spread into the rich soils of Alabama, Louisiana, Mississippi, and Texas as emigrants from the Southeast scrambled to settle land and supply the booming demand of the British textile industry for raw cotton. By 1860, the majority of the nation's slaves, now numbering 4 million, were laboring on cotton plantations located primarily in the lower South.

The natural growth of the mainland slave population—a feature unique in the New World—belied the harsh conditions of North American slavery. Because the slave system was above all a labor system predominantly geared toward staple-crop production, the majority of slaves were subjected to a grueling, nonstop seasonal work routine. The cotton season began with planting in the spring and continued through chopping and hoeing during the long, hot summer; picking, ginning, and shipping in the fall and winter; and in the late winter, clearing new ground and repairing buildings, tools, and cotton gins in preparation for the next planting season. At the same time, slaves planted corn, raised hogs, and cultivated vegetable gardens to supplement the monotonous diet supplied by the planters. Given this intense work regimen, the lazy, dozing slave of the popular plantation legend was certainly a myth.

Such an intense work regimen in a disease-ridden environment took an enormous toll on the health and welfare of slaves. Planters maintained their slaves in conditions little beyond the level of subsistence and bare material support. Although the average diet for adolescents and adults, consisting largely of corn and other grains, sweet potatoes, and pork, was generally "sufficient to maintain body weight and general health," slaves were widely susceptible to diseases of malnutrition such as beriberi, pellagra, tetany, rickets, and kwashiorkor (Fogel 1989, 137, 134). The limited diet exacted the highest cost from children. Low birth weights resulted from the undernourishment and overwork of pregnant women, and early weaning of infants significantly increased the risks to infant health and mortality. Height and weight data indicate that slaves suffered from severe protein-calorie malnutrition primarily in early childhood, increasing their susceptibility to diarrhea, dysentery, whooping cough, respiratory diseases, and worms. Such conditions made slave infants and children twice as likely to die as their white counterparts (Fogel 1989, 143). Nor did the danger of disease end if a slave managed to survive childhood. Intense work, the threat of injury from punishment, and poor sanitary conditions made slaves vulnerable to illnesses throughout their lives.

To survive the relentless work regimen and its effects on health, slaves engaged in a variety of acts of resistance to planters' efforts to exploit their labor. On a few significant occasions, resistance took the form of rebellious plots or uprisings—Nat Turner's 1831 revolt is the most notable example—though some recent scholarship has suggested that other famous slave rebellions were less actual plots than they were panics on the part of slave owners. In any case, such revolutionary challenges to planter hegemony were rare and faced overwhelming odds against success. Far more frequent and concerted was a day-to-day resistance—"shirking, destruction of tools, stealing, malingering, spoiling of crops, slowdowns, and other deliberate forms of sabotaging production"—that constituted an ongoing struggle between planters, who sought to control and exploit their workforce as completely as possible, and slaves, who refused, as far as they were able, to give the planters everything they demanded (Fogel 1989, 157).

Slaves' daily struggle to resist exploitation, to improve their conditions, to acquire whatever education and skills they could come by, and to supplement their diets was greatly abetted by a resilient family, community, and cultural life beyond the fields. Although slave marriages had no status in law in any southern state, slaves married, had children, raised families, and viewed family life as a basis for resistance to an otherwise dehumanizing system. Most masters encouraged marriage out of religious conviction and because they viewed such unions as a means of controlling overt rebelliousness, yet they did not recoil from dividing families through sale. Slaves' community life and culture offered an additional means of solace and resistance to the harsh conditions of plantation labor. Particularly on larger plantations, slaves fashioned a culture that melded elements of disparate ethnic ancestries into a sense of shared pan-African heritage and that emphasized kinship, created work songs and spirituals, told folktales of the weak outwitting the strong, and adapted a form of Christianity that held out the hope of spiritual deliverance from a bleak world of bondage.

National politics reflected the tensions created by the expansion of slavery and the ongoing struggle between masters and slaves on the plantations. Contention over the metaphor of impoverishment played no small role in the resulting conflict. In midcentury, the expansion of slavery into the western territories ultimately destroyed a political party system that was built on cross-sectional party alliances and contributed fundamentally to a divisive sectional politics that resulted in the devastating Civil War of 1861–1865.

In widening northern antislavery circles during the antebellum period, slavery came to symbolize the backwardness of the South in contrast to the dynamic economy of the industrializing North. In the 1850s, the newly formed northern Republican Party based its "free soil, free labor" appeal to voters on the necessity of protecting western territory from the blighting effects of slavery.

For their part, southerners claimed that taking their slave property into western territory was not only a right guaranteed by the Constitution but also a social necessity if the South was to avoid dangerous imbalances in Black-white population ratios. The natural expansion of the slave population also convinced southerners that the worst New World excesses—the cruelty of the intercontinental slave trade and the brutal conditions of West Indian sugar plantations—were not characteristic of southern slavery. Accordingly, southerners developed a vigorous body of racist propaganda that defended slavery as a "positive good" for Blacks themselves, for the South, and for the nation as a whole. At a time when the capacity of the northern economy to absorb and sustain impoverished immigrants seemed highly questionable to many, the southern pro-slavery argument opportunistically claimed that slavery could successfully compete with free labor both in agriculture and in some forms of manufacturing and could still provide a more generous alternative to the impoverishing "wage slavery" characteristic of England and the North. In 1857, a reactionary defender of slavery, George Fitzhugh, wrote that "our negroes are confessedly better off than any free laboring population in the world" (Fitzhugh [1857] 1960, 201).

Slaves themselves, less convinced of their welfare, put the lie to any notion that they were "confessedly better off" under slavery when they deserted their plantations by the thousands during the Civil War. From the vantage point of the present, there can be no doubt that slavery's mistreatment of African Americans hindered the long-term development of the South. As economic historian W. Elliot Brownlee has written, "The heritage of slavery is seen most clearly when we define our modern problem as one of absorbing the unskilled and undereducated into a society that places prime value on the attainment of skills and whose growth is tied to high levels of investment in people" (Brownlee 1988, 250). The slave South's systematic underinvestment in training and education for slaves beyond the most rudimentary skills—a situation that hurt the prospects of ordinary whites as well—has contributed fundamentally to the persistence of poverty in the United States.

Jay Carlander

See also: African Americans; Indentured Servitude; Malthusianism; Nineteenth Century; Racial Segregation; Racism; Sharecropping; Work Ethic

References and Further Reading

Berlin, Ira. 1998. *Many Thousands Gone: The First Two Centuries of Slavery in North America*. Cambridge, MA, and London: Belknap Press/Harvard University Press.

Blassingame, John. 1979. *The Slave Community: Plantation Life in the Antebellum South*. 2d ed. New York and Oxford: Oxford University Press.

Brownlee, W. Elliot. 1988. *Dynamics of Ascent: A History of the American Economy*. 2d ed. Belmont, CA: Wadsworth.

Engerman, Stanley L. 2000. "Slavery and Its Consequences for the South in the Nineteenth Century." In *The Cambridge Economic History of the United States*, vol. 2, *The Long Nineteenth Century*, ed. Stanley L. Engerman and Robert E. Gallman, 329–366. Cambridge: Cambridge University Press.

Fitzhugh, George. [1857] 1960. *Cannibals All! or, Slaves without Masters*. Ed C. Vann Woodward. Cambridge, MA, and London: Belknap Press/Harvard University Press.

Fogel, Robert William. 1989. *Without Consent or Contract: The Rise and Fall of American Slavery*. New York and London: Norton.

Genovese, Eugene D. 1976. *Roll, Jordan, Roll: The World the Slaves Made*. New York: Vintage Books.

Morgan, Edmund S. 1975. *American Slavery American Freedom: The Ordeal of Colonial Virginia*. New York and London: Norton.

Stampp, Kenneth M. 1956. *The Peculiar Institution: Slavery in the Ante-Bellum South*. New York: Vintage Books.

Slum Clearance

See Housing Policy; Urban Poverty; Urban Renewal

Social Contract

See Citizenship; Liberalism; Republicanism

Social Darwinism

In 1859, Charles Darwin published *The Origin of Species*, in which he presented his theory of biological evolution. Debunking creationism and other positions asserting the centrality of humanity in the universe, Darwin concluded from his research that the evolution of species was not the invention of intelligent design but was instead the result of natural selection—what became popularly known (although the terminology did not originate with Darwin) as "the survival of the fittest." Species fortunate enough to possess characteristics that enabled them to adapt to a hostile environment survived and then transmitted their traits to future generations; less fortunate or weaker species simply died off. As Darwin feared and predicted would occur, social thinkers began to (mis)apply his theory of evolution to human society. British sociologist Herbert Spencer was the leading and most renowned advocate of what would later be called "Social Darwinism." Spencer argued that the progress of humanity demanded that those people whose weaknesses showed them to be unfit to survive in the struggle for existence should be left to die off. His ideas were immensely influential, attracting a substantial following in the United States, and justified a cruel indifference to the plight of the poor and other less fortunate people in society. Social Darwinism also led to specious theories of racial supremacy, culminating in the 1930s with the rise of Nazism.

Spencer and his followers were proponents of classical liberalism, decrying government intervention in social and economic life. Even before the publication of Darwin's groundbreaking book, Spencer called for the abolition of poor laws, of national education, of a central church, and of all regulation of commerce and factories on the grounds that these interferences stymied social progress. For Spencer, progress depended on the movement from the homogeneous to the heterogeneous, from the simple to the complex. He and his followers believed that small, minimalist—or laissez-faire—government would promote progress because it maximized individual freedom and in turn stimulated social complexity. Similarly, Social Darwinists also advocated free-market capitalism, a system they believed sparked individual achievement and ingenuity and promised enhanced specialization and a complex division of labor. Laissez-faire government, they argued, would benefit society by letting the free market grow unfettered and by rewarding the most ingenious and deserving. Government regulation, on the other hand, would stand in the way of society's "natural" evolution and progress because its reforms and social protections would impede the competitive forces separating the weak from the strong.

The Social Darwinist understanding of progress was chillingly amoral, lacking any kind of sympathy for human suffering or recognition of the social origins of inequality. Social Darwinists grafted the fierce struggle for biological existence onto human society and came to accept the notion that "Might makes right." Accommodating the needs of the weak and pitiful merely served to enervate the human race. In the wake of Spencer's laissez-faire political philosophy, theories emerged about the superiority of certain races or ethnicities. A particularly egregious example is the rise of pseudosciences like eugenics, which, setting its sights on the genetic perfection of humankind, sought to prevent the supposedly weak and unfit from transmitting their traits to future generations.

Vestiges of Social Darwinism can be found in social and political thought to this day. Charles Murray, the author of *Losing Ground* and coauthor of *The Bell Curve,* is a conservative intellectual who asserts that social welfare programs perpetuate social pathologies not only by protecting people from the consequences of their own behavior but by ignoring the genetically based intellectual inferiority of the poor. These and other modern reformulations of Social Darwinist thought continue to influence those who reject systemic or structural explanations of poverty and social inequality.

Robert J. Lacey

See also: Malthusianism; Racism

References and Further Reading

Degler, Carl N. 1991. *In Search of Human Nature: The Decline and Revival of Darwinism in American Social Thought.* New York: Oxford University Press.

Hofstadter, Richard. 1955. *Social Darwinism in American Thought.* New York: Braziller.

Social Gospel

In the late nineteenth and early twentieth centuries, a group of American Protestants preaching what became known as the Social Gospel began to raise new concerns and to offer novel solutions for the nation's various social problems. Increasing economic inequality, abysmal health care, dangerous working conditions, exploitation of workers, and unrestrained, rapid urban growth brought clerics out of their churches and onto the streets. The Christian gospel, they believed, was not just about a person's relationship with God but was also about his or her social relationships: God sought to redeem society as well as individuals. Proponents of the Social Gospel, both clerics and laypeople, became key crusaders in Progressive-Era reform efforts for justice by integrating faith with the social, political, and economic issues of the era.

Christian faith and social reform have often gone hand in hand in American history. The temperance movement and the abolition of slavery were two of many early-nineteenth-century reform movements led by Protestants. After the Civil War, new issues arose that challenged preachers and theologians to reconceptualize their faith to make it relevant to a world in rapid transition. Friction defined the relationship between capital and labor, while the nation's population exploded. Millions of people abandoned the countryside for urban life, and immigrants flooded the nation's burgeoning cities, which proved incapable of meeting the increasing demands. Innovative technology and more efficient business practices combined with the maturing Industrial Revolution to reshape the American economy. Disillusioned by the human impact of such unprecedented industrial and urban growth, a group of Protestant preachers and laypeople carved out a place for themselves as reform leaders and social critics. Although resolutely middle-class, they tried to identify with and speak up for the poor, in the hope of curbing the injustices of the era.

A number of factors influenced Social Gospel leaders. Although the movement developed in specifically American ways, European Christians had been facing similar problems for decades. Christian social movements from all over the world produced a body of writings that suggested concrete solutions to modern problems and related religion to city life. As they had in so many other areas during the Progressive Era, Americans seeking solutions to the nation's problems frequently looked back to Europe for inspiration and for models. Christian social scientists raised new questions about their burgeoning disciplines, seeking to apply ethical and often explicitly religious ideas to their analyses of the world they inhabited.

Ideologically and theologically, Social Gospel leaders composed the "modernist" wing of American Protestantism. Modernists were broadly characterized by their efforts to keep their faith up-to-date with the latest scientific and philosophical movements, as opposed to fundamentalists, who more often isolated themselves from the culture around them. The modernists emphasized the possibility of redemption and the essential goodness of humanity, whereas the fundamentalists stressed sin and God's judgment. Social Gospel advocates were interested not in a traditional faith that might be irrelevant to modern conditions but in one that adapted to new, constantly evolving, social circumstances. They had an exalted view of society, believing that God was not only transcendent but also immanent through it. The person and actions of Jesus Christ were central to their ideology. In contrast to groups that placed more emphasis on the God of the Old Testament or on the writings of Paul, these Christians gave the character, words, and work of Christ preeminence. Finally, they were committed to a millennial ideal. They believed that by their efforts, God's kingdom could be restored on earth, a belief that gave the movement a utopian tinge. Such a presupposition led some Christians to defend and advocate American expansionism. If God chose America to usher in his kingdom, they believed, then America had an obligation to build its institutions around the globe. Although the movement was diverse, these themes tended to drive the optimism of the modernists, who sought to live like Christ while wrestling with the relationship between faith and culture. Other groups, like the Salvation Army, also looked to Christ as a model for social reform but rejected the liberal theological ideas of the modernists.

Post-Victorian changing gender roles influenced the Social Gospel movement. During the nineteenth century, liberal Protestant churches had become the province of women, who dominated the pews and often made up a significant majority of the nation's various reform groups. However, by the early-twentieth-century Progressive Era, male ministers were seeking to bring men back to church. They developed a concept of "muscular Christianity," which asserted that Jesus had been a socially active, rough-handed carpenter, a virile, strong, authoritative figure who served as a model for modern Christian man. "Muscular" Christians were not afraid to live the strenuous life, and they attacked society's problems with all their might. Although women continued to be the primary constituencies of Progressive-Era reform groups, muscular Christian preachers did succeed in attracting to church more men, who channeled their vigor into social reform on urban streets.

The Social Gospel influenced many of the classic Protestant denominations, but its most obvious expressions surfaced through interdenominational organizations. The Men and Religion Forward Movement of 1911–1912 (which linked muscular Christianity with the Social Gospel) and the Federal Council of the Churches of Christ were two leading organizations with strong Social Gospel components. At its organizing meeting in 1908, the Federal Council of Churches adopted a "social creed," which outlined many tenets of the Progressive-Era reforms, including a declaration for the rights of workers and a call for the abolition of child labor and for a living wage. Through such interdenominational agencies, the movement accomplished many things. The Social Gospel faithful revived Protestant liberalism and reshaped the role of church in society. Religiously inspired men and women established schools for all ages to educate the new urban public, while settlement houses were built for the poor. Northern churches also created schools in the South for African Americans, who otherwise received little help. Some leaders immersed their churches in such political issues as suffrage, prohibition, and expansionism, while others were subtler about their politics. Social action groups, missionary societies, and student organizations were established or expanded under the auspices of the Social Gospel. From church pulpits, in seminaries, on street corners, and in the academy, movement leaders attempted to convert all who would listen to a new way of life.

Although the Social Gospel developed as laypeople and church leaders struggled together, it was clerics who gave the movement its earliest and most definitive form. Three influential initial leaders of the movement were Washington Gladden, Josiah Strong, and Charles M. Sheldon. Gladden began his reformist career as a journalist and then accepted Congregational pastorates in Springfield, Massachusetts, and Columbus, Ohio. As a minister, he resolved to use faith as a weapon against corrupt business, a determination that surfaced in a series of lectures he delivered while in Massachusetts. The talks, collected and published as *Working People and Their Employers* (1876), suggested that business leaders had a responsibility to treat their employees more justly. At the same time, Gladden worked to modernize theology and plunged into explosive debates on such topics as biblical inerrancy.

Gladden next took a pulpit in Columbus, Ohio, where he became one of the most powerful preachers in the nation. His sympathies with labor intensified as he watched Ohio coal executives, some of whom were leading members of his church, ruthlessly fight their workers and attempt to undermine labor unions during major strikes. Committed to the Golden Rule (the admonition to treat others as you want to be treated) as a principle needed in American business, he sided with workers against the wealthier members of the church. He also adopted other causes, including the quest for public ownership of utilities and critiques of American capitalism. Gladden ultimately wrote over three dozen books and gained a tremendous following.

Josiah Strong was more controversial. Also ordained a Congregational minister, Strong organized numerous conferences that focused on Social Gospel themes. He sought to include as many Protestant groups as possible in his work and helped establish the Federal Council of Churches, yet some of his views were contentious. His most famous book, *Our Country: Its Possible Future and Its Present Crisis* (1885) defined seven issues that "threatened" the United

States, including increasing Roman Catholicism, immigration, and socialism. Ascribing to a Social Darwinist "scientific" racism, a patronizing ideology found among many but not all Progressive-Era reformers, he believed that Anglo-Saxon Protestant Americans should "civilize" the rest of the nation and then the world. Influenced by muscular Christianity, Strong also wrote a book on Christian manliness, as had Gladden.

Yet another Congregationalist minister, Charles M. Sheldon, had an enormous influence on American Christianity. From his pulpit in Topeka, Kansas, Sheldon worked to alleviate the problems of the common person. He lived at times with different social groups, seeking to understand the hardships they faced and to encourage reform in a variety of areas. In a novel entitled *In His Steps* (1897), which became one of the nation's best-selling books, he articulated a simple solution to the world's problems. The book traces the life of a small congregation that is energized by its pastor who asks his congregants to do one thing before they make any decision: to ask themselves "What would Jesus do?" and then to act accordingly, regardless of the consequences. Sheldon's fictional congregation transformed its city, reflecting his hope that just such an approach could transform America. Legions of Christians, liberal and conservative, have asked themselves "What would Jesus do?" ever since.

Building on the work of these Social Gospel architects, Walter Rauschenbusch became the most influential popularizer of the movement. As the pastor of a German Baptist Church in New York's Hell's Kitchen, Rauschenbusch encountered the worst characteristics of urbanization. Daily confrontations with starvation, unemployment, injustice, crime, and despicable health conditions left him dissatisfied with his traditional theological training. Like clerics before him, he sought to apply his faith to these overwhelming problems and began emphasizing the construction of the kingdom of God on earth. He eventually became a seminary professor, where he had the opportunity to develop and publish what he had learned from his experiences in Hell's Kitchen. His most famous book, *Christianity and the Social Crisis* (1907) catapulted him into the national spotlight and made him the nation's leading Social Gospel proponent. Over the rest of his life, he continued publishing influential books on social justice and developed a systematic theology that provided the foundation for Christian social action.

The work of laypeople was also essential for the Social Gospel's success. Jane Addams and Richard Ely were two of the movement's leading lay proponents. Addams was raised a Quaker and was educated at Rockford Female Seminary. While traveling in Europe, she witnessed both the negative effects of industrialization and the various methods that reformers were using to attack social problems, which inspired her to work for similar reform at home. In Chicago, she established Hull House, a settlement house, to help provide for the basic needs of the city's poor and to expose the middle class to the plight of the nation's workers. Although less explicit about her faith than were the clerics, Addams evidenced a strong commitment to many of the same themes and issues raised by liberal Protestants, viewing Jesus as a seminal figure.

Richard Ely was an Episcopalian, an economist, and one of America's best-known and distinguished university professors. He sought to integrate Christian faith with economics and worked to apply his training to building a more just society. He believed that the core of faith could be reduced to two things: loving God and loving one's neighbor. His early work sought to explain and defend America's struggling labor movement, and he went on to help found the American Economic Association with Gladden. Ely was popular at church conferences and became a sought-after speaker. His efforts to balance political economy with religion helped model the integration of faith with the burgeoning social sciences.

Despite Progressive-Era faith that the kingdom of God was at hand, World War I quenched the optimism of many Social Gospel reformers. Although the movement lasted well into the twentieth century and influenced later reformers, such as Martin Luther King Jr., the radical, uninhibited conviction that the kingdom of God could be achieved on earth slowly began to fade. Although the Social Gospel movement did not deal with issues of race or gender as thoroughly as it might have, what it did accomplish was remarkable. In an age of reform, Social Gospel leaders provided the moral and religious basis for the quest for justice.

Matthew A. Sutton

See also: Christian Fundamentalism; Hull House; Protestant Denominations; Settlement Houses; Social Darwinism

References and Further Reading

Handy, Robert, ed. 1966. *The Social Gospel in America, 1870–1920*. New York: Oxford University Press.

Marty, Martin. 1986. *Modern American Religion*. Vol. 1, *The Irony of It All, 1893–1919*. Chicago: University of Chicago Press.

Putney, Clifford. 2001. *Muscular Christianity: Manhood and Sports in Protestant America, 1880–1920*. Cambridge, MA: Harvard University Press.

White, Richard, and C. Howard Hopkins. 1976. *The Social Gospel: Religion and Reform in Changing America*. Philadelphia: Temple University Press.

Social Science

See Poverty, Statistical Measure of; Poverty Line; Poverty Research; Social Surveys

Social Security

The term "social security" was coined in the 1930s during the Great Depression and was quickly adopted by lawmakers as the title for the landmark Social Security Act of 1935 (originally labeled the Economic Security Act). Most often credited to the prominent social insurance advocate Abraham Epstein, the term was meant to convey the value and necessity of collective, *public* responsibility for providing people with a basic level of protection against the hazards of the market and against life-cycle risks. Although the Social Security Act of 1935 created other key safety net programs as well, the term "social security" has subsequently come to refer to the Old Age, Survivors', and Disability Insurance (OASDI) program and stands as a testament to that program's importance.

Social Security today is the largest and broadest safety net program, and it is also widely considered to be the nation's most successful one. Nearly all working Americans and their families are covered by the program, and more than 45 million Americans currently receive Social Security benefits. Retirees and their surviving spouses make up the largest category of beneficiaries, but Social Security is far more than a retirement income security program. It also insures families against catastrophic income loss due to the disability or premature death of a breadwinner. Social Security relieves the adult children of retired beneficiaries of much of the financial and emotional burden of providing income support for their aging parents.

Although Social Security benefits are hardly lavish, the program has succeeded admirably in its income support objectives. For the middle quintile of retired couple beneficiaries, whose yearly household incomes range from approximately $14,000 to about $22,000, Social Security benefits account for roughly two-thirds of total household income. Thus, for typical retired beneficiaries, Social Security benefits dwarf the proportion of household income derived from all other sources combined, including private pensions, personal savings, and earnings from work.

Among especially vulnerable retiree subgroups, including African Americans, Hispanics, women, and older retirees (who are disproportionately women), dependence on Social Security as a source of household income is even greater than for the remainder of the retiree population. More than half of all retired women age sixty-five and up are widowed, divorced, or never married. Among the Social Security beneficiaries in this group, Social Security provides seventy-two cents of every income dollar; 26 percent have no other source of income but Social Security (AFL-CIO n.d., 13). Social Security is also vital for the fast-growing contingent or nonstandard workforce, including part-time, temporary, and independent contract workers, because few nonstandard workers are covered by private pension plans (Jorgensen and McGarrah 2001). Although the United States lags far behind other industrialized nations in the provision of other social benefits, such as health care, the proportion of retiree household income derived from Social Security in the United States is typical of other industrialized nations. According to a recent study of public and private retirement income security systems in the United States, Japan, and five major European countries, the national public pension system provides a percentage of retiree household income that ranges from a low of 58 percent (Italy) to a high of 83 percent (Germany) (Weller 2001). The United States is right near the middle of this range. On the other hand, the wage replacement rate (the ratio of Social Security benefits to preretirement wages) tends to be lower in the United States than in other industrialized countries.

Nevertheless, Social Security plays a crucial role in reducing poverty among its beneficiaries. Were it not for their monthly benefit checks, nearly half of all elderly Social Security recipients would be in poverty. With Social Security, only 8 percent are in poverty. Prior to Social Security, most workers worked until they died. Those who were too ill or infirm to work often became wards of their adult children or of private charities or were forced to end their days in poorhouses maintained by county governments. The advent of Social Security changed that radically for the better, enabling millions of Americans to retire with dignity and at least a modest level of financial security.

Three features of the structure of Social Security benefits in the United States deserve special mention: Benefits are guaranteed for life, they are adjusted annually to compensate for the erosive effects of inflation, and they are calculated using a formula that replaces a larger share of the earnings of low-wage workers than of high-wage workers.

The lifetime guarantee means that it is impossible for retirees or their surviving spouses to outlive their Social Security benefits, no matter how long they live. Since workers cannot know how long they will live after they retire and since increasing life expectancies are allowing Americans to live longer in retirement, a guaranteed lifetime benefit is a vital feature of a program that seeks to ensure retirement income security. This feature sets Social Security apart from personal savings and many private pension plans, both of which can be and often are depleted by long-lived retirees or their surviving spouses. A large and growing proportion of private pension plans are of the defined-contribution variety, in which a retirement lump sum accumulates in a pension account during an employee's working career. Once the employee retires and his or her account has been depleted, the private pension is gone. It is possible to convert personal savings or private pension lump sums into lifetime benefits by purchasing an annuity from an insurance company, but it is very costly to do so. Moreover, unlike bank deposits, annuities are not federally guaranteed if the insurance company that sold them defaults; instead, there is a patchwork of often poorly funded state guarantee programs.

Of equal importance is the automatic annual adjustment of Social Security benefits to offset the corrosive effects of inflation. This provision was implemented in the 1972 amendments to the Social Security Act, which greatly enhanced the antipoverty effects of the program. Passed at a time when "runaway inflation" was beginning to erode the value of wages and social welfare benefits, cost-of-living adjustments proved crucial to reducing elderly poverty rates. Even the modest inflation rates of recent years would, over time, erode the value of Social Security benefits were it not for these annual adjustments. Without annual inflation adjustments, at 3 percent inflation, retirement benefits would lose a third of their value over fifteen years and nearly half their value over twenty years. Retirees whose benefits kept them out of poverty when they first retired would find themselves pushed far below the poverty line. Social Security's annual inflation adjustments are becoming even more important, as people live longer and spend more years in retirement. This feature of Social Security is unmatched by most other forms of retirement income; nor does it apply to most other public safety net programs. Very few private pension plans adjust benefits to offset the impact of inflation. Annuities that protect beneficiaries against the effects of inflation are simply unavailable on the private insurance market.

Social Security is especially important to low-wage workers. The formula for calculating a low-wage worker's Social Security benefits weights his or her earnings higher than the earnings of high-wage workers in the determination of benefits. As a result, although high-wage workers receive higher monthly benefits than low-wage workers with equivalent work histories, the benefits received by low-wage workers represent a higher percentage of their preretirement earnings. This feature of the program has played a major role in alleviating poverty among Social Security beneficiaries.

Social Security is much more than a retirement program; it also provides income support to workers in the event of disability and to the young children and spouses of a worker who dies. For a twenty-five-year-old average-earnings worker with a newborn, Social Security's disability protection is equivalent to a $220,000 disability insurance policy. For a twenty-five-year-old average-earnings worker with a spouse and two young children, Social Security's survivor's benefit equates to $374,000 in life insurance. Given Social Security's zero risk of default, guaranteed lifetime benefits, and protection against inflation, comparable protection simply is not available at any price in the private insurance market (Social Security Administration 2001).

These disability and survivors' insurance provisions of Social Security are especially important to African Americans and Hispanic Americans and are largely responsible for keeping nearly 1 million children under age eighteen above the poverty line. As a result of these family insurance features of Social Security, 26 percent of the program's African American and 20 percent of its Hispanic American beneficiaries are children, as are 10 percent of its white beneficiaries (Rawlson and Spriggs 2001).

Social Security delivers its important benefits with remarkable efficiency. More than ninety-nine cents of every revenue dollar available to finance the program is paid out to beneficiaries. The program's administrative overhead rate of less than 1 percent compares very favorably with the 12 to 14 percent overhead rates typical of private insurers. Several factors account for Social Security's low overhead. As a social insurance program, coverage under Social Security is nearly universal. Private insurers, by contrast, spend large sums on underwriting—essentially, the process of determining whether a prospective customer is or is not a good insurance risk. Private insurers incur costs of managing a diverse investment portfolio, including real estate, stocks, and bonds; Social Security, by contrast, invests its reserves in special government bonds virtually without cost. Private insurers pay their top executives the huge salaries typical of large corporations; the Social Security Administration compensates executives much more modestly.

The program is financed primarily by payroll taxes paid by covered workers and their employers and by self-employed persons. Taxes for 2001 were paid on the first $80,400 of wages and salaries, at the rate of 6.2 percent by employers and 6.2 percent by employees. During 2000, Social Security's receipts (taxes plus interest) exceeded the amount paid out in benefits by $153 billion; this excess of receipts over benefits represents a surplus that was credited to the Social Security Trust Fund, where it is invested in special interest-bearing government bonds. The program currently is expected to continue running surpluses every year until 2025, by which time the Trust Fund balance is projected to reach $6.5 trillion (Board of Trustees 2001, 159).

The law requires Social Security's trustees to make seventy-five-year forecasts of revenues and benefit outlays. These forecasts are published annually each spring. Such long-range forecasts inevitably require guesswork, and their results can vary greatly with small changes in underlying assumptions about such variables as life expectancy or economic growth twenty-five or fifty years in the future. Accordingly, the trustees publish three forecasts, based on optimistic, pessimistic, and middle scenarios, rather than a single forecast. Most media and policy attention, however, is focused on the forecast derived from the middle scenario.

Based on the latest middle-scenario forecast, the trustees project that revenues will be sufficient to pay full benefits promised under current law until 2038. From 2039 until the end of the seventy-five-year forecast period in 2075, revenues are projected to be sufficient to pay 70 percent of promised benefits. It should be noted, however, that the shortfall forecast to begin in 2039 is a pessimistic projection that may not materialize (Baker and Weisbrot 1999).

Critics of Social Security, from President George W. Bush to influential right-wing think tanks, such as the Heritage Foundation and the Cato Institute, have seized upon the conjectured post-2038 shortfall to undermine public confidence in the future of the program. Indeed, in 2001, President Bush appointed a commission that even seeks to undermine public confidence that benefits will be paid out of the enormous surpluses that Social Security will accumulate through 2025 (Baker 2001).

President Bush's commission and other critics allege that workers today who pay taxes throughout their working careers to finance Social Security will face a bankrupted program that will not be able to pay the benefits promised to them when they retire. The solution they offer is to replace Social Security in whole or in part with a privatized system of individual investment accounts. Since these accounts will be in the worker's own name and will be financed by the worker's own contributions, workers need never fear that their accounts will be taken away. Furthermore, the critics allege, by investing their account balances in the stock market, workers will earn high returns on their investments, thereby stretching their retirement funds much further than would be possible under today's Social Security.

Leading financial services firms, such as State Street Bank, Mellon Bank, and Merrill Lynch, have quietly funded the assault on Social Security. It is estimated that these and other firms stand to reap $12 billion over the next ten years from management fees derived from administering individual accounts if partial privatization becomes a reality.

The defenders of Social Security have put forth powerful counterarguments against privatization, but they are not as well financed as their adversaries, and it is unclear at this writing whether they will prevail. First, the diversion of even a modest portion of current Social Security payroll taxes into private individual accounts will trigger a huge financing crisis requiring deep benefit cuts, tax increases, or government borrowing—the very things privatization advocates claim they want to avoid. Whether benefit cuts come in the form of an increase in the retirement age or a reduction in annual cost-of-living adjustments, or are across-the-board, American workers, retirees, and their families would lose heavily. An increase in the retirement age would penalize workers in such physically demanding industries as construction and health care and would be especially harsh for African American males due to their low life expectancy. Any reduction in cost-of-living adjustments would be especially harsh for older women, pushing many of them below the poverty line.

Second, individual accounts invested in the stock market are completely unsuitable as a replacement for Social Security. Social Security, as noted earlier, provides a lifetime benefit guarantee, annual cost-of-living adjustments, and a benefit calculation formula advantageous to low-wage workers. Furthermore, Social Security's disability and survivors' insurance features help insulate family incomes against the loss of a breadwinner. Private individual accounts possess none of these crucial features. To make matters worse, account balances would fluctuate with the stock market and even with the prices of individual stocks. Workers with identical work histories and earnings would face radically different retirement prospects depending on whether the stock market was up or down when they retired and on their luck or skill as investors. Privatization, in short, would replace Social Security's vital social insurance features with a lottery (Harrington 2001).

Of course, Social Security as it currently exists is not perfect, and improvements in it are needed. Some feminists, for example, have criticized the program for its patriarchal structure and advocate increased benefits for older women who face high poverty rates despite Social Security (Ghilarducci 2001). The payroll tax that finances the program weighs heavily on lower-income workers. Furthermore, the eligibility rules for disability benefits have been made too restrictive and should be revised. Concerns about post-2038 solvency could be addressed, in large part, by raising or eliminating the cap that currently exempts earnings in excess of $80,400 from payroll taxes. Privatization, however, would move Social Security further away from these and other needed improvements.

Sheldon Friedman

See also: Old Age; Social Security Act of 1935

References and Further Reading

Aaron, Henry J., and Robert D. Reischauer. 2001. *Countdown to Reform: The Great Social Security Debate*. Rev. and updated ed. New York: Century Foundation Press.

AFL-CIO. N.d. "Strengthening Social Security: A Guide for Working Families." Publication No. O-SSS01.0998-25.

Baker, Dean. 2001. "Defaulting on the Social Security Trust Fund Bonds: Winners and Losers." Briefing paper, Center for Economic and Policy Research. July 23. Washington, DC.

Baker, Dean, and Mark Weisbrot. 1999. *Social Security: The Phony Crisis*. Chicago: University of Chicago Press.

Board of Trustees, Federal Old-Age and Survivors' Insurance and Disability Insurance Trust Fund. 2001. *The 2001 Annual Report*. March 19. Washington, DC: GPO.

Ghilarducci, Teresa. 2001. "Rising Expectations: Women, Retirement Security, and Private Pensions." In *The Future of the Safety Net: Social Insurance and Employee Benefits*, ed. Sheldon Friedman and David Jacobs, 165–186. Champaign, IL: Industrial Relations Research Association.

Harrington, Brooke. 2001. "Investor Beware: Can the Small Investor Survive Social Security Privatization?" *The American Prospect*, September 10, 20–22.

Jorgensen, Helene, and Robert McGarrah. 2001. "Contingent Workers: Health and Pension Security." In *The Future of the Safety Net: Social Insurance and Employee Benefits*, ed. Sheldon Friedman and David Jacobs, 225–238. Champaign, IL: Industrial Relations Research Association.

The Nation. Social Security-related articles. http://www.thenation.com/directory/view.mhtml?t=00040403.

Rawlson, Valerie, and William Spriggs. 2001. "Social Security: A True Family Value." In *The Future of the Safety Net: Social Insurance and Employee Benefits*, ed. Sheldon Friedman and David Jacobs, 101–118. Champaign, IL: Industrial Relations Research Association.

Social Security Administration. 2001. "Basic Facts." January. http://www.pueblo.gsa.gov/cic_text/fed_prog/socsecbf/socsecbf.html.

Weller, Christian E. 2001. "Programs without Alternative: Public Pensions in the OECD." In *The Future of the Safety Net: Social Insurance and Employee Benefits*, ed. Sheldon Friedman and

David Jacobs, 15–71. Champaign, IL: Industrial Relations Research Association.

Social Security Act of 1935

The Social Security Act of 1935, signed into law by President Franklin D. Roosevelt, remains the most comprehensive social policy creation in American political history. By combining several programs into one law, the act effectively established an entire social welfare apparatus, intended to protect, eventually, the majority of American citizens from economic insecurity. Of the major components of the statute, two were contributory programs geared toward full-time employed individuals: Old Age Insurance (OAI, which has come to be called "Social Security") for retired workers, and Unemployment Insurance (UI), for those who lost their jobs. Eligibility for either depended on a worker's previous employment status, length and constancy of presence in the workforce, and level of earnings. Two others, Old Age Assistance (OAA) and Aid to Dependent Children (ADC), were public assistance programs aimed at nonemployed individuals considered deserving. The potential of the Social Security Act to alleviate poverty was curtailed, at the outset, by features of policy design that effectively excluded most men of color and the majority of women from the contributory programs. Policymakers amended the law in 1935, transforming OAI into Old Age and Survivors' Insurance (OASI), thus including the wives or widows and dependent children of primary beneficiaries. Over time, additional amendments and demographic changes have made the contributory programs more inclusive and redistributive, though stratifying features remain.

Unlike programs and rules established in earlier eras that clearly distinguished between citizens on the basis of sex or race, such as protective labor laws for women or Jim Crow segregation laws, the Social Security Act was free of discriminatory language. The fact that eligibility for some programs depended on work status while others did not guaranteed a gendered division in program coverage. Public officials in the Roosevelt administration did not intend, however, to establish a higher and lower tier of social provision. In the context of the 1930s, the programs geared to white men appeared least likely to succeed: Both OAI and UI lacked precedents in the United States and relied on unconventional financing arrangements, but OAA and ADC built on preexisting programs and adhered to the established grant-in-aid model.

In the course of implementation, however, the program coverage became stratified in a manner that was gendered and racialized, functioning as income-maintenance programs especially for white males and their families while doing little to keep people of color or single or divorced white women out of poverty. These outcomes were attributable in part to financing distinctions between the programs: OAI and UI were "contributory" programs, funded through automatic payroll taxes, while OAA and ADC depended on repeated appropriations of funds from general government revenues, controversial processes in which the question of whether recipients were "deserving" was constantly revisited. The different administrative arrangements for the programs, national versus primarily state-level authority, also proved deeply divisive.

Reformers in the United States had long desired to create social programs resembling those established in most European nations by the late nineteenth century. They finally found their political opportunity in the midst of the Great Depression as unemployment skyrocketed and state and local forms of social provision were strained to the breaking point. Numerous social movements rallied for government to establish more comprehensive and more enduring programs than relief. A widespread grassroots populist movement known as the Townsendites championed monthly payments of $200, drawn from taxes, to every individual sixty and over on the condition that the money be spent within the month as a means to spur the economy. Left-wing supporters of the Lundeen Bill, or "Workers' Bill," believed that a universal unemployment compensation plan should be financed by general taxation instead of by employee contributions, which they feared would raise prices, lower wages, and hurt consumers. Despite the diversity of their proposals, the activists were united in their desire for programs featuring fairly universal coverage, administration by national government, and financing through general revenues. In all of these regards, their proposals differed vastly from the Roosevelt administration's initial plans for lasting measures of social provision.

President Roosevelt disliked the prospect of long-term general relief; he believed it would have ill effects on recipients, place too heavy a toll on government revenues, and be subject to the vacillation of politics. He envisioned instead that work-related social insurance would serve as the cornerstone of his program. He also acknowledged the necessity of some forms of public assistance, so long as they were crafted narrowly to apply to particular groups of "deserving" recipients. He called for a plan that involved coordinated efforts by national and state governments.

In June 1934, Roosevelt appointed a cabinet committee, the Committee on Economic Security (CES), to study economic security issues, develop recommendations, and draft legislative proposals to be sent to Congress. CES chair and secretary of labor Frances Perkins, her assistant Arthur J. Altmeyer, and CES director Edwin Witte all shared Roosevelt's guiding assumptions about the appropriate design for programs. All three had worked at the state level for social reform—Perkins in New York and the others in Wisconsin—and they retained a belief in considerable state-level authority for social programs. They wanted to build on the foundations of programs already established in many states during the early twentieth century: About half the states had enacted old-age pensions, forty-five had mothers' pensions laws, and only one state—Wisconsin—had unemployment compensation. The three leaders also shared considerable intellectual ties with both the social insurance approach and the social work tradition as epitomized by public assistance.

Of the four major programs in the Social Security Act, Old Age Insurance—later known simply as "Social Security"—was the only one endowed with a strictly national, unified administrative authority. The program was spearheaded by a law professor from the University of California, Barbara Nachtrieb Armstrong, whom Witte had hired to be director of planning for the old-age security staff. Armstrong had recently published a book entitled *Insuring the Essentials: Minimum Wage Plus Social Insurance, a Living Wage Program*, in which she firmly endorsed social insurance as a critical tool for preventing poverty and argued that public assistance programs for the elderly robbed them of their dignity. Armstrong parted ways with the CES leaders, however, on the issue of state-level authority. She and her subcommittee, including Princeton University economist J. Douglas Brown, were convinced that only a fully national system of social insurance could make benefits in old age a meaningful right. The members argued that given the mobility of the population, a federal-state program would present administrative difficulties while a national system would ensure quicker and fuller coverage of the population and superior compliance. Controversy ensued, as Perkins expressed discomfort with the proposal and the counsel to the CES claimed it would be unconstitutional. Armstrong's approach prevailed after she consulted several esteemed scholars of constitutional law, each of whom approved it.

In contrast to popular movements that promoted flat benefits financed by government revenues, the financing scheme and mildly progressive benefits arrangement that the CES officials designed for OAI were fairly conservative. Roosevelt and Secretary of the Treasury Henry A. Morgenthau insisted on the use of insurance-style financing principles. Armstrong and her colleagues planned for employers and employees to contribute to retirement funds according to a regressive combination of a flat payroll tax rate and a ceiling on taxable wages. Benefits would be figured according to a graduated scheme that corresponded to prior earnings, but those who had the lowest incomes would receive higher benefits in proportion to their earnings than would those who had earned more. Because only 25.4 percent of women in the late 1930s participated in the paid labor force at any given time, compared to 79 percent of men, and because women workers tended to have intermittent employment histories or to work part-time due to their domestic roles, they were much less likely than were men to qualify for the work-related programs (Mettler 1998, 26).

Given widespread support for expansion of old-age pensions and because OAI would take some years to establish, the CES bestowed on Old Age Assistance the prominent position of Title I in the legislative proposal. Planned as a federal grant-in-aid to the states, the program was designed to spur states that had not done so already to create programs for the elderly, while prompting states that had already acted to boost their benefit levels. National government would be required to provide funds for one-half of the benefits, up to fifteen dollars per month. In order to receive federal monies, states would be required to implement programs statewide rather than only in certain localities.

The design of unemployment insurance triggered more controversy than did all the other components of the Social Security Act combined. Policy leaders battled over the degree of national authority and uniformity that such a program should feature. Perkins and top CES officials espoused a tax-offset scheme in which employers would be subject to a uniform national payroll tax but individual states themselves would have administrative authority. States could opt for a plan that featured specific accounts for each business (a plant-reserves approach) or a pooled-funds approach. CES staff, the Advisory Counsel, and, once again, Barbara Armstrong all favored a more fully national system. As a compromise, they offered support for a "subsidy plan" in which states would have to comply with administrative standards established by the federal government. In the end, Perkins pushed CES members to decide the issue, and they opted for the tax-offset arrangements, requiring all employers to pay an unemployment tax on covered employees but leaving all matters regarding benefit levels and eligibility criteria to the individual states.

Policy officials also aimed to build upon mothers' pensions, state-level programs aimed at assisting mothers and children who had lost their male breadwinner. Such programs enjoyed a positive reputation, and officials believed that their inclusion within the Social Security Act would help gain political support for the more unfamiliar features of the package. Aid to Dependent Children (ADC) was planned in the Children's Bureau of the Department of Labor, whose leaders had long argued that national government could play an important role in modernizing social programs by offering funds to states and elevating standards. Katharine Lenroot, acting chief of the bureau and the daughter of a Wisconsin state legislator, drafted the program in collaboration with Martha Eliot, chief medical officer. They designed a federal grant-in-aid program that would enhance and extend mothers' pensions by offering federal funds to assist those states that planned statewide programs in keeping with federal rules. At the same time, states would retain considerable authority for administering their programs. Lenroot and Eliot hoped that such arrangements would promote the development and professionalization of state-level welfare departments generally. They also believed that

Message to Congress on Social Security, President Franklin Roosevelt, January 17, 1935

Three principles should be observed in legislation on [social security]. First, the system adopted . . . should be self-sustaining in the sense that funds for the payment of insurance benefits should not come from the proceeds of general taxation. Second, excepting in old-age insurance, actual management should be left to the States subject to standards established by the Federal Government. Third, sound financial management of the funds . . . should be assured by retaining Federal control over all funds. . . .

I recommend the following types of legislation looking to economic security:

1. Unemployment compensation.
2. Old-age benefits, including compulsory and voluntary annuities.
3. Federal aid to dependent children through grants to States for the support of existing mothers' pension systems and for services for the protection and care of homeless, neglected, dependent, and crippled children.
4. Additional Federal aid to State and local public health agencies and the strengthening of the Federal Public Health Service.

. . . An unemployment compensation system should be constructed in such a way as to afford every practicable aid and incentive toward the larger purpose of employment stabilization.

This can be helped by the intelligent planning of both public and private employment [and] by correlating the system with public employment so that a person who has exhausted his benefits may be eligible for some form of public work. . . .

In the important field of security for our old people, it seems necessary to adopt three principles: First, non-contributory old-age pensions for those who are now too old to build up their own insurance. . . . Second, compulsory contributory annuities which in time will establish a self-supporting system. . . . Third, voluntary contributory annuities by which individual initiative can increase the annual amounts received in old age. . . .

We cannot afford to neglect the plain duty before us. I strongly recommend action to attain the objectives sought in this report.

the educational component of the program, through which social workers would instruct poor women in child rearing and in domestic skills, was essential and would be handled best by local officials.

In Congress, the administration's bill was considered by the House Ways and Means Committee and the Senate Finance Committee, both dominated by southern Democrats. Throughout the New Deal years, southern congressmembers offered strong support for federal spending but opposed measures that might threaten the prevailing racial hierarchy. Arguing for states' rights, they consistently sought to limit the extent of national programs within the Social Security Act and to undermine CES efforts to impose national standards on the states. Following warnings from Secretary Morgenthau about the potential administrative difficulties involved in providing social insurance to agricultural, domestic, and temporary workers, the House committee dropped such workers from coverage in OAI. Given patterns of occupational segregation, these exclusions disproportionately withheld old-age insurance from African Americans, Latinos, and Asian Americans. Women of all races similarly were deprived of coverage when religious and nonprofit organizations successfully argued that they could not survive if they had to cover their employees,

President Roosevelt signs Social Security Bill, 1935. (Library of Congress)

who were predominantly women who worked as teachers, nurses, and social workers. All such exclusions under OAI were applied to UI as well, and in addition, workers employed twenty weeks or fewer per year were dropped from coverage.

The House Ways and Means Committee proceeded to make the public assistance measures even more reliant on state-level authority than administration officials had planned by weakening some of the few federal standards the CES had included in the bill. Members voted to strike language that would have mandated that states provide minimum benefits, for "assistance at least great enough to provide . . . a reasonable subsistence compatible with decency and health." Instead, states were left with considerable discretion, required only to provide assistance "as far as practicable under the conditions in each State" (S. 1130, sec. 42, Seventy-fourth Cong., 1st sess., quoted in Abbott 1966, 279). ADC benefits were set at an especially low level and did not include benefits for mothers, and the matching principle only required the federal government to pay one-third of what states offered, compared to the one-half the federal government paid under OAA. In addition, representatives abolished requirements that civil servants charged with administering Social Security Act programs be hired according to merit system principles. Finally, Congress insisted that a quasi-independent board be established to administer the national components of programs, quashing CES plans for the Department of Labor to be in charge. Overwhelming majorities of each house voted in favor of the bill, and President Roosevelt signed it into law on August 14, 1935.

The Social Security Board (SSB) was established as the agency charged with overseeing the

Presidential Statement Signing the Social Security Act, Franklin D. Roosevelt, August 14, 1935

Today a hope of many years' standing is in large part fulfilled. The civilization of the past hundred years, with its startling industrial changes, has tended more and more to make life insecure. Young people have come to wonder what would be their lot when they came to old age. The man with a job has wondered how long the job would last.

This social security measure gives at least some protection to thirty millions of our citizens who will reap direct benefits through unemployment compensation, through old-age pensions and through increased services for the protection of children and the prevention of ill health.

We can never insure one hundred percent of the population against one hundred percent of the hazards and vicissitudes of life, but we have tried to frame a law which will give some measure of protection to the average citizen and to his family against the loss of a job and against poverty-ridden old age.

This law, too, represents a cornerstone in a structure which is being built but is by no means complete. It is a structure intended to lessen the force of possible future depressions. It will act as a protection to future Administrations against the necessity of going deeply into debt to furnish relief to the needy. The law will flatten out the peaks and valleys of deflation and of inflation. It is, in short, a law that will take care of human needs and at the same time provide the United States an economic structure of vastly greater soundness.

I congratulate all of you ladies and gentlemen, all of you in the Congress, in the executive departments and all of you who come from private life, and I thank you for your splendid efforts in behalf of this sound, needed and patriotic legislation.

If the Senate and the House of Representatives in this long and arduous session had done nothing more than pass this Bill, the session would be regarded as historic for all time.

administration of Social Security Act programs at the national level. Arthur Altmeyer was appointed chair of the SSB. Under his leadership, the agency quickly became a major player in steering the subsequent development of the law.

Over the next few years, the future of Old Age Insurance appeared in doubt. The distribution of benefits was not scheduled to begin until 1942, though collection of payroll taxes would commence in 1937. Leaders of the Republican Party and the business community assailed the financing arrangement that permitted the federal treasury to hold the high levels of government reserves that accumulated from contributions to the program. Meanwhile, the public assistance program for the elderly began to flourish, as more than 7,000 Townsend clubs created a fervor in many states for generous benefits and for broader coverage than the law required. SSB officials became concerned that OAA would thwart the development of the more fiscally conservative contributory program.

The Senate Finance Committee recommended the formation of an Advisory Council to study the possibility of alterations to the existing law. The council was chaired by J. Douglas Brown, who had assisted Armstrong in formulating OAI for the CES. Altmeyer offered the committee recommendations that would liberalize OAI in some regards, making it more generous and expansive than the 1935 law had permitted.

The Advisory Council of 1937–1938 planned several measures to transform the national, contributory program into the primary source of social benefits for the elderly. The council suggested that the full government reserve plan, under attack from all sides, be abandoned in favor of a pay-as-you-go financing system assisted by government revenues. It advised that benefits should commence earlier than planned, in 1940 instead of 1942. As a means of increasing average benefits, the council proposed changing the benefit formula to relate to average monthly wages before retirement rather than to average cumulative wages.

Most fundamentally, the Advisory Council proposed an immense expansion of OAI program coverage that would include benefits for the wives of retired beneficiaries and for the widows and children of deceased beneficiaries. Council members understood such benefits not as a social right for women but, rather, as a means of strengthening men's capacity to perform their assigned gender role of providing for their families, even after their deaths. The Advisory Council proposed that familial benefits be correlated directly to the benefit levels of primary beneficiaries. The wage-oriented structure of taxes and benefits would remain intact, with payments for wives and widows scheduled to be less than husbands' benefits but also graduated on the basis of husbands' former earnings. Retired workers whose wives were sixty-five or older were to receive "supplementary allowances" amounting to an extra percentage of the benefits for their wives. Widows were to receive benefits equal to three-quarters of the benefits their husbands would have received.

Although including married women in the contributory program on a noncontributory basis, the council also proposed to disqualify those same women from receiving benefits based on their own participation in the paid workforce. The system would be organized so that a married woman would be eligible for either a wife's allowance or a benefit based on her own previous earnings, whichever would be larger. Given the differential in average wages between men and women, women's earned benefits would typically be smaller than 50 percent of their husbands'. In opting for the wives' allowance, however, they would gain nothing from the payroll taxes they themselves had paid into the system. No provisions were made for spousal or survivors' benefits for husbands, denying working women the opportunity to provide for their husbands in retirement or death.

Congress readily enacted the recommendations as law, so women married to men covered by OAI became beneficiaries of OASI. The rules for coverage of wives and widows did not require evidence of reproductive labor but, rather, were based entirely on marital status in relation to covered men. Divorced women were excluded from coverage, and states were given flexibility regarding recognition of common-law marriages and waiting periods after divorce before a new marriage would be recognized. Also, new stipulations about minimum participation in the contributory program meant that workers who earned especially low wages or worked on a part-time basis—disproportionately men of color and women—became more likely to be excluded from direct coverage in the contributory program.

The amendments of 1939 did not change the national government's authority in the contributory program for the elderly. In the course of implementation, OAI became striking for its national uniformity, distinct from the other programs. Although occupational and earning criteria and marital status were the only distinctions formally inscribed in law, they had lasting implications in terms of race and gender. The mostly white, male primary beneficiaries enjoyed the advantages of clear, impartial, and routinized procedures administered by a single tier of government. In addition, those women who were married to covered men became endowed with measures of security—albeit at lower levels than their partners—in a realm where standardized procedures were the norm and where benefits were considered a right.

Although Old Age Assistance had originally

been understood as an honorable program aimed to reward elderly people for their earlier service to society, over time, coverage became increasingly stigmatizing. Owing to its grassroots support, OAA benefits remained higher on average than benefits under the contributory old-age program until 1950, by which time national administrative officials had pushed successfully to enhance the latter program. The 1939 amendments made the OAA's procedural rules more demanding by giving states authority to use means testing to determine program benefit levels. Eligibility standards and benefits varied substantially from one state to another, and decisions about coverage were made by social workers who exercised a high degree of discretion. Over time, the differences in coverage and delivery between old-age and survivors' insurance, on the one hand, and old-age assistance, on the other, stratified the fates of women, depending largely on their race and marital status, and of men, depending on their race and occupational status.

The politics of implementation transformed Unemployment Insurance into a program that was experienced very differently depending upon one's employment status, and consequently, upon one's sex and race. Administrators worked successfully to improve the level and duration of benefits for those at the upper end of the wage scale, mostly white men. States balked, however, when the SSB urged them to raise benefits for low-paid workers, meaning most women as well as most men of color. In addition, while the eligibility status of white males was generally determined on the basis of the national rules alone, states developed an extra set of eligibility hurdles that applied to low-wage workers and women, in particular, when they sought to qualify for benefits. One variant of the state-level rules measured "attachment to the labor force" on the basis of recent work history and earnings levels and thus discriminated in a subtle manner. Another set of rules denied benefits to individuals whose unemployment was related to "domestic reasons," such as pregnancy, childbirth, or marital obligations; these directly disqualified women on the basis of their gender roles. As a result, for well-paid, mostly white male beneficiaries, UI benefits were effectively nationalized and standardized, but for low-wage workers, especially women, the benefits were administered entirely at the state level, where applicants encountered a labyrinth of eligibility rules that made access to benefits difficult.

ADC became, in the course of implementation, the program least able to extend rights of social citizenship to its beneficiaries. It was the most decentralized of all of the major programs in the Social Security Act, providing states with the least incentive and assistance to develop programs and to raise standards. Though the policy design of OAA was not very different from that of ADC, OAA benefited at least initially from strong grassroots support on the part of the Townsend organization and other groups struggling to improve conditions for the elderly. Lacking such support, ADC benefits grew little, and the administration of the program came to take on the worst features of the mothers' pensions program. In determining client eligibility, for example, "suitable home" rules were used to scrutinize the lives of potential beneficiaries, evaluating their child-rearing and housekeeping abilities and the school and church attendance of their children. In addition, some states and localities used "man in the house" rules to withdraw aid from women suspected of or found to have "male callers." Such investigations were often conducted through "midnight raids" by local officials (Bell 1965).

Over time, the Social Security Act was altered again, as Congress included more of the workforce in the contributory programs and later the courts disallowed some forms of discretion in the public assistance programs. Throughout the mid-twentieth century, coverage within the state-run public assistance programs became increasingly inferior to coverage under OASI and to higher wage earners' experience of UI. As a result, the women and minority men still disproportionately relegated to such programs were governed differently as social citizens than were those who had gained access to nationalized social benefits. Even today, African American women are less likely than white women to qualify for spouse and widow benefits, and when they do qualify, the racial wage gap means that their benefits are significantly lower than those of white women. In addition, middle- and upper-class women are far more likely than lower-class women to receive spousal or widows' benefits; in effect, the benefits heighten class inequality (Meyer 1996). The framework of the American welfare state, as established by the Social Security Act, has perpetuated poverty among some social groups even as it has lifted or kept others out of poverty.

Suzanne Mettler

See also: Aid to Families with Dependent Children (ADC/AFDC); Dependency; Deserving/Undeserving Poor; Federalism; Gender Discrimination in the Labor Market; Great Depression and New Deal; Means Testing and Universalism; Old Age; Racism; Social Security; Townsend Movement; Unemployment Insurance; Welfare Administration; Welfare Policy/Welfare Reform

References and Further Reading

Abbott, Grace. 1966. *From Relief to Social Security*. New York: Russell and Russell.

Altmeyer, Arthur J. 1968. *Formative Years of Social Security*. Madison: University of Wisconsin Press.

Bell, Winifred. 1965. *Aid to Dependent Children*. New York: Cambridge University Press.

Cates, Jerry. 1983. *Insuring Inequality: Administrative Leadership in Social Security, 1935–54*. Ann Arbor: University of Michigan Press.

Derthick, Martha. 1979. *Policymaking for Social Security*. Washington, DC: Brookings Institution.

Gordon, Linda. 1994. *Pitied but Not Entitled: Single Mothers and the History of Welfare, 1890–1935*. New York: Free Press.

Lieberman, Robert. 1998. *Shifting the Color Line: Race and the American Welfare State*. Cambridge, MA: Harvard University Press.

Mettler, Suzanne. 1998. *Dividing Citizens: Gender and Federalism in New Deal Public Policy*. Ithaca, NY: Cornell University Press.

Meyer, Madonna Harrington. 1996. "Making Claims as Workers or Wives: The Distribution of Social Security Benefits." *American Sociological Review* 61, no. 3: 449–465.

Perkins, Frances. 1946. *The Roosevelt I Knew*. New York: Harper and Row.

Skocpol, Theda, and Edwin Amenta. 1985. "Did Capitalists Shape Social Security?" *American Sociological Review* 50 (August): 572–578.

Witte, Edwin. 1963. *Development of the Social Security Act*. Madison: University of Wisconsin Press.

Social Service Review

First published in March 1927, the *Social Service Review* continues to be the leading journal in the field of social work. Sophonisba Breckinridge and Edith Abbott, professors at the School of Social Service Administration of the University of Chicago, founded the journal as a venue for research about social work and social problems. Reflecting the interests of Breckinridge and Abbott, who had both earned Ph.D.s at the University of Chicago and had spent time at the Hull House settlement, the journal emphasized research on social problems and advocacy for specific welfare policies. It published work in sociology, economics, political science, and history as well as contributions from social workers active in the field.

During the Depression, the journal, then edited by Edith Abbott's sister Grace Abbott, advocated an expansion of public welfare, federal rather than local administration of New Deal programs, and the hiring of social workers to run relief agencies. In the wartime and postwar periods, the journal continued to call for a larger role for the federal government in welfare, including international relief. With the push for greater professionalization of social work in the 1950s, the journal redefined itself as a publication by and for social workers, including more articles on the casework process and on social work education. At the same time, it remained the most scholarly of social work journals, and in the following decades it returned to its earlier multidisciplinary emphasis.

Breckinridge's article from the first issue, excerpted below, shows the journal's support for federal welfare policy and institutions.

Sarah Case

See also: Hull House; National Association of Social Workers (NASW); Philanthropy; Settlement Houses; Social Work; Welfare Administration

In substantially every state there is some provision for meeting [public welfare] needs, but in no two states are the agencies alike; and the great variety and lack of uniformity of treatment . . . causes every suggestion of possible federal intervention to have a very great interest for the student of welfare problems. . . .

In a situation involving such a burden for the taxpayer, fraught with such danger for the helpless and inarticulate groups under care, and involving the right of every citizen to be assured that the standard of care and of expenditures for which as a taxpayer he is responsible is not below the standard set by modern humane and civilized communities, the possibility suggests itself of developing on a national scale the services which have proven reasonably effective on a state-wide scale and which could be enormously stimulated and assisted by the service of a national authority. The fundamental service is, of course, that of securing uniform accurate comparable records, intelligently analyzed and made use of to stimulate those states whose standards are especially low. None of the proposals for the creation of a national department of public welfare contemplates any service of this kind. It is, however, clear that until such records and reports are available and until an agency exists equipped to stimulate, to inform, to direct, and to guide a national program on the basis of a national body of fact analyzed with a national purpose in view, the American public-welfare administration must remain chaotic, fragmentary, uneven, and inadequate, possessing neither of those features to which it is entitled by its public character, namely, comprehensiveness and continuity. And nothing less than continuous, comprehensive, and progressive service in this field can be satisfactory to those who compose the professional group in social service.

Source: Sophonisba Breckinridge, "Frontiers of Control in Public Welfare Administration," *Social Service Review* 1, no. 1 (March 1927): 84, 98–99.

Social Surveys

Social surveys are the systematic collection of data on a specific subject. From approximately 1890 to 1935, social surveys in the United States often encompassed broad topics, a whole city, or a very large sample of a target population. After World War II, surveys increasingly became more quantitative, narrower in their definition of populations, and more focused. Surveys were initially relatively infrequent events and were conducted face-to-face, but surveys now permeate daily life and increasingly occur over the telephone.

The earliest social surveys were done by governments taking a census of their people. Great Britain conducted an early count of its population and was the origin of many concepts associated with empiricism and methodology to collect data. Starting in 1790, the U.S. census has occurred every ten years and provided information affecting government services and funding.

In France from the middle to late nineteenth century, the work of Frederick LePlay focused on family budgets and social amelioration. At the end of this period, Emile Durkheim attacked LePlay's approach, and Durkheim's emphasis on objective science combined with statistics was accepted as more valid than LePlay's applied work. Durkheim's definition was increasingly accepted by many survey researchers in the United States during the 1930s.

In Britain, Charles Booth's seventeen-volume study of *The Life and Labour of the People in London* (1889–1903) became a landmark survey that mapped the relationship among poverty, work, community, and social life. Booth's work influenced many sociological surveys until the mid-1930s. This can be clearly seen in the seven-volume *New Survey of London Life and Labour* (1930–1934) conducted by the London School of Economics.

Booth's work profoundly influenced the writing of Hull House residents, who surveyed their Chicago neighborhood to help people in poverty understand their social patterns and become empowered to initiate social changes. *Hull-House Maps and Papers* (1895) helped legitimate what is called "the social survey movement," which followed this model of connecting everyday people with data collection about social issues affecting them. Women played a central role in these surveys and in using them to empower the people whose lives were studied, as well as to advocate for social reform. Thousands of social surveys were conducted; some of the most famous ones concerned urban crime. By linking the occurrence of social problems to objectively measured social and economic conditions, the survey movement played an important role in debunking the widely held notion that poverty and other social "pathologies" could be blamed on the behavior of the poor.

The government often helped organize and fund these massive studies. Thus, the nineteen-volume *Report on Condition of Woman and Child Wage-Earners in the United States* (1910–1913) was a model of such an effort. Government bureaus—for women, children, immigrants, and labor—amassed data and connected it to governmental decisions and politics. Women often staffed these bureaus and continued the social survey tradition in a wider public arena.

A split between academically based social sciences and other fields, such as social work and urban planning, appeared during the 1920s and 1930s. These groups debated the nature of objectivity and expertise and the relationships to "respondents" and funding. Philanthropic foundations such as the Russell Sage, Ford, and Rockefeller Foundations also increasingly paid for massive social surveys over this period.

Until the mid-1930s, broadly defined social surveys often included a combination of firsthand investigation using the case method and statistics to analyze various aspects of a community. This blend of qualitative ground-level research and more detached, quantitative research had theoretical and ameliorative consequences—among them, a capacity to interpret statistical findings through the lens of day-to-day community experience. By the 1930s, the use of strictly quantitative techniques was becoming more common and was increasingly associated with a Durkheimian definition of science, "objectivity," and the expert. Survey researchers less frequently allied themselves with the poor and the populations studied and increasingly aligned themselves with powerful interests.

This distance between researchers and respondents rapidly increased after World War II. The growth in statistical sampling techniques and computers combined to popularize a redefinition of social surveys as methods to collect numerical data on a population. Researchers and other experts in politics, government, and policy-making used these data with little or no input from the poor.

Survey institutions emerged during this period and focused on obtaining funding for continuous surveying of many groups, particularly those experiencing what experts called "social problems." They defined these pathologies as emerging from the poor and not from the economy, racism, or sexism. Concepts such as the "culture of poverty" explained the poor as people with faulty ways of life and ideas. Ghettoization of segregated populations of the poor, of African Americans, and of female-headed households also grew. During the 1960s, the differences between social surveyors and the poor sometimes exploded into angry confrontations. Poor people increasingly suspected the motives of researchers who took data from the people they studied but returned little if anything.

In the 1970s, a "poverty research industry" became more established and continues to this day. This bureaucratic enterprise has increasing prestige within the academy, which sponsors survey institutions to garner billions of dollars in grants from a wide range of agencies, foundations, and private donors. Academic training is allied with and often subsidized by this process.

On a smaller scale, a "participatory action research movement" coexists with this industry and continues the alliance between social surveyors and community interests. Feminist methods for data collection, problem solving, and politics also create an alternative arrangement between experts and the poor. Once again, community action aligns with training and social research for and by the poor, which they can use for their own liberation. Such training increasingly crosses national boundaries and is part of the international effort to decolonize nation-states. Massive amounts of data are increasingly available over the Internet and can potentially help poor people gain access to social facts affecting their lives. These vital efforts are offset, however, by the widespread conservative attitudes and politics that dominate the contemporary poverty research industry.

Mary Jo Deegan

See also: Hull House; *Hull-House Maps and Papers; The Philadelphia Negro;* Pittsburgh Survey; *Poverty;* Poverty Research; *Survey* and *Survey Graphic*

References and Further Reading

Bulmer, Martin, Kevin Bales, and Kathryn Kish Sklar, eds. 1991. *The Social Survey in Historical Perspective, 1880–1940*. Cambridge: Cambridge University Press.

Carpenter, Niles. 1934. "Social Surveys." In *Encyclopedia of the Social Sciences*, ed. Edwin A. Seligman and Alvin Johnson, 162–165. New York: Macmillan.

Durkheim, Emile. 1938. *The Rules of Sociological Method*. 8th ed. Trans. by Sarah A. Solovay and John H. Mueller and ed. by George E. G. Catlin. Chicago: University of Chicago Press. Originally published in French, 1895.

Feagin, Joe R., and Hernan Vera. 2001. *Liberation Sociology*. Boulder, CO: Westview Press.

O'Connor, Alice. 2001. *Poverty Knowledge: Social Science, Social Policy, and the Poor in Twentieth-Century U.S. History*. Princeton: Princeton University Press.

Reinharz, Shulamit. 1992. *Feminist Methods of Social Research*. New York: Oxford University Press.

Report on Condition of Woman and Child Wage-Earners in the United States. 1910–1913. 19 vols. Prepared under the direction of Chas. P. Neill. Serial Set 5685–5703. Washington, DC: GPO.

Residents of Hull House. 1895. *Hull-House Maps and Papers*. New York: Crowell.

Social Work

Social workers help individuals, families, groups, and communities deal with social problems and individual difficulties, including poverty. Social work is a broad profession with many subgroups and areas of practice. It is part of a social service system in which informal, voluntary, for-profit, and public sectors interact in complex ways. Although social workers vary in the methods they use, the populations they work with, the settings in which they practice, and levels of professional education, they are drawn together by a common code of ethics and a basic mission and set of values. This mission includes helping meet "the basic human needs of all people, with particular attention to the needs and empowerment of people who are vulnerable, oppressed, and living in poverty" (National Association of Social Workers [NASW] 1999, 1). Historically, social work was the predominant profession working with poor people, yet controversies over the centrality of this role to social work and about the best way to help the poor have haunted the profession from its early years to the present.

Several major debates have dominated the history of social work. One relates to the appropriate balance between professionalization and service. Another is whether problems like poverty are best dealt with by working with individuals and families or by focusing on the community and the political arena. A third is about the efficacy of public versus private approaches to meeting individual and group needs.

Although "doing good"—in the form of almsgiving, charitable acts, and providing shelter for the less fortunate—has been going on for centuries, social work as a profession first began to emerge in the United States in the late 1800s. From the 1860s on, America rapidly transformed itself from a largely rural society to an urban industrial giant. Rural Americans and European immigrants were drawn to the cities, seeking streets of gold. What they often found were low-paying jobs and crowded slums. As poverty and social problems grew, Catholic and Protestant clergy and laypeople developed systems for visiting the poor in their homes, offering moral guidance and attention to economic needs. Voluntary associations of both white and African American women created orphanages, community libraries, and similar institutions and promoted social reforms. At the same time, states experimented with a new "scientific institution," epitomized by the large, well-regulated asylum for the mentally ill. These three movements—visitation of the poor, women's club work, and creation of the scientific institution—led to new ideas and techniques for responding to such social problems as poverty. This in turn bolstered a belief among Americans that effective responses were possible.

By the 1880s, two new movements had emerged, building on the above precedents. The Charity Organisation Society (COS) focused on a new "scientific" charity, while the social settlement labored to reform society and to strengthen urban communities. The COS developed in reaction to the proliferation of small private charities. The movement's founders felt that the home visitors of those charities failed to carefully investigate recipients and that the charities lacked coordination. To keep poor families from receiving help from multiple sources, the COS sought to coordinate the work of all charities in a particular locality through a central registry of applicants and recipients. COS promoters believed that poverty was caused by individual defects, such as idleness and drunkenness. Haphazard charity only furthered the dependency of the poor. The solution was to develop a cadre of voluntary "friendly visitors," generally well-to-do women, who would investigate families, offer assistance in finding jobs and locating short-term support from churches and other sources, and serve as good moral examples for the poor.

As the movement grew, it became apparent that the COS approach could not stem the growth of poverty. Charitable societies found themselves giving direct cash payments to the poor. Also, as the pool of volunteer visitors became insufficient to meet the need, charities began replacing them with paid workers, who were a major forerunner of professional social workers. Like the volunteers before them, they were chiefly white Protestant women, often college-educated, for whom paid charity work was a socially acceptable endeavor. The administrators of the charity societies were almost entirely men.

The social settlement was another response to poverty and rapid urban growth, focusing particularly on immigrants. The prototype of this new invention was Toynbee Hall, a live-in laboratory in a London slum where young male university students studied the lives of the poor and engaged in social reform. Translated to the United States, the model appealed particularly to young, college-educated women, but unlike the COS, both women and men worked in and headed the new settlements. Jane Addams's Hull House, established in Chicago in 1889, exemplified the combination of research, service, and reform that characterized much of the U.S. settlement movement. Beginning with the notion of becoming good neighbors to the poor, Hull House residents soon discovered structural elements of poverty: exploitation of immigrant workers, inadequate wages, and substandard housing. They responded by establishing a day nursery, a club for working girls, cultural programs, and meeting space for neighborhood political groups. They took reform beyond the neighborhood, pressuring the city to improve housing and services (for example, garbage collection), supporting labor unions, and becoming involved in local politics. Hull House tried to support the cultural heritage of its immigrant neighbors and established the Immigrants' Protective League to deal with exploitation.

Not all settlements were like Hull House. Some focused on Americanizing the immigrants in their communities and were less committed to social reform. Most, including Hull House, did not accept African Americans in their programs, although Jane Addams was an early member of the National Association for the Advancement of Colored People. African Americans established their own settlement houses as part of a parallel social welfare system that discrimination had forced upon them.

Most settlements focused on the social rather than individual causes of poverty. This put them at odds with charity workers, who considered settlements an ineffective response to individual dependency. But the rift between the groups has been overemphasized by those seeking neat ideological cubbyholes. For example, COS leader Josephine Shaw Lowell appreciated the importance of structural factors in the poverty of certain types of people, including widows and orphans. Mary Richmond, the influential director of the Baltimore COS, deplored the "'socially mischievous' antagonism between the social worker and the social reformer" (quoted in Trattner 1999, 256–257) and forecast modern social work's stress on the interaction between the social and the personal in her call for the "sympathetic study of the individual in his social environment" (quoted in Leighninger 2000, 54). As the two groups drew closer together, the notion of a distinct occupation—social work—began taking shape. A rudimentary form of public welfare social work emerged with the hiring of experienced workers from private charities to help administer the new mothers' pensions programs, established in many states by 1915 (Crenson 1998). Hospitals and schools also employed people who by then were beginning to be called "social workers." Many of these workers mingled at the national meetings of the National Conference of Charities and Corrections (NCCC), a gathering place for administrators and staff members of state institutions, private charity organizations, and settlements. Work with individuals and families, now called "casework," became more systematic. Finally, formal training for the new field had arrived; close to twenty professional schools of social work existed by 1920.

This new field was hardly cohesive, however. It struggled both with a definition of its boundaries and scope—what common threads ran through its endeavors?—and with the question of whether it constituted a "true profession." In an attempt to find answers to these questions, the NCCC invited Abraham Flexner, an authority on graduate professional education, to address the 1915 conference. Flexner's speech "Is Social Work a Profession?" catalogued the reasons why the answer had to be "no." Flexner noted the vastness of the field, its lack of clear and specific goals, and the fact that social work had not yet developed a meaningful educational program. Most important, he observed that social workers dealt with their cases by summoning the necessary experts, such as the doctor, the teacher, or the legislator, rather than by applying their own expertise. Social workers were mediators, not independent professionals (Flexner 1915). Flexner's remarks energized many social workers in their pursuit of professional standing. They strove to develop specialized knowledge and techniques. Since the most accessible and prestigious sources in this area, such as psychological theories, focused on the individual, the recent rapprochement between reformers and caseworkers began to fray. In the 1920s, casework was in the ascendancy, the country was less tolerant of social reform, and the private social agency became the most prestigious setting for social work practice. Although settlements still existed and although social workers were also employed in public welfare institutions, hospitals, and other settings, the social agency set the tone for scientific professional development. Social workers still worked with the poor, but from a narrower perspective.

Events in the 1930s forced attention back to economic and social forces. Social workers were among the first to witness the toll the Great Depression took, not only on the traditional poor but also on working- and middle-class families. Social workers recently schooled in the wonders of Sigmund Freud found individual casework approaches futile in the face of hunger and unemployment. As they faced clients much like themselves, they rediscovered the importance of structural factors in dependency. Social workers joined other groups in demanding a federal response to unemployment. The field developed a radical, union-based wing, but even the mainstream professional organization, the American Association of Social Workers, adopted a program in 1933 that stressed "the redistribution of wealth and power through reconstruction of socio-economic institutions" (Weismiller and Rome 1995, 2307).

Social workers testified in congressional hearings on public relief, and most supported President Franklin D. Roosevelt's creation of the Federal Emergency Relief Administration (FERA) under fellow social worker Harry Hopkins. But the particular interest of many lay in institutionalized programs that would create permanent systems of support for children, the elderly, and those with disabilities. The School of Social Service Administration at the University of Chicago was one of the few schools that had promoted public social work in the 1920s. Dean Edith Abbott felt the profession "should provide scientific knowledge about social welfare problems and lead the way in improving institutional responses" to poverty and unemployment (quoted in Leighninger 1987, 79–80). Edith's sister Grace Abbott headed the U.S. Children's Bureau, established in 1912 to investigate the health and well-being of the country's children. With the backing of secretary of labor and social worker Frances Perkins, the Abbotts and other social workers played key roles in developing the Aid to Dependent Children (ADC) portion of the Social Security Act of 1935.

Another social worker, Jane Hoey, directed the new ADC program along with programs to provide assistance to the poor elderly and the blind. Hoey promoted hiring professional, master's-level social workers for the implementation of these programs in the states. Large numbers of social workers, trained and untrained, had been drawn into the public system under the FERA, which did not allow private agencies to dispense public funds. Master's-level social workers were in short supply. To meet the staffing demands of the new public services, many state universities developed undergraduate social work programs. The existence of two degree levels caused much dissension within social work; the bachelor's of social work (B.S.W.) was finally accepted as a professional degree by the National Association of Social Workers (NASW) in 1969.

In the aftermath of the New Deal, most private agencies retreated to family casework and individual counseling. Public social work struggled to find its role: Was it to engage in casework or to provide economic aid and help clients develop resources for dealing with the structural causes of poverty? The casework response predominated, but a somewhat broader approach emerged in the 1962 "service amendments" to the Social Security Act. Social workers, along with social policy experts like Wilbur Cohen and Elizabeth Wickenden, took center stage in developing this new approach. The amendments provided federal matches to states for rehabilitative services, including casework, foster care, and community work programs.

However, the service approach was soon eclipsed by the community-building and social action focus of President Lyndon B. Johnson's War on Poverty. Although individual social workers engaged in community organizing and worked in programs like Head Start and the Job Corps, the profession as a whole was not prominent in shaping the new antipoverty agenda. Sensitized by the civil rights movement, social workers did increase awareness of the influence of racism on America's public welfare system. And at the end of the 1960s, NASW amended its bylaws to stress the profession's obligation to use "both social work methods . . . and social action" to prevent poverty (quoted in Trattner 1999, 345).

The last several decades have presented continued challenges to social work's attempt to promote effective responses to poverty. Reagan-era attacks on social programs and the abandonment of much of the public welfare safety net under President Bill Clinton have engaged the profession in many rearguard actions. Today, only 1 percent of NASW members work in public welfare. The majority work in private agencies, and about 15 percent engage in full-time private clinical practice. Yet these figures are misleading. The public welfare and Medicaid systems now contract out much of their work with poor clients to private agency and solo practitioners. The question is not whether social workers have abandoned the poor but whether they are engaged in a systematic effort to grapple with the causes of poverty. Current lobbying for sensible welfare reform by NASW and other social work groups holds some hope that such an effort may yet emerge.

Leslie Leighninger

See also: Charity Organization Societies; Hull House; National Association of Social Workers (NASW); Settlement Houses; U.S. Children's Bureau

References and Further Reading

Crenson, Matthew A. 1998. *Building the Invisible Orphanage: A Prehistory of the American Welfare System*. Cambridge, MA: Harvard University Press.

Flexner, Abraham. 1915. "Is Social Work a Profession?" *Proceedings of the National Conference of Charities and Correction*, vol 42. Boston: Press of Geo. H. Ellis.

Leighninger, Leslie. 1987. *Social Work: Search for Identity*. Westport, CT: Greenwood Press.

———. 1999. "The Service Trap: Social Work and Public Welfare Policy in the 1960s." In *The Professionalization of Poverty: Social Work and the Poor in the Twentieth Century*, ed. Gary R. Lowe and P. Nelson Reid, 63–88. New York: Aldine.

———. 2000. *Creating a New Profession: The Beginnings of Social Work Education in the United States*. Washington, DC: Council on Social Work Education.

Lubove, Roy. 1969. *The Professional Altruist: The Emergence of Social Work as a Career, 1880–1930*. New York: Atheneum.

National Association of Social Workers (NASW). 1999. *NASW Code of Ethics*. Washington, DC: National Association of Social Workers Press.

Trattner, Walter I. 1999. *From Poor Law to Welfare State: A History of Social Welfare in America*. 6th ed. New York: Free Press.

Weismiller, Toby, and Sunny Harris Rome. 1995. "Social Workers in Politics." In *Encyclopedia of Social Work*, ed. Richard L. Edwards and June Gary Hopps, 19th ed., vol. 3, 2305–2313. Washington, DC: National Association of Social Workers Press.

Socialist Party

Founded in 1901, the Socialist Party of America (SPA) addressed the questions of poverty and social welfare through electoral politics. Socialists did not accept the common belief that most poverty was due to such individual failings as intemperance, vice, or laziness. They largely blamed poverty on capitalism's inherent inequalities. They saw poverty as inevitable in a society organized around the appropriation of workers' labor by their employers, allowing a few to accumulate huge fortunes at the expense of many. For socialists, charity was not the answer. Instead, they believed that the social ownership of the means of production would eradicate the poverty of progress. Robert Hunter's characterization of the poor in *Poverty* (1904) influenced many socialists.

The Socialist Party's first campaign for the presidency was a ticket of Eugene Debs and Benjamin Hanford. Eugene Debs founded the Socialist Party of America. (Library of Congress)

The Socialist Party's predecessor, the Social Democracy of America, initially looked to communitarianism to help the poor. Its leaders, ex-directors of the American Railway Union, devised a scheme, called "colonization," to pack a sparsely populated state like Washington with socialist sympathizers and take over its political infrastructure. They endorsed colonization because it offered a promising means to help railroad workers who had been blacklisted after the 1894 Pullman Strike.

Colonization quickly proved unfeasible, and socialists turned exclusively to electoral politics. They disagreed, however, as to what this meant. Some viewed it as an educational strategy with the long-term goal of building a revolutionary, class-conscious proletariat; others viewed it as a real opportunity to win elections in the present. This disagreement had major implications for how socialists would manifest their social program. Were they to present a platform with immediate demands, which offered the possibility of short-term solutions to capitalism's worst abuses, or one without them, focusing instead on socialism's ultimate goal of establishing the cooperative commonwealth? They decided on the former course, but not without conflict. They advocated collective ownership, unemployment relief, shorter working days, the abolition of child labor, and compulsory insurance.

During the SPA's heyday, Eugene V. Debs served as its presidential standard-bearer. He ran in 1900, 1904, 1908, 1912, and 1920. He envisioned a society where workers would receive the full fruits of their toil and the opportunity to enjoy those fruits. In his writings and speeches, Debs railed against capitalism for perpetuating a system of stark inequality. He decried the deleterious effects of poverty not only on the body but on the human spirit. His outspokenness brought him the scorn of President Theodore Roosevelt, who called Debs an "undesirable citizen."

It also led to his imprisonment in 1918 for an antiwar speech he gave in Canton, Ohio. At his sentencing hearing, he identified with those whom his accusers held in contempt: "While there is a lower class I am in it; while there is a criminal element, I am of it; while there is a soul in prison, I am not free" (quoted in Salvatore 1982, 295). He served three years. Prisoner 9653 ran the 1920 presidential campaign from his cell, receiving 3 percent of the total vote cast. Upon his release, he devoted himself to rebuilding the SPA and pushing for the penal system's overhaul. In his posthumously published book *Walls and Bars* (1927), Debs addressed the criminalization of poverty, arguing that poverty itself was responsible for a majority of incarcerations.

In 1910, Wisconsin voters elected the first socialist to congress, Victor L. Berger, signaling for many a new era in American politics. At its peak, in 1912, the SPA had 100,000 dues-paying members. That year, Debs received 900,000 votes, 6 percent of the total cast. The SPA had also made great inroads at the state and municipal levels. All told, over 1,000 socialists had been elected to public office, including 2 state senators, 17 state representatives, 56 mayors, 145 aldermen, and 160 councilmen. The party had 323 newspapers and periodicals spreading its message, including the *Appeal to Reason*, which had at its peak at least 400,000 weekly subscribers. In 1905, the *Appeal* serialized Upton Sinclair's *Jungle*, which prompted passage of the Pure Food and Drug Act the next year.

Socialism had a far greater impact than its numbers suggest. The socialist threat fueled labor and other reform efforts during the Progressive Era. An increasing number of business leaders and policymakers began to see that it was better to concede a little rather than to risk everything. Indeed, progressivism owed a great debt to socialism: Socialism both contributed to progressive programs and caused middle-class people, scared of the alternative, to vote for the reformists. Socialists made wages, working hours, pensions, and unemployment national political issues. They would remain matters of national debate for the rest of the century.

Government repression and factionalism led to the SPA's precipitous decline during and after World War I. Yet the movement did not die. Wisconsin constituents returned Berger to Congress three times during the 1920s. In 1928, Norman Thomas, the "conscience of America," became the party's new presidential standard-bearer. He had especially strong appeal among intellectuals and college students, whose support brought him over 800,000 votes in 1932. His platform more closely reflected what would soon become the New Deal than did Franklin D. Roosevelt's. Thomas used his prominence to bring national attention to the plight of southern sharecroppers and helped organize the Southern Tenant Farmers Union in 1934. After 1948, he supported Democratic presidential candidates.

The socialist legacy of Debs and Thomas remained alive largely through Michael Harrington, whose book *The Other America* (1962) inspired policymakers to take another look at the persistent problem of poverty. Harrington, like Thomas, supported Democratic Party candidates, looking to push their program further to the left. Refusing to acknowledge socialism's failure, Harrington remained committed to the idea that democratic social change was possible and, like his socialist forebears, used his speeches and writings to galvanize Americans to have a similar optimistic faith in humankind.

Jason D. Martinek

See also: Communist Party; *The Jungle; The Other America; Poverty;* Progressive Era and 1920s

References and Further Reading

Johnpoll, Bernard K., and Lillian Johnpoll. 1981. *The Impossible Dream: The Rise and Demise of the American Left*. Westport, CT: Greenwood Press.

Salvatore, Nick. 1982. *Eugene V. Debs: Citizen and Socialist*. Urbana: University of Illinois Press.
Shannon, David A. 1955. *The Socialist Party of America: A History*. New York: Macmillan.
Weinstein, James. 1984. *The Decline of Socialism in America: 1912–1925*. New Brunswick, NJ: Rutgers University Press.

Society for the Prevention of Pauperism

Formed in 1818 in New York City, the Society for the Prevention of Pauperism sought to respond to the growing problem of poverty in the early republic through moral education of the poor. Poverty, the organization believed, represented both individual failing and a threat to social stability. The society's board of directors included five members of the Corporation of the City, allowing for public participation and the contribution of municipal funds. Reflecting the contemporary view that individuals were responsible for their own hardship, the society focused on improving character and teaching self-reliance. The group created committees to investigate what it viewed as the leading causes of poverty, including idleness, intemperance, lotteries, prostitution, pawnbrokers, gambling, ignorance, and charitable institutions. Like the later charity organization societies, they viewed charities that indiscriminately gave relief with skepticism, believing they encouraged dependency and further weakened recipients' moral fiber. Only friendly visiting and moral instruction, they maintained, would truly aid and uplift the poor.

The following, an excerpt from the "Report on the Subject of Pauperism to the New-York Society for the Prevention of Pauperism" (1818), reflects the combination of moral conviction and investigation that informed what was then considered the leading edge of charitable work.

Sarah Case

See also: Charity; Charity Organization Societies; Dependency; Poorhouse/Almshouse; Relief

We were not insensible of the serious and alarming evils that have resulted, in various places, from misguided benevolence, and imprudent systems of relief. We know that in Europe and America, where the greatest efforts have been made to provide for the sufferings of the poor, by high and even enormous taxation, those sufferings were increasing in a ratio much greater than the population, and were evidently augmented by the very means taken to subdue them.

We were fully prepared to believe, that without a radical change in the principles upon which public alms have been usually distributed, helplessness and poverty would continue to multiply—demands for relief would become more and more importunate, the numerical difference between those who are able to bestow charity and those who sue for it, would gradually diminish, until the present system must fall under its own irresistible pressure, prostrating perhaps, in its ruin, some of the pillars of social order. . . .

The great and leading principles, therefore, of every system of charity, ought to be, First, amply to relieve the unavoidable necessities of the poor; and Secondly, to lay the powerful hand of moral and legal restriction upon every thing that contributes, directly and necessarily, to introduce an artificial extent of suffering. . . .

The indirect causes of poverty are as numerous as the frailties and vices of men. They vary with constitution, with character, and with national and local habits. Some of them lie so deeply entrenched in the weakness and depravity of human nature, as to be altogether unassailable by mere political regulation. They can be reached in no other way, than by awakening the dormant and secret energies of moral feeling.

Source: "Report on the Subject of Pauperism to the New-York Society for the Prevention of Pauperism," February 4, 1818. Reprinted in of *First Annual Report*, Society for the Prevention of Pauperism in New York City, 1818, in June Axinn and Herman Levin, eds., *Social Welfare: A History of the American Response* to Need, 3d ed., 69–70 (White Plains, NY: Longman, 1992), 63–64.

Soup Kitchens

See Antihunger Coalitions; Food Banks; Hunger; Nutrition and Food Assistance; Salvation Army; Voluntarism

Southern Poverty Law Center

The Southern Poverty Law Center (SPLC), a nonprofit law firm in Montgomery, Alabama, was founded in 1971 by local attorneys Morris Dees and Joe Levin. From its inception, the SPLC's goal was to use law to address the roots of Black poverty, broadly defined. However, the SPLC is best known for its innovative litigation strategy to challenge hate groups, particularly the Ku Klux Klan. The center's $7 million judgment against the United Klans of America in 1987—and the SPLC's subsequent enforcement of that and other judgments—are widely acknowledged to have forced the Klan into bankruptcy, shutting down its open operations in the South.

Morris Dees, a graduate of the University of Alabama School of Law, had already made a name as a successful entrepreneur and book publisher when he decided to shift his professional focus to civil rights law. After selling his business, he used the proceeds to establish the SPLC with his law partner and fellow Alabaman, Joe Levin. Civil rights activist Julian Bond, a founder of the Student Nonviolent Coordinating Committee, was the center's first president.

Early cases taken on by the SPLC focused on a range of issues, from defending poor Blacks against criminal prosecutions to integrating the local newspaper's weddings section and promoting sex equality. In 1973, Joe Levin argued *Frontiero v. Richardson* (411 U.S. 677 [1973]), a landmark women's rights case challenging benefits preferences given to men in the military, before the U.S. Supreme Court. More recently, the SPLC challenged the state of Alabama's reinstitution of prison chain gangs and, utilizing popular education techniques, developed a comprehensive tolerance education program.

The SPLC's Klanwatch project was started in 1980 to counteract the backlash against the civil rights movement that was fueling increased Klan activity. However, the center's courtroom successes against the Klan in the 1980s exposed Dees and other SPLC employees to retaliation. In 1983, the center's offices were set on fire by Klan members. Nevertheless, the SPLC continued its efforts, with Dees's direct-mail experience playing an important role in maintaining the center's financial stability.

As Klan activity in the South decreased as a result of the center's efforts, the SPLC focused more broadly on using litigation to combat hate crimes. For example, in 1989, the center sued three skinheads who clubbed to death an Ethiopian refugee in Portland, Oregon; in 1995, the SPLC sought to hold antiabortion leader John Burt liable for the death of David Gunn, a doctor shot and killed outside an abortion clinic. The latter case was settled prior to trial for an undisclosed amount. However, anti-Klan litigation is still a major focus of the SPLC's litigation. In 1998, the center secured a $37.8 million judgment against the Christian Knights of the Ku Klux Klan, based on their destruction of churches.

The center's office in Montgomery is the site of the Civil Rights Memorial, which celebrates the memory of forty individuals who died during the civil rights movement. The memorial was designed by Maya Lin, creator of the Vietnam Veterans Memorial.

Martha F. Davis

See also: Civil Rights Movement; Legal Aid/Legal Services; Poverty Law

References and Further Reading

Dees, Morris, and Steve Fiffer. 1991. *A Season for Justice: The Life and Times of Civil Rights Lawyer Morris Dees*. New York: Scribner's Sons.

Stanton, Bill. 1991. *Klanwatch: Bringing the Ku Klux Klan to Justice*. New York: Grove Weidenfeld.

Taylor, Damon Henderson. 1999–2000. "Civil Litigation against Hate Groups Hitting the Wallets of the Nation's Hate-Mongers." *Buffalo Public Interest Law Journal* 18: 95–145.

Speenhamland

The term "Speenhamland" refers both to a specific period in the history of the English poor laws and to a particular welfare practice. The period encompasses the years between 1795 and 1834. The practice was for local parish officials to supplement the wages of rural workers to ensure that they could afford enough bread to feed all family members. Critics of the English poor laws insisted that this particular practice dominated relief practices across the entire historical period and that it produced catastrophic results: both a population explosion among the rural poor *and* a precipitous decline in rural wages. They have insisted that a measure intended to help the rural poor ended up hurting the very people that it was intended to help. However, scholarly work since the 1960s has undermined the claim both that wage supplements were widespread and that they had the consequences attributed to them.

England's "preindustrial welfare state" originated in the sixteenth century; it gave local governments—parish authorities—the responsibility to assist those without the means to support themselves. There was considerable variation both across localities and across time in the specific rules for providing assistance, but there was a long history of aiding the unemployed as well as orphans, the infirm, and the aged. As commercial activity intensified in the second half of the eighteenth century, there were significant increases in aggregate relief outlays, greater controversy, and more intense experimentation with new welfare policies.

In 1795, county squires in Speenhamland in Bedford County agreed to a measure to supplement the wages of agricultural workers. They established a minimum-income scale depending on family size and the price of bread. The idea was that wages would be supplemented by parish assistance when they fell below the minimum. However, the measure was passed when England faced the threat of famine because of two consecutive years of bad harvests and obstacles to expanding food imports. The rapid rise in the price of bread—the central item in both rural and urban working-class diets—had already led to food riots, and local authorities were desperate to calm the situation for fear that revolutionary action would jump the English Channel from France to England.

The use of a bread scale was only one of a variety of expedients that local authorities used to reduce the threat of widespread starvation and revolt. Some parishes used funds to purchase wheat that they resold to the poor at below-market prices, and there was also a dramatic expansion in private charitable efforts to feed the hungry. Parallel measures were also taken in 1802–1803 and in 1812, when similar conditions also produced dramatic increases in food prices. Historians generally agree, however, that most of these antifamine measures were of brief duration; they were abandoned as soon as prices returned to traditional levels.

Nevertheless, critics of the poor laws seized on the Speenhamland decision as indicating a fundamental shift in social policy. Their argument was that before Speenhamland, assistance was limited to groups who were outside the labor force: small children, the infirm, and the aged. Speenhamland marked an expansion of the recipient population to include men in their prime working years. This shift, critics alleged, "pauperized" rural workers because their income was no longer a direct consequence of their own work efforts. British philosopher

Thomas Malthus developed this critique of the poor laws—without specific references to Speenhamland—as early as 1798. His argument was taken up by both religious and secular writers, who agitated throughout this entire period for abolition of the system of poor relief.

But such a break in poor law practices did not actually happen in 1795; assistance to the able-bodied had a long history. Moreover, the claim that poor relief contributed to laziness or reduced work effort seems fanciful, since assistance was provided in small face-to-face communities. Nevertheless, these arguments gained greater force because of changes in the English countryside that occurred as the Napoleonic Wars wound down between 1813 and 1815. Except for famine years, the period from 1795 to 1813 had been relatively positive for the rural poor. The wartime economy led to an expansion of wheat production, and a tight labor market produced an upward trend in wages. But the end of the war brought both a significant contraction in wheat production and a dramatic increase in rural unemployment. Since many of the rural poor could no longer earn income in rural crafts or by grazing animals on the common, the result was intense hardship and another dramatic increase in poor law outlays as local authorities struggled to handle the distress. Assistance most often took the form of relief payments to the households of unemployed workers and a variety of schemes to put the unemployed to work on private farms or in public works projects.

Contemporary welfare critics tended to treat all these new forms of assistance as simple variants of the Speenhamland bread scale; they were seen as further indicators of the pauperization of the able-bodied. Moreover, these critics blamed the existence of surplus population not on structural changes in the economy but on increases in the birthrate, which they attributed to the perverse incentives of poor law policies. As Malthus had argued earlier, why should the poor limit their fertility when they were assured by the parish of additional assistance to keep their children alive?

These criticisms were systematically elaborated by the royal commission that investigated the English poor laws in 1834 and proposed much of the language of the New Poor Law that was enacted later in the same year. The new legislation sought to abolish all outdoor relief for the able-bodied, and it established the principle of "less eligibility": The conditions for receiving assistance had to be less attractive than the jobs that were available on the labor market. The logic of the Royal Commission Report has been cited repeatedly in campaigns against outdoor relief in both England and the United States in both the nineteenth and twentieth centuries.

But the claims that poor relief in the Speenhamland period had perverse consequences are not supported by historical evidence. First, the bread scale was not actually implemented on a broad enough basis to have had the consequences that are attributed to it. Second, in both the periods of famine and of high unemployment, the basic reality is that poor law outlays helped the rural poor survive periods of extreme hardship that resulted from economic processes over which they had no control. Third, the claim that poor relief contributed to higher fertility rates is still unproven after more than 200 years. In fact, the evidence is quite clear that birthrates began to decline well before the change in welfare regimes in 1834.

Fred Block

See also: Malthusianism; Poor Laws; Relief; Welfare Policy/Welfare Reform

References and Further Reading

Block, Fred, and Margaret Somers. Forthcoming. "In the Shadow of Speenhamland: Social Policy and the Old Poor Law." *Politics and Society*.

King, Steven. 2000. *Poverty and Welfare in England 1700–1850: A Regional Perspective*. Manchester, UK: Manchester University Press.

Malthus, T. R. [1798] 1985. *An Essay on the Principle of Population*. London: Penguin.

Snell, K. D. M. 1985. *Annals of the Labouring Poor:*

Social Change and Agrarian England, 1660–1900. Cambridge: Cambridge University Press.

Steinbeck, John

See The Grapes of Wrath

Sterilization Abuse

See Birth Control; Eugenics

Strikes

See Great Depression and New Deal; Industrialization; Nineteenth Century; Service and Domestic Workers; Trade/Industrial Unions

Supplemental Security Income

Supplemental Security Income (SSI) is a federal assistance program providing cash payments to the nation's elderly and disabled poor. Administered by the Social Security Administration (SSA), the program uses eligibility criteria and benefit levels that are uniform throughout the nation, and its payments—like Social Security benefits—are indexed to rise with inflation. In 2001, SSI paid benefits averaging $394 per month to approximately 6.7 million individuals, including 880,000 disabled children (Social Security Administration 2001, 33, 34). SSI is a rarity among American income support programs in that it provides a nationally uniform income floor for the nation's poor—albeit one open only to a limited number of the poor.

Congress created SSI in 1972 by nationalizing the existing state public assistance programs for the aged, blind, and disabled. Legislators wanted SSI to serve as an income supplement for Social Security beneficiaries whose social insurance checks were too meager to provide an adequate income. SSI, therefore, was modeled on Social Security's retirement and disability insurance programs, in that individuals qualify for SSI if they are over age sixty-five or if they have a long-term physical or mental impairment that prevents employment. Children are eligible for SSI if they have a "marked and severe" impairment. As is the case with Social Security Disability Insurance (SSDI), state agencies conduct the determinations of disability for SSI. Unlike Social Security, SSI applicants need not show a history of work and payroll contributions. Instead, they must meet the program's income and assets tests; benefits are paid from general revenues rather than from the retirement or disability trust funds. In order to qualify for SSI, a person must not have income that exceeds the maximum federal benefit level (currently $540 for an individual and $817 for a couple per month) or assets valued over $2,000 for individuals and $3,000 for couples. Because eligibility for SSI does not require previous attachment to the workforce, the program's disabled recipients tend to be younger than beneficiaries of SSDI.

When SSI was enacted, lawmakers expected it to serve a largely aged clientele, and in 1974, almost two-thirds of recipients were elderly. Over time, however, SSI developed into a program primarily for the disabled. Today four out of every five SSI recipients are eligible on the basis of disability, not age (Social Security Administration 2001, 19). Among disabled recipients of SSI, two-thirds do not receive Social Security checks but instead rely on SSI as their primary source of income (U.S. House of Representatives 2000, 250). Thus, although initially intended as a supplement for the aged, SSI has become a major source of income support for individuals with disabilities, especially for children and adults with little or no work history at all.

Because SSI served recipients who policymakers assumed were incapable of work, it was for most of its history not embroiled in the sharp ideological divisions over welfare dependency that came to typify the political debates over social policy in the 1970s and 1980s. As the number of disabled recipients began to increase after 1983, however, the program became controversial. There were several reasons for this growth. First, in 1984, Congress passed the Social Security Disability Benefits Reform Act, which made it more difficult for the SSA to removed disabled persons from the Social Security rolls. The act, moreover, required the SSA to issue regulatory changes that made it easier for disabled applicants, especially those with mental disorders, to become eligible for disability benefits. Second, the federal courts also pushed the SSA to relax its disability criteria. In particular, the U.S. Supreme Court case of *Sullivan v. Zebley* (493 U.S. 521 [1990]) had a far-reaching impact on SSI. In *Zebley*, the Supreme Court struck down the SSA's regulatory standards for determining childhood disability and directed the SSA to implement more lenient standards. Shortly thereafter, the number of children receiving SSI tripled, peaking in 1994 at nearly 1 million children. These political developments, combined with a weakening economy and other factors, led to a surge in program enrollment and expenditures. Between 1985 and 2000, the number of disabled persons receiving SSI more than doubled, from 2.6 million to over 5.4 million. In terms of real dollars, program expenditures doubled (U.S. House of Representatives 2000, 261, 268).

Accompanying this expansion were three developments in the 1990s that made SSI increasingly unpopular among lawmakers. First, the growth in the number of recipients was most dramatic among groups of the disabled who are often considered less "deserving" of assistance, including adults with mental illness, drug addicts, alcoholics, children with behavioral and emotional troubles, and noncitizens. Second, the media ran several stories alleging widespread fraud and abuse in the program. These stories claimed (1) that drug addicts and alcoholics were using their SSI checks to sustain their habits, (2) that parents were encouraging their children to "act crazy" and fail in school so that they could qualify for SSI, (3) that unscrupulous translators were coaching immigrants on how to fake psychiatric disorders, (4) that adult children were bringing their aged parents to the United States only to enroll them on SSI rather than supporting them once they were in the country, and (5) that prisoners were drawing SSI checks while behind bars. Though government investigators failed to find any evidence of widespread fraud, these anecdotal stories worried many legislators. Finally, rates of exit from the SSI rolls due to rehabilitation decreased, leading some legislators to criticize the SSA for not placing enough emphasis on returning to work.

In 1995 and 1996, Congress enacted a number of measures designed to slow growth in the SSI program. These included provisions that tightened children's eligibility for SSI and that removed legal immigrants, drug addicts, and alcoholics from the program. Lawmakers also instituted tougher penalties for individuals who committed fraud. In 1997, however, amid pressure from state governments and immigrant groups, Congress restored SSI benefits to legal immigrants who had been in the country before August 1996.

Because of the restrictive measures, the number of individuals receiving SSI payments leveled off after 1997. Nonetheless, despite these retrenchment efforts, SSI remains a vital source of income support for impoverished individuals who would otherwise fall through the cracks in the American social safety net.

Jennifer L. Erkulwater

See also: Disability; Disability Policy; Social Security; Welfare Policy/Welfare Reform

References and Further Reading

Burke, Vincent, and Vee Burke. 1976. *Nixon's Good Deed*. New York: Columbia University Press.

Derthick, Martha. 1990. *Agency under Stress*. Washington, DC: Brookings Institution.

Social Security Administration. 2001. *Annual Statistical Supplement, 2001*. Washington, DC: GPO.
U.S. House of Representatives, Committee on Ways and Means. 2000. *Background Material and Data on Programs within the Jurisdiction of the Committee on Ways and Means, 2000*. Washington, DC: GPO.

Survey *and* Survey Graphic

The *Survey* (1912–1952) and *Survey Graphic* (1921–1948) were complementary publications that fostered thoughtful and wide-ranging discussion of social welfare issues for much of the first half of the twentieth century. Whereas the *Survey* was oriented toward social workers and other social welfare professionals, *Survey Graphic* was intended for the socially conscious lay reader. Both magazines covered topics of interest to progressive reformers, including labor, poverty, international affairs, public health, immigration, and federal and state social welfare legislation. Often these topics intersected with broader questions of race, class, and gender.

The *Survey* began in 1897 as *Charities*, the philanthropic review of the New York Charity Organization Society. Journalist and social welfare activist Paul Kellogg joined the staff of *Charities* in 1902, later becoming editor when the magazine merged with another magazine associated with the settlement movement to become *Charities and the Commons*. In 1907, Kellogg moved to Pittsburgh to oversee the Pittsburgh Survey, a pathbreaking sociological study, funded by the newly established Russell Sage Foundation, of an American city. *Charities and the Commons* was renamed the *Survey* in 1912 because Kellogg wanted the magazine to embody the same commitment to progressive social science he developed in the Pittsburgh Survey.

Kellogg created *Survey Graphic* in 1921 to serve as a companion to the *Survey* and to compete with other journals of public opinion such as the *Nation*. *Survey Graphic* treated many of the same issues that the *Survey* did, but with a more popular approach that embraced art, illustration, and photography as alternative ways to communicate about social welfare. Both magazines valued progressive principles of social intervention and believed in the authority of social scientific expertise. The views of progressive public intellectuals, such as Jane Addams, Louis Brandeis, Alain Locke, and John Dewey, were featured regularly in the magazines. During the 1920s, *Survey Graphic* featured a special issue on the farm crisis well before the agricultural depression was widely apparent, and it explored the emerging public health concern about heart disease. During the 1930s, *Survey Graphic* routinely published socially conscious art and photography, featuring the work of the social realists, Lewis Hine, and Dorothea Lange. In the years before a fully formed civil rights movement emerged, *Survey Graphic* covered African American political and cultural life in its now-famous March 1925 special issue, "Harlem: Mecca of the New Negro" (edited by Alain Locke), as well as in two special issues on race and segregation published during and just after World War II.

By the late 1940s, financial difficulties necessitated a merger between the two magazines, but the merged magazine was never able to identify a coherent audience. It ceased publication in 1952.

Cara A. Finnegan

See also: Charity; Charity Organization Societies; Philanthropy; Picturing Poverty (I); Pittsburgh Survey; Poverty Research; Settlement Houses; Social Work

References and Further Reading

Chambers, Clarke. 1971. *Paul U. Kellogg and the* Survey: *Voices for Social Welfare and Social Justice*. Minneapolis: University of Minnesota Press.
Katz, Michael B. 1996. *In the Shadow of the Poorhouse: A Social History of Welfare in America*. Rev. ed. New York: Basic Books.

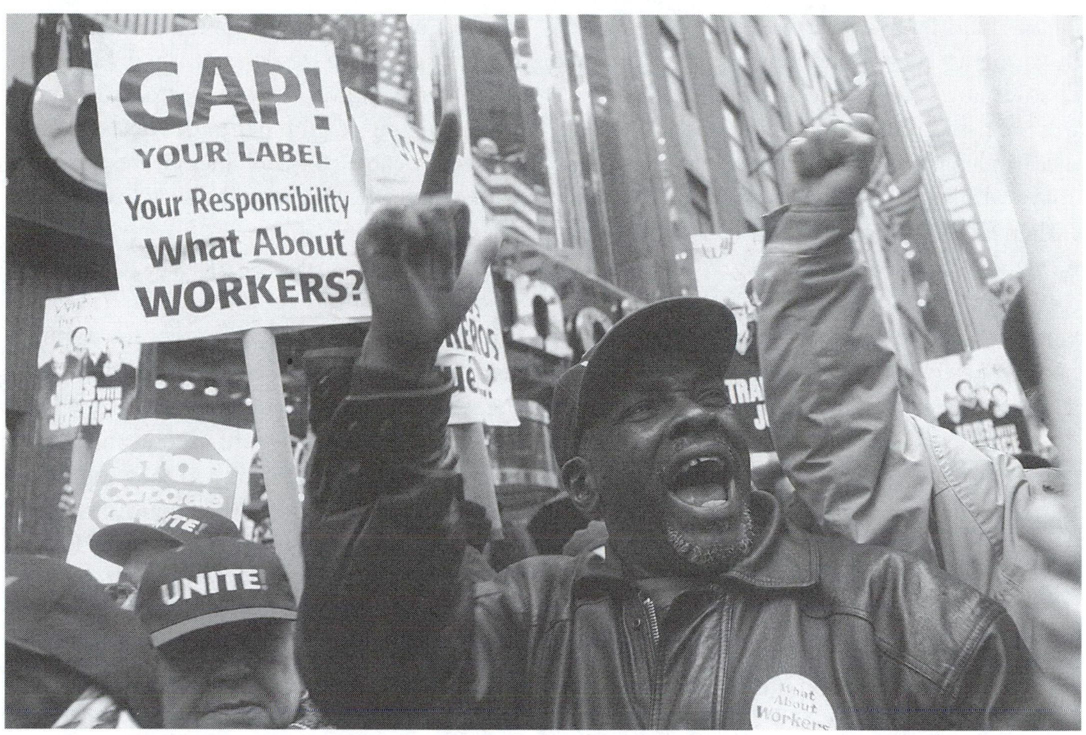

Members of the AFL-CIO, along with other labor organizations, hold a protest across from the Gap in midtown Manhattan to bring attention to exploitation of sweatshop workers by the Gap. A sign held by a demonstrator reads, "GAP! Your label, your responsibility, what about workers?" (Lorenzo Ciniglio/Corbis)

Sweatshop

The words "sweatshop" and "sweating system" can be dated to the end of the nineteenth century. They were first used by factory inspectors to describe—and criticize—conditions in a garment industry undergoing massive changes in the face of immigration from eastern and southern Europe, although the relationship between the word "sweat" and arduous, physically draining work has a longer history that can be traced even to Shakespeare.

The association of sweated work with garment production and, in particular, the labor of immigrant women was forged in the early nineteenth century in New York. Women, frequently Irish immigrants, took home bundles of garments, often destined for western or slave markets, to finish in their homes. Pay was low and was often withheld.

Between the 1840s and the 1880s, however, garment production steadily moved out of workers' homes and into ever-larger factories. Industrial changes combined with rapid immigration to reverse this trend by the late 1880s, shifting production from large factories to the smaller, difficult-to-regulate shops that became indelibly associated with the term "sweatshop." The invention of the sewing machine in 1846 and of the cutting knife (which allowed the cutting of multiple pieces of cloth) in 1876 encouraged cheap mass production and dramatically reduced the need for skilled workers. Starting around 1880, thousands of Jews from eastern Europe and, later, Italians expanded the ranks of garment workers in cities like Boston, Chicago, Cleveland, and

New York. Many Jews arrived with experience in garment production, and, like their Italian counterparts, they were desperate for paying work. These immigrants sought jobs in the garment industry, often working for friends or relatives who had emigrated to the United States earlier. Wages plummeted with the arrival of newcomers who had no alternative but to work for low pay, while the number of hours immigrants labored increased. Larger factories could not compete with smaller shops that hired only a few immigrant workers and cost only about fifty dollars to open. The industry became dominated by small "outside," or "contractor," shops that took in bundles of garments from larger manufacturers or retailers. The owners of these shops—frequently impoverished immigrants themselves—would bid for contracts and would sometimes further subcontract out bundles. Profits were literally "sweated" from workers.

Thus, in 1888, New York factory inspectors coined the term "sweating system" to describe and denigrate these small, contractor shops. For these American inspectors, as well as for critics in Great Britain who also used the term, the sweatshop was an immigrants' workshop that often doubled as a living space and that featured low pay, long hours, and shocking sanitary conditions. By the 1890s, the sweatshop had become a target for social reformers and public health advocates, if only because they worried that clothing manufactured in sweatshops could infect middle-class consumers with disease. In an era when immigrants were understood as distinct races, critics also worried that the cramped conditions, dusty atmosphere, and perceived immorality of sweatshop conditions would lead to the racial "degeneration" of Jews and Italians. Native-born, white inspectors often understood the sweating system to be at least in part a byproduct of Jews' and Italians' racial inferiority, manifest in the immigrants' alleged comfort with filth.

Beginning in the 1880s, armed with fears of epidemic disease and racial degradation, reformers were able to pass some of the most powerful factory inspection legislation to date. However, there were simply too few inspectors to enforce the stringent requirements of the laws, and inspectors came to see alliances with organized workers as the only means of eradicating the sweatshop.

Immigrants also came to describe their workplaces as sweatshops. Yet while inspectors focused on the moral and racial failings of immigrants, Jewish and Italian workers described the sweating system as the result of exploitation and built a powerful labor movement around the goal of its eradication. Starting in the 1880s and accelerating after 1900 with the founding of the International Ladies' Garment Workers' Union (ILGWU) and led initially by Jews, workers led several strikes seeking to regulate garment production. Finally, in 1910, at the conclusion of a strike in New York, workers, in alliance with factory inspectors, signed an agreement with manufacturers that allowed for the inspection and regulation of garment shops. Similar kinds of agreements were signed across the country, and the number of contractor shops declined dramatically. However, in regulating sweatshops and the garment homework that remained an integral part of the sweating system, union leaders and social reformers also sought to restrict the employment of working women. By the end of the 1910s, union leaders and inspectors were cautiously declaring victory over the sweatshop. Within a decade, though, and reflecting a decline in the Progressive reform impulse, employers began skirting regulations and workers were again bemoaning the return of the sweatshop.

The New Deal of the 1930s brought a renewed offensive against the sweatshop. The Fair Labor Standards Act of 1938 helped establish a minimum wage and a maximum workweek and brought the federal government into the regulation of the garment industry. With new efforts spearheaded by the government and by unions, whose membership had grown to nearly 400,000 by 1934 (about two-thirds of the garment industry workforce), the number of contractor shops declined by 26 percent between 1936 and 1940.

The gains of the 1930s, however, began to be reversed in the 1960s. In a reprise of earlier patterns, the arrival of new immigrants—this time first from Puerto Rico and then from Central and South America and Southeast Asia—once again spurred the growth of contractor shops that hired between twenty and forty workers. Because many of these new workers were and remain undocumented immigrants, they were hesitant to call on factory inspectors to help improve working conditions. Some employers even use the threats of deportation to coerce workers to accept miserable wages. At the same time, especially after 1970, the American garment industry has been affected by competition from abroad. The increasingly globalized garment industry has led to a dramatic decline in wages and conditions and has spurred a fall in union membership.

By the 1990s, the conditions of garment workers in America and abroad had become the focus of renewed campus and labor activism. The raiding of a sweatshop in El Monte, California, in 1995 where Thai immigrants worked in slavery led to government hearings about the contracting practices of major retailers. At the same time, the efforts of groups like United Students against Sweatshops, the National Labor Committee, and the Union of Needletrades, Industrial, and Textile Employees (UNITE) (formed in 1995 from the merger of the ILGWU and the Amalgamated Clothing and Textile Workers Union) focused attention on employers such as Nike, Wal-Mart, Kathie Lee Gifford, and Walt Disney, as well as on universities that license their logos to clothing manufacturers. In addition to supporting worker organizing in the United States and abroad, these efforts have urged the adoption of standards of conditions and have demanded independent monitoring. As the sweatshop has become the center of activism, its meaning is no longer restricted to the garment industry. Indeed, the sweatshop has become a metaphor for exploitative conditions, whether in the clothing, electronics, trucking, or other industries.

Daniel E. Bender

See also: Fair Labor Standards Act (FLSA); Immigrants and Immigration; Trade/Industrial Unions

References and Further Reading

Bender, Daniel. 2003. *From Sweatshop to Model Shop: Anti-Sweatshop Campaigns and Languages of Labor, 1880–1934*. New Brunswick, NJ: Rutgers University Press.

Green, Nancy. 1997. *Ready-to-Wear and Ready-to-Work: A Century of Industry and Immigrants in Paris and New York*. Durham, NC: Duke University Press.

Ross, Andrew, ed. 1997. *No Sweat: Fashion, Free Trade, and the Rights of Garment Workers*. New York: Verso.

T

Tax Policy

Tax policy plays a central role in social welfare provision in the United States. It serves as a mechanism both for distributing (and redistributing) income and wealth across the broad population and for financing government social programs. Tax policy can also be used—and has been increasingly in recent decades—to manage economic growth and to provide subsidies for activities ranging from business investment to child rearing.

Government social programs, including welfare and Social Security, must be financed by tax revenue. In the United States, federal, state, and local governments share responsibility for spending on social services. All must overcome resistance to taxes by individuals and business interests in order to finance social programs and other government responsibilities. The result is a complex mixture of revenue sources and overall levels of taxation much lower than those in most industrial democracies; only Japan, South Korea, and Australia pay a smaller proportion of their gross domestic product in taxes. The American welfare state not only provides a significantly lower level of benefits than do comparable industrialized countries, but the burden of most taxes in the United States falls most heavily on lower-income groups (regressive taxation).

Three major factors account for the low level and regressivity of U.S. taxes. First, the political influence of business interests and the wealthy has led to lower tax rates and the heavy use of tax expenditures or deductions to offset their taxes. Second, in a federal system, competition among states, cities, and metropolitan areas leads to lower taxes as each jurisdiction tries to attract businesses and population. Third, the United States has lower levels of spending on social programs than do the European countries. In the United States, resistance to taxes by wealthy individuals and businesses has made it difficult to expand welfare benefits or to provide new ones, such as health care (although the relatively small size of the American welfare state is accompanied by higher levels of spending on defense).

Federal Taxes

At the federal level, in 2000, 50 percent of revenue derived from the individual income tax (see the accompanying table). Income tax rates were sharply progressive in the 1950s and 1960s, with high-income earners paying rates as high as 91 percent on earnings over $200,000. Under the presidencies of Ronald Reagan (1981–1988) and George H. W. Bush (1989–1993), however, the top tax rates on high-income earners declined to only 31 percent. The top rate was increased to 36 percent under President Bill Clinton's 1993 budget plan to reduce the federal deficit. But President George W. Bush (2001–) instituted a series of major tax cuts in 2001, which will further reduce the tax rates on high-income earners. His administration has also pledged to phase out the federal estate tax, which taxes large inheritances, by 2010. This tax currently applies only to estates worth over $1 million and the change will thus benefit only the richest 1 percent of Americans.

Table 1

Sources of tax revenue, 1960–2000

	1960	*2000*
Federal		
Personal income	44.0%	49.6%
Corporate income	23.3	10.2
Payroll	15.9	32.1
Excise taxes	12.6	3.4
Estates, customs, other	4.2	4.7
State		
Personal income	30.1	34.2
Corporate income	8.3	6.8
General sales	40.1	33.0
Excise taxes	5.6	8.7
Lotteries, gambling	0.7	2.7
License fees	6.0	6.2
Other	9.2	8.4

Source: Statistical Abstract of the U.S.

Revenue from the corporate income tax in 2000 accounted for only 10 percent of federal revenue, down from 23 percent in 1960. Personal and corporate income tax revenue is greatly reduced by a broad array of tax deductions, or loopholes, for home mortgages, health benefits paid by employers, pension contributions, and charitable giving. Sizable tax breaks are available for businesses as well, to encourage activities such as business investment, timber harvesting, and the installation of pollution reduction equipment and to offset business losses. Critics claim that such business deductions constitute "corporate welfare" and that the value of these deductions (estimated at between $100 billion and $200 billion annually) is far greater than society's gain from the business investment they are meant to encourage, and far larger than spending on many federal social and educational programs.

Working Americans also pay Social Security payroll taxes on their wages; their employers pay a matching rate. In 2001, this was 7.65 percent. This is a flat-rate tax with no deductions or exemptions allowed. It is highly regressive, since anyone earning more than a fixed amount ($80,000 in 2001) pays no Social Security taxes on the income above that fixed amount. This means that billionaires pay no more in Social Security taxes than do many working professionals. Since the early 1980s, the payroll tax has increased significantly to help meet expected shortfalls in the Social Security and Medicare trust funds when the large baby boom generation reaches retirement age. In 1994, the payroll tax was increased by 1.5 percent to help finance Medicare, the federal program that covers part of hospital and medical costs for those over age sixty-five; this increase does apply to all wage earners. The percentage of federal revenues that came from the payroll tax doubled, from 16 to 32 percent, between 1960 and 2000 (see the accompanying table). But excise tax revenue from cigarettes, gasoline, furs, and other luxury items constituted a smaller share of federal revenues in 2000 than it did in 1960.

The federal Earned Income Tax Credit (EITC) was established in 1975 to offset the adverse effects of increased Social Security and Medicare payroll taxes on working-poor families and to strengthen work incentives. The EITC is a refundable credit that is administered through the Internal Revenue Service (IRS). Because it is refundable, the EITC is used not only to reduce a family's income tax liability but also to supplement its household income. The amount by which the credit exceeds taxes owed is paid as a refund. If a family has no income tax liability, the family receives the entire EITC as a refund.

The EITC for families with children provides an average credit of more than $1,900 and (as of 2001) covers families with incomes up to $27,400 or $31,200, depending on the number of children in the family. By contrast, the EITC for workers without children provides an average credit of approximately $200 and ends when income reaches $10,400. Some 98 percent of overall EITC benefits go to families with children, with 2 percent going to working individuals and married couples who are not raising minor children.

Since 1975, the EITC has been increased several times to further offset the effects of federal payroll taxes on low-income families. It was greatly expanded during the Clinton administration to assist many former welfare (Aid to Families with Dependent Children) recipients who, under Temporary Assistance for Needy Families, have been pushed into the workforce. Support for the EITC has come from across the political spectrum, with conservatives such as former president Ronald Reagan among its strong supporters; Reagan called the EITC "the best anti-poverty, the best pro-family, the best job creation measure to come out of Congress" (Greenstein and Shapiro 1998). Recent studies have confirmed the effectiveness of the federal EITC in supporting work and in alleviating child poverty. The EITC now lifts more than 4 million people, including over 2 million children, out of poverty each year, and it has become the nation's most effective antipoverty program for working families.

State and Local Taxes

At the state level, sales taxes provide the major source of revenue (see the accompanying table). Rates in 2001 ranged from 2 to over 8 percent. A few states (Delaware, Montana, New Hampshire, Oklahoma, and Oregon) have no sales taxes. Ten states, mostly in the South, tax food. States also levy excise taxes on liquor, cigarettes, or gasoline, even though these (and taxes on food) tend to be highly regressive since low-income families spend a higher proportion of their incomes on these items.

Forty-three states have income taxes. Four states (California, Delaware, Montana, and Vermont) have moderately progressive rates, but in other states rates are flat regardless of income. Most state income taxes allow fewer deductions or exemptions than does the federal income tax, but Rhode Island and Vermont allow their residents to calculate their state taxes as a fixed percent of their federal tax liability.

States have also increased their use of lotteries, which tend to be regressive since the poor, the less educated, and the elderly are those most likely to participate. And states have also expanded their reliance on legalized gambling. In 1973, only Nevada permitted casino gambling and only seven states had lotteries; by 1999, all states except for seven (mostly in the Bible Belt) had lotteries. Riverboat gambling or casinos have also been legalized in twenty-six states and on Native American reservations. Although gambling may attract tourist dollars from residents of other states, it also produces negative social consequences, such as addiction and corruption, and likewise tends to be a regressive (although "voluntary") tax.

State government revenue collections rise and fall with the state of the economy. Thus, during times of recession, such as 1990–1991 and 2001–2003, sales and income tax revenues decline, even though demands for welfare and unemployment increase during economic downturns. But unlike the federal government, states cannot rely on deficit spending; all but Vermont are legally obligated to submit balanced budgets, and state borrowing is also constrained by constitutional limits. Therefore, many state and local governments are forced to *increase* taxes during a recession as well as to cut back on services. Recent cuts in federal domestic spending, as well as "unfunded mandates"—federal legislation or regulations that are not accompanied by federal funds for implementation—for such policies as pollution abatement, disability access, and prison improvements have also forced state and local governments to find new sources of revenue.

Local Taxes

Local governments (including school districts) receive nearly three-quarters of their revenue from property taxes. Some local governments also assess income taxes or wage taxes and may add a percent or two onto the state sales tax rate. Many communities offer a "homestead exemption" so that poor or elderly home owners pay less in property taxes. But local governments cannot tax state or federal property or the holdings of nonprofits or religious institutions (although in some communities, nonprofits pay fees for some public services). Local governments must thus rely on state or federal aid. Large cities in particular face serious constraints on revenues. A few, such as New York and Philadelphia, have enacted wage taxes in order to gain revenue from suburbanites who work or enjoy recreation in the city but live elsewhere. A handful of other cities, such as Indianapolis and Nashville, have merged city-county or metropolitan-area governments, which offer a broader tax base. But such consolidations are usually strongly opposed by suburban governments.

High property tax rates in California in 1978 led to the passage of Proposition 13, which drastically reduced property taxes. Tax revolts in other states as well have led to limitations on both taxing and spending. User charges are currently the fastest-growing source of state and local government revenue. Only those persons who actually use a given government service, such as toll roads, college tuition, water and sewerage, or garbage collection, actually pay for it. User fees are usually regressive, since low- and moderate-income earners make more use of public services. Recent sharp increases in tuition at state colleges and universities have put the cost of higher education beyond the reach of many working- and middle-class families.

State and local personal income and property taxes are allowed as itemized deductions in computing federal income taxes. Citizens for Tax Justice (1996) reported that after federal deductions, the average state and local tax on the richest 1 percent was 5.8 percent of their income, but on average, the poorest 20 percent of Americans spent 12.5 percent of their incomes on state and local taxes. Thus, overall, the regressivity of state and local taxes offsets the modestly progressive federal income tax.

To offset these regressive taxes, ten states began to offer EITCs in the 1990s, a move supported by businesses as well as by social service advocates. Despite the economic expansion in the late 1990s, many children in families with parents in the paid labor force remained poor. State EITCs, like the federal EITC, are meant to help reduce poverty among workers with children. Further, with large numbers of welfare recipients entering the workforce, state EITCs complement welfare reform by helping low-wage workers support their families as they leave public assistance.

Susan B. Hansen

See also: Earned Income Tax Credit (EITC); Health Policy; Social Security; Welfare Policy/Welfare Reform; "Working Poor"

References and Further Reading

Center on Budget and Policy Priorities. Web site. cbpp.org. Cited November 17, 2002.

Citizens for Tax Justice. 1996. *Who Pays? A Distributional Analysis of the Tax Systems in All 50 States*. Washington, DC: Institute on Taxation and Economic Policy.

———. Web. site. Cited November 21, 2002.

Greenstein, Robert, and Isaac Shapiro. 1998. "New Research Findings on the Effects of the Earned Income Tax Credit." http://www.cbpp.org/311eitc.htm.

Hansen, Susan B. 1983. *The Politics of Taxation: Revenue without Representation*. New York: Praeger.

Levi, Margaret. 1988. *Of Rule and Revenue*. Berkeley and Los Angeles: University of California Press.

Peterson, Paul E. 1995. *The Price of Federalism*. Washington, DC: Brookings Institution.

Steinmo, Sven. 1993. *Taxation and Democracy:*

Swedish, British, and American Approaches to Financing the Welfare State. New Haven: Yale University Press.

Teacher Corps

The Teacher Corps, established as part of the Higher Education Act of 1965, no longer exists. As part of the flood of legislation in the 1960s aimed at improving the opportunities for disadvantaged children in America, the Teacher Corps concept was explicitly aimed at bringing young socially and politically liberal "change agents" into public schools that demonstrated need. These change agents were to be recruited from the ranks of recent college graduates (and particularly, within this group, minorities) with backgrounds in the liberal arts and nontraditional fields; they were meant to infuse the public high school system with new ideas and new teaching techniques. In addition to training recruits, the federal government supplied short-term and modest grants to schools participating in the program. The goals of the corps as originally envisioned were bold: to reform the educational establishment by challenging its inflexibility and introducing to it a fresh and idealistic group of young teachers.

However, the program encountered substantial difficulties, and, after many changes and iterations, it was eventually scrapped in the 1980s under President Ronald Reagan. Many states continued or created state Teacher Corps programs, which met with far greater success and support and continue to operate today. In 1989, while a senior at Princeton, Wendy Kopp dreamed up the concept of a philanthropically funded organization that would, in time, realize many of the goals of the earlier program. The program came to be known as Teach for America, the "national corps of outstanding college graduates of all academic majors and backgrounds who commit two years to teach in urban and rural public schools and become lifelong leaders in the effort to ensure that all children in our nation have an equal chance in life" (Congressional Hispanic Caucus Institute 2004). Since its creation in 1990, more than 9,000 individuals have participated in the program, teaching over 1.25 million students.

Support for a renewed federally funded Teacher Corps program still exists in some quarters. In 2001, Senator Hillary Rodham Clinton proposed the National Teacher Corps and Principal Recruitment Act. Though the legislation has been hung up in committees since its introduction, if enacted, the act would create scholarships and other financial incentives in order to recruit 75,000 teachers a year in order to meet the growing needs of public schools in certain subject areas and districts.

Rebecca K. Root

See also: Education Policies; Peace Corps; Voluntarism; Volunteers in Service to America (VISTA)

References and Further Reading

Congressional Hispanic Caucus Institute. 2004. "Fellowships outside Washington, DC." http://www.chci.org/chciyouth/publications/04directory/dir_outsidefellow.pdf.

Corwin, Ronald G. 1973. *Reform and Organizational Survival: The Teacher Corps as an Instrument of Educational Change*. New York: John Wiley and Sons.

Teach for America. Web site. www.teachforamerica.org.

Temperance Movement

The temperance movement promoted moderation in the use of or abstinence from alcoholic beverages, deriving momentum largely from alcohol's association with such social ills as poverty and family violence. Although early in the movement, temperance forces distinguished between distilled spirits, which they believed to be harmful, and fermented and brewed drinks such as wine and beer, which many believed to be safe, eventually most temperance groups attempted to abolish both the manufacture and sale of all alcoholic drinks. The movement

Board of Directors, Anti-Saloon League of America, Indianapolis, April 9, 1924. (Library of Congress)

gained strength throughout the nineteenth century and into the early twentieth, culminating in the passage of the Eighteenth Amendment establishing Prohibition in 1919. Although Prohibition was repealed in 1933, the temperance movement effected numerous permanent legislative and social changes, especially with regard to women. After the repeal of Prohibition, temperance organizations continued, although generally in smaller numbers and different forms.

By the turn of the nineteenth century, unrestrained alcohol consumption came to be seen as a major societal problem. During this period, citizens drank more alcohol than at any other time in U.S. history. Clean water was scarce, and alcohol was generally believed to have nutritional value. Spirits were inexpensive—less costly, for example, than tea or coffee. In addition, drinking distilled alcohol had become patriotic because it supported home industries. Large quantities of grain were cumbersome and costly to move great distances, so surplus grains from the West were difficult to transport for sale in the East. And fruits rotted in transit. Farmers converted products into beverage alcohol, which could be shipped in much less space without fear of decay. However, as consumption of alcohol increased, so did social ills, and groups formed in opposition to excessive consumption of alcohol, constituting what came to be labeled the "temperance movement."

Quakers and Methodists began to question the pervasive use of alcohol, promoting moderation and self-discipline. Members of other religious groups joined the movement early in the nineteenth century, popularizing the idea that intemperance and immorality were associated. Physicians also began to question long-held beliefs about the health benefits of alcohol, recommending alternative beverages. Benjamin Rush, perhaps the most respected American physician of the century, spoke widely to medical students and to the public at large about the dangers of alcohol. The public increasingly expressed disgust with public drunkenness and concern about alcohol's addictive qualities.

Poverty and other economic concerns provided a primary focus for gathering support for the temperance movement. Industrial and political leaders became concerned about the high consumption of alcohol because it led to workers' unemployability, absenteeism, and tardiness. They also worried about drunkards' diminished resources and, therefore, reduced capacity to invest in the growth of the new nation, as well as the cost to the community in providing economic support for impoverished children. Workers and their unions decried intemperance as a deterrent to self-respect and argued that money spent on inessentials such as intoxicating beverages also decreased workers' prospects for prosperity. Reform groups condemned the penury that could be suffered by families, who were dependent on the men in their lives for economic security. For example, in its fourth annual report (1831), the American Temperance Society attributed three-quarters of all "pauperism, crimes, and wretchedness" to the 60 million gallons of spirits consumed annually and claimed that alcohol "beggared more families [. . .] than all other vices put together."

Because of widespread poverty and abuse within alcoholic families, women and children were seen primarily as innocent victims of intemperance, providing women an ideal issue around which to organize. By midcentury, women were joining men's temperance organizations in large numbers and forming their own temperance unions. By the last quarter of the century, women had become the primary promoters of reform in the name of temperance; their largest organization, the Woman's Christian Temperance Union (WCTU), marshaled hundreds of thousands of women to seek temperance legislation and other major reforms on behalf of women.

Until the mid-nineteenth century, nearly every state denied personal and real property rights to married women. Alcoholic men might sell or lose all family property through unemployment, gambling, or other profligacy, even if that property had been brought to the marriage by the wife. If a woman sought employment to support herself and her children after her husband had become alcoholic, her husband could demand that the employer pay her wages directly to him. The recognition that men's intemperance impoverished women and children and left them with no other means of protection permitted women to argue for social, legislative, and judicial reform and to insist on women's need for suffrage as self-protection. Women's compelling arguments based on the temperance issue facilitated changes in legislation governing personal and real property rights, ownership of wages and children, physical abuse, oversight of women prisoners, and age of sexual consent. In addition, women's temperance organizations, especially the WCTU, provided a primary force for passage of the Nineteenth Amendment giving women the right to vote.

Great changes in drinking patterns resulted from the temperance movement. Reasons for major societal change are always complex, and the reduced costs of alternative beverages and the need for sobriety in industrial employment as well as other factors contributed to a reduction in excessive inebriation. However, the temperance movement played a major role in altering drinking habits. Intoxication, generally accepted as legitimate social behavior at the beginning of the nineteenth century, was broadly frowned upon throughout the second half of the century. Consumption of alcohol fell by nearly three-quarters from 1830 to 1850, and there was a gradual shift from distilled spirits to beer among drinkers after midcentury.

Today, the WCTU, the largest women's organization in the nineteenth century, exists in greatly reduced numbers. New variants of earlier movements have formed: Mothers Against Drunk Driving (MADD) brings together those who have lost children or other loved ones at the hands of intoxicated drivers to work for legislative and cultural changes with regard to alcohol consumption, as did the WCTU. Alcoholics Anonymous, like a similar nineteenth-century group known as the Washingtonians, unites those with problematic dependence on alcohol to fight addiction together. Some religious denominations continue to oppose the use of intoxicating beverages. Statistics suggest that three of ten drinkers became chronic alcoholics in the early nineteenth century; today experts estimate that three in two hundred do so. Although Prohibition is generally seen as a failed effort, changed attitudes toward intoxication and laws affecting women and children have been permanent.

Carol Mattingly

See also: Feminisms; Nineteenth Century; Progressive Era and 1920s; Protestant Denominations

References and Further Reading

Blocker, Jack. 1989. *American Temperance Movements: Cycles of Reform*. Boston: Twayne.

Mattingly, Carol. 1998. *Well-Tempered Women: Nineteenth-Century Temperance Rhetoric*. Carbondale: Southern Illinois University Press.

Rorabaugh, W. J. 1979. *The Alcoholic Republic, an*

American Tradition. New York: Oxford University Press.

Tyrrell, Ian. 1979. *Sobering Up: From Temperance to Prohibition in Antebellum America, 1800–1860*. Westport, CT: Greenwood Press.

Temporary Assistance for Needy Families (TANF)

See Aid to Families with Dependent Children (ADC/AFDC); Welfare Policy/Welfare Reform

Tenant Organizing

Tenant organizing emerged as one strategy in the struggle against poverty in the nineteenth century, when renters in rural and urban areas began to mobilize to protest high rents, poor living conditions, and unjust leases imposed by often-distant landlords. Based on tactics such as withholding rent ("rent strikes"), resisting eviction, suing landlords, and taking over abandoned sites ("squatting"), tenant organizing should be understood as an economic and political response to poverty, segregation, maldistribution of land, and the structural shortage of decent-quality, affordable land and housing.

In 1845, more than 10,000 tenant farmers from eleven counties in eastern New York engaged in full-scale revolt against their landlords, refusing to pay rent and challenging landlords in court. Six years in the making, this massive rent strike protested a centuries-old legal provision that tied tenants to the land. Lawyers called their tie "lease in fee," but the farmers called it "voluntary slavery" and "unhallowed bondage." The tenants emerged victorious, ending the lease in fee that had kept many of their households in poverty.

This famous strike was one of many attempts by tenants in the nineteenth century to redefine the tenant-landlord relationship and improve the quality of housing. It drew on a transatlantic discourse that challenged traditional property rights as well as on republican notions of civic virtue. In spite of the 1845 victory, tenants across the nation remained at a disadvantage in tenant-landlord relations. During the turbulent urban and industrial expansion after the Civil War, low-cost urban housing was typically shabby and sometimes dangerous, lacking adequate air, light, and clean water—as Jacob Riis and other reformers documented and publicized. Rural housing was no better. In both areas, there was always a housing shortage for workers. By the turn of the twentieth century, the right of the landlords and their agents to determine and collect rents on units had been firmly established in law, while the rights of renters were few.

Although most tenant actions were individualized, collective actions surged as the nation became more urbanized and housing conditions deteriorated, particularly among the most vulnerable and poor. These actions drew on a tradition of transatlantic protest and, for those in poverty, on an understanding that the high rents they paid were just as much to blame for their financial hardship as were the low incomes they received for their labor. In addition to rent strikes, tenants worked with labor unions, boycotted landlords and buildings, and joined together to prevent evictions. Very few tenants participated in Progressive-Era housing reforms. Though women and socialists led these actions, it was not uncommon for children and the elderly to participate. The majority of these dramatic actions stopped once tenants had achieved their goals. Some such actions, however, led to more sustained efforts linking labor unions and ethnic organizations in limited dividend and cooperative housing projects.

During the Great Depression of the 1930s, renters continued to collectively fight evictions and rent collectors and were often assisted by the growing ranks of the unemployed. Formal and informal tenant associations addressed grievances at the building and city levels and sometimes demanded rent reductions from landlords who had profited from rents and speculation. Urban renters also joined New Deal liberals, labor unions, and radicals in the call for federal public housing, viewing the program as a way to create jobs, decent-quality housing, and communities where tenant organizing would not only continue but spill over into surrounding neighborhoods. In the South, white and Black tenant farmers formed the Southern Tenant Farmers Union and the Sharecroppers' Union, among other associations, to win better leases and higher crop prices and to prevent evictions caused by federal programs to reduce crop production. African Americans also used these associations to fight for civil rights with the assistance of Socialist Party and Communist Party workers and white allies. Whether in urban or rural areas, tenant organizing during the capitalist crisis highlighted how the maldistribution of land, the power of landlords, and rent contributed to poverty and political inequality.

Neither government nor private home construction during the capitalist crisis of the 1930s met the nation's housing needs. This shortage worsened during World War II with the massive migrations of workers and their families from the rural South to cities in the North and West. Landlords were quick to raise rents, absorbing wage gains. Nonwhite renters faced the greatest housing hardships because they generally earned less than whites and, from San Francisco to Detroit to Miami, were excluded from many neighborhoods by racially restrictive covenants and by whites who staged both peaceful and violent demonstrations. Wartime housing shortages produced a wave of housing rallies and tenant organizing across the nation, action that helped expand public housing and federal rent control in congested housing areas.

After World War II and the passage of the 1949 Housing Act, urban renewal projects produced an upsurge of tenant activism. Targeting nonwhite and poor neighborhoods, directors of urban renewal agencies and the public officials who assisted them earned a reputation for destroying vibrant communities and replacing affordable housing with freeways, shopping centers, luxury apartments, and convention centers. Given the persistence of racial discrimination in housing and employment and given the shortage of decent affordable housing in many nonwhite communities, tenants blended their anti–urban renewal attacks with demands for legislation to ensure fair and open housing and employment. Housing discrimination kept nonwhites and the poor away from the schools and social networks through which better jobs were distributed and thus maintained social, racial, and economic inequality. Members of tenant associations became more diverse in terms of race, ethnicity, and income groups after the war, though women continued to outnumber men in the fight to preserve rent control, enforce building codes, improve maintenance and services, and expand the amount of government-assisted, low-income housing.

Tenant organizing contributed to the social and political movements in the United States and around the world in the 1960s. To be sure, tenants still organized around grievances with landlords and for legislation and programs favorable to tenants, but they also addressed such issues as useful jobs, health care, ending discrimination, and peace. In some cities, public housing authorities offered tenants meeting space, funding, and technical advice to increase participation in policymaking, while President Lyndon B. Johnson's administration supplied organizers and lawyers through Community Action Programs and Legal Aid. Some tenants, impatient with government housing programs and inspired by the radical discourses of the 1960s, organized squats that refurbished abandoned buildings with sweat equity and then ran them cooperatively and democratically for use rather than speculation and profit.

Even though President Richard M. Nixon and all succeeding administrations slashed federal spending for community action, the protest culture, political networks, and institutions nurtured in the previous two decades of tenant activism remained intact in many communities. Through local associations and their national federation, the National Tenant Union (founded in 1980), tenants continued to address century-old issues, from improving their buildings to promoting politicians and legislation. As the nation's environmental movement grew, tenants resisted private and public projects that posed environmental and health hazards to their communities. Occasionally, these protests took place in middle-income neighborhoods, but they have sprung increasingly from nonwhite and poor communities whose residents refused to continue being exposed to a disproportionate share of pollution. Public housing tenants built citywide umbrella associations and created the National Tenant Organization to advocate for them. Although a few tenant association leaders have been co-opted, others have improved public housing policy, have demanded greater resident hiring, and have beaten back attempts to displace tenants without adequate replacement housing. More recently, tenants have protested plans to privatize public housing projects.

Tenant organizing at the turn of the twenty-first century has been as challenging as ever, for private and public landlords have many tools to curtail tenant activism: well-funded local, regional, and national associations; a culture and legal system that privileges property rights and profit over human rights; access to police and marshals; and databases for screening the credit and "character" of tenants. Moreover, tenants still have trouble sustaining organizations and movements after victories, and their associations suffer from high turnover rates among members. But because rent remains one of the greatest contributors to poverty, tenants continue to organize.

John Baranski

See also: African American Migration; Communist Party; Community Organizing; Housing Policy; Legal Aid/Legal Services; *Progress and Poverty;* Property; Racial Segregation; Urban Renewal; U.S. Department of Housing and Urban Development; Wealth

References and Further Reading

Blackmar, Elizabeth. 1989. *Manhattan for Rent, 1785–1850*. Ithaca, NY: Cornell University Press.

Kelley, Robin. 1990. *Hammer and Hoe: Alabama Communists during the Great Depression*. University of North Carolina Press.

Lawson, Ronald, with the assistance of Mark Naison. 1986. *The Tenant Movement in New York City, 1904–1984*. New Brunswick, NJ: Rutgers University Press.

Tennessee Valley Authority

A public corporation established in 1933, the Tennessee Valley Authority (TVA) reshaped the landscape of the Tennessee River valley, creating a system of navigable waterways and sources of fertilizer and electricity for the seven-state valley region. It also built a new way of life for the inhabitants of the nation's most impoverished communities, providing cheap power, new sources of employment and wealth, and enhanced public services, even if the authority's original vision of a stable, sustainable rural Southeast never materialized. After World War II, TVA became the template for multiuse, regional development programs around the United States; eventually, U.S. policymakers exported the model to Asia and South America.

An act of Congress chartered TVA to generate and distribute hydroelectric power, erect dams for flood control, produce fertilizers, control erosion, and build a navigable waterway from the headwaters of the Tennessee River near Knoxville to its confluence with the Ohio River at Paducah, Kentucky. But the authority's scope envisioned much more than a vast program of public works. TVA sought to uplift the region's impoverished rural folk, improving nutrition, health care, recreational opportunities, and education. It also promoted conservation and attracted new industries to the American Southeast.

TVA was born in January 1933 when President-elect Franklin D. Roosevelt toured Muscle Shoals, Alabama, with Senator George Norris of Nebraska, the great old warhorse of progressive reform and campaigner for public power. During World War I, the federal government had constructed Wilson Dam on the Tennessee River to produce nitrates for munitions. The dam was not completed until after the Armistice, and private utilities, in league with the administrations of Calvin Coolidge and Herbert Hoover, repeatedly frustrated Norris's plans to generate public hydroelectric power. The sad disparity between the gleaming technical might of the unused dam and the dark, kerosene-lit poverty of the Tennessee River valley prompted Roosevelt to more dramatic action than Norris had ever imagined.

Two workers with the Tennessee Valley Authority operate jackhammers. The TVA, a program covering the entire Tennessee Valley and parts of Alabama and West Virginia, was established during the New Deal administration of President Franklin D. Roosevelt to control flooding and use dams to provide power. (Arthur Rothstein/Corbis)

Over the course of its first decade, the Tennessee Valley Authority dramatically altered its approach to regional development and social welfare. The early TVA hoped to restore a sound agricultural economy without manufacturing, unsightly urban growth, or fundamental change on the farms. Indeed, TVA officials generally interpreted the Great Depression as a warning against the dangers of industrialization. At the same time, they saw rural poverty as a land use problem rather than an economic one. Better agricultural practices and swifter access to markets lay at the core of TVA's early efforts.

This "Decentralization Program" achieved limited success. Operating in the nation's poorest region, the authority refused to challenge either local political prerogatives or traditional economic arrangements. The TVA constructed dams, harnessed hydroelectric power, and manufactured fertilizer, but it hardly affected the economic structure of the Southeast or succored its impoverished people.

In 1938, soon after President Roosevelt focused new attention on southern poverty, the Tennessee Valley Authority changed direction, taking the lead in the federal government's drive for southern industrialization. TVA's first chairman, Arthur E. Morgan, was ousted; Morgan's rival and successor was David E. Lilienthal. Under Lilienthal, the TVA abandoned the "phosphate philosophy" of economic growth—the idea that small, rural-oriented industries could strengthen the agricultural economy and raise living standards while preserving the area's rural character.

As the World War II defense buildup proceeded, TVA recruited large manufacturing plants to the region. TVA also promoted rural electrification and pressed for further industrialization of the valley region, especially the development of large-scale, finished-products industries. Among the TVA's wartime achievements was the development of new manufacturing processes for aluminum. The authority assembled a team of scientists for this project, and its success dramatized the economic benefits of industrial research. This stimulated the South's postwar love affair with scientific research, helping to develop the kind of technological community the region had never possessed. At the same time, it shifted the authority's priorities toward regional economic growth, often to the benefit of newly arrived businesses and skilled workers, and away from improving the welfare of the valley's poorest residents.

The record of economic progress in the Tennessee River Valley in the decade after 1938 seemed to confirm TVA's confidence in manufacturing-based growth. The authority could hardly claim the entire credit for the valley area's gains in nearly every economic indicator, gains that, after all, reflected the national economic revival. Nevertheless, the authority did point with pride to the valley's relative gains over the nation and the rest of the South, both in indices of manufacturing growth and in general economic progress. The early vision of a valley inhabited by small, decentralized rural industries had faded into the reality of an industrializing region. By 1946, most wage earners in the region toiled in cities of 10,000 or more people.

"If we are successful here," FDR (1933) had proclaimed, "we can march on, step by step, in a like development of other great natural territorial units within our borders." After Roosevelt's death, President Harry S Truman's administration envisioned TVA as the model for similar river valley authorities on the Missouri, the Columbia, and other American rivers. But these ambitious programs never won congressional approval on the size and scope imagined by their backers. In later years, Lilienthal and many other TVA veterans took their expansive vision overseas, joining multipurpose river-development projects in Asia, Africa, and Latin America. In 1964, in an effort to transpose the New Deal TVA vision to war-torn Vietnam, President Lyndon B. Johnson offered to establish a multibillion-dollar Mekong River Authority in Indochina if North Vietnam would desist from its efforts to reunite Vietnam under a communist regime.

By that time, TVA had become a shadow of its earlier self. When Dwight D. Eisenhower had assumed the presidency in 1953, his administration had reined in the TVA, limiting the scope of its social welfare, education, and economic development programs. It became mainly a power company and dam-building operation. The authority remained deeply committed to a New Deal model of conservation that stressed industrial development and found itself the enemy of a new environmentalist ethos. When TVA pressed for the construction of Tellico Dam on the Little Tennessee River during the 1970s, a massive public works project that threatened the habitat of an endangered fish called the snail darter, the agency's transformation was complete. The most far-reaching, experimental, and comprehensive effort to revive a laggard region and its impoverished people had become a symbol of pork-barrel politics and bureaucratic insensitivity.

Bruce J. Schulman

See also: Great Depression and New Deal; *Report on Economic Conditions of the South;* Rural Poverty

References and Further Reading

Grant, Nancy L. 1990. *TVA and Black Americans: Planning for the Status Quo*. Philadelphia: Temple University Press.

Lilienthal, David E. 1977. *TVA: Democracy on the March*. Westport, CT: Greenwood Press.

Norris, George W. 1972. *Fighting Liberal: The Autobiography of George W. Norris*. Lincoln: University of Nebraska Press.

Roosevelt, Franklin D. 1933. "Message to Congress Suggesting the Tennessee Valley Authority." April 10. http://www.fdrlibrary.marist.edu/odtvacon.html.

Schulman, Bruce J. 1991. *From Cotton Belt to Sunbelt: Federal Policy, Economic Development, and the Transformation of the South, 1938–1980*. New York: Oxford University Press.

Selznik, Philip. 1949. *TVA and the Grass Roots: A Study in the Sociology of Formal Organization*.

Berkeley and Los Angeles: University of California Press.

Think Tanks

See New Right; Poverty Research

Title VII

See Civil Rights Acts, 1964 and 1991

Townsend Movement

The Townsend movement, a popular mass movement of the Great Depression, was dedicated to the enactment of a national system of old-age pensions called the Townsend Plan. In the fall of 1933, unemployed physician Francis E. Townsend of Long Beach, California, proposed that the federal government should pay pensions of $150 a month (later raised to $200 a month) to all citizens over the age of sixty who agreed to retire and spend the money in thirty days; the pensions would be paid for by a national sales or "transaction" tax. He promised that his plan would bring full employment and universal prosperity, eliminating the need for the New Deal welfare and job programs, which he viewed as expensive, wasteful, and destructive to beneficiaries' self-esteem. In January 1934, Townsend and real estate developer Robert Clements launched Old Age Revolving Pensions, Ltd., with the goal of building support for his plan. By the end of 1935, the organization claimed more than 2 million members and had collected approximately 20 million signatures on petitions calling for the Townsend Plan's immediate enactment (Holtzman 1975, 49; Burg 1999, 103–104, 232).

Though dismissed by most economists and policymakers—including President Franklin D. Roosevelt—as unsound and potentially ruinous to the economy, the Townsend Plan found a large following among the aged. The onset of the Great Depression had intensified the financial insecurity of the nation's growing elderly population; the nation's elderly were living longer but often lacked work or savings sufficient to support themselves. The rash of bank failures and the scarcity of jobs also made it difficult for families to care for their needy older relatives. Townsend's promise of generous, immediate assistance proved appealing to financially insecure old people, their families, and those sympathetic to the plight of the impoverished elderly.

Townsend's plan challenged many of the basic assumptions underpinning early-twentieth-century old-age social welfare policy. For example, the notion that the government would undertake the financial support of its older citizens contradicted the widely held belief that families should care for their aging relatives. Likewise, the demand for federal pensions sought to nationalize a form of public relief that had traditionally been administered by state and local governments. Townsend also proposed that old-age assistance should be granted to all older citizens as an entitlement for a lifetime of service to the nation rather than as a form of stigmatized charity meted out to those deemed sufficiently poor and deserving. Perhaps most radical, Townsend desired $200 a month for all American citizens, regardless of their race, gender, place of residence, marital status, or work history. In short, Townsend repudiated the meager benefits, fragmentation, and inequities of the old-age relief of his day by demanding a national pension program that would provide generous, dignified, universal benefits to all older citizens.

Although the Townsend Plan bill introduced in January 1935 never had serious prospects of passage (it was defeated in the U.S. House of Representatives by a vote of 206 to 56), the size and fervor of the lobbying campaign launched on its behalf brought national attention to the Townsend Plan and posed an electoral threat to politicians across the North and West. The Townsend movement's rise also coincided with the introduction of the Roosevelt administration's Economic Security Bill (subsequently modified into the Social Security Act of 1935), providing a natural point of comparison for politicians debating the contours of the nation's first federal old-age social welfare system. Critics of the Economic Security Bill noted the Townsend Plan's superior coverage and benefits, and some conservative politicians even used their support of the Townsend Plan to camouflage their opposition to other welfare proposals. Supporters of the Economic Security Bill used comparison with the Townsend Plan to highlight the moderate nature and fiscal soundness of their bill and to suggest that its passage provided the best way to undercut support for the Townsend Plan. The powerful presence of older Americans demanding Townsend's vision of generous and dignified benefits thus influenced the atmosphere and terms of debate surrounding the creation of Social Security.

Though the passage of Social Security did little to diminish the enthusiasm of the Townsendites, support for the movement fell sharply in 1936 due in part to negative publicity generated by a congressional investigation that revealed the large profits earned by the movement's leaders and the unscrupulous methods used by some of its organizers. Francis Townsend's alliance with demagogic popular leaders such as the Reverend Gerald L. K. Smith and Father Charles Coughlin, along with his harsh criticism of FDR, caused further dissension within the movement. The recession of 1937–1938 helped revive interest in the Townsend Plan enough to make it a factor in the midterm election of 1938 and to win a second vote on the Townsend Plan in the House of Representatives in 1939 (it was defeated 302–97), but the onset of World War II led to its long-term decline. Wartime full employment, the prosperity of the postwar era, the death of aged members, and the increasing availability of old-age benefits diminished the organization's ranks to fewer than 32,000 members by 1952 (Holtzman 1975, 49). Nevertheless, Townsend maintained his reputation as a representative of older Americans, advocating for more generous old-age benefits until his death at ninety-three in 1960. New senior citizen organizations such as the American Association for Retired Persons (AARP) emerged in the subsequent decades, continuing the tradition of senior citizen political activism pioneered decades earlier by Townsend and the Townsend movement.

Steven B. Burg

See also: Ageism; Old Age; Social Security; Social Security Act of 1935

References and Further Reading

Bennett, David. 1969. *Demagogues in the Depression: American Radicals and the Union Party, 1932–1936*. New Brunswick, NJ: Rutgers University Press.

Brinkley, Alan. 1982. *Voices of Protest: Huey Long, Father Coughlin, and the Great Depression*. New York: Vintage Books.

Burg, Steven. 1999. "The Gray Crusade: The Townsend Movement, Old Age Politics, and the Development of Social Security." Ph.D. diss., University of Wisconsin, Madison.

Holtzman, Abraham. 1975. *The Townsend Movement: A Political Study*. New York: Octagon Books. Originally published New York: Bookman Associates, 1963.

Trade/Industrial Unions

The union movement has not merely pursued income gains for its membership but has also advanced a critique of workers' powerlessness on the job and of inequality in the labor market, politics, and the community. Beginning with the first Industrial Revolution in the early nineteenth century, workers have combined their voices and actions in organizations they hoped would counter the economic power and workplace control wielded by employers. By the mid-twentieth century, unions also had become important partners in the welfare state and proponents of social policies that promote economic security.

Although unions characteristically organized workers within capitalism, some of their claims generated a radical critique of the capitalist marketplace. In the lexicon of early-nineteenth-century male workers, workingmen sought a "competence," that is, a steady remunerative job that paid enough to support a family even during layoffs. Concentrations of economic power that interfered with this competence sometimes aroused opposition, in the name of democracy, to developing capitalism. Similarly, the labor movement's mid-nineteenth-century critique of "wage slavery" embodied not just a derogatory comparison between white and Black labor but also the promise that good wages would generate the conditions necessary for industrial freedom itself.

During the half century between the onset of antebellum industrialization and the rise of the craft unions that dominated the American Federation of Labor at the end of the nineteenth century, American labor organizations saw themselves as part of a broad social reform movement concerned with the abolition of slavery, the reduction of child labor, and the political empowerment of millions of immigrants into the urban, industrial polity. Printers, railroad engineers, machinists, shoemakers, iron workers, textile operatives, brewery workers, carpenters, and cigar makers developed locally powerful unions that sought to raise wages and regularize working conditions in their respective trades and occupations. But these unions were episodically functioning institutions that could not rely on their own power to sustain wages even of the best-paid male workers. Given the deflationary pressures and the drive for managerial control that pushed nominal wages down during the decades after the Civil War, many of these unions were forced into violent strikes designed to defend the working-class incomes in an entire community. This was the dynamic that transformed the railroad strikes of 1877 into a mid-Atlantic insurrection; likewise, in the 1892 lockout at the Homestead plant when Carnegie Steel abrogated a contract, the well-paid iron rollers of the Amalgamated Iron and Steel Workers Union won solid backing from the vast majority of more poorly paid workers.

Craft unions were the backbone of the union movement from the mid-1880s, when they founded the American Federation of Labor (AFL), to 1932. Craft unions were organized on the basis of worker skills and trades. The AFL also included a few industrial unions—in the needle trades and in coal mining—which organized everyone in an industry regardless of his or her particular job and irrespective of skill. Reflecting the bias of the crafts, the official policy of the AFL itself was that of "voluntarism," which rejected government minimum-wage and unemployment insurance programs (for male adults). The AFL held to this view into the 1930s, in part because the federation considered unions to be the wellspring of self-reliance and "manly independence," in part to avoid inviting interference by a hostile government, and in part to enhance the presumptive attractiveness of union wages and working conditions. This led to a radical division between the interests of a highly paid stratum of unionized workers and the bulk of the working population—usually more than 90 percent—who enjoyed few social protections or state-mandated income standards. Indeed, AFL craft union leaders, most from the British Isles or northern Europe, saw African Americans, the new immigrants from southern and eastern Europe, and those from Mexico and East Asia as a kind of lumpen proletariat unsuitable for trade union membership. Although socialist and syndicalist rivals to the dominant craft leadership of the AFL put forward a quite different vision, the union movement of the early twentieth century did little to link itself directly to a program that might have reduced poverty.

Even if the AFL set its interests apart from those of the majority of the male working class, it also participated in the patriarchal exclusion and protection of women workers. The "family-wage" ideal the AFL espoused in the Progressive Era assumed a male breadwinner. The federation viewed women workers as transients in the labor market and therefore unorganizable, and while it supported equal-pay legislation and protective labor legislation for women, it did so because these policies would prevent women workers from undercutting male wages. Despite the hostility of the AFL to the economic and organizational interests of women as workers, some women workers mobilized on their own and with the help of allies in the Women's Trade Union League and the Industrial Workers of the World.

The New Deal and its aftermath transformed the character of American trade unionism and the social program it advanced. In the twenty years after 1933, trade union membership soared more than fivefold, reaching about 35 percent of the wage-earning population by the mid-1950s. More important, many of these new workers were enrolled in huge new unions that effectively organized the key industries of mid-twentieth-century America: coal, steel, auto, longshoring, rubber, electrical products, and trucking. Although many companies in these industries had traditionally been high-wage employers, others were not: The organization of East Coast garment shops, California canneries, New England textile mills, and big-city department stores helped double the effective wage in these occupations. Likewise, the turn away from day and casual labor in maritime work, first on the West Coast and later in the East, eliminated the skid row districts in many port cities, eventually generating a cohort of extremely well-paid workers on sea and shore.

The new industrial unions successfully pursued three programs that materially reduced income instability and insecurity among the working population, many from those very racial and ethnic groups that had been disdained by the old AFL. First, unions like the United Auto Workers and the United Steelworkers negotiated seniority schemes that gave millions of ordinary workers a property right in their job, thus generating in the middle years of the twentieth century the dignity-enhancing "competence" first sought by the shoemakers and textile hands of the antebellum era. Second, these same industrial unions successfully negotiated pay increases that disproportionately benefited the lowest-paid stratum of the workforce, thereby flattening the wage hierarchy and generating the material conditions necessary for a mass consumer society. Nonunion firms like Kodak, IBM, and the large financial and insurance institutions followed the "patterns" established in heavy industry, if only to forestall unionization of their own employees. Real wages in the United States doubled between 1940 and 1970. Massive productivity enhancements proved to be responsible for some of this growth, but the relatively equitable distribution of this technological dividend is largely attributable to the existence of a powerful union movement.

One major change that followed the rise of industrial unions and the labor-friendly measures of the New Deal administration was the shift in overall union attitudes regarding government policies toward labor relations and social welfare. The unions of the New Deal era became forceful advocates of a rise in the social wage, through the labor contract for their members as well as through social policies that would benefit the unorganized. Government programs that lifted the real income of the entire working class lowered the incentive for corporate flight to low-wage regions and made collective bargaining seem like a sure path to routine and incremental progress in wages and working conditions. Postwar unions were, therefore, strong advocates of an increase in the minimum wage, of Social Security, and of the establishment of a system of national health insurance. During the 1960s, key progressives from the world of labor, including Walter Reuther, Michael Harrington, and Willard Wirtz, proved staunch advocates of President Lyndon B. Johnson's War on Poverty.

During the 1960s, some unions also began organizing among those poverty-wage sectors of the working class that had been largely excluded by New Deal–era labor laws and social policies and by many pre–New Deal unions. Union support for incorporating low-wage workers was not universal, because some unions, especially from the crafts, resisted job training and apprenticeship programs and regulations designed to open employment opportunities to men of color. But, led by the American Federation of State, County, and Municipal Employees (AFSCME), other unions played the key role in raising the pay of at least 3 million local government clerks, janitors, and sanitation workers, the last, most notably, in the famed 1968 Memphis strike that proved the occasion for the assassination of Martin Luther King Jr. Likewise, Hospital Workers Local 1199 conducted a vigorous set of strikes and organizing campaigns in New York and other East Coast cities, which helped transform the political economy of the health care sector, thus lifting it out of the world of philanthropic charity, for employees and patients alike. Finally, in California, Florida, New Jersey, and Texas, the unions sought to organize the migrant labor force in agriculture, for generations an icon of poverty-level work and degradation. This task proved largely ineffective in the East, but in California the United Farm Workers, led by the charismatic Cesar Chavez, won political and organizational support to make it possible for unionized agricultural workers to secure a wage and enjoy living conditions above the federal poverty line.

Despite a decline in union membership since the 1970s, unions have actually grown in the public and service sectors in which women are disproportionately employed. Whether in order to attract women members to union membership or in order to represent them, unions have made important contributions to legal and policy challenges to women's disproportionate poverty. This union role did not develop automatically; rather, it was the result of mobilizing by working-class feminists within unions—through the Coalition of Labor Union Women (CLUW), for example—who put problems of gender inequality at work and in the labor market on the union agenda. Since the mid-1970s, when CLUW was formed, public-sector and service-sector unions, such as AFSCME and the Service Employees International Union, have spearheaded efforts to make affordable child care available to more workers and to close the gender wage gap through comparable-worth policies.

Deindustrialization, global competition, and the growth of political and managerial hostility to organized labor slashed union membership rolls, economic leverage, and policy influence during the years after 1978. Poverty wages and sweatshop conditions reappeared in industries—such as meatpacking, the garment trades, urban janitorial service, and even commercial construction—that had once been thoroughly unionized. Pattern bargaining—whereby unions seek similar wage and benefit arrangements across an industry or sector—lost its pace-setting potency, thus generating a new wave of wage inequality between workers in the union sector and those outside it. In the 1950s, the weekly earnings of production workers in "miscellaneous manufacturing" stood at about two-thirds of those in the major automobile firms; by the end of the 1980s, those earnings had dropped to less than 50 percent. Likewise, the real value of the minimum wage and of unemployment insurance payments fell steadily after 1968 because the unions and their liberal allies lacked the political influence to sustain them.

Under these conditions, the trade unions can no longer rely upon collective bargaining mechanisms to advance the interest of their members or of their larger working-class constituency. By the early twenty-first century, many of the most dynamic labor organizations, including the Service Employees International Union and the Hotel Employees and Restaurant Employees Union (HERE), have generated political alliances and mobilizing strategies that put the unions at the center of a broad reform coalition that fights for living-wage legislation, universal health insurance, higher minimum wages, and the social regulation of transnational capital.

Nelson Lichtenstein

See also: Agricultural and Farm Labor Organizing; Fair Labor Standards Act (FLSA); Family Wage; Living-Wage Campaigns; Service and Domestic Workers; Sweatshop

References and Further Reading

Davis, Mike. 1986. *Prisoners of the American Dream: Politics and Economy in the History of the U.S. Working Class*. London: Verso.

Freeman, Joshua 2000. *Working-Class New York: Life and Labor since World War II*. New York: Free Press.

Kessler-Harris, Alice. 2003. *Out to Work: A History of Wage-Earning Women in the United States*. 20th anniversary ed. New York: Oxford University Press.

Lewis, Ronald. 1987. *Black Coal Miners in America: Race, Class, and Community Conflict, 1780–1980*. Lawrence: University Press of Kentucky.

Lichtenstein, Nelson. 2002. *State of the Union: A Century of American Labor*. Princeton: Princeton University Press.

Murolo, Priscilla, and A. B. Chitty. 2003. *From the Folks Who Brought You the Weekend: A Short, Illustrated History of Labor in the United States*. New York: New Press.

Transportation Policy

Since at least the turn of the twentieth century, transportation policy has strongly influenced how and where America's poor live, work, and play. In the first decades of that century, most large and medium-size cities boasted outstanding mass transportation systems. Privately owned but publicly regulated electric streetcar and steam railroad systems provided affordable service that allowed a wide range of urban residents to travel to sites of employment and recreation. However, beginning in the 1920s and throughout the country, mass transportation systems—on which the urban poor depended—began a long decline. Public policy at the local, state, and federal levels encouraged this decline in the decades to come, while simultaneously subsidizing the growth of private automobile use and road building. The results of these policy choices have had far-reaching consequences for America's poor.

The lack of adequate financial assistance, coupled with public regulations and taxes, contributed to the difficulties of private mass transit operators. Many lines went out of business, and in most cases where local governments took over aging mass transit systems, decades of decreasing service and increasing fares followed. Meanwhile, huge public subsidies were devoted to roads and cars. Public road building accelerated in the 1920s, but the federal Interstate Highway Act of 1956 proved most significant, both in the expansion of road building and in the accompanying decline of mass transit. Providing 90 percent federal funding for highways built by states, the 1956 legislation amounted to the largest public works program in American history and literally and figuratively placed in cement the nation's automobile-focused transportation policy.

The building of the federal interstate highway system during the following decades had vast and wide-ranging consequences for poor people in the United States. For some among the rural poor, the highways provided new opportunities and diminished the isolation of life away from fast-growing metropolitan areas. As the interstate system made the movement of goods by truck rather than by train increasingly efficient and inexpensive, numerous kinds of private employers took advantage of the new transportation system by locating enterprises near highways in rural areas, where labor, land, and tax costs were often lower. In addition to bringing work to once-remote areas, the interstate highways also stimulated the reverse process, allowing the rural poor to reach nearby large towns and cities more quickly and reliably and to take advantage of economic and social opportunities that were farther afield. At the same time, the reliance on the highway system as an avenue of opportunity put a premium on private car ownership, an asset sometimes beyond the reach of the rural poor.

The new highways affected the lives of poor and working-class people in metropolitan areas even more significantly. First, the construction of highways in urban areas required the demolition of large numbers of homes and businesses in roadway rights-of-way. According to one estimate, interstate highway building destroyed 330,000 urban housing units between 1957 and 1968, and the state and local officials choosing highway routes frequently selected paths that disproportionately harmed poor and minority neighborhoods (Mohl 1993). For example, in Florida, relatively poor, usually African American communities in Jacksonville, Miami, Orlando, Saint Petersburg, and Tampa all experienced serious disruption as the result of highway building. And in innumerable instances around the nation, new roads that skirted the edges of low-income neighborhoods created both daunting physical barriers separating the poor from their more affluent neighbors and harmful air- and noise-pollution health hazards.

The interstate highway system also played an important role in deconcentrating the economic life of metropolitan areas away from urban centers and toward suburban peripheries, encouraging plant relocation as well as the massive boom in suburban shopping malls and other commercial activities that drew business away from central cities. The growing suburbanization of industry and commerce affected poor and working-class urban dwellers profoundly, albeit less directly, by reducing their access to many available jobs. The inconvenient or nonexistent city-to-suburb public transportation options available in most metropolitan areas and the scarcity of low-income housing opportunities in most suburban areas combined to increase commute times and dependence on cars. Those among the urban poor who could not afford to buy, maintain, and insure a reliable automobile were effectively cut off from the rapidly growing suburban labor market. Residential segregation compounded the problem for people of color, who were barred by a powerful combination of racial covenants, discriminatory real estate and lending practices, and racist attitudes from moving to—and often from getting jobs in—growing suburban areas.

In addition to altering the physical and economic environment, the building of new highways contributed to a new political environment. Especially by the mid-1960s and later, community-based citizens' groups were beginning to mobilize in opposition to road builders' plans to condemn and clear land in low-income urban neighborhoods; such organizing in turn created a powerful venue for residents to express their anger with city development policies and decision-making processes. When fighting alone, poor communities still lost many more highway battles than they won. But when they were part of a larger coalition, some notable victories occurred. In metropolitan Boston, for example, groups representing the urban poor, working-class ethnic neighborhoods, suburban environmentalists, and large educational institutions combined in the early 1970s to convince state officials to cancel the remaining highways planned for the area and shift substantial state resources to public transportation instead. Furthermore, the many highway fights—along with other simultaneous conflicts such as those over urban renewal projects and over the control and use of federal antipoverty funds—contributed to the beginning of a new political era in many cities in which community participation increased significantly and the concerns of poor neighborhoods could not be as easily ignored.

Despite an altered political culture, however, the public transportation systems that the urban working classes relied on disproportionately continued to suffer in the 1970s, 1980s, and 1990s. Legislation passed by Congress, especially in the mid-1970s and early 1990s, provided small new financial boosts to these mass transit systems, but the overwhelming bias of public policy continues to favor the private automobile and the publicly subsidized roads on which it travels.

Peter Siskind

See also: Housing Policy; Racial Segregation; Rural Poverty; Urban Poverty; Urban Renewal

References and Further Reading

Jackson, Kenneth. 1985. *Crabgrass Frontier: The Suburbanization of the United States*. New York: Oxford University Press.

Mohl, Raymond A. 1993. "Race and Space in the Modern City: Interstate 95 and the Black Community in Miami." In *Urban Policy in Twentieth-Century America*, ed. Arnold R. Hirsch and Raymond A. Mohl, 100–158. New Brunswick, NJ: Rutgers University Press.

Rose, Mark H. 1990. *Interstate: Express Highway Politics, 1939–1989*. Knoxville: University of Tennessee Press.

Twenty Years at Hull-House, *Jane Addams*

In 1889, Jane Addams (1860–1935) and her colleague, Ellen Gates Starr, moved to Chicago to open a settlement house in the Nineteenth Ward, a neighborhood teeming with immigrants from over twenty different ethnic backgrounds. They opened the doors of Hull House in the fall with the intention of teaching literature and the arts to the people in the neighborhood. These classes in "high" culture were well attended from the outset, and Hull House grew in popularity and scope, eventually offering courses through the University of Chicago Extension and more practical classes such as English, American government, cooking, and sewing. Twenty years later, Jane Addams wrote a memoir of her experience as the director of the most renowned and influential settlement house in America: *Twenty Years at Hull-House* (1910). In it, she subtly offered a progressive social philosophy framing poverty and urban squalor as systemic social and economic problems and not merely the result of individual failure.

The dual educational program at Hull House served people who already had a basic education and aspired to higher learning and people, especially recent immigrants, who needed help to prepare for citizenship and to acquire basic skills to improve their employment opportunities. Addams's discussion of the cultural offerings at Hull House debunked the presumptions of elitists, who doubted that the "unwashed masses," especially those born abroad, could appreciate classes on Shakespeare or classical music. Her colorful anecdotes portrayed her neighbors as intellectually curious, insightful, and sensitive to the refinements of high art. Addams artfully admonished her readers to remember that poverty can by no means be a fair measure of a person's intellect or morality.

Though Addams betrayed an elitist preference for refined and educated people, she also told stories that often subverted these elitist prejudices. She often depicted her neighbors as having more wisdom than the teachers visiting Hull House and made snide remarks about priggish college professors who were unable to make their knowledge accessible and relevant. Addams rejected the paternalistic attitude characteristic of the many settlement houses that sought to "cure" the lower classes of their ignorance and crudeness. Addams believed that all citizens would benefit not only from the knowledge of high culture but also from the experience of material struggle. Of a decidedly democratic disposition, Addams argued that both upper and lower classes benefited from contact with one another. Avoiding the self-righteous polemic in favor of artful storytelling, she tried to convince her largely middle- and upper-class readership that they had just as much to learn from the poor and foreign-born as these people did from them.

Addams's observations of her neighbors taught her that even their most disturbing behavior was often a rational reaction to a destructive social environment. Eschewing moralizing of any kind, Addams ascribed social pathologies to an inadequate social and economic system, never to the inferior character of an individual or group. Her critique of the system notwithstanding, Addams never embraced a particular ideology and asserted that the complexity of each individual experience, and of social problems in general, precluded the application of a particular formula to bring about a solution. She favored the messiness of democracy and cooperative effort.

Addams continued her work as a reformer and advocate but gradually moved on from Hull House and toward efforts to promote democracy and peace internationally, for which she was awarded the Nobel Peace Prize in 1931.

Robert J. Lacey

See also: Hull House; *Hull-House Maps and Papers;* Maternalism; Maternalist Policy; Progressive Era and 1920s; Settlement Houses

References and Further Reading

Addams, Jane. 1999. *Twenty Years at Hull-House: With Autobiographical Notes*. Edited and with an introduction by Victoria Bissell Brown. Bedford Series in History and Culture. Boston: Bedford/St. Martin's Press.

Polacheck, Hilda Satt. 1989. *I Came a Stranger: The Story of a Hull-House Girl*. Urbana: University of Illinois Press.

"Underclass"

The term "underclass" is both a synonym for poverty and a term used to blame poor Americans for their poverty. It was originally coined by the Swedish economist Gunnar Myrdal (Myrdal 1963) to describe poor people whose jobs had disappeared and who were being driven out of the economy and to the very bottom of the class hierarchy. Journalists and social scientists later added the connotation of blame, using "underclass" as a term for poor people whom they painted as lazy, promiscuous, drug addicted, and criminal and as preferring welfare over work and single motherhood over marriage. Like another widely recognized blaming term, "the undeserving poor," "underclass" carries with it the implication that the poor are not deserving of help. Indeed, "underclass" is a particularly vicious term because it sounds technical and scientific even as it is used to blame people.

Blaming terms function as labels that cover the entire person, leaving no room for redeeming features. Blaming terms can be divided into two kinds: *popular* and *professional*. Widely used popular blaming terms of the past include "paupers," "ne'er do wells," "tramps," and "the dregs." Today's popular blaming terms include "bums" and "welfare queens." These are used in public, but in addition, there are, and always have been, a much larger number of private blaming terms. Most of them are so profane and hateful that they are never used in public or in print.

"Underclass" has always been strictly a professionals' term. A handful of politically liberal social scientists first began to use Myrdal's term in the late 1960s in order to call attention to the structural, principally economic, shifts underlying poverty as sizable numbers of urban factory and other blue-collar jobs disappeared. For the small number who used it this way, Myrdal's term had the attraction of capturing the extreme economic marginalization of a segment of the working class under the impact of industrial restructuring.

Before long, however, and especially during the ghetto disorders of the late 1970s, "underclass" came to be used as a blaming term to label a subgroup of supposedly alienated, culturally deviant inner-city residents. As such, it started to replace the "culture of poverty," the then-dominant professionals' blaming term. "Underclass" was also applied almost entirely to poor African Americans and Latinos, and as a result it became a racial code word.

No one knows who first redefined "underclass" from a synonym for the poverty-stricken to a term blaming the poor, or whether it was a journalist, social scientist, or someone else. In any case, the initial adopters of the blaming term were mainly politically conservative social scientists, social critics, and intellectuals. They pointed to what they saw as the failure or the unwillingness of the poor to act in accord with mainstream or middle-class values, a deficiency that social scientists call "deviant behavior" and that conservatives believe is a major cause of poverty. They ignored the research findings that most poor people shared mainstream American values but that many lacked the jobs, incomes, or economic security required to live in mainstream ways. They simply could not afford to be middle-class.

Journalists rarely used "underclass" in Myrdal's sense, using it, instead, almost entirely in the blaming sense and adopting it at about the same time as the social scientists did. The journalists' accusations of the poor resembled those employed by the social scientists, but this should not be surprising, for these accusations are hoary old stereotypes of the poor that were applied during the nineteenth century to poor German, Irish, Italian, Polish, and Jewish immigrants. Similar stereotypes have been traced back at least to the Middle Ages but are probably much older than that.

The journalists made the term "underclass" more publicly visible, especially during the mid-1980s when the arrival of inexpensive crack cocaine in the ghettos drove up rates of street crime, including murder, especially by drug buyers and sellers. Indeed, the number of poor people assigned to the underclass by the news and other media increased sufficiently to turn the underclass into a national problem, after which several government agencies and private foundations provided funds to undertake studies of "underclass behavior."

The visibility of the term seems also to have had an effect on its definition. Perhaps because of its attention-getting quality, writers began to employ it as an alternative term for the poor or to use it without defining it at all, leaving readers (and perhaps themselves) guessing whether they were describing or blaming the poor.

The popularity of "underclass" as a blaming term peaked in the late 1980s and early 1990s, when the country's economy was in trouble. As the economy improved, more poor people found jobs and had less reason to use crack, and fewer people and organizations found it necessary to blame the poor. Since the mid-1990s or thereabouts, both definitions of "underclass" have been employed in the news media, but so far in the twenty-first century, the term seems to be in decline. This may be related to the elimination of the federal welfare program in 1996, a change that forced large numbers of poor people into the minimum- (and subminimum-) wage jobs that were created during the economic boom of the 1990s. Even though many of the poor workers were earning less than they did while they were on welfare, they could no longer be accused of "dependency" or blamed for refusing to work.

The future of "underclass" is unpredictable. Maybe its popularity will increase again, especially in a recession, when many become even poorer than they already are. Then rates of homelessness, family breakdown, crime, and the like will go up again, and so will the demand for a blaming term. Eventually, however, a change of economic and political conditions or the invention of an attention-getting new word could relegate "underclass" to the pile of obsolete terms for the poor.

Herbert J. Gans

See also: African American Migration; Deserving/Undeserving Poor; Poverty Research; Puerto Rican Migration; Urban Poverty

References and Further Reading

Auletta, Ken. 1982. *The Underclass*. New York: Random House.

Gans, Herbert J. 1995. *The War against the Poor: The Underclass and Antipoverty Policy*. New York: Basic Books.

Katz, Michael M. 1989. *The Undeserving Poor: From the War on Poverty to the War on Welfare*. New York: Pantheon Books.

Myrdal, Gunnar. 1963. *Challenge to Affluence*. New York: Pantheon Books.

Undocumented Immigrants

See Day Labor; Domestic Work; Immigrants and Immigration; Immigration Policy; Informal Economy; Migrant Labor/Farm Labor; Sweatshop

The Unemployed Worker *and* Citizens without Work, *E. Wight Bakke*

The two-volume work *The Unemployed Worker* and *Citizens without Work* (1940) is a classic of Depression-era social science, based on path-breaking research by Yale University sociologist and later professor of economics E. Wight Bakke. Expanding upon survey methods he had developed in research on unemployed workers in early 1930s England, Bakke undertook a massive eight-year study in New Haven, Connecticut, of what was to remain the decade's overriding social concern: the impact of extended joblessness on individual workers as well as on the very fabric of economic and social life, as measured and observed in the unemployment and welfare offices, union halls, commercial enterprises, civic institutions, and—most poignantly—in the households of unemployed men. Although Bakke had no way of anticipating the unprecedented length or severity of the Great Depression when he started his research in the early 1930s, his approach was uniquely well suited to capturing the unfolding dramas, crises, and eventual "readjustments" made by workers and their families as they grappled with what he aptly dubbed in his subtitle, "the task of making a living without a job." Combining quantitative survey techniques with ethnography, participant observation, intensive case studies, and personal interviews—all conducted with a select sample of workers over the course of several years—he offered a carefully nuanced picture of unemployment as a life-altering experience for individual workers, whose very identities were wrapped up in work and earning, as well as for their families, surrounding neighborhoods, and communities.

Accompanying his subjects through the frustrations of futile job searches and unyielding employment offices, Bakke vividly portrayed the gradually escalating material and psychological effects of economic insecurity—often presented in the words of his subjects—while also tracing the strategies they devised to get by. Shattering the pernicious myth that these workers had grown lazy and dependent on "the dole," he took readers through the often painful and humiliating steps workers would take to stretch their resources and pick up extra income—such as borrowing from or relying on earnings from family members, including their wives and children—before turning to public assistance. He also offered powerful testimony to the impact on family and community life, showing, among other things, that families were devastated but more often than not resilient in adapting to the displacement of the traditional male breadwinner. In striking contrast to later commentators, who would treat this as the beginning of an inevitable descent into family "disorganization" and pathology, Bakke found that the best-adjusted families were those in which the husband had come to accept the greater economic autonomy and household authority of their income-generating wives.

The more fundamental message of Bakke's study, however, was that the days of individualistic economic "self-reliance"—if ever a reality—were long since gone, while the task of maintaining the conditions of economic opportunity and security was the joint responsibility of government, private-sector employers, and collectively organized workers. In the passage excerpted below, Bakke takes note of the emergence of working-class consciousness and its implications for the way Americans thought about traditional values and future social policy.

Alice O'Connor

See also: Family Wage; Great Depression and New Deal; Labor Markets; Poverty Research; Unemployment

References and Further Reading

Bakke, E. Wight. 1940a. *The Unemployed Worker: The Task of Making a Living without a Job*. New Haven: Yale University Press.

———. 1940b. *Citizens without Work: A Study of the Effects of Unemployment upon the Workers' Social Relations and Practices*. New Haven: Yale University Press.

The weight of evidence in the observations we have made in New Haven is that the solidification of a working class is well on the way. This fact has an important bearing on social and economic policy. It means that the satisfaction of human demands will be undertaken by the development of practices and institutions, which have a class character and that economic and political arrangements must take account of the fact of class stratification. Security will be increasingly sought through bargaining between groups. Working-class groups will continue the process perfected by other social groups to use government as a lever toward greater security. This increasing reliance on organization and government is no indication of the decay of self-reliance. It is a form of self-reliance that substitutes collective for individual skills. Class organization and class pressure become the developed means for escaping dependence and providing self-maintenance. The development here charted is not one from self-reliance to dependence, it is from individual to collective self-reliance.

Source: E. Wight Bakke, *Citizens without Work: A Study of the Effects of Unemployment upon the Workers' Social Relations and Practices* (New Haven: Yale University Press, 1940), 105.

Unemployment

The unemployment rate measures the fraction of people who want a job and cannot find one. Unemployment and poverty are related because earnings from work in the paid labor force are the main source of income for most working-age people and their dependents. Employment status also determines eligibility for such major social welfare protections as Social Security retirement and survivors' benefits. Whenever unemployment rises, household incomes fall and poverty rates increase, as does the overall level of economic insecurity.

Each month the Bureau of Labor Statistics (BLS), which is part of the U.S. Department of Labor, calculates the unemployment rate. The bureau arrives at this figure from telephone surveys of 60,000 households that it conducts during the third week of each month. These households are chosen to try to mirror the main characteristics of the entire U.S. population. The BLS asks questions of each household in order to find out who is working, who is not working but looking for work, and who is neither working nor looking for work. It uses the responses to these questions to compute monthly unemployment figures.

The labor force is defined as those who want jobs—the sum of those people working and those people without jobs who have been looking for work. The labor force is a subset of the entire population; it excludes all people who do not want a job. Some of these people have retired, some have decided to be a stay-at-home parent, some are in school, and some are too young to work.

The unemployment rate is the percentage of the labor force unable to find work. On the first Friday of each month, the BLS releases the results of its survey from the previous month. For the year 2002, the unemployment rate was 5.8 percent, the average of the twelve monthly unemployment rates for the year. This was an increase of 1.8 percentage points from 2000, the end of the 1990s economic boom (U.S. Department of Labor Bureau of Labor Statistics).

Many economists have criticized the way the official unemployment rate gets computed. For starters, it ignores discouraged workers, those people who want a job but who have not looked

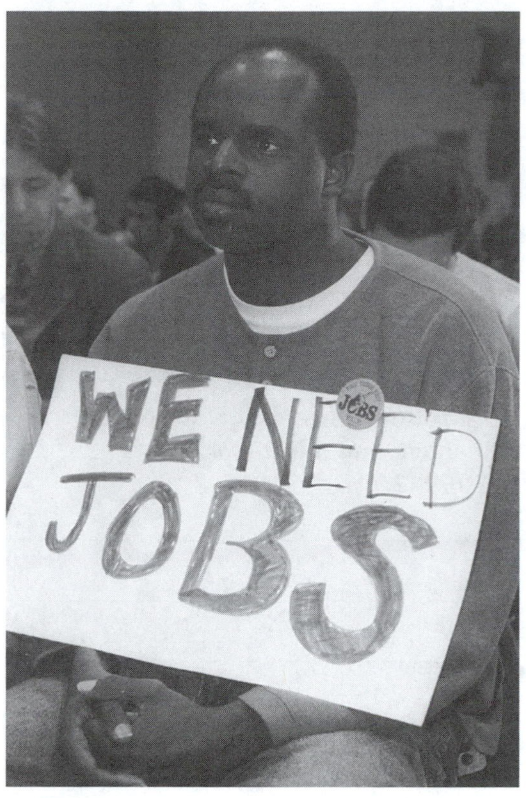

Unemployed workers want unemployment insurance, but mostly they want jobs. (Photographer: Rick Reinhard. Courtesy of National Employment Law Project: www.nelp.org)

for work because employers are not hiring. It also counts as fully employed someone who can only find a part-time job but would like a full-time job. And the survey has been criticized for not accurately reflecting the U.S. population. For example, households that are so poor that they do not own telephones or have homes cannot be surveyed by the BLS. Yet these two groups are much more likely to have unemployed adults, since the lack of jobs and income is a main reason for not having a phone and being homeless.

Despite these criticisms, most economists think that the published unemployment rate provides a good index of the U.S. unemployment problem. Although not perfect, it still provides a good measure of the extent to which the economy cannot create jobs for those who want to work. Moreover, since mismeasurement problems stay relatively the same over time, the unemployment rate provides an excellent measure of unemployment trends. When published figures go up, we can thus be pretty confident that the actual unemployment rate is rising, and vice versa.

Figure 1 presents a historical picture of U.S. unemployment from 1929 to 2001. Unemployment was at its highest levels during the Great Depression of the 1930s, averaging 20 to 25 percent of the labor force. World War II then brought unemployment rates down to under 2 percent. Unemployment rates remained at relatively low levels during the 1940s, the 1950s, and the 1960s. Several recessions in the 1970s, 1980s, and early 1990s pushed up the national unemployment rate. The prolonged economic expansion of the 1990s then reduced unemployment to 4 percent in 2000 from 7.5 percent in 1992. Then the recession of 2001, which was followed by a prolonged period of slow economic growth, pushed the unemployment rate up to 6 percent in the first half of 2003 (U.S. Department of Labor Bureau of Labor Statistics).

Figure 1

U.S. unemployment rates, 1929–2001

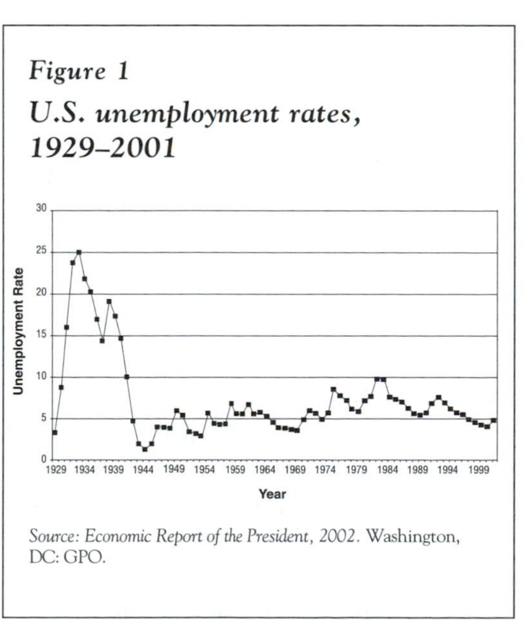

Source: Economic Report of the President, 2002. Washington, DC: GPO.

Figure 1 presents only average unemployment figures. But what is true on average is not true of all the parts of the whole. Some groups experience much higher rates of unemployment while other groups tend to have below-average unemployment rates.

As Figure 2 shows, racial minorities have significantly higher unemployment rates than do whites; they are a bit more than two times as likely as whites to be unemployed. For example, in 2001, the white unemployment rate was 4.2 percent, whereas for Blacks and other minorities the unemployment rate was 8.7 percent. Economists have several explanations for this phenomenon. Some attribute the difference to discrimination against minorities. Others attribute higher minority unemployment to lower levels of education, experience, and job skills.

Figure 2

U.S. unemployment rates for minority and white workers, 1959–2001

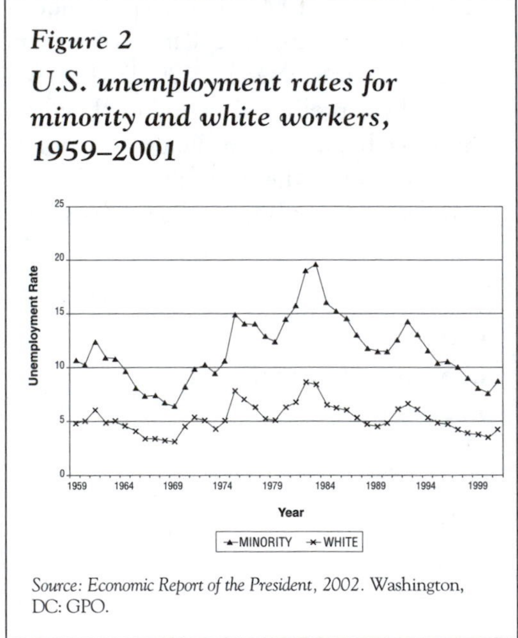

Source: Economic Report of the President, 2002. Washington, DC: GPO.

Teenagers are also more likely to be unemployed than are adults. In large part, this stems from their lack of steady employment experience and from the fact that younger workers tend to be last hired and first fired. Figure 3 compares the unemployment rates for workers twenty years old and over (both male and female) to the rates for teenagers (both male and female). Although the lines tend to rise and fall together, teens experience around three to four times the unemployment that adults do. For example, in 2001, teen unemployment was 14.7 percent while for everyone else the unemployment rate was 3.9 percent (U.S. Department of Labor 2000).

Figure 3

U.S. unemployment rates for teenage and adult workers, 1959–2001

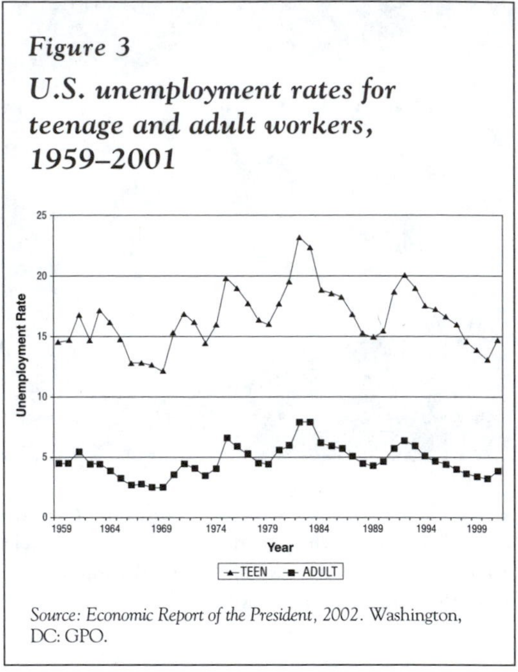

Source: Economic Report of the President, 2002. Washington, DC: GPO.

Combining the results for Blacks and for teenagers, Black teens are around eight times more likely to be unemployed than white adults. The actual figures from 2001 drive home this point: Unemployment was 3.7 percent for adult whites but a whopping 27.8 percent for Black teens.

The unemployment situation of women is somewhat more complicated. Until the early 1980s, the unemployment rate for women usually exceeded that of men by a small amount—close to 1 percentage point. Since then, the two have been close to equal, as Figure 4 shows; sometimes females have experienced slightly higher unemployment than males, and in other

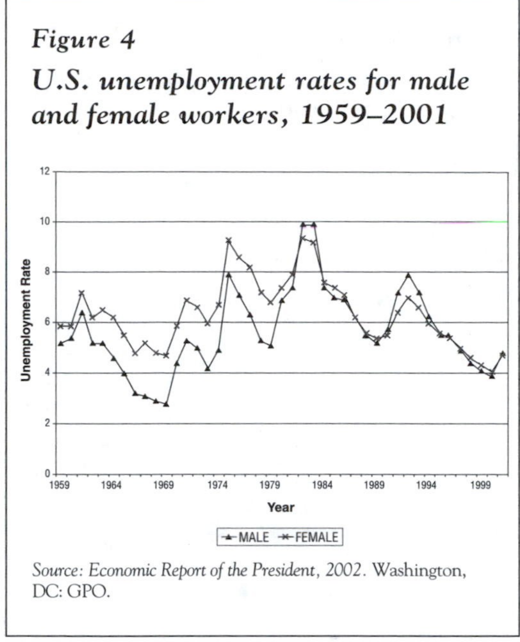

Figure 4
U.S. unemployment rates for male and female workers, 1959–2001

Source: Economic Report of the President, 2002. Washington, DC: GPO.

years female unemployment rates have been lower than male unemployment rates.

Unemployment would not be such a traumatic experience if unemployment lasted for a short period of time. If laid-off workers could quickly find another job, they would be able to return to their normal life with minimal disruption and minimal loss of income. However, when unemployment lasts for a long period of time, households are likely to run out of government benefits (such as unemployment insurance), use up any savings they had put away for the proverbial rainy day, and exhaust their ability to borrow money from friends and relatives. It is these long bouts of unemployment that spell disaster for individuals and households. Typically, whenever the overall unemployment rate rises, the duration of unemployment for individuals also rises. This makes rising unemployment a recipe for financial disaster, and it is one important reason why unemployment and poverty are related to one another.

But there are other reasons that higher unemployment rates lead to higher poverty rates. Excluding those people who are retired, the main source of income for virtually every household turns out to be the wages derived from work. At times of high unemployment, many individuals lose their jobs and their incomes entirely. Others lose their jobs and are forced to take part-time work. With less work comes less income. Because wage income is so important to household income, whenever unemployment rises there tends to be an increase in poverty. To be sure, employment does not guarantee incomes above the poverty line, as is demonstrated by the problem of millions of employed people who receive below-poverty wages. However, in the United States especially, without income from a job it is much harder for households to maintain a standard of living above the poverty line.

But the relationship between poverty and unemployment is just not a one-way street. Unemployment can lead to poverty, but poverty can also lead to unemployment. Poor households may not be able to afford the reliable transportation needed to take them to work every day, and so they can easily lose their job. Poor individuals are also unlikely to be able to afford the child care necessary to allow them to go off to work. Similarly, the poor may put off medical care and may not be able to eat well, leading to health problems that result in the loss of a job or the inability to hold down a job. If extreme poverty leads to homelessness, it can make it harder to find employment when job applications ask for a current address and phone number.

There are also long-term trends that need to be considered. Children are especially hurt when they grow up in poor families. Poor children do not perform well in school and have higher dropout rates. This is compounded by the fact that poorer communities are less likely to attract high-quality teachers and have less control over their schools. For these reasons, among others, poor children are more likely to grow up to be unemployed (and thus poor) adults (Sexton 1961).

Figure 5 looks at the relationship between the overall poverty rate in the United States and the overall unemployment rate in the United States. The figure makes it clear that these two measures are somewhat related. In the 1960s and the 1990s, both unemployment and poverty fell. And during the recessions of the early 1980s and early 1990s, both the unemployment and poverty rates rose.

But several factors keep poverty and unemployment rates from always moving together. First, government benefits like unemployment insurance and welfare provide income to people without jobs. Although welfare does not, in most instances, bring income above poverty levels, it does provide a temporary measure of protection that may be combined with other income sources. Second, poverty measures are derived from household incomes, whereas unemployment rates measure the experiences of individuals. Many people are members of households with more than one adult. When one adult loses a job, others may continue working and manage to keep household income above the poverty line. This factor has become increasingly important over time as more and more women have entered the labor force. Third, as we saw above, the overall unemployment rate can fall or be artificially low due to a rise in the number of discouraged workers who are no longer looking for work and are thus not meaured in the official statistics, but this does not necessarily mean that jobs and income are increasing. Finally, since the United States measures poverty in absolute terms, economic growth should reduce the U.S. poverty rate over time. In contrast, there is no long-term trend in the rate of unemployment, and no reason to expect unemployment rates to fall as living standards rise. We can see the effects of these forces in Figure 5. Unemployment rates climbed in the 1970s, but poverty rates remained relatively stable due to rising government benefits, more workers per household, and rising living standards on average.

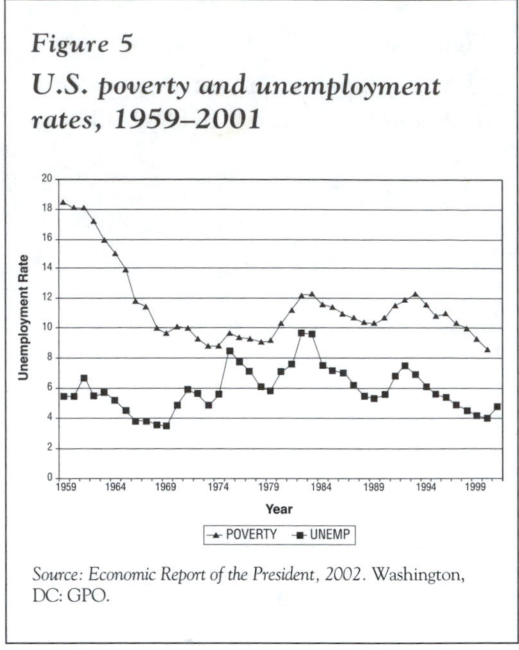

Figure 5

U.S. poverty and unemployment rates, 1959–2001

Source: Economic Report of the President, 2002. Washington, DC: GPO.

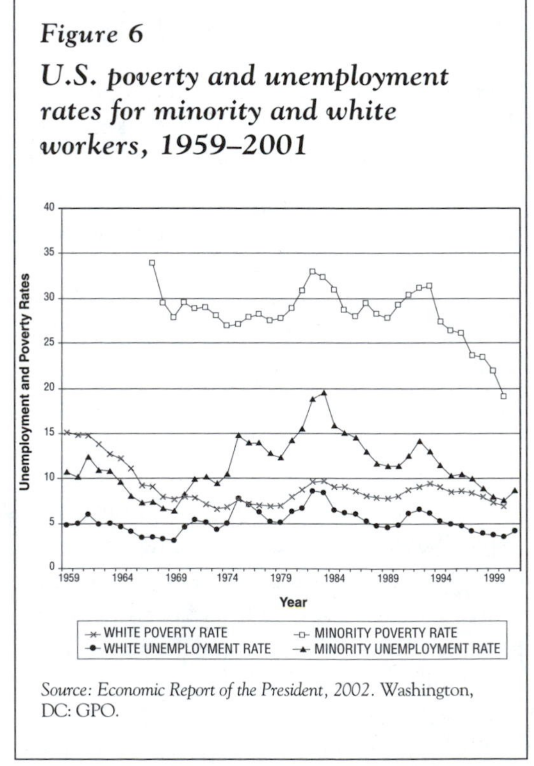

Figure 6

U.S. poverty and unemployment rates for minority and white workers, 1959–2001

Source: Economic Report of the President, 2002. Washington, DC: GPO.

Figure 7

U.S. poverty and unemployment rates for male workers, 1959–2001

Unemployment and Poverty Rates

Year

MALE UNEMPLOYMENT RATE — MALE POVERTY RATE

Source: Economic Report of the President, 2002. Washington, DC: GPO.

Figure 8

U.S. poverty and unemployment rates for female workers, 1959–2001

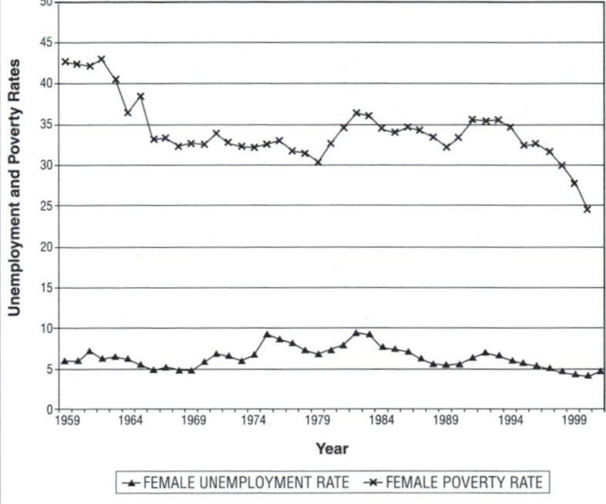

Source: Economic Report of the President, 2002. Washington, DC: GPO.

Figure 6 looks at the relationship between unemployment and poverty by race. The poverty figures here are for households headed by Blacks, since the U.S. Census Bureau has not calculated poverty rates for all minorities stretching back over long periods of time. Like the overall figures, the relationship between unemployment and poverty for both whites and minorities in Figure 6 is rather close, more so for minorities than for whites. This is partly because minorities are less likely than whites to have other sources of income that can be used during times of unemployment. As a result, job loss is more likely to result in poverty for minorities than for whites.

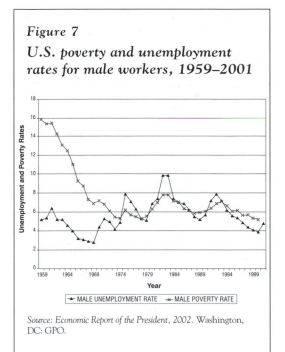

Finally, Figures 7 and 8 show the relationship between unemployment and poverty by gender. These relationships are noticeably weaker than the race relationships and the overall relationship between poverty and unemployment. For example, Figure 7 shows male unemployment rates rising sharply in the 1970s while poverty rates for households headed by a male fell. This occurs because all married couples are considered to be a household headed by a male. When one adult loses his or her job, other adults in the household can pick up the slack and keep the household out of poverty. This occurred with great frequency in the 1970s as women entered the labor force in large numbers.

Unfortunately, the Census Bureau does not collect information on poverty rates for households headed by teenagers. However, for some of the reasons discussed above, teen unemployment and poverty rates for households headed by teens will probably be closely related.

Steven Pressman

See also: Economic/Fiscal Policy; Employment Policy; Feminization of Poverty; Labor Markets; Poverty, Statistical Measure of; Social Security Act of 1935

References and Further Reading

Blank, Rebecca, and Alan Blinder. 1986. "Macroeconomics, Income Distribution, and Poverty." In *Fighting Poverty: What Works and What Doesn't*, ed. Sheldon Danziger and Daniel Weinberg, 180–208. Cambridge, MA: Harvard University Press.

Economic Report of the President, 2002. Washington, DC: GPO.
Sexton, Patricia. 1961. *Education and Income*. New York: Viking.
U.S. Department of Labor. 2000. "Report on the Youth Labor Force." http://www.bls.gov/opub/rylf/rylfhome.htm.
U.S. Department of Labor. Bureau of Labor Statistics. Web site. http://data.bls.gov/cgi-bin/surveymost.

Unemployment Insurance

Unemployment insurance, also referred to as unemployment compensation, is the chief governmental program of income support for unemployed individuals in the United States. Unemployment insurance is not means-tested; rather, it addresses poverty by providing income support as a matter of right to laid-off workers (O'Leary and Rubin 1997, 164–165). In recent nonrecession years, state unemployment insurance (UI) benefits and payroll taxes each annually amounted to $20 billion or more, with benefits considerably higher during economic downturns as a result of greater numbers of recipients and of benefit extensions (U.S. Department of Labor 2002a, 5).

The related goals of the UI program are to provide involuntarily unemployed workers with adequate, temporary income replacement and to automatically stabilize the economy by using accumulated trust funds to maintain consumer spending levels during an economic downturn. Secondary goals include supporting the job search of unemployed individuals by permitting them to find work that matches their prior experience and skills and enabling employers to retain experienced workers during layoffs (Advisory Council on Unemployment Compensation 1995, 27–30).

Unemployment insurance is a federal-state social insurance program. Established in the United States with the passage of the 1935 Social Security Act, federal law (now including the Federal Unemployment Tax Act) provides employer tax incentives and federal administrative funding to states with unemployment insurance laws conforming to the basic federal framework. In response to these federal incentives, all states have established and maintained state unemployment insurance laws since the passage of the federal enabling legislation (Blaustein 1993, 149–153, 158–159).

In order to achieve the UI program's goals, adequate weekly benefits must reach sufficient numbers of laid-off workers for a sufficient period. Otherwise, unemployed workers are unable to maintain sufficient consumer spending to support economic activity in their communities while they are looking for suitable jobs. On these counts, unemployment insurance programs in the United States are more limited than government assistance programs provided for unemployment in other developed nations (Storey and Neisner 1997, 615–625; Advisory Council on Unemployment Compensation 1995, 33–36).

Qualifications for regular unemployment insurance benefits are set almost entirely in state (and not federal) laws. Expressed in their most basic terms, eligibility rules require prior work history and willingness to work. Disqualification from benefits is imposed for separations from employment for reasons considered voluntary. The most common disqualification provisions are for leaving work without good cause, for discharges due to misconduct, and for refusals of work (Blaustein 1993, 278–283; Advisory Council on Unemployment Compensation 1995, 91, 101–123). Over the life of the program, state laws have become more restrictive in their treatment of workers separated from employment for reasons other than layoffs, especially those out of work due to quits and discharges (Blaustein 1993, 283–287).

State unemployment insurance laws also control the levels and duration of regular benefits. The basic duration of regular state benefits in the United States is twenty-six weeks. This generalization largely applies to laid-off workers with a substantial period of employment prior to their unemployment; part-year or part-time workers are not always eligible for the full number of benefit weeks. Only eight states (Connecticut, Hawaii, Illinois, Maryland, New Hampshire, New York, Vermont, and West Virginia) and Puerto Rico currently pay unemployment to all laid-off workers for a full twenty-six weeks; in other states, the maximum duration of benefits depends upon the particular formula employed in state laws. Massachusetts and Washington State currently have a maximum duration of up to thirty weeks of regular benefits (U.S. Department of Labor 2002b). During periods of higher unemployment, benefit extensions are typically provided for a specified number of weeks. In the past four recessions, Congress has adopted temporary, federally funded extension programs (Blaustein 1993, 228–241).

Weekly benefits generally come to around 35 percent of lost wages, on average, for unemployed workers (see Figure 1), with higher-wage workers having a lower rate of wage replacement because their benefits are capped at weekly maximums, which are set by state laws. These national averages mask considerable variability in unemployment benefits from state to state. In 2002, maximum weekly unemployment insurance benefits ranged from $210 in Alabama to $512–$768 in Massachusetts (depending on the number of dependents) (U.S. Department of Labor 2002b). Average weekly benefits in the United States in June 2002 were $258 (U.S. Department of Labor 2002c), a below-poverty level in many of the lower-benefit states.

Unemployment insurance is not paid to all unemployed workers. Some are separated for disqualifying reasons, some have insufficient earnings to qualify, and some do not apply. Although experts have debated the precise reasons, there has been a generally noted decline in receipt of unemployment insurance benefits in the United States since the 1950s, with a marked decline in the 1980s (see Figure 2). The reasons given for this decline in the proportion of unemployed individuals receiving unemployment

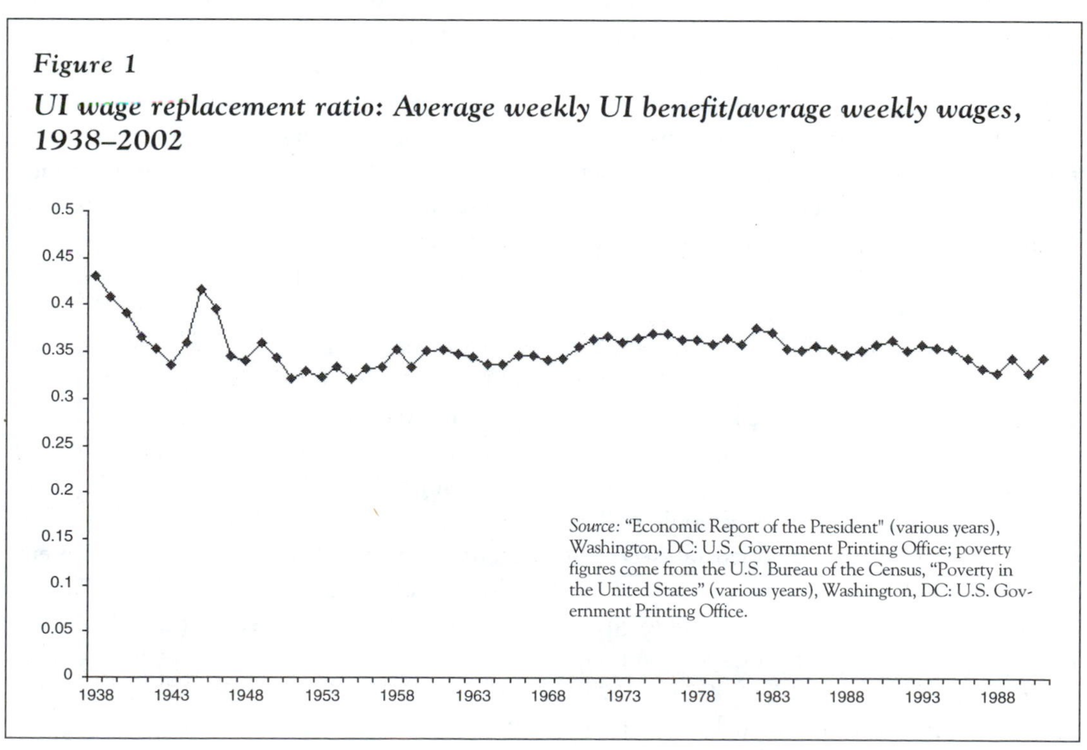

Figure 1

UI wage replacement ratio: Average weekly UI benefit/average weekly wages, 1938–2002

Source: "Economic Report of the President" (various years), Washington, DC: U.S. Government Printing Office; poverty figures come from the U.S. Bureau of the Census, "Poverty in the United States" (various years), Washington, DC: U.S. Government Printing Office.

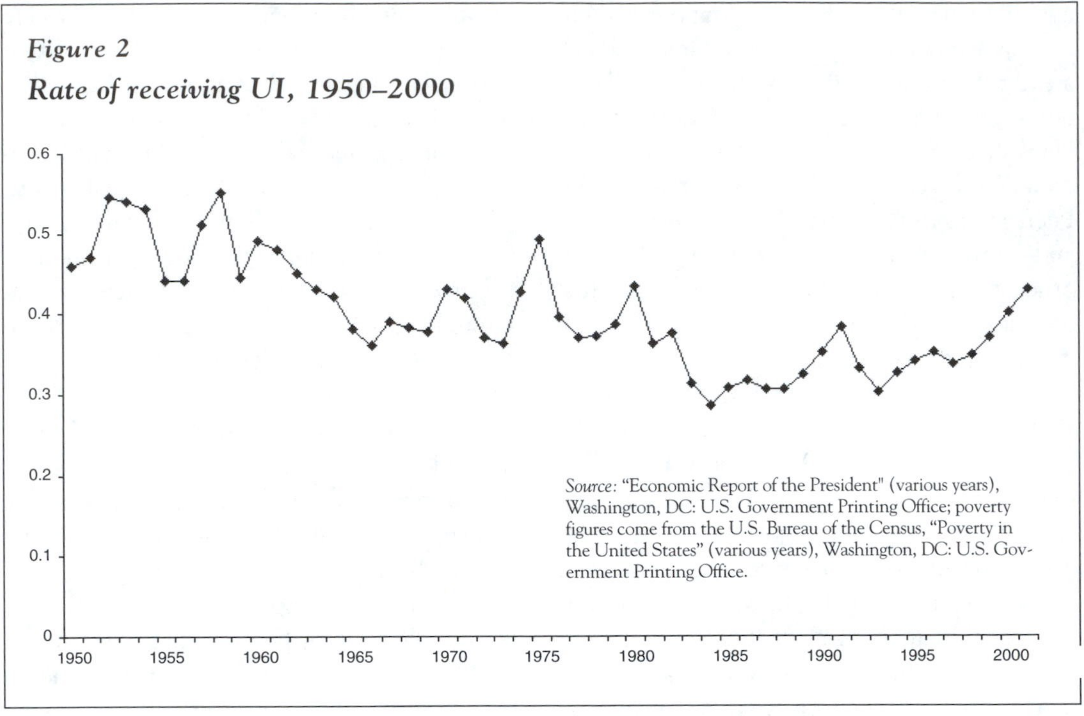

Figure 2
Rate of receiving UI, 1950–2000

Source: "Economic Report of the President" (various years), Washington, DC: U.S. Government Printing Office; poverty figures come from the U.S. Bureau of the Census, "Poverty in the United States" (various years), Washington, DC: U.S. Government Printing Office.

insurance include more restrictive state laws and penalties, changes in unionization rates and manufacturing employment, and shifts in the geographic location of unemployment (Advisory Council on Unemployment Compensation 1996, 44–49). In addition, the expansiveness or restrictiveness of the administrations in different states is probably a factor in the range of variation in benefit receipt (Vroman 2001, 102–103, 134–135).

Low-wage and contingent employees experience more unemployment, yet they receive unemployment insurance benefits at levels below their participation rates in the labor market. A recent study of mid-1990s data found that "low-wage workers were twice as likely to be out of work as higher-wage workers but only half as likely to receive UI benefits" (General Accounting Office 2000, 13).

The New Deal origins of unemployment insurance still affect current rules governing eligibility for and disqualification from benefits. To a significant degree, many unemployment insurance rules reflect the male-breadwinner model of households that was prevalent at the founding of the program. This model presumed a nonworking spouse available to perform child care and other domestic tasks. Current unemployment insurance rules adversely affect female workers disproportionately because they must leave work due to domestic responsibilities or limit their work search to conform to these responsibilities (McHugh and Koch 1994, 1422–1436).

Unemployment insurance is financed by both state and federal payroll taxes, which are imposed on employers falling within legal definitions of covered employment. Federal laws defining employment cover the employees of most private employers (Advisory Council on Unemployment Compensation 1995, 163). State unemployment insurance laws are free to cover employment that is not subject to federal taxation, and a number of states have broader definitions of covered employment (Blaustein 1993, 162).

Nonemployees, mainly independent contractors and self-employed individuals, are not covered by unemployment insurance programs. Another major exception in coverage is made for some agricultural laborers (Blaustein 1993, 278; Advisory Council on Unemployment Compensation 1995, 163–167, 169–171). There are also a number of specific occupational exclusions and inclusions in both federal and state laws (U.S. Department of Labor 2002d, tables 1.1–1.11).

Private employers pay a tax rate imposed upon these taxable wages that is partially established by valid claims filed by their former employees, a process known as "experience rating" (Advisory Council on Unemployment Compensation 1995, 73–89). State unemployment insurance payroll tax structures vary, but generally employers with little or no history of layoffs owe far less than employers with prior claims; in many states, employers with no history of layoffs pay no tax (U.S. Department of Labor 2002b).

Nonprofit and governmental employers generally reimburse state trust funds for any benefits paid to their employees and do not pay experience-rated unemployment insurance taxes (Advisory Council on Unemployment Compensation 1995, 163, 167–168). Nonprofit and governmental employers also do not pay the federal unemployment tax (Advisory Council on Unemployment Compensation 1995, 167).

An international comparison of programs reveals three distinctive features of U.S. unemployment insurance programs: First, unlike all other unemployment insurance programs in major developed nations, these programs in the United States are administered by the states rather than the national government (Storey and Neisner 1997, 603–604). As a result, competition between the states over employer tax and program benefit levels provides considerable restrictive pressures on unemployment insurance programs in the United States (Advisory Council on Unemployment Compensation 1996, 28–34). Second, in the United States, employers pay virtually all the costs of unemployment insurance programs, whereas in other countries, employees usually share a considerable, if not equal, portion of unemployment insurance financing (Storey and Neisner 1997, 604–609). This translates to considerable employer "ownership" of unemployment insurance programs in government deliberations about the cost and scope of the program. Third, state unemployment insurance taxes are set by experience rating in the United States, unlike programs in all other developed nations, which use flat taxes (Storey and Neisner 1997, 607). Some analysts feel that using experience rating to determine unemployment taxes heightens the concern of U.S. employers regarding unemployment insurance eligibility and benefit levels, because these factors have a direct impact on their payroll tax levels (Advisory Council on Unemployment Compensation 1996, 99–112).

Richard W. McHugh

See also: American Association for Labor Legislation; Economic/Fiscal Policy; Social Security Act of 1935; Unemployment

References and Further Reading

Advisory Council on Unemployment Compensation. 1995. *Unemployment Insurance in the United States: Benefits, Financing, Coverage*. Washington, DC: U.S. Department of Labor.

———. 1996. *Defining Federal and State Roles in Unemployment Insurance*. Washington, DC: U.S. Department of Labor.

Blaustein, Saul J. 1993. *Unemployment Insurance in the United States: The First Half Century*. Kalamazoo, MI: Upjohn Institute.

General Accounting Office. 2000. *Unemployment Insurance: Role as Safety Net for Low-Wage Workers Is Limited*. Washington, DC.

McHugh, Richard W., and Ingrid Koch. 1994. "Unemployment Insurance: Responding to the Expanding Role of Women in the Work Force." *Clearinghouse Review* 27: 1422.

O'Leary, Christopher J., and Murray A. Rubin. 1997. "Adequacy of the Weekly Benefit Amount." In *Unemployment Insurance in the United States: Analysis of Policy Issues*, by Christopher J. O'Leary and Stephen A. Wandner. Kalamazoo, MI: Upjohn Institute.

Storey, James R., and Jennifer A. Neisner. 1997. "Unemployment Compensation in the Group of Seven Nations: An International Comparison." In *Unemployment Insurance in the United States: Analysis of Policy Issues*, by Christopher J. O'Leary and Stephen A. Wandner. Kalamazoo, MI: Upjohn Institute.

U.S. Department of Labor. 2002a. *UI Outlook: President's Budget*. Washington, DC: Employment and Training Administration, Office of Workforce Security, Division of Actuarial Services. http://workforcesecurity.doleta.gov/unemploy.

———. 2002b. *Significant Provisions of State Unemployment Laws*. Washington, DC: Employment and Training Administration, Office of Workforce Security.

———. 2002c. *Summary Data for State Programs, by State, Report Period between 06/01/02 and 06/30/02*. Washington, DC: Employment and Training Administration, Office of Workforce Security. http://workforcesecurity.doleta.gov/unemploy.

———. 2002d. *Comparison of State UI Laws*. Washington, DC: Employment and Training Administration, Office of Workforce Security.

Vroman, Wayne. 2001. *Low Benefit Recipiency in State Unemployment Insurance Programs*. Washington, DC: Employment and Training Administration, Office of Workforce Security.

Unions

See Agricultural and Farm Labor Organizing; Fair Labor Standards Act (FLSA); Service and Domestic Workers; Trade/Industrial Unions; Wagner Act

Urban Poverty

Urban poverty refers to poverty in cities, which is distinguished from rural or suburban poverty by its concentration, its conspicuousness, its causes, and its racial and ethnic composition. Most poor people in the United States do not live in central cities, but a disproportionately high percentage of central-city residents are poor. In 2001, the Census Bureau counted approximately 32.9 million poor people in the United States, of whom some 13.4 million (or 40.7 percent of all poor people) lived in central cities, compared to about 12.1 million (36.8 percent of the poor) in suburbs and 7.5 million (22.8 percent) in rural areas (percentages and populations do not add precisely because of rounding). However, while 11.7 percent of all Americans were poor in 2001, 16.5 percent of people living in central cities were poor, compared to 8.2 percent of people in suburbs and 14.2 percent of people in nonmetropolitan areas (Proctor and Dalaker 2002, 8–9). Over the course of American history, urban poverty has probably attracted a disproportionate share of commentary as well, for a variety of reasons. Urban poverty carries with it distinctive problems, such as dense living conditions, poor sanitation, and the diseases that can result. Furthermore, because the rich and poor live relatively close to one another in cities, the difficulties of the urban poor are especially evident to those who are better off. This fact has helped make cities the birthplaces of many important innovations in poor relief, ranging from poorhouses to settlement houses. It has also made cities the setting for a whole host of social investigations into the nature and sources of poverty—investigations often distorted by sensationalistic images of the poor. In attempting to explain the inequalities of urban life, many observers have divided the poor into categories of "deserving" and "undeserving." These categorizations have often drawn upon and contributed to racial and ethnic stereotypes, reflecting the large number of immigrants and, since the early twentieth century, of African Americans among the urban poor. Yet the attempt to distinguish the worthy from the unworthy poor has never corresponded to reality: Urban poverty has historically been the result of structural and economic conditions rather than of individual or behavioral characteristics.

In the eighteenth century, cities in British North America generally enjoyed lower rates of poverty than those of England. Nonetheless, economic inequality and poverty were important problems in American cities from colonial days: In Philadelphia in 1772, one in four mariners, laborers, sawyers, and carters received poor relief (Smith 1990, 174). In many ways, preindustrial urban poverty established patterns that would be followed for decades or even centuries. Urban working people faced frequent unemployment caused by cyclical or seasonal economic downturns, epidemic disease, injuries, and political turmoil.

The practice of public poor relief in eighteenth-century cities derived largely from British precedent, which emphasized kin responsibility for the poor where possible and public responsibility for the local poor in other cases (under "settlement laws," nonlocal poor were not supposed to be aided; rather, they were to be sent back to their place of legal residence). City governments offered both outdoor relief, in which poor people were aided in their own homes, and indoor relief, in which the destitute were placed in an institution such as a poorhouse. Several cities built workhouses during the colonial period as a way of recouping some of the costs of aiding the poor and discouraging the able-bodied poor from seeking relief. Despite such early attempts to distinguish the deserving from the undeserving poor, some historians have seen this as a period when prevailing attitudes toward the poor were relatively benign: Poverty was viewed as an integral part of God's plan for humanity.

In the postcolonial period and the early nineteenth century, structural changes in the industrializing economies of cities such as New York and Philadelphia took a toll on working-class urban residents. Jobs formerly performed by a single worker were subdivided into individual tasks in new factories and large workshops. The result was the de-skilling of much artisanal work, the rise of sweated—that is, sweatshop—labor, and a growing class of men who were dependent on wages and vulnerable to economic contractions.

For those excluded from or segregated within the industrial labor market, conditions were even worse. For poor urban women, industrialization meant the decline of household production and the need to earn money in a labor market sharply segregated by sex. Among African Americans, a few prospered, but the majority were kept out of industrial jobs and forced into menial labor. The arrival of impoverished immigrants, particularly the Irish fleeing the Great Potato Famine of the 1840s, augmented the ranks of the urban poor.

Both indoor and outdoor aid underwent a transformation during the first half of the nineteenth century. Poor relief became less accepting of poverty as a facet of divine providence and more condemning of the poor as lazy and intemperate. Private antipoverty associations such as the New York Association for the Improvement of the Condition of the Poor (established in 1843) sought to correct what reformers saw as the degenerate domestic habits of the poor. Poorhouses reached a peak of popularity among reformers during this period, and although more people received outdoor assistance than indoor, the asylum was an important symbolic statement of the aim to reform the poor through isolation and regimentation.

The late nineteenth and early twentieth centuries were a peak period for urbanization and industrialization in the United States, as well as a high point in immigration to American cities. Millions of poor immigrants from southern and eastern Europe arrived during this period, and most settled in cities, typically in neighborhoods characterized by poor paving and sanitation, overpriced housing, and high population densities. These new arrivals faced harsh conditions at work as well, including long hours, frequent unemployment, and wages that failed to keep pace with the rising cost of living. To make ends meet, many men "tramped," traveling in search of work, and many families moved, took in boarders, cut back on consumption, went into debt to local grocers or landlords, got help from kin or friends, or sent additional wage earners (most commonly children) into the workforce.

As a last resort, many turned to relief, but this became increasingly difficult as advocates of "organized charity" in the 1870s and 1880s attacked public outdoor relief for "demoralizing" the poor and for being too costly. By sending well-off native-born women as "friendly visitors" to monitor the condition of relief applicants, the charity organizers hoped to eliminate fraud and redundancy in charitable giving and to aid only the truly deserving, while "uplifting" the poor and introducing immigrants to American ways. In several cities, including Philadelphia and Brooklyn, the charity organizers succeeded in eliminating public outdoor relief altogether in the 1870s.

The depression of 1893, the worst the nation had yet seen, revealed to many the shortcomings of the charity organizers' individualistic and moralistic approach to poverty. The economic shock provided fertile ground for a growing movement of "progressive" reformers who stressed poverty's environmental and societal causes. Simultaneously, new understandings of child development helped create support for tenement reform, child labor and compulsory-education legislation, juvenile courts, and other reforms aimed at improving the lives of the urban poor through "child-saving." Settlement houses, such as Jane Addams's Hull House in Chicago, provided an important base for middle-class reformers, particularly young, college-educated women, who aimed to help the poor through the emerging professions of social science and social work.

The era around the turn of the twentieth century was a time of tremendous physical growth and restructuring for cities. Although poor and working-class European immigrants continued to cluster in "ghettos," electric trolleys and automobiles allowed wealthier members of ethnic communities as well as native-born urbanites to live in new "streetcar suburbs" in less densely settled areas of the industrial metropolis. The major exception to this pattern was African Americans, who left the rural South for the urban North by the hundreds of thousands during and after World War I and found themselves tightly segregated in both housing and labor markets.

The Great Depression of the 1930s transformed both the experience of and the response to poverty in American cities. By the summer of 1933, unemployment in the United States had reached 24.9 percent, but in many cities the problem was even more severe: In Toledo, Ohio, unemployment reached 80 percent (Katz 1996, 207). Private charities, ethnic mutual insurance societies, and municipal welfare systems were overwhelmed by the increase in demand for relief.

President Franklin D. Roosevelt's New Deal provided relief and work to millions of impoverished city dwellers. The Works Progress Administration employed more than 3 million people within a year of its 1935 creation, many of them building roads, public buildings, and other infrastructure improvements in the cities where they lived (Katz 1996, 236). For workers in the private sector, the Wagner Act (1935) provided an important tool for organizing and bargaining with employers. The resulting union contracts protected many workers from the frequent encounters with poverty that had for more than a century been virtually inseparable from wage labor.

In the decades following World War II, cities underwent tremendous demographic, economic, and spatial transformations that profoundly shaped the character and scope of urban poverty. Demographically, the Great Migration of African Americans that had begun in World War I picked up again with considerable force during and after World War II. Between 1940 and 1970, 5 million Blacks left the South for northern and western cities (Katz 2001, 39). At the same time, an even greater number of whites, encouraged by federally subsidized loans and by highways constructed with federal funds, left central cities in a comparable "great migration" to the suburbs. The net effect was to deplete the populations of northern and midwestern cities and to transform their racial composition: Between 1950 and 1970, Philadelphia changed from 18 to 34 percent Black, and Detroit from 16 to 44 percent Black (Massey and Denton 1993, 45). During the same years, nearly 40 percent of the population of Puerto Rico left for cities on the U.S. mainland, principally New York (Davis 2001, 124).

As Black and Puerto Rican migrants were arriving in search of opportunity, however, many of the high-paying industrial jobs they sought were moving elsewhere. Enticed by federal tax and procurement policies, the interstate highway system, more advantageous state labor laws, and cheap land, corporations moved jobs from northern central cities to the suburbs, to the Sun Belt, and overseas. Between 1967 and 1987, Philadelphia lost 64 percent of its manufacturing jobs, and Chicago lost 60 percent (Wilson 1997, 29). Some of the lost manufacturing jobs were replaced by service-sector work, but unskilled service jobs tended to be less unionized, less stable, and less well paid than industrial work. Thus, low-wage workers saw their real incomes drop in the late twentieth century. A large class of working poor people emerged in cities throughout the country, alongside even larger numbers of the unemployed (those looking for work) and the jobless (discouraged workers no longer looking). And while both housing and employment opportunities moved increasingly to the suburbs, African Americans remained largely in central cities, confined by a housing market segregated by race.

Martin Luther King Jr. and others within the African American civil rights movement insisted that the nation address the segregation and poverty that affected Blacks in the urban North. Partly in response to these demands, President Lyndon B. Johnson instituted a War on Poverty that included a variety of measures for relieving conditions in American cities. The Community Action Program, created in 1964, and the Model Cities program, rolled out in 1966, required that poor people themselves participate in administering the federal funds. Though innovative, these programs received relatively little funding and frequently met with opposition from local politicians. These programs proved to be ineffectual in averting the riots that killed scores of people and damaged hundreds of millions of dollars' worth of property in Black ghettos throughout the country in the summers of 1964 through 1968.

The industrial decline at the root of the unemployment in Black ghettos also undermined municipal tax bases, putting pressure on city services, particularly in the wake of New York City's brush with bankruptcy in 1975. In the 1980s, the ascendance of right-wing politics in statehouses and in Washington, D.C., led to cuts in aid to cities already suffering from fiscal austerity and facing new problems, such as AIDS, crack cocaine addiction, and a sharp rise in homelessness. These years also saw cuts in a variety of federal social welfare programs serving millions of urban residents. Food stamps, school lunches, Medicaid, and Aid to Families with Dependent Children (or "welfare") were all cut back during the Republican presidency of Ronald Reagan. It was Democrat Bill Clinton, however, who signed the Personal Responsibility and Work Opportunity Reconciliation Act in 1996 and thus ended the entitlement to welfare and forced many city dwellers off relief rolls and into poverty-wage jobs.

As the twenty-first century began, race remained a crucial component of urban poverty. African Americans, particularly in large cities, remained highly segregated residentially and at much greater risk than whites for unemployment and poverty. In 2000, some 7.9 million people, most of them Black and urban, lived in census tracts in which more than 40 percent of the residents were poor (Jargowsky 2003, 4). These neighborhoods often also suffered from crime, drug use, and low educational attainment.

At the same time, the problem of urban poverty cannot be reduced to a stereotypical portrayal of a Black "underclass" living in an inner-city ghetto. Urban poverty is not simply Black and white: Since immigration laws were reformed in 1965, many poor immigrants, particularly from Mexico, the Caribbean, and Southeast Asia, have swelled the ranks of the urban poor in cities across the country. Nor is poverty defined simply by race and ethnicity. Women remain at higher risk for poverty than men, and age is also a major factor. Now, however, it is not the old but the young who are at greatest risk: In 1995, 36 percent of inner-city children under age six were poor, compared to 16 percent of young children in suburbs (Katz 2001, 39).

Michael B. Kahan

See also: African American Migration; Charity Organization Societies; Deserving/Undeserving Poor; Economic Depression; Globalization and Deindustrialization; Homelessness; Immigrants and Immigration; Industrialization; Puerto Rican Migration; Racial Segregation; Settlement Houses; "Underclass"; Urban Renewal; U.S. Department of Housing and Urban Development

References and Further Reading

Davis, Mike. 2001. *Magical Urbanism: Latinos Reinvent the U.S. City*. Rev. ed. New York: Verso.

Jargowsky, Paul A. 2003. *Stunning Progress, Hidden Problems: The Dramatic Decline of Concentrated Poverty in the 1990s*. Washington, DC: Brookings Institution.

Katz, Michael B. 1996. *In the Shadow of the Poorhouse: A Social History of Welfare in America*. Tenth anniversary ed. New York: Basic Books.

———. 2001. *The Price of Citizenship: Redefining the American Welfare State*. New York: Henry Holt.

Massey, Douglas S., and Nancy A. Denton. 1993. *American Apartheid: Segregation and the Making of the Underclass*. Cambridge, MA: Harvard University Press.

Newman, Katherine. 1999. *No Shame in My Game: The Working Poor in the Inner City*. New York: Knopf and Russell Sage Foundation.

Proctor, Bernadette, and Joseph Dalaker. 2002. *Poverty in the United States: 2001*. U.S. Census Bureau. Washington, DC: GPO.

Smith, Billy G. 1990. *The "Lower Sort": Philadelphia's Laboring People, 1750–1800*. Ithaca, NY: Cornell University Press.

Wilson, William Julius. 1997. *When Work Disappears: The World of the New Urban Poor*. New York: Vintage Books. Originally published New York: Knopf, 1996.

Urban Renewal

The term "urban renewal" is sometimes used generically to refer to any public or private effort to redevelop an urban area, and at other times it refers to a specific federal program that existed from 1949 until 1974. This entry will address both the specific program of that name and some of its successor programs that have pursued similar goals.

The federal urban renewal program was proposed after World War II as a response to the rapid decline in industrial, commercial, and residential activity that was overtaking most American cities. Local civic leaders desperately wanted federal assistance so that they could respond to this decline with various redevelopment initiatives. A temporary coalition between business interests and supporters of housing for the poor led to the passage of the Housing Act of 1949, which created the urban renewal program and authorized substantial funding for new public housing units to replace those demolished by earlier urban renewal projects.

Under the urban renewal program, cities were provided federal funds, with which they were to acquire land in "blighted" areas of the city, demolish buildings, relocate residents, and redevelop the land for new uses. Cities had to provide one-third of the cost, which was usually met through local public works projects. States also had to pass laws enabling localities to utilize the power of eminent domain to acquire "blighted" properties.

New York City: Urban renewal in Harlem. 1930s photograph. (Bettmann/Corbis)

The housing goals of urban renewal were soon subordinated to the redevelopment goals for two principal reasons. First, public housing was unpopular both in Congress and at the local level, so many fewer units were funded than were authorized in 1949, and those that were developed often faced stiff local opposition. Second, local officials placed their highest priority on revamping their central business districts with new private and public developments, and they often wanted to move low-income people away from the downtown area rather than to improve their neighborhood living conditions.

Therefore, over the life of the urban renewal program, many more low-income households were displaced than were provided replacement public housing. In addition, until 1970, relocation benefits were grossly inadequate, so poor households had difficulty obtaining housing in the private sector. Displacement also resulted in the destruction of neighborhood ties and traditions that had sustained low-income families. Particularly hard-hit were African Americans, whose neighborhoods were disproportionately bulldozed and whose relocation opportunities were limited by racial discrimination. The extremely high concentration of African Americans in public housing was, in part, the result of urban renewal.

Urban renewal was also criticized for failing to achieve downtown redevelopment goals. Many massive projects were isolated from their surroundings and resulted in a loss of human scale within downtown areas. Yet even if projects had been better designed, they probably would have failed to counter the strong economic and social pressures driving the exodus of retail and commercial activity to the suburbs.

In response to a growing chorus of protest, the goals of the urban renewal program were substantially modified by the Housing Act of 1968. It was more strictly targeted to residential renewal, replacement housing requirements were tightened, and localities were encouraged to use rehabilitation, rather than clearance, where possible. Also reducing the negative impact of the program was the passage of the Uniform Relocation Act of 1970, which substantially increased relocation benefits for those displaced by this and other federal programs.

However, by the early 1970s, the program remained sufficiently unpopular that it became one of the targets of President Richard Nixon's efforts to redesign and reduce the federal commitment to revitalizing cities. With the passage of the Housing and Community Development Act of 1974, it and several other programs were combined into the Community Development Block Grant (CDBG). The CDBG program uses a formula, rather than a lengthy application process, to distribute funds, and it gives local officials wide discretion in how to spend its funds. Whereas urban renewal was criticized for obliterating low-income neighborhoods, CDBG has often been accused of ignoring them in favor of other local projects and of spreading funds to communities that have less pressing needs. However, the bulk of CDBG funds are targeted at lower-income areas and are primarily used for housing rehabilitation rather than clearance. The Housing Act of 1990 supplemented CDBG with another housing block grant, the Home Investments Partnership (HOME) program.

Another successor to the urban renewal program was the Urban Development Action Grant program, created during President Jimmy Carter's administration in 1978. This program was targeted at central-city economic redevelopment, and it required substantial leveraging of federal funds with private investment. It never reached the scale of the earlier program, and it was often criticized for unfairly subsidizing some businesses at the expense of others. President Ronald Reagan's administration persuaded Congress to abolish this program in 1988.

Currently, most redevelopment of downtown areas is carried out with private funds, augmented by state and local government support through such mechanisms as development bonds and tax increment financing (TIF) districts. Some federal CDBG funds are also used for this purpose. (When local elites consider attracting a particularly desirable industry or when they are especially committed to a large project, such as a sports stadium, state and local subsidies can become quite large.) Private developers, such as James Rouse, developed creatively designed retail centers that successfully lured downtown workers in to eat and shop, capitalizing on the fact that throughout the postwar central-city decline, the central business district had retained its function as an administrative center. These centers were also supported by a growing emphasis on tourism, which became a major new downtown economic force. The redevelopment projects of the 1980s and 1990s tended to be more modest in scope than the urban renewal projects of the 1950s and 1960s, therefore generating less displacement, although the demolition of single-room-occupancy hotels for some of these projects was found to contribute to homelessness.

President Bill Clinton attempted to revive federal support for declining areas through the Urban Empowerment Zone program (1994), but little new federal funding accompanied this effort. In addition, federal housing assistance programs continue to be funded at levels far below the extent of need. In many residential areas, nonprofit community development corporations (CDCs) piece together multiple public and private funding sources to create affordable housing and limited commercial redevelopment. However, reduced federal funding means that their efforts reach only a small portion of those in need of affordable housing.

R. Allen Hays

See also: Housing Policy; Racial Segregation; Urban Poverty; U.S. Department of Housing and Urban Development

References and Further Reading

Hays, R. Allen. 1995. *The Federal Government and Urban Housing: Ideology and Change in Public Policy*. 2d ed. Albany: SUNY Press.

Judd, Dennis R., and Todd Swanstrom. 1998. *City Politics: Private Power and Public Policy*. New York: Longman.

Stone, Clarence N., and Heywood T. Sanders, eds. 1987. *The Politics of Urban Redevelopment*. Lawrence: University Press of Kansas.

U.S. Agency for International Development (AID)

The U.S. Agency for International Development (AID) is the federal government agency responsible for overseeing the implementation of U.S. bilateral foreign aid. It was officially created by an executive order of President John F. Kennedy in 1961 as part of the Foreign Assistance Act, but the agency's goals were established earlier. The Marshall Plan reconstruction of Europe after World War II set the pathway for future projects to help countries recovering from disasters, attempting democratizing reforms, and climbing out of poverty. U.S. AID was organized to unify previous aid efforts by combining the work of the Export-Import Bank on currency issues, the Department of Agriculture's surplus distribution programs, the International Cooperation Agency's economic and technical assistance, and the Development Loan Fund's strategic loan programs. U.S. AID does not administer military aid.

Today, U.S. AID has an annual budget of $6 billion and, under the guidance of the Secretary of State, operates programs in more than seventy-five countries. The agency itself describes its raison d'être as to "advance U.S. foreign policy objectives by supporting economic growth, agriculture and trade; global health; and democracy, conflict prevention and humanitarian assistance" (U.S. AID, "About USAID"). The agency has claimed many victories in the decades since its inception. According to the agency's Web site, over 3 million individuals are saved each year thanks to U.S. AID's immunization projects, and its family planning programs have improved the lives of 50 million couples worldwide. Regional projects have met with great success as well; millions of South African deaths were prevented by U.S. AID action to deter a massive famine in 1992, and approximately 21,000 Honduran families have been educated about cultivation techniques that have already reduced soil erosion there by 70,000 tons.

However, there are both limitations to and criticisms of U.S. AID's work. First, and contrary to the belief of the vast majority of Americans, only 0.5 percent of the U.S. federal budget is devoted to nonmilitary foreign aid. This clearly curtails the scope of possibility for U.S. AID. Second, some argue that the goals of the agency are misguided and are too rooted in a concern for U.S. business interests. For example, the agency has targeted $15 million since the early 1990s on developing the energy sectors of poor nations. Environmentalists and other critics point out that most of this money is spent on fossil fuels rather than on cleaner and renewable alternatives. The United States has captured by far the largest share of these mushrooming markets for private power. In addition, U.S. foreign aid has sometimes been used as a carrot to entice vulnerable nations to adhere to U.S. foreign policy goals, a fact long criticized by third world nations. A notable instance was Kennedy's Alliance for Progress, which extended U.S. AID monies to Latin American nations friendly to both anticommunism and U.S. businesses.

Nevertheless, U.S. AID has fulfilled an important role in extending assistance to many of the neediest communities in the world. By highlighting the suffering of underdeveloped nations, the centrality of development to sustaining peaceful and prosperous relations worldwide, and the vast improvements that even small infusions of aid money can make when administered appropriately, U.S. AID continues to perform a vital service.

Rebecca K. Root

See also: Peace Corps; World Bank

References and Further Reading

Mickelwait, Donald, Charles Sweet, and Elliott Morss. 1979. *New Directions in Development: A Study of U.S. AID*. Boulder, CO: Westview Press.

U.S. AID. "About USAID." http://www.usaid.gov/about_usaid/.

———. Web site. http://www.usaid.gov.

Zimmerman, Robert. 1993. *Dollars, Diplomacy, and Dependency: Dilemmas of U.S. Economic Aid*. Boulder, CO: Lynne Rienner.

U.S. Children's Bureau

The U.S. Children's Bureau (CB) is a federal government agency devoted to research and advocacy on behalf of the nation's children. The CB was created by Congress in 1912 at the urging of a national network of women reformers and their male allies. Originally charged with the investigation of child life, the bureau expanded its scope over the following decades to include the administration of programs devoted to maternal and child health, the regulation of child labor, and services for disadvantaged children. Although the CB was not conceived as an antipoverty agency, its studies consistently highlighted the devastating effects of low family incomes on children, and its staff designed government programs—most especially Aid to Dependent Children—to support poor children. Until 1946, the CB maintained a high profile among those concerned with the welfare of children. Thereafter, the agency lost status and jurisdiction: By 2002, it was housed in the Administration for Children and Families in the U.S. Department of Health and Human Services, and its focus was narrowed to abused and neglected children and foster care.

The CB emerged in the ferment of early-twentieth-century progressive reform. Progressivism comprised a set of mostly middle-class responses to problems that reformers believed were caused by the increasing pace of immigration, urbanization, and industrialization. Eager to establish new places for themselves in the world, educated women not only participated in but also effectively led a spectrum of these reform campaigns, especially those intended to improve the lives of women and children. Lillian Wald and Florence Kelley, activists in New York, hatched the idea of a federal agency devoted to collecting and disseminating information about the nation's children. As early as 1903, the two women began drawing allies into their hopes for such an agency, arguing that Americans could not make sound decisions about the welfare of children if they did not have knowledge of children's condition or of the results of existing programs to improve children's lives. Finally, in 1912, their efforts resulted in creation of the U.S. Children's Bureau, situated in the Department of Labor.

As soon as the bureau was created, women reformers urged President William Howard Taft to appoint a woman to head the agency. Ultimately, he acquiesced and appointed the women's nominee, Julia Lathrop, as the CB's first head and the first woman to run a federal agency. Lathrop mostly hired women for her new bureau, making it a female stronghold in the overwhelmingly male federal government.

During its first two decades, the CB's most significant achievements related to maternal and infant health. The bureau's first research projects revealed that the United States had some of the highest maternal and infant mortality rates in the industrialized world and that high infant mortality rates correlated with poverty. Unable directly to reduce poverty, however, the CB attempted to intervene where it could by providing preventive health care services for mothers. Outlined in the Maternity and Infancy Act (1921), this program funded state health education initiatives for pregnant women and babies. The funds especially supported the work of itinerant public health nurses, who set up temporary clinics in the remotest areas of many states to examine pregnant women and babies and to offer mothers information on how best to preserve their own and their children's health. The CB administered this program—sometimes identified as the country's first federal social welfare measure—until 1929.

By that time, the CB was deeply involved in issues explicitly related to poverty. When the stock market crashed in 1929, the CB emerged as the federal agency best informed on the effects of unemployment and the inadequacy of existing relief efforts. The bureau then participated in shaping the founding legislation of the U.S. welfare state: the Social Security Act (1935) and the Fair Labor Standards Act (1938). Best known for establishing old-age insurance and unemployment compensation for many American workers (mostly white men), the Social Security Act created several other programs as well. The CB designed four of them, and they constituted the agency's most significant antipoverty programs. These programs included services for crippled children; a revived maternal and infant health program exclusively for impoverished mothers, especially in rural areas; and services for children with special needs. The CB administered all of these programs.

The most important of the bureau's contributions, however, was Aid to Dependent Children (ADC), which provided funds to the states for the sustenance of children whose fathers could not support them. Although the CB believed that adequate wages for men constituted the best antipoverty program, its administrators recognized that sometimes families were without a male breadwinner. ADC aimed to spare mothers in these unfortunate families from the labor market. Though created by independent professional women, the program promoted their firm belief that most women would be economic dependents of men and should care for their children without recourse to professional child care providers. As a means-tested program, ADC stigmatized its recipients in a way that other Social Security programs did not. Against the bureau's will, the newly established Social Security Board administered ADC.

A longtime opponent of child labor, the CB fared better in relation to the Fair Labor Standards Act. The bureau implemented the provision that prohibited child labor in industries engaged in interstate commerce.

In 1946, the CB began to lose power. A federal reorganization moved it from the Department of Labor to the Federal Security Administration, leaving work on child labor to the Department of Labor. In 1969, the bureau was buried deeper in the federal bureaucracy and lost its health programs to the Public Health Service. Since that time, the CB has focused primarily on research and advocacy for children with special needs.

Robyn Muncy

See also: Aid to Families with Dependent Children (ADC/AFDC); Child Welfare; Child-Saving; Fair Labor Standards Act (FLSA); Family Wage; Maternalism; Social Security Act of 1935; U.S. Department of Health and Human Services; U.S. Department of Labor; Welfare State

References and Further Reading

Bremner, Robert, et al., eds. 1974. *The United States Children's Bureau, 1912–1972*. New York: Arno Press.

Lindenmeyer, Kriste. 1997. *A Right to Childhood: The U.S. Children's Bureau and Child Welfare, 1912–1946*. Urbana: University of Illinois Press.

Muncy, Robyn. 1991. *Creating a Female Dominion in American Reform, 1890–1935*. New York: Oxford University Press.

U.S. Department of Health and Human Services

The U.S. Department of Health and Human Services (HHS), originally the Department of Health, Education, and Welfare (HEW), was created in 1953 as the first cabinet-level office for social welfare programs, and it has played a primary role in shaping and administering federal programs that affect low-income people, notably Aid to Families with Dependent Children (AFDC, now Temporary Assistance for Needy Families, TANF). HHS also administers other means-tested public assistance programs, social insurance programs and medical insurance programs, and a range of other programs affecting low-income people, including Medicaid, child care programs, and child welfare programs. Although many HHS programs address the problems faced by low-income persons, over the years none has come under greater scrutiny or attracted more controversy than the AFDC program, or "welfare." Since the mid-1970s, HHS leadership has been closely focused on pursuing welfare reform to "end welfare as we know it" and replace it with limited income support in return for work.

Historically, HEW/HHS has addressed poverty in two ways, via social insurance and public assistance, with different results.

Social insurance, including Old Age, Survivors', Disability Insurance (Social Security), and Medicare, is overseen by the Social Security Administration within HHS. Entitlements to pensions in old age or disability have been granted to wage earners on the basis of their employment or relationship to someone who is employed. Social insurance has historically served those with regular full-time employment in specified fields and occupations, leaving out large numbers of domestic and agricultural workers, service workers, and part-time workers. As a result, its beneficiaries have been disproportionately white and male; many nonwhites, recent immigrants, unskilled and less educated workers, and women have been overlooked. Poverty has been greatly reduced among those covered by social insurance, but not among those not included.

HEW/HHS has addressed citizens not covered by social insurance through means-tested public assistance programs, or "welfare." Unlike social insurance programs, public assistance has served those unable to work, not expected to work, or not engaged in regular wage labor. Until 1957, HEW/HHS's largest federal welfare program was Old Age Assistance. Since then, AFDC has been the largest and best-known federal welfare program, and it has been the focus of HEW/HHS initiatives with regard to low-income people.

Over time, HEW/HHS has addressed welfare in different ways and has exerted varying influence on the overall federal agenda regarding poverty.

During the 1950s and early 1960s, HEW was the main federal bureaucracy overseeing programs helping low-income Americans. Although headed by business leaders and politicians, the department's Bureau of Public Assistance (renamed the Bureau of Family Assistance and then the Welfare Administration) was dominated by social workers. Through their influence in this period, HEW expanded federal public assistance programs and redirected them toward a social service approach called "rehabilitation." In 1962, the Public Welfare Amendments institutionalized a rehabilitative approach to AFDC, providing welfare clients with federally funded services aimed at promoting self-support. These amendments marked HEW's first step directly linking welfare with work, as the self-support services were aimed at employment.

In the 1960s, social workers' influence over welfare waned, changing the way HEW addressed the poor. In 1967, President Lyndon B. Johnson's administration eliminated the Welfare Administration, headed by social worker Ellen Winston, and replaced it with a new agency called Social and Rehabilitative Services, headed by a vocational education and rehabilitation expert named Mary Switzer, a woman whom Johnson expected to pursue work-based welfare reform more aggressively. As a result, HEW passed the 1967 Work Incentive Program (WIN), linking welfare more closely to work.

During the second half of the 1960s, the War on Poverty—the largest federal intervention in the field of poverty since the New Deal—bypassed HEW in favor of a new federal bureaucracy, the Office of Economic Opportunity (OEO). This reduced HEW's influence upon the overall federal poverty agenda. The OEO avoided the social work perspective of HEW, eschewing social services in favor of training and jobs programs. In addition, OEO avoided association with welfare programs and poor single mothers. This outcome left HEW with little role to play in a broader assault on poverty, save for administering AFDC.

In the late 1960s and 1970s, HEW policy for the poor on welfare shifted directions several times.

Under Johnson, HEW attempted to replace welfare with a guaranteed minimum income. This effort continued in a different form, the Family Assistance Plan, under President Richard M. Nixon, but was defeated in 1972. In the end, HEW expanded and guaranteed income support only for the needy elderly, blind, and disabled through the passage of Supplemental Security Income (SSI), leaving needy single mothers on AFDC without guaranteed income support.

At the same time, HEW also began a research initiative that led to yet another approach to welfare reform. In 1965, the office of Assistant Secretary of Program Evaluation (ASPE) was created in HEW to direct research on HEW programs and poverty. Throughout the 1970s and 1980s, ASPE pursued a research agenda based on microeconomic analysis of welfare programs and on intense research on the behaviors of welfare clients and the poor. This intense scrutiny of the poor coincided with conservatives' attacks on welfare clients and welfare programs, accelerating the process already under way within HEW/HHS of using welfare to force poor women into the labor market.

In the 1980s and 1990s, HEW, renamed HHS, consistently pursued welfare reform that required poor women to work. Under President Ronald Reagan's Republican administration, this goal derived from cost-cutting priorities and a belief among HHS leadership that welfare encouraged "loafing" and "immoral behavior." The 1981 Omnibus Budget Reconciliation Act and the 1988 Job Opportunities and Basic Skills program reflected these beliefs. In the 1990s, President Bill Clinton's HHS leadership presided over an effort to reform welfare that it could not control. Although HHS wanted to pursue welfare-to-work goals through well-funded services to welfare clients, the Clinton administration and Congress passed the 1996 Personal Responsibility and Work Opportunity Reconciliation Act, abolishing AFDC and replacing it with TANF, a program that offers limited income assistance and services while imposing work requirements and strict lifetime time limits on welfare participation.

Jennifer Mittelstadt

See also: Aid to Families with Dependent Children (ADC/AFDC); Poverty Research; Social Security; War on Poverty; Welfare Policy/Welfare Reform

References and Further Reading

Berkowitz, Edward, and Kim McQuaid. 1988. *Creating the Welfare State: The Political Economy of Twentieth-Century Reform*. New York: Praeger.

O'Connor, Alice 2000. *Poverty Knowledge: Social Science, Social Policy, and the Poor in Twentieth-Century U.S. History*. Princeton: Princeton University Press.

Patterson, James. 1994. *America's Struggle against Poverty, 1900–1994*. Cambridge, MA: Harvard University Press.

U.S. Department of Health, Education, and Welfare. 1972. *A Common Thread of Service: A Historical Guide to HEW*. Washington, DC: GPO.

U.S. Department of Housing and Urban Development

The U.S. Department of Housing and Urban Development (HUD) was created in 1965 with the elevation of the Housing and Home Finance Agency (HHFA, which had administered the public housing program, the Federal Housing Administration, and the urban renewal program since the late 1940s) to a cabinet-level department. The director of the HHFA, Robert Weaver, became the first secretary of HUD and the first African American to serve in a cabinet post. Its most important functions are (1) to oversee federally assisted housing programs for the poor, such as public housing and housing vouchers; (2) to oversee the Federal Housing Administration (FHA) program of assistance to moderate-income home buyers; (3) to oversee federal community development programs such as urban renewal and Community Development Block Grants; (4) to enforce laws protecting racial and other minorities from housing discrimination and promoting fair housing; and (5) to promote research and development of new ideas for community development and housing.

HUD was born in an atmosphere of controversy. The administrations of Presidents John F. Kennedy and Lyndon B. Johnson were eager to create and expand programs that would benefit their urban political base and that would reach out to African Americans newly empowered and enfranchised by the civil rights movement. However, most southern Democrats and Republicans were opposed to these initiatives, and it was only with the extraordinary Democratic majorities in both houses of Congress created by the 1964 election that President Johnson was able to push through the creation of this department. From the beginning, the legitimacy of the department and its funding levels were tied to the level of presidential and congressional support for urban initiatives. Unlike some other federal departments, HUD does not have a politically powerful constituency that enables it to withstand ideological changes in leadership.

The complex and contradictory pieces that make up the department reflect the conflicting goals of federal urban redevelopment and housing policies. The FHA was created during the Great Depression to revive the middle-class housing market by providing federal insurance for long-term, low-down-payment mortgages. It really came into its own after World War II, as FHA loans helped build the suburbs. However, the FHA ignored central-city neighborhoods and reinforced the discrimination against people of color that was prevalent in the private banking industry. In the late 1960s, new programs were created to reorient the FHA toward making loans in disadvantaged areas, but the FHA's corrupt or incompetent administration of these programs produced scandals in many cities. Despite these difficulties, the FHA continues to play an important role in mortgage lending.

The public housing program was created in 1937 to house people whose incomes were too low to benefit from FHA programs and to provide substitute housing for those in the path of slum-clearance efforts. Although the program provided much better housing to many low-income persons than they could have obtained on the private market, it was plagued by funding, design, and site-selection problems. Middle-class neighborhoods vehemently resisted the construction of public housing, so such housing was usually built in already poor areas. The high-density high-rises that were typical of public housing were not conducive to the creation of stable, safe, low-income communities. Therefore, the program has brought much controversy to HUD. During the last five years, HUD has been demolishing many high-density public housing projects. The intention is to replace them with mixed-income communities, but the extent to which displaced tenants will benefit from the new housing is not clear.

Criticism of public housing led to the creation in the 1960s and 1970s of HUD programs that utilized assistance to private developers and landlords to create housing for the poor. The Section 8 program, created in 1974, became the largest and most successful of these programs. It encompassed both new construction and assistance to tenants living in existing units. During President Ronald Reagan's administration, the new construction element was phased out, and emphasis was placed entirely on Section 8 vouchers that subsidize the rent of low-income tenants. Current problems with HUD vouchers include a low level of voucher funding relative to the need and the inability of the payment standard upon which assistance is based to keep up with rising housing costs.

Enforcement of fair housing laws became a responsibility of HUD with the passage of the Housing Act of 1968. Through the first twenty years of this role, HUD's enforcement mechanisms were weak, often simply involving negotiations between the offending parties and those filing the complaint. Several court cases put pressure on HUD and on local housing authorities to use federally assisted housing in ways that did not reinforce racial segregation, but intense local opposition again made enforcement difficult. Finally, in 1988, HUD was granted much more vigorous enforcement mechanisms, and promoting fair housing remains a high priority within the department. Unfortunately, despite HUD's efforts, the vast majority of Americans still live in racially segregated neighborhoods.

The urban renewal program was created in 1949 to counter the decline of the central cities in the face of suburbanization. From the program's inception until the passage of the Housing Act of 1968, most cities used the funding to displace low-income residents to make room for large commercial or public works developments. The 1968 act reoriented the program to renewing low-income areas and to creating, rather than destroying, low-income housing. However, the program fell victim to the reevaluation of all HUD programs during the moratorium on HUD spending declared by President Richard M. Nixon's administration in 1973–1974. It was replaced with the Community Development Block Grant (CDBG) program, which emphasized housing rehabilitation and was thus less devastating to low-income neighborhoods. However, CDBG replaced the competitive grant process with a formula entitlement that distributed funding to a larger number of communities, some of which had less severe problems than the larger central cities where urban renewal had been concentrated. CDBG also gave cities considerable discretion as to how funds could be spent, thus reducing HUD's micromanagement of local efforts.

Over its entire history, HUD has oscillated between more centralized and less centralized control over local housing and redevelopment authorities. Concerns with instances of local corruption and incompetence have led to increased oversight, but subsequent concerns with too much bureaucratic rigidity have led to relaxation of federal control. HUD has also oscillated between serving the interests of the poor and serving the interests of local officials and their allies in the private sector. By acquiescing to local desires to displace and segregate the poor, HUD contributed to its reputation for failing to create decent housing and neighborhoods in which the poor could live. By getting too cozy with private developers, the department became associated with various scandals that tarnished its reputation. However, the overwhelming national need for affordable housing has kept HUD programs alive, despite frequent criticism. Its budget was drastically curtailed in the 1980s and has remained low ever since, but efforts to abolish it have been unsuccessful. It continues to provide much-needed community development assistance, it provides a number of programs to address homelessness, and its vouchers provide desperately needed reductions in housing costs to those households lucky enough to make it to the top of lengthy waiting lists.

R. Allen Hays

See also: Community Development; Homelessness; Housing Policy; Racial Segregation; Tenant Organizing; Urban Renewal

References and Further Reading

Burt, Martha R. 1992. *Over the Edge: The Growth of Homelessness in the 1980s*. New York: Russell Sage Foundation.

Hays, R. Allen. 1995. *The Federal Government and Urban Housing: Ideology and Change in Public Policy*. 2d ed. Albany: SUNY Press.

Koebel, C. Theodore, ed. 1998. *Shelter and Society: Theory, Research, and Policy for Nonprofit Housing*. Albany: SUNY Press.

Yinger, John. 1995. *Closed Doors, Opportunities Lost*. New York: Russell Sage Foundation.

U.S. Department of Labor

On March 4, 1913, the day of Woodrow Wilson's inauguration, President William Howard Taft signed a bill into law establishing a cabinet-level Department of Labor designed, according to the act creating the department, "to foster, promote and develop the welfare of working people, to improve their working conditions, and to enhance their opportunities for profitable employment" (Grossman 1973, 3). The new department combined four existing bureaus (the Bureau of Labor Statistics, the Bureau of Immigration, the Bureau of Naturalization, and the Children's Bureau) with the newly formed U.S. Conciliation Service. Through its long, varied, and often controversial career, the Department of Labor has functioned as an investigator, regulator, mediator, and law enforcer.

President Woodrow Wilson nominated William Wilson (no relation)—a congressman and a member of the United Mine Workers union who had been one of the chief advocates for the new department—as the first secretary of the Department of Labor. During the Wilson administration, the department assumed an active role. Labor conflicts and the need to retool industry for war led to a dramatic assertion of wartime federal government power in labor relations. In April 1918, Secretary Wilson's Department of Labor established the War Labor Administration, whose strongest component was the War Labor Board (WLB). The WLB frequently injected itself into controversial labor conflicts, often siding with workers and labor organizations. Also during World War I, the Women in Industry Service (the predecessor to the Women's Bureau) and the Division of Negro Economics emerged as venues for investigations that focused on women and Black workers, who were entering the industrial workforce in unprecedented numbers.

In contrast to the vigorous World War I years, the 1920s were grim years for the Department of Labor. Congress slashed the department's funding, and James J. Davis replaced Wilson as secretary of labor. Davis had little of Secretary Wilson's willingness to insert the department into controversial aspects of the ever-changing labor question. Vigorous demands by worker and reform organizations, however, led to the formation of the Women's Bureau within the Department of Labor. Advocates of a permanent bureau to investigate the condition of Black workers had less success in institutionalizing the Division of Negro Economics, which disappeared in 1921.

Between World War I and 1940, a majority of the department's resources were devoted to immigration and naturalization issues. Secretary Davis's administration vigilantly enforced the dramatic restrictions on immigration promulgated in the Immigration Act of 1921. According to Department of Labor historian Jonathon Grossman, Davis created a border patrol "trained in law, investigation techniques, fingerprinting, jiujitsu, the use of firearms, and tracking and trailing" to stop illegal immigrants from entering the United States. In 1930 alone, the patrol "caught 269 smugglers of aliens and 20,815 aliens" (Grossman 1973, 25). In the late 1930s and early 1940s, much of the responsibility for immigration issues was transferred to the Department of Justice.

In 1947, however, President Harry S Truman transferred control of the Bracero Program—a World War II executive agreement between the United States and Mexico that allowed the U.S. government to recruit, screen, and transport to the United States temporary agricultural workers—from the Department of Agriculture to the Department of Labor. Following the war, the Bracero Program increasingly came under attack as a farm subsidy that exploited Mexican farmworkers. In 1948, the federal government transferred the costs of recruitment and transportation of temporary workers to the farmers who employed the workers. In 1950, the President's Commission on Migratory Labor, chaired by Secretary of Labor James P. Mitchell, concluded that Bracero farmworkers lived in "virtual peonage." The Bracero Program survived mounting criticism until 1964, when Congress terminated it.

The Great Depression and President Franklin D. Roosevelt's New Deal reinvigorated the Department of Labor. To fill the secretary's position, FDR nominated Frances Perkins, who became the first woman to hold a cabinet-level office. After reorganizing the Bureau of Immigration, Perkins led the effort to establish the Civilian Conservation Corps (CCC), one of the more ambitious efforts in the "relief" phase of the New Deal. Perkins also chaired the administration's Committee on Economic Security and Unemployment Insurance, which developed and promoted FDR's most ambitious New Deal policies. Within the CCC structure, the department assumed responsibility for the recruitment of the urban unemployed to work on a variety of conservation projects. By the time the program ended in 1942, the CCC had employed some 3 million workers. The department played a key role in a number of other New Deal employment policies. In 1933, Congress passed the Wagner-Peyser Act establishing the U.S. Employment Services (USES) within the Department of Labor. The USES functioned as a national employment agency aimed at connecting workers with jobs. Another Department of Labor–administered policy during the New Deal was the Fair Labor Standards Act (1938), which established a minimum wage and a forty-hour workweek for manufacturing workers.

When FDR died in April 1945, Perkins resigned from the department in order to direct the Civil Service Commission. Lewis B. Schwellenbach replaced Perkins at a time of dramatic labor unrest and institutional reorganization within the Department of Labor and the federal government. The Bureau of Employment Security (formerly the U.S. Employment Service) and the Apprentice-Training Service became permanent agencies within the department, while the Children's Bureau moved out of the department. With the passage of the Taft-Hartley Act in 1947, the U.S. Conciliation Service moved out of the department and became the Federal Mediation and Conciliation Service. Meanwhile, the Bureau of Labor Statistics, the Labor Standards Division, the Women's Bureau, and the Wage and Hour and Public Contracts Division maintained their stations within the department, but often with drastic cuts in funding. Schwellenbach passed away suddenly in August 1948 and was replaced by Massachusetts governor Maurice J. Tobin, whose connections to organized labor and influence in Massachusetts immediately bolstered Truman's waning election hopes. Between 1948 and 1952, the department regained much of the funding it had lost in the backlash against labor unrest following World War II.

As part of President Lyndon B. Johnson's War on Poverty, the department under Secretary W. Willard Wirtz and succeeding secretaries established a dizzying array of employment and training bureaus and services to help retrain workers whose skills had become obsolete and to train poor workers for jobs where there was work. Many of these programs focused on urban neighborhoods with historically high unemployment or little industry. The most prominent, expensive, and controversial of them, the Job Corps, was established in 1967 with the aim of removing "at-risk" urban youth from their communities and placing them in a residential training center for at least six months. By 1968, nearly 33,000 young people were enrolled in the Job Corps.

In the 1970s, in a trend toward increasing its regulatory power, the department's purview expanded to include the health, safety, and retirement plans of the nation's workers. In 1970, with the passage of the Occupational Safety and Health Act, Congress gave the department the power to establish and enforce the act. To take on this new and ambitious task, the department established the Occupational Safety and Health Administration (OSHA), which enforced the law in states that did not develop OSHA-approved plans. In 1974, Congress passed the Employee Retirement Income Security Act (ERISA) authorizing the Department of Labor to regulate pension and retirement plans.

G. Mark Hendrickson

See also: Employment Policy; Great Depression and New Deal; Progressive Era and 1920s; Welfare State

References and Further Reading

Gamboa, Erasmo. 1990. *Mexican Labor and World War II: Braceros in the Pacific Northwest, 1942–1947*. Seattle: University of Washington Press.

Grossman, Jonathon. 1973. *The Department of Labor*. New York: Praeger.

MacLaury, Judson. 1988. "History of the Department of Labor, 1913–1918." http://www.dol.gov/asp/programs/history/hs75menu.htm.

Sealander, Judith. 1983. *As Minority Becomes Majority: Federal Reaction to the Phenomenon of Women in the Work Force, 1920–1963*. Westport, CT: Greenwood Press.

U.S. Department of Labor. 1963. *The Anvil and the Plow: A History of the United States Department of Labor, 1913–1963*. Washington, DC: GPO.

Vagrancy Laws/ Settlement Laws/ Residency Requirements

Poor people have historically been subject to various criminal and regulatory measures restricting their freedom of movement and eligibility for public assistance. Vagrancy laws have imposed criminal sanctions for a range of loosely defined conduct, such as idleness and moving from place to place without a visible means of support. Settlement laws have tied receipt of public assistance, or "poor relief," to membership in a local community and have authorized the removal of indigent outsiders. Residency requirements, a successor to settlement laws, have similarly made assistance conditional on an established period of residency but have not authorized the forced removal of those ineligible for relief.

Vagrancy laws were first enacted in England after the Black Plague epidemic of the fourteenth century to address the severe labor shortages caused by the collapse of feudal estates. These statutes prohibited increases in wages and restricted the movement of workers to ensure a supply of cheap labor. Wandering became a crime, as did begging. As social and economic changes led to the displacement of large segments of the population during the next several centuries, the emphasis of vagrancy laws shifted from requiring individuals to work in a fixed place to protecting the countryside against financial strain, social unrest, and criminal activity. Vagrancy laws became increasingly punitive and served as the criminal law component of the Elizabethan poor laws, enforcing restrictions on movement by those without a visible means of support, requiring the able-bodied poor to work, and outlawing begging.

Vagrancy laws were adopted in colonial America to regulate the effects of poverty, to prevent crime, and to protect communities against perceived threats to the moral order. In a society where poor relief was a local responsibility, vagrancy laws restricted the availability of assistance. Vagrancy laws required the able-bodied to work, discouraged idleness, and prohibited begging. Vagrants could receive a range of penalties, including corporal punishment, imprisonment, confinement in a workhouse, and involuntary indenture. Vagrancy laws thus illustrate the ways that criminal justice overlapped with the poor laws.

The vagueness of vagrancy laws has made them an effective form of social control. During the nineteenth century, vagrancy laws were used against hoboes, tramps, and the unemployed. The police also employed vagrancy laws to restrict the activities of undesirable types, such as gamblers and prostitutes, and to make preventive arrests based on suspicion. In the South, vagrancy laws helped enforce the repressive

Black Codes intended to control former slaves after the Civil War. In a recent incarnation of vagrancy laws, police employed an antiloitering statute to target members of urban street gangs.

As American society became increasingly urbanized, local governments relied on vagrancy laws not only to prevent criminal conduct but also to "clean up" skid row and commercial areas of cities, to institutionalize mentally ill people, and to abate nuisances. As late as the 1960s, most states still punished vagrancy, and vagrancy laws accounted for a large percentage of criminal arrests. Vagrants were generally tried summarily, without a formal indictment or the right to a jury trial.

During the 1960s, several developments began to undermine vagrancy laws. There was a growing recognition that vagrancy laws were being used as a tool against minority communities and civil rights activists. The U.S. Supreme Court's 1963 decision in *Gideon v. Wainwright* (372 U.S. 335) guaranteeing legal representation for indigent individuals helped make possible legal challenges to vagrancy statutes. Several state and federal court decisions invalidated vagrancy laws as unlawful discrimination against the poor. In its 1972 decision in *Papachristou v. City of Jacksonville* (405 U.S. 156), the Court struck down a local vagrancy ordinance as an overly broad prohibition of seemingly innocent conduct. In a subsequent decision, the Court invalidated a California loitering statute requiring any person wandering the street to produce credible identification upon request by a police officer.

Despite these decisions, however, state and local governments continued to address poverty, mental illness, drug addiction, and other social problems through criminal laws. Vagrancy laws have taken on new forms. For example, cities have increasingly focused on "quality of life" offenses to stem urban crime and neighborhood decay. Prominent social scientists compared vagrants to broken windows in a building: Though harmless when viewed individually, together they can destroy.

The outbreak of modern mass homelessness during the 1980s and 1990s contributed to the revival of vagrancy laws in cities throughout the country. Numerous measures essentially criminalized homelessness by restricting the right of individuals to use public spaces like parks or to solicit money in public, either through broad bans or through narrower rules prohibiting begging at transportation hubs. Cities also increased their efforts to expel homeless people by conducting sweep operations that led to arrests for offenses like camping on public land or sleeping in public. Although legal challenges to these antihomeless activities have been brought on the grounds that they violate the right to equal protection under the law, the prohibition against cruel and unusual punishment, and the right to travel, the challenges have had mixed success. Given their protean nature, vagrancy laws have proven to be among the most enduring legacies of the English poor law system.

Like vagrancy laws, settlement laws also originated in England. The Act of Settlement of 1662 authorized local justices of the peace to remove any person from a parish who had arrived within the preceding forty days and who was determined either to need relief or possibly to need relief in the future. If removed, the person was returned to his or her place of settlement (his or her last place of residence or place of birth). To establish settlement in a parish, an individual needed to own or rent property and pay taxes. Settlement laws reflected a punitive attitude toward the poor, led to the removal of thousands of people each year, and sharply limited geographic mobility and economic opportunity.

Settlement laws were adopted by the American colonies. As in England, they provided that individuals could receive relief only in their place of legal settlement and authorized removal of the nonsettled poor. Settlement laws, however, varied considerably in their organization and structure. Colonies in New England adopted "warning out" systems in which local officials authorized the removal of individuals who lacked settlement and threatened to become a financial burden on the town. Other colonies, such as New York, adopted a "passing on" system in which nonsettled indigents were conveyed by constables from one town to the next until they reached their place of settlement. Those who returned after being expelled could be prosecuted as vagabonds and interned in workhouses or houses of correction. In some colonies, individuals could obtain settlement by remaining in the town for a specified period of time without being ordered removed; in others, they could obtain settlement by vote of the town or by holding a public office. As the number of transients grew, settlement laws became an increasingly important means of social control and significantly limited geographic mobility. Together with vagrancy laws, settlement laws restricted the class of people eligible for relief and limited the financial obligations of towns in a system where poor relief was a local responsibility.

During the nineteenth century, states assumed greater responsibility for the cost and administration of poor relief. A new class started to emerge of poor people who were the financial obligation of the state rather than of the locality. State control over poor relief increased with the growth of immigration during the 1830s and 1840s as immigrants who were barred from relief in towns under the settlement laws turned to the state for assistance. Settlement laws also imposed significant administrative burdens. These laws became increasingly complex and led to frequent—and costly—litigation between local governments over support obligations. In addition, settlement laws were undermined by increasing moral opposition to their cruelest features, such as the removal of old and sick paupers in the middle of winter. Furthermore, the growing movement to place poor people in institutions like poorhouses and workhouses rather than providing them relief in their homes (which was known as "outdoor relief") undercut the settlement law system.

The Great Depression witnessed a resurgence of the practice of excluding and removing poor people as a dramatic increase in interstate migration prompted a backlash among states fearful of their ability to absorb an influx of migrants. Although most displaced farmers and factory workers migrated in search of employment rather than public assistance, states were concerned about increasing demands on their poor-relief systems. Many states sought to prevent the entry of poor migrants and to return them to their last place of residence. Twenty-seven states enacted statutes creating "border patrols." Some went further, attempting to criminalize the knowing importation of paupers into their jurisdiction. The effort by states like California to exclude "Okies" and other migrants gained notoriety in works like John Steinbeck's *Grapes of Wrath*.

The Depression, however, also prompted successful legal challenges to the restrictions. In its 1941 decision in *Edwards v. California* (314 U.S. 160), the Supreme Court invalidated a California statute prohibiting the importation of paupers into the state, noting that under the U.S. Constitution's commerce clause, California could not isolate itself from the impact of the Depression. More broadly, the decision reflected a rejection of the idea that welfare was a local matter and a reconsideration of the link between poverty and immorality. The "theory of the Elizabethan poor laws," the Court stated, "no longer fits the facts." After *Edwards*, states largely ceased relying on exclusion or removal to restrict migration and instead resorted to rules that made assistance conditional on the fulfillment of durational residency requirements.

These residency requirements, however, also eventually came under attack. In 1969, the U.S. Supreme Court declared unconstitutional several state statutes that made welfare benefits contingent upon the satisfaction of durational residency requirements. Such restrictions, the Court stated in *Shapiro v. Thompson* (394 U.S. 618), violated poor people's constitutional right to travel freely among the states. The Court, however, never said that *every* restriction would violate that right, and more modest waiting periods, including up to sixty days, remain in force in some states.

Recent welfare reforms signal a return to the punitive and exclusionary practices of the past. Like the English poor laws of 400 years ago, the Personal Responsibility and Work Opportunity Reconciliation Act of 1996 (PRWORA) employs coercive tactics to force the able-bodied poor to work and devolves power to local governments and officials. Poor people must now comply with strict work requirements to receive welfare benefits, unless they fall within certain narrow exceptions. Although refusal or failure to work is no longer enforced through criminal vagrancy laws, punitive measures are still employed, ranging from conditions on the receipt of benefits to the outright denial or termination of assistance. PRWORA has also attempted to revive residency requirements by authorizing states to limit a family's welfare payments to the amount received in another state if the family has resided in the new state for less than one year. Although the Supreme Court declared such a limitation unconstitutional in its 1999 decision in *Saenz v. Roe* (526 U.S. 489), attempts to limit benefits through residency requirements still retain political and popular support and will probably continue given the increasing decentralization of the country's welfare system. Finally, by restricting receipt of various benefits by certain groups of immigrants, PRWORA echoes the settlement laws' restrictions on assistance to strangers and outsiders.

Jonathan L. Hafetz

See also: Crime Policy; Deserving/Undeserving Poor; Dust Bowl Migration; *The Grapes of Wrath;* Homelessness; Poor Laws; Poorhouse/Almshouse; Poverty Law; Relief; Welfare Policy/Welfare Reform

References and Further Reading

Adler, Jeffrey S. 1989. "A Historical Analysis of the Law of Vagrancy." *Criminology* 27: 209–229.

Foote, Caleb. 1956. "Vagrancy-Type Law and Its Administration." *University of Pennsylvania Law Review* 104: 603–650.

Friedman, Lawrence M. 1993. *Crime and Punishment in American History*. New York: Basic Books.

Herndon, Ruth W. 2001. *Unwelcome Americans: Living on the Margin in Early New England*. Philadelphia: University of Pennsylvania Press.

Katz, Michael B. 1986. *In the Shadow of the Poorhouse: A Social History of Welfare in America*. New York: Basic Books.

Quigley, William P. 1996. "Work or Starve: Regulation of the Poor in Colonial America." *University of San Francisco Law Review* 31: 35–83.

Stephen, James F. 1883. *A History of the Criminal Law of England*. London: Macmillan.

The Vanishing Black Family: Crisis in Black America, *Bill Moyers*

The Vanishing Black Family is a controversial documentary made by journalist Bill Moyers in 1986 that helped revive and give an aura of liberal respectability to once-discredited ideas about a deviant, self-perpetuating "culture of poverty" gripping African American inner-city neighborhoods.

Bill Moyers, a domestic policy adviser to President Lyndon B. Johnson in the 1960s and since then a prominent TV documentarian, was considered sympathetic to the plight of the downtrodden in the mid-1980s when his film exploring the causes and consequences of Black poverty appeared. *The Vanishing Black Family* invited viewers to go where most had never gone before—the inner city—which Moyers explained was a polite term for the ghetto. The film became extremely influential partly because it incorporated a number of perspectives that many white Americans recognized and believed. These included providing a middle-class white man to conduct a kind of tourist curriculum in the folkways of poor people of color and promoting an explanation for poverty based solely on observations of poor people's behavior. The documentary completely eclipsed larger social, economic, and political causes of poverty in the United States.

Most prominently, *The Vanishing Black Family* built on and updated Daniel Patrick Moynihan's 1965 report *The Negro Family: A Case for National Action*. Over the course of the TV documentary, Bill Moyers asked again and again, "Why is this happening?" Why are young African American men unemployed and irresponsible? Why are young African American women having babies, one after the other, long before they are prepared to be mothers? And most important, why are these young people avoiding marriage? Throughout the film, Moyers presented the institution of marriage as the key to prosperity; without marriage, according to Moyers, these young people were doomed to lives of misbehavior and poverty.

In Moynihan's 1965 version of the Negro (the prevailing term at the time) family, young men were passive and defeated, robbed of their masculinity by overaggressive "matriarchs." In Moyers's update, the males were portrayed as "predators" and "hustlers." The girl-mothers appeared as madonnas, filled with love, devotion, and fear for their children, struggling day after day through lives sanctified by maternity.

At the end of the documentary, Moyers asked community "elders" why this was happening, and the documentarian featured answers that focus on individual failure. Elders suggested that African American youth misbehaved because they lacked religious values, because their psychological profile was missing the capacity for guilt, because the welfare system sapped personal initiative, because they indulged in too much sex.

Overall, Moyers depicted a perverse world where middle-class rituals sanctifying family had been ruined: Mother's Day in the ghetto was the depraved celebration of the arrival of welfare checks. Father's Day marked the birth of a hustling father's third son, a child he would never support.

As Moynihan had twenty years earlier, Moyers explicitly denied and implicitly ignored racism, job loss associated with deindustrialization, race-specific unemployment rates and wage rates, substandard educational opportunities and housing, and lack of day care—all characteristics of mid-1980s Newark, New Jersey, the hometown of the young people in the film—when he assigned blame for poverty. Each young man in the documentary was described as "killing time." Each young woman recognized that having a baby was the only accomplishment she could expect in this world. Moyers never explored how and why public policies and employment practices consigned young African Americans to these lives.

Rickie Solinger

See also: *Losing Ground*; Moynihan Report; Picturing Poverty (II); Racism; Welfare Policy/Welfare Reform

References and Further Reading

Gilens, Martin. 1999. *Why Americans Hate Welfare: Race, Media, and the Politics of Antipoverty Policy*. Chicago: University of Chicago Press.

Mink, Gwendolyn. 2002. *Welfare's End*. Rev. ed. Ithaca, NY: Cornell University Press. Originally published 1998.

Mink, Gwendolyn, and Rickie Solinger. 2003. *Welfare: A Documentary History of U.S. Policy and Politics*. New York: New York University Press.

Veterans' Assistance

Veterans' assistance encompasses the varied array of pension, health, educational, and other social welfare benefits accorded to war veterans and their family members.

The history of U.S. social provision is one of classifying individuals and groups into categories of those "deserving" and "undeserving" of government benefits. Veterans' assistance is not just an important example of this; it is the precedent for all federal entitlement programs. Although it is commonly assumed that veterans have always held a special, privileged position in U.S. policy, historically this is not true. Veterans' benefits have varied widely. Veterans of some wars have been treated poorly; those of others, very well. World War II veterans' benefits were uniquely generous and comprehensive.

The first federal U.S. entitlements, passed in 1818, were pensions for disabled or indigent veterans of the Revolutionary War. (Before this, the Continental Congress had enacted pensions and land grants only for disabled veterans, leaving funding to the states [Department of Veterans Affairs 1997, 2].) With the establishment of the 1818 pensions, which included financial need as a criterion for being eligible for benefits, Congress gave individuals a right to public assistance. As Laura Jensen has pointed out, "these benefits foreshadowed the future of U.S. social provisioning by establishing highly discretionary, *selective* entitlements as the distinct *form* of policy solution that would be utilized to address the nation's wide variety of issues of personal socioeconomic well-being." The system created "legal categories of citizens based upon their possession of chosen—not intrinsic—criteria of 'deservingness'" (Jensen 1996, 386).

These benefits were passed only after great debate and conflict. Some, including President James Monroe, argued for life pensions just for service; others argued against the idea that military status should confer any special government recognition. The Continental Congress had favored officers as a strategy to keep the army together, but this was in opposition to the egalitarian ideals of the war. Opponents argued for a break with the European tradition of a military whose leadership was drawn from the aristocracy, in favor of the citizen-soldier ideal. The dissent against pensions was a reaction against the idea of establishing a system in which some citizens would be privileged over others (Jensen 1996, 366–369, 370, 372–379). Later, in 1832, pensions were expanded to include not just disabled or indigent veterans but other veterans of the Revolution and of the Indian wars and the War of 1812 as well. In 1836, pensions were extended to those veterans' widows (Jensen 1996, 386).

Civil War benefits were more generous than those of earlier wars, but not initially. The 1862 General Pension Act provided for veterans of the Union Army and for their widows, children, and dependents. The primary benefit took the form of disability payments. In addition, veterans were given priority in the Homestead Act for land in the West. Homes were opened to care for disabled and indigent veterans, regardless of whether their disabilities had been incurred in the war. Initially, payments were distributed according to rank and disability. In 1873, this was changed to payments based only upon disability. Benefits were further broadened in 1890, with the Dependent Pension Act, which gave pensions to veterans unable to perform manual labor. Any Union veteran who had served honorably for ninety days was eligible, even if his disability was not related to the war. The Sherman Act of 1912 granted pensions to all Union veterans of the Civil War and the Mexican War, regardless of disability, once they reached age sixty-two. Confederate disabled and indigent veterans and their widows were given pensions by their states (Department of Veterans Affairs 1977, 3–6; Skocpol 1992, 110, 139).

As Theda Skocpol has noted, Civil War pensions, initially a limited system for veterans disabled in war and for their dependents or widows, became "an open ended system of disability, old-age, and survivors' benefits for anyone who could claim minimal service time on the northern side of the Civil War." It resulted in a "social security system for those U.S. citizens of a certain generation and region who were deemed morally worthy of enjoying generous and honorable public aid" (Skocpol 1992, 102).

World War I benefits focused on rehabilitating disabled veterans and on making discharge payments. Those unable to work at all were eligible for ongoing payments. In 1924, the World War Adjusted Compensation Act (1924), commonly known as the Bonus Act, provided for payments for service, depending upon the number of days a veteran had served. The larger bonuses, for those serving more than fifty days, were in the form of insurance certificates scheduled to be paid in 1945. In 1931, a new law enabled veterans to borrow up to 50 percent of the value of the certificates. The unemployment and poverty of the Great Depression motivated some veterans to form a mass movement that became known as the Bonus Army to seek earlier payment of the promised bonuses. In 1932, between 15,000 and 40,000 men marched on Washington to call attention to their plight and to demand payment. They were met with hostility, and after spending months encamped in tent cities just across the Anacostia River from the Capitol, they were violently forced to disperse by the U.S. Army. It was not until 1936 that Congress authorized payment (Department of Veterans Affairs 1997, 6–11).

The benefits for veterans of World War II conferred by the federal government in the Servicemen's Readjustment Act of 1944, more commonly known as the G.I. Bill of Rights or the G.I. Bill, were very generous and comprehensive, in stark contrast to those for veterans of earlier wars. The bill was broadly inclusive. Anyone who had served in the military for ninety days and who had been discharged honorably was eligible, whether or not he or she had been in combat. At the same time, the distribution of benefits reflected the exclusions and restrictions in the military and in the broader society. For example, the number of African Americans in the military was limited to 10 percent of the total, reflecting their representation in the U.S. population, and the proportion of women in the military, 2.1 percent, was far lower than their proportion in the nation.

Benefits under the G.I. Bill were unprecedented in scope and included fifty-two weeks of unemployment compensation; tuition grants for four years of postsecondary or vocational education with stipends for living expenses (grants were higher for those with dependents); access to free health care; access to investment capital, including a housing ownership program that provided government-guaranteed mortgages with no required down payment; and a similar loan program for a farm or business (Department of Veterans Affairs 1997, 13–16, 32). Additional lifetime stipends were established for those who had service-related injuries, regardless of financial need. Also, the federal government and many states and municipalities established hiring preferences for veterans.

As of 1956, half of World War II veterans—almost 8 million—had used the education and training benefit. Of these, 2.23 million went to college, 3.48 million went to other schools, 1.4 million took on-the-job training, and 690,000 were trained in farming. In 1947, veterans made up 49 percent of all college enrollment. In addition, 5.32 million veterans used the unemployment allowance, and 3.78 million used the loan benefit. As a result, many stayed out of the labor force, at a time when high unemployment was feared, and were then better prepared to enter the workforce later (Department of Veterans Affairs 1997, 14; Ross 1969, 124).

A congressional cost-benefit analysis of just the college benefits estimated that for each dollar spent, the economic benefit to the nation (in terms of economic output) was between $5 and $12.50. Furthermore, the increased taxes veterans paid, due to higher earnings during their lifetimes, more than paid for the program. In addition, Veterans Administration surveys have shown that only 35.7 percent of veterans questioned reported that they could have purchased a home without the G.I. Bill; of those who used the benefit, 41.6 percent were white and 37.8 percent were Black (Veterans Administration 1980, 54). These are impressive figures, especially considering that Blacks were limited to 10 percent of the military and often experienced discrimination in real estate and banking.

Authors and groups disagree about the origins of the unprecedented—and unrepeated—generosity of the G.I. Bill. The Roosevelt administration, members of Congress, and the American Legion were deeply worried about a postwar return to the Great Depression; the prospect of 16 million unemployed veterans raised concerns that there might be civil unrest and even revolt (Olson 1974, 20–21). Some scholars credit the G.I. Bill to President Franklin D. Roosevelt's planning agency, the National Resources Planning Board (NRPB), which proposed postwar benefits for the whole population (Merriam 1944; Ross 1969, 123). The American Legion, organized by a group of World War I veterans, claims credit for the G.I. Bill (other veterans' groups sought more limited assistance), and some authors agree, emphasizing their very well-organized lobbying and public relations campaign (Skocpol 1997, 106; Bennett 1996). The Legion also lobbied successfully to vest control of all benefits in a single agency, the Veterans Administration. Some proposals included benefits for all; some, only for veterans and war production workers. The bill that passed provided benefits only for those in the military. Veterans of subsequent wars received less generous benefits than did World War II veterans.

The 6.8 million Korean War veterans received benefits similar to but more limited than those of their World War II counterparts. The education allowance did not completely cover the cost of education; it paid up to three years of a stipend, but no longer paid tuition to schools. This benefit was used by 2.4 million veterans. The home, farm, and business loan program continued and was used by 1.8 million people. This time, the states, rather than the federal government, administered the unemployment allowance (Department of Veterans Affairs 1997, 17, 20).

The benefits Vietnam War veterans received were even less generous. Of the 9.2 million persons in the military, 3.1 million had been deployed to Southeast Asia; as a group, their needs were great. A larger percentage of Vietnam survivors had disabilities, compared to those of earlier wars. In addition, Vietnam veterans returning home in the 1970s faced rising unemployment, inflation, and recessionary conditions that paralleled the unemployment problems that veterans of World War I had experienced. Nevertheless, education benefits were much less generous than those offered to World War II or Korean War veterans. One month of assistance in exchange for each month served was given to those who had served 180 days on active duty. Of those eligible, 5.5 million veterans used the benefit. Home loan programs continued, and severely disabled veterans could apply for mortgage insurance to cover loans to modify their houses. Exposure to Agent Orange (dioxin) resulted in a number of health problems for those who had been in Vietnam. The Veterans Administration denied this at first and gave no assistance. Later, in 1978 and 1981, additional access to care was established. Finally, in 1991, the number of illnesses that were presumed to be related to exposure to Agent Orange was broadened, expanding eligibility for service-related disability payments (Department of Veterans Affairs 1997, 20, 22; Severo and Milford 1990).

In the 1980s, while the country was not at war and was operating with an all-volunteer military, a shift in veterans' assistance took place. Previously, benefits had been enacted for the particular veterans of each war. Now, although not as generous as in the past, some benefits were created as enlistment enticements. For the unemployed veteran, job-training assistance was transformed into reimbursements to employers for a training period, and the education benefit became a contributory program. The 1984 Montgomery G.I. Bill provided $300 per month for up to thirty-six months in exchange for three years of active duty and reduced pay for the first year of service (Department of Veterans Affairs 1997, 27).

Persian Gulf veterans' benefits, passed in 1991, granted educational assistance, medical care, housing loans, and unemployment compensation. Following considerable controversy, those with chronic illnesses thought to be related to exposure to toxic agents during the Gulf War, after 1993, could receive care at special Veterans Administration Gulf War referral centers and, after 1994, could receive compensation (Department of Veterans Affairs 1997, 31–32).

Although the level and inclusiveness of veterans' assistance have varied from war to war, some general themes have affected what veterans are granted. First, there was ideological struggle over whether veterans should have any status different from other citizens. This conflict continued from the Revolutionary War through the 1930s. Later, a prominent issue was how returning veterans would affect the country, which depends both on how large a proportion of the population was in the military and on the economic state of the country after the war. This was obvious in the case of World War II benefits and was further illustrated by the lesser benefits received by Korean War and Vietnam War veterans. In addition, the prevailing attitude toward government spending in a given period affects benefits. A good contrast is World War I veterans, who struggled during a time of fiscal conservatism, and World War II veterans, who returned during a period of Keynesian economic thinking, when government spending was seen as a positive influence on the economy. In the twentieth century, the popularity of a given war also may have influenced assistance for its veterans.

Ann M. Robbart

See also: Bonus Army; Deserving/Undeserving Poor; G.I. Bill

References and Further Reading

Bennett, Michael. 1996. *When Dreams Came True: The GI Bill and the Making of Modern America*. Washington, DC: Brassey's.

Department of Veterans Affairs. 1997. "VA History in Brief." VA 80-97-2. Washington, DC: GPO.

———. Web site. http://www.va.gov.

Jensen, Laura S. 1996. "The Early American Origins of Entitlements." *Studies in American Political Development* 10: 360–404.

Merriam, Charles. 1944. "The National Resources Planning Board: A Chapter in American Planning." *The American Political Science Review* 38, no. 6: 1075–1088.

Olson, Keith. 1974. *The GI Bill, the Veterans, and the Colleges*. Lexington: University Press of Kentucky.

Ross, Davis. 1969. *Preparing for Ulysses: Politics and the Veterans during World War II*. New York: Columbia University Press.

Severo, Richard, and Lewis Milford. 1990. *The Wages of War: When America's Soldiers Came Home—From Valley Forge to Vietnam*. New York: Simon and Schuster.

Skocpol, Theda. 1992. *Protecting Soldiers and Mothers: The Political Origins of Social Policy in the United States*. Cambridge, MA: Harvard University Press.

———. 1997. "The GI Bill and U.S. Social Policy, Past and Future." *Social Philosophy and Policy* 14, no. 2: 95–115.

Veterans Administration. 1980. "National Survey of Veterans: Summary Report." Washington, DC: GPO.

Vocational Education

Vocational education encompasses a variety of educational experiences aimed at preparing students for paid and unpaid work by focusing on practical and applied study. Since the 1860s, the U.S. government has sought to fund vocational education programs in order to meet a number of social and economic goals.

The first federal legislation embracing the concept of vocational education was the Morrill Act of 1862, which created the first land-grant institutions of higher education in response to the growing perception in the country that the demands of the agricultural and industrial sectors of the economy were beyond the capacity of the students of the time. Land-grant schools did not offer merely skills-oriented apprenticeship-type programs; rather, they sought to combine a broad educational foundation for their students with a focus on the skills necessary to solve the problems relevant to agriculture and industry more broadly. Their purposes overall were to educate future farmers and agricultural technicians in methods to expand agricultural productivity; to teach future homemakers the necessary skills for improved nutrition, child care, and the other "domestic arts"; and to prepare future engineers and technicians to meet the demands of the rapidly growing industrial economy. The Smith-Lever Act of 1914 set in place the principle that the national government would bear half the responsibility for financing vocational education at the postsecondary level, usually through matching grants between the state and national governments.

It was the Smith-Hughes Act of 1917, however, that made vocational education a national program common in many public secondary schools across the country. This act represented a new assertiveness by the national government over the content of public education and was, in many ways, a product of the Progressives' demands for reforms to both improve the lives of American citizens and imbue them with "American" values and habits. These reformers were concerned that the large immigrant populations living in and entering the country were failing to adopt the "superior" health, hygienic, and homemaking practices that many Progressives saw as vital to the creation of a strong American public. In light of this, they sought to use new vocational education programs to combine the previous economic aims of the land-grant system with social and cultural engineering goals: teaching male immigrants to become more skilled in areas of manual labor, molding female immigrants into proper American homemakers, and "Americanizing" all immigrant groups. These reformers were also responding to the very real problems of inadequacies in the public education available to both immigrant and nonimmigrant communities, the stark disparities in spending on education along gender lines (with much less money being dedicated to home economics than to the "manly" sciences), and persistent illiteracy and poor health in

Standing at a stove, a student chef prepares soups in the kitchen as part of vocational training at Lane Community College. Eugene, Oregon. (Bohemian Nomad Picturemakers/Corbis)

recent immigrant communities. By teaching children—and through them, if not directly, teaching their parents—the basics of nutrition and child rearing, these reformers believed they were serving humanitarian purposes as well as engaging in cultural reform. The Smith-Hughes Act required states to establish boards for vocational education and institutionalized the separation of vocational education from other areas and approaches to education.

In the 1960s, vocational education took on new life with the Vocational Education Act of 1963, signed into law by President Lyndon B. Johnson, and with a series of related acts throughout the 1960s and 1970s designed to expand and improve vocational education programs in light of the changing demands of the labor market and the needs and wishes of those in search of employment. Vocational education was now made available to a much larger population, including high school students, the unemployed and underemployed, nontraditional students, and students with special needs. Increased attention was given to the demands of minorities, the emotionally and physically challenged, and the incarcerated population, among other groups. By the 1980s, major efforts had been made to reform vocational education in order to minimize its earlier cultural and gender biases, to refocus programs to include technology and the new skills important to the contemporary economy, and to move more control of these programs into the orbit of the states or local educational agencies—and their budgets. Reforms in the 1980s, on the other hand, were spurred primarily by a sense that the U.S. labor force was performing poorly compared to that of other countries and that this lack of competitiveness stemmed from low standards and poor delivery of educational services. Stricter requirements for student performance and a prioritization of national standards for assessing educational programs were the watchwords of the day.

In the 1990s, several new pieces of legislation shaped the evolution of vocational education. The Carl D. Perkins Vocational and Applied Technology Education Act of 1990 was the first piece of legislation to attempt to reintegrate vocational and academic education, thereby emphasizing the education of well-rounded individuals. The School-to-Work Opportunities Act of 1994, on the other hand, emphasized cooperative relationships between vocational education and employers. Businesses often invest directly in vocational education programs, and students often spend part of their schooling working at actual employment sites. Finally, changes to the nature and structure of welfare programs in the United States in 1996 meant that nearly all welfare recipients were required to find employment after two years, thereby pushing issues of vocational education, retraining programs, and labor flexibility to the fore.

The vocational education programs of today are very different from those of 1917. "Home economics" has been replaced by "family and consumer sciences," courses in which both male and female students (though still fewer males than females) learn about managing household accounts and develop parenting skills built on modern models. The "mechanic arts" of a century ago have been replaced with "trade and industrial education" classes that emphasize familiarity with new technologies, workplace skills, and business practices. Agricultural education has, since the 1960s, included study of agribusiness and agriscience as well as of the primary issues of production. Outside of family and consumer sciences, men are still overrepresented in vocational education programs. And while much of the prejudiced social-engineering aspect of early vocational education has been eliminated, some argue that the focus on meeting employers' labor force requirements has taken precedence over the value of education in its own right. Some fear, too, that vocational education programs tend to keep certain groups trapped in lower-paying employment tracks. These questions will remain important as the institution of American vocational education continues to evolve in the decades to come. In the meantime, it continues to expand the opportunities of many Americans by giving them the skills and training necessary for better-paying jobs and therefore higher standards of living.

Rebecca K. Root

See also: Education Policies; Employment and Training; Welfare Policy/Welfare Reform; Workfare

References and Further Reading

Gordon, Howard. 1999. *History and Growth of Vocational Education in America*. Boston: Allyn and Bacon.

Kliebard, Herbert. 1999. *Schooled to Work: Vocationalism and the American Curriculum, 1876–1946*. New York: Teachers College Press.

Mink, Gwendolyn. 1995. *Wages of Motherhood: Inequality in the Welfare State, 1917–1942*. Ithaca, NY: Cornell University Press.

Techniques. Journal of the American Vocational Association.

Voluntarism

Voluntarism is the principle that services should be provided not by the government but by private efforts that are not motivated by the pursuit of profit. Self-help, charity, and benevolence are all examples of voluntarism in the field of social welfare. Although civic participation and volunteering are often celebrated as central to American society, the history of social provision documents a more complex and shifting mix of government, for-profit, and voluntary provision of care. Early almshouses and institutions for the poor were typically established by governments, usually state, county, or local. Voluntary or charitable efforts were also an important component of the mix of social provision, but they were often targeted at specific groups defined by religion, ethnicity, or local residence. Such arrangements posed problems of "philanthropic particularism," the provision of charitable care to some populations and not others. When charity was extended across class lines or ethnoreligious differences, conflicts might arise from the perceived condescension of "benevolent ladies" or "friendly visitors" as well as from fear that charity would be used to encourage religious conversion or cultural assimilation. To the present, however, many voluntary activities have remained entwined with public social provision.

By the beginning of the twentieth century, American social provision was embedded in a complex network of public agencies and voluntary organizations. Public funds for health care and orphans often took the form of subsidies to private charitable organizations, making it sometimes difficult to distinguish between the "voluntary" and "public" elements of social provision. Nevertheless, fraternal orders and ethnic associations were significant providers of health care, insurance, and charity prior to the establishment of large-scale public programs for the care of the needy and dependent. Orphanages, homes for the aged, and hospitals were often established and maintained through the efforts of voluntary organizations.

The New Deal programs of Social Security and Aid to Dependent Children consolidated the ascendance of public spending and social service professionals over volunteers and charitable organizations. But this shift to government provision was far from complete. During the 1960s, the creation of community action agencies and the mandate for "maximum feasible participation of the poor" created new opportunities for cooperation between government and nonprofit agencies. Since the 1970s, a range of policy initiatives—from decentralization to "faith-based" service provision—have increased the potential for voluntarism to reestablish its once-central place in the web of American social provision. These programs have also created opportunities for members of disadvantaged communities to establish careers in activism or to gain skills for other forms of paid labor through participation in community activities (Naples 1998; Warren 2001). In fields such as child protective services, public agencies may depend on volunteers to fill the lower rungs of the labor force; these experiences or internships, in turn, facilitate acceptance into professional training programs that may lead to paid employment in those same public agencies. Such quasi-voluntaristic programs of community development both deliver services directly and provide opportunities for employment and skill development within disadvantaged communities.

Given these combinations of public funding and community organization, individual volunteers must obviously be distinguished from voluntary organizations. Although "voluntary organization" is often used loosely to indicate a wide range of charitable, membership, or mutual organizations, many of those working in these organizations receive wages and therefore are not "volunteers" in the strict sense. The contemporary nonprofit sector depends on both forms of labor; estimates for the United States in the 1980s indicate that nonprofit organizations received labor equivalent to that of 6 million full-time workers from volunteers, which amounted to between 60 and 70 percent of the total full-time equivalents working in the sector (Weisbrod 1988, 132). Until recently, it has been necessary to estimate these numbers because the U.S. government has not systematically tracked volunteer labor; as of 2002, however, the Current Population Survey (CPS) included volunteer labor in its household survey and found that 59 million persons over sixteen years old had volunteered "through or for organizations" in the preceding year. This amounted to 27.6 percent of the civilian population outside of institutions. Survey results on volunteering vary widely (many are considerably higher than the CPS results), with some including informal help to others or using lists of associations or activities to prompt responses.

Despite the varying estimates of the quantity of volunteering, research has illuminated the question of who volunteers (Wilson 2000). Individuals with more education are more likely to volunteer. Volunteering has a more complex relationship with work. People outside the labor force—the unemployed and homemakers—volunteer at lower rates; work, it appears, is an important context in which people encounter opportunities or invitations to volunteer. Among workers, however, there are complex relationships between income or occupational status and the rate or hours of volunteering. More extensive social networks—including the ties of marriage and parenthood—also increase the rate of volunteering. Patterns of volunteering vary by age (falling in young adulthood, peaking in middle age), gender (women are slightly more likely to volunteer), and race (although many of these differences disappear when income is taken into account). Economists have also addressed the question of whether public programs "crowd out" charitable donations and volunteering, but the results are mixed (Weisbrod 1988).

Other debates focus on why Americans engage in voluntary activities and with what consequences (Skocpol and Fiorina 1999). Starting with Alexis de Tocqueville's *Democracy in America* (based on his visit in the 1830s), associations have been understood as central to American society and politics. Voluntary activities—whether charitable or not—are believed to both expand sympathy for or understanding of others and cultivate organizational skills that support participation in formal politics. Consequently, changing patterns of membership in voluntary organizations—particularly the decline of the large fraternal orders and civic organizations that were prominent from the late nineteenth through the mid-twentieth centuries—have been taken as symptoms of a dangerous change in the political engagement of American citizens. This contention has been hotly contested, and other scholars (Wuthnow 1998) have documented changes in the character if not the quantity of volunteer participation. Volunteers are now less likely to make durable commitments to a single organization and more likely to participate on a project basis that is more compatible with patterns of work and family that include dual-earner families, highly scheduled children, and frequent commuting or residential mobility.

Elisabeth S. Clemens

See also: Charitable Choice; Charity; Citizenship; Community-Based Organizations; Community Chests; Mutual Aid; Nonprofit Sector; Philanthropy; Privatization

References and Further Reading

Naples, Nancy A. 1998. *Grassroots Warriors: Activist Mothering, Community Work, and the War on Poverty*. New York: Routledge.

Skocpol, Theda, and Morris P. Fiorina, eds. 1999. *Civic Engagement in American Democracy*. Washington, DC: Brookings Institution; New York: Russell Sage Foundation.

Warren, Mark R. 2001. *Dry Bones Rattling: Community Building to Revitalize American Democracy*. Princeton: Princeton University Press.

Weisbrod, Burton A. 1988. *The Nonprofit Economy*. Cambridge, MA: Harvard University Press.

Wilson, John. 2000. "Volunteering." *American Review of Sociology* 26: 215–240.

Wuthnow, Robert. 1998. *Loose Connections: Joining Together in America's Fragmented Communities*. Cambridge, MA: Harvard University Press.

Volunteers in Service to America (VISTA)

Volunteers in Service to America (VISTA) is one of three major projects that fall under AmeriCorps, one of the most important national service organizations in the United States. Over 100,000 individuals have served impoverished communities through VISTA's full-time, one-year programs by working through nonprofit organizations to address the many needs of low-income areas and their residents. In exchange, participants receive an education award to pay back student loans or to fund future college education and are sometimes granted a small stipend and benefits.

A proposal for a domestic service program originally put forward by President John F. Kennedy shortly after the creation of the Peace Corps was defeated by Congress, but VISTA was finally created in 1964 as part of President Lyndon B. Johnson's War on Poverty and the Economic Opportunity Act. During the 1960s, VISTA participants helped establish the nation's first Head Start and Job Corps programs and were active in the migrant worker camps of California, the poorest regions of the Appalachians, and various inner cities. During the 1970s, VISTA was reorganized as part of the new ACTION agency, which also included the Peace Corps and the senior service programs. VISTA also began to focus on recruiting trained professionals, including architects, lawyers, and doctors, to expand their services into new areas, such as renovation of low-income housing, advocacy of legislative reforms, and the provision of community health service. In the 1980s, that focus changed: Community self-help and citizen participation now formed the backbone of VISTA projects. In 1986, the VISTA Literacy Corps was established to promote adult education; since that time, literacy has become one of VISTA's main efforts, with over one-fourth of all VISTA members working in literacy programs (Potee and Zelson).

The 1990s also saw major changes for VISTA. In 1993, President Bill Clinton signed the National Service Trust Act, which reorganized VISTA once again, this time as part of the new AmeriCorps program, thereby creating the new AmeriCorps*VISTA program. AmeriCorps is part of the Corporation for National Service, which also oversees Learn and Serve America and the National Senior Service Corps. AmeriCorps*VISTA has continued VISTA's dedication to impoverished communities and boasted approximately 6,000 volunteers serving in over 2,000 different local programs in 2001. In fiscal year 2002, the program had a budget of $85 million, with over $5 million donated by local sponsors. New projects include the Entrepreneur Corps, established in 2002, which attempts to match volunteers with business experience with low-income populations to develop financial skills and establish small businesses.

Rebecca K. Root

See also: AmeriCorps; Peace Corps; Voluntarism; War on Poverty

References and Further Reading

AmeriCorps: VISTA. Web site. www.americorps.org/vista/index.html.

Potee, Deb, and John Zelson. "Brief History of VISTA." VISTA Living History. www.friendsofvista.org/living/hist.html.

Reeves, T. Zane. 1988. *The Politics of the Peace Corps and VISTA*. Tuscaloosa: University of Alabama Press.

Schwartz, Martin. 1988. *In Service to America: A History of VISTA in Arkansas 1965–1985*. Fayetteville: University of Arkansas Press.

Voting Rights Act, 1965

Although the Fifteenth Amendment prohibits race-based deprivation of the right to vote, southern states had erected barriers to voting such as poll taxes and literacy tests that served as proxies for race-based disenfranchisement. The seminal Voting Rights Act of 1965 sought to end all means and manner of racial disenfranchisement and to ensure that democratic representation would be available to all. The Voting Rights Act was signed into law by President Lyndon B. Johnson on August 6, 1965. Because of legal challenges, it gained a quick review by the U.S. Supreme Court, which upheld its constitutionality in 1966 in the *South Carolina v. Katzenbach* (383 U.S. 301) decision. Since its initial adoption, the act's provisions have been extended in 1970, 1975, and 1982. Further, its Section 2 provisions on vote dilution and Section 5 provisions on preclearance were significantly amended in 1982. The act, one of the legislative accomplishments of the civil rights movement, is widely credited with politically empowering racial and linguistic minorities, many of them among the poor, so that their political representation is much closer to parity than it was in any period preceding the law.

The Voting Rights Act followed by one year the landmark 1964 Civil Rights Act, which included voting access in some of its provisions (Titles I and VIII). The weaker 1957 and 1960 Civil Rights Acts also had voting protections, as does the Fifteenth Amendment to the Constitution. To overcome southern resistance to earlier efforts to ensure the right to vote, the Voting Rights Act explicitly stated that "no voting qualification or prerequisite to voting, or standard, or practice, or procedure shall be imposed or applied by any State or political subdivision to deny or abridge the right . . . to vote on account of race or color" (Section 2:a). Section 2 has been most used to fight against such election structures as multimember and at-large districts, which tend to dilute the effects of minority voting.

At the time the Voting Rights Act was passed, numerous discriminatory voter registration and election procedures were in effect. In addition to literacy tests, poll taxes, and at-large districts, some southern states gave registrars discretion to require certain voter applicants to pass "understanding tests" showing their reading comprehension of the state constitution, and some states imposed long residency requirements and required personal voter registration at county courthouses that were both intimidating venues and far from home. These practices had been occurring for over a century, despite numerous federal court decisions on the illegality of such similar practices as white primaries and grandfather clauses (U.S. Department of Justice 2001, 1). States responded to findings that certain procedures were illegal by replacing those procedures with equally discriminatory alternative ones. The selective application of such procedures by white election officials resulted in significant Black disenfranchisement.

The Voting Rights Act initially put all or parts of seven southern states, among other jurisdictions, under its coverage and made these

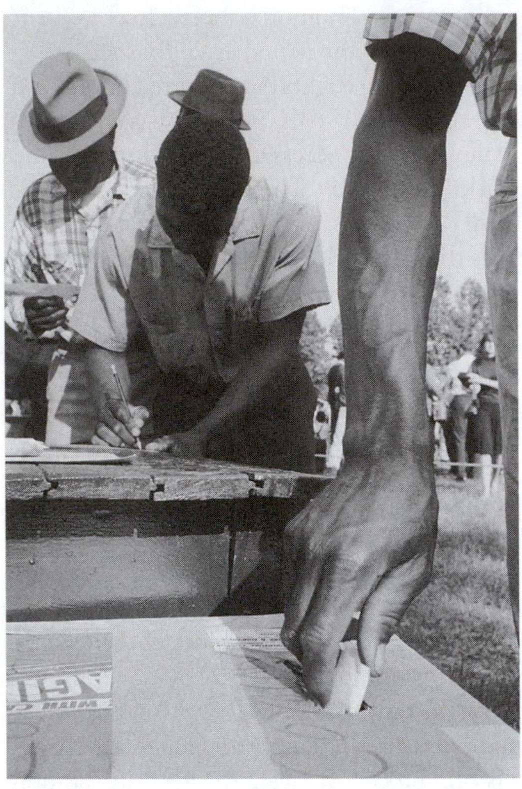

African American men fill out their ballots and drop them in ballot boxes in Alabama after enactment of the Voting Rights Act of 1965. **(*Flip Schulke/Corbis*)**

jurisdictions subject to Department of Justice enforcement because of past discriminatory practices. A ban on voting practices that discriminated against language minorities was added to Section 2 with the 1975 amendments, along with bilingual assistance requirements. This amendment expanded the coverage of the act to include additional southern states (Texas and parts of Florida) as well as states in the West and Southwest (Arizona, California, parts of Colorado, and South Dakota) and Alaska (Grofman, Handley, and Niemi 1992, 21).

Two of the immediate results of the Voting Rights Act were the introduction of federal voting examiners to oversee the registration process and the suspension of literacy tests in the South. Under Section 3, federal voting examiners or federal observers could be sent to any state or jurisdiction to enforce the Fifteenth Amendment. Literacy or other tests or devices were eliminated in Section 4 in seven southern states (Alabama, Georgia, Louisiana, Mississippi, South Carolina, Texas, and Virginia) and the parts of North Carolina that used them. After Section 2's prohibition of practices intended to dilute minority votes, the most important part of the act in terms of its muscle and impact is Section 5, enforcement. Section 5's preclearance requirement mandated that no voting changes could be implemented in covered jurisdictions without federal approval. Section 5 preclearance approval would only be granted to jurisdictions showing their changes were not discriminatory in intent or impact. From 1965 to 1982, 815 of 35,000 submitted changes were ruled objectionable (Davidson 1984, 16). Section 5 of the Voting Rights Act was last renewed for twenty-five years in 1982 and will be up for reauthorization in 2007. Parts of twenty-two states have been covered since 1975 by the law's "triggering" formula based on where racial and language-minority voting discrimination has existed in the past (Days and Guinier 1984, 173). Other noteworthy parts of the act include Section 10's prohibition of the poll tax "as a precondition to voting" and Section 12's monetary and criminal sanctions for violations of sections of the act.

In March 1965, only 36 percent of voting-age Blacks in the South, compared to 73 percent of voting-age whites in the South, were registered to vote (Grofman, Handley, and Niemi 1992, 21). As a result of the Voting Rights Act, Black and Latino voters have made huge gains in registration and turnout, as well as in the election of minority local, state, and federal officials, though they are still significantly underrepresented in many covered jurisdictions (Davidson 1984, 10–15; Grofman, Handley, and Niemi 1992, 23–26). Illustratively, the number of Blacks holding political office nationwide grew from 1,500 in 1970 to 7,300 in 1990, a 400 percent increase (Pildes 1994). However, the number of

Black elected officials has remained stagnant at slightly less than 2 percent of all elected officials since the 1990s, and they are concentrated primarily at the municipal level (Joint Center of Political and Economic Studies 2000). Given the persistent gap between poor people's registration and voting rates and those of the nonpoor, social, geographic, and political impediments to full participation by the poor remain, even as legal barriers have been torn down. In 2000, those earning under $15,000 lagged more than 20 percentage points behind the 66 percent and 57 percent, respectively, registration and voting rates reported for all Americans (U.S. Census Bureau 2002). Poor people's underparticipation in the electoral process undoubtedly has an impact on the quality of representation they receive. And given the racial distribution of poverty, the informal disenfranchisement of the poor disproportionately constrains the electoral participation of people of color.

Cheryl M. Miller

See also: Civil Rights Acts, 1964 and 1991; Civil Rights Movement; Racial Segregation; Racism; Slavery

References and Further Reading

Davidson, Chandler. 1984. "Minority Vote Dilution: An Overview." In *Minority Vote Dilution*, ed. Chandler Davidson, 1–23. Washington, DC: Howard University Press.

Days, Drew S., and Lani Guinier. 1984. "Enforcement of Section 5 of the Voting Right Act." In *Minority Vote Dilution*, ed. Chandler Davidson, 167–180. Washington, DC: Howard University Press.

Grofman, Bernard, Lisa Handley, and Richard Niemi. 1992. *Minority Representation and the Quest for Voting Equality*. New York: Cambridge University Press.

Joint Center for Political and Economic Studies. 2000. *Black Elected Officials: A National Roster 2000*. Table 1. Washington, DC: Joint Center for Political and Economic Studies.

Pildes, Richard. 1994. "The Price of Colorblindness." *Washington Post*, April 16.

U.S. Census Bureau. 2002. "Voting and Registration in the Election of November 2000." Table 9: "Reported Voting and Registration of Family Members, by Race, Hispanic Origin, and Family Income: November 2000." Internet release date: February 27, 2002. http://www.census.gov/population/www/socdemo/voting/p20-542.html.

U.S. Department of Justice. 2001. "Introduction to Federal Voting Rights Laws." http://www.usdoj.jgov/crt/voting/intro.htm. Accessed December 17.

Wages

See Earned Income Tax Credit (EITC); Fair Labor Standards Act (FLSA); Family Wage; Labor Markets; Minimum Wage; "Working Poor"

Wagner Act

On July 5, 1935, President Franklin D. Roosevelt signed the Wagner Act (also referred to as the National Labor Relations Act [NLRA]) establishing the institutional and legal framework for collective bargaining that endured through the twentieth century. Senator Robert Wagner (D–New York) sponsored the NLRA as a replacement for the National Industrial Recovery Act, which the U.S. Supreme Court had ruled unconstitutional. In a dramatic shift away from federal government opposition to unions, the act explicitly outlawed "unfair labor practices" such as company unions and yellow dog contracts, forced employers to recognize and bargain in good faith with duly elected organizations representing workers (though it did not force the parties to agree to a contract), and, at least on the surface, protected workers engaged in union organizing from employer retaliation.

According to historian Michael Katz, FDR's labor legislation provided the major alternative to the "patchy, inadequate social insurance policies" that made up the New Deal's "semiwelfare state" (Katz 1986, 250). For many workers, this incomplete welfare system worked. The skyrocketing number of employees who joined unions pushed union and nonunion wages higher and slightly redistributed the burden of economic risk in the employee-employer relationship. Between 1933 and 1945, the number of workers represented by unions increased from 3 million to 14 million, approximately 30 percent of the workforce. These gains for labor were concentrated in manufacturing industries, where, by 1947, nearly two-thirds of the workforce was covered by union contracts.

Not surprisingly, business groups such as the National Association of Manufacturers and the Chamber of Commerce strenuously objected to the Wagner Act. However, opposition came from other corners as well. The National Association for the Advancement of Colored People and the National Urban League feared that the Wagner Act's move toward union-only shops would limit employment options for African American workers by codifying craft unions' existing exclusionary practices. The act could have legally remedied this problem, but according to New Deal historian David Kennedy, "Senator Wagner and the act's other sponsors . . . failed to accept suggested amendments that would have defined racial discrimination by

In the first test of the Wagner Act, officials from the National Labor Relations Board watch as workers of the Jones and Laughlin steel mill vote whether the Steel Workers Organizing Committee will be their sole bargaining agency. **(Bettmann/Corbis)**

unions as an 'unfair labor practice'" (Kennedy 1999, 307). In practice, however, increased rates of unionization benefited the increasing number of African American industrial workers who, largely because of organizing by the newly formed Congress of Industrial Organizations in the steel and automobile industries, gained a measure of economic security. The Wagner Act did much less for workers in domestic and agricultural occupations that employed a high percentage of Black and Latino workers. As they did with the Fair Labor Standards Act of 1938 and the Social Security Act of 1935, southern legislators excluded domestic and agricultural occupations from coverage under the Wagner Act.

The Wagner Act transformed the government's role in labor-management relations. To determine the proper and exclusive bargaining unit to represent workers, the Wagner Act established the National Labor Relations Board (NLRB). With the formation of the NLRB, the Wagner Act created a system by which workers could choose and the state could certify an organization to represent employees in negotiations with employers. The board immediately came under attack from employers, who challenged the legality of federal regulation of relations between employees and privately held companies. In *National Labor Relations Board v. Jones and Laughlin Steel Corporation* (301 U.S. 1 [1937]), the U.S. Supreme Court found that the "refusal to confer and negotiate has been one of the most prolific causes of strife." According to the Court, the Wagner Act's framers had aimed to minimize industrial strife. For the majority, Chief Justice Charles E. Hughes wrote, "The theory of the act is that free opportunity for negotiation with accredited representatives of employees is likely to promote industrial peace." By portraying unions as vehicles for industrial peace, the Court dramatically reversed its previous characterization of unions as institutions that by their very nature threatened to interfere with the flow of commerce. Though the Wagner Act contributed to organized labor's important gains, many unionists protested that this emphasis on stability inhibited workers' ability to organize for more fundamental changes in the American workplace.

From the outset, the board was a political institution subject to significant change in direction and membership. In 1939 and 1940, under protest from both employers and the American Federation of Labor (AFL), the board underwent significant congressional scrutiny that resulted in the removal of important board members and the reorganization of the board under the leadership of William Leiserson, who helped to craft long-standing board policies and procedures. With the passage of the Taft-Hartley Act in 1947, Congress further reorganized the board by transferring its prosecution and investigation responsibilities to the newly created General Counsel, an independent body not part of the NLRB and appointed by the president with the consent of the Senate. Currently, the board has five seats, each appointed by the president with the consent of the Senate to a five-year term.

Since its passage, the number of workers covered under the Wagner Act has been subject to constant judicial review and legislative amendment. For example, in the early 1970s, the Supreme Court expanded the NLRB's jurisdiction to include government and health care workers. Rulings that narrowly defined workers to exclude wide categories of employees who were designated as managers and supervisors, however, dramatically limited the number of workers eligible to join unions.

G. Mark Hendrickson

See also: Agricultural and Farm Labor Organizing; Fair Labor Standards Act (FLSA); Service and Domestic Workers; Trade/Industrial Unions

References and Further Reading

Cohen, Lizabeth. 1990. *Making a New Deal: Industrial Workers in Chicago, 1919–1939*. Cambridge: Cambridge University Press.

Gross, James. 1974. *The Making of the National Labor Relations Board: A Study in Economics, Politics, and the Law*. Albany: SUNY Press.

———. 1981. *The Reshaping of the National Labor Relations Board: National Labor Policy in Transition*. Albany: SUNY Press.

Katz, Michael B. 1986. *In the Shadow of the Poorhouse: A Social History of Welfare in America*. New York: Basic Books.

Kennedy, David M. 1999. *Freedom from Fear: The American People in Depression and War, 1929–1945*. New York: Oxford University Press.

Tomlins, Christopher. 1985. *The State and the Unions: Labor Relations, Law, and the Organized Labor Movement in America, 1880–1960*. Cambridge: Cambridge University Press.

War on Poverty

Begun officially in 1964, the War on Poverty was an ambitious governmental effort launched by President Lyndon B. Johnson's administration to address the problem of persistent poverty in the United States. Over the next decade, the federal government—in conjunction with state and local governments, nonprofit organizations, and grassroots groups—created a new institutional base for antipoverty and civil rights action and, in the process, highlighted growing racial and ideological tensions in American politics and society. Marked by moments of controversy and consensus, the War on Poverty defined a new era for American liberalism and, along with other initiatives encompassed within Johnson's Great

Society, added new layers to the American welfare state. Legislatively, the first two years were the most active. Between Johnson's State of the Union address in 1964—when he declared "unconditional war on poverty"—and the liberal setbacks suffered in the congressional elections of 1966, the Johnson administration pushed through an unprecedented amount of antipoverty legislation. The Economic Opportunity Act (1964) provided the legislative basis for the Office of Economic Opportunity (OEO), the new federal agency dedicated to fighting poverty, as well as for a host of new antipoverty programs, including the Job Corps, Volunteers in Service to America (VISTA), Upward Bound, Head Start, Legal Services, the Neighborhood Youth Corps, the Community Action Program, the college work-study program, Neighborhood Development Centers, small-business loan programs, rural programs, migrant worker programs, remedial education projects, local health care centers, and others. The antipoverty effort, however, did not stop there. It encompassed a range of Great Society legislation far broader than the Economic Opportunity Act alone. Other important measures with antipoverty functions included an $11 billion tax cut (Revenue Act of 1964), the Civil Rights Act (1964), the Food Stamp Act (1964), the Elementary and Secondary Education Act (1965), the Higher Education Act (1965), the Social Security amendments creating Medicare and Medicaid (1965), the creation of the Department of Housing and Urban Development (1965), the Voting Rights Act (1965), the Model Cities Act (1966), the Fair Housing Act (1968), several job-training programs, and various urban renewal–related projects.

The War on Poverty was complex in its origins, its implementation, and its impact. Its programs and philosophies were born out of the political discomfort caused by the persistence of poverty amid the abundance of post–World War II America, the vexing questions of citizenship raised by the civil rights movement, and decades of social scientific thought about poverty and social reform. With the War on Poverty, American liberalism's insistent optimism and deep faith in expertise encountered a domestic crisis of race, social order, and political economy comparable in scope only to the Civil War and the Great Depression. The administrations of Presidents John F. Kennedy and his successor Lyndon B. Johnson became the primary organizers of the government's response to that crisis. To deal with concern that poverty threatened American progress, these administrations pushed hard for economic growth that could create full employment and for social reform that could enable the poor to gain access to what President Johnson called "the good life."

The political will necessary for a major antipoverty initiative intensified in the early 1960s. Part of that intensification came from the moral and organizational groundswell of the civil rights movement. Another part grew from the so-called rediscovery by policymakers and the mainstream media of poverty as an urgent social and political issue. Leading the rediscovery were several exposés by journalists and social reformers. President Kennedy was reportedly moved by Homer Bigart's 1963 *New York Times* series on Appalachian poverty and a review, published in *The New Yorker,* of Michael Harrington's searing book *The Other America* (1962). Harrington's book offered a stunning portrait of an allegedly separate, forgotten America populated by an estimated 50 million poor Americans. For Kennedy, those works probably compounded a concern about poverty that had been roused during a 1960 campaign visit to depressed coal regions in West Virginia. Whatever motivated Kennedy, his administration put in motion a process that became the foundation for Johnson's War on Poverty.

During President Kennedy's lifetime, however, that process yielded scant benefits for the poor. Like his administration's involvement with civil rights, the efforts against poverty were piecemeal, hesitating, and limited to relatively safe political terrain. The Area Redevelopment Act (1961) mainly provided infrastructure and job-training assistance in economically "depressed" regions. Kennedy established a slightly more substantial record through wage policies, an experimental food stamp program, and the Manpower Development and Training Act (1962). The longest-lasting efforts came in the background work for a tax cut that stimulated economic growth and the work of the President's Committee on Juvenile Delinquency and Youth Crime (PCJD). The PCJD embraced several ideas and developed important strategies that guided much of the later War on Poverty. Its leaders, who included Robert F. Kennedy, Kennedy's close friend David Hackett, and several influential academics and social reformers, were especially captivated by the concept of community action, which maintained that poor people, especially in urban neighborhoods, should be organized and empowered in the struggle against poverty to demand the services, education, jobs, and, most controversially, political representation they needed for access to opportunity and full citizenship. In formulating this idea, they drew heavily on sometimes conflicting strands of social thought: on the one hand, sociological and anthropological theories that emphasized the internal "disorganization" and lack of "competence" in poor communities and the culturally reinforced "cycle of poverty" that poor people found themselves in; on the other, the "opportunity theory" associated with sociologists Richard Cloward and Lloyd Ohlin that focused on the structural economic and political barriers poor people faced. Community action proponents also drew on influential demonstration projects such as the multilayered attack on poverty and juvenile delinquency found in Cloward's Mobilization for Youth project in New York City and the Ford Foundation's Gray Areas project, which funneled resources into target areas in a select number of cities.

The War on Poverty was also influenced by economists based in the Kennedy/Johnson Council of Economic Advisors (CEA). Schooled in the economic theories of John Maynard Keynes, they were convinced that the key to fighting poverty was government-stimulated economic growth and full employment. In 1963, CEA chairman Walter Heller organized a task force to start planning what was initially envisioned as an "attack" on poverty, with an eye toward making this a major theme in the 1964 presidential campaign. After the tragic assassination of President Kennedy in November 1963, Johnson embraced the idea and made it his own. After a series of meetings with Heller and other key economic advisers at his ranch in late December 1963, Johnson decided to escalate and enlarge the antipoverty effort and to make community action one of its centerpieces. Approximately two weeks later, in his 1964 State of the Union address, Johnson made this decision public with his famous metaphorical declaration of "unconditional war." This War on Poverty quickly grew into a multifaceted attempt to attack the intertwined causes of poverty. Wanting to do more than ameliorate the symptoms of poverty, policymakers sought reform in a wide range of areas, including education, housing, health, employment, and civic participation. Antipoverty planners tried to provide poor people access to the American "good life" by offering them a "hand up" rather than a "handout." This required economic measures to stimulate growth and employment opportunities, they thought, but it also required local action and individual initiative. Early antipoverty warriors, especially in the OEO, placed great responsibility on local people and had great hopes of the skills and vision of people at ground level. This expectation encouraged thousands of distinctive battles against poverty throughout America. It also ensured that the War on Poverty would expose far more social, political, and economic problems than it could fix.

In early 1964, the two most pressing priorities of President Johnson's antipoverty agenda involved passing a massive tax cut designed to

8/20/1964—Washington, DC: President Johnson hands a pen, used in signing the $947.5 billion "War on Poverty" bill, to Peace Corps director Sargent Shriver, whom Johnson nominated to head the program. At right, looking on, is Robert Weaver, administrator, Housing and Home Finance Agency, later Secretary of the Department of Housing and Urban Development (HUD). (Bettmann/Corbis)

stimulate the economy and organizing a task force to shape the War on Poverty. The tax cut passed Congress in February and contributed to a major economic expansion. The task force—headed by R. Sargent Shriver, the director of the highly popular Peace Corps and the brother-in-law of the slain President Kennedy—established the basis for the Economic Opportunity Act (EOA) that Johnson signed in August 1964. The EOA was a remarkable piece of social welfare legislation that many contemporaries considered *the* War on Poverty. Premised on improving economic opportunity instead of providing cash transfers or creating a New Deal–style jobs program, the antipoverty legislation created a long list of programs designed to help individu-

State of the Union Address, Lyndon B. Johnson, January 8, 1964

. . . This budget, and this year's legislative program, are designed to help each and every American citizen fulfill his basic hopes—his hopes for a fair chance to make good; his hopes for fair play from the law; his hopes for a full-time job on full-time pay; his hopes for a decent home for his family in a decent community; his hopes for a good school for his children with good teachers; and his hopes for security when faced with sickness or unemployment or old age.

Unfortunately, many Americans live on the outskirts of hope—some because of their poverty, and some because of their color, and all too many because of both. Our task is to help replace their despair with opportunity.

This administration today, here and now, declares unconditional war on poverty in America. I urge this Congress and all Americans to join with me in that effort.

It will not be a short or easy struggle, no single weapon or strategy will suffice, but we shall not rest until that war is won. The richest Nation on earth can afford to win it. We cannot afford to lose it. One thousand dollars invested in salvaging an unemployable youth today can return $40,000 or more in his lifetime.

Poverty is a national problem, requiring improved national organization and support. But this attack, to be effective, must also be organized at the State and the local level and must be supported and directed by State and local efforts.

For the war against poverty will not be won here in Washington. It must be won in the field, in every private home, in every public office, from the courthouse to the White House.

The program I shall propose will emphasize this cooperative approach to help that one-fifth of all American families with incomes too small to even meet their basic needs.

Our chief weapons in a more pinpointed attack will be better schools, and better health, and better homes, and better training, and better job opportunities to help more Americans, especially young Americans, escape from squalor and misery and unemployment rolls where other citizens help to carry them.

Very often a lack of jobs and money is not the cause of poverty, but the symptom. The cause may lie deeper—in our failure to give our fellow citizens a fair chance to develop their own capacities, in a lack of education and training, in a lack of medical care and housing, in a lack of decent communities in which to live and bring up their children.

But whatever the cause, our joint Federal-local effort must pursue poverty, pursue it wherever it exists—in city slums and small towns, in sharecropper shacks or in migrant worker camps, on Indian Reservations, among whites as well as Negroes,

als develop marketable skills, political power, and civic aptitude. The legislation established the OEO, a new bureaucracy under the control of the president that oversaw the Community Action Program, the Job Corps, and VISTA and initiated such programs as Head Start and the federal legal services program. Other EOA programs, such as the Neighborhood Youth Corps, Adult Basic Education, and rural loan programs, were placed under the control of traditional executive departments.

Other parts of the War on Poverty were located outside the Economic Opportunity Act framework and, in the long term, probably had more impact on the lives of Americans. Those programs and legislation certainly accounted for far more expenditures than did the programs of the Office of Economic Opportunity, which

among the young as well as the aged, in the boom towns and in the depressed areas.

Our aim is not only to relieve the symptom of poverty, but to cure it and, above all, to prevent it. No single piece of legislation, however, is going to suffice.

We will launch a special effort in the chronically distressed areas of Appalachia.

We must expand our small but our successful area redevelopment program.

We must enact youth employment legislation to put jobless, aimless, hopeless youngsters to work on useful projects.

We must distribute more food to the needy through a broader food stamp program.

We must create a National Service Corps to help the economically handicapped of our own country as the Peace Corps now helps those abroad.

We must modernize our unemployment insurance and establish a high-level commission on automation. If we have the brain power to invent these machines, we have the brain power to make certain that they are a boon and not a bane to humanity.

We must extend the coverage of our minimum wage laws to more than 2 million workers now lacking this basic protection of purchasing power.

We must, by including special school aid funds as part of our education program, improve the quality of teaching, training, and counseling in our hardest hit areas.

We must build more libraries in every area and more hospitals and nursing homes under the Hill-Burton Act, and train more nurses to staff them.

We must provide hospital insurance for our older citizens financed by every worker and his employer under Social Security, contributing no more than $1 a month during the employee's working career to protect him in his old age in a dignified manner without cost to the Treasury, against the devastating hardship of prolonged or repeated illness.

We must, as a part of a revised housing and urban renewal program, give more help to those displaced by slum clearance, provide more housing for our poor and our elderly, and seek as our ultimate goal in our free enterprise system a decent home for every American family.

We must help obtain more modern mass transit within our communities as well as low-cost transportation between them. Above all, we must release $11 billion of tax reduction into the private spending stream to create new jobs and new markets in every area of this land.

These programs are obviously not for the poor or the underprivileged alone. Every American will benefit by the extension of social security to cover the hospital costs of their aged parents. Every American community will benefit from the construction or modernization of schools, libraries, hospitals, and nursing homes, from the training of more nurses and from the improvement of urban renewal in public transit. And every individual American taxpayer and every corporate taxpayer will benefit from the earliest possible passage of the pending tax bill from both the new investment it will bring and the new jobs that it will create. . . .

received an initial appropriation of slightly less than $1 billion and experienced only marginal increases after that. The food stamp program, for instance, fed hungry Americans and eventually reached almost 10 percent of the population and 60 percent of the poor. Medicare subsidized health care for the elderly (with almost 40 million enrollees in 2000 according to the Centers for Medicare and Medicaid Services), while Medicaid provided access to health care for the poor. The Elementary and Secondary Education Act provided money to local school districts, which were supposed to use the funds to help their poor students. The Higher Education Act eased the financial burdens of millions of college students. The Civil Rights Act and the Voting Rights Act empowered the federal government to enforce tough new antidiscrimination measures. The Fair Housing Act established an important base of law to combat housing discrimination.

The program that generated the most intense controversies and came to dominate the politics of the early War on Poverty was the Community Action Program (CAP). Envisioned as a foundation of the War on Poverty in 1964, the CAP offered the most promise for reform but also the most potential for turmoil. The basic idea behind the program was to stimulate the creation of new, community-based agencies to come up with and administer comprehensive antipoverty plans geared to the special needs of local communities. These local agencies, which would apply for federal funding through the OEO, were required by law to provide for the "maximum feasible participation" of poor people in designing and implementing these plans. This requirement was meant to prevent local politicians from dominating and controlling the use of the new antipoverty funds, and OEO officials were initially determined to follow through on this promise. For this reason, and because of the OEO's commitment to shaking up the local status quo, ensuring maximum feasible participation proved to be the most contentious part of the War on Poverty. In theory, and in reality in some places, OEO funding for community action agencies involved the distribution of not only money but power to poor people and their representative organizations, putting them in a position to challenge traditional federal, state, and local bureaucracies. By requiring the "maximum feasible participation of the poor" in community action agencies, the Economic Opportunity Act substantially elevated the role of marginalized people and set off a daring policy experiment. And because so many local power struggles and inequities were bound up with race, community action, like the broader War on Poverty, became inextricably intertwined with the struggle for racial equality.

Almost immediately after the initiation of the Community Action Program in August 1964, the innovative program stirred a storm of protest, particularly from some southern white leaders, who wished to preserve African American subordination, and from entrenched local politicians and social service leaders, who found their power threatened by newly empowered people and organizations. Angered by the turmoil CAP was causing and politically threatened by influential big-city mayors, President Johnson ordered the OEO to reign in the more combative community action agencies and to cooperate with local officials. This was the first of many steps taken to control and contain what some saw as the radicalism of community action but others saw as a matter of basic justice and access to opportunities that were being denied. Added regulations reduced the flexibility envisioned in the original Community Action Program and narrowed the meaning of maximum feasible participation to a concise mathematical formula. Through the Green Amendment of 1967, Congress effectively required that city halls and established civic leaders give their approval to actions of community action agencies. Eventually, preapproved "national emphasis" programs rather than locally generated programs came to dominate the work of community action agencies. Further changes arose from the intensification of urban civil disorder after 1965. Urban unrest narrowed the War on Poverty and turned the OEO and the CAP into major antiriot endeavors. By 1969, over 1,000 community action agencies were in operation, and they offered ready-made organizations capable of dealing with tension on the streets. In that role, according to several studies, the OEO proved relatively effective at calming tensions and reconfiguring attention paid to American ghettos. With modified structures and functions, community action agencies generally became much less controversial and developed into accepted social welfare institutions delivering fairly specific services. In this instance, as in other War on Poverty programs, attacks on the CAP did not kill the entire project. Even after the federal program was eliminated in 1974, it was evident that the CAP had left a lasting and widespread institutional legacy of community-based antipoverty organizations. In 1999, the U.S. Department of Health and Human Services reported that 96 percent of all counties in the United States had operating community action agencies or their equivalent.

Despite aggressive attacks on the War on Poverty in the 1968 presidential campaign, the Republican administration of President Richard Nixon continued many of its key programs and actually expanded the welfare state through the liberalization of the food stamp program, the indexing of Social Security to inflation, and the passage of the Supplemental Security Income (SSI) program for disabled and elderly Americans. Politically, however, the Nixon administration did a great deal to undermine the War on Poverty. In 1973, as one of a series of "reorganizations" that had already left the OEO much diminished and much less activist in orientation, Nixon replaced the OEO with the much weaker Community Services Administration and redistributed control over antipoverty programs to more traditional federal bureaucracies—in effect, bringing the formal War on Poverty to an end. The Nixon administration also launched a "New Federalism" initiative, in which the federal government shifted more authority over social welfare to state and local governments. This more decentralized vision for federalism was most fully realized during the administration of President Ronald W. Reagan, which replaced the Community Services Administration with the Community Services Block Grant system, redesigned job training, cut back the food stamp program, and initiated what some scholars have called a "War on Welfare."

The legacies of the Community Action Program and the rest of the War on Poverty remain a subject of contentious debate. Generally, the War on Poverty has been most often remembered for its political controversies and its failure to live up to its own stated goal of ending poverty in the United States. Assessments of its accomplishments and limitations, however, have tended to differ according to the political affiliation and ideological orientation of the interpreter and the spirit of the times. One example is the debate over the reasons for a substantial decline in the Black poverty rate, from 55 percent of all African Americans in 1959 to 33 percent in 1970, and for a drop in the overall U.S. poverty rate, from 22 percent to 12 percent in same time period (in 2000, the rate for African Americans was 22 percent and the overall rate was 11 percent) (U.S. Census Bureau 2003). Critics of the Great Society have tended to credit the decline in poverty to economic growth spurred by American entrepreneurship, while blaming the Great Society for impeding further economic growth. Defenders have tended to argue that the Great Society was crucial for the economic growth and directly helped move people out of poverty. Even those who applaud the many initiatives of the War on Poverty agree, however, that in the broader scheme of things it was more a skirmish than the all-out attack promised in presidential rhetoric. Modestly funded from the very beginning, it quickly fell victim to the artificial austerity imposed by spending demands from the much more rapidly escalating war in Vietnam. Hastily planned programs were subject to corruption and, under the spotlight of constant and intense scrutiny, scandal. Even the most popular programs, such as Head Start, have never been sufficiently funded to reach all who are eligible for their services. There is also some question over whether, given its primary emphasis on services to individuals and communities, the War on Poverty could ever have lived up to its lofty promise: It did not redistribute much wealth or address deep structural problems in the American economy, and those options were not seriously considered, except by those on the fringes. Equally important, the goal of ending poverty was quickly overshadowed, not only by the demands and growing controversy over Vietnam but also by the economic downturn of the 1970s and the political appeal of welfare reform.

In the 1980s and 1990s, disagreements over the legacies of the War on Poverty and the Great Society became especially intense. President Reagan and others on the political right convinced many that the War on Poverty represented a failure of big government. Instead of helping alleviate poverty, they argued, its programs supposedly encouraged sloth, dependency, crime, single parenthood, and unproductive citizenship. Conservative critics, led by Charles Murray in his 1984 book *Losing Ground*, charged that most of the programs were misguided, mismanaged attempts at social engineering in which liberal overspending stifled market-based solutions and covered up for the faults of individuals. Defenders of the Great Society retorted that social programs—despite being fragmented, underfunded, and besieged—had helped lower the poverty rate, reduce disorder, and absorb the shock from baby boomers entering the job market. Those defenders pointed out that most Americans have favored most of the Great Society's programs. In that regard, support for the Great Society's contributions to the welfare state—especially elements with formidable popular backing, such as Medicare, Head Start, Social Security expansion, and education funding—limited the effect of conservative assaults.

Two presidential moments hint at the political distance traveled by the War on Poverty since its inception. In President Johnson's first State of the Union address (1964), the roughhewn Texas Democrat declared an "unconditional war on poverty in America." With eager bravado, he promised not to rest "until that war is won." His audience thundered in ovation. Almost a quarter of a century later, in President Reagan's final State of the Union address (1988), the smooth, good-looking California Republican announced that in America's War on Poverty, "poverty won." His audience rumbled with laughter. The applause and the laughter on all sides may continue until some combination of time, domestic crisis, and movement building generates renewed political will to mount a major antipoverty initiative.

Kent B. Germany

See also: Area Redevelopment Act; Civil Rights Movement; Community Development; Community Organizing; *Economic Report of 1964;* Education Policies; Employment and Training; Federalism; Food Stamps; Health Policy; Housing Policy; Juvenile Delinquency; Legal Aid/Legal Services; *Losing Ground;* New Right; North Carolina Fund; *The Other America;* Peace Corps; U.S. Department of Housing and Urban Development; Volunteers in Service to America (VISTA); Welfare Policy/Welfare Reform

References and Further Reading

Davies, Gareth. 1996. *From Opportunity to Entitlement: The Transformation and Decline of Great Society Liberalism*. Lawrence: University Press of Kansas.

Gillette, Michael, ed. 1996. *Launching the War on Poverty: An Oral History*. New York: Twayne.

Katz, Michael B. 1989. *The Undeserving Poor: From the War on Poverty to the War on Welfare*. New York: Pantheon Books.

Matusow, Allen J. 1984. *The Unraveling of America: A History of Liberalism in the 1960s*. New York: Harper and Row.

Murray, Charles. 1984. *Losing Ground: American Social Policy, 1950–1980*. New York: Basic Books.

O'Connor, Alice. 2001. *Poverty Knowledge: Social Science, Social Policy, and the Poor in Twentieth-Century U.S. History*. Princeton: Princeton University Press.

Quadagno, Jill. 1994. *The Color of Welfare: How Racism Undermined the War on Poverty*. New York: Oxford University Press.

Schwarz, John E. 1983. *America's Hidden Success: A Reassessment of Twenty Years of Public Policy*. New York: Norton.

U.S. Census Bureau. 2003. "Table 3: Poverty Status of People, by Age, Race, and Hispanic Origin: 1959–2002." Current Population Survey, Annual Social and Economic Supplements. http://www.census.gov/hhes/poverty/histpov/hstpov3.html.

Wealth

Defined in strictly material terms, wealth is the ownership of assets that generate income or have market value, including land or other forms of real estate; savings; stocks, bonds, and similar financial assets; and tangible capital such as equipment and manufacturing plants. But wealth can also be understood in terms of the social and economic advantages, political power, and cultural values with which it has historically been associated. Thus, although some argue that the definition of wealth should include marketable skills, education, and other aspects of human capital and claims on social insurance benefits, these assets do not carry the same significance in terms of class status and social standing as do property or financial assets. And it is in the power, status, and prestige factors as well as in its material dimensions that wealth—specifically its unequal distribution and concentration—has been of such great consequence to the history of poverty and social welfare in the United States.

The pursuit of wealth has been a powerful, in some ways defining, force in American history and political economy: From the earliest European settlers seeking to aggrandize imperial fortune to succeeding generations of immigrants in search of the "American dream" of opportunity and upward mobility, the notion of America as a land of abundance and comparative economic freedom has been both a significant drawing point and keynote of national identity, reaching an apotheosis in the image of the United States as the "affluent society" in the decades following World War II. But there is an equally characteristic tradition that draws on sometimes overlapping political, ideological, and moral sensibilities to raise fundamental concerns about the dangers of wealth concentration and inequality, and that tradition has fueled efforts to regulate, redistribute, or otherwise democratize wealth holding in the United States and to prevent the wealthy from crystallizing into a political and economic ruling class. The tension between these two impulses has been played out in shifting patterns of wealth distribution; in efforts to regulate its accumulation, distribution, and political power; in debates over the public and private obligations of wealth, as exemplified especially in the emergence of organized philanthropy as an expression of institutionalized wealth stewardship; and in shifting attitudes toward the wealthy and the symbols of wealth accumulation that have become part of the cultural landscape at various times.

American wealth distribution has always been unequal, although the degree, nature, and consequences of inequality have undergone significant transformations over time. Moreover, the full dimensions of wealth inequality cannot be understood apart from the broader social and economic conditions within which it occurs. By most measures—as well as by contemporaneous assessments—wealth in colonial America was more equally distributed than in Europe, and indeed, more than in any subsequent period in U.S. history, with just under 13 percent of wealth concentrated in the hands of the top 1 percent of wealth holders and approximately one-half in the hands of the top 10 percent. Subsequent periods show a far more uneven distributional picture, with sustained periods of rising or persistent inequality followed by briefer periods during which wealth distribution leveled out somewhat. Historical research shows a sharp rise in wealth concentration and inequality through the first half of the nineteenth century. That rise was stemmed during the 1860s by the impact of Civil War and the emancipation of slaves, but it was soon followed by the tremendous accumulation of individual and corporate fortunes that marked the end of the century as the Gilded Age. As a result, in 1912, on the eve of World War I, more than half of the nation's wealth was concentrated among the top 1 percent of wealth holders and an estimated 90 percent among the top 10 percent (Huston 1998, 84).

The closing decades of the twentieth century saw a similarly dramatic rise in measured wealth inequality, which has continued through the early years of the new millennium and stimulated talk of a new Gilded Age. After reaching post–World War II lows of 25–30 percent in

Andrew Jackson, Bank Veto, July 10, 1832

In July 1832, President Andrew Jackson vetoed legislation that would have renewed the Bank of the United States, which was originally chartered in 1791 amid great controversy but subsequently gained acceptance within the political establishment. Nevertheless, as Jackson's veto message indicates, to its opponents the bank had come to symbolize the corrupting influence of large accumulations of wealth. With its explicit appeal to populist and class interests, Jackson's speech has been seen as a democratic manifesto against the looming threat of an aristocratic "money power," wielding undue influence on the political process and threatening to undermine democracy.

It is to be regretted that the rich and powerful too often bend the acts of government to their selfish purposes. Distinctions in society will always exist under every just government. Equality of talents, of education, or of wealth can not be produced by human institutions. In the full enjoyment of the gifts of Heaven and the fruits of superior industry, economy, and virtue, every man is equally entitled to protection by law; but when the laws undertake to add to these natural and just advantages artificial distinctions, to grant titles, gratuities, and exclusive privileges, to make the rich richer and the potent more powerful, the humble members of society—the farmers, mechanics, and laborers—who have neither the time nor the means of securing like favors to themselves, have right to complain of the injustice of their Government. There are no necessary evils in government. The evils exist only in its abuses. If it would confine itself to equal protection, and, as Heaven does its rains, shower its favors alike on the high and the low, the rich and the poor, it would be an unqualified blessing. In the act before me [to recharter the Bank of the United States] there seems to be a wide and unnecessary departure from these just principles.

Source: Andrew Jackson, Bank Veto, July 10, 1832, in *Andrew Jackson vs. Henry Clay: Democracy and Development in Antebellum America*, ed. Harry L. Watson (Boston and New York: Bedford Books, 1998), 187.

the early 1960s, the share of wealth garnered by the rich shot up to 40 percent for the top 1 percent and nearly 85 percent for the top 20 percent of wealth owners (the figures are substantially higher for stock market and investment wealth). These gains at the top occurred even as absolute wealth holdings diminished for the remaining 80 percent of U.S. households and dropped substantially for the bottom two-fifths (Wolff 1998; Keister 2000). Today, in a stark departure from its Revolutionary-era origins, the United States has the dubious honor of boasting the highest rates of wealth (and income) inequality in the industrialized world.

Of course, considering these trends in light of the broader dimensions of inequality deepens and in some ways complicates the picture of wealth inequality while cautioning against the impulse to designate any given period a "golden age" of relative egalitarianism in wealth distribution. Considering the bigger picture also underscores the multiple ways in which the concentration of wealth among the few has historically been linked to the growth and deepening of poverty among the many. Thus, colonial and Revolutionary-era wealth—although less concentrated among a top elite than in other periods—was largely confined to the minority of free white men who were property owners. Women, legally subordinate to and disentitled to wealth ownership apart from their husbands, faced legal as well as social barriers to independent wealth holding until the late nineteenth century. In addition to land, a substantial and growing amount of wealth from the colonial through the Civil War years was in the form of slave-holding (Wright 1986). Both slave labor and the slave trade contributed to the fortunes of individuals and corporations alike. In this and other ways, including the appropriation of Native American land through conquest and other means, wealth was generated from the mass impoverishment of people of color, while wealth distribution was patterned on subordination along the lines of class, race, and gender.

In contrast, the extreme polarization of wealth that has been accelerating since the 1980s has occurred within a context of more widespread overall wealth ownership (for most households, this takes the form of home ownership or savings accounts) and fewer formal, officially sanctioned barriers based on status. Contrary to the claims of those who would defend the status quo, however, this hardly amounts to a democratization of wealth. For one thing, in an economy that requires greater levels of education and training as well as access to consumer markets for basic goods, some form of wealth ownership represents an increasingly necessary point of financial leverage for ensuring basic opportunity and security. For all but those at the very top of the distribution, wealth ownership is less a source of privilege than a basic economic stakehold, a source of security as well as access to educational and related opportunities. Meanwhile, the proportion of households with no measurable assets has been rising since the 1980s, leaving as many as one-quarter of American families locked out of the protections and opportunities accorded on the basis of wealth ownership. Moreover, as even modest wealth ownership has become a requisite of economic and social citizenship, racial and gender gaps remain quite substantial (Keister 2000; Oliver and Shapiro 1995). And important changes in the forms of wealth ownership have put its benefits out of reach for many. Today, wealth is more corporate and globalized and is held in the form of financial assets from investments in the stock market. It is also, as much as ever, reliant on the existence and persistence of low-wage labor, in the United States and around the world.

Although conservative social theorists such as William Graham Sumner and, more recently, George Gilder have justified wealth inequality as a reflection of differences in individual ability and entrepreneurial acuity, scholars have pointed to a range of structural and political factors in explaining patterns of distribution over time. Some analysts point to the role of economic transformation, positing, in variations on the famous hypothesis put forward by economist Simon Kuznets (1955), that such major periods of economic modernization as the Industrial Revolution or the rise of the high-technology information economy create more inequality in their initial stages as part of the normal course of restructuring but eventually level out as more people become positioned to benefit from change. Others, more controversially, argue that wealth inequality is a necessary and desirable spur to economic growth and, conversely, that measures to promote greater equity suppress growth—an argument at odds with the experience of the post–World War II decades, when declining wealth inequality coincided with sustained economic growth. Historians have also emphasized the crucial role played by law and public policy in encouraging wealth accumulation and shaping its form and distribution: On the one hand, for example, are the controversial chartering of the National Bank in 1791 (seen to favor northern mercantile and financial interests), public subsidies that enabled private corporations to generate huge profits from activities such as railroad building, and legal decisions favoring the interests of capital and limiting its regulation. On the other hand are measures to bring land and home ownership within reach of the unmonied masses, such as the Homestead Act of 1862 and the Federal Housing Administration home mortgage provisions initiated in 1934.

But the question that has most consistently preoccupied observers, both as cause and consequence of wealth inequality, is the consolidation of enormous political and economic power in the hands of an identifiable elite devoted to its own aggrandizement and perpetuation. Such a group has been variously embodied in the European landed aristocracy, the colonial-era merchants chartered and under the protectorate of the British monarchy, the primarily northeastern banking and financial "money interest" behind the National Bank, or the fabulously wealthy corporate giants, "robber barons," and bankers of the late nineteenth and early twentieth centuries—the John D. Rockefellers, Andrew Carnegies, J. P. Morgans, Andrew Mellons, and others whose financial and business maneuverings earned them Theodore Roosevelt's famous epithet "malefactors of great wealth."

It was largely in response to the persistent but changing face of wealth concentration that reformers, beginning with the Revolutionary generation, first established and later refined the principles guiding provisions for protecting the "general welfare" against the designs of monied elites. From the outset of the new republic, these included prohibitions against European traditions of aristocratic inheritance as well as against centralized "big government" lest it operate in collusion with the rich. Indeed, in an era still charged by memories of the British East India Company (the target of the Boston Tea Party) and in which the "common man" was not a wage worker but a small proprietor, farmer, or independent artisan, limited government, "free enterprise," and "laissez-faire" were embraced as the safeguards of economic independence and democracy.

By the late nineteenth century, the situation was quite the reverse, as reformers increasingly turned to government regulation to rein in the great corporate trusts and monopoly capitalists who were overwhelming smaller competitors while themselves embracing the doctrine of laissez-faire and championing the cause of unregulated market growth. Laissez-faire, in the context of vast and monopolistic enterprises—many of them built with the help of government subsidies—was serving to undermine free enterprise and equal opportunity and weigh the scales in favor of *Wealth against Commonwealth*, as Henry Demarest Lloyd called it in the title of his influential 1894 screed against corruption. Laid bare in the writings of Lloyd, Ida Tarbell, Upton Sinclair, Frank Norris, and other muckraking journalists and novelists of the Progressive Era, the power and unethical business and labor practices of wealthy corporate monopolists became the target of congressional hearings and modest antitrust and regulatory legislation beginning in the 1890s. The work of such writers also helped fuel growing popular and political support for the establishment, after decades of struggle, of the progressive federal income tax (by the Sixteenth Amendment to the U.S. Constitution, ratified in 1913) and the permanent federal estate or inheritance tax in 1916.

Although various reform and redistributionist movements met with fierce resistance, they also spawned efforts to put a more beneficent face on wealth. The best-known of these was an essay entitled "Wealth" by steel tycoon Andrew Carnegie, published in the *North American Review* in 1889 and widely reprinted as "The Gospel of Wealth." Referring to the growing gap between rich and poor as "essential for the progress of the race," Carnegie argued that the rich should use their "surplus" wealth—over and above what was necessary for a life of comfort—for social betterment by administering it for "the common good" during their lifetimes (Carnegie 1889, 653, 658). Carnegie carried out his own mandate with highly visible projects such as municipal libraries for "working men"—even as Carnegie-employed Pinkerton detectives were using violence to quash labor organizing in his own steelworks. More significant, along with John D. Rockefeller and Margaret Olivia Sage (wife of railroad millionaire Russell Sage and founder of the philanthropy that bears his name), Carnegie took part in establishing the first generation of large-scale, general-purpose philanthropies. Greeted with skepticism as efforts to shelter large accumulations of capitalist wealth from taxation, these corporate foundations were able to diffuse such criticism with funding for such widely sanctioned endeavors as scientific research, education, and the arts.

If organized philanthropy put a beneficent face on great industrial fortunes, it also helped consolidate and institutionalize the influence of wealth in civil society and in the broader culture. This was increasingly apparent in charity and social work, where philanthropy made a concerted effort to set standards of training and professionalization, but it also extended to education, the arts, social sciences, and other fields. Translating much older ideas of elite stewardship into professional endeavor, philanthropists put their wealth into the business of cultural uplift—for the poor, as well as for the working and middle-class general public—far more than into addressing the roots of economic and social inequality. As self-appointed arbiter of "the common good," philanthropy seemed to lend credence to the idea that the existing system, of highly unequal wealth accumulation and distribution, would ultimately ameliorate disparities between rich and poor.

The post–World War II decades were comparatively complacent regarding problems of wealth and poverty. The disparities of earlier generations had not disappeared, but for several reasons they did diminish somewhat. One was the rising standard of living brought about by the combination of sustained economic growth, rising incomes among middle-class and unionized working-class earners, the expansion of mass consumerism, and the protections against economic insecurity established by the New Deal welfare state. The benefits of economic growth, in an era marked by broadly based wage gains and even modestly redistributive social policies, were more widely shared than in the past. Also significant was the vast expansion of home ownership—and hence, wealth ownership—among white working-class and middle-class households as a result of New Deal–initiated home mortgage guarantees and the benefits for World War II veterans provided by the G.I. Bill. And while these signposts of mass affluence helped paper over the persistence of considerable disparities in wealth and income, Cold War anticommunism played a powerful role in muzzling dissent. Amid the Cold War propaganda battles that pitted American "people's capitalism" against Soviet communism, talk that could be construed as fomenting "class warfare" was labeled subversive or anti-American and suppressed. Indeed, when foundations such as Rockefeller and Carnegie and the recently established Ford Foundation came under attack at the height of Joseph McCarthy's Red Scare, it was not as scheming protectorates of great capitalist fortunes but as hubs of a "liberal establishment" conspiring to foist vaguely socialist ideas of redistribution and "welfare statism" onto an unsuspecting public. In this atmosphere, liberals themselves looked to economic growth and full employment, far more than they did to redistribution, as the answers to enduring economic disparities. Social critics who sought to puncture the idealized vision of the "affluent society" by pointing to powerful networks of corporate wealth or to deep-seated racial disparities in home ownership and the "American Dream" remained on the margins of political debate.

It is against that backdrop—of diminishing wealth inequality in the postwar period and of complacency about enduring disparities—that the late-twentieth-century return to Gilded Age patterns of polarized wealth distribution has been received by some as a shocking and unexpected reversal of fortune and by others as a sign, as Andrew Carnegie might have said, of "the advancement of the race." Indeed, in these polarized reactions to the ever more visible concentrations of wealth among the very rich, a handful of corporate giants, and the globalized networks of first world economies, we can see an important aspect of the trend toward polarization. Shifts in power—away from labor and toward capital, away from locally based independent producers and toward large multinational corporations, away from institutions of democratic governance and toward privatized, market-based mechanisms of distribution—have helped fuel the rise in inequality. Along with these shifts, there has been an accompanying shift in ideological and political alignments that has helped advance an explicitly pro-wealth doctrine and policy agenda (Phillips 2002).

Cultivated within the think tanks, legal institutes, foundations, academic departments, and journals that form the intellectual backbone of the conservative New Right, this pro-wealth agenda is grounded in "supply-side" economics and in what some have described as a new Social Darwinism. It is hostile to government regulation and social provision and to the rights of labor to organize, and it has revived the idea of laissez-faire and free markets as the basis of economic freedom. Its deregulatory policies have encouraged the massive corporate merger wave since the 1980s while severely weakening the political standing of wage earners and consumers alike. And since the 1980s, it has mounted an assault not only on the New Deal/Great Society welfare state but on the very idea of progressive taxation that has infused economic policy with at least a modicum of fairness for nearly a century. In a radical departure from the Revolutionary-era, republican imprimatur against the concentration and dynastic inheritance of wealth, it has orchestrated the elimination of the estate tax—which affects only the very wealthy—by 2011, as well as a major redistribution of the tax burden from the very rich to the vast majority (Gates and Collins 2002).

Save for sporadic outcries over excessive CEO compensation, over the role of big money in politics, and over the cascading array of enormously costly corporate and financial scandals that have continued to unfold since the late 1990s, the broader consequences of wealth inequality have been largely absent from public and political debate. Some regard this as itself a consequence of the influence of wealth in both political parties. However, more popular explanations have pointed to the power of enduring cultural values of individualism, economic entrepreneurship, and self-reliance and, in particular, to the power of a cultural mythology that honors the rags-to-riches stories and the self-made man images that have surrounded those who develop great fortunes, from the immigrants John Jacob Astor and Andrew Carnegie to Microsoft founder Bill Gates. Nevertheless, in the past, those very same values have also been invoked to curb the excesses and overweening, enterprise-quashing power of concentrated wealth, even as the proverbial success story has been made possible by the very public provisions and amenities that the new gospel of wealth now seeks to undermine.

Alice O'Connor

See also: Capitalism; Globalization and Deindustrialization; "Gospel of Wealth"; Income and Wage Inequality; Philanthropy; *Progress and Poverty;* Property; Republicanism; Slavery; Social Darwinism; Wealth, Distribution/Concentration

References and Further Reading

Beckert, Sven. 2001. *The Monied Metropolis: New York City and the Consolidation of the American Bourgeoisie, 1850–1896*. New York: Cambridge University Press.

Carnegie, Andrew. 1889. "Wealth." *North American Review* 148 (June): 653–664.

Gates, William H., Sr., and Chuck Collins. 2002. *Wealth and Our Commonwealth: Why America Should Tax Accumulated Fortunes*. Boston: Beacon Press.

Gilder, George. 1981. *Wealth and Poverty*. New York: Basic Books.

Huston, James. 1998. *Securing the Fruits of Labor: The American Concept of Wealth Distribution*. Baton Rouge: Louisiana State University Press.

Keister, Lisa. 2000. *Wealth in America: Trends in Inequality*. New York: Cambridge University Press.

Kuznets, Simon. 1955. "Economic Growth and Income Inequality." *American Economic Review* 45: 1–28.

Lloyd, Henry Demarest. 1894. *Wealth against Commonwealth*. New York: Harper and Row.

Oliver, Melvin, and Thomas Shapiro. 1995. *Black*

Wealth/White Wealth: A New Perspective on Racial Inequality. New York and London: Routledge.

Pessen, Edward. 1990. *Riches, Class, and Power: America before the Civil War*. New Brunswick, NJ: Transaction Books.

Phillips, Kevin. 2002. *Wealth and Democracy: A Political History of the American Rich*. New York: Random House.

Williamson, Jeffrey G., and Peter H. Lindert. 1980. *American Inequality: A Macroeconomic History*. New York: Academic Press.

Wolff, Edward. 1998. "Recent Trends in the Size Distribution of Household Wealth." *Journal of Economic Perspectives* 12: 131–150.

Wright, Gavin. 1986. *Old South, New South: Revolutions in the Southern Economy since the Civil War*. New York: Basic Books.

Wealth, Distribution/Concentration

Wealth ownership is concentrated in the hands of a small minority of the U.S. population. Wealth, or net worth, is the value of a person's assets less his or her debts. For a typical family, assets include the home, savings and checking accounts, and other investments. Wealthier families also own stocks, bonds, investment real estate, and business assets. Liabilities typically include mortgage debt as well as student loans, car loans, and other consumer debt. Between the 1960s and 1990s, total household wealth grew from $8 trillion to nearly $24 trillion (all dollar values are 2000 dollars, converted using the Consumer Price Index), and the number of billionaires in the Forbes 400 rose from 85 to 267. Although total wealth has increased, wealth has become more concentrated in recent decades. The implications of severe and growing inequality are apparent when the advantages of wealth ownership are considered. Wealth provides current use value (as in the ownership of a home), generates more wealth when it is invested, provides a buffer during financial emergencies, and can be passed to future generations. Moreover, wealth may increase political influence, educational and occupational opportunities, and social advantages for both current and future generations.

The average wealth owned by American families has grown considerably since the mid-1960s. In 1962, the mean net worth for an American family was $152,000, rising to $223,000 by 1983 and $283,000 by 1998. There were years during those decades in which family wealth did not grow, particularly during the 1970s; however, when measured on average, American families got much richer between the 1960s and 1980s. Yet what according to these measures may appear to be a story of growing affluence masks a more disturbing reality of growing disparity in the distribution of wealth ownership. This disparity can be illustrated by looking at the difference between two different wealth indicators. The first is mean, or average, wealth holdings, which are calculated by dividing total overall wealth by the number of families in the United States. This estimate is relatively high because a small number of extremely large fortunes skew the distribution of wealth and bring the average up. The second indicator is median wealth, which shows the midpoint of wealth ownership for American families. The median value of a family net worth in 1962 was about $41,000, meaning that one-half of American families had more and one-half had less than that amount in wealth. This figure rose to $57,000 in 1983 and to $64,000 in 1998, indicating that a great deal of the substantial growth of average wealth was realized by those at the top. Likewise, growth in the percentage of households with zero or negative net worth suggests that not all families enjoyed increases in their well-being. Indeed, more than one-quarter of all families had no wealth as recently as 1998.

Since the early 1920s, the top 1 percent of wealth holders have consistently owned an average of 30 percent of total family wealth. During economic downturns, the distribution of wealth appears more equal. However, studies of wealth mobility suggest that it is rare for families to move upward in comparative wealth holding and that eras of relative equality reflect deflated asset prices more than improvements in the well-being of the majority of the population. The top 1 percent of wealth owners owned an average of 30 percent of total net worth between 1922 and the early 1950s. During the 1950s, economic prosperity brought with it increased wealth inequality, and by the late 1950s, estimates suggest that the top 1 percent of households owned nearly 35 percent of total wealth. Inequality was not as dramatic during the 1960s and 1970s due to an extended stock market slump and the growth of welfare programs such as Aid to Families with Dependent Children and Social Security, but it increased again starting in the 1980s and continued through the 1990s.

Recent trends in wealth inequality are particularly startling. The top 1 percent of wealth owners owned nearly 40 percent of net worth and nearly 50 percent of financial assets in the late 1980s and 1990s. During this period, the top 1 percent enjoyed two-thirds of all increases in financial wealth. Moreover, while wealth inequality was consistently more severe throughout Europe for many decades, by the early 1990s, the United States had surpassed all industrial societies in the extent of family wealth inequality. Perhaps most striking is the decline in the wealth of the poorest 80 percent of households. The wealth of this group decreased by more than 2 percentage points, from 18.7 percent of total wealth in 1983 to 16.4 percent in 1989. Moreover, nearly all growth in real wealth between 1983 and 1989 was accumulated by the top 20 percent of wealth holders, who gained 2.3 percentage points in their total wealth holdings, from 81.3 to 83.6 percent. The Gini coefficient, an indicator of the degree of inequality, increased from 0.85 in 1989 and 1992 to 0.87 in 1995. (The Gini coefficient ranges from 0 to 1, with 0 indicating perfect equality and 1 indicating perfect inequality. Conceptually, if a single household owned all the wealth, the Gini would equal one.) These estimates indicate that wealth inequality is extremely severe and that it worsened considerably after 1962.

Racial inequality in wealth ownership is among the most extreme and persistent forms of stratification in the United States. Blacks and Hispanics, in particular, own considerably less wealth than whites. In 1992, while median Black income was about 60 percent of median white income, median net worth for Blacks was only 8 percent of median net worth for whites. In that same year, 25 percent of white families had zero or negative assets, but more than 60 percent of Black families had no wealth. Longitudinal estimates suggest that between 1960 and 1995, whites were twice as likely as were minorities to have more wealth than income and nearly three times as likely to experience wealth mobility. Minorities are also underrepresented among the very wealthy. In 1995, 95 percent of those in the top 1 percent of wealth holders were white, while only 1 percent were Black. The wealth position of other minorities has attracted less attention, but there is evidence that the wealth accumulation of whites also exceeds that of Hispanics and Asians.

Data limitations have made the study of wealth mobility very difficult, but recent data improvements have allowed researchers to provide unprecedented detail in their estimates of wealth ownership. These data have revealed that levels of wealth inequality are so extreme that many people own essentially no wealth, even though assets are one of the most central indicators of well-being. Although wealth inequality remains a fundamental and critical social problem, improved understanding of the problem may help with developing ways to alleviate it.

Lisa A. Keister

See also: Capitalism; Classism; Economic Theories; Economic/Fiscal Policy; Income and Wage Inequality; Wealth

References and Further Reading

Keister, Lisa A. 2000. *Wealth in America*. New York: Cambridge University Press.

Oliver, Melvin O., and Thomas M. Shapiro. 1995. *Black Wealth/White Wealth*. New York: Routledge.
Wolff, Edward N. 1998. "Recent Trends in the Size Distribution of Household Wealth." *Journal of Economic Perspectives* 12: 131–150.

Welfare Administration

The political history of welfare is one not only of embattled policies but also of embattled administration. Welfare administration has developed unevenly and inconsistently, buffeted by competing impulses toward localism and centralization, public and private provision, professionalization and bureaucratization, simplification and complexity. Caught amid these crosscurrents and an enduring ambivalence about the provision of relief itself, public welfare bureaucracies have often drawn the ire of politicians, taxpayers, and the poor families that rely on them for assistance.

Contemporary arrangements for welfare administration have their roots in the localism and moralism that were distinctive features of the British poor laws and colonial welfare provision. In the United States, care of the poor was largely a secular function of town governments, whose locally appointed "overseers of the poor" dispensed relief. Administrative practices informally established a moral hierarchy for assistance, boarding out widows of higher social standing to homes in the community and sending widows of less exalted standing to work in Houses of Industry and their children to work on farms, where, it was reasoned, they would benefit from the fresh country air. Local administration of relief, reflecting the burden relief placed on the local property tax, utilized strategies to prevent in-migration, for example, "warning out" citizens from other communities who might try to establish residency without adequate economic support.

As industrialization and immigration swelled the ranks of the poor toward the end of the nineteenth century, relief remained both limited and local. Two private forms of welfare—charity organization societies and settlement houses—began to emerge in the gaps of public provision. Both offered aid to the needy, creating a private sphere for "welfare work" and developing practices that combined material assistance with social intervention. Although different in tone and mission, both types of organization anticipated the uneasy mix of "cash and care" that would come to infuse welfare provision as it developed into a major public function.

Mothers' pensions, sometimes heralded as the first great welfare reform of the twentieth century, may be viewed more modestly as an incipient system for providing income support to poor families. Administratively, the program was a bridge from local poor law arrangements to a new form of state-based social insurance. Welfare financing moved up the governmental ladder, with state governments assuming a greater share of welfare costs. This eased somewhat the fiscal constraints created by tying relief to the local property tax. However, local units of government retained administrative authority for relief giving, including the considerable power of administrative gatekeeping. Local boards and commissions continued to make case-by-case decisions on who would receive aid, using moralistic standards similar to those practiced in the nineteenth century to limit support largely to "worthy widows" and to exclude mothers of color and many noncitizen immigrants. In the ten years after mothers' pensions were first established in 1911, forty states passed similar legislation. However, administrative gatekeeping practices minimized the potential impact of these laws. By 1930, less than 3 percent of potentially eligible families received aid. Of those receiving aid, 82 percent were the families of widows, 96 percent of them white.

In the wake of the Great Depression, as economic deprivation spread through much of the nation, poverty briefly lost its stark moral stigma. President Franklin D. Roosevelt's New Deal responded, in part, by creating the Aid to Dependent Children (ADC) program within the Social Security Act of 1935. ADC constituted a marked departure from existing forms of provision, bringing the federal government into the picture, largely in the realm of financing but also in establishing the basic parameters for welfare eligibility. The law provided a subsidy to existing state aid programs, reimbursing them for up to six dollars for payments to one child and four dollars for each additional child. Although the federal program was small at its start, it opened the way to an enlarged federal role over time. In the domain of administration, ADC made a significant concession to past practices, leaving control in the hands of the states.

This element of continuity reflected not only incrementalism at work but also the political sensitivities of the period. ADC sidestepped potentially explosive political issues by permitting states to set their own eligibility and administrative standards, effectively shielding local gatekeeping practices from federal intrusion. State administrative autonomy permitted southern states to prevent most minorities from obtaining access to assistance and enabled all states, northern and southern, to adapt provision to the requirements of local economic interests (for example, suspending aid during harvest seasons and keeping benefits lower than the wages available in the least desirable jobs).

Beginning in the late 1950s, restrictive gatekeeping practices caught the attention of federal officials, undoubtedly made more attentive by the burgeoning civil rights movement. One of the more flagrant state practices was to deem as "unsuitable" those homes in which unmarried women had children. Once a household was designated unsuitable, its welfare benefits could be cut. When the state of Louisiana adopted this tactic, the racial implications were hard to miss: White families made up only 5 percent of the homes the state deemed unsuitable. The federal government blocked this practice, issuing an administrative rule (the Flemming rule, named for then secretary of health, education, and welfare Arthur S. Flemming) prohibiting states from withholding support from children simply because they were "illegitimate." These types of administrative tactics were not limited to southern states. In another infamous case, the small city of Newburgh, New York, used its administrative discretion to block access to welfare by requiring adult welfare recipients to "muster" at the local police station for their welfare checks and by threatening to investigate applicants' home environment and to remove children from homes found unsuitable.

Federal officials were troubled by blatantly restrictive and racially skewed state practices and were broadly concerned about the professional adequacy of state welfare bureaucracies. Social workers and their professional associations joined with the antipoverty warriors of President John F. Kennedy's administration to make the case that fighting poverty required more than the provision of income. They argued that fighting poverty required social services that could prevent families from becoming poor and could rehabilitate others who were mired in poverty. In effect, they reintroduced the notion that "cash" should be coupled with "care," an approach practiced in the old settlement houses and charity organization societies. The way to reduce welfare caseloads, they argued, was to expand social services and to professionalize state welfare staff.

These views informed the Social Security Act Amendments of 1962, under which the federal government provided grants to states to reform welfare administration and build professional service capacity. States quickly took advantage of the grant program, using it to channel public funds to private social service providers (an early form of privatization). However, they also found loopholes in the grant language that allowed them to substitute federal funds for preexisting state administrative activities. Consequently, millions of federal grant dollars poured into states, but with no discernible effect either on the professional stature of the bureaucracy or on rapidly rising caseloads. In 1967, the services strategy was pronounced a failure, and the grant program was terminated.

Nevertheless, the issue of professionalism in service provision remained on the agenda, pursued in the form of a narrower federal initiative encouraging states to separate social service and public assistance functions. In effect, this created a new domain for the social work profession in the specialized field of child welfare services, while leaving to generalists and nonprofessionals the increasingly bureaucratized functions of administering the Aid to Families with Dependent Children (AFDC) program (formerly ADC).

When the much-remarked "welfare explosion" hit in the late 1960s and early 1970s, state welfare administration came under renewed political attack. Rising caseloads were viewed as a political problem, although they might have been taken to indicate that poor families long excluded from welfare were finally gaining access to support. Rising caseloads were also viewed as indicating a failure in state gatekeeping practices, now seen as insufficiently restrictive. As welfare became available to a growing population of African Americans and female-headed households, state welfare provision was widely decried as "a mess" and "a nightmare" overwhelmed by "waste, fraud, and abuse."

Growing state caseloads created a drain on the federal treasury because AFDC provided states an open-ended federal subsidy for state benefit expenditures. As costs mounted, the federal government began to search for ways to assert control. President Richard M. Nixon's administration proposed a Family Assistance Plan that would have controlled the outflow of federal dollars by providing a fixed amount of support for state welfare payments. It also would have simplified welfare administration, emphasizing cash transfers and streamlining the terms of assistance.

In the wake of the plan's defeat in the early 1970s, the administration turned to administrative reform as a way to stem the growth of welfare, initiating a federal audit system called "quality control" to crack down on sloppy state practices and on what the administration believed to be overly generous welfare provision. Quality control audits seemed to indicate that millions of dollars in cash assistance were being paid out improperly. However, the error rate was both overestimated and skewed. It treated all paperwork mistakes as if they produced payment errors, although many of them involved only missing documents that did not change a family's actual eligibility for aid. The error rate also counted only excess payments; it did not record underpayments or failure to pay benefits to eligible families.

Quality control provided an instrument for federal intrusion in state welfare administration, using the threat of fiscal penalties to prod states to tighten up gatekeeping practices in order to reduce error rates that had reached double digits in some states. Under pressure to bring error rates down to 4 percent by 1982, states erected new process-driven gatekeeping practices. These practices replaced the overtly moralistic and race-based restrictions of previous eras, making procedural compliance the new mark of a virtuous client. Those who had difficulty navigating complex new procedural demands were deemed "uncooperative" and denied benefits.

Administrative reform modestly helped control caseload growth. Perhaps more significantly, it advanced processes of deprofessionalization and bureaucratization initiated earlier as part of the separation of service functions from income transfer functions. Although error rates dropped, administrative reform was not sufficient to insulate state welfare agencies from an emergent new critique in the 1980s. Both welfare policy and administrative practices were blamed for continued welfare use (often referred to as "dependency"). Some critics even caricatured the reformed welfare bureaucracy as too streamlined, toeing the line on procedural rules but still making welfare too readily available. The conservative version of this critique called on welfare agencies to intervene more actively in the lives of the poor to dissuade them from using welfare for income support and to demand work in return for aid. The liberal version of this critique called for a return to a services strategy, this time focused on supporting work as an alternative to welfare.

These critiques were embedded in a broader political challenge to welfare, which precipitated a series of incremental changes, eventually culminating in a complete overhaul of welfare policy. Beginning in the 1980s, the federal government gave states authority to change aspects of policy and practice in order to promote work. The Work Incentive (WIN) Program demonstrations, the Job Opportunities and Basic Skills (JOBS) provisions of the Family Support Act of 1988, and a variety of work-oriented programs operated under waivers from federal rules. Implicit in these initiatives was a vague notion of a newly reformed style of administration that expanded state authority, eschewed the bureaucratization of the previous era, and focused on achieving behavioral change through an unspecified mix of social services, persuasion, and strongly enforced work requirements.

These piecemeal efforts to transform state welfare administration were codified into federal law in 1996 with the replacement of AFDC by Temporary Assistance for Needy Families (TANF). TANF explicitly redirected authority from the federal level to the states and emphasized work requirements over income assistance. Under the banner of devolution, states received federal financing through flexible block grants and were accorded wide discretion over the dispensation of assistance and the imposition of work rules.

However, the degree of state-level autonomy should not be overstated. Like prior federal legislation, TANF used federal fiscal incentives and disincentives to direct state administrative practices toward meeting specific objectives. The strongest fiscal incentives were attached to the objectives of caseload reduction and enforcement of work requirements. To a more modest degree, federal law also prodded state agencies to discourage childbearing and to encourage marriage by welfare recipients, a reminder of the "morality work" of early-twentieth-century welfare provision. In short, after decades of efforts to reform administration by simplifying the rules and reducing bureaucratic discretion, TANF reintroduced complexity and expanded discretion in welfare administration.

Devolution has made it difficult to characterize contemporary administration in any coherent way. TANF allowed states to vary widely in their administrative practices. Although targeted fiscal incentives, in effect, held states accountable for meeting caseload and "work activity" quotas, they did not hold states accountable for how they met them. In some states and counties, administration continued largely under the auspices of the same public agencies—and indeed, the same agency staff—that had previously administered welfare under AFDC. In other instances, TANF spurred privatization, for the first time turning many public welfare functions—case processing and work-related services—over to for-profit enterprises. Private, nonprofit agencies also expanded their role in many states, especially in the operation of welfare-to-work programs. Although some advocates championed privatization as a way to bring more professional expertise to welfare administration, there has been little consistency in the standards states have required of private providers. In addition, in some states, the fragmentation of provision among a growing number of public and private agencies has produced instability in institutional arrangements, with contracted providers moving in and out of the public welfare system. Privatization has also raised new problems of coordination, accountability, and equity in administration.

At the beginning of the twenty-first century,

the mission and methods of welfare administration remain a work in progress. The complexity of the administrative task reflects its functional and political ambiguities: Welfare administration is part dispenser of income, part dispenser of morality, and part dispenser of social services. It is in this context that welfare provision has developed an uneven history and faces an uncertain future.

Evelyn Z. Brodkin

See also: Aid to Families with Dependent Children (ADC/AFDC); Federalism; Hull House; Maternalist Policy; Settlement Houses; Social Security Act of 1935; Welfare Policy/Welfare Reform; Welfare State

References and Further Reading

Brodkin, Evelyn Z. 1986. *The False Promise of Administrative Reform: Implementing Quality Control in Welfare*. Philadelphia: Temple University Press.

Derthick, Martha. 1970. *Uncontrollable Spending for Social Services Grants*. Washington, DC: Brookings Institution.

Handler, Joel, and Ellen Jane Hollingsworth. 1971. *The "Deserving Poor": A Study of Welfare Administration*. Chicago: Markham.

Simon, William. 1985. "The Invention and Reinvention of Welfare Rights." *Maryland Law Review* 44.

Steiner, Gilbert. 1971. *The State of Welfare*. Washington, DC: Brookings Institution.

Trattner, Walter F. 1994. *From Poor Law to Welfare State*. 5th ed. New York: Free Press.

Welfare Capitalism

"Welfare capitalism" is a term that must be defined on two levels. First, it refers to social welfare benefits and health, safety, or leisure programs offered in the private sector through the workplace. These are programs established and directed by employers in market-based economies. More broadly, welfare capitalism must also be seen as a continuing management strategy for negotiating political and economic demands from workers and the regulatory state. In the United States, welfare capitalism has historically expanded when government has extended its involvement in labor and social welfare matters. Thus, when it comes to the unique mix of private and public social welfare benefits in the United States, business and government cannot be thought of as inversely proportional, with one sector expanding as the other contracts. Private welfare schemes have historically developed, expanded, and contracted in tandem with public ones.

In the early twentieth century, American business managers in large-scale corporate enterprises, racked by two decades of labor strife, began preaching a new industrial relations doctrine. Liberal business leaders called on firms to strive for a harmony of interests between capital and labor and to address the source of workers' anxiety or frustration: economic insecurity. Leading industrialists believed that the best way to achieve a new class accord was not through collective representation for workers but through the assumption by each firm of some obligation for its own workers' well-being, either inside or outside the workplace. Known as "welfare work," this rather broadly and loosely defined program relied on employee benefits that ranged from company cafeterias and lunch plans to athletic activities, picnics, English-language and home economics classes, company housing, and company doctors. Some employers offered pecuniary forms of welfare work—loans, savings plans, profit-sharing plans, or accident relief funds. Some company owners, such as George Pullman, established entire towns, complete with company housing, stores, churches, and athletic teams. Companies offered different benefit mixes and approached welfare work with a variety of motivations and expectations. Some executives believed that welfare work improved productive efficiency, that these programs would inspire the employee to become a better worker, whether more efficient, healthier, or more loyal. Others sought to avoid labor upheaval and to discourage unionization; still others hoped to attract and keep skilled workers. In all cases, however, welfare work was a strategy to retain complete managerial control over the terms of employment.

Although ostensibly a means of alleviating workers' economic distress, welfare capitalism prior to the New Deal emphasized workforce efficiency more than individual economic security. Often, company welfare benefits were meant to be the carrot that would convince workers to accept the stick of faster, mechanized production systems, such as the assembly line. Qualifying for Henry Ford's famed five-dollar-a-day compensation or for profit-sharing bonuses entailed conforming to proper social and deferential behavior both inside and outside the workplace. Pension consultants and welfare capitalist proponents urged firms to adopt company-provided old-age pensions as a means to move older workers out of the workplace, thereby eliminating less fit employees who could not run the machinery as fast as younger workers. Moreover, until the 1930s, firms with industrial pension programs almost always provided their own in-house plans rather than using actuarially based and funded insurance policies or annuities. Whether small or large, the majority of companies failed to make any systematic effort to put monies aside for the purpose of paying benefits. The firm could then decide at the moment of a worker's retirement how much he or she would receive or whether he or she would receive any benefits at all. Management could and did base these decisions on personal characteristics, such as work performance, cooperation with foremen, absentee and tardiness records, participation in labor disturbances, or even conduct outside the workplace. Company plans rarely included any surviving spouse's benefits. The case of old-age pensions points to a broader pattern: Rather than being a real source of economic security for workers, welfare capitalism functioned as a program of nonwage incentives used to compel workers to conform to greater mechanization and automation and to a much faster pace of work. Moreover, this tendency to think in terms of managerial rewards and gratuities rather than employment rights became a permanent part of corporate employers' and commercial insurers' view of industrial relations and social welfare.

The work of historian Andrea Tone has revealed the gender politics inherent in welfare capitalism. In the early twentieth century, state legislatures passed new laws that circumscribed employers' authority and protected workers, including maximum-hours laws, minimum-wage laws, and certain occupational safety laws. However, thanks in part to U.S. Supreme Court rulings overturning more generalized protective laws (*Lochner v. New York*, 198 U.S. 45 [1905]) while upholding them when targeted on women (*Muller v. Oregon*, 208 U.S. 412 [1908]), these laws applied exclusively to women workers. Some states also had new widows' pensions, potentially removing women from the workforce. In response, and in efforts to contain the threat of further regulations, employers offered "welfare capitalism as an alternative to welfare statism" (Tone 1997) and sought to regain their prerogatives and control over employment rules by presenting themselves as protectors of female workers and caretakers of their welfare. In contradiction to reformers' claims that the industrial workplace harmed women's health, employers offered the industrial workplace as a site of female uplift and reform, establishing washrooms, cafeterias and hot lunches, toilet facilities, home economics classes, and physical exercise for women workers. Conversely, claiming that public regulation and welfare provision robbed male workers of their manly virtue, independence, and breadwinning role, employers offered male workers savings and loan plans, profit-sharing plans, athletic teams, and housing loans. In neither case, however, did these programs ensure job security or living wages. Male and female workers continued to experience regular periods of unemployment, underemployment, indebtedness, and the need for public relief.

In the 1920s, welfare capitalist employers shifted their emphasis toward pecuniary welfare benefits. One of the most effective and long-lasting of these benefit programs was group insurance, a new type of private social insurance policy that would become the basis of the modern employee benefits system. Insurance companies originally devised group insurance for employers to provide life insurance coverage for a large group of employees under one group risk factor; individual employees did not have to pass a medical examination to be included in the plan. Like other welfare capitalist measures, group life insurance was promoted as a measure that would improve relations between capital and labor. Insurers and employers presented such private social insurance as a solution to economic insecurity that was apolitical, rational, and organized. "Expert" managers and actuaries could make the decisions on behalf of working people but without the interference of the masses. Group insurance did indeed respond to a real need, bringing life insurance and funeral benefits to many workers who did not have any life insurance or who could not maintain their own policies over a number of years. At the time, over 40 percent of wage earners had no life insurance policies, and many industrial workers could not obtain individual coverage because industrial diseases, occupational injuries, and poor health prevented them from passing the necessary medical exams. Life insurance companies categorically denied individual policies to workers in designated hazardous industries. More generally, until the advent of employer-based group insurance, low-wage industrial workers were considered "uninsurable risks" by the major insurance companies. This designation served as a form of racial as well as class exclusion and was routinely applied to African Americans, Asians, and Mexicans regardless of the jobs they held.

And yet employer-provided group insurance was partial at best, extending principally to white male workers, who were more likely than nonwhites to work in companies that made some effort to regularize employment and stabilize production. By extending "insurability" to only one category of workers, namely white, urban workers, group insurance deepened the cleavages of class and race already built into insurance underwriting and the labor market.

These cleavages in welfare capitalism extended to gender as well. Both group insurance and company pensions rested on long-term employment and uninterrupted employment. Thus, women workers were far less likely to qualify for insurance benefits, since they worked in part-time jobs or in seasonal jobs that regularly laid off workers at particular points in the year. Women periodically removed themselves from the paid labor market to take care of children or sick relatives. Therefore, as long as insurance remained tied to workforce participation—essentially the rest of the twentieth century—women had a great deal of trouble qualifying for benefits.

By the time Franklin D. Roosevelt took office as president in early 1933, one-quarter of the American working population was unemployed. After three years of despair and passivity—broken sporadically by communist-orchestrated demonstrations—unemployed workers and families without income began actively demanding some governmental support where there was no opportunity to work. In this climate of political upheaval, grassroots political movements—especially movements of the elderly unemployed—and the Roosevelt administration pushed government responsibility for economic security to the center of national politics. And yet, far from disappearing, welfare capitalism persisted as a business strategy for adapting to pressure from workers and from the federal government during the Great Depression and the New Deal era. Insurance companies began to convince employers that, although discontinuing company programs might seem an effective economic response, the most effective political response was to follow through on the promises of welfare capitalism. Although there was an iconoclastic group of corporate executives calling for government social insurance programs, most voices from within the business community believed government solutions could be avoided if business made private options more dependable and realistic.

With the passage of the Social Security Act in 1935, the grassroots movements and New Dealers generated an ideology of collective economic security and publicly provided social insurance, as well as new policies of government regulation of labor relations. Insurers and welfare capitalist employers quickly adapted to the new welfare state, offering private, company plans as "supplemental social security." In order to promote the idea of supplementation, they had to argue that government pensions were inadequate. Life insurance executives from large and small companies all stressed the utter insufficiency of Social Security retirement pensions, arguing that individual private insurance policies or employee benefits were necessary supplements. Thus, rather than rejecting or fighting the welfare state outright, welfare capitalists helped disseminate the concept, to use Sanford Jacoby's term, of the "basic welfare state": one that provided a minimal, basic level of protection that would not cover all needs and thus left the rest to private institutions (Jacoby 1997, 206–210).

The latter half of the 1930s marked a period of growth and adaptation of private pensions and welfare capitalism. This new wave of industrial pensions helped preserve the notion of the paternalistic employer who cared for his employees' needs beyond the workplace, and it continued to serve the earlier functions of welfare capitalism. Although new employer-provided pensions were more likely to be insured and funded than were pre-Depression pensions, they still retained the one-sided characteristics of their predecessors. Management chose to implement them, chose what the amounts would be, chose the carrier, and retained the right to discontinue them.

Welfare capitalists also had to adapt to the emerging power of organized labor. The New Deal gave the ascendant union movement new legal backing in the 1930s. By the end of World War II, new Congress of Industrial Organizations (CIO) unions had organized most of the basic industry and transportation sectors. Under the terms of the National Labor Relations Act (1935), employers would have to negotiate with unions and sign labor-management contracts. Yet while business executives of the 1940s and 1950s did have to make decisions about labor policy in a new political and economic context, they chose the old strategy for generating employee loyalty: establishing and expanding their own private welfare state. Indeed, by enhancing company-provided benefits, employers wanted to check any further expansion of the New Deal, especially government intervention in the employment relation. They also wanted to check the growth of the union movement.

For employers, the unilateral purchase of commercial group insurance proved to be the key to containing union power and union political goals. Commercial insurers had now expanded group insurance plans to include hospital insurance, surgical insurance, disability wage compensation, and limited medical insurance. Again, since the employer was the only legal policyholder, employers could control the choice of insurance carrier, the type of policy, the benefits, and the percentage of costs paid by the workers. Insurance companies helped rejuvenate welfare capitalism after World War II by offering to "tailor" health insurance policies to fit the needs of each employer, laying the roots of the current balkanized system of health insurance coverage in the United States. Employers could choose the hospital services that would be covered, the percentage of reimbursement, and the amount of an employee's contribution to the plan. The employer could keep all the dividends on the policy. Indeed, in both unionized sectors and nonunionized sectors, management could make these decisions without input or revision from a union or other group representing employees.

The postwar employee benefits system retained two essential aspects of welfare capitalism. Insurers made no attempt to allow an employee to convert from a group policy to an individual one if she or he left the job. As Equitable Life group insurance policies claimed, "employee privileges on termination of employment" were "none" (quoted in Klein 2003, 228). Thus, employee benefits tied workers to a particular company and made all other family members dependent on the worker. Such a welfare system was inherently patriarchal and unequal. Because they designed health insurance as part of the family wage—a single (usually male) breadwinner and dependent family—insurers forged a health care system in which numerous persons had no direct claim to medical care. Their only claim to medical coverage was through a wage earner. Managers and insurers became partners in defining what constituted health security, shifting its focus away from the New Deal emphasis on national standards and toward a multitude of isolated, firm-specific welfare sites. More than ever, group insurance and welfare capitalist personnel programs, as Jacoby has written, could highlight the difference between security inside the firm and insecurity in the outside labor market (Jacoby 1997).

Although for a generation the employment-based benefits system brought many workers an unprecedented level of economic security and access to health care, it soon widened wage and income disparities among workers rather than closed them. Inequality inhered in coverage for family members, especially if they were not in the waged labor force. Family members usually received lesser benefits than the covered worker, such as fewer days in the hospital and more excluded procedures, and faced stricter rules about preexisting conditions. Even in unionized sectors, coverage for family members varied from place to place. For the vast majority of the American workforce, the lags in family coverage have persisted into the present.

The reliance on private employer benefits as an essential supplement to public provision also generated inequities between different groups of workers. To benefit from the supplemental security system, one had to work in industries covered by both the public and the private social security system. Until the 1970s, the majority of African American women worked in industries that were covered by neither. By the mid-1950s, African American men and some African American women had begun to move into urban manufacturing jobs and under the umbrella of the New Deal social security system. Yet just as Black workers had the possibility to obtain union-negotiated health insurance, life and disability insurance, and pensions, employers undercut these gains with labor strategies of automation and relocation. As major industrial employers pursued automation beginning in the mid-1950s, Black workers bore the brunt of displacement and layoffs. Companies such as General Motors and Ford Motors relocated plants to suburbs and small communities where Blacks could not follow. For African Americans, the limited welfare state and private supplementation would both mirror and solidify unequal patterns of economic opportunity.

Indeed, the patterns of racial and regional inequality inherent in welfare capitalism remained in place throughout the twentieth century. For the most part, the industries that did not offer private welfare benefits prior to World War II still do not. The South still lags behind the Northeast and the West. Nor have benefits ever been fully extended to African Americans or Latinos. By the end of the 1980s, only 47 percent of African Americans had private, employment-related health insurance, and at the end of the twentieth century, employment-based coverage finally reached just 50 percent of African Americans. Throughout the 1990s, the number of uninsured women grew steadily, rising to 21.3 million. About 42 percent of Latinos have employment-based health insurance, but 37 percent have neither public nor private health insurance of any kind (Klein 2003, 267). The distribution of health coverage remained tied to the distribution of good jobs, and the distribution of good jobs has not changed sufficiently for women, African Americans, or Latinos. As long as labor markets remain segmented, private employment-based social welfare will not compensate for those inequalities; it reinforces them.

The degree to which private employer benefits adequately supplement public social welfare has also been contingent upon the power of organized labor, both at the bargaining table and in garnering political support for regulatory legislation. During the two decades following World War II, this power—albeit limited—was at its height. With each round of bargaining in the 1950s and 1960s, employers granted enumerated increases—adding on a few more surgical procedures, additional hospital days, physician's office visits, maybe coverage for eyeglasses and root canals—within a limited framework that foreclosed labor's capacity to challenge any existing economic relationships, whether in industrial relations or in the delivery of health care. Thus, as long as business executives faced a countervailing weight—unions or the state—the incentive to bargain upward remained. In the 1970s, the tables turned, and bargaining started going in the other direction; "bargaining for security" became a downward spiral of concessions and losses.

Similarly, for two generations the public and the private welfare systems grew in tandem, offering a greater level of benefits to millions of Americans. After 1979, this trend would reverse, and the number of Americans covered by private pensions and health insurance began a steady, uninterrupted decline. After dropping to 38 percent of the private-sector workforce in 1980, private pension coverage fell to 31 percent by 1987 and below 30 percent in the 1990s. This trend toward diminished employer coverage occurred during a time of cutbacks and retrenchment in the public-sector safety net as well. Thus, as the New Deal state is dismantled, less than one-third of Americans receive private old-age pensions from their employers. In private-sector employment, only 25 percent of women workers participate in a pension plan. Minimum-age requirements and service requirements still hinder most women from ever actually qualifying for benefits. They receive only 22 percent of total private pension income (Ghilarducci 1992, 12; Witkowski, Castro, and Song 2002).

Proponents of social welfare privatization have argued that if the role of the government in social welfare provision is reduced or eliminated, business will fill the gap. This conclusion ignores history. In fact, business firms increased their commitment to corporate social welfare programs when government itself expanded its social welfare and labor intervention roles.

Fragmentation and inequality became just as characteristic of the private welfare system as of the public one. The public Social Security old-age pensions, however, have become universal. Still, most of the public policies enacted since the late 1970s have been aimed at propping up or patching up the leaky private welfare system. Yet neither private health insurance nor private pensions have moved any closer to universal coverage; nor will they. Health insurance coverage has never covered more than 69.6 percent of the workforce. The historical and ideological legacy of the American public-private welfare state—that of the basic welfare state, contained and limited, with all other needs met by private sources—continues to dominate policy proposals and legislation.

Jennifer Klein

See also: Capitalism; Privatization; Social Security; Social Security Act of 1935; Trade/Industrial Unions; Wagner Act; Welfare State

References and Further Reading

Ghilarducci, Teresa. 1992. *Labor's Capital: The Economics and Politics of Private Pensions*. Cambridge: MIT Press.

Jacoby, Sanford M. 1997. *Modern Manors: Welfare Capitalism since the New Deal*. Princeton: Princeton University Press.

Klein, Jennifer. 2003. *For All These Rights: Business, Labor, and the Shaping of America's Public-Private*

Welfare State. Princeton: Princeton University Press.

Licht, Walter. 1998. "Fringe Benefits: A Review Essay on the American Workplace." *International Labor and Working-Class History*, no. 53 (Spring): 164–178.

Stone, Deborah A. 1993. "The Struggle for the Soul of Health Insurance." *Journal of Health Politics, Policy and Law* (Summer): 286–317.

Tone, Andrea. 1997. *The Business of Benevolence: Industrial Paternalism in Progressive America*. Ithaca, NY: Cornell University Press.

Witkowski, Kristine, Charita Castro, and Xue Song. 2002. *The Gender Gap in Pension Coverage: What Does the Future Hold?* Washington, DC: Institute for Women's Policy Research.

Zahavi, Gerald. 1983. "Negotiated Loyalty: Welfare Capitalism and the Shoeworkers of Endicott Johnson, 1920–1940." *Journal of American History* 70, no. 3 (December): 602–620.

Welfare Law Center

The Welfare Law Center is a not-for-profit, public interest law firm that advocates for the right to adequate income support to meet basic human needs and to foster healthy human and family development. The center, which is based in New York City, engages in litigation and policy advocacy on behalf of applicants for and recipients of public benefits throughout the United States. It also provides support to grassroots organizations concerned with welfare issues and to legal services organizations and other lawyers for the poor. The center's work focuses on food stamps, Medicaid, and child care as well as on programs providing direct cash assistance. The center concentrates on removing unlawful substantive and procedural barriers to access to benefits created by the federal, state, and local governments. Henry A. Freedman has directed the center since 1971.

Known for its first thirty-one years as the Center on Social Welfare Policy and Law, the center was founded in 1965 by Edward V. Sparer, one of the founders of modern poverty law. Sparer envisioned the Welfare Law Center as a "backup" center that, in conjunction with the National Welfare Rights Organization, would coordinate and organize a national litigation strategy to effectuate welfare rights. Originally affiliated with the Columbia University School of Social Work, the center received funding from the Legal Services Program of the Office of Economic Opportunity. The Welfare Law Center served as the model for a network of over a dozen other backup centers funded by the Legal Services Program dealing with particular issue areas.

The Welfare Law Center played a major role in most of the Supreme Court cases that established welfare rights as a legal concept. Center director Lee Albert, who succeeded Sparer, argued the landmark case of *Goldberg v. Kelly* (397 U.S. 254 [1970]), which established that welfare benefits are a form of "property" under the due process clause of the Constitution. The center was also deeply involved in such cases as *King v. Smith* (392 U.S. 309 [1968]), striking down state "substitute father" rules that rendered families ineligible for Aid to Families with Dependent Children (AFDC) if the mother cohabited with a man, and *Shapiro v. Thompson* (394 U.S. 618 [1969]), in which the Court held that state durational residency requirements in the AFDC program violated the constitutional right to travel. After a period of initial success, however, decisions of the Supreme Court on welfare issues took a more negative turn for recipients. The center was on the losing end in decisions in *Dandridge v. Williams* (397 U.S. 471 [1970]), which upheld a household cap on AFDC benefits, and *Jefferson v. Hackney* (397 U.S. 821 [1972]), which rejected a challenge to disparities in assistance provided to the elderly and to families with children. In 1979, however, the center won a significant victory in *Califano v. Westcott* (443 U.S. 76 [1979]), in which the Supreme Court held unconstitutional a statutory provision limiting AFDC eligibility for two-parent households to situations where the father, but not the mother, was recently unemployed.

As the idea of a coordinated litigation strategy to establish a constitutional right to welfare benefits appeared increasingly unrealistic, the center redirected its efforts at enforcing rights to procedural fairness and challenging restrictive state eligibility standards that violated federal statutory law. The center also increasingly focused on providing training and support to legal services lawyers around the country.

The Welfare Law Center severed its affiliation with Columbia University in 1971. In 1995, as part of the dramatic cuts and restrictions in legal services funding that followed the shift to Republican control of Congress, the Welfare Law Center lost the federal funding that it had received through the Legal Services Corporation. As a result, the center is now wholly funded through donations, grants, and attorneys' fee awards.

Matthew Diller

See also: Legal Aid/Legal Services; New Property; Poverty Law; Welfare Rights Movement

References and Further Reading

Davis, Martha F. 1993. *Brutal Need: Lawyers and the Welfare Rights Movement, 1960–1973.* New Haven: Yale University Press.

Reich, Charles. 1964. "The New Property." *Yale Law Journal* 73: 733–787.

Personal Responsibility and Work Opportunity Reconciliation Act, *Public Law 104-193, 1996*

Title I—Block Grants for Temporary Assistance for Needy Families

Sec. 101. <42 USC 601 note> Findings.

The Congress makes the following findings:

(1) Marriage is the foundation of a successful society.

(2) Marriage is an essential institution of a successful society which promotes the interests of children.

(3) Promotion of responsible fatherhood and motherhood is integral to successful child rearing and the well-being of children.

(4) In 1992, only 54 percent of single-parent families with children had a child support order established and, of that 54 percent, only about one-half received the full amount due. Of the cases enforced through the public child support enforcement system, only 18 percent of the caseload has a collection.

(5) The number of individuals receiving aid to families with dependent children (in this section referred to as "AFDC") has more than tripled since 1965. More than two-thirds of these recipients are children. Eighty-nine percent of children receiving AFDC benefits now live in homes in which no father is present.

(A)(i) The average monthly number of children receiving AFDC benefits—

(I) was 3,300,000 in 1965;
(II) was 6,200,000 in 1970;
(III) was 7,400,000 in 1980; and
(IV) was 9,300,000 in 1992.

(ii) While the number of children receiving AFDC benefits increased nearly threefold between 1965 and 1992, the total number of children in the United States aged 0 to 18 has declined by 5.5 percent.

(B) The Department of Health and Human Services has estimated that 12,000,000 children will receive AFDC benefits within 10 years.

(C) The increase in the number of children receiving public assistance is closely related to the increase in births to unmarried women. Between 1970 and 1991, the percentage of live births to unmarried women increased nearly threefold, from 10.7 percent to 29.5 percent.

(6) The increase of out-of-wedlock pregnancies and births is well documented as follows:

(A) It is estimated that the rate of nonmarital teen pregnancy rose 23 percent from 54 pregnancies per 1,000 unmarried teenagers in 1976 to 66.7 pregnancies in 1991. The overall rate of nonmarital pregnancy rose 14 percent from 90.8 pregnancies per 1,000 unmarried women in 1980 to 103 in both 1991 and 1992. In contrast, the overall pregnancy rate for married couples decreased 7.3 percent between 1980 and 1991, from 126.9 pregnancies per 1,000 married women in 1980 to 117.6 pregnancies in 1991.

(B) The total of all out-of-wedlock births between 1970 and 1991 has risen from 10.7 percent to 29.5 percent and [**2112] if the current trend continues, 50 percent of all births by the year 2015 will be out-of-wedlock.

(7) An effective strategy to combat teenage pregnancy must address the issue of male responsibility, including statutory rape culpability and prevention. The increase of teenage pregnancies among the youngest girls is particularly severe and is linked to predatory sexual practices by men who are significantly older.

(A) It is estimated that in the late 1980's, the rate for girls age 14 and under giving birth increased 26 percent.

(B) Data indicates that at least half of the children born to teenage mothers are fathered by adult men. Available data suggests that almost 70 percent of births to teenage girls are fathered by men over age 20.

(C) Surveys of teen mothers have revealed that a majority of such mothers have histories of sexual and physical abuse, primarily with older adult men.

(8) The negative consequences of an out-of-wedlock birth on the mother, the child, the family, and society are well documented as follows:

(A) Young women 17 and under who give birth outside of marriage are more likely to go on public assistance and to spend more years on welfare once enrolled. These combined effects of "younger and longer" increase total AFDC costs per household by 25 percent to 30 percent for 17-year-olds.

(B) Children born out-of-wedlock have a substantially higher risk of being born at a very low or moderately low birth weight.

[**2112] (C) Children born out-of-wedlock are more likely to experience low verbal cognitive attainment, as well as more child abuse, and neglect.

(D) Children born out-of-wedlock were more likely to have lower cognitive scores, lower educational aspirations, and a greater likelihood of becoming teenage parents themselves.

(E) Being born out-of-wedlock significantly reduces the chances of the child growing up to have an intact marriage.

(F) Children born out-of-wedlock are 3 times more likely to be on welfare when they grow up.

(9) Currently 35 percent of children in single-parent homes were born out-of-wedlock, nearly the same percentage as that of children in single-parent homes whose parents are divorced (37 percent). While many parents find themselves, through divorce or tragic circumstances beyond their control, facing the difficult task of raising children alone, nevertheless, the negative consequences of raising children in single-parent homes are well documented as follows:

(A) Only 9 percent of married-couple families with children under 18 years of age have income below the national poverty level. In contrast, 46 percent of female-headed households with chil-

continues

Personal Responsibility and Work Opportunity Reconciliation Act (*continued*)

dren under 18 years of age are below the national poverty level.

(B) Among single-parent families, nearly 1/2 of the mothers who never married received AFDC while only 1/5 of divorced mothers received AFDC.

(C) Children born into families receiving welfare assistance are 3 times more likely to be on welfare when they reach adulthood than children not born into families receiving welfare.

(D) Mothers under 20 years of age are at the greatest risk of bearing low birth weight babies.

(E) The younger the single-parent mother, the less likely she is to finish high school.

(F) Young women who have children before finishing high school are more likely to receive welfare assistance for a longer period of time.

(G) Between 1985 and 1990, the public cost of births to teenage mothers under the aid to families with dependent children program, the food stamp program, and the medicaid program has been estimated at $120,000,000,000.

(H) The absence of a father in the life of a child has a negative effect on school performance and peer adjustment.

(I) Children of teenage single parents have lower cognitive scores, lower educational aspirations, and a greater likelihood of becoming teenage parents themselves.

(J) Children of single-parent homes are 3 times more likely to fail and repeat a year in grade school than are children from intact 2-parent families.

(K) Children from single-parent homes are almost 4 times more likely to be expelled or suspended from school.

(L) Neighborhoods with larger percentages of youth aged 12 through 20 and areas with higher percentages of single-parent households have higher rates of violent crime.

(M) Of those youth held for criminal offenses within the State juvenile justice system, only 29.8 percent lived primarily in a home with both parents. In contrast to these incarcerated youth, 73.9 percent of the 62,800,000 children in the Nation's resident population were living with both parents.

(10) Therefore, in light of this demonstration of the crisis in our Nation, it is the sense of the Congress that prevention of out-of-wedlock pregnancy and reduction in out-of-wedlock birth are very important Government interests and the policy contained in part A of title IV of the Social Security Act (as amended by section 103(a) of this Act) is intended to address the crisis.

Welfare Policy/ Welfare Reform

The history of welfare in the United States includes the story of local relief and charity practices during the eighteenth and nineteenth centuries as well as the provision of in-kind benefits such as food stamps during the late twentieth century. But what we've come to call "welfare" refers to a twentieth-century policy innovation designed for poor mothers and children in families without fathers. State and local mothers' pensions enacted during the Progressive Era were the first welfare policies; they were later nationalized in the Aid to Dependent Children (ADC) program of the New Deal, expanded in the Aid to Families with Dependent Children (AFDC) program during the 1960s, and replaced by the Temporary Assistance for Needy Families (TANF) program of the 1990s.

At its inception, welfare's focus on children and child-raising by mothers distinguished it from ordinary relief. According to the poor law tradition and the U.S. preference for individual self-help, relief for people who were considered "employable" was a temporary gesture and not intended as an alternative to participation in the labor market. Able-bodied aid recipients were understood to be capable of earning a living through wages. Such persons might need aid because their wages were too low to survive on them; or they might need aid due to economic depression or other causes of unemployment that were beyond the individual's control. But even if recipients' need could be explained by economics, most able-bodied poor were believed, in the end, to be morally responsible for their own poverty and their own support. Hence relief generally was stingy, so as not to encourage malingering; and it was disciplinary, so as not to encourage dependency.

In contrast, welfare was designed to keep (primarily) widowed mothers out of the labor market so that they could devote themselves to raising their children. The economic dependency of single mothers and children was assumed and approved; the problem was not that they were dependent, but that without a breadwinner in the home, single mothers and children had no one to depend on.

Nevertheless, many of the negative assumptions about the poor that powered the politics and policy of relief also powered the politics and policy of welfare, both at its origins and in the present day. A core assumption has been the idea that the poor fall easily into immorality and improvidence. It followed that welfare should discriminate between mothers who were virtuous or deserving and those who were not. It further followed that the home lives of recipients should be monitored for moral lapses and that recipients should receive guidance in managing family matters.

Promoted by the National Congress of Mothers as well as by upper-middle-class women reformers such as Jane Addams, Florence Kelley, and sisters Grace and Edith Abbott, mothers' pensions were first enacted by state governments during the second decade of the twentieth century and were implemented by localities. An alternative to the established practice of warehousing half-orphans in institutions, mothers' pensions affirmed the view that the mother-care of children was the best form of care.

Although states' policies varied, most shared common purposes, assumptions, and contradictions. Recognizing that many single mothers could not both provide care for children and earn an income to support them, state pension policies—at least in theory—made it possible for mothers to meet their caregiving responsibilities by providing a surrogate for a husband's income. In practice, however, states were stingy in setting benefit levels and most mothers were not able to support their families on pensions alone. Nor were all mothers who needed pensions invited to receive them. Pensions provided economic support only to "the best" mothers, even so regulating their dietary, kinship, and other cultural conditions to ensure their continued worthiness as mothers. Pension policies thus recognized the value of care only when mothers met certain cultural, racial, and moral standards.

Mothers' pension initiatives yielded two enduring legacies. One was that while all mothers performed the work of caregiving, the value of that work depended on the culture, race, and morality of the caregiver. The other was that even mothers who enjoyed social approbation and support had to earn and defend it by submitting to social controls. The Aid to Dependent Children program of the New Deal inherited these legacies.

Created by the Social Security Act of 1935, ADC (later renamed Aid to Families with

Dependent Children, or AFDC) nationalized mothers' pension policies by providing for joint federal-state funding of welfare benefits and by requiring states to hew to certain administrative rules in exchange for federal dollars. Though the welfare measure—Title IV of the Social Security Act—did not specify moral criteria for welfare participation, it gave states the opportunity to impose such criteria by delegating administration and management to them. States took old rules from mothers' pension statutes—rules against nonmarital motherhood and heterosexual cohabitation, for example—and folded them into the new federal policy.

The welfare system set up in the 1930s was hardly an ideal system. For one thing, not all mothers who needed welfare were permitted to receive it, as states retained the discretion that had characterized mothers' pension programs under the new federal arrangement. As a result, even mothers who qualified for assistance had to suffer surveillance and interference in their lives as a condition of aid. Still, at the end of the 1930s, the prevailing image of recipients was that they *did* deserve their benefits.

Amendments to the Social Security Act in 1939 changed the profile of welfare. Under the amendments, widowed mothers with minor children who had been in durable marriages to men who qualified for the Social Security insurance system were placed in a different kind of welfare program—Survivors' Insurance. Benefits under the program were national, regular, automatic—and far more generous than welfare. Moreover, widowed beneficiaries and their minor children did not have to convince welfare agencies that they deserved their benefits; they just *did*, by virtue of their status as survivors of socially insured fathers.

Creation of the Survivors' Insurance program removed widows, especially white widows, from the welfare system. Gradually, welfare became a program for mothers who were divorced, had never married, or had been married to the wrong men: By 1961, only 7.7 percent of welfare mothers were widows. When the pitiful but blameless white widow left welfare for Survivors' Insurance, the stigma of welfare began to congeal.

By the end of the 1940s, the subject of welfare assistance had become sharply and explicitly politicized. On one side were those who focused on the needs of poor mothers and their children—and on how ADC could address those needs. On the other were people who focused first on the bad behavior of ADC recipients and potential recipients and then on ways to make sure that ADC payments were reserved for the "worthy poor."

At the beginning of the decade, the Aid to Dependent Children program appeared well defined, well funded, and stable. Federal administrators collaborated with state officials to oversee an assistance program that provided sustenance to a population of "helpless" poor mothers and their children. Many of the first generation of welfare administrators and policy experts believed through the 1940s that the Social Security Act had established welfare assistance as a statutory right of the poor. They understood welfare assistance as a combination of money payments and services.

Most important to the first generation of federal-level experts was the idea that poor mothers had a "right to choose aid" if taking a job might cause their children to be neglected or cared for inadequately. Even after the beginning of World War II, when many single mothers of young children responded to their own economic needs and to the wartime labor shortage by entering the workforce, the War Manpower Commission endorsed this "mothers' right." Also during the war, the Federal Bureau of Public Assistance was critical of local welfare agencies that put pressure on poor mothers of young children to go to work. Federal officials argued that welfare benefits should be high enough so that these mothers could stay home with their children. One welfare expert in the early 1940s observed that a mother's application for day care services for her children was a sign that she may need ADC so that she could remain at home to care for them. Another expert disapproved of programs that hired poor mothers to take care of the children of other mothers working outside of their homes: "It would have been much more useful to pay them to take care of their own children," social welfare pioneer Grace Abbott wrote. At the end of World War II, ADC was still serving a population that resembled its original target. Only 10 percent of the recipients were unwed mothers; almost 80 percent were white.

Endorsing the goals of the 1939 Social Security Act Amendments, President Franklin Roosevelt referred in his 1944 State of the Union address to an economic "bill of rights" for the American people, a guarantee of "security and prosperity for all—regardless of station, race, or creed." In the spirit of this vision of democracy, the Bureau of Public Assistance worked throughout the 1940s to increase the proportion of nonwhite recipients on the welfare rolls; between 1942 and 1948 the proportion rose from 21 percent to 30 percent. People of color were much more likely in the forties to receive welfare benefits in northern states than in the South. For example, in Illinois, 173 out of 1,000 Blacks were ADC recipients. In North Carolina, despite near-complete impoverishment of the Black population, only 14 out of 1,000 Blacks received benefits.

The presence of new recipients-of-color on the rolls and occasional federal pressure on the states to extend ADC to people of color stimulated some states to intensify their efforts to keep the welfare rolls as white as possible. During the 1940s, states gradually crafted and formalized exclusionary criteria for participation in ADC. Many southern states used work rules to restrict participation of African Americans. A field supervisor in one state wrote, "The number of Negro cases is few due to the unanimous feeling on the part of the staff and board [of the welfare agency] that there are more work opportunities for Negro women and to their intense desire not to interfere with local labor conditions. The attitude that they have always gotten along and that 'all they'll do is have more children' is definite." In 1943 in Louisiana, the state welfare agency adopted a formal rule requiring that no ADC applicant would be granted assistance as long as she was needed in the cotton field; this rule included children as young as seven years old.

States also adopted rules governing the intimate lives of recipients, which gave the local welfare agencies additional grounds for excluding certain populations. In Michigan, ADC mothers had to sign an affidavit promising, "I will not have any male callers coming to my home nor meeting me elsewhere under improper conditions." In states around the country, various forms of "suitable home" laws cropped up—rules that excluded from welfare eligibility women who had children outside of marriage, or were suspected of having sexual relations while on welfare, or any of a number of other "nonconforming" behaviors.

Recognizing the trend in many states toward targeting specific populations with exclusionary rules, the Federal Bureau of Public Assistance sent state welfare agencies a cautionary letter in 1945, strongly recommending that the states repeal "suitable home" eligibility conditions. Most state officials ignored the suggestion, preferring instead to apply the rules to contain the increasing number of nonwhite recipients, as well as the rise in absent-father, unwed-mother-headed households and in the number of "illegitimate" children receiving welfare. A number of state legislatures and welfare officials also resisted federal interference with their political and policy preferences ("states' rights")—a position that preserved white southern control of the local racial order.

Notwithstanding various state efforts to curtail certain mothers' participation in welfare, in 1950 Congress added a caregiver/mother benefit to the ADC payment. That same year, Congress also gestured its concern about single-mother families. As part of a child support amendment, Congress mandated welfare agencies to "provide prompt notice to appropriate law enforcement officials of the furnishing of aid to dependent children in respect of a child who has been deserted or abandoned by a parent." In 1951, Congress focused sharply on the welfare confidentiality policy that since 1939 had promised that agencies would not publicize the identities of recipients. Democratic and Republican governors around the country supported ending this protection, and Representative Burr V. Harrison of Virginia spoke for many of his colleagues when he claimed that "criminals, illegitimate children, prostitutes and Cadillac owners are receiving welfare payments in some states because of the Federal ban on publication of the relief rolls." In a development that demonstrated how politicized and stigmatized welfare had become, Congress revoked recipients' confidentiality guarantee in a measure promising states that the federal welfare contribution would not be withheld if a state opened its rolls to public scrutiny, as long as the list of names disclosed was not used for commercial or political purposes.

Although Congress invented new federal stipulations regarding welfare during the 1950s, it also expanded welfare eligibility and allocations—beginning with the addition of the grant for mothers. Congress was responding to studies that showed increased need because of population growth, rising incidence of divorce and births outside of marriage, and inflation, among other factors. In 1954, federal eligibility rules opened ADC up to 10 million previously excluded agricultural and domestic workers. As a result, the number of families receiving ADC increased year by year. Many of the new families were African American, not surprising since for much of the 1950s, the unemployment rate for Blacks was twice the rate for whites.

Over the course of the 1950s, the states, the Congress, the federal welfare bureaucracy, and local welfare agencies carved out strong positions on welfare eligibility. By the 1960s, federal-state, Black-white tensions over welfare provision and administration intertwined with the national conflict between civil rights and states' rights.

In 1960, Louisiana governor Jimmie Davis, facing school desegregation orders in New Orleans, signed legislation that disqualified 23,000 "illegitimate" children from public assistance in one day. This act made welfare a national issue. Welfare opponents condemned "undeserving" African American women and their families; others questioned the heartlessness of legislatures willing to starve little children. The Louisiana situation even brought international attention to the welfare problem in the United States; a group of women in England arranged for an airlift of food and supplies to disqualified families in the state.

The Louisiana statute drew criticism from the Federal Bureau of Public Assistance and the secretary of the Department of Health, Education, and Welfare. But because the federal government was unwilling to stand staunchly against this assertion of states' rights, states continued to regulate the number of Blacks on welfare rolls by approving variants of illegitimacy statutes and suitable home laws.

The next year, 1961, national attention was drawn north when the city manager of Newburgh, New York, issued thirteen rules designed to exclude Blacks from public assistance rolls in that small mid-Hudson city—despite the fact that most Newburgh recipients were white and the fact that the city was actually spending much less than its welfare budget. In Louisiana, Newburgh, and in every region of the country in the early 1960s, politicians railed against illegitimate children and women who gave birth to ever more of them. Yet at this time, 4 percent of all children in the United States were "illegitimate," and only one-half of 1 percent were illegitimate and receiving welfare.

The federal government responded to the increasingly racialized politics of welfare (renamed Aid to Families with Dependent Children, or AFDC) in the states by shifting the gaze of national policy to remedying the shortcomings of individuals and addressing family problems. The 1961 legislation creating the AFDC-UP (Unemployed Parent) option affirmed the heteronormative two-parent family headed by a male breadwinner. AFDC-UP made benefits available to households headed by able-bodied men who could not meet their breadwinner duties due to unemployment. (By the end of the decade, twenty-five states had adopted the program but, altogether, fewer than 100,000 families received benefits from this program.)

The 1962 Social Security Amendments are remembered for having stressed "rehabilitation" of poor families through services provided by welfare agencies. For the first time, welfare policy suggested that benefits would assist mothers only temporarily, while they prepared for jobs. In concert with this idea, the 1962 amendments provided $5 million for day care centers for the children of low-income working mothers. Katherine Oettinger of the federal Children's Bureau calculated that this allocation represented $1.25 for each of the 4 million under-six children of working mothers.

The 1962 federal legislation experimented with the idea that poor women could be trained to support their families through employment, but many state and local welfare regulations in the early 1960s were predicated on the notion that women were and ought to be *dependent* persons. For example, a Washington, D.C., regulation indicated that if a woman's need for assistance was a result of her unwillingness to be with her husband, the welfare department would not accept her claim of neediness.

Further indicating the tension between purported federal principles and state practices, the 1962 Social Security Amendments wrote into law the federal government's willingness to continue federal funds even for states that had suitable home laws of which the government disapproved, as long as the state provided for adequate care and assistance for the children involved. Thus, an "illegitimate" child could not be cut off assistance, but could be treated differently from a "legitimate" child.

Between 1950 and 1964, the number of persons covered by ADC almost doubled, from 2.2 million to 4.3 million. The increase was due to the addition of the caregiver benefit in 1950, escalating rates of divorce and desertion, growing numbers of woman-headed households, and other demographic trends. By the end of the 1950s, African Americans accounted for well over a third of welfare enrollments, while women of all races composed the vast majority of adult recipients. The contradiction between poverty and personhood for most mothers on welfare made welfare policy an important women's issue. But in this moment of national struggle between white supremacy and racial justice, welfare was dragooned into racist, not gender, politics.

Taking cues from politicians while also giving cues to the electorate, the media began to portray the poor primarily through pictures of African Americans, and to pair African American images with the most negative aspects of poverty. One scholar has found that this trend began in 1964, and by 1967, 72 percent of the time, illustrations of the poor in newspapers and magazines pictured Blacks, while Blacks, in fact, made up only 30 percent of the poor in the United States. These media practices fueled white racism and stoked hostility toward welfare expenditures and against paying taxes that supported ever-larger welfare rolls.

Talk of a "welfare crisis" during the mid-1960s fed off popular stereotypes of the welfare system and of welfare recipients. This dynamic was reinforced by ostensibly social scientific research done by Assistant Secretary of Labor Daniel Patrick Moynihan, which attributed poverty in Black communities to Black family culture. The Moynihan Report, published in 1965, blamed matriarchy in African American communities for a "tangle of pathology" that included poverty and dependence on welfare.

Although it had no explicit policy recommendations, the Moynihan Report was used to support the idea that welfare undermined the normative two-parent, male-headed family and that stringent behavioral and moral stipulations were needed in welfare policy—both to reform recipients and to secure the program for the "worthy" poor.

During this period, welfare recipients began to mobilize around a claim for welfare rights. Frustrated by the tortures of the welfare system and by the stigma others stamped on them for needing economic assistance, welfare recipients all over the country organized grassroots groups under the auspices of the National Welfare Rights Organization (NWRO). These groups worked on local, state, and national levels to improve welfare benefits, housing, employment opportunities, the public image of poor mothers on public assistance, and other conditions of life. At the same time, activist lawyers began to pursue litigation to establish the rights of poor people to receive public assistance and to be treated with dignity, even though they were welfare recipients.

In 1965, Edward Sparer, one of the most important of these welfare rights lawyers, proposed a bill of rights for recipients to guarantee (1) the right to privacy and protection from illegal search; (2) the right to freedom of movement and choice of residence; (3) the right to choose one's own standard of morality; and (4) the right to freedom to refuse work relief without suffering penal or other improper consequences. In order for recipients to be able to claim these rights, Sparer and his colleagues determined, they would have to successfully challenge state statutes and local practices controlling the lives of welfare recipients. They would have to challenge the legitimacy of residency laws, "man in the house" rules, midnight raids, work-relief practices, inadequate money grants, and the absence of due process protection. In 1968, welfare rights lawyers argued *King v. Smith* (392 U.S. 309)—an ultimately successful effort to overturn the Alabama "man in the house" rule—all the way to the Supreme Court; this was the first time a welfare case had been heard by the highest court in the land. A number of welfare cases followed, a crucial few of which established national constitutional standards for recipients and restrained the discretion of state-run welfare programs.

In tandem with Supreme Court decisions recognizing certain welfare rights, the electoral and legislative politics of "welfare reform" caught hold. In the context of the civil rights movement and the welfare rights movement, and in reaction against the expansion of welfare funding and participation, "welfare reform" meant welfare without rights, restricted participation, and states' rights.

The late 1960s and early 1970s saw a number of legislative campaigns to make discretionary state policies, then under challenge in the courts, part of the federal policy mandate. In 1967, public welfare amendments introduced a new emphasis on biological fathers' financial responsibility for families with a provision calling upon states to establish paternity for all AFDC families. Vowing to "make papa pay," this provision was aimed against welfare "matriarchs," against welfare's so-called disincentives to marriage, and against "illegitimacy." The 1967 amendments also introduced the Work Incentive (WIN) program to encourage adult recipients' movement into the labor market. Although the WIN program gave job training and placement priority to men, not mothers, its adoption marked the beginning of a thirty-year effort to force mothers to leave welfare for the labor market.

The popularity of welfare reform was not lost on Richard Nixon, who became president in January 1969. A Republican who regularly criticized federal solutions to local problems, Nixon nonetheless proposed the centralized Family Assistance Plan (FAP) as an alternative to the established AFDC program. At the heart of the proposal was a national minimum income that would apply to all families but that was primarily aimed at aiding low-wage, male-headed, two-parent families. Nixon calculated that large numbers of workers—11 or 12 million of whom were not covered by minimum-wage regulations in 1970—might be courted into the Republican Party with FAP's minimum-income promise. At the same time, FAP would deflect income assistance policy from allegedly undeserving single mothers to the presumably more deserving "working poor," thereby accomplishing a watershed welfare reform. Ultimately, a collection of strange bedfellows—southern conservatives (who saw that FAP income supplements would undermine cheap local labor markets), northern liberals, and the National Welfare Rights Organization, among others—killed the Family Assistance Plan.

This legislative failure, combined with widespread negative assessments of many features of welfare policy, encouraged many Americans to believe that the situation could never be salvaged. Policymakers and recipients alike judged the Work Incentive program a failure. Of several million recipients eligible for WIN services, ultimately only a tiny percentage were placed in jobs, and many of those had to work in dead-end jobs for salaries below minimum wage. In California, women brought a class-action suit against the program because men were given priority in WIN training programs.

Also, many policymakers claimed that the "income disregard" provision (which allowed recipients to set aside a small portion of their earned income in determining benefits) created by the 1967 Social Security Amendments was a failure because it provided an opportunity for many poor women to elevate their incomes above women with full-time jobs and no assistance. Congress made little headway in funding adequate child care, and President Nixon ultimately vetoed the comprehensive child care bill passed by Congress in 1971. Many politicians found themselves in the awkward position of simultaneously demanding that poor mothers enter the workforce, condemning publicly funded day care schemes, and praising middle-class mothers who stayed home with their young children.

By the second Nixon administration (1973–1974), policy discussions focused on cost cutting, work requirements, stricter eligibility rules, and the need for substantial allocations of resources for antifraud initiatives. In 1975, Congress fundamentally altered welfare by making a mother's cooperation in the establishment of paternity a condition of receiving a welfare benefit.

Despite the popularity of promises to reform welfare, especially among candidates for high office, the mandatory establishment-of-paternity provision was the only major change to welfare during the 1970s. Perhaps the American public's ambivalence was a major obstacle. A 1977 *New York Times*/CBS News poll indicated that almost 60 percent of Americans disapproved of government-sponsored welfare programs. But when it came to evaluating specific programs—food stamps, AFDC, health care—four-fifths of those polled, both the liberals and the conservatives, wanted these forms of assistance to continue. Not until the presidential candidacy and election of Ronald Reagan in 1980 did antiwelfare politics fully congeal.

Indeed, the election of Ronald Reagan to the presidency in 1980 propelled antiwelfare forces into ascendancy for the rest of the century. A longtime foe of welfare as governor of California, Reagan established himself as a national antiwelfare leader when he fought President Nixon's Family Assistance Plan by arguing that it would make welfare profitable for the poor. As an aspiring presidential candidate in 1976, Reagan expanded his antiwelfare repertoire when he propagated the myth of a Chicago "welfare queen" who had allegedly scammed $150,000 from the welfare system using multiple aliases, addresses, and Social Security cards and claiming four dead husbands. Although numerous politicians had played the welfare card since the 1960s, Reagan's victory over Democrat

Jimmy Carter in 1980 was the first time an antiwelfare reformer had won the White House.

Reagan's prescriptions for welfare reform were most notable for their emphases on reducing federal social spending, eliminating welfare fraud, requiring labor market work, and restoring states' rights. But his presidency also opened political space for antiwelfare punditry about the values, behavior, and reproductive decisions of the poor.

Reagan's main legislative initiative in welfare policy came in 1981, when the Omnibus Budget Reconciliation Act (OBRA) he pushed through Congress changed the way resources and earned income were counted in determining recipients' eligibility and benefits—to their disadvantage. OBRA also contained provisions authorizing states to stiffen work requirements and to promote workfare.

In addition to these legislative revisions of AFDC, Reagan advanced right-wing plans to make welfare the template for its "family values" agenda. By the mid-1980s, right-wing intellectuals, think tanks, and Christian fundamentalists had given coherence and prominence to the view that welfare fostered welfare dependency by encouraging recipients to avoid work and to continue having "illegitimate" babies as a way to get benefits. "Family values" proponents enjoyed an official imprimatur when President Reagan convened the White House Working Group on the Family and appointed Gary Bauer, then undersecretary of education and later president of the Family Research Council, as its chair. They also claimed social scientific authority for their claims—despite the preponderance of evidence to the contrary—in antiwelfare polemics such as Charles Murray's *Losing Ground* (1984) and in a steady stream of policy briefs from conservative think tanks such as the Heritage Foundation.

Over the course of the 1980s, the idea that the need for welfare was a measure of the poor moral choices of recipients circulated widely, priming the antiwelfare consciousness of policymakers and voters. By the late 1980s, restrictive welfare rules and incentives gained currency as states took advantage of Reagan administration proposals that welfare policy should regulate the behavior of the poor. To facilitate initiatives by the states, the Reagan administration, which favored devolution to the state and local levels, expanded and expedited waivers that allowed states to deviate from federal AFDC eligibility criteria and to conduct so-called experiments to find ways of moving people off the rolls. Among the most popular state initiatives was the "family cap," which withheld welfare benefits from a child conceived or born to a mother while she was on welfare.

Whether because of the insidious osmotic power of the Moynihan Report or because of the logical prowess of Charles Murray in his *Losing Ground*, the specter of "illegitimacy" aroused interest in correcting welfare's "perverse incentives" among Democrats as well as Republicans. In addition, the fact that increasing numbers of women were working outside the home, at least part-time, led many Democrats—including feminists—to argue that welfare mothers *should* do so. For both Republicans and Democrats, arguments about reproduction, work, and welfare were loaded with racially drawn gender expectations and judgments about who should have babies under what conditions and about which women were workers first and which women could be mothers on their own terms.

In 1988, bipartisan interests in welfare reform came together in the Family Support Act (FSA), which was shepherded through Congress by Senator Daniel Patrick Moynihan (D–New York), who had been a central figure in welfare politics since the publication of his infamous report. The act amended AFDC by adding stiffened work requirements, job-training provisions, work supports, and stronger child support enforcement mechanisms. Under the act, states were supposed to match federal expenditures for services and supports as well as for benefits. Success of this reform accordingly would depend in part on the states' willingness to invest in each recipient's transition from welfare to work. It also would depend on the willingness of the labor market to pay living wages and to accommodate the family needs of parents, especially single mothers, as well as on the willingness of government to deliver promised social supports such as child care.

The Family Support Act was a major welfare reform, as it broadened and deepened the employment goals of welfare policy. Despite the major changes it portended, however, the FSA did not end the war on welfare. The precarious and regressive economic recovery of the 1980s gave way to recession by the beginning of the 1990s. Welfare participation reached new highs, which in turn fueled taxpayer resentment against recipients and generally churned racist politics against the poor. By 1992, many voters would again be receptive to a presidential candidate's pledge to overhaul welfare.

After twelve years of Republican control of the White House, Democrat Bill Clinton won the presidency in 1992. Feminists, civil rights activists, other progressives, and mainline Democrats all cheered the election for ending the long conservative siege of government and democracy. The Democrats' return to the presidency did not place liberal or progressive goals high on the national agenda, however. Clinton was a "New Democrat" with roots in the conservative wing of the Democratic Party. In addition, he brought into national government the biases he had developed as governor of Arkansas: a frustration with national rules governing welfare programs, confidence in local control, and a commitment to state flexibility.

As president, Clinton did promote the appointment and election of unprecedented numbers of people of color to high governmental office and he did defend basic abortion rights for women, two causes associated with liberal Democrats. But in language more familiar to Republicans than to Democrats, he declared an end to "big government" and "welfare as we know it." Rather than produce a sharp policy and political turn away from the antiwelfare demonology of the 1980s, Clinton's election raised the attack on welfare and on mothers who need it to a shrill pitch. Clinton's own plans to reform welfare did differ in some important ways from the Republican approach: Clinton favored job training and social supports to "make work pay." But Clinton and the Republicans were in agreement that existing welfare policy was a behavioral and moral hazard, that welfare policy should engineer the lives of the poor, and that states could do a better job than the federal government had done in setting strict and disciplinary terms for welfare participation. The election of a Republican majority in Congress in 1994 ensured that the most punitive imaginable version of welfare reform would prevail. But it was Clinton's election in 1992 that began the end of welfare.

The crescendo to end welfare in the 1990s reflected more than conservative party politics. Some progressives criticized AFDC for being too stingy and cumbersome, as well as for failing to provide promised transitional supports to mothers who sought participation in the labor market. Although few progressives actually called for the end of welfare, some—including some feminists—agreed with the antiwelfare mantra that mothers should "move from welfare to work." Although criticisms of welfare came from diverse political quarters and carried very different policy implications, the breadth of criticism meant that it would be difficult to rescue welfare from the bipartisan pincers of punitive welfare reform.

Antipoverty advocates for women and children did try, as did grassroots welfare rights activists. A few feminists also mobilized in opposition to punitive welfare reform, some among them defending welfare as essential economic recognition and support for the important work of caregiving. These points of view were not salient in the national discussion about welfare reform, however. Welfare rights activists were shunted to the margins of policy discussion, and those feminist groups that mobilized did not succeed in gaining the attention of the media or even garner much support from the feminist rank and file.

Racism entered the debate both tacitly and overtly, usually intersecting with moralistic discourse regarding gender behavior and the roots of poverty. Much of welfare reform's racial politics played out around the icon of the Black single mother, said to be immoral in her own right as well as the cause of numerous social ills. Thus, for example, the same conservative politicians who pressed for stringent work requirements for welfare recipients (stereotyped Black) also insisted that "family values" dictated that middle-class married mothers (stereotyped white) ought to leave paying jobs to stay home to care for their young children. This argument drew from a racially bifurcated gender expectation that Black women would support their families through wage work at low-paying jobs (including caring for other women's children) while privileged white women would rely on husbands for their income (and in some cases on Black nannies to help raise their children). Racist ideas also stoked the war on "illegitimacy" and fueled the campaign to exclude noncitizen immigrants from receiving welfare and other social supports.

Even though "work" was the ostensible goal of welfare reform, pervasive concerns about "illegitimacy" and disdain for poor single motherhood placed marriage, reproduction, and family formation at the center of the welfare debate. The 1996 Personal Responsibility and Work Opportunity Reconciliation Act (PRWORA), which replaced AFDC with the Temporary Assistance for Needy Families program, codified the view that welfare policy should reward and punish the intimate decisions and behavior of poor single mothers.

President Clinton signed the PRWORA into law in August 1996. In addition to promoting marriage and requiring financial relationships between biological parents, the new legislation eliminated the federal entitlement to assistance to those who qualified, imposed a five-year lifetime time limit on participation in the federal TANF program, severely restricted the eligibility of noncitizen immigrants to receive benefits, and required labor market "work activities" of adult recipients. Education and training can satisfy the work requirement only in restricted circumstances, while caregiving work for one's own children does not count as work at all. In fact, under the PRWORA, the only welfare mothers who may work inside the home raising children are married mothers.

Although the PRWORA established harsh national rules regarding work participation, paternity establishment and child support enforcement, and the eligibility of immigrants, the new law also created fifty separate welfare programs when it replaced the AFDC funding structure with block grants to states. Within states, welfare programs can be further decentralized, as in California and Colorado, where counties define their own programs. The consequences of this decentralization spill over into other social welfare programs. For example, many local welfare agencies do not ensure continued Medicaid and food stamp benefits to recipients who leave welfare or who never make it onto welfare because they are "diverted" from it. In addition, sanction policies (punishments) vary widely: Some counties or states remove families from welfare the first time they violate a rule while other counties and states stage their sanctions or do not sanction the same violations. Further, workfare participants receive varied degrees and quality of training depending on where they live, and welfare-to-work participants in some states are routed through churches while those in other states are routed through corporations.

The scale of devolution and differentiation in the new welfare system makes monitoring it a considerable challenge. Although it is possible to measure aggregate caseload reduction—50 percent since the mid-1990s—comprehensive data that would tell us the fate of recipients and former recipients are more difficult to come by. This is one reason why official pronouncements that welfare reform is a "success" have been accepted at face value. As a result, few policymakers have contested the fundamental structure and principles of TANF. Although some policymakers are concerned that TANF has not cured poverty among current and former welfare recipients, few argue that it is the TANF program itself that perpetuates poverty.

The 1996 TANF legislation required that the program be reauthorized in 2002. In 2002 and then again in 2003, the Bush administration piggybacked additional welfare reforms onto TANF reauthorization bills. If enacted, the Bush proposal would ratchet up the work requirement by increasing the number of weekly hours a recipient must engage in work activities, by increasing the percentage of the caseload a state must enroll in work activities, and by requiring states to develop work plans for all recipients. These new requirements will weigh harshly on single mothers, who already have a hard time juggling wage work and care work under the current work requirement, especially given inadequate provision of child care. In contrast, married mothers (and fathers) will not be expected to wholly abandon children for the labor market. Under the Bush plan, married families and single-mother families will be subject to the same hourly work requirement (now a proposed family work requirement), and, as under the 1996 law, only one parent in a married family will need to engage in work activities.

This preference for married families marks another radical shift in welfare, which began as a program to support independent mothers. Currently contemplated policy goes beyond favoring married families to actively promoting marriage itself. The second major element of the Bush proposal for TANF reauthorization is "marriage promotion." Current law already promotes marriage by making it a goal of TANF. Proposals put forth by the Bush administration in 2002 and 2003 aim to accomplish that goal by offering states $1.8 billion over five years to promote marriage and by requiring that states develop plans for doing so.

Feminists, welfare rights activists, and other progressives have mobilized against this patriarchal tide. Although some progressives primarily are interested in reforming the TANF framework so as to improve job training, education, and job supports for recipients so that they can leave welfare for family-supporting wages, welfare rights activists and some feminists have been working also to reconsider the TANF framework altogether. From their point of view, the welfare system not only ought to improve poor mothers' choices and prospects in the labor market but also ought to support mothers' caregiving work in their own families. Recognition and support for caregiving would advance mothers' economic security and, in turn, their capacity to make independent choices about wage work, about personal safety, and about intimate life. Without such support, poor mothers are punished for parenting alone, for having children while unmarried, and for being poor. Their children, meanwhile, are punished for being born to the wrong mothers.

Gwendolyn Mink and Rickie Solinger

[This essay was first published in a different format in Gwendolyn Mink and Rickie Solinger, *Welfare: A Documentary History of U.S. Policy and Politics* (New York University Press, 2003).]

See also: Aid to Families with Dependent Children (ADC/AFDC); Dependency; Deserving/Undeserving Poor; Maternalism; Maternalist Policy; Poor Laws; Poverty Law; Welfare Administration; Welfare Rights Movement; Welfare State; Workfare; see also the extracts from the following court cases (in sidebars to the entry Poverty Law): *King v. Smith* (1968); *Shapiro, Commissioner of Welfare of Connecticut, v. Thompson* (1969); *Goldberg v. Kelly* (1970); *Dandridge v. Williams* (1970); *Saenz v. Roe* (1999)

References and Further Reading

Mink, Gwendolyn. 2002. *Welfare's End*. Rev. ed.

Ithaca, NY: Cornell University Press. Originally published 1998.

Mink, Gwendolyn, and Rickie Solinger. 2003. *Welfare: A Documentary History of U.S. Policy and Politics*. New York: New York University Press.

Welfare Rights Movement

I am not ashamed of being on welfare and fighting for my right to be helped as a human being. My reasons are too important to make me feel the least bit ashamed. I am fighting for the right to an education and for the future of my children. But shame on those rich people who get tax breaks. Shame on those corporations that get welfare money but they call it grants and subsidies. Shame on those politicians who get thousands of dollars of free money to pay their debts, while at the same time taking money away from America's poor children. . . . And shame on those who pass laws that affect the lives of people they couldn't even imagine being in the place of.

—*Cathy Ortega, Boston welfare rights activist*

Poverty is particularly a "women's issue." Obviously, it is a men's issue too, but the nature of the economy and the structure of the U.S. polity mean that women are especially vulnerable to poverty due to their culturally assigned (and often desired) roles as primary caregivers for children and for sick, disabled, or elderly relatives. This means that simple employment strategies to alleviate poverty, such as increasing wages and benefits, are often inadequate to address women's economic and social needs. Because of this special relation to poverty, many women from a variety of backgrounds have historically joined together to fight poverty and to demand "welfare rights" as a means to fully address their needs as women.

The National Welfare Rights Organization

The National Welfare Rights Organization (NWRO) was the first group to make a claim specifically for "welfare rights." The NWRO was a direct outgrowth of the African American civil rights movement and arose from efforts of the broader movement to expand democracy at home and to end the U.S. war in Vietnam. The organizing efforts of George Wiley, Johnnie Tillmon, Faith Evans, and many Black and (some) white women created an organization that fought to expand the economic and social rights of poor families. The NWRO struggled on many fronts—through grassroots protests, through legislative advocacy, and through litigation that would win basic constitutional protections for welfare recipients.

Beginning in 1966 and for approximately ten years, the NWRO established a presence in most major urban areas, including Boston, Chicago, Cincinnati, Columbus, Cleveland, Los Angeles, Newark, New York City, Philadelphia, Trenton, and Saint Louis. Nationally and locally, it received funds from a variety of sources, including church-based sources, private foundations, and even some federally funded local Community Action Programs. Different groups in different regions employed differing organizing models, most but not all under the auspices of the NWRO.

Over time, several parallel and evolving arguments emerged from local welfare rights organizing efforts and at NWRO national meetings. One line of analysis asserted civil rights claims to fair treatment by and equal access to welfare. Another line of analysis emphasized the role of welfare in manipulating the low-wage labor supply. A third line of analysis argued that welfare mothers should be supported as caregivers for their own children. Together these analyses produced a "welfare rights" strategy that demanded improved access to and democratic influence over state welfare systems, as well as higher and more reliable benefits.

Four major circumstances provided the context and justification for welfare rights organizing, which the leaders explicitly presented as a legitimate part of the ever-widening movement for democratic rights and social justice that characterized the period. First, poverty in the North was concentrated in urban neighborhoods, where poor people commonly endured the abuses and inadequacies of public services.

Second, the interconnections among public housing, public health, public schools, and the welfare systems led to an understanding of the interrelatedness of issues affecting poor people. This was especially true for women in the movement, since mothers were already the ones dealing with the housing authorities, the welfare workers, the teachers, and the social service workers. Shared experience, anger, and sophistication made local organizing feasible.

A third context for welfare rights organizing was the problem of racism in the welfare system. Black women, in particular, organized to fight exclusion and discrimination but also to make real alliances with those poor white women who were in the system with them. As Guida West (1987) and Jackie Pope (1989) both document well, Black women were often treated worse by welfare workers than were white women and were often denied options that were available to white women. At the same time, since the system was inadequate, punitive, and invasive toward all participants, wider coalitions could be forged for economic justice for families Black and white.

A fourth condition for the welfare rights movement was provided by the simultaneous growth of the Community Action and Model Cities programs, along with local responses to the urban rebellions and police riots of the late 1960s. These brought a range of new, activist social agencies and young activists into urban neighborhoods across the country. Poverty programs pursuing their mandate for "maximum feasible participation" by poor constituents provided a critical base of resources and recruitment for the emerging welfare rights movement.

For many who were a part of it, the welfare rights movement was a life-changing experience. Local, state, and national meetings provided a heady mix of stories of injustice, examples of incredibly brave and creative organizing efforts, and intense strategy and policy debates. Local efforts were usually focused on finding and enrolling members, naming abuses, identifying allies, and finding ways for welfare mothers to get more benefits and stop abuse by the system. State and national meetings tried to spread the word and coordinate strategy. Allied litigation soon won from the U.S. Supreme Court constitutional assurances of due process and certain basic liberties for recipients and judicial recognition that welfare was an entitlement due to all individuals who met the program's income requirements. By the early 1970s, policy and organizing initiatives could imagine the possibility of a national guaranteed income, with a mandated federal structure for recipient input.

The effort to achieve a guaranteed income in the early 1970s, while initially supported by a wide coalition of social justice groups, devolved into a predictably conflicted effort over how much to compromise and what to demand. Allies, advocates, and welfare rights leaders disagreed over what to do about President Richard M. Nixon's surprise proposal for a Family Assistance Plan (FAP). The FAP would have created a national floor under family benefits, but one that was extremely low and that was attached to a work requirement. Twice the proposal failed in Congress, due in part to opposition from liberals influenced by NWRO demands for more adequate benefits, work opportunities rather than work requirements, and more adequate representation for welfare recipients in the system. By 1974, the issue was essentially dead, as Watergate loomed and advocates moved on to other issues.

Activists and advocates offer many explanations for the demise of the NWRO and related organizations, including the lack of a sustained national focus after the defeat of FAP and an ensuing lack of resources. Some simply blame the general collapse of radicalism and of liberal allies in the labor movement and the Democratic

Party. Although Martin Luther King Jr.'s leadership in a Poor People's Campaign and march in 1968 has been seen as a validation of the welfare rights approach, his death and the strategic confusions that resulted from the campaign weakened the focus of the NWRO. Gender- and class-based struggles over leadership also played a part in the decline of the organization, as Guida West (1987) observed in her important study of the welfare rights movement. Finally, the untimely death of an already-discouraged Wiley helped seal the fate of the national movement, even though he had already stepped down from official leadership.

Still, welfare rights organizations and local and statewide organizing efforts did not die out completely after the mid-1970s. Many small local groups maintained themselves with support from local antipoverty organizations, churches, or the public colleges that many welfare recipients attended. Individual leaders stayed involved or moved to other local antipoverty initiatives, so the issue of welfare itself seldom disappeared. But the welfare rights movement as such was never a powerful national force after the end of NWRO. The major later effort to revive it with a National Welfare Rights Union in 1987, while important, was unable to achieve the national level of attention or progressive support of the earlier movement. Although a welfare rights movement of the proportions of the movement of the 1960s and 1970s has not emerged in recent years, by the late 1990s, a solid network of local organizations had developed, greatly enhanced by the ability to organize electronically. Responding to the 1996 welfare law, organizations such as the Welfare Made a Difference Campaign and Montana's Working for Equality and Economic Liberation (WEEL)—and many others—have kept welfare rights issues alive.

Antipoverty Activism since the 1980s

Although the welfare rights movement of the 1960s and 1970s did not win a right to welfare or income security, through a combination of litigation and protest, it did secure certain rights for recipients and did make welfare more accessible to people who needed it. But these successes were not inexorable. By the late 1980s, the victories of the earlier movement were in jeopardy. Antipoverty activists were unable to defeat or defang successive waves of federal welfare reform, immigration reform, child welfare reform, and criminal justice reform that took away rights and worsened the everyday conditions of poor people. Punitive policies, at both federal and state levels, pushed antipoverty advocates into defensive postures, fighting to preserve programs tainted by racist stereotypes of their recipients' "dependency," by growing heteronormative moralism, and by attacks on "big government." In such a climate, almost all the actors became unsure about what strategic and tactical goals could have any likelihood of success, however success was defined.

Traditional professional antipoverty advocacy continued through such organizations as the Children's Defense Fund and the National Association of Social Workers. Such liberal advocacy groups have tried to address family and child poverty via lobbying and professional education. Joined by national legal advocacy groups, most notably the Center for Law and Social Policy (CLASP), these groups perfected a style of information dissemination, teleconferencing, and targeted lobbying that kept those concerned about policy issues well informed.

During the campaign to reform welfare in 1995–1996, some mainstream women's organizations tried to speak out on issues related to women's poverty, although many were unable to arouse interest from their rank-and-file contributors or members. The NOW Legal Defense and Education Fund (NOW-LDEF) played a key role in education and advocacy, while national leadership of the National Organization for Women protested punitive proposals. Women's research organizations also participated in the welfare debate, conducting and

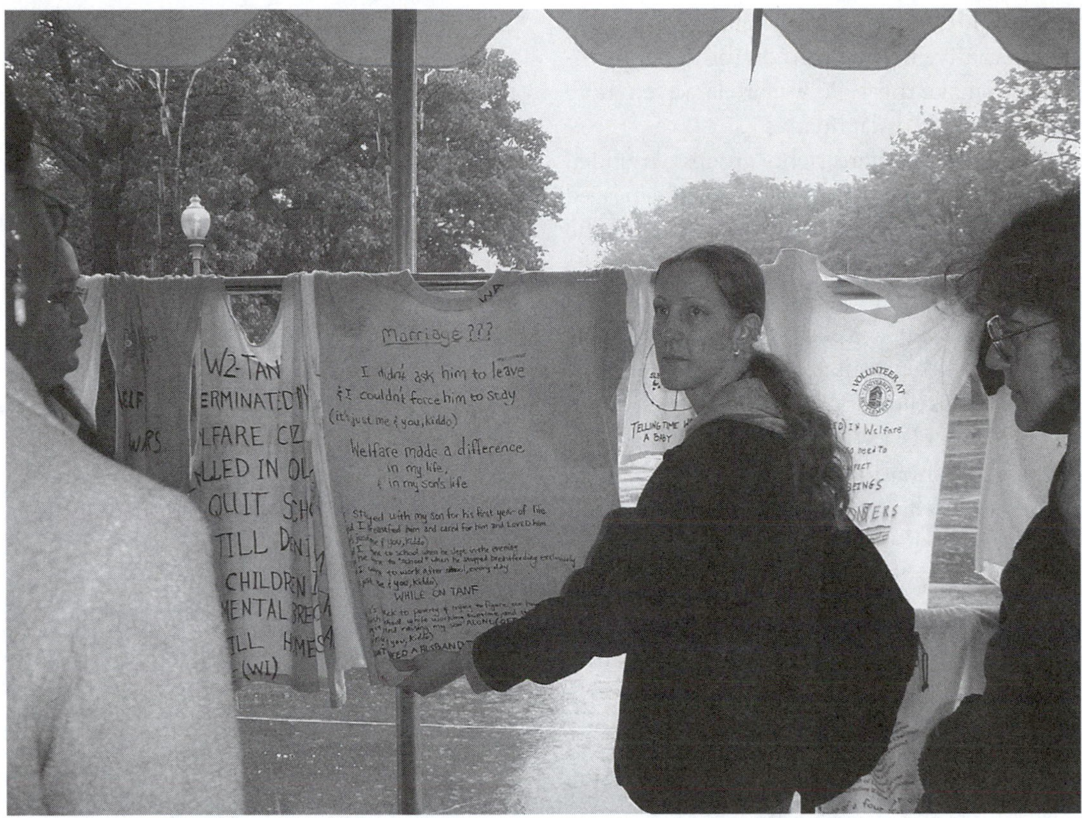

At "Shirts Off Our Backs Day" in Upper Senate Park on Capitol Hill, the Welfare Made a Difference Campaign displayed shirts on which poor mothers had written of their experiences in poverty and on welfare. Recipients and former recipients read the shirts to demonstrate their opposition to Republican proposals to make welfare more restrictive, meager, and disciplinary, October 27, 2003. (Photo courtesy of Gwendolyn Mink)

publishing studies that debunked stereotypes and exposed how bad the situation was for low-income women. Beginning in 1995, a group of feminist scholars and social welfare advocates mobilized in the Women's Committee of 100, the only feminist group specifically devoted to fighting for welfare justice and against punitive welfare reform. Grassroots groups, such as Jedi Women, Welfare Warriors, and the Kensington Welfare Rights Union, actively campaigned against proposals to end welfare.

These efforts failed, and in 1996 the Aid to Families with Dependent Children program was replaced by the Temporary Assistance for Needy Families (TANF) program. As new welfare provisions took effect following enactment of the 1996 welfare law, groups have mobilized around efforts to secure rights, opportunities, and protections for TANF participants. For example, NOW-LDEF organized and administered the Building Opportunities Beyond Welfare Reform (BOB) Coalition, which has aided communication among antipoverty advocates, some unions, some religious groups, domestic violence activists, child care advocates, immigrant rights groups, and others. Supported by most participants in the BOB Coalition, NOW-LDEF worked with the Welfare Made a Difference Campaign and the Women's Committee of 100 in 2001 to help draft progressive welfare legislation (H.R. 3113, 107th Congress, 1st sess.) as an alternative to the Bush administration's proposal to make the 1996 welfare law even more restrictive and disciplinary.

Grassroots welfare rights groups abounded in the late 1990s as individual recipients engaged the harsh new welfare system established by the 1996 Personal Responsibility and Work Opportunity Reconciliation Act. More established groups, such as the Kensington Welfare Rights Union and the Welfare Warriors, continued their work, as did national networks such as the Every Mother Is a Working Mother group. New regional organizations such as Grassroots Organizing for Welfare Leadership (GROWL) and the Western Regional Organizing Coalition (WROC) mobilized a strong presence in national policy discussion about how to pursue welfare justice in the new legislative environment. In addition, antipoverty activism remained prominent in related policy arenas: child care, job training and employment flexibility, and meaningful health care. These issues emerged as part of poor women's agendas at countless conferences and meetings where advocacy strategies and organizing tensions were the source of both dialogue and struggle.

Welfare advocacy in the early twenty-first century is not popular. Media interest and opportunities have waned, yielding the floor to the antiwelfare cause. Internet communication through organizations such as the Welfare Law Center's LINC Project tries to counter media bias, though the LINC Project cannot make up for poor people's lack of access to the media. But the LINC Project does allow groups to share information on legislation, litigation, and events across state and county lines.

One of the few remaining independent, national antipoverty media sources is *Survival News, the National Welfare Rights Newspaper,* the official newspaper of the National Welfare Rights Union, still published twice a year. *Survival News* provides welfare rights groups an avenue to inform recipients about their rights and supply them with survival tips, to compare welfare policies, to document their activities, and to honor their leaders. Welfare rights groups are encouraged to write articles and poems and to send pictures describing the situation in their home states. However, each year fewer groups are able to submit the desired free-flowing and detailed articles due to limited funding, staffing, and time. In addition, *Survival News* itself constantly struggles to maintain adequate funding. Although it is a collective staffed by volunteers and does not maintain office space, funding to purchase and maintain the necessary equipment and supplies and to sponsor special projects is constantly sparse. Yet in spite of the numerous mounting challenges, the newspaper has gained international recognition among grassroots activists and their allies.

The economic downturn at the beginning of the twenty-first century and the perception that welfare reform "worked" have severely limited the funding resources for all types of direct welfare rights organizing. Many welfare rights groups have folded due to lack of funding and to the increasing work requirements for their members—rules that impede women's ability to attend meetings and organize. Few organizations still have paid staff to train and assist members. As national organizations that have traditionally been allies experience diminishing returns from their funding sources, their ability and willingness to fund low-income women's attendance at conferences and symposiums have fallen off dramatically. As a result, welfare rights groups across the country have had their ability to share organizing strategies and experiences seriously limited.

Beyond the resource limitation, however, the most discouraging aspect of the post–welfare reform era has been the lack of willingness of liberal and left allies to argue for welfare rights as a basic part of the fight against poverty and as an essential element of a socially secure society. The struggle for welfare rights has historically rested on the recognition that without worker organizing and governmental intervention in the market, jobs in a capitalist society will never offer family wages; that caregiving is socially valuable work; and that there is a public obligation to provide economic support to women for undertaking what many often see as their primary obligations as parents. But these facts and commitments have been obscured by the assertion by many in the antipoverty community that an employment-based strategy is the only feasible way to win economic assistance for families. From this point of view, welfare should be a wage supplement for labor-market workers rather than income support for family caregivers.

Although the future of welfare rights may be precarious, the history of the welfare rights movement is an impressive and shining example of what has been possible despite the limits of democracy and capitalism in the United States. Knowing the history is vital to any continued organizing efforts because history reveals that poor women working together can make a difference. The courageous leaders who asserted their right to be treated with respect challenged the system and worked with allies effectively enough to allow a campaign for a guaranteed income to be seen as a feasible strategy. And the welfare rights activists of the 1960s paved the way for improved income benefits, along with such programs and services as food stamps, Medicaid, and fuel assistance. Still, in the first decade of the new century, welfare rights groups struggle just to survive, to document their experiences, and to share strategies and tactics with one another. Members become discouraged with low attendance at protest demonstrations and rallies, which produce scant media attention and little political influence. Many poor women drift away as the struggle to survive overtakes them, and they search for other ways to be more effective. At the same time, few advocates or political leaders dare speak of welfare rights, and almost none seems willing to argue for mothers' rights to choose the kind of work they do, whether inside or outside of their family, as a basic aspect of social security.

Ann Withorn and Diane Dujon

See also: Aid to Families with Dependent Children (ADC/AFDC); Capitalism; Civil Rights Movement; Family Structure; Feminisms; New Property; NOW Legal Defense and Education Fund; Poverty Law; Racism; Sexism; Welfare Policy/Welfare Reform; see also the extracts from the following court cases (in sidebars to the entry Poverty Law): *King v. Smith* (1968); *Shapiro, Commissioner of Welfare of Connecticut, v. Thompson* (1969); *Goldberg v. Kelly* (1970); *Dandridge v. Williams* (1970); *Saenz v. Roe* (1999)

References and Further Reading

Abramovitz, Mimi. 1996a. *Regulating the Lives of Women*. 2d ed. Boston: South End Press.

———. 1996b. *Under Attack. Fighting Back*. New York: Monthly Review Press.

Abramovitz, Mimi, and Ann Withorn. 1999. "Playing by the Rules: Welfare Reform and the New Authoritarian State." In *Without Justice for All: The New Liberalism and Our Retreat from Racial Equality*, ed. Adolph Reed, 151–173. Boulder, CO: Westview Press.

Albelda, Randy, and Nancy Folbre. 1996. *The War on the Poor: A Defense Manual*. New York: New Press.

Albelda, Randy, and Ann Withorn. 2002. *Lost Ground*. Boston: South End Press.

Bennett, J., and B. Laslett. 1991. "Gender, Social Reproduction, and Women's Self Organization: Considering the US Welfare State." *Gender and Society* 5, no. 3 (September): 311–333.

Dujon, Diane, and Ann Withorn, eds. 1996. *For Crying out Loud: Women's Poverty in the United States*. Boston: South End Press.

Fisher, Robert. 1994. *Let the People Decide: Neighborhood Organizing in America*. 2d ed. Boston: Twayne.

Gordon, Linda, ed. 1991. *Women, the State, and Welfare*. Madison: University of Wisconsin Press.

———. 1994. *Pitied but Not Entitled*. New York: Free Press.

Kotz, Mary, and Nick Kotz. 1977. *A Passion for Equality: George Wiley and the Welfare Rights Movement*. New York: Norton.

Mandell, Betty Reid, and Ann Withorn,.1993. "Keep on Keeping On: Welfare Rights Organizing in Massachusetts." In *Mobilizing for Change*, ed. Robert Fisher and Joel Kling. Thousand Oaks, CA: Sage.

Marable, Manning. 1991. *Race, Reform, and Rebellion: The Second Reconstruction in Black America, 1945–1990*. Jackson: University Press of Mississippi.

Mink, Gwendolyn, ed. 1999. *Whose Welfare?* Ithaca, NY: Cornell University Press.

Naples, Nancy, ed. 1998. *Community Activism and Feminist Politics*. New York: Routledge.

Ortega, Catherine. 1998. "Who Makes These Laws?" *Survival News* (Winter): 7.

Piven, Frances Fox, and Richard A. Cloward. 1972. *Regulating the Poor*. New York: Vintage Books.

———. 1986. *Poor People's Movements: Why They Succeed and How They Fail*. 2d ed. New York: Viking.

Pope, Jacqueline. 1989. *Biting the Hands That Feed Them: Grassroots Organizing of Women on Welfare*. New York: Praeger.

Ryan, Charlotte. 1991. *Prime Time Activism*. Boston: South End Press.

West, Guida. 1987. *The Welfare Rights Movement*. New York: Praeger.

White, Deborah Grey. 1999. *Too Heavy a Load: Black Women in Defense of Themselves, 1894–1994*. New York: Norton.

Withorn, Ann. 1996a. "Fulfilling Fears and Fantasies: The Role of Welfare in Rightwing Social Thought." In *Re-Reading the Right*, ed. Amy Ansell. Boulder, CO: Westview Press.

———. 1996b. "Why Do They Hate Me So Much?" *American Journal of Orthopsychiatry* (November).

———. 1999 "Not for Lack of Trying: The Fight against Welfare Reform in Massachusetts." Center for Women in Politics occasional paper. Fall. Boston: University of Massachusetts.

Welfare State

Welfare states are a primary apparatus of rule in capitalist democracies. Welfare states provide cash and in-kind benefits, such as Social Security and food stamps. They provide subsidies for housing, education and training, and low-wage work. They regulate wages and labor standards. They also provide, subsidize, or regulate services related to people's well-being, such as medical care, child support enforcement, legal advice, discrimination and abuse prevention and remediation, and job training. Some welfare states serve as the employer of last resort. During economic downturns, as part of countercyclical government spending to stimulate the economy, public works programs can be important aspects of the antipoverty programs of welfare states. Military expenditures are additional means some welfare states use to manage capitalist economic development. Politicians and administrators generally build and support welfare states in the wake of crises in employment and profitability that shake the middle and working classes, in response to calls for a safety net for the poor, out of fear of massive social unrest or revolution, and in response to international threats to domestic security. As a result, the extent and generosity of welfare benefits depend at least as much on politics and demands from social movements as on economics and the level of resources available to "provide for the common welfare."

Welfare states are contradictory. The primary contradiction is that welfare states are economic hostages to capitalist enterprise. Welfare states depend for revenue on capitalism, yet capitalism generates, or at least aggravates, the inequality, poverty, and alienation that welfare states are supposed to remedy. Welfare states are vulnerable to political backlash if they enable large numbers of people to subsist without engaging in wage work. Because they are beholden to capital, welfare states can seldom risk implementing policies—such as generous benefits for the long-term unemployed or for women caring for significant people in their lives—that undermine work discipline, capitalist profitability, and the social control functions of providing for the poor.

Another contradiction of the welfare state is the fact that people of all classes and income levels potentially benefit from social provision, redistribution, regulation, subsidies, domestic and international security, and services. The more universal the benefits, the broader the political appeal of welfare programs. Welfare programs are politically vulnerable to the degree that they narrowly target benefits to "the truly needy"—often stigmatized segments of the population. Welfare states also face a contradiction between rights and relief, between entitlement (based on citizenship) and eligibility (based on work effort, marriage, or other evidence of docile compliance with the status quo). Moreover, the basis of demands—that is, a living wage as a right versus poor relief to prevent riots—may place conflicting pressures on administrators and politicians in welfare states. Thus, although politicians respond most to insistent demands, policymakers prefer to reward conformist rather than disruptive people and social movements.

The apparatus of rule known as welfare states consists of *institutions*, *capacities*, and *ideologies*. The *institutions* of welfare states generally include legislatures, courts, administrative bureaucracies, prisons, armed services and police, schools, and public health services. Welfare states vary in their juridical, administrative, military and paramilitary, and therapeutic *capacities*. All seek to impose specific ways of making and enforcing law and legal decisions, to determine crime and punishment, to monopolize war making and regulate firearms, to protect private property, and to manage local and global interests in territory and commerce. Welfare states also define and protect public health and rehabilitation, determine who is sick or crazy, and license experts with the power and authority to diagnose, treat, and quarantine. In welfare states, the characteristic *ideologies*, or sets of ideas and ways of talking about how politics and power operate, typically include distinctions between the worthy and unworthy poor, notions of entitlement and need, implicit or explicit social contracts between providers and beneficiaries or recipients of transfers and services, and assumptions about the relative value of military service, wage work, and care work.

The United States has had a conspicuously meager and punitive set of programs for the poor. Historically, the United States has been a laggard builder and a precocious reformer and dismantler of welfare state programs. The U.S. welfare state started officially in 1935 with the passage of the Social Security Act, a central plank of President Franklin D. Roosevelt's platform for the New Deal. The major predecessors of the U.S. welfare state were pensions for Civil War veterans and state-level mothers' aid programs, both of which were considered public compensation for having sacrificed earnings ability for dutiful service to country or family.

The benefits called "welfare" in the United States have been consistently and closely targeted at the people at greatest risk of poverty: the old, the young, people with temporary or permanent illness or disability, the unemployed, and unmarried mothers. This targeting has made it easy for U.S. politicians and taxpayers to vilify both welfare recipients and welfare programs. Following in the footsteps of Republican President Ronald Reagan, who ran up record government deficits and blamed them on Cadillac-driving "welfare queens," Democratic president Bill Clinton signed the law that "ended welfare as we [knew] it" in 1996. In so doing, Clinton eliminated the cheapest but most politically vulnerable part of the U.S. welfare state: the entitlement to cash benefits for unmarried mothers and their children. Thus concluded sixty years of modest U.S. policy efforts to mitigate inequality and poverty for mothers and children, the people whose relationships to the labor market are the most precarious.

Nonwelfare programs based on the principle of social insurance, or worker contributions to benefits that will be drawn later, have been less vulnerable to attack. Politicians routinely if begrudgingly extend unemployment insurance during hard times. Medicare expansion, not contraction, engages serious policy debate in the early twenty-first century. And national politicians can talk about universalizing health coverage without being hooted off the stage. The different political status accorded programs the public believes have been earned by participants marks the degree of stratification in the welfare state. Nevertheless, antigovernment, neoliberal proposals that would undermine the more protected programs of the welfare state do enjoy serious consideration. Proposals to privatize Social Security are high on Republican agendas, for example, precisely because privatization would destroy the core program of the U.S. welfare state.

Scholars debate the extent to which welfare states seek to ameliorate poverty because they can afford it, because reformers consider it morally correct, because social provision is an effective means of social control, because politicians sometimes cannot afford *not* to, or for some combination of these reasons. In order to understand the late rise and relatively weak character of the U.S. welfare state and the recent efforts to dismantle it, one must comprehend two complementary dynamics. First is the degree to which U.S. welfare state policies and programs aggravate or ameliorate inequalities of class, race, and gender. Second is the extent to which race, gender, and class organize U.S. welfare state institutions, capacities, and ideologies.

The U.S. welfare state contributes importantly to the social construction of poverty and the poor. Through "needs talk," welfare state administrators, politicians, and social scientists distinguish poor people from everyone else and also distinguish the "worthy" from the "unworthy" poor. For example, in the United States, "worthy" welfare recipients are generally those not expected to be able to earn enough to fulfill their needs. Expectations about "availability for work" and about earnings vary enormously across time and region and by race, gender, and immigration status. Over the span of the twentieth century, for instance, the U.S. welfare state viewed white, native-born children sometimes as earners expected to contribute their wages to the household budget and sometimes as innocent dependents who should not suffer poverty because of the economic or moral failings of their parents.

Furthermore, the professionals who seek simultaneously to serve the poor, promote their own expertise, and reform the welfare state have used eligibility criteria and other everyday bureaucratic practices to maintain racial segregation, reinforce conventional notions of motherhood and fatherhood, enforce work discipline, and otherwise reproduce inequalities of gender, race, birth status, and class. Regulations and program implementation have reproduced racist and sexist assumptions about "work readiness" and sexual respectability for mothers, selectively benefiting some groups, such as native-born, white, celibate widows, at the expense of others. Jobs disproportionately filled by people of color and immigrants (for instance, domestic work and agricultural labor) have been excluded from eligibility for welfare state benefits.

Welfare states contribute to the meaning and consequences of poverty, racism, nativism, and women's subordination. At the same time, race, gender, and class organize welfare states and their approaches to poverty. Divisions of labor, levels of resources, and access to power in welfare state institutions are structured by race and gender, for example, to the extent that racism and sexism organize personnel practices, professional opportunities, and political clout within the welfare state. The U.S. welfare state is divided into two distinct tiers, which further organize welfare by race and gender. The benefits and services associated with masculine citizenship activities—being a soldier or a worker—are relatively generous entitlements. They are administered with minimal intrusion, little stigma, and no requirement that recipients prove need in order to meet eligibility criteria. In sharp contrast, the benefits and services associated with feminine citizenship activities—being a mother or other care provider—are stingy, intrusive, stigmatized, and subject to stringent tests for eligibility. For instance, welfare recipients in the United States in the 1950s and 1960s were subject to late-night searches under a "man in the house" rule that enforced celibacy on poor single mothers. At both tiers, services and benefits reward conformity and punish women and men who stray from race- and class-specific norms. Finally, race, class, and gender difference and dominance inform welfare state ideologies such as the rhetoric of "family values," the notions of rugged individualism that blame poor people for their plight, and categories that distinguish the "truly needy" from "welfare cheats."

Compared to the welfare states in other capitalist democracies, the United States has had only fragmented and weak programs and has been reluctant to address poverty and inequality through systematic political intervention. The U.S. welfare state shares these features with other "liberal" countries in which markets and families are more important sites for obtaining welfare than are states and social programs. Welfare states in some other countries make it easier for people to reconcile their potentially conflicting obligations to meet their needs through market earnings and to provide for the well-being of others through unpaid care work in families. Strong left-labor parties in some countries allow welfare states to maintain more generous benefits in the face of pressure from business interests. In still other countries, coalitions among business, labor, church, and government promote different work and family arrangements through welfare state programs, practices, and policies. Countries vary in the degree to which they emphasize markets, families, voluntary organizations, or states in the overall package of welfare. However, both individual country case studies and comparative analyses show that all welfare states both organize and are organized by class and race. In addition, welfare states seldom include provisions for enhancing women's physical safety, sexual integrity and agency, access to complete reproductive health care, or other markers of genuine commitment to reducing women's dependence on and subordination to men.

Recent reforms of the welfare state in the United States have had two types of impacts. First, they affect the quality of everyday life for poor people. Work requirements and time limits, the central features of the 1996 welfare reforms, can make economic survival more precarious for families and individuals, making it harder to provide food and housing, to pay the bills, to maintain physical and mental health, and to secure women's safety from men's violence and control. Second, welfare reforms change the rules of the game and the material bases of struggles over work, relationships, privilege, and equality. Dismantling welfare shifts the balance of power between workers and employers in favor of business interests. Welfare reforms have racially disparate impacts and systematically reproduce racist notions of worthiness, need, and job-readiness. Increasingly oppressive and exploitative class, race, and gender rules and relations are all "impacts of welfare reform." Poor people and their advocates therefore have to explore new coalitions in order to fight back.

Lisa D. Brush

See also: Domestic Violence; Employment Policy; Federalism; Gender Discrimination in the Labor Market; Health Policy; Liberalism; Maternalist Policy; Privatization; Social Security; Social Security Act of 1935; Welfare Policy/Welfare Reform

References and Further Reading

Abramovitz, Mimi. [1988] 1996. *Regulating the Lives of Women: Social Welfare Policy from Colonial Times to the Present*. Rev. ed. Boston: South End Press.

Brush, Lisa D. 2003. *Gender and Governance*. Walnut Creek, CA: AltaMira Press.

Esping-Andersen, Gøsta. 1999. *Social Foundations of Postindustrial Economies*. Oxford: Oxford University Press.

Gordon, Linda, ed. 1990. *Women, the State, and Welfare*. Madison: University of Wisconsin Press.

Mink, Gwendolyn. 1994. *Wages of Motherhood: Inequality in the Welfare State, 1917–1942*. Ithaca, NY: Cornell University Press.

Neubeck, Kenneth J., and Noel A. Cazenave. 2001. *Welfare Racism: Playing the Race Card against America's Poor*. New York: Routledge.

O'Connor, Julia, Ann Shola Orloff, and Sheila Shaver. 1999. *States, Markets, Families: Gender, Liberalism, and Social Policy in Australia, Canada, Great Britain, and the United States*. Cambridge: Cambridge University Press.

Piven, Frances Fox, and Richard A. Cloward. [1971] 1993. *Regulating the Poor: The Functions of Public Welfare*. Updated ed. New York: Vintage Books.
Skocpol, Theda. 1992. *Protecting Soldiers and Mothers: The Political Origins of Social Policy in the United States*. Cambridge, MA: Harvard University Press.

Welfare-Made-a-Difference Campaign

See Welfare Policy/Welfare Reform; Welfare Rights Movement

What Social Classes Owe to Each Other, William Graham Sumner

William Graham Sumner, born in 1840, was a prominent proponent of Social Darwinism, the late-nineteenth-century belief that Charles Darwin's theories of natural selection, as translated by Herbert Spencer into the doctrine of "survival of the fittest," applied to human society. A graduate of Yale University, Sumner trained as a minister and became an Episcopal clergyman before joining the faculty of his alma mater as a professor of social science. In his lectures and books, Sumner argued in favor of laissez-faire economics and against government intervention in economics or social welfare. Like other Social Darwinists, he explained the growing social and economic inequality of the period—including the growth of an industrial working class, the development of urban slums, and ever more extreme differences in income—as a reflection of immutable natural laws of social development. Sumner viewed inequality as natural and inevitable, the result of differences in ability and willingness to work. For him, the vast wealth amassed by corporate leaders was the result of their talent as managers of people and capital rather than of the exploitation of underpaid labor. The poor, he believed, were not victims; rather, they were underachievers, held back by their laziness, lack of intelligence, or indulgence in alcohol. Welfare programs, therefore, represented an attempt to remake the natural order of society.

In the passage below, Sumner discusses his view that economic inequality is part of human life, conceding only that members of all classes should have the opportunity to rise above their circumstances.

Sarah Case

See also: Malthusianism; Self-Reliance; Social Darwinism

If words like wise and foolish, thrifty and extravagant, prudent and negligent, have any meaning in language, then it must make some difference how people behave in this world, and the difference will appear in the position they acquire in the body of society, and in relation to the chances of life. They may, then, be classified in reference to these facts. Such classes always will exist; no other social distinctions can endure. If, then, we look to the origins and definition of these classes, we shall find it impossible to deduce any obligations which one of them bears to the other. The class distinctions simply result from the different degrees of success with which men have availed themselves of the chances which were presented to them. Instead of endeavoring to redistribute the acquisitions which have been made between the existing classes, our aim should be to increase, multiply, and extend the chances. . . . The yearning after equality is the offspring of envy and covetousness, and there is no possible plan for satisfying that yearning which can do aught else than rob A to give to B; consequently all such plans nourish some of the meanest vices of human nature, waste capital, and overthrow civilization.

Source: William Graham Sumner, *What Social Classes Owe to Each Other* (New York and London: Harper and Brothers, 1883. Reprint 1920), 167–168.

Women, Infants, and Children (WIC) Program

See Hunger; Maternalist Policy; Nutrition and Food Assistance

Work Ethic

The work ethic is a culturally constructed set of norms that refer to one's ideological orientation toward labor. As such, the work ethic can be understood as both an attitude and a set of habitual actions. Those who possess the work ethic are said to be focused, diligent, efficient, responsible, personally accountable, self-disciplined, and self-regulating. Some believe that those who possess the work ethic will be materially self-supporting. Individual failure to manifest the work ethic is understood, particularly by political conservatives, as the root cause of poverty. Those who hold this position also argue that social provision corrupts the recipient's will to work and that the renewal of the work ethic is a solution to poverty and welfare "dependency."

The Western version of the work ethic has its origins in biblical text. Specifically, after the Fall from God's grace, work became a form of punishment for man's sinful nature. Building on this view during the Protestant Reformation, John Calvin and Martin Luther positioned work as a profession of faith and a form of service to God. Work was understood as a calling or vocation, and dutiful work practice as a religious duty.

The Puritan sects that immigrated to North America in the seventeenth century believed strongly in the link between faith and disciplined work practice. Adherence to the work ethic was a key component of Puritan self-understanding. Some of the earliest efforts to instill the work ethic in others date back to Puritan efforts to transform the labor practices of Native Americans living near the Massachusetts Bay Colony. In a widely influential theory, German sociologist Max Weber argued that the Puritan's belief system, which stressed one's duty to work and understood success in work as indicative of salvation, reinforced a set of self-denying habits and ascetic practices that eventually helped foster the rise of industrial capitalism.

The work ethic had its origins in religious belief, and these connections remain visible today in faith-based approaches to social welfare provision. Nevertheless, in the eighteenth century, the American work ethic took a secular turn. This was due in large part to the writings of Benjamin Franklin. Franklin championed thrift, industry, and self-discipline. He saw these values as the first step in the creation of a successful persona that one could use to enter the public sphere of democratic politics. Indeed, it was Franklin who forged the connection between the work ethic and democratic citizenship. In his annually produced *Poor Richard's Almanac* and in his *Autobiography*, Franklin lay the groundwork for a narrative that connects hard work, self-discipline, financial success, class mobility, and full political membership. This narrative remained prominent and can be seen in popular literature of the nineteenth century, especially in such books for children as the McGuffey's Readers and the writings of Horatio Alger. Notably, the secular version of the American work ethic, with its promise of material reward and full citizenship, was being consolidated at the same time that Black chattel slavery, the organization of labor through the systematic use of force and violence, was also being solidified in the United States.

The advent of the Industrial Revolution tested America's adherence to the work ethic and the assumption of a natural link between the work ethic and democratic citizenship. Some argue that work ethic ideology fits fairly well with smallholder agrarian and craft economies. In these economic systems, the worker has some control over work organization, can see the product that is created, and can use leisure time to pursue politics. Thomas Jefferson celebrated the link between preindustrial labor and democratic politics in his depiction of the hardworking yeoman farmer as the ideal democratic citizen. With the advance of industrialization, the combination of harsh working conditions and workers' alienation from the product being produced led intellectuals and labor leaders to doubt that the work ethic as a set of beliefs and practices could be sustained. Yet despite massive technological change and periods of severe economic downturn, the work ethic persisted, principally as a narrative, suggesting that disciplined work behavior would lead to material reward.

Work norms and expectations of financial reward became a narrative shared by a range of immigrant groups, who used it to mark themselves as loyal American citizens. And yet, although for some the work ethic was deployed as a narrative of assimilation, specific ethnic and racial groups have historically been stereotyped and stigmatized as having a poor work ethic or as being lazy—specifically Native Americans, Irish immigrants, and, most persistently, African Americans emancipated from slavery.

Early-twentieth-century social commentators and social reformers linked poverty to a failure of the work ethic. Accordingly, social interventions such as poorhouses, orphanages, and settlement houses were designed in part to alter their subjects' values by teaching the work ethic. These programs were designed to break personal and group norms and instill a sense of individual striving and a desire for class mobility. The view that poverty was rooted in an individual's failure to adhere to the work ethic diminished somewhat in the wake of the massive market failures and unemployment of the Great Depression. With the partial expansion of the welfare state in the 1930s, there was a greater understanding of poverty as a systemic rather than individual failure.

Though the emergence of the welfare state in the early twentieth century disrupted the hegemony of the work ethic narrative to some degree, the notion that the work ethic is the proper way for the individual to relate to the economy and gain material provision has never been fully displaced. The conservative critiques of welfare provision that began circulating in the 1970s and 1980s again argued that the expansion of income supports was due to a failure of work discipline. In this view, cash supports generated "welfare dependency" and a "culture of poverty," which undermined "mainstream" norms of striving and personal responsibility. The work requirement component of the Personal Responsibility and Work Opportunity Reconciliation Act of 1996 can be understood as an effort to change recipients' norms and values by mandating work. The assumption driving this component of the law is that engaging in the practice of wage work engenders the acquisition of new work norms, thereby instilling an ideological commitment to the work ethic.

Anne M. Manuel

See also: Americanization Movement; Malthusianism; Poor Laws; Poorhouse/Almshouse; Puritans and Puritanism; Self-Reliance; Social Darwinism; Workfare

References and Further Reading

Franklin, Benjamin. 1961. *The Autobiography and Other Writings*. New York: Signet.

Weber, Max. 2002. *The Protestant Ethic and the Spirit of Capitalism*. Los Angeles: Roxbury.

Workers' Compensation

Workers' compensation is a state-based system of no-fault insurance for work-related injuries. Established in early-twentieth-century legislation that laid important groundwork for the American welfare state, this system replaced workers' right to sue employers directly for work accidents with an insurance-based model. Although workers' compensation laws vary by state, virtually all require employers to pay for insurance providing injured workers with disability benefits, medical benefits, and death benefits. Traditional theory distinguishes workers' compensation from "welfare" programs by describing it as earned compensation for workers rather than government charity for the poor. Consistent with historical gender and race stratification of American welfare, workers' compensation originally focused on securing the income of industrial workers, who were predominantly (though not exclusively) white men. But despite the favored status of workers' compensation, in practice it has a long history of failing to adequately protect many injured workers. And after a period of benefit expansion, at the end of the twentieth century, most states adopted broad reforms that significantly restricted workers' rights to compensation.

In the typical structure of workers' compensation, state administrative agencies oversee the benefit claims process and resolve disputes. Private commercial companies provide a large portion of workers' compensation insurance, although many large employers self-insure. Some states also offer insurance through public funds, and in a few states these public funds are the exclusive insurers. Although most claims are for medical expenses alone, the most costly claims involve cash disability benefits for lost work time, divided into temporary and permanent benefits. Cash disability and death benefits generally cover about two-thirds of lost wages up to a weekly maximum based on a percentage of the state's average wage. For some permanent injuries, states determine benefit amounts according to a fixed payment schedule regardless of individual income loss.

Workers' compensation developed in response to a crisis in the late-nineteenth-century law governing accidental workplace injury. Injured workers generally could not recover damages from employers in court because of legal rules holding workers responsible for avoiding accidents. But when states began to ease these rules and to increase employers' risk of high damage awards, many business leaders joined some labor advocates and social reformers in supporting a change to a "social insurance" system drawn from European models. Between 1911 and 1920, most states adopted workers' compensation laws that gave employers responsibility for compensating accidental injuries "arising out of and in the course of employment," regardless of fault, and in exchange limited compensation to lost income and medical costs instead of broader damage awards. Proponents argued that this "bargain" would benefit society by reducing wasteful litigation and by spreading the costs of occupational risks to employers and consumers.

Although the new scheme allowed many injured workers (or their survivors) to receive some compensation relatively quickly and easily, from the beginning, state laws failed to cover many workers and many kinds of injuries. For the first several decades after the passage of workers' compensation laws, most states narrowly interpreted the concept of accidental injuries to exclude many gradually developing disabilities and many occupational illnesses. During its early decades, workers' compensation generally did not compensate medical expenses or else restricted benefits to limited and often poor-quality treatment provided by employers or insurers. By the late 1950s, many states had expanded their programs to cover more employees and more injuries and to provide less restrictive medical benefits. But by this time, rising wages had outpaced disability benefit maximums, so benefits typically replaced a much smaller share of workers' lost earnings than they had when workers' compensation began.

These falling benefit levels, along with continuing concern about inadequate workplace safety, spurred political pressure for federal intervention. In the Occupational Safety and Health Act of 1970, Congress established a national commission to review state workers' compensation programs, along with a new system for regulating work hazards. Concluding that benefits were inadequate and inequitable, in 1972 this bipartisan commission issued a series of recommendations for more complete coverage of workers and injuries, including occupational illness, and for raising benefit levels. Recognizing that competition among states for business impeded political support for adequate benefits, the commission recommended that the federal government establish a national program if states failed to meet the recommended standards. Although most states did take steps to expand benefits over the next decade, overall these efforts fell significantly short of the recommendations.

By the late 1980s, expanded benefits contributed to steeply rising insurance costs. When employers demanded relief, some states modified their traditional practice of allowing insurance companies (protected from antitrust law) to cooperatively fix prices in a largely self-regulating process. As state regulators began to control insurance prices, insurers complained that their business was unprofitable. States relying on private commercial insurers faced a crisis as these insurers left the market or moved large numbers of employers into special insurance pools structured to temporarily protect individual insurers from high claims costs. Many of these special pools, along with some states' government-run insurance funds, ran up high deficits. In a number of states, many employers turned to alternative insurance sources, including group self-insurance pools and new state funds, some of which controlled costs through innovative programs for safety, reemployment, and claims deterrence. Insurance companies blamed their high deficits on regulatory rate controls and excessive benefits, and they joined with some employer groups in a national campaign for law reforms. This campaign used anecdotal evidence to frame the problem as one of widespread claims fraud, and insurance companies and employers complained that expanded benefits allowed undeserving beneficiaries to substitute "welfare" for work responsibility. By the early 1990s, most states responded to such ongoing political pressure by adopting comprehensive legal changes designed to scrutinize claims more aggressively and to give workers more responsibility for reducing their own injury costs. These reforms often limited covered injuries and illnesses, workers' protections in claims disputes, and disability benefit levels for permanently injured workers. The reforms restored insurers' profits and eased employers' costs but left many seriously injured workers with increased poverty and stigma and made it harder for them to challenge denials of claims.

Martha T. McCluskey

See also: American Association for Labor Legislation; Disability Policy; Social Security; Welfare Capitalism

References and Further Reading

Fishback, Price V., and Shawn Everett Kantor. 2000. *A Prelude to the Welfare State: The Origins of Workers' Compensation*. Chicago: University of Chicago Press.

McCluskey, Martha T. 1998. "The Illusion of Efficiency in Workers' Compensation 'Reform.'" *Rutgers Law Review* 50: 657–941.

Workfare

Workfare is a social policy of mandatory work programs for welfare recipients or, more generically, the process of work-oriented welfare reform. The neologism "workfare," coined in the late 1960s, is the contraction of "work" and "welfare." Workfare has become a powerful signifier of the prevailing method and philosophy of welfare reform in the United States. Work-based or work-enforcing welfare policies have been favored by politicians on the right for some considerable time, bolstered by the perennial concern that welfare entitlements with no strings attached erode the employment habits, job skills, and work ethics of the poor. Support for workfare-style policies widened during the 1980s, however, as centrist liberals became increasingly convinced of the argument for "tough love" approaches to welfare reform. The Personal Responsibility and Work Opportunity Reconciliation Act (PRWORA) of 1996 would later crystallize this bipartisan commitment, replacing the federal entitlement to welfare with a post–New Deal system of time-limited cash benefits and strict work requirements. Characterized by some as "welfare repeal," the PRWORA could also be regarded as a "workfare settlement" in that it embodies a defining objective of helping and hassling welfare recipients into the job market, offering minimal support for those who fail its work tests. Crucially, the underlying goals of such workfare regimes are no longer focused on straightforward poverty alleviation, since the fate of many of those leaving the welfare rolls has been *working* poverty. Workfare policies are instead addressed to the problem of "welfare dependency," whose solutions are defined in terms of encouraging or enforcing work.

Concretely, the term "workfare" is applied to programs that require welfare recipients to work—in public-sector jobs, in private workplaces, or in community placements—in exchange for benefits. More generally, it has become associated with a wide range of policy measures designed to improve the "employability" and work orientations of welfare recipients, typically through job-training programs and job search assistance. These measures are regarded as "workfarist" when they are used in the context of compulsion or strict benefit conditionality. Beyond these literal meanings, though, workfare is now recognized as a symbol of U.S.-style (or neoliberal) welfare reform. In its most abstract sense, the term "workfare state" denotes an inversion of the principles and practices of the welfare state, as the notion of (social) rights and entitlements gives way to a new emphasis on (personal) responsibility and obligation (Peck 2001). Whereas welfare stood for the principles of needs-based entitlement and standardized treatment, workfare stands for market-based compulsion, selectivity, and local discretion. Whereas welfare stood for passive income support, workfare stands for active labor market inclusion. And whereas welfare constructed its subjects as claimants, workfare reconstitutes them as job seekers.

Reflecting this increasingly generic usage, the reach and resonance of workfare have increased over time. What began as a specific program reform within the Aid to Families with Dependent Children (AFDC) system during the 1970s acquired a wider significance during the 1980s when President Ronald Reagan's administration made resources available for "demonstration projects," with the intent of propagating workfare-style initiatives. At this time, a distinction was drawn between "hard" and "soft" variants of workfare: The former emphasized strict policies of penalties and a no-nonsense approach; the latter was couched within a more supportive philosophy, seeking to build the human capital of welfare recipients through education and training investments. The Family Support Act (FSA) of 1988 represented a compromise between these two approaches, embedding the general principles of work-oriented welfare in the federal system.

The work program associated with the FSA, Job Opportunities and Basic Skills (JOBS), achieved no more than mixed results, its implementation being hampered by a slowing economy and growing political impatience on the part of state governors. This was the context for Bill Clinton's presidential campaign pledge to "end welfare as we know it," a fateful slogan that would come to epitomize the workfarist drift in U.S. welfare policy. With the Republican takeover of Congress in 1994, the language of welfare reform became more shrill, just as the attendant policy proposals became progressively more radical. In the lexicon of the ascendant Republican Right, "welfare" was associated with unambiguously negative terms like "decay," "failure," and "waste," whereas "workfare" was to be constituted as an "optimistic, positive, governing word" alongside "opportunity," "moral," and "hard work" (Peck 2001).

More than a war of words, the real battle in the mid-1990s was over the content and likely consequences of policy. In the wake of the passage of PRWORA, the responsibility for the new system passed to the fifty states, and most adopted approaches that emphasized rapid "labor force attachment." In the context of generally buoyant job markets, unprecedented numbers of welfare recipients left the welfare rolls in the late 1990s, further bolstering the confidence of workfare advocates and adding to the allure of the "American model" in international policy debates (Lodemel and Trickey 2001). Yet the economic slowdown that began in 2001 raised new questions about the efficacy of an approach that is self-evidently predicated on the ready availability of jobs. Although this faltering performance may have tarnished the image of workfare, the immediate prospects of a shift in policy away from the workfare model remain remote. On the contrary, workfare has apparently become established as a social policy counterpart to labor market "flexibility" policies. In the context of a continuing trend toward short-term, unstable, "contingent" jobs, workfare policies exhibit a primitive logic: They purposefully mobilize workers for (minimum) wage work, holding them close to the labor market in a persistently job-ready state. In a sense, they provide a forced (or "activated") labor supply for the labor market's least desirable, lowest-paid jobs. Although the prosaic reality of workfare may be to replace poverty-on-benefits with poverty-in-work, advocates like Lawrence Mead (1997) continue to insist that a much deeper *social* and moral problem is being tackled: the postindustrial phenomenon of "worklessness."

Jamie Peck

See also: Aid to Families with Dependent Children (ADC/AFDC); Contingent Work; New Right; *Regulating the Poor;* Welfare Policy/Welfare Reform; Welfare State; Work Ethic; "Working Poor"

References and Further Reading

Lodemel, Ivar, and Heather Trickey, eds. 2001. *An Offer You Can't Refuse: Workfare in International Perspective*. Bristol, UK: Policy Press.

Mead, Lawrence M., ed. 1997. *The New Paternalism: Supervisory Approaches to Poverty*. Washington, DC: Brookings Institution.

Peck, Jamie. 2001. *Workfare States*. New York: Guilford Press.

Rose, Nancy E. 1995. *Workfare or Fair Work: Women, Welfare, and Government Work Programs*. New Brunswick, NJ: Rutgers University Press.

"Working Poor"

"Working poor" is a term used in the press, among policy analysts and advocates, and in political debates to refer to people who have below-poverty income despite being employed in the paid labor force. Although the term has frequently been used to draw attention to the persistence of poverty wages and exploitative labor conditions as well as the work ethic of poor people, the "working poor" have also been deployed in contrast to welfare recipients, reinforcing stereotyped imagery of the latter as "dependent," "nonworking," and otherwise "undeserving."

Most people living in poverty are working and do not receive public assistance even when it is available. This has been true throughout the history of welfare provision. Nonetheless, one major anxiety associated with welfare historically is that it will undermine people's commitment to work. Therefore, welfare has most often been structured so as to constrain the degree to which providing aid will diminish work effort. A panoply of practices have evolved over time to buttress the expectation that recipients should take work over welfare as often as possible. These practices have reinforced the tendency to distinguish the "working poor" from the "welfare poor," casting a positive light on the former at the expense of the latter. This invidious distinction fails to take into account the fact that often, throughout the history of welfare, many of the working and nonworking poor were the same people at different points in their struggle to overcome poverty. The distinction has also done much to marginalize mothering by denigrating mothers who stay at home with their children and are not taking paid employment. In particular, single mothers receiving public assistance in order to stay at home with their children have been stigmatized, in no small part because of the historical valorization of the working poor.

The welfare population has always been a minority of those persons living in poverty. Most people who are poor do not rely on public assistance but instead are in families with wage workers. The main sources of poverty for these people historically have been low wages and unemployment. Nonetheless, the dominant welfare policy discourse has de-emphasized wage deficiency and labor market insecurity, focusing instead on welfare as a disincentive to work. As systems of public aid developed to replace almsgiving in the nineteenth century, work requirements were common. "Indoor relief" in the form of the poorhouse where work was required was the most often preferred. "Outdoor relief," provided to families in their homes, was extended reluctantly, and only when labor markets failed seriously and the numbers of destitute families multiplied dramatically. Subject to intense criticism, outdoor relief was eventually seen as something that had to be structured according to the principle of "less eligibility," which held that benefits were to be below the wages for the lowest-paying jobs. As welfare systems developed in the modern era, they became increasingly articulated with the requirements of the labor market and were increasingly structured to limit the extent to which they might undermine work.

When welfare was liberalized, it was often in the name of aiding families who lacked a wage earner. In the early-twentieth-century United States, mothers' pension programs spread across the states to support "widowed" mothers in staying at home with their children. These programs formed the basis of the welfare system codified in the Social Security Act of 1935 and later known as Aid to Families with Dependent Children (AFDC), which itself was repealed in 1996 and replaced by the more limited Temporary Assistance for Needy Families (TANF). The 1996 repeal was driven in part by concern that welfare had come to undermine wage work among single mothers and the fathers of their children. It was also accompanied by inflammatory rhetoric pitting the "working" against the "welfare" poor. Time limits and work requirements were imposed on the receipt of TANF. The goal of aiding single mothers to stay at home to care for their children was de-emphasized in favor of the goal of promoting work.

This retrenchment of public assistance took place even though much available research indicated that welfare's negative effect on work effort was minimal. Most poor families preferred work in the paid labor force over welfare, and most continued to work even when welfare was made more readily and generously available. In addition, much research had indicated that many welfare recipients worked at least part-time and that the distinction between the working and nonworking poor was overdrawn. Nevertheless, the rhetoric of welfare reform had successfully pushed past these nuances to imply, in melodramatic terms, that there was a sharp divide between the working and nonworking poor. Another point lost in the debate as it was structured was that mothering is a form of work that has important value for society and needs to be supported in those cases where families are unable to provide for themselves. The emphasis on work during the reform debates emphasized paid employment outside the home and further marginalized single mothers who stay at home to care for their children.

In the United States, the focus on reducing welfare dependency has led to increased efforts to aid the working poor by enhancing public policies that help "make work pay." In particular, in recent years, there have been dramatic increases in the Earned Income Tax Credit (EITC) that allow low-wage workers to supplement their wages with payments from the federal government. Some states have added to these policies as well. Nonetheless, wage deficiency and unemployment still plague labor markets in the United States and remain the primary sources of poverty. In the face of resistance to raising the minimum wage at the federal level, living-wage campaigns have spread across the country since the 1990s, trying to bring about local policies that will boost pay scales. These campaigns have had some victories, but the poverty stemming from wage inadequacy persists. Most welfare recipients leaving welfare for work under the new policies remain in poverty several years after leaving welfare.

Sanford F. Schram

See also: Aid to Families with Dependent Children (ADC/AFDC); Dependency; Deserving/Undeserving Poor; Earned Income Tax Credit (EITC); Living-Wage Campaigns; Relief; Self-Reliance; Welfare Policy/Welfare Reform; Work Ethic

References and Further Reading

Edin, Kathryn, and Laura Lein. 1997. *Making Ends Meet: How Single Mothers Survive Welfare and Low-Wage Work*. New York: Russell Sage Foundation.

Mead, Lawrence. 1992. *The New Politics of Poverty: The Nonworking Poor in America*. New York: Basic Books.

Newman, Katherine. 1999. *No Shame in My Game: The Working Poor in the Inner City*. New York: Knopf.

Works Progress Administration (WPA)

As an alternative to direct relief, President Franklin D. Roosevelt's Executive Order 7034 (1935) created the Works Progress Administration (WPA, renamed the Work Projects Administration in 1939) to distribute funds appropriated by Congress in the Emergency Relief Appropriations Act of 1935. The public service work provided by the WPA earned it the support of many unemployed workers, who regained a sense of dignity that had been compromised by the hard times of the Great Depression. Along with other New Deal programs, the WPA contributed to workers' conception of the federal government as a vehicle to advance economic security and workplace justice. New Dealers such as WPA head Harry Hopkins described the WPA as part of a general shift in the organization of the U.S. economy. According to Hopkins, "The time . . . when industry and business can absorb all able-bodied workers seems to grow more distant with improvements in management and technology" (quoted in Kennedy 1999, 375). In its eight-year history, the WPA allocated more than $11 billion and employed some 8.5 million workers. Three-fourths of the WPA's budget went toward funding infrastructure construction; the other quarter was allocated to a range of art, education, and historic-preservation projects. Between 1935 and 1943, WPA workers constructed or repaired some 572,000 miles of roads, 67,000 miles of city streets, 124,000 bridges, 8,000 parks, 125,000 public buildings, and 350 airports.

In its cultivation of art and preservation of folk traditions, stories, and music, the WPA often publicized the economic and social hardships of a wide range of American citizens. The WPA included four often-controversial arts programs that frequently drew attention to social injustice and the impact of the Great Depression on American workers and families. The Federal Art Project commissioned murals, often of working people, in public buildings and hired artists to conduct art classes. The Federal Music Project recorded and preserved regional folk music traditions and sponsored concerts heard by some 50 million Americans. The Federal Theatre Project performed classic and contemporary theater for some 30 million people before Congress abolished it in 1939, accusing it of promoting race mixing and FDR's New Deal agenda. The Federal Writers' Project hired writers for a wide range of tasks, from interviewing former slaves to compiling guidebooks of cities and roads of the United States.

Not surprisingly, given its ambitious and controversial mission, the WPA received considerable criticism from a wide range of conservatives, who thought the program undermined private industry, and worker advocates, who thought it provided insufficient relief to the nation's poor. The struggle over the WPA highlighted longstanding debates in U.S. welfare policy regarding the "deserving" versus the "undeserving" poor and the role of state, local, and federal government in providing relief. Labor advocates, workers, and reformers decried the low wages and inadequate aid the WPA and other New Deal programs provided to unemployed workers and their dependents. For the millions of unemployed who did find work with the WPA, wages, referred to as "security wages," fell somewhere between wages in the private sector and sustenance. Labor union leaders saw the low wages allotted to WPA workers as a threat to organized labor's bargaining position. Other worker advocates criticized the program for the discrepancies between the wages of skilled and unskilled workers, the failure of the program to advance workers' training, and the program's requirements for WPA employment. Despite its sizable budget, the WPA did not provide employment for all eligible workers. Unemployed workers had to be certified as eligible for WPA work, a certification that did not guarantee employment. Some estimates suggest that the WPA employed only a quarter of the eligible unemployed workers. In addition, regulations limited employment in the WPA to one person per family, which prevented many women from obtaining WPA jobs (women workers made up less than 20 percent of the WPA workforce). Republicans and some conservative Democrats lambasted the WPA for its wasteful use of tax dollars and its propensity for paying workers for doing unnecessary work or no work at all. Republican political foes accused FDR, not without some justification, of using the WPA as a new means of rewarding political patronage.

The regional and racial discrepancies in WPA wages drew fire from civil rights advocates. In the South, racial wage differentials left some southern African American workers with much smaller wages than their white southern counterparts. The low-skilled and physically demanding work frequently assigned to Black workers compounded their frustrations over low wages. Nonetheless, Black workers made up a disproportionately high number of WPA workers (between 15 and 20 percent of the WPA workforce), and FDR's executive order banning discrimination in WPA hiring amounted to one of his administration's most aggressive civil rights actions.

In early 1937, as the economy showed tenuous signs of recovery, WPA opponents in Congress slashed funding for it and other relief programs. This cut in "emergency" programs exacerbated the effects of the economic collapse of 1937, when production fell more than 40 percent and unemployment climbed. In response to the "Roosevelt Recession," Congress approved FDR's additional spending measures, which restored some of the funding to the WPA. The WPA continued until 1943, when a coalition of Republicans and southern white Democrats succeeded in eliminating the agency.

G. Mark Hendrickson

See also: Great Depression and New Deal; Public Works Administration; Relief

References and Further Reading

Brinkley, Alan. 1996. *The End of Reform: New Deal Liberalism in Recession and War.* New York: Vintage Books.

Cohen, Lizabeth. 1990. *Making a New Deal: Industrial Workers in Chicago, 1919–1939*. Cambridge: Cambridge University Press.

Howard, Donald Stevenson. 1943. *The WPA and Federal Relief Policy*. New York: Russell Sage Foundation.

Katz, Michael B. 1996. *In the Shadow of the Poorhouse: A Social History of Welfare in America*. New York: Basic Books.

Kennedy, David M. 1999. *Freedom from Fear: The American People in Depression and War, 1929–1945*. New York: Oxford University Press.

Patterson, James T. 2000. *America's Struggle against Poverty in the Twentieth Century*. Cambridge, MA: Harvard University Press.

World Bank

The International Bank for Reconstruction and Development (IBRD) was established following a conference at Bretton Woods in 1944 (which also led to the creation of the International Monetary Fund). The conference debates and the bank's Articles of Agreement contain no references to poverty or to related notions such as living standards or equity. Today, the World Bank Group comprises, in addition to the IBRD, the International Development Association (IDA), the International Finance Corporation (IFC), the Multilateral Investment Guarantee Agency (MIGA), and the International Centre for Settlement of Investment Disputes (ICSID).

The principal lending vehicle for the bank's poverty agenda is IDA, a soft loan window created in 1960. Between 1960 and 2002, IDA, whose funds have been periodically replenished by industrialized countries, has lent about $135 billion. Until the creation of IDA, the IBRD, which raises its resources on global financial markets and whose loans are at near-market rates, was constrained from lending to poor countries because of their perceived lack of creditworthiness. Nor did the bank lend to poverty-oriented projects with high social rates of return, because a low financial rate of return rendered them "unbankable." In contrast, IDA credits are lent only to countries whose per capita incomes are below a certain level, and the loans have a nominal service charge and long maturities. Still, until the late 1960s, the bank barely touched on the subject of poverty and continued to focus on economic growth as the key to poverty reduction. The shift from a market-disciplined, "productive investment" approach toward an increasingly social, need-based definition of its goals had started with the switch from reconstruction to development banking, but became more pronounced in the late 1960s.

It was during the 1970s, however, that the institution set out in earnest on an ambitious path of poverty-oriented social engineering, seeking to improve on the economic and political processes that, in many developing countries, appeared to be shortchanging the poor in the distribution of benefits from growing production. Those efforts to help the poor, over and above the promotion of growth, came to be understood, in a stricter sense, as "poverty alleviation." Whereas poverty reduction through growth has been the bank's constant, if mostly implicit, pursuit, poverty alleviation in the more ambitious sense of providing more than a "trickle-down" effect has followed a more eventful course in the bank's history. During this period, it initially promoted a redistribution-with-growth strategy, focusing first on small farmers and subsequently on the urban poor. Later in the decade, it tried to push for a basic human needs approach to poverty alleviation.

A hiatus followed in the early 1980s. The economic crisis afflicting many of the bank's borrowers led to a focus on policy-based adjustment lending, overshadowing the bank's poverty reduction objectives—although this new focus was rationalized as enabling the bank to address more effectively the relationship between poverty and the policy environment. Critics, however, charged that adjustment lending exacerbated poverty by making governments cut social expenditures. The bank's poverty objective again became a central issue in the late 1980s, and with the end of the Cold War, the bank's poverty agenda came to be increasingly influenced by donor governments, legislatures, nongovernmental organizations (NGOs), and the media, with IDA replenishments being the principal leverage.

At the end of 1991, the bank's staff operational manual affirmed that "sustainable poverty reduction" was the institution's "overarching objective." Externally, poverty reduction became the benchmark by which its performance as a development institution began to be measured. Loan approvals were linked to a country's commitment to poverty reduction. New goals sprang up. Although addressing the problem of inadequate income, or "poverty," remained a central objective, the bank began to focus on the relevance to poverty of a host of other issues: gender equality, the universal right to education, protection or security against hunger, minimum nutrition and health standards, the environment, the right not to be forcibly resettled, the suffering caused by natural disasters and wars, socially vulnerable groups, indigenous peoples, the special claim of sub-Saharan Africa, safety nets for the victims of macroeconomic adjustment programs, and the AIDS crisis.

Significantly, the bank began to stress the relationship between political variables in borrowing countries and the impact of those variables on the poor. "Governance," or the quality of government and corruption issues, was now debated openly. Rather than dealing exclusively with governments, the bank began to work with civil society and NGOs in implementing its antipoverty programs. And acknowledging that the fungibility of public resources meant that money channeled to a government might or might not go to its official objective, the bank began to use public expenditure reviews to influence the overall budgetary priorities of borrowing governments. In the new millennium, the bank emerged as the largest external source of financing for programs in education and HIV/AIDS in poor countries.

Have poverty reduction and development been distinct objectives for the bank? For the most part and throughout its history, the bank has seen the promotion of economic growth as its principal means of bringing about poverty reduction. The institution has encouraged such growth as much by financing the expansion of productive capacity as by seeking to improve the way in which capacity is used. Underlying these activities is a strong assumption that growth in output eventually benefits a majority of the population or, at least, increases a nation's capacity to reduce poverty within its borders. Over much of its lifetime, however, the bank has thought that it should and could do better than rely on economic growth and trickle-down effects to help the poor. Growth, it came to believe, could be made more beneficial to poor people by redesigning the geographical, sectoral, factor-mix, and other aspects of production so that the benefits of additional output might accrue more directly to the poor.

It would be tempting to conclude that the bank made almost steady progress in learning about and addressing poverty. However, its agenda and intellectual prognosis have had greater shifts than can be reflected in its lending operations, which have in practice been subject to a number of constraints. For the most part, the principal contribution made by the bank to poverty reduction has been the result of its general support for economic stability and development rather than of its many efforts to bring about more direct poverty alleviation. Although the poor have made up a declining proportion of the world's total population through the bank's life, the institution continues to be strongly criticized for its actions (or inaction) in light of the persisting scale and intensity of global poverty. In part, the bank has itself to blame, for promising far more than it can deliver. But in part, it is also a convenient scapegoat for both borrowing and industrialized countries whose own actions are a much bigger part of the problem.

Devesh Kapur

See also: Globalization and Deindustrialization; U.S. Agency for International Development (AID)

References and Further Reading

Ayres, Robert. 1983. *Banking on the Poor: The World Bank and World Poverty*. Cambridge: MIT Press.

Easterly, William. 2002. *The Elusive Quest for Growth*. Cambridge: MIT Press.

Kapur, Devesh, John Lewis, and Richard Webb. 1997. *The World Bank: Its First Half Century*. Vol. 1, *History*. Vol. 2, *Perspectives*. Washington, DC: Brookings Institution.

Mason, Edward, and Robert Asher. 1973. *The World Bank since Bretton Woods*. Washington, DC: Brookings Institution.

Young Men's Christian Association (YMCA)

The Young Men's Christian Association (YMCA) is an international network of community-based organizations whose stated mission is "to put Christian principles into practice through programs that build healthy spirit, mind, and body for all" (YMCA). Originally founded to assist and convert the young men flocking into cities in the nineteenth century, the YMCA long emphasized Bible reading rather than antipoverty activism; after a brief spate of social activism, it has become a family-focused community organization. From the 1870s through the 1920s, the YMCA ran programs for working men in tandem with corporate employers. During the Great Depression, local YMCAs provided unemployed men with services such as fitness programs, medical assistance, education, job training, and recreation. During the 1930s and 1940s, the national YMCA tentatively embraced a more liberal stance, though never to the extent the YWCA did. YMCA social welfare activity peaked in the late 1960s and early 1970s, influenced by the Student YMCA, its college organization, which was highly active on social justice issues. Today, besides providing transient low-cost housing, many local YMCAs serve as ecumenical community centers for both sexes. They provide nonprofit day care, programs for underprivileged youth, and reasonably priced fitness facilities. YMCAs began forming in U.S. cities in the 1850s, inspired by the new British YMCA and by American evangelical revivalists. Most YMCA programs focused on keeping men from such vices as alcohol and tobacco, and they increasingly emphasized physical fitness and camping as ways to build rugged, "masculine" men who adhered to Christian values of sobriety and hard work.

The YMCA long avoided taking public stands on social issues, initially resisting the direction of the Social Gospel movement, efforts by concerned members, and activities by some locals. Focused on individual salvation, from 1880 to 1915 it passed no resolutions about public affairs. Some local YMCAs were more active, though; the Cleveland YMCA fought for improved government treatment of underprivileged "delinquent" boys, built public bathhouses in tenement areas, organized public relief for the neediest, and founded the city's first public playground. In 1919, by a narrow margin, the national YMCA adopted the Social Ideals of the Churches, a prominent Social Gospel creed, marking the start of a serious crisis over the YMCA's purpose and techniques. In the 1920s, it faced pressure to embrace social reform both from some prominent YMCA staff members and from an increasingly activist student membership. It began offering summer programs in which students learned about industrial problems by taking jobs in industry and discussing issues with their coworkers.

Up through the 1920s, the YMCA offered extensive programs for working-class men that focused on maintaining what it called a "zone of agreement between the employer and employee" (Hopkins 1951, 478). In 1894, it refused an American Federation of Labor request for classes on labor problems and training for labor leaders. Seeking to build Christian character and to keep workingmen away from radicalism, the YMCA's "industrial" programs offered Bible-centered education, library and gym access, and wholesome recreation. These programs drew hundreds of thousands of men, including, by 1915, 150,000 Catholics. The first and most substantial program targeted transient railroad workers; others served workers in iron, steel, mining, cotton, lumber, and several other industries. Employers initially funded the programs, though member fees paid an increasing proportion of the costs. At some YMCAs, railroad workers changed the programs to suit themselves—insisting, for instance, on playing billiards (against YMCA policy) and contesting companies' use of YMCA facilities to house strikebreakers. At the same time, many workers apparently embraced the YMCA's idealized vision of sober, industrious Christian manhood. Dozens of "colored" YMCAs served working-class Black men; there, the focus on Christian manhood had additional implications. Black urban elites founded YMCAs to challenge racial stereotypes; they hoped that by showing whites African Americans who were model Christian men, they would earn respect and, eventually, equality (they abandoned this approach after World War II). Through the 1920s, the YMCA's industrial programs remained focused on bringing boys and men to Christ. These programs all but disappeared during the 1930s. The YMCA's Industrial Department never was as strongly sympathetic to workers and their movements as that of the YWCA.

The 1930s brought more liberal YMCA rhetoric, and sometimes action. In 1931, it adopted an "open platform" policy committing it to maintain discussion of social issues from all perspectives and to promote education for a greater social justice. Numerous local associations used this policy to fight for civil rights and free speech and to draw underrepresented people into public discussion and education groups. In 1935, abandoning the "zone of agreement" policy of its first five decades, the YMCA created a National Public Affairs Committee to educate and advocate for social justice issues, including better labor and racial conditions. Problems remained: In 1941, only 14 percent of local YMCAs engaged in public affairs education; in 1942, the YMCA's own Black secretaries accused it of severe discrimination in its programs and employment.

In the postwar period, the YMCA suffered something of an identity crisis. Even as it adopted an interracial charter in 1946, many locals balked at racially integrating. Urban whites were moving to suburbs, and suburban YMCAs began focusing on families rather than on single men. Simultaneously, inner-city YMCAs and the Student YMCA forced the national association to face urban poverty and racism; the YMCA responded in the 1960s by supporting civil rights and launching numerous programs to help the poor. In 1972, the YMCA proposed dropping its goal of converting young men in favor of fighting social problems. In order to fund programs for low-income people, it sought federal aid for the first time; it also relaxed its moralizing about drinking, smoking, and profanity in order to make its facilities more broadly welcoming. After the Vietnam War, it returned to an individualistic focus, offering fitness and other self-improvement programs.

Dorothea Browder

See also: African American Migration; Civil Rights Movement; Community Chests; Community-Based Organizations; Employment and Training; Housing Policy; Juvenile Delinquency; Missionaries; Protestant Denominations; Social Gospel; Temperance Movement; Young Women's Christian Association (YWCA)

References and Further Reading

Hopkins, C. Howard. 1951. *History of the Y.M.C.A. in North America*. New York: Association Press.

Mjagkij, Nina. 1994. *Light in the Darkness: African Americans and the YMCA, 1852–1946*. Lexington: University of Kentucky Press.

Mjagkij, Nina, and Margaret Spratt, eds. 1997. *Men and Women Adrift: The YMCA and the YWCA in the City*. New York: New York University Press.

Winter, Thomas. 2002. *The YMCA and Workingmen, 1877–1920*. Chicago: University of Chicago Press.

Young Men's Christian Association (YMCA). Web site. http://www.ymca.net/index.jsp.

Young Women's Christian Association (YWCA)

The programs of the Young Women's Christian Association (YWCA) for working-class and poor women, dating back to the mid-nineteenth century, originally emphasized evangelism. A changing membership and broader cultural developments have altered them significantly. Deeply held religious belief motivated many YWCA leaders and members, and at key times, their interpretation of the YWCA's religious goals led them to embrace controversial positions about racial and class issues. Through the nineteenth century, the YWCA was composed of middle-class Protestant women who sought to "save" workingwomen from urban evils. From 1910 through the 1940s, the YWCA facilitated a nationwide workingwomen's movement, assisted immigrant families, and lobbied for labor and civil rights legislation. From midcentury onward, it particularly emphasized racial justice. Today, its mission is "to empower girls and women and to eliminate racism"; it carries out its mission with attention to low-income women and lobbies extensively for related programs and policies. The YWCA is the largest U.S. provider of both nonprofit day care and shelter services to women and their families. It also offers low-income women employment training and placement, domestic violence prevention programs and domestic violence treatment, and financial literacy programs. The YWCA represents more than 2 million girls and women in more than 300 affiliated locals.

Arising in the 1850s in the United States and Britain alongside the YMCA, the YWCA initially brought together well-off evangelical Protestant women concerned about the many women migrating to cities for work. It sought to keep them from prostitution and to bring them to Christ. From the northeastern United States, the movement spread across the country in the 1860s. Early YWCAs provided workingwomen with boarding homes, employment training and placement, domestic science classes, physical education, libraries, and noontime Bible classes in factories. In 1907, two national YWCA movements merged into one, run by a national board.

Around this time, the YWCA began incorporating Social Gospel ideology and drawing in more workingwomen. In 1908, it created an Industrial Department. In 1911, it started publicly advocating for living-wage laws and protective labor laws for women. During World War I, the YWCA provided shelter, recreation, and assistance to more than 300,000 women war workers. After the war, it joined other female reformers and policy intellectuals to convince the U.S. Department of Labor to continue studying women's needs; many YWCA staff members served in the resulting Women's Bureau.

Beginning in the second decade of the twentieth century, tens of thousands of workingwomen and their middle-class allies used the YWCA to build a multiracial, national industrial movement (causing considerable internal turmoil). The YWCA's Industrial Department offered them lobbying power, education, and crucial social and political networks. Locally, workingwomen met weekly in "industrial clubs." Initially a top-down continuation of the YWCA's traditional mission, the clubs changed their goal after members began to run them. At a time when few labor unions admitted women, the clubs provided a place to discuss wages and working conditions and to develop leadership skills that many later used in the labor movement. They also provided exercise, recreation, medical checkups, and sex education classes, including birth control. Attracting staff who were further to the left politically than most YWCA board members, the Industrial Department served as a path into activism for middle-class women. By 1918, more than 800 industrial clubs had sprung up, with more than 30,000 members from various religious backgrounds. Ultimately, membership reached nearly 60,000, and tens of thousands more women attended club meetings without joining. In 1919, a YWCA staff member designed a program to train women labor leaders, offering courses on women in industry and on economic and political history. Immensely popular, the program soon added training in leadership, public speaking, parliamentary procedure, and writing. In 1920, the Industrial Department membership convinced the YWCA National Board to sign on to the Social Ideals of the Churches, a prominent Social Gospel creed, and insisted that it endorse collective bargaining, a controversial stance for many board members. From the 1920s through the 1940s, the YWCA's workingwomen held annual regional and national summer conferences, inviting labor leaders, workingwomen's advocates, theologians, scholars, and health experts to lecture and lead discussions. The conferences drew nearly 1,000 industrial club representatives annually—African American, Asian American, Mexican American, white, and immigrant; unionized and nonunionized; Catholic, Protestant, and Jewish.

Beginning in 1921, the YWCA's Industrial Department also played a central role in founding, staffing, and recruiting for a number of two-month summer schools for working-class women. The schools ran through the 1940s and fostered many labor activists. Each summer, the schools brought together hundreds of workingwomen from a range of backgrounds, occupations, and regions to exchange perspectives; to learn about economics, history, and labor activism; and to play, swim, write and perform plays, and stargaze. Women from YWCA industrial clubs successfully fought to overturn racially exclusive admissions policies at some schools and to include domestic workers in their programs.

African American women constantly pushed the YWCA to live up to its professed Christian embrace of all races, and they did not except programs for workingwomen. In 1915, the YWCA held the first interracial conference ever in the South, in Louisville, Kentucky, to discuss programs for African American women workers. It greatly expanded such programs during World War I, and by 1919, a special secretary oversaw forty-five wartime service and recreation centers serving 12,000 Black women workers. The YWCA's workingwomen initially included African Americans in their national conferences; local and regional gatherings gradually included women of color, and when Japanese American members were interned during World War II, fellow members protested and kept in touch with them. Industrial club members often brought more racially liberal ideas from conferences back to conservative communities. The clubs and conferences welcomed women who performed paid household work—often the only work women of color could find. During a period when labor organizers and labor laws tended to ignore household workers, the YWCA lobbied for them and helped them organize. Industrial clubs' advocacy for household workers caused considerable tension in some local YWCAs, whose middle-class members resented any interference in their own employment practices.

In the postwar period, race became a primary focus for the YWCA. In 1946, it adopted an interracial charter committing it to integrate and to fight racism in the broader society. Although the national association took great strides, some all-white local associations disaffiliated, and others tried to ignore the call to integrate. In 1970, responding to efforts by a group of 500 Black women, the YWCA adopted as its "One Imperative" the elimination of racism "wherever it exists and by any means necessary" (YWCA, "Eliminating Racism"). Dorothy Height, an extremely prominent advocate for African American women, served on the National Board from 1944 to 1977 and was instrumental in YWCA racial justice programs.

Dorothea Browder

See also: African American Migration; Civil Rights Movement; Community-Based Organizations; Employment and Training; Feminisms; Housing Policy; Living-Wage Campaigns; New Left; Protestant Denominations; Service and Domestic Workers; Social Gospel; U.S. Department of Labor; Young Men's Christian Association (YMCA)

References and Further Reading

Frederickson, Mary. 1984. "Citizens for Democracy: The Industrial Programs of the YWCA." In *Sisterhood and Solidarity: Workers' Education for Women, 1914–1984*, ed. Joyce L. Kornbluh and Mary Frederickson, 75–106. Philadelphia: Temple University Press.

Harper, Elsa. 1963. *Fifty Years of Social Action in the YWCA*. New York: National Board of the Young Women's Christian Association of the United States.

Mjagkij, Nina, and Margaret Spratt, eds. 1997. *Men and Women Adrift: The YMCA and the YWCA in the City*. New York: New York University Press.

Salem, Dorothy. 1990. *To Better Our World: Black Women in Organized Reform, 1890–1920*. Brooklyn, NY: Carlson.

Weisenfeld, Judith. 1997. *African American Women and Christian Activism: New York's Black YWCA, 1905–1945*. Cambridge, MA: Harvard University Press.

Young Women's Christian Association (YWCA). "Eliminating Racism, Empowering Women." http://www.ywca.org/site/pp.asp?c=btIRK9OXG&b=23377.

———. Web site. http://www.ywca.org.

Index

About the Editors

Gwendolyn Mink is the author of *Welfare's End* and *The Wages of Motherhood: Inequality in the Welfare State*, which won the Victoria Schuck Book Award from the American Political Science Association.

Alice O'Connor is associate professor of history at the University of California, Santa Barbara. Her published works include *Poverty Knowledge: Social Science, Social Policy, and the Poor in Twentieth-Century U.S. History* and she is coeditor of *Urban Inequality: Evidence from Four Cities*.